MISSION 66

MISSION 66

MODERNISM AND THE NATIONAL PARK DILEMMA

ETHAN CARR

UNIVERSITY OF MASSACHUSETTS PRESS   AMHERST

IN ASSOCIATION WITH LIBRARY OF AMERICAN LANDSCAPE HISTORY   AMHERST

Copyright © 2007 by University of Massachusetts Press
All rights reserved
Printed in China

LC 2006037077
ISBN-13: 978-1-55849-587-6
ISBN-10: 1-55849-587-8

Designed by Jonathan D. Lippincott
Set in New Baskerville and Neutra Text
Printed and bound C&C Offset Printing Co., Ltd.

Library of Congress Cataloging-in-Publication Data
Carr, Ethan, 1958-
    Mission 66 : modernism and the National Park dilemma / Ethan Carr.
    p. cm.
    "In association with Library of American Landscape History, Amherst."
    Includes bibliographical references and index.
    ISBN-13: 978-1-55849-587-6 (cloth : alk. paper)
    ISBN-10: 1-55849-587-8 (cloth : alk. paper)
1. Park facilities–United States–Design and construction–History. 2. Park
facilities–United States–Maintenance and repair–History. 3. National
parks and reserves–United States–Design. 4. United States. National Park
Service–History. 5. Landscape design–United States–History. 6. Modern
movement (Architecture)–United States. I. Library of American
Landscape History. II. Title. III. Title: Mission sixty-six.
    SB486.F34C37 2007
    333.78'30973–dc22
                                                                2006037077

Publication of this book was made possible by a generous grant
from Furthermore: A Program of the J.M. Kaplan Fund
and generous support from Mr. and Mrs. Michael Jefcoat.

333.78
C

FOR SARAH AND MARION

CONTENTS

The subject of this book is Mission 66, a decade-long planning, landscape, and architecture initiative begun in 1956 that transformed the national parks in the United States into the form we know them today. Ethan Carr's meticulously detailed, at turns gripping, study of this billion-dollar program of the National Park Service is the first comprehensive analysis of the topic. In it, he examines the roots, planning, and execution of a program whose very title captured a postwar sense of urgency and almost military purpose.

The impetus for Mission 66 was the deteriorating condition of America's national parks, which had received little attention during World War II and were being visited by unprecedented numbers of people. By the early 1950s, crowded roads, jammed parking lots, inadequate visitor facilities, and poor maintenance were undermining almost every aspect of park visitors' experience. Inspired by the vision and purpose of the National Park Service founders, Conrad "Connie" Wirth, a graduate of the landscape ar-chitecture program at Massachusetts Agricultural College, proposed a ten-year program that would not only rehabilitate the aging system but vastly expand it. Wirth's initiative was timed to conclude with the fiftieth anniversary of the founding of the National Park Service in 1966. Eisenhower liked the look of the program and approved it in every detail, including its mammoth budget.

In addition to the physical legacy of Mission 66—the vast increase in parklands and campgrounds, as well as new roads, worker housing, visitor centers, and other user amenities—the initiative can also be credited with catalyzing the modern environmental movement that began in the 1960s, largely in opposition to it. At the heart of this conflict was a profound disagreement over the purposes of America's national parks. As Carr points out, the founding fathers of the National Park Service were, first and foremost, motivated to provide scenic enjoyment to the American people, and the progenitors of the second wave of park development—Wirth, his landscape architect Thomas C. Vint, and the other protagonists in the Mission 66 story—firmly believed that their own actions were in keeping with this original mission.

As concern about the preservation of wilderness grew, however, far-ranging construction projects of the Mission 66 program, particularly new roads and road improvements, were seen as a direct threat to parklands, not only because they would alter scenic landscapes but because they would greatly increase public access to them. The debate was about wilderness and, as Carr notes, "how wilderness would be defined, designated, and protected in the postwar period." The opposition of prominent wilderness advocates, including Ansel Adams, who spoke out against a signal Mission 66 project, the widening of Tioga Road in Yosemite National Park, provoked a battle that helped transform the Sierra Club from a mountain hiking club to a major player in the modern environmental movement. The Wilderness Preservation Act passed in 1964 was another paradoxical legacy of Mission 66.

Carr's study also illuminates the thinking behind the now ubiquitous park building known as the "visitor center," an invention of the Mission 66 architects, who found inspiration in the new shopping centers of the time. In Carr's view, these buildings, despite their modernist trappings, were also manifestations of early park system philosophies and purposes. As part of a larger analysis of the meaning of the national parks for the American people, Carr examines the public outcry the structures' sleek lines and industrial materials provoked among those accustomed to the more familiar rustic style of the

1920s and 1930s. Many of these buildings, now almost a half-century old, are facing their own structural crises, and park managers who favor demolishing and replacing them are butting heads with preservationists who see in these modernist structures icons of architectural and cultural significance. *Mission 66* will help frame this debate by offering a broad, historical context in which to understand and appreciate these aging buildings and the designed landscapes surrounding them.

At the present moment of crisis in our national parks, deferred maintenance, overuse, and abuse once again threaten the integrity of the system. We're hopeful that Carr's book will be widely read and that his thoughtful conclusions will prompt future planning which frankly acknowledges the philosophical dilemma inherent in maintaining our National Parks—a system charged simultaneously with protecting scenic resources and making them freely accessible to millions of visitors. As Carr writes, "The story of Mission 66 is a reminder that the parks are reservoirs of national identity, history, and imagination as well as ecosystems. Their vast symbolic power has been constant but has also constantly shifted in meaning."

Mission 66 is also a significant work of scholarship. The author's training as a landscape architect and park historian is manifest on every page of his text. *Mission 66* is very much in keeping with other books published by LALH, which address topics from parks and parks systems to subdivisions to town planning to country estates.

I am very grateful to Ethan Carr for offering LALH an opportunity to publish this important book and for the care with which he prepared every element of it—from the text to its two hundred illustrations to the captions that describe them. I believe that *Mission 66* expands the LALH list in significant regards. Randall J. Biallas of the National Park Service was instrumental in facilitating the publishing arrangement that brought *Mission 66* to print, and I am grateful to Randy for his persistence in seeing it through. A generous grant from Furthermore helped cover the costs of the extensive illustration program and the index by Kevin Millham. I am grateful to Joan K. Davidson, founder and director of Furthermore, for the foundation's underwriting of this and other LALH projects, and to Mr. and Mrs. Michael Jefcoat for their generous gift in support of this book.

I thank Amanda Heller for her fine editing and Mary Bellino for her copyediting and proofreading in later stages, and I am grateful to Jonathan Lippincott for his imaginative modernist design. Jack Harrison, production manager of University of Massachusetts Press, has seen this project through its final stages of production, and I am grateful to him and all the members of the Press staff, including director Bruce Wilcox, for their continued enthusiasm for our program. In the end, it is the Trustees and supporters of the Library of American Landscape History who make our work possible, and it is to them that I direct my deepest thanks.

LALH

Library of American Landscape History, Inc., a nonprofit organization, produces books and exhibitions about North American landscape history. Its mission is to educate and thereby promote thoughtful stewardship of the land.

ACKNOWLEDGMENTS

Numerous institutions and individuals have supported and guided this project over the more than five years it took to complete. Randall J. Biallas, chief historical architect of the National Park Service, was one of the first to identify the need for a more complete historical context in which to assess the potential historical significance of Mission 66 architecture and landscape architecture. His original vision and sponsorship resulted in Sarah Allaback's report, *Mission 66 Visitor Centers: The History of a Building Type* (Washington, DC: Government Printing Office, 2000), and in this book. In large part thanks to Randy's leadership, numerous listings in the National Register of Historic Places and three National Historic Landmark designations for Mission 66 buildings and districts have already been made.

At the beginning of this project, the topic was also approved as a subject for Ph.D. research in the department of landscape architecture at the Edinburgh College of Art. I am indebted to Professor Catharine Ward Thompson, whose initial interest, suggestions, and encouragement helped me develop appropriate research questions and methodology. Professor Simon Bell, as my primary supervisor, clarified the purposes and requirements of doctoral research. I am deeply grateful to them both for their contributions to this project, which in a longer and somewhat different form they approved in 2006 as my Ph.D. thesis. I also thank my thesis examiners, Professor Miles Glendinning (Edinburgh College of Art) and Professor Keith N. Morgan (Boston University) for their valuable critique and insights.

While writing this book this book I taught in the department of landscape architecture and regional planning at the University of Massachusetts, Amherst. Department chair Jack F. Ahern made it possible for me to be able to write and teach full time. Without his support and friendship I could not have done both. My colleagues at the University of Massachusetts history department, professors David H. Glassberg and Marla R. Miller, gave me invaluable advice and instruction on historical theory and research methodology. A number of talented University of Massachusetts graduate students also assisted me in several research tasks, including going through National Archives records in Philadelphia and Washington and conducting an oral history project. I especially acknowledge Patricia Alesi, Donna Lilborn, and Trinidad Rodriguez for these contributions.

In addition to funding much of the research for this book, the National Park Service enlisted a committee of scholars and professionals to review the work. I am indebted to this extraordinary group for their observations and comments. Former deputy director of the National Park Service, John J. Reynolds, was a rich source of information, perspective, and understanding of the role of national parks in American society. Professor Richard Longstreth (George Washington University) suggested changes that improved overall structure and content. National Park Service historians Timothy Davis, Barry Mackintosh, and Rodd Wheaton also made comments that resulted in important improvements. Professor Richard Guy Wilson (University of Virginia) and Elizabeth Barlow Rogers shared their expertise and gave personal support and advice, for which I am particularly grateful. Other members of the National Park Service peer review committee to whom I owe a debt include: Randall J. Biallas, Robert W. Blythe, Shaun Eyring, Heidi Hohmann, Denis P. Galvin, David H. Glassberg, Elaine Jackson-Retondo, Lucy Lawliss, Dwight T. Pitcaithley, Paul Schullery, John Sprinkle, Donald L. Stevens Jr., Stephanie S. Toothman, and Sherda K. Williams.

Many individuals in archives and national parks all over the country were generous with their time and observations. The most comprehensive textual and photographic records of Mission 66 are conserved at the National Park Service's Harpers Ferry Center, Harpers Ferry, West Virginia. David Nathanson guided me through the textual records of the National Park History Collection at Harpers Ferry, an archive that he has developed into an indispensable resource for anyone interested in national park history. Thomas DuRant shared his amazing knowledge of the National Park Service Historic Photo Collection. Without their help, it would have been impossible for me to fully utilize the textual and photographic records at Harpers Ferry.

I am grateful to the staff of the American Heritage Center of the University of Wyoming, Laramie, for their help in using the Conrad L. Wirth Collection. Scott Pawlowski assisted me with the National Park Service records at the Technical Information Center in Denver, another vital repository of agency records. The National Archives in College Park, Maryland, conserves Record Group 79, the official administrative records of the National Park Service. Conrad Wirth's official papers became available only in the middle of this project, and in general the records of the postwar decades have not yet received the same level of organization that makes prewar federal records far easier to use. Record Group 79, both in College Park and in the regional branches of the National Archives, however, remains an essential source of records relating to Mission 66.

Since many records of the recent past have

not yet been accessioned to the National Archives, individual park archives (and even working files) were very significant sources of information. At Yellowstone National Park, Harold Housley led me through the park's records, and park historian Lee H. Whittlesey took time to discuss Mission 66. At Yosemite National Park, Linda Eade assisted me at the Yosemite Research Library, and park historian Jim Snyder shared his great knowledge of Mission 66.

At Carlsbad Caverns National Park, Robert J. Hoff guided me through the park's archives, and at Everglades National Park, Nancy J. Russell did the same. Anyone who has done this type of research knows how vital this help was. At Big Bend National Park, Thomas Alex gave needed assistance. For Grand Canyon and Petrified Forest national parks, Amanda Zeman shared her research on postwar national park development. For other western region parks, Elaine Jackson-Retondo and Len Warner did as well. At Cape Cod National Seashore, Hope Morrill provided guidance to park records, and William P. Burke conveyed the significance of that park's history both to me and to a large group of University of Massachusetts students.

Dozens of individuals participated in oral history interviews that were part of the research for this book, and I thank them all. In particular, Theodore J. Wirth described his memories of his father (and grandfather), as did Robert J. Vint of his father. Former director George B. Hartzog Jr. was generous with his time. William C. Everhart, Denis P. Galvin, Theresa Wood, and other former National Park Service officials and employees shared memories, information, and their network of "alumni" contacts.

The photographs of Jack E. Boucher appear throughout this text. His remarkable career as a National Park Service photographer—which began during Mission 66—continues today with the Historic American Buildings Survey. Boucher's work demands more thorough consideration than can be given here. The artistic quality of his images, however, speaks for itself.

I am honored and grateful that the Library of American Landscape History selected this book to be part of its prestigious list of publications. Executive director Robin Karson's comments and suggestions have been invaluable. The book greatly benefited from Amanda Heller's editing and Jonathan Lippincott's design. At the University of Massachusetts Press, I am grateful to Bruce Wilcox for his enthusiasm and support.

Sarah Allaback, whose research on national park visitor centers (cited above) remains the most cogent source on these buildings, provided observations, information, and expertise throughout this project. We are also married, and so my debt is profoundly personal as well as intellectual. This book is dedicated to her and to our daughter Marion.

MISSION 66

A typical American family visiting a national park, as depicted in 1958 by Park Service officials. The image was part of a narrated slide show, "Mission 66 in Action," shown to thousands of park visitors. NPS History Collection.

"THE PEOPLE WHO USE THE PARKS"

The developed areas of the U.S. national park system as it exists today are mainly the result of two busy periods of modernization overseen by the National Park Service. While older parks such as Yellowstone, Glacier, and Grand Canyon boast hotels and other remnants of the railroad era, the construction of the modern national park system really got under way in the mid-1920s, when Congress began making generous appropriations for the development of public facilities in national parks, particularly for park roads. This was the "rustic" era of park architecture and landscape design, when Park Service designers and engineers developed a unique approach to "harmonious" site development and "landscape engineering." During the 1930s the agency oversaw the expansion and development not only of the national park system but of almost every state park system as well. Then World War II, followed by reduced postwar budgets, caused an extended hiatus in federal park spon-

sorship. When Congress was again ready to ratchet up park spending in the mid-1950s, a second major wave of national park development occurred. This postwar era of development was structured around a ten-year program proposed in 1955 by Park Service director Conrad L. Wirth. Characterized by Wirth as "MISSION 66," the program was intended to modernize, enlarge, and even reinvent the park system by 1966, the fiftieth anniversary of the National Park Service.

Mission 66 was essentially an audacious budget proposal that persuaded Congress to increase national park appropriations immediately and to provide further increases over the next decade. The program responded to a generally perceived crisis that resulted from an extended period of low park funding combined with heavy public use of the park system. During the late 1940s and early 1950s, the Cold War and the Korean War helped keep national park budgets

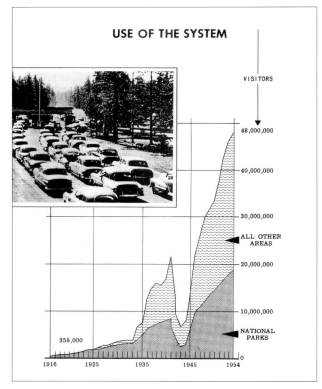

USE OF THE SYSTEM

VISITORS

48,000,000

40,000,000

30,000,000

ALL OTHER
AREAS

20,000,000

10,000,000

NATIONAL
PARKS

358,000

1916   1925   1935   1945   1954

Contemporary Park Service graphics illustrating how postwar park budgets did not keep pace with the "use of the system." NPS History Collection.

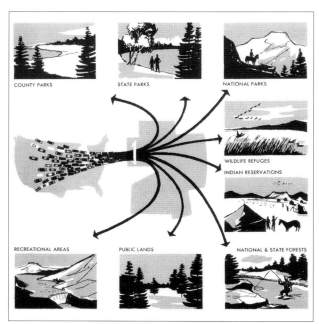

COUNTY PARKS   STATE PARKS   NATIONAL PARKS

WILDLIFE REFUGES

INDIAN RESERVATIONS

RECREATIONAL AREAS   PUBLIC LANDS   NATIONAL & STATE FORESTS

A page from *Our Heritage* (1956). NPS History Collection.

near pre–World War II levels: $32 million in 1955, for example, compared to $26 million in 1939. Adjusted for inflation, budgets were lower in the 1940s and early 1950s than they had been in the 1930s.[1] In addition, the Civilian Conservation Corps (CCC), the Public Works Administration (PWA), and the other New Deal programs abolished in 1942 were not resumed, crippling the ability of the Park Service (and most state park departments) to build and maintain roads, trails, bathrooms, or any other visitor facilities. But as soon as wartime rationing and travel restrictions ended in 1945, a flood of visitors inundated state and national parks. In Yellowstone, more than 1 million visits were recorded annually beginning in 1948, up from an all-time high of 500,000 in 1940 (and from a wartime low of 86,000 in 1944). The numbers continued to climb to unprecedented levels. In 1955 there were 56 million visits to the national park system, compared to 17 million in 1940; yet Park Service budgets had remained at or below prewar levels despite the enormous increase.[2]

By the late 1940s a ruinous combination of low budgets and unprecedented numbers of visitors had depreciated the experience of national parks for millions. In the developed zones of parks, or "frontcountry," people found traffic jams, long lines outside bathrooms, overflowing parking lots, and no available accommodations or campgrounds. With too few rangers, superintendents could not adequately protect their parks, much less staff their museums and interpretive programs. Many park concessioners had suffered economically during the Great Depression and had shut down during World War II. Now they struggled unsuccessfully to reopen aging and inadequate hotels and restaurants for the sudden tide of visitors. Both the Park Service and park concessioners were forced to manage far larger numbers of people with far fewer staff. Limited public facilities in poor repair, little or no office space or support, and a shortage of decent housing for employees made their tasks more onerous. In other words, almost immediately following the end of the war in August 1945, national park managers were exposed to the overcrowding, limited budgets, understaffing, and other difficulties that have continued, to a greater or lesser degree, to the present day.

The continued trend toward automobile use over rail transportation intensified an already profound dilemma. At Yosemite Valley, where three quarters of visitors were arriving by car by 1919, the "All-Year" highway opened in 1926. By 1944 the Yosemite Valley Railroad, which had served the gateway town of El Portal since 1907, was sold for scrap. Even parks that had a tradition of "motor coach" connections to nearby rail stations ended those services as national passenger rail lines atrophied and disappeared. By 1950, up to 99 percent of visitors to the national park system were arriving in their own cars or in increasingly popular "drive-yourself" rentals.[3] Just finding room to drive and park millions of automobiles became a chronic and worsening problem in the country's most popular national parks. The sheer number of cars made providing even basic services problematic.

Newton B. Drury, the director of the Park Service during and after World War II, was perhaps the most preservation-oriented director in the history of the agency. He was also apparently comfortable with reduced budgets, especially

The Park Service used this image of park visitors waiting to use an outhouse in several brochures in the mid-1950s. NPS Historic Photo Collection.

This photograph of traffic congestion in Yellowstone was taken by park superintendent Edmund Rogers to document postwar conditions in his park. NPS Historic Photo Collection.

Postwar traffic at a Yosemite entrance station. NPS Historic Photo Collection.

Yellowstone superintendent Edmund Rogers (left) with Park Service director Newton Drury. NPS Historic Photo Collection.

for construction. "We have no money," he reportedly told the Sierra Club board of directors. "We can do no harm."[4] But the truth of this sentiment was soon called into question. High levels of visitation combined with a lack of supervision, parking lots, and bathrooms, it turned out, could do great harm, at least to park features anywhere near a road. The greatest harm being done in the postwar period, however, was to the public's experience of the parks. The degradation of the experience eroded the national park idea itself. The Park Service could not simply abdicate its responsibility for enabling visitors to have meaningful and enjoyable experiences of the country's most scenic and historic places. With millions of automotive tourists overwhelming the limited "rustic" facilities of a previous era, quantities of both ideas and money were needed if the parks were to remain cultural icons, revered by the same public that now threatened their viability. In the early 1950s the scandalous condition of developed areas in many national parks became a favorite subject of columnists and editorial boards. Bernard DeVoto started the trend with a 1953 column in *Harper's* magazine provocatively titled "Let's Close the National Parks." Pointing out the deficiencies in national park budgets and staff, DeVoto observed that "homeopathic measures will no longer suffice." He estimated that at least $250 million over five years would be needed if the parks were to retain "a proper level of safety, attractiveness, comfort, or efficiency." Since no such sum was forthcoming

Crowded camping conditions in Yosemite Valley (top row) and in Sequoia National Park (below left), as photographed by Park Service personnel in 1953. NPS Historic Photo Collection.

Attempting to give an interpretive program in an overcrowded space at Shiloh National Military Park, Tennessee. NPS Historic Photo Collection.

from Congress, he suggested closing as many of the parks as necessary, for their own protection. In 1954 and 1955 other articles appeared in national magazines with titles such as "National Parks: Tomorrow's Slums?," "The Shocking Truth about Our National Parks," and "Twenty-four Million Acres of Trouble."[5]

The tone and content of such criticism suggested that the Park Service had not met its obligation to the public, and even to its own employees, to provide basic services and facilities. The agency seemed unable to regain its position as the country's chief "recreational planning" and landscape preservation organization. There was no way to compensate for the loss of emergency spending programs, especially the CCC and the PWA, which had become vital supplemental sources of labor and construction money during the 1930s. In the postwar political context, a more conservative

By the 1950s many CCC-era buildings were considered substandard, including housing and a comfort station at Grand Canyon (right), and a maintenance building at Zion (below). NPS Historic Photo Collection.

Congress condemned "New Dealism" in any form, making it unlikely that Franklin Roosevelt's enthusiasm for national park expansion and development would be easily rekindled. Harry Truman shared little of Roosevelt's personal enthusiasm for conservation programs. In any case, politically he could ill afford to propose the sort of public park initiatives that had been among the most vivid symbols of his predecessor's social idealism. While Congress kept Park Service appropriations low, Truman further hobbled the agency by advancing policies at the Department of the Interior (the bureaucratic home of the Park Service) that favored dam building and economic growth over conservation programs.

These were the challenges facing Conrad L. Wirth when he became National Park Service director near the end of 1951. Wirth had been born into the world of park planning and management. His father, Theodore, was a famous superintendent of the Minneapolis park system and a friend of leading park planners and advo-

Photographs by Jean Speiser for the NPS Women's Organization documenting substandard employee housing in the Lake area of Yellowstone in 1956. NPS Historic Photo Collection.

Originally built by the CCC, a campground circle and a park road in Glacier National Park symbolized the need for revitalization. NPS Historic Photo Collection.

cates of the day. After studying landscape architecture under Frank A. Waugh at the Massachusetts Agricultural College, Conrad Wirth went to work for the Park Service in 1931 with a personal recommendation from one of his father's admirers, Frederick Law Olmsted Jr. Wirth began as the agency's "chief land planner," a powerful position in which he investigated the suitability of various areas for inclusion in the expanding park system. After 1933 he directed the Park Service's CCC activities in state parks, a massive program involving thousands of employees which grew to be larger than the rest of the Park Service programs combined. Wirth was a consummate New Dealer and a key figure in expanding the role of his agency in national resource planning.[6] Despite his best efforts, however, Wirth failed to persuade Congress to make the CCC a permanent program, and so he lost the main source of his funding and bureaucratic power in 1942.

The inauguration of Dwight D. Eisenhower and the end of the Korean War in 1953 put in motion the changes that would lead to Mission 66. As the armed forces demobilized and recession threatened, Eisenhower looked more favorably on public works spending that would stimulate the economy. The bad press the national parks were receiving was also being noticed. After more than three years as director of the Park Service, Wirth decided the hour had come, and he suddenly proposed a ten-year capital program to modernize and expand the national park system. He assembled key staff into special "working" and "steering" committees and instructed his park superintendents to begin preparing "prospectuses" of the work they

needed done in their parks. Within eight months they had outlined the scope of the Mission 66 program, including preliminary budget estimates. The name of the program (Wirth's inspiration) captured the desired sense of a crisis, but it did so by evoking the wartime urgency of a "mission," not a return to New Deal social programs. In any case, the name and the image proved effective. Eisenhower personally endorsed Mission 66 after Wirth presented the program at a cabinet meeting in January 1956. That spring Congress indicated a willingness to go along with the request for over $700 million for the ten-year program by increasing the agency's budget for fiscal year 1957 to $68 million, up from $32 million in 1955. Further increases led to annual budgets in excess of $100 million by 1962. The planning and policy initiative of Mission 66 proved to be the most effective means of increasing Park Service appropriations since the New Deal emergency spending legislation of the 1930s.[7]

By 1966 Congress had spent about $1 billion on land acquisition, new staff and training, general operations, and all types of construction activity in national parks. Seventy new "units" of the park system were authorized between 1956 and 1966. The Park Service constructed or reconstructed thousands of miles of roads and hundreds of miles of trails. Many parks received adequate water, sewer, and electric service for the first time. Hundreds of park residences, administration buildings, comfort stations, and other buildings for public use and park administration were built. Mission 66 expanded and professionalized Park Service staff and established new "training centers." Above all, Mission

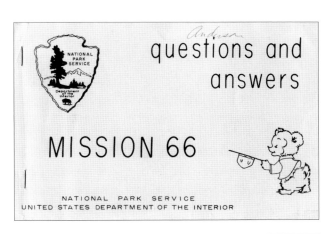

By 1957 a number of Park Service publications attempted to describe Mission 66 to the public and shape perceptions of the program. NPS History Collection.

This image from "Mission 66 in Action" (1958) shows a typical park's staff, including rangers in their postwar uniforms. NPS History Collection.

The arrowhead logo, as approved by Wirth in 1952. NPS History Collection.

66 funded more than one hundred "visitor centers," a new building type invented by the agency's planners and architects, which was at the heart of revised "master planning" goals for the parks. A new identity for the agency was forged, represented by a new idiom of park architecture and by the "arrowhead" agency logo, introduced in 1951 and featured prominently on buildings, publications, and redesigned uniforms.[8] Although the development (or, as was often the case, the redevelopment) of national parks on this scale was almost always beset by controversy, in the end Mission 66 accomplished much of what Wirth intended: the reinvention of the national park system and the National Park Service—and to some extent the national park idea—to meet the exigencies of postwar American society.

Mission 66 was greeted with enthusiasm by Congress, government officials, and many preservationists. From the beginning, however, the program was also criticized for emphasizing capital construction as a one-dimensional solution to the complex social and environmental problems park managers were facing. Critics also complained that Mission 66 construction abandoned the architectural theory and building technology of the rustic era. Distinctive new buildings adapted various strains of postwar American modernism to the programmatic and aesthetic requirements of the national parks. Postwar park architecture made full use of steel, concrete, prefabricated elements, unusual fenestration, climate control, and other aspects of contemporary architecture.[9] The new park architecture also expressed contemporary planning ideas. The visitor center, for example, bore similarities to shopping centers and urban cultural centers, since it also sought to make centralized services accessible to large numbers of people arriving in cars. The interstate highway system also influenced Mission 66 road design and sometimes determined the locations of developed areas in the parks. For preservationists who decried these changes in the American landscape in general, seeing their expression in the frontcountry of national parks was deeply disturbing. If Mission 66 began in an atmosphere of intense optimism, the program soon led the Park Service into bitter controversy as the postwar environmental movement began to take shape and exert its strength. Mission 66 hastened the advent of environmentalism by creating genuine concern that the Park Service was "overdeveloping" parks while failing to take other steps to preserve "wilderness."

But for Conrad Wirth, his chief landscape architect Thomas C. Vint, and the other planners and designers of Mission 66, these critics over-

Park Service "chiefs" in February 1956. Left to right, seated: Eivind Scoyen, Lawrence Merriam, Conrad Wirth, Thomas Allen, Hillory Tolson, Thomas Vint; standing, Howard Baker, Elbert Cox, Hugh Miller, Daniel Tobin, Ronald Lee, Ben Thompson, Sanford Hill, Edward Zimmer. Photo by Abbie Rowe, NPS Historic Photo Collection.

looked the fundamental challenge at the heart of managing national parks. From Vint's point of view, merely designating parks as wilderness would not "solve the national park problem" because "our national park law includes the words 'for the benefit and enjoyment of the people.'"[10] Whether in the case of scenic or historic places, Vint believed that preserving a place as a park required providing for public access. In the 1950s, either this compromise would be renegotiated to serve a larger public, or public access would have to be significantly restricted in some way. Wirth, Vint, and many of their colleagues recoiled at the idea that parks would no longer be truly public landscapes, preserved for the benefit of the public at large. They felt that they could expand and adapt the national park system, increase its capacity, provide meaningful experiences of the nation's natural and historical heritage, and still preserve that heritage for future generations. They realized, however, that procedural and even cultural changes would be required of their agency in order to meet new challenges. Wirth exhorted his colleagues to reconsider all aspects of their professional activities. "Nothing was to be sacred," he later recalled, "except the ultimate purpose to be served. Man, methods, and time-honored practices were to be accorded no vested deference. Old traditions seemed to have determined standards far beyond their time."[11]

If it implemented new planning procedures and design concepts, however, Mission 66 also remained profoundly committed to facilitating public enjoyment of the parks. Wirth again and again insisted that Mission 66 should be seen as a "conservation" program, not a "development" program, that ultimately would preserve and not destroy "wilderness." But he also made it clear that he believed the "parks were for the people," and that preservation outside the context of public enjoyment was simply not what the parks or the Park Service was intended to achieve. When Wirth's father, Theodore, died in 1949, Frederick Law Olmsted Jr. wrote a letter of condolence that Wirth would later say best expressed the philosophy of park making to which he had dedicated himself and his agency. Both of their fathers, Olmsted began, had shared "a deep-seated, constant and compelling interest in and sympathy with, the *people* using the parks." Park work involved understanding how people derived pleasure from a particular park and "guiding them by every available means to get the best values from their use of it." Without this concern for "the *people* who use the parks," and for determining how they could be "induced to use them with greater benefit to themselves," park management was an "academic and sterile" exercise. This was the most important idea, Olmsted concluded, to be learned from "your father's life work, and that of my father."[12]

Six years later, Wirth and his seasoned staff launched Mission 66, confident in their abilities and experience, as well as in the tradition and theory of American park making that they represented. Their confidence perhaps made it more difficult to anticipate the storm of controversy that loomed ahead, as environmental organizations pressed for less, not more, public access to parks. Mission 66 came to symbolize, fairly or not, a willingness to sacrifice the integrity of park ecosystems for the sake of enhancing the merely superficial appreciation of scenery by crowds of people in automobiles. Olmstedian theory had little appeal to those who saw the recreational use of parks as the primary agent of their destruction. Wirth would step down as director at the beginning of 1964, two years before his program was to have been completed. Congress passed the Wilderness Act the same year, a signal victory for advocates pressing for the total protection of natural areas from any kind of development, including park development.

Mission 66 was the last major period of intense activity and profoundly new ideas to find expression in a systemwide program of national park development. Regardless of how one judges the legacy of Mission 66, a close examination of the era is warranted. We would not recognize the developed areas of the national parks today without the visitor centers, roads, housing, and other facilities acquired and built during these years. Mission 66 greatly enlarged the park system and expanded entire categories of parks, including national recreation areas and national seashores. For better or worse, the national park system and the National Park Service today are still in many ways artifacts of Mission 66, and park managers still face the same dilemma that Mission 66 attempted to solve.

As Mission 66–era facilities age and require rehabilitation or replacement, the Park Service will need to assess their potential historical significance.[13] There are also lessons to be learned from an earlier generation of ambitious park planners who were so sure of their values and methods that they failed to anticipate profound shifts in the always complex relationship between the American public and its national parks. The story of Mission 66 is a reminder that the parks are reservoirs of national identity, history, and imagination as well as ecosystems. Their vast symbolic power has been constant but has also constantly shifted in meaning. Today more visited than ever before, the parks continue to be reinvented by the very act of visiting. It remains to be seen if today's park managers will successfully mediate and enhance future relationships between parks and their publics, or if they too will be restricted by the calcification of their own ideals.

PART I

MISSION 66: PLANNING

CHAPTER 1

NEWTON DRURY AND THE "DILEMMA OF OUR PARKS"

Although Mission 66 was presented to the public in 1956 as a dramatic new initiative, the program responded to severe pressures on the national park system that had already been analyzed and lamented for years. Many aspects of Mission 66, in fact, were first suggested in the 1930s. But the program responded, above all, to the events, realities, and trends of the first postwar decade. Examples of modernist national park architecture first appeared in the 1940s, and many basic assumptions that became cornerstones of Mission 66 planning were elaborated during that decade. The story of Mission 66, therefore, really begins in 1945, as the dismal postwar situation described as "the dilemma of our parks" rapidly unfolded.

Newton B. Drury became the fourth director of the National Park Service in 1940, following the departure of the depression-era director, Arno B. Cammerer. Like Stephen T. Mather and Horace M. Albright, the influential first two di-

rectors of the Park Service, Drury was a native Californian and a University of California graduate. Born in 1889, he was just a year older than Albright, and they graduated together in the Berkeley class of 1912. Like Albright, he was trained as a lawyer but never practiced. Following service in World War I, Drury started a public relations firm. Like Mather, who had made a fortune earlier in life promoting borax, he proved to be an adept spokesman and publicizer, first of products, then of causes.[1]

In 1920 Drury became the first executive director of the Save-the-Redwoods League, a conservation organization that sought to preserve remaining stands of coast redwoods in California. The preservation of the redwoods had become a national cause, and Drury worked closely with John C. Merriam, Madison Grant, and other Progressive Era conservationists from across the country who had been among the founding members of Save-the-Redwoods in

Park Service Director Newton Drury (left) with Secretary of the Interior Julius Krug (center) and Assistant Secretary (and later Krug's successor) Oscar Chapman in 1949. Photo by Abbie Rowe, NPS Historic Photo Collection.

1918. Drury became a well-known figure himself, raising private funds and lobbying for state appropriations to acquire redwood groves and make them parks. In 1927 Drury led the public relations and lobbying efforts for legislation that established the California State Park Commission. The act also authorized a survey of potential park sites and allowed for a $6 million park bond act, subject to approval by public referendum. Drury then led a consortium of interests in a massive publicity campaign in favor of the bond act, which was eventually supported by dozens of automobile clubs and chambers of commerce, as well as by both local and national conservation organizations. The voters approved the bond with a large majority. From 1929 until 1940, Drury served the State Park Commission as acquisitions officer while also directing Save-the-Redwoods. In both his private

and public capacities Drury worked closely with figures such as Mather and Albright (who had been advocating a "redwood national park" since 1918) and Frederick Law Olmsted Jr., the author of the 1929 California state park plan.[2]

Drury's experience obviously made him an excellent candidate for the job of directing the Park Service, and in fact he was first offered the job in 1933, when Albright, who had become the agency's second director in 1929, resigned. Drury declined the offer at that time, citing personal reasons. His deep involvement in the creation of California's state park system was no doubt a project he was reluctant to leave. Drury also was a Republican, and (again like Albright) may have questioned the expansive role for federal government that Roosevelt championed. Drury may have had other concerns about taking over the Park Service as well. Although he clearly shared background, experience, and values with Mather and Albright, he also identified with a more rigorous group of preservationists, often dismissed by Park Service officials as "purists," who since the 1920s had been concerned about the effects of automotive access made possible by national park development. Albright opposed Drury's appointment as Park Service director in 1933, favoring associate director Arno Cammerer as a safer choice to continue the agency's policies. Roosevelt's new secretary of the interior, Harold L. Ickes, preferred Drury, a choice that may even then have indicated his desire for new priorities at the agency.[3] Albright got his way and Cammerer was promoted, but only after Drury declined the job.

Criticism of Park Service policy had flared almost as soon as the agency was created. In the 1920s unprecedented numbers of motorists crowded Yosemite Valley, the south rim of the Grand Canyon, the Paradise Valley area of Mount Rainier, and other popular national park destinations. What can be described as the modern, organized campaign for "wilderness" began in the 1920s, and it was in large part a reaction—as the creation of the Park Service had been—to the vast expansion of outdoor recreation and tourism made possible by the automobile.[4] For those who considered Yosemite Valley already "spoiled," or who condemned the "ballyhoo" at the south rim of the Grand Canyon, the policies of the new Park Service were at least in part to

The 1903 Roosevelt Arch at the Gardiner entrance to Yellowstone. The words inscribed in the arch, often quoted by Thomas Vint and other Park Service officials, are from the 1872 federal legislation that created the park. Author's photo.

blame.[5] The question of how to define and pre-serve wilderness was widely discussed in the 1920s. By the end of the decade both the Park Service and the U.S. Forest Service responded to criticism and made attempts to become better stewards of the remaining inaccessible lands under their jurisdiction. Several historians describe the story of early Forest Service wilderness designations for Trappers Lake, Colorado, and the Gila National Forest, New Mexico.[6] Contemporary with these events, the Park Service was also struggling with various administrative "wilderness" designations as part of the master planning process developed by chief landscape architect Thomas Vint. Vint supported the "protective attitude toward wilderness values" that he observed growing by that time, but he also felt that his mandate "included the words 'for the benefit and enjoyment of the people.'"[7] The master plans drawn up by Vint and his colleagues during the late 1920s and 1930s typically restricted development in a park to a narrow road corridor, while outside of these "developed areas" the plans usually zoned the remaining areas of the park as "wilderness." This zoning designation required that the area remain "undeveloped" except for hiking and stock trails, a few backcountry ranger cabins, and perhaps fire roads.[8] But like the Forest Service's "L-20 regulation," which protected wilderness in national forests, such an administrative decision could easily be changed at the discretion of the land management agencies.

The rapid pace of national and state park development in the 1930s exacerbated concerns about whether the Park Service could preserve wilderness while it developed parks. The initiation of the New Deal transformed the agency. The Civilian Conservation Corps in particular undertook a tremendous amount of work in the national parks and developed dozens of state park systems. All of this CCC park work was done under the direction of the Park Service, specifically of a young Conrad Wirth, who proved adept at rapidly organizing a large bureaucracy, as well as at the delicate task of "cooperating" with state authorities while maintaining strict control over budgets and design standards. Thomas Vint's design staff at the Park Service grew from 16 in 1933 to 220 in 1936, and that number still did not include hundreds of architects, landscape architects, and engineers working in the state park CCC camps under Wirth. Park Service budgets rose steadily from about $10 million in 1933 to more than $25 million in 1939, but work relief programs funded park development far beyond these appropriations. By 1940 the CCC, the PWA, the Civil Works Administration (CWA), and the Works Progress Administration (WPA) had funneled an additional $218 million into national park construction. By that time the number of units in the park system had grown from 63 to 161. The combination of federal funding sources and the extensive cooperation between federal, state, and local park agencies made the 1930s a unique era in American park history.[9] Such an infusion of resources would not be repeated, even under the generous construction and land acquisition budgets of the Mission 66 program.

Clearly not everyone was happy with the role of the Park Service as the nation's leading "recreational planning" agency. Robert Sterling

Thomas Vint (front row right of center, hands in coat pockets) ca. 1938 with his design staff on the roof of the Department of the Interior building in Washington. Architect Cecil Doty is on Vint's right and landscape architect Ernest Davidson is on his left. NPS Historic Photo Collection.

Yard at the National Parks Association, Robert Marshall at the Wilderness Society, Arthur Newton Pack at the American Nature Association, and Rosalie Edge at the Emergency Conservation Council, among others, organized around a common vision of "wilderness" that precluded any kind of development, including park development. The advocates of this new landscape ideal insisted that the true mandate of the Park Service was to preserve the integrity of "primeval wilderness," not to facilitate automotive touring, camping, or any of the increasingly popular activities described as "outdoor recreation." While Park Service officials had seen only strength in the typological and geographical expansion of the park system, critics in the 1930s felt that the many historical sites, state parks, and national recreation areas being acquired by the agency degraded true national park standards. And for early wilderness supporters, public recreation itself was the greatest threat to wilderness values. In 1935 the creation of the Wilderness Society, directed by the charismatic Robert Marshall, signaled a new level of organization and maturity in the movement to keep the last inaccessible, wild places in the United States truly remote and completely undeveloped. In 1936 the National Parks Association, with a coalition of other organizations, suggested designating the older, larger parks as a "National Primeval Park System," declaring that "the original system" had been "lost . . . among innumerable recreational activities, local, regional and national, assigned to the National Park Service."[10] And in 1938

Newton Drury and the Save-the-Redwoods League opposed a plan to create a "redwoods national park," which had been a goal of the League since its creation in 1918. Apparently they feared the consequences of transferring state park land to the Park Service to create the new national park.[11]

By the end of the 1930s a growing number of preservationists believed that the National Park Service had failed to protect wilderness aggressively enough. These proto-environmentalists were advocating an ideal of wilderness which implied that preservation should be for its own sake, not for the sake of public enjoyment. Society would be better served by assuring that the last truly inaccessible areas of the nation remained in isolation, even if this meant that the general public would never see or appreciate them. As the meaning and purpose of preservation shifted for these advocates, ideas about what exactly was to be preserved were also changing. For example, by the 1920s many biologists were reaching a new understanding of the role of predators in the overall health of wildlife populations, and therefore condemned federal and state land management agencies, including the Park Service, that remained committed to the extirpation of wolves, coyotes, and mountain lions.[12] Charles C. Adams and other scientists of the Ecological Society of America had begun to advocate the preservation of "primitive landscapes" in their "natural condition," by which they meant specifically that the ecological relationships between populations of plants and animals would be undisturbed by any human activity or presence.[13] This was a very different kind of landscape reservation than the national park had ever been, and it implied a different understanding of what "natural" conditions were and how they should be perpetuated. For ecologists and other scientists, the success of wilderness preservation would be measured by the degree to which an area remained "pristine," without any indications of human history or influences. Scenic preservation, still the fundamental goal and philosophy of the Park Service, was not enough if it failed to maintain the diversity and integrity of native plant and animal populations. Even if visitor facilities were designed in an aesthetically harmonious, or "rustic," idiom, they still could destroy vital habitat. Once nature was defined more in terms of ecological science than landscape aesthetics, the "preservation and improvement" of natural areas (to quote the 1864 Yosemite grant legislation) became an increasingly complex and contradictory mandate.

The wilderness ideal was not really new in the 1930s, nor was it strictly a response to the perceived overdevelopment of national parks during the New Deal. Nineteenth-century figures such as John Muir had always argued that preservation should be for its own sake, and as numerous historians have shown, the poetic concept of wilderness can be traced to ancient origins. But the ideal gained converts and increased its appeal during the 1930s. Even with greatly expanded national and state park systems, ever larger numbers of visitors crowded popular scenic destinations, many of which had seemed, just a few years earlier, relatively remote. But their status and development as parks opened them to a broader, larger public and to the impacts of such use. The underlying premise that landscapes could be preserved by developing them as public parks began to erode. For some, preservation entailed something more (or actually less) than what the Park Service was doing.

One very powerful holder of such convictions was Harold Ickes himself, the cantankerous secretary of the interior and public works spending czar under Roosevelt. In the course of the 1930s Ickes often chafed under Park Service policies he felt were being perpetuated by Cammerer, Wirth, Vint, and other Park Service officials in Washington, as well as the cadre of superintendents in the parks. Despite the fact that Ickes was in charge of administering many of the appropriations that funded park development, he often managed to be a hero to "purists" by taking their side against his own agency. Ickes's personal contempt for Cammerer, his Park Service director, was well known, and this helped the secretary distance himself from Park Service actions when he felt the need to do so.[14]

Ickes was a master at having it both ways. The Park Service was kept busy, for example, building popular automotive parkways and dramatic roads throughout the 1930s. Projects such as the Blue Ridge Parkway and the Trail Ridge Road in Rocky Mountain National Park, considered showcases of "landscape engineering," were extremely popular among the always growing numbers of people visiting parks by car. But while Ickes took credit for federal largesse on the one hand, he regularly condemned the construction of roads in the parks on the other. As early as 1934 he admonished national park superintendents assembled in Washington with the observation that the parks had "too many roads" and "ought to be for people who . . . wander about and have . . . a renewed communion with nature." He felt that the agency was "getting alienated from that ideal."[15] Indeed, the assembled Park Service officials were at that moment mobilizing the largest park development campaign in history, replete with roads and entire "park village" plans. Ickes himself was very much in charge of that mobilization. But at the same time he pleaded that the agency was beyond his control. "Ever since I came to Washington I have been trying to impress the National Park Service with the fact that not only do we not want to have any more roads but that we have too many as it is," he wrote in 1938 in response to a letter from a landscape architect and preservationist, Jens Jensen, who was worried about Park Service plans for the upper Mississippi. "I have been trying to modify some of these policies because I do not agree with them any more than you do. . . . [A]ll I can hope to do is slow down the pace."[16] After 1934, any road proposals for national parks required the personal approval of the secretary, who clearly distrusted the Park Service in this regard.[17] This strategy of disavowal also held for other areas of policy—from concession contracts to interpretive programming—in which Ickes could condemn, when convenient, the "Mather men" for their intransigence and adherence to "tradition" while still acquiescing to major park developments and reaping the political dividends of their popularity. In this behavior Ickes set a pattern that would be followed by Interior officials throughout the Mission 66 era.

Ickes's harshest conservation battles were fought over new parks brought into the system in the 1930s. In these cases he fervently insisted that he would hold the line on the development of roads or any other kinds of park facilities. Ickes demanded a greater role in shaping development policies for the new "wilderness parks" (an unofficial designation), such as Everglades (Florida, 1934), Big Bend (Texas, 1935), Olympic (Washington, 1938), and Kings Canyon (California, 1940). The first park to include explicit wilderness protection in its legislation was Grand Teton National Park (Wyoming), which was established in 1929 with language that precluded the construction of any roads, hotels, or other lodging. The legislation in this case, however, responded to the concerns of dude ranchers worried about competition more than a desire to preserve wilderness.[18] At Isle Royale National Park in Michigan, the park legislation of 1931 depended on the acquisition of private land by the state, since Congress was unwilling to fund directly the acquisition of private land for

park purposes. As a result Isle Royale National Park only became a reality in 1940. Although its legislation did not specifically prohibit road building, its remote, insular situation made it a perfect case for Ickes to state categorically in 1938 that the new park would "have no roads."[19]

But for most historians, the first true "wilderness park" was Everglades National Park, because in this case the 1934 legislation was shaped by the wilderness debates of the time. The extraordinary bird populations of South Florida, and the bloody history of their exploitation and attempted protection, were bound to influence any discussion of a national park in the area. The "river of grass" was an awesome landscape, but it lacked specific scenic features or dramatic tourist attractions typical of earlier national parks. The character of the landscape and its importance as habitat suggested that it should become a different kind of park, one left in a "primitive" or "wilderness" condition. How

The Shark Valley observation tower in Everglades National Park and the "river of grass" as seen from the tower's viewing platform. Author's photos.

View of the surrounding desert through "the window," Chisos Basin, Big Bend National Park.
Author's photo.

exactly park planners would achieve this was a question that would be put off until the state of Florida finished the acquisitions of private land in 1947.[20] As was the case with many of the wilderness parks of the Ickes years, the ultimate disposition and physical management of the Everglades would only be resolved—and debated—later, as part of the Mission 66 program. The situation was similar at Big Bend National Park, which was established in 1935 but with property acquisition by the state of Texas not finished until 1944. The original legislation for the park was supported by local business interests and many citizens of surrounding towns in anticipation of the economic stimulus that could follow from the development of a national park. From the first plans that were drawn up in the mid-1930s, however, the Park Service acknowledged the constraints of working in an "untouched wilderness area," and although a lodge was developed in the Chisos Basin, the overall level of development, and the impact of the park on local economies, remained restrained, even during Mission 66.[21]

The creation of Olympic National Park was entwined in the long and fierce battles over the enormous potential wealth represented by the dense, mature expanses of fir, hemlock, spruce, and cedar that made up the temperate rain forest of the Olympic Peninsula. Following the park legislation of 1938, the Park Service became embroiled in a series of attempts—some of them successful—to continue logging anyway. Park Service planners began to offer projects for tourist development partly as a means to placate local businesses and chambers of commerce. In the process they incurred the wrath of their own secretary of the interior. "It is the intention to keep this park, so far as possible, in a wilderness area . . . a natural park," Ickes instructed in a 1938 rebuke.[22] Conflicting visions over how Olympic should be managed as a "wilderness park" would live on to become controversies during the Mission 66 program. Similar concerns incited debates over the future of Kings Canyon National Park. Early versions of that park's 1940 legislation contained provisions limiting road and concession development. Although these were eventually stricken, Kings Canyon stayed true to Ickes's hope that it remain a wilderness park, free of development of any kind, including roads and park development.[23]

The term "wilderness park," which became a common if unofficial usage at the Park Service by the mid-1930s, defied precise definition. National parks had always been created "for the benefit and enjoyment of the people," as Thomas Vint often pointed out, and that mandate implied "improvements" that both enabled and controlled public access. But wilderness was defined in the 1930s as an area that would remain roadless forever, therefore limiting public access to those willing and able to undertake extended hiking or stock trips. While such backcountry users were dedicated preservationists,

they were also a tiny minority of national park visitors. Nevertheless, the need to resolve the potentially conflicting programs of the "wilderness park" was postponed. World War II put an end to most park construction appropriations in 1942, and budgets continued to be limited between 1945 and 1955. Mission 66 funding, however, reawakened expectations for expanded visitor facilities in parks. At the same time, organized wilderness advocates of the postwar period pressed for greater preservation of wilderness, precisely by forgoing such development plans. The Mission 66 program never fully reconciled these competing ideas of national park management. It was during the postwar period that it first became a commonplace to refer to the "paradox" of making national parks available for "public enjoyment" while at the same time preserving them as "wilderness."

For Conrad Wirth and his recreational planners, however, increased capacity for public enjoyment could still be accommodated by the park system, as long as facilities were well designed and the system was appropriately expanded. While Ickes was promoting wilderness parks in the 1930s, Wirth and his army of CCC recruits were building entire categories of state and national parks that were unapologetically oriented toward recreational use.[24] National recreation areas, for example, were planned and built through an interbureau agreement with the Bureau of Reclamation specifically to develop the potential of large reservoirs for boating, camping, and swimming. Lake Mead National Recreation Area (Nevada, 1936) behind Hoover Dam set the precedent for a national park area conceived almost entirely

Hopewell Village (now Hopewell Furnace) National Historic Site, Pennsylvania, as photographed in the 1960s. NPS Photo by Jack E. Boucher.

around the demand for access by recreationists. National seashores were planned for areas that could also expect intense levels of recreational use. A 1935 Park Service survey identified at least twelve seashores to be added to the national park system in order to assure public access to the last great beaches still relatively unaffected by private ownership and resort construction. Cape Hatteras National Seashore in North Carolina was the first of its type when it was authorized in 1937; but once again the state's acquisition of private land was not completed until after the war.[25] Both new types of recreational parks, national recreation areas and national seashores, would become signatures of the Mission 66 era. Their origins, however, lay in the rich recreational planning legacy of the New Deal.

The roots of important postwar national historical parks also went back to projects that were planned or under way by the late 1930s. In 1933 Roosevelt transferred a host of Civil War battlefields and other historic sites to the jurisdiction of the Park Service, vastly expanding the agency's role as a curator of historic sites. In 1935 Congress passed the Historic Sites Act, authorizing the Park Service to undertake a national survey of historic sites and structures for possible addition to the national park system. The same year a large portion of the St. Louis waterfront was designated a national historic site under the terms of the act, a first step in the creation of what would become the Jefferson National Expansion Memorial. The Salem Maritime National Historic Site in Massachusetts and Hopewell Village in Pennsylvania were both designated in 1938. By that time the Park Service was also involved in proposals for a national historical park centered on Independence Hall in downtown Philadelphia; in 1948 Congress passed legislation creating Independence National Historical Park, which would become the most significant of all Mission 66–era historical parks.

By 1940, when Arno Cammerer retired after a heart attack, the national park system had increased greatly in size but even more so in complexity. The small and unique organization that Mather and Albright nurtured in the 1920s had grown into one of the most influential bureaucracies of the New Deal. New wilderness parks, national recreation areas, and urban national historical parks had compounded the already challenging task of centrally managing such a disparate group of properties. With the departure of his long-suffering Park Service director, Ickes was determined to end the succession of "Mather men" who had run the agency thus far. He considered several candidates, including New York City's park commissioner Robert Moses, who if nothing else would have brought his own strong stamp and a new sense of identity to the agency. But Ickes decided to return to his first choice for the job, Newton Drury.[26] Despite his personal and biographical closeness to Mather and Albright, many people believed that Drury represented a very different philosophy. His reputation as a preservationist was such that when David R. Brower (later executive director of the Sierra Club) heard of his appointment, he "wept for joy," believing that it was "the beginning of a new era" in national park management.[27] In his choice of Park Service director Ickes sent a clear signal to members of the Sierra Club, the Wilderness Society, the National Parks Association, and all the wilderness advocates of the previous decade that their concerns were understood.

But whatever plans Drury might have had in accepting the job seven years after first turning it down, they were quickly obscured by the war in Europe. Drury's first annual report was already filled with wartime priorities, such as cooperating with the War Department to provide access to parks for troops on leave.[28] From the beginning of his time in Washington, the reality of managing the national park system also clearly tempered Drury's "purist" tendencies. In the early 1940s Drury drafted a letter to Robert Sterling Yard, one of the most formidable wilderness advocates of the era, attempting to explain "the wilderness problem as we are faced with it." Drury defended his agency, pointing out that "with a development policy, based on Master Plans of each area, and governed by restraining hands," the parks already benefited from the highest level of protection. At that time, Drury considered congressional designation of wilderness areas in national parks "futile." It might also interfere with access to backcountry areas for firefighting and other purposes. Drury insisted that in most western parks (the particular concern of Yard and other advocates), development had remained within the same footprint since Mather's day, and that "no new roads have been built into new ground that were not projected at that time. . . . It is an astonishing fact that the Public Works Program of the 30s was largely a rebuilding program." Drury was as sympathetic a director as wilderness advocates were ever to have. He nevertheless chided Yard, insisting that national parks required no further official wilderness designation beyond what was implied by their status as parks, telling him, "It is the hope of the National Park Service that National Park Status is the safest classification wild land can attain for its protection in a natural condition for future generations."[29] Drury's arguments summarized a Park Service philosophy that Albright had articulated in the 1920s, and that would be repeated by Wirth in the 1950s in defense of Mission 66. Drury may have been more convincing at the time, however, since he seemed perfectly satisfied with his agency's drastic budget reductions during World War II, which ensured that his agency could indeed "do no harm."

Drury proved to be a director well suited to the special conditions of wartime. In 1942, as park visitation plummeted, the agency was reduced to a skeleton staff both in parks and in regional offices. The Washington office (including the director) was removed to Chicago to free up space for more vital war purposes. Drury was kept busy, nevertheless, because his talents as a preservation advocate were soon badly needed. When timber, stock, and mining interests exploited patriotic sentiment and tried to force open national parks to commercial uses, Ickes and Drury were able to turn aside much of the attempted profiteering, with some exceptions. For Drury this was a familiar kind of preservation battle. One of Drury's first tasks as director in 1940 had been determining how to assess applications for permission to mine, log, and graze livestock in the parks by groups already ostensibly involved in defense industries. He instituted protocols for differentiating true wartime emergencies from cynical efforts at exploitation, procedures that helped

the Park Service avoid charges of impeding the war effort. Drury was willing to put "the resources of the national parks . . . unreservedly at the disposal of the armed forces and the war production" but only when it was proved that other sources were completely unavailable; "park resources" were to be used solely "as a last resort." Drury insisted that applications should come from designated federal defense agencies or from private corporations that had documented evidence of relationships to such an agency. The burden of proof was on applicants to demonstrate the absolute necessity of their request by considering, and exhausting, specified alternatives. Applicants were also required to propose mitigations that would minimize the effects of their requests on "park values" and landscapes.[30]

The most sought-after wartime resource was the Sitka spruce of Olympic National Park, prized as "airplane lumber" for its high strength-to-weight ratio. Ickes and Drury allowed logging in the Queets River corridor, which at the time was still in the process of being added to the park. This and further incursions by the logging industry into Olympic seriously damaged Drury's reputation with wilderness advocates and led to a bitter feud with Ickes. Drury was soon enduring the same abuse that any Park Service director was likely to receive under Ickes, and the personal recriminations (Ickes's preferred means of exonerating his own actions) only intensified once the secretary left office in 1946.[31] Other wartime encroachments, such as salt mining in Death Valley, tungsten mining in Yosemite, and the salvaging of dead chestnut trees in the Appalachian parks, seem to have produced less political fallout. Drury was also quick to make use of the symbolic power of the parks in their own defense, for example, by allowing the Ahwahnee, the grand rustic hotel in Yosemite Valley, to become a naval hospital in 1943. Thousands of men and women in the armed services visited parks for rest and relaxation, and numerous parks served as training grounds. Drury was also credited with keeping grazing in parks near prewar levels, despite pressure from ranchers eager to capitalize on wartime beef prices. Grass was a far less lucrative resource than "airplane lumber" and therefore more easily preserved; a Park Service study also pointed out that the potential grazing land in the national park system was irrelevant to the war effort, making up well under 1 percent of the national total available.[32]

Drury's preservationist attitude, as well as an inherently conservative style, proved to be a combination well suited to the emotional debates of a nation at war. When the fighting ended in 1945, however, his agency was immediately plunged into an increasingly unfamiliar world, in which the dynamics of Progressive Era controversies—such as "utilitarian" use of resources versus the preservation of "aesthetic" values—were swept away by a new generation of pressures and threats. In 1946 an already perplexed Drury reported that following the lifting of travel restrictions in August, "the floodgates of travel opened immediately. For months there-

The Ahwahnee in Yosemite Valley, designed by Gilbert Stanley Underwood, opened in 1927. NPS Historic Photo Collection.

after all previous monthly records for numbers of visitors were broken." Drury did not attempt to disguise the fact that both Park Service and concessioner facilities were insufficiently staffed and in poor, sometimes inoperative condition. Those in charge of "on-the-ground management of the parks," he reported, had "made an effort to meet the demands put on them that deserves full recognition." The tone of the report suggested that those efforts had not met with success. "The unprecedented wave" of park visitors, he suggested hopefully, "accepted cheerfully the inconveniences of a period of reconversion," although "facilities and services to the public during 1945–46 were not—and could not be—up to the usual park standards."[33]

Drury became acutely aware of what he would soon describe as the "dilemma of our parks," which resulted from of a number of postwar factors and trends. For one thing, the end of the CCC in 1942 meant that thousands of maintenance workers would not be returning to work, even after the postwar labor shortage abated. All the work performed by CCC recruits before the war could not possibly be accomplished by the much smaller number of regular Park Service employees returning from the war, who now also enjoyed a forty-hour workweek, down from forty-eight before the war. New Deal spending programs, such as the PWA, had funded many park improvements, including roads, buildings, campgrounds, and museums. The CCC had provided not only construction labor but often maintenance personnel for completed facilities as well.[34] In 1946 it was doubtful that the conservative Eightieth Congress would continue to invest in parks, or even sustain the investments already made. Labor, housing, and construction materials were all in short supply, in any case, not only in the parks but also nationally. At the same time, the "floodgates" had opened: after 1945 parks across the system began to break their visitation records every year. Understaffed and underfunded, the parks nevertheless entered an era of unprecedented use, taking on an even more prominent place in the individual lives and collective imaginations of the American public. In the five years since Drury had taken on the job, the social, political, and economic realities of managing the national park system had changed forever.

By 1947, when Drury and the rest of the central office of the Park Service finally were allowed to move back to Washington, other changes affected the director's relative influence within the Department of the Interior. Important decisions involving the parks increasingly occurred at the level of the secretary of the interior (or assistant secretaries), leaving Drury to deal with the consequences of policies without having an active hand in making them. The director was often reduced to a role of merely pointing out the increasingly untenable situation of his park system. In 1947, for example, he observed that "never have the inadequacies of the development of the National Park System been so highlighted." He estimated that $110 million was needed for road modernizations, as was another $120 million to complete the Blue Ridge and other parkway projects already under way. Another $110 million would need to be invested directly by the government in concessioner facilities. Drury estimated that it would take an additional $45 million every year for seven years to address the situation. Despite his repeated calls for a "comprehensive program of development and improvement," construction budgets during those years totaled less than a third even of his conservative proposal. In 1949 Drury estimated the development backlog at almost $500 million; Congress appropriated a little more than $14 million for park construction that year. Legislators were understandably preoccupied with the costs of the Cold War, the Korean War, and the reconstruction of Europe. Drury's calls for multiyear construction authorizations—essentially the basis of Mission 66 seven years later—were ignored. While other domestic public works projects were funded, they reflected congressional priorities for housing, highways, and dam construction, which were spending categories the Truman administration perceived to be more direct forms of economic stimulus.[35]

Drury may have had credibility with the "purists," but the only reason he did not initiate a major modernization of the parks himself was that he never got the funding he requested. Throughout his tenure as Park Service director, he made it clear that he believed that national parks were to be preserved for the enjoyment of the public. In 1946 he described his essentially Progressive Era "park idea" in a long memorandum to Ickes. For Drury, the superlative scenic and biological importance of certain places made "public enjoyment" their most efficient use. The first priority of the Park Service was therefore to maintain "inviolate protection" from "lumbering, grazing, mining, hunting, water development, or other industrial uses." The second priority was "planned development" for

human use. Such development should be kept to a minimum and "designed to harmonize" with its setting. But development was not described as an impairment itself, as long as these conditions were met. "The designation 'national parks' rather than 'reservations,' or 'preserves,' or 'refuges,'" he elaborated, implied that "these areas are for the enjoyment of the people," although certainly this "enjoyment" needed to be distinguished from the mere "physical recreation" that might be available "in less distinguished natural environments."[36] Drury remained committed to traditional Park Service ideology, and he believed that his agency had an obligation to ensure that the American people had opportunities for meaningful experiences of the scenery and history held in trust for them in their national parks.[37] Drury's ambivalence about official wilderness designations in national parks and his support of Mather's concession policies further indicated his conservative management philosophy. Only occasionally did comments about the "element of human erosion" in parks reveal that he had begun to believe that visitation itself, and the development that made it possible and convenient, was becoming as great a threat to parks as the dam construction and logging he had fought since the beginning of his career in conservation in 1920.[38]

Despite Drury's best efforts to describe the overwhelming conditions his park managers faced, he never managed to raise the concern for national parks above the other, admittedly more dramatic events and issues of the day. In 1949 Drury published an article titled "The Dilemma of Our Parks," in which he summarized many of his frustrations. The parks, he said, were "still victims of the war . . . over-crowded and understaffed." More funds were needed for their "protection and development," two priorities he saw not as in conflict but as mutually supportive. "Whether we like it or not," he continued, the "enjoyment of 'the scenery and the natural and historic objects and the wildlife' in the national parks . . . is in large degree dependent on the 'physical plant' we provide." Drury repeatedly argued for the "modernized and enlarged utilities" that were required for visitor safety and the protection of park landscapes and resources. Congress, he urged, must increase appropriations, since New Deal spending had ended but public use had grown to unimagined levels.[39] These were essentially the arguments that would be made for Mission 66; but in the 1940s they went unheeded by both Congress and the Truman administration.

The controversy that ended Drury's Park Service career, however, did not involve angry concessioners, unprecedented numbers of visitors, lack of staff, inadequate budgets, or the other elements of the "dilemma of our parks." Drury's return to California in 1951 (to run California's state parks for the next eight years) was instead brought about by one of the oldest of threats to national parks: a dam building controversy. Dam construction was one aspect of the New Deal that Truman and postwar Democrats in Congress were continuing enthusiastically. For much of the West, the politics of water decided party affiliations and national elections, and even Republicans were willing to forsake fiscal conservatism to support grand plans for the impounding and distribution of western river water. While the Park Service had stagnated in the 1940s, the Bureau of Reclamation (a sister agency at the Department of the Interior) expanded rapidly, as Truman and Congress proved willing to fund massive studies and dam construction projects. Throughout the late 1940s Drury was kept busy on the one hand trying to keep Bureau of Reclamation surveyors out of national parks, and on the other overseeing the planning of national recreation areas around new reservoirs proposed by that bureau, as well as by the Army Corps of Engineers.

Since 1934 Conrad Wirth had been in charge of planning those new recreation areas in cooperation with the Bureau of Reclamation. In 1941 Drury and Wirth on behalf of the Park Service entered into an interbureau agreement with the Bureau of Reclamation to undertake a new kind of "recreational study" investigating the potential of the entire Colorado River basin for public recreation. The study, done with consulting landscape architect Frederick Law Olmsted Jr. and others, became a prototype for a series of multi-disciplinary "river basin studies" that documented and analyzed historical, archaeological, and recreational resources. They were funded mostly through the large budgets of the Bureau of Reclamation and the Army Corps of Engineers. Wirth was soon planning for the recreational potential of scores of new reservoirs being proposed by federal dam builders in the Central Valley of California, the Missouri, Colorado, and Columbia river basins, and other areas. Wirth used this opportunity to recover at least a portion of the national recreational planning role his department had enjoyed during the New Deal. The recreation areas planned around new reservoirs were, like many state parks of the 1930s, oriented toward outdoor recreation and facilities for boating, swimming, and automotive access. Drury and Wirth did not envision adding the majority of the new sites to the national park system, since many were not considered of "national significance." They were instead reprising the Park Service's role as an agency that cooperated with other branches of federal and local government to provide expertise in different types of recreational developments, including state parks and recreation areas. Wirth also rationalized his agency's involvement in dam projects, insisting that the Park Service was "in a better position to protect areas within the National Park System," since it could "keep abreast of plans and investigations" of the dam building agencies.[40] Since the river basin studies also included archaeological surveys of areas scheduled to be flooded, they were undertaken under the authority of the 1935 Historic Sites Act as well as the 1936 Park, Parkway, and Recreational-Area Study Act. By 1952 at least sixty reservoir and river basin reports had been completed under Wirth's supervision, and together they covered about a third of the total area of the United States. His New Deal ambitions still very much with him, Wirth insisted that his river basin studies should be only the beginning of a "new nation-wide study . . . [for a] park and recreation plan for the whole nation."[41]

But at the same time this important new role for the agency was being developed, Drury was also fighting federal dam proposals that would have affected Grand Canyon, Glacier, Mammoth Cave, Big Bend, Kings Canyon, and other national parks.[42] Despite the growing partnership with the dam building agencies, the pre-

vention of dam construction in national parks was one of the Park Service's oldest priorities. Since the battle over the Hetch Hetchy Valley in Yosemite thirty years earlier, national park advocates had vehemently resisted building reservoirs in existing national parks, although they were less opposed to adding new recreation areas to the national park system, even though such areas included reservoirs. The loss of the Hetch Hetchy Valley to a reservoir project in 1913 had been an impetus for the creation of the Park Service in 1916. During the 1920s Stephen Mather turned back dam proposals for Yellowstone and elsewhere in part by arguing that public enjoyment—of the kind his agency made possible—was a more valuable use for parklands. Drury undoubtedly had strong misgivings over the partnership with dam building agencies, as historian Richard West Sellars has shown.[43]

But while Drury successfully turned aside most of the dam proposals that would have affected national parks in the 1940s, one project in particular became a source of controversy. The events and issues that swirled around this project led to Drury's departure from the Park Service and helped shape the immediate political context for the planning and initiation of Mission 66. The Bureau of Reclamation's massive Colorado River Storage Project, a system of dams in the upper Colorado watershed, had at its center a large reservoir in Echo Park, a particularly scenic area of Dinosaur National Monument. Although Dinosaur was technically a monument and not a park, and although most park and wilderness advocates had never visited this remote region on the Utah-Colorado border at the confluence of the Green and Yampa rivers, the incursion of a dam into a unit of the national park system could not be allowed if the integrity of the system as a whole was to be protected. Several recent histories establish that the struggle over the proposed Echo Park dam influenced and even instigated the postwar environmental movement. Wilderness advocates, nonprofit outdoors clubs, scientists, magazine editors, and a broad range of other concerned individuals and groups all rallied around the threatened Echo Park, and in the process they permanently changed the politics of preservation.[44]

The relationship of the Park Service to this nascent environmental movement was troubled from the outset. In this case the trouble began by 1941, when the Colorado River basin study by Wirth and Olmsted had first been authorized through the interbureau agreement with the Bureau of Reclamation. When the study was finished in 1946, the authors recommended against transforming Echo Park into a reservoir and recreation area, stating that the plans would "deplorably alter . . . the wilderness qualities" of Dinosaur National Monument. They noted that the first duty of the Park Service was to make "the protection of the natural and archeological values of the area the controlling factors in administering it." But the report also allowed that the dam could be justified if it were "clearly shown . . . that it would be of greater benefit to the whole nation to develop the area for water storage and power than to retain it in a natural state," at least leaving a door open for future debate likely to occur in Congress. They also suggested that if the wilderness character of the monument would suffer on the one hand, "on the other hand . . . [the dam] would undoubtedly produce other recreational opportunities."[45]

The idea of accepting the construction of the dam (and effectively redesignating Dinosaur National Monument as a national recreation area) had been at least discussed by Park Service officials in the 1930s, leading Bureau of Reclamation engineers to develop surveys and plans during the 1940s under an assumption that the Park Service could be made to go along with their plans.[46] As partners in the planning for recreational land uses in the Colorado River basin, Drury and Wirth had allowed the investigations for the Echo Park project to proceed. This proved to be a tactical error. During the postwar period attitudes among wilderness advocates hardened against the dam, and the Park Service scrambled to revise its own stand on the issue. Drury and Wirth spoke out repeatedly against the dam in the late 1940s, but the plans had been allowed to go too far, and the project had built up strong political support. In 1950 Truman and Secretary of the Interior Chapman officially endorsed it. Once again, Drury was in a position not of shaping Park Service policy but of attempting to deal with the consequences of decisions made higher up in the Department of the Interior. In this case the resulting friction with Secretary Chapman led to Drury's resignation in 1951.[47]

The Echo Park dam proposal ultimately failed, but when it did it was because of the opposition of public and of private nonprofit environmental groups—the National Parks Association, the Sierra Club, and the Wilderness Society—not that of the Park Service. Drury's opposition to the Echo Park dam came too late and meant too little to the activists on the front-lines. Wilderness advocates learned to do without the Park Service in the Echo Park fight. The lesson carried over to their struggle for federal wilderness legislation, which the Park Service also did not support. The Echo Park dam was defeated in 1956, the same year a coalition of many of the same preservation groups introduced the first "wilderness bill" in Congress, later to become the 1964 Wilderness Act. It was also the same year that Conrad Wirth launched Mission 66, a radically different response to the postwar pressures on public lands. Nonprofit environmental groups and the Park Service both inaugurated eras of increased strength and great expansion in 1956. They were, however, headed on very different courses.

Newton Drury was the first Park Service director to encounter the complex postwar issues that to some degree have occupied park managers ever since. The vastly increased use of the park system, for example, and the reduced in-fluence and function of the Park Service within the federal bureaucracy both continued to challenge Drury's successors. Negotiations to renew concessioner contracts and secure new private investment for concession improvements became ever more difficult. Wilderness advocates and early environmentalists, while supportive of the general goals of the Park Service, often differed on key assumptions about the purposes of preservation, and therefore on specific policies for managing parks. The postwar social and demographic trends that precipitated many of these issues—such as population growth, automobile ownership, and low-density urbanization—only intensified in the 1950s. After Drury's departure for California in 1951, the "dilemma of our parks" that he had described did not dissipate but grew more ominous and intractable. This was the backdrop against which Conrad Wirth would organize and conduct Mission 66.

CHAPTER 2

CONRAD WIRTH AND POSTWAR "RECREATIONAL PLANNING"

In April 1951 Secretary of the Interior Oscar Chapman named Arthur E. Demaray, a longtime Park Service employee now near retirement, director of the Park Service. Demaray's appointment recognized his contributions as an assistant to every director since Stephen Mather. The choice also allowed Chapman to minimize the controversy caused by Newton Drury's departure. Opponents of the Echo Park dam seized upon Drury's resignation as an indication that Chapman was forcing the Park Service further into recreational development at the expense of its mandate to protect inviolate wilderness.[1] By abetting the transformation of Dinosaur National Monument into a national recreation area (or its equivalent), the Park Service would be allowing a pristine wilderness under its care to be destroyed by dam construction. Chapman probably already had Conrad Wirth in mind as Drury's replacement, but replacing Drury directly with Wirth—who was in charge of

recreational planning—would have been a further incitement to opponents of the Echo Park dam. In any case, Demaray retired that December, and Chapman then replaced him with Wirth as the sixth director of the agency.

If Chapman or anyone else thought Wirth would be amenable to the sacrifice of Dinosaur, he misconstrued not simply Wirth's position on the Echo Park controversy but his entire background and philosophy of park planning. Conrad Louis Wirth, known as "Connie" by his colleagues, was a longtime Park Service stalwart. He had been hired by Horace Albright in 1931 and spent his early career working in the Washington office, which then consisted of about twenty-five employees, including many "Mather men" such as Albright, Vint, Arno Cammerer, and Arthur Demaray. Wirth also knew many leading park planners and advocates through his father, Theodore, a well-known figure in the American park movement. Theodore Wirth was born in Switzerland in 1863 and emigrated to the United States in his twenties after studying landscape design and horticulture in Paris and London. In the 1880s he worked for Calvert Vaux as a gardener and arborist in Central Park, and later was supervisor of Riverside Park, also in New York. In 1894 he moved to Frederick Law Olmsted's hometown of Hartford, Connecticut, to run the municipal parks department there. He established his reputation as the "dean" of American park superintendents in Minneapolis, where he oversaw the management and expansion of the municipal park system from 1906 to 1935. Minneapolis was favored with a remarkable park system begun in the 1880s under the landscape architect Horace W. S. Cleveland. For almost thirty years Wirth oversaw the realization of what remains today one of the finest park systems in the country. His son was born in the superintendent's residence in Hartford's Elizabeth Park in 1899 and grew up in the superintendent's residence in Lyndale Park, Minneapolis.[2]

As an adolescent, Conrad Wirth attended military school in Wisconsin. From there he went on to study landscape architecture with his "father's choice of teachers," Frank A. Waugh, a landscape architect from Wisconsin who had established a landscape degree program at the Massachusetts Agricultural College (later the University of Massachusetts, Amherst) in 1903. Wirth was no more than an average student, but he maintained the strong interest in sports and other extracurricular activities that he had developed in military school. He graduated with a bachelor of science degree in landscape architecture in 1923 and moved to San Francisco, where he went to work for nurseryman Donald

McLaren, the son of John McLaren, the Scottish superintendent of Golden Gate Park, who was another close friend of his father. After two years of this apprenticeship, Wirth moved to New Orleans and started his own landscape architecture firm with a partner. The new business did well at first, mainly in the design of subdivisions for land developers. But the development boom soon turned to bust on the Gulf Coast and elsewhere, and by 1927 Wirth was out of business. At that point he again relied on his father's connections and moved to Washington, where Frederick Law Olmsted Jr. secured him a job with the National Capital Park and Planning Commission in 1928. In 1931 Albright offered him a transfer to the Park Service's Washington office, where Wirth became assistant director in charge of the Branch of Lands, or "chief land planner," in 1931.[3]

Wirth remained in the Washington office of the Park Service for the next thirty-three years, finally running the agency from 1951 until 1964, the longest tenure of any director before or since. But it was his first decade in Washington that shaped many of his future attitudes and policy decisions. Wirth was only one of what would soon be hundreds of landscape architects idled by the depression who would come to work for the Park Service. The transformation of the agency began in the spring of 1933, when Roosevelt introduced his idea for the mobilization of a "peacetime army." Roosevelt conceived of the CCC to conserve the human and natural resources of the nation at a time when unemployment among young men, and natural disasters such as the Dust Bowl drought, seemed to imperil both. The CCC was quickly organized, with the War Department, the Department of Labor, and other agencies all taking part and sharing the enormous costs. The conservation work itself was to be directed in national forests by the Forest Service, and in national, state, and some county and municipal parks by the Park Service.

In his position as chief land planner, Wirth had been in charge of investigating possible additions to the national park system for the previous two years. He now became the principal liaison to dozens of state governments, many of which had virtually no state parks, but which were rapidly acquiring land (at depression prices) in order to take advantage of the federal government's offer to develop them with CCC labor and funds. With the assistance of Herbert Evison, formerly the executive director of the National Conference on State Parks, Wirth oversaw and reviewed all planning, design, and construction undertaken by the Park Service's CCC state park program with "cooperating" local park agencies. Wirth maintained strong centralized control over the quality and design standards of the park developments rapidly undertaken all over the country. Park designers and construction superintendents, whether they were working for local agencies, the CCC, or directly for the Park Service, had their work reviewed by traveling Park Service inspectors, and ultimately by Wirth himself in Washington. Local agencies that did not meet the standards set by Wirth risked not having CCC camps and associated funding assigned to them. Hundreds of architects, engineers, and landscape architects worked in state park CCC camps as designers, supervisors, and foremen. By 1941 more than 560 state, county, and municipal parks had

Conrad Wirth in 1933. Photo by George A. Grant, NPS Historic Photo Collection.

been created or redeveloped by Wirth's program, in partnership with 140 state and local park agencies.[4]

The New Deal catapulted the Park Service into a national recreational planning and state park development agency, one that was to a considerable degree run by Wirth. The rapid expansion of budgets and activities required a regionalization of the agency. By 1935 there were eight state park "regions" within the Park Service, headed by regional directors who were mostly former state park officials.[5] In 1936 Cammerer consolidated his agency's CCC programs, bringing together Wirth's state park program and the national park CCC camps all under Wirth's control. That year Congress passed the Park, Parkway, and Recreational-Area Study Act (drafted under Wirth's direction), which expanded and legitimized the Park Service's role in national recreational planning in cooperation with state agencies. The act also authorized the Park Service to assemble a national plan for the recreational use of public lands in every state, using CCC funds and labor. The Land Planning Committee of the National Resources Board gave the Park Service responsibility to produce that agency's national recreation plan, *Recreational Use of Land in the United States*, which it published in 1938.[6] Wirth's prewar recreational planning activities culminated in 1941, when the Park Service published *A Study of the Park and Recreation Problem of the United States*, a report that summarized and analyzed recreational land use data collected over the previous eight years.[7] By 1940, when Drury arrived in Washington, Wirth had personally transformed the Park Service into a regionalized national planning organization, working with government partners in every state to coordinate the recreational use of federal and state lands. By the end of the New Deal, Wirth was a seasoned and effective bureaucrat with a personal reputation for strong leadership, political savvy, and an ability to impart idealism and enthusiasm to his agency's employees.

In the meantime, Thomas Vint, who was only five years older than Wirth and had been the

chief landscape architect of the Park Service since 1927, remained the agency's overall chief of planning and design. Vint was more involved in landscape and architectural design, which had always been his strength, rather than administration. Nevertheless, in 1933 he moved from San Francisco to Washington to head up a centralized Branch of Plans and Designs, which oversaw the depression-era work being done in the national parks themselves. Vint's former San Francisco "field office" became the "western division" of his design branch, under the supervision of his assistant, landscape architect William G. (Bill) Carnes. An "eastern division" was headed by another close friend of Vint's, architect Charles E. Peterson, who moved from Philadelphia to Washington.[8]

For those concerned that the Park Service was abandoning its mandate to preserve wilderness in favor of increased national park development and the design of state parks, national seashores, and national recreation areas, the regionalization, expansion, and diversification of the bureaucracy in the mid-1930s were ominous signs. The controversy that might have resulted from New Deal park development, however, was cut short by the entry of the United States into World War II. Following the attack on Pearl Harbor, Congress rapidly terminated the emergency spending measures that had been the basis of public works and conservation programs. Debates over the stewardship of park wilderness and the limits of recreational development would only be rekindled in earnest when Congress once again approved major national park appropriations, almost fifteen years later, under the banner of Mission 66.

Thomas Vint ca. 1945. Photo by George A. Grant, NPS Historic Photo Collection.

But in 1942 the most crucial question for the Park Service, and for Wirth in particular, was whether the CCC would be terminated or made a permanent agency. With Ickes's approval, Wirth had been drafting the legislative outlines for a permanent CCC since at least 1936. Roosevelt personally supported the idea and made detailed suggestions for the proposed organization.[9] The effort was cut off by the coming war. Already in 1940 CCC funds and equipment were being diverted to the military, and in 1942 Congress ordered the complete liquidation of the CCC camps. Wirth continued to work on legislation for a new CCC, however, and in 1943 he completed a comprehensive report for Ickes in which he documented the achievements of the CCC and recommended that a new "Conservation Corps" be created after the war. Persuasive and replete with organizational details for the proposed agency, Wirth's report made it clear that he would be the key figure in planning a permanent postwar youth conservation effort.[10] But like Ickes's ambitious plans for a unified federal "Department of Conservation," the idea of a permanent CCC never achieved congressional support. The departure of Ickes in 1946 ended the effort.

Part of the reason why Wirth worked so hard to institutionalize the CCC was that he hoped to preserve the basis of the Park Service's function as a national recreational planning agency. Although Wirth had support from Roosevelt, as well as Ickes and other key New Dealers, Drury did not support making the CCC a permanent force in the American landscape. Whether he had political concerns about the expansion of the federal government or merely wanted to continue to assure that his agency could "do no harm," Drury insisted in 1943 that the "unskilled labor" of the CCC was no longer needed and should be replaced by "private contractors" after the war.[11] By 1946, in any case, Wirth was engaged in dozens of river basin and reservoir studies, and so had found another source of bureaucratic support for his multistate recreational planning. But without a replacement for the CCC and other New Deal spending programs, the Park Service remained crippled. Faced with a bewildering new array of pressures on the parks, Drury was discovering that in its weakened position, his agency was forced to respond to policy being set elsewhere at the Department of the Interior—whether on park concessions or proposed dam projects—and was often unable to set its own course.

In 1950, after Truman and Secretary of the Interior Chapman endorsed the Echo Park dam, Drury decided that he would rather lose his job than preside over what promised to be the largest violation of the national park system since 1913. Under the circumstances, it was even more imperative for Wirth to find a way to oppose the dam as vigorously as he could. After all, he had overseen the plans for dozens of recreation areas around new reservoirs going back to the 1930s, and especially since 1941. The activists now fighting the Bureau of Reclamation's plans for Dinosaur could easily have perceived him as a collaborator who had undermined his own agency's duty to protect the integrity of the national park system. If for no other reason, Wirth's astute political sensibilities would have led him to oppose the Echo Park proposal. There were other, more personal reasons to demonstrate his opposition as well. Wirth needed to show that he understood the difference between appropriate recreational development and development that was out of place—that in fact became "deplorable"—when it inappropriately altered the character of a scenic or wilderness area. Wirth's entire philosophy of recreational planning depended on the ability to make such distinctions. He had summarized his methodology as early as 1935, when his state park CCC operations (and criticisms of them) were beginning to reach a peak. Parks should be considered in two categories, Wirth suggested, "conservation" and "recreation." The two types of parks might be separate or linked, or "one might even completely surround the other, forming a multiple-use area"; but the two types of landscape needed to be separate and distinct, since the wrong kind of recreational development would destroy the value of an area set aside for conservation. To know where recreational developments were needed and appropriate, extensive statistical, demographic, and natural resource information of the type that filled his river basin plans needed to be gathered, analyzed, and used as the basis for informed decisions.[12]

Since the mid-1930s, wilderness advocates had attacked Wirth's recreational planning as nothing more than "overdevelopment," or indiscriminate destruction of pristine scenic areas. They insisted that the Park Service could not develop recreation areas and also be an adequate steward of wilderness. If Wirth were to abet the destruction of Echo Park, it would be impossible to refute such claims. The credibility of his entire approach to park planning and management was at stake. Since the publication of his and Olmsted's 1946 report on the Colorado River basin, Wirth had maintained that Dinosaur National Monument was not appropriate for development as a recreation area. When he became Park Service director in December 1951, he continued to speak out against the dam in numerous articles and at public meetings. He did not shrink from traveling to Vernal, Utah, and other communities in the area that fiercely supported the dam and were outraged at his opposition. As the new Park Service director, Wirth was criticized in Utah and by the project's backers in Congress. But he was not fired. In fact, Chapman was already reconsidering his 1950 decision to support the dam, in part because of the strong negative response it had generated from an increasingly broad coalition of opponents. Wirth's opposition to the dam was longstanding and the result of deeply held convictions, but his timing was also fortuitous. He was able to reinforce his credibility with conservation groups at a critical moment without suffering consequences at the Department of the Interior.[13]

Frederick Law Olmsted Jr. was another influential opponent of the Echo Park dam proposal. Olmsted's credentials as a scenic preservationist were impressive and unique. Born in 1870, the younger Olmsted had grown up in his famous father's office and home in Brookline, Massachusetts, and had participated in major landscape design and park planning projects at an early age. He had been an influential opponent of the Hetch Hetchy reservoir proposal in 1913, citing his father's 1865 plan for Yosemite Valley in defense of the irreplaceable value of such scenery.

At the 1950 congressional hearings on the fate of Echo Park, Olmsted could speak with authority on the superlative character of the scenery: he was one of only two opponents testifying who had actually visited the remote site, which he had done twice in the 1940s while in his seventies.[14] The relationship between Olmsted and Wirth was clearly important to both. Wirth owed his career to the elder landscape architect, and like Vint and others at the Park Service, he often looked to him as a direct link to Olmstedian tradition and as an unimpeachable authority on park management. For his part, Olmsted had a profound interest in the Park Service going back to 1916, when he had drafted the key portions of the legislation that created the agency. Through his work as a frequent consultant, as a member of the Yosemite National Park Board of Expert Advisors, and as a mentor to both Wirth and Vint, he continued to influence the practice of Park Service landscape architecture and park planning until his death in 1957.

Olmsted's letter of condolence and encouragement to his accomplished young protégé was thus written at a time when the Echo Park controversy was reaching a crucial point. The letter emphasized that parks were set aside and preserved for a purpose: to allow public enjoyment without permitting any use that would compromise scenery or wildlife. At Echo Park, Olmsted and Wirth were faced with a classic "impairment" (to quote Olmsted's contribution to the 1916 Park Service legislation) of a national park: a vast reservoir that would destroy the dramatic landscape of desert canyons and unusual geologic features. While a recreation area could be developed around such a reservoir, by far the

Frederick Law Olmsted Jr.
National Archives, RG 79.

more appropriate choice for a unit of the national park system would be to leave the park in its "natural condition" by devising a "master plan" for public use. Such park development might include carefully sited roads, trails, campgrounds, administrative facilities, and possibly overnight accommodations; but it would not necessarily constitute an impairment if the facilities were properly designed and limited to specific areas. In fact, development as a park would be the best assurance that any proposals for true impairments, such as private resort development, dam construction, mining, logging, or grazing, for example, would be condemned by the public, and therefore by Congress. Park development could preserve places "unimpaired," in other words, "for the people."

This overall philosophy of what constituted an "impairment" of a park landscape and what it meant to "preserve" landscapes for "public enjoyment" can be characterized as Olmstedian theory. Frederick Law Olmsted Jr. reiterated this ideology of public park making, which was first described by his father in his 1865 recommendations for Yosemite Valley. This was the professional theory that guided Wirth throughout his career. But neither Olmsted nor Wirth recognized at the time that extractive industries and dam construction (Echo Park notwithstanding) would not remain the primary threats to national parks in postwar American society. As the numbers of visitors to national parks continued to climb, the presence of the public itself would itself increasingly be perceived as a devastating form of impairment. The idea of preservation for the sake of public enjoyment became, for many, a sinister paradox. The theoretical basis of the U.S. park movement was shifting in the 1950s. The results of this change were evident by the early 1960s, as a rising generation of advocates and politicians ushered in an era of "New Conservation" along with legislation such as the 1964 Wilderness Act and the 1966 Historic Preservation Act. If this change had been under way to some degree since the 1920s, its most dramatic moments coincided, and often conflicted, with the implementation of Mission 66.

To understand the influence of what would soon be described as the "environmental movement" on the one hand and the contrasting philosophical basis of the Mission 66 program and postwar national recreational planning on the other, both must be seen in the context of the dramatic changes occurring in the nation's landscape and society at the time. Between 1940 and 1960 the United States grew from 132 million to 180 million people, with virtually the entire increase occurring in cities and, especially, postwar "suburbs." Growth was particularly evident in California and the other ten western states, where the total population doubled from 14 million to 28 million. During the same period, individual average annual earnings rose nationally from $1,300 to $4,700. A larger, more affluent, and more urban population indulged an unrelenting appetite for outdoor recreation and new automobiles, often in combination. Americans spent almost $4 billion on recreation in 1940 but more than $14 billion in 1955. Passenger car registrations rose from 27 million to 52 million during the same years.[15] Leisure time steadily increased as the five-day workweek became standard, while the proportion of income spent on housing and other necessities decreased from 33 percent in 1947 to 23 percent in 1967.[16] As the opportunities for discretionary travel and recreation increased even beyond the growth in population, enormous new pressures on rural scenic areas, mountains, beaches, lakes, and rivers—any sites that could be used for vacation or resort purposes—were inevitable. The demographic trends of the postwar period would have meant great changes for the national park system whether the Mission 66 program had been put forward or not.

The fate of the national parks, as public parks, was linked to the size, character, and habits of the public that used them and (it was hoped) supported congressional policies and budgets that kept them viable. But the parks also formed an integral part of a larger, distinctly modern American landscape that was, as a whole, also changing rapidly. Again, national parks could not have escaped change during this period, as sprawling urbanization and the interstate highway system produced entire new geographic contexts for them. Better roads, faster cars, and growing cities in the Southwest, the Rocky Mountains, and on the West Coast made many western national parks almost as easy to reach as eastern parks. Postwar patterns of urbanization and transportation made the entire national park system far more accessible than it had ever been before. National park development constituted a part—as did tracts of residential development, shopping centers, and highway construction—of an overall modern landscape that was beginning to reach its ultimate extent across the entire continent during the postwar decades. In this sense, the history of the modernization of national park landscapes must be seen in the context of the modernization of the American landscape generally, including contemporary trends in housing subdivisions, commercial and corporate "centers," and interstate highway engineering.

Several histories analyze the most salient aspect of postwar U.S. landscape history: the "suburbanization" of the nation.[17] The vast expansion of cities during this period assumed low-density patterns that quickly took them into surrounding towns, counties, and unincorporated areas. Ubiquitous, sometimes vast subdivisions of detached single-family tract housing covered entire regions. The resulting communi-

ties were politically and physically decentralized, and they perplexed planners, who coined neologisms—conurbation, megalopolis, sprawl, metro city—for this expanded form of the American metropolis. Low-density patterns of urbanization were hardly a novelty in the United States, but the postwar suburb reached an entirely new scale. Housing demand had built up during the years of the depression and World War II, and returning veterans and their families created an insatiable market. Builders responded, and the great majority of the houses being built were outside the political limits of major cities. Like many other cities, New York and San Francisco, for example, actually lost population between 1950 and 1960, but their standard metropolitan statistical areas (or SMSA, another new coinage) gained 12 percent and 24 percent, respectively.[18] The expanded metropolis became a type of city never seen before. The scale of residential building dwarfed historical precedent. Well over 1 million housing starts were recorded every year beginning in 1946, with 1.5 million each in 1954 and 1955. The total value of residential structures (in constant 1994 dollars) rose from $163 billion in 1940 to $714 billion in 1960. By that year, 43 percent of the housing units in the United States were less than twenty years old.[19]

The historic postwar housing boom was fueled by the intense postwar housing shortage. Twenty years of low housing production, 15 million returning veterans, and an increase in marriage and birth rates resulted in many families "doubled up" in houses or apartments, or living with relatives. The shortage of housing in national parks mirrored a national condition, and was particularly comparable to the situation on U.S. Army and other military bases all over the country. In 1949 *Life* magazine documented "scandalous" substandard and overcrowded living conditions for military families. That year Congress acted with unprecedented legislation that created a partnership with private industry to build new military housing.[20] A shortage of Park Service staff housing figured prominently in the postwar "crisis" in the national parks as well. As Mission 66 got under way, Congress proved willing to make direct appropriations for park housing, as it did for military housing, and Wirth finally was able to address the long-standing need. The design and construction of Mission 66 houses in national parks would be determined, as it had for the military, by federal requirements and by the economics of the postwar building industry. Not surprisingly, Park Service architects turned to standard plans for two- and three-bedroom ranch houses, built with materials and construction technology readily available and familiar to local builders. Standard plans, streamlined construction techniques, prefabricated components, and flexibility in materials were absolutely necessary if national park housing was to be built within the set cost per unit Congress required. The Park Service adopted the ranch house for many of the same reasons it had earlier used the bungalow type: it represented an achievable and efficient standard for housing, and it embodied what occupants were likely to perceive as a desirable setting for the conduct of modern family life. But while the bungalow of the 1920s fit in with the rustic imagery of Vint's master plans, the Mission 66 ranch house of the 1950s announced a new approach to park planning intended to respond to the changing social and geographic contexts of the parks.

Other aspects of postwar suburbanization affected Mission 66 and national recreational planning and design as much as the proliferation of tract subdivisions and changes in the residential construction industry. As people abandoned older cities for new communities on the urban periphery, they did not leave the city behind so much as they brought it with them. While earlier suburbs had been residential enclaves populated mainly by a professional or business class that commuted to a central city, postwar patterns of urbanization dispersed not only residential neighborhoods but entire industries, corporate headquarters, and vast retail complexes as well. The result was not an enclave apart from the city but an extension of it: postwar suburbs included places to live, work, shop, and enjoy leisure activities—the components of a city—set in urbanized landscapes that covered entire regions.

As migrating Americans turned their cities inside out, one of the first requirements for their new way of life was the establishment of retail and commercial centers that could serve a dispersed population. By the early 1950s planners and developers were building hundreds of what the architect Victor Gruen called "the new building type . . . shopping centers."[21] While a few early examples of suburban retail complexes had been built since the 1920s (and even earlier), in 1950 there were still only around one hundred mostly small shopping centers in the United States. But as retailers followed their customers out to their new tract house communities, more than 7,500 shopping centers were built between 1950 and 1965.[22] Developers located and planned shopping centers based on the assumption that the great majority of customers would arrive in their own automobiles. The automobile brought great mobility and personal freedom to millions in the postwar years. But the convenience of the private car evaporated if destinations were not convenient to major roads and equipped with abundant parking. The successful model for shopping centers called for parking areas for thousands of cars, closely juxtaposed with but completely segregated from a purely pedestrian shopping environment. If widespread automobile ownership made the shopping center possible (even necessary), the experience of shopping once out of the car was calculated for convenient walking. "One-stop shopping" and the pedestrian mall were necessitated, ironically, by the near total dependence on the automobile in daily patterns of living. Once in the shopping center, people could expect to find a full range of products and services in an efficient, compact plan, completely unhindered by the automobile traffic that was so much a part of the rest of their lives. To address the sheer size of new retail buildings and parking structures, architects borrowed from industrial architecture and employed structural solutions, such as pre-stressed concrete and prefabrication, that reduced costs and construction time. Purpose, economics, structural systems, and contemporary tastes all contributed to the design of shopping centers that, from a distance, had the appearance of giant boxes, cylinders, or other abstract geometric forms.[23]

Retailers were not the only businesspeople to see the advantages of moving from older downtown districts to the urbanizing edges of metropolitan areas. By the early 1950s many corporations had decided to abandon their office and industrial space in downtown buildings in order to relocate nearer to the residential areas where many of their employees now lived. The automobile, according to one architect in 1947, "made the skyscraper obsolete." Low horizontal buildings set in large campuses on the edge of the city were a more desirable and more efficient alternative.[24] In 1952 *Fortune* magazine asked, "Should management move to the country?"[25] Many corporations, some experiencing periods of enormous profits and growth, had already answered the question.[26] By 1951 the Connecticut General Life Insurance Company had decided to relocate five miles outside Hartford in a starkly modernist headquarters building, designed by Gordon Bunshaft and completed in 1957. It was set in what had been until then a farm; the surrounding landscape was redeveloped to resemble a scaled-down eighteenth-century English private park. General Foods also decided to move, in 1951, from Manhattan to outlying Westchester County. The choice was a result of corporate growth as well as considerations of cost and employee convenience.[27] A shift in architectural style accompanied the moves; even insurance companies gave up the Colonial style for modernist architectural imagery. Perhaps the most important example of all was the General Motors Technical Center, outside Detroit, designed by Eero Saarinen and landscape architect Thomas Church, two leading figures of American modernist design. The stunning structures and geometricized layout of the campus created a sensation, from the publication of initial designs in 1945 through the completion of the project about ten years later.[28] Soon there were scores of examples of "the corporate neighbor in the suburb," relocated to "corporate parks," which, like contemporary retail complexes, featured easy arterial road access, extensive parking, and modernist architectural design. Big business, getting bigger every year, "moved to the country" along with so much of the rest of American society.[29]

The dramatic commercial success of shopping centers and the decision by many corporations to relocate their headquarters to the outer city significantly influenced American architectural and landscape design in general in the 1950s. Planners, designers, and others in the construction business were inevitably drawn to the place where so much new development was occurring: the suburban edges of metropolitan areas. New commissions, programs, and clients, as well as new construction materials, techniques, and economics, all were bound to change architectural and landscape design. At the Park Service, professional staff could not ignore these trends and remain effective, or even competent. As in any other design office, they worked within the social, economic, and technical contexts of their day. The proliferation of the automobile, the expansion of suburban cities, and the availability of labor-saving construction technology all affected proposed development in the national parks as much as construction anywhere else. Mission 66 needed to be planned within the limits of what would be acceptable and affordable in the eyes of Con-

gress and the public, with the participation of available architectural consultants and construction contractors. It could hardly be surprising that the centerpiece of Mission 66 would be a major new type of park facility: a large, centralized building, modernist in its architectural inspiration, with easy highway access, generous parking, and "one-stop" convenience. The new concept had many names at first, reflecting its complex, unified program. In 1956 Conrad Wirth personally insisted on the designation that he felt best captured its essential purpose and character, and it became known as the "visitor center."[30]

No element of the postwar landscape more directly indicated the connections between national parks and the changing geography around them than the development of automotive highways. No other aspect of the postwar landscape more directly influenced the condition and fate of national parks or the priorities and structure of Wirth's program. Parks and roads together already had a long and intertwined history of federal policy and funding. In 1916, the same year Congress created the Park Service, it passed the Federal-Aid to Highways Act, which authorized $75 million for state highway improvements and initiated the commitment to public highway funding that continues to the present day.[31] Mather and Albright began lobbying for a similar level of commitment to improve national park roads, which were not covered by the federal highway money because they were noncommercial (roads in national forests did allow commercial traffic and so were included). In 1924 Congress responded, authorizing $7.5 million for national park roads over three years, almost doubling the total existing Park Service budget for 1925 to more than $3 million. Albright, in particular, had succeeded in linking the need for national park development to the federal aid highway program, bringing his agency's appropriations to a whole new level. He argued that the situation in the parks had become untenable because improved state highways and national forest roads made it easier than ever before to drive *to* national parks but not *in* them. The thousands of visitors arriving by car found that road conditions deteriorated—sometimes dramatically—as soon as they entered a park. Inevitably these tourists demanded not only improved park roads but also campgrounds, comfort stations, and other infrastructure for traveling and camping by automobile. Mather and Albright presented the modernization of the national park system in the 1920s as a necessary adjunct to the subsidization of the nation's highways. They effectively, if unofficially, linked the relative levels of federal highway spending to national park budgets.[32] As federal aid to highways increased in the 1920s, Park Service construction budgets also grew. During the New Deal, highway and park improvements ranked first and second in total dollars spent on public works construction. But the implications and potential of this association between federal highway and federal park development were not fully realized until 1956, when Congress passed unprecedented federal aid legislation funding the interstate highway system, and Conrad Wirth responded the same year with his Mission 66 proposal.

Throughout the twentieth century, the federal government developed both highways and parks in tandem, as the two principal components of a modern national public landscape. In both cases Congress became involved as soon as Americans took to the road in automobiles. The Bureau of Public Roads (BPR), established in 1918 through a reorganization of the old Office of Public Roads, subsequently set the engineering standards and most of the policy for how the federal aid highway program was implemented. In 1924 the BPR formed an important partnership with the Park Service, which allowed the parks agency to impose its own aesthetic considerations on road construction in the national parks while at the same time relying on BPR engineers to ensure that new roads were well engineered and that their construction was well supervised. The interbureau agreement resulted in a series of national park roads that combined the landscape architect's concern for park preservation and the experience of scenery with the engineer's requirements for high construction standards. Congress was also more willing to make park appropriations knowing that the BPR would be an active partner in managing the construction of roads such as Going-to-the-Sun Road in Glacier National Park, Trail Ridge Road in Rocky Mountain National Park, and the Zion–Mt. Carmel Road in Zion National Park.[33]

By the mid-1930s the New Deal had poured hundreds of millions of dollars into highway construction, and the BPR, in partnership with state highway agencies, had overseen the construction of a numbered system of "primary" roads across the country. These were the roads that brought unprecedented millions of automotive tourists to the national parks. But the BPR also began to encounter criticism, much as the Park Service did at about this time. In the case of the nation's highways, however, some critics felt that the BPR had done too little, not too much, to accommodate the automobile. The increased number of automobiles on the road and the high speed at which they traveled were already making even the federal aid highways obsolete. Two-lane highways engineered for speeds of 30 miles per hour, without limited access (meaning that cars could enter and exit at many curb cuts along the road), were unsafe for larger numbers of heavier vehicles that could travel at 50 to 70 miles per hour. In urban areas the national system had done little to ameliorate chronic traffic congestion, which worsened everywhere as the number of car and truck registrations climbed.

By the late 1930s many planners and elected officials favored dramatic proposals for urban expressways and interstate toll roads that effectively bypassed the BPR. They were aware of the new "superhighway" autobahns in Germany and came to believe that a system of express highways—with intersecting traffic carried over or under the roadway and access limited by entrance and exit ramps—would be the only means of alleviating the dangerous and congested condition of American roads. Several states began their own plans for toll-financed superhighways, the Pennsylvania Turnpike (first section opened 1940) being the first, and the New York State Throughway (first section opened 1948) the most ambitious.[34] The popularity and economic success of the early turnpikes and throughways suggested that a national system of such roads would be heavily used. In 1944 Congress held hearings that historian

Bruce Seely calls "the most comprehensive discussion on roads in this country to that date."[35] The result was the Federal-Aid Highway Act of 1944, which authorized a forty thousand–mile "national system of interstate highways," to be financed half by the federal government and half by the states.

The proposed locations of the interstate system were established by 1947, but the exact means of funding construction was not yet determined. Other priorities of the Truman administration, particularly military involvement in Korea, delayed the federal commitment that would be needed to complete the superhighway system. A national consensus for highway improvement existed by the early 1950s, but it was far from clear exactly what to do about it.[36] In the meantime, phenomenal numbers of new cars and trucks were being put on the road. By the late 1940s American highways—like American national parks—were generally perceived as critically overcrowded and in need of dramatic expansion and improvement. Highways and parks were overcrowded for the same reasons: more Americans than ever before could afford to buy cars and did, and more Americans chose to live in a manner that made the use of automobiles essential. By 1955 more than 60 million motor vehicles were registered in the United States, double the number in 1945.[37] But the capacity of the nation's roads, including national park roads, had not doubled or even increased significantly in many areas.

The truce in Korea and a postwar downturn in the economy, in addition to the rising numbers of trucks and automobiles on American roads, made the reorganization of the federal aid highway program a high priority for Dwight D. Eisenhower when he assumed office in 1953. As a former general, Eisenhower understood the power of modern highways to move people and goods. He also strongly believed that improved transportation—specifically the construction of a new interstate highway system—would be the foundation of stable economic growth and widespread prosperity in the United States for decades to come. But the cost would be great, and the congressional politics surrounding highway legislation were complex and easily misjudged. In 1954 Eisenhower asked an old friend and colleague, former general Lucius D. Clay, to head an advisory committee to make recommendations on how to shape highway policy. In January 1955 Clay's committee reported to Congress that a "national highway program" of limited-access superhighways would require a $25 billion commitment by Congress in order to cover a 90 percent share of construction costs over the next ten years. Clay urged that the federal share of the bill be financed through the sale of bonds, to be liquidated by the proceeds of the federal gasoline tax. Other highway planners and advocates lobbied for a system financed by tolls. Congress considered many different funding and highway planning strategies over the next year and a half. In its 1956 federal aid highway legislation, Congress finally decided to create a "highway trust fund," separate from the rest of the federal budget, financed by setting aside proceeds from an increased gasoline tax solely for that purpose. The Federal-Aid Highway Act of 1956 also abandoned the typical pattern of annual or biennial highway authorizations and instead authorized $25 billion over the next ten years to cover 90

percent of the construction costs of what it described as the "National System of Interstate and Defense Highways."[38]

The interstate highway legislation of 1956 initiated what is often characterized as the largest and most expensive public works project in history. No federal policy or law since the 1785 Federal Land Ordinance had as great an impact on the American landscape. Rural regions of the country became less isolated, while entire city neighborhoods were demolished as "expressways" were routed directly through them, hastening the already unbridled movement of people and businesses to the suburbs. The interstates altered the demographics of the entire nation, as California and the Sunbelt cities of the South and Southwest grew around the framework of the new highways. The interstate highways stimulated the economy to an even greater degree than Eisenhower could have imagined. As moving goods by truck became cheaper and more flexible, freight costs declined, and businesses were able to relocate to more advantageous locations, whether just outside town or across the country. Few aspects of American life and landscape would be unaffected by the combination of widespread automobile ownership and a national system of superhighways on which to drive them.

If parks and roads were two related aspects of the modern topography taking shape across the continent, it followed that the unprecedented federal road building would affect national parks in particular. Park Service officials, including Wirth and Vint, knew firsthand how federal aid highway modernization had affected the park system in the 1920s and 1930s. They could not have missed the significance, for their own efforts, of the debates leading up to the 1956 highway legislation. The interstate highway plans demanded that Wirth and the Park Service react, just as Horace Albright had responded in 1924 to the original federal aid program. To a significant degree, Mission 66 was that new response. Even its overall concept and bureaucratic structure were influenced by the interstate highway debate. In his memoirs, Wirth describes how, in order to break the cycle of inadequate annual appropriations, "one weekend in February 1955" he was trying to imagine "what Congress wanted to hear."[39] Lucius Clay's report, titled *A Ten-Year Highway Program,* had been submitted to Congress the month before.[40] Although Wirth does not mention Clay's proposal or interstate highways in general, the essence of the Mission 66 proposal was also to present a massive ten-year modernization program that would be conceived outside the traditional scope of annual budget authorizations. In the case of Mission 66, however, Wirth would not prepare legislation to be debated in Congress; he simply described a policy initiative to be approved administratively by the secretary of the interior, and ultimately by President Eisenhower himself. Once the outlines of the program were approved, Mission 66 became a means to persuade Congress to increase Park Service budgets greatly over an extended period. But since Mission 66 was not based on new legislation, such as the Federal-Aid Highway Act of 1956, it did not actually entail a multiyear authorization of funds, and certainly not a "trust fund" of dedicated tax receipts. Despite its reputation as a ten-year development program, Mission 66 would be accomplished through—and

would remain subject to—the annual congressional appropriations process.

Mission 66 was not just a response to the emerging Federal-Aid Highway Act, although the proposals leading to that legislation influenced the timing and structure of Wirth's initiative. As Wirth considered the postwar "dilemma" of the parks and their changing geographic setting, he also faced strident and widespread dissatisfaction with what many considered the degenerating quality of the national park experience. By 1955 public anger over the conditions in national parks had reached a crescendo. An entire journalistic genre had emerged, as dozens of reporters and editorialists decried the "shocking truth" about the parks. The postwar criticism really began as a continuation of some of the "purist" assertions of the 1930s: the parks were being destroyed by overuse and automotive tourism. But in the early 1950s this criticism was often supported, not denied, by Park Service officials. Articles such as "Yosemite's Beauty Fast Disappearing," by *Los Angeles Times* writer Martin Litton (who was also a board member of the National Parks Association) appeared in large-circulation magazines and newspapers and quickly found a receptive public. Writing in his 1952 article "Yosemite can't take it any more," Litton quoted the park's superintendent, Carl P. Russell, suggesting that "the natural appeal of the valley . . . will be gone in another fifty years" as a result of increasing numbers of tourists.[41] Another National Parks Association Member, Paul Shepherd Jr., insisted that "something was amiss" in the way the public was using parks. Shepherd bemoaned the commercialization and rapid pace of park visits, and felt that "a large majority of visitors [were] unaware of the peculiar meaning . . . of the parks." The increasingly affluent "American tourist," in constant search for novelty and leisure activities, was described, in terms previously reserved for dam builders and loggers, as a powerful and destructive threat. Shepherd did not think that more money for parks was the answer. "More money to handle more people" would only mean "greater pressure" on parks. He concluded, "Time has shown our parks to have a maximum carrying capacity and intrinsic qualities which render an indiscriminate recreational policy obsolete."[42]

But these opinions urging more "discriminating" approaches to park planning (published typically in *National Parks Magazine* and *Living Wilderness*) soon were drowned out by articles in magazines with far greater readership. And for commentators such as Bernard DeVoto, more money definitely was part of the solution to the postwar park dilemma. A western historian and novelist, and one of the most influential columnists of his day, DeVoto was originally from Ogden, Utah. As a leading opponent of the Echo Park dam, he had become a national voice on western conservation issues. His essay "Let's Close the National Parks," which appeared in his *Harper's* magazine column, "The Easy Chair," in 1953, incited outrage among a large and diverse group of readers. Echoing much of the reasoning Newton Drury had laid out four years earlier, DeVoto insisted that "a lack of money has now brought our national park system to the verge of crisis." Perhaps less concerned with whether an increasingly disaffected and angry public fully appreciated the "peculiar meaning" of the parks, he noted that campgrounds were "slums," roads

and trails dangerous, and staff housing "antiques or shacks" that would "produce an egg shortage if you kept chickens in them." Congress had asked the Park Service to operate "a big plant on a hot-dog-stand budget," and as a result the parks were "beginning to erode away." DeVoto was sure that Congress would not appropriate what he considered adequate funds ($250 million over five years) to address the crisis, and therefore there was only one alternative: "The national park system must be temporarily reduced to a size for which Congress is willing to pay." He urged that Yellowstone, Yosemite, Grand Canyon, and Rocky Mountain national parks be closed, and that the army patrol them until they could safely be reopened. Perhaps then an outraged public would finally bring the "nationally disgraceful situation to the really serious attention of the Congress which is responsible for it."[43]

Over the next two years, other major magazines such as the *Saturday Evening Post* and *Reader's Digest* investigated conditions in national parks and published feature articles that stressed overcrowding and inadequate facilities. But the articles did not blame the Park Service; in fact they almost always cited the unselfish dedication of park staff attempting to work under impossible conditions. Unlike earlier critiques, which were aimed at Park Service policy, the press that followed DeVoto's column blamed Congress for not giving the agency enough funds to do its job. Park superintendents—or often Wirth himself—were interviewed and provided much of the information for these articles, and it was clear that the Park Service did not regret this kind of negative publicity. But a decidedly different popular image of the national parks was taking shape in the years that immediately preceded Mission 66. "Make sure you are prepared for almost anything in the way of personal discomfort, annoyance, and even danger," warned *Travel* magazine, which suggested that $500 million would be needed over five years to bring the parks out of their "slum-like depths."[44] The *Saturday Evening Post* suggested that "the people are wearing out the scenery," while *Reader's Digest* described a "perversion" of the national park idea in Yosemite Valley. The popular media had never before described the national parks in such harsh terms. The overcrowding and deterioration of developed areas were also presented as an indicator of the condition of the parks overall. The poor condition of the frontcountry, in other words, was usually not considered separately from the ecological health of the backcountry. The biological health of the parks rarely caught the attention of journalists at the time. When they described the parks as "eroding away," they were referring to dangerous roads and trails, slum-like campgrounds, and overcrowded restaurants and hotels. In fact, in many parks, which had yet to experience the effects of the "backpack boom" of the next decade, the backcountry was probably not as devastated as the frontcountry experience suggested. Magazine articles appearing in 1954 and 1955, however, claimed that "human erosion" caused by rising numbers of visitors and low Park Service budgets was "destroying the parks," without making such a distinction. In almost every case, the articles suggested that massive park budget increases should be made to pay for road repairs, campground development, and other construction to better accommodate the growing numbers of visitors and cars. The estimates for the total cost of such a modernization of the system steadily rose from DeVoto's $250 million to $600 million, estimated for addressing the "backlog" of needed park development by 1954.[45]

Some authors also suggested that a complete reorientation of Park Service policy should accompany increased appropriations for modernization and construction. *Reader's Digest* argued for eliminating "resort activities," including many overnight accommodations, and getting back to the "traditional policy and functions" of the Park Service, which implied fewer "amusements" and better-preserved opportunities for more reflective, direct appreciation of scenery away from roads and hotels. The *Saturday Evening Post* stressed the reform of concession contracts as a big part of the answer, noting that Wirth had already secured better terms and increased capital investments from concessioners since becoming director in 1951.[46] For both of these articles, Wirth clearly was supplying estimates of the "backlog" of capital investment and suggesting his own ideas for policy initiatives such as concession reform. He was quoted extensively in these and other articles, and the *Saturday Evening Post* included a short biography of Wirth and a description of his efforts to keep the system together despite congressional indifference. Wirth himself popularized certain characterizations—such as the parks' being "loved to death"—to describe a "seemingly hopeless situation."[47]

Wirth may not have personally orchestrated the media interest in national parks, but he successfully used it to shape the public debate between 1953 and 1955 on the condition of the parks. Most authors disturbed about the future of the system wondered why Congress would not make larger appropriations, not whether some sort of limit should be imposed on the number of park visitors. A 1955 article titled "Crisis in Our Parks" followed a familiar formula, deploring the overuse and crowded condition of public facilities and then laying the blame on Congress for failing to pay for more development. Wirth's 1953 testimony to the House appropriations subcommittee was quoted at length: "It is hard for me . . . to understand why during times of prosperity; times of great advancement in our economic conditions; times of advancement in our standard of living, yes, in times when individuals are getting so much social and economic benefit out of their great scenic and historic treasures, we are unable to get even the bare necessities to protect these treasures. Treasures that in themselves play an important part in our progress as a nation."[48] In his first years as director, Wirth succeeded in depicting the postwar crisis in the national park system largely as one of inadequate funding, not a case of too many visitors. In the process he also enhanced his own image as a dedicated and disinterested public servant fighting against congressional apathy. The magazine writers who followed Bernard DeVoto's lead might have found reason to condemn the Park Service leadership, but they ended up portraying a dedicated agency facing imposing challenges with too few resources.

The relationship between the public and the national parks, and the public's expectations and perceptions of the Park Service, were shifting in the mid-1950s. Beginning in 1953 the po-

litical context in which the Park Service operated was changing decisively as well. The Cold War, the Korean War, and other dramatic international events of the period had prevented national parks from becoming a central concern for the Truman administration, and Truman showed little interest in conservation issues in any case. The Eisenhower administration brought its own political priorities to the Department of the Interior. Wirth was one of the few Interior agency heads to be retained when Eisenhower took office in 1953; he was described by the new secretary of the interior, James Douglas McKay, as one of the officials who gave government service "the prestige it deserves."[49] But if McKay felt that the Park Service's expertise and tradition put the directorship above partisan considerations, he nevertheless immediately appointed members of his staff to a "management study committee" to recommend a complete reorganization of the agency. McKay admitted that the parks were underfunded, but he also believed that reorganizing the bureaucracy could "increase efficiency" and so alleviate some problems in the parks without substantial budget increases.[50]

In December, McKay's study committee recommended that the Park Service reduce the size of the Washington and regional offices and decentralize authority for management decisions to park superintendents. By February, Wirth had an approved plan for the Washington office that reduced it slightly in size. In May he issued "delegation orders" describing the increased authority of the regional directors and park superintendents in making management decisions for the parks.[51] These measures appear to have had a minimal effect on Park Service operations, though they did comply with the administration's desire to reduce the size of government. But Wirth also used the reorganization as an opportunity to consolidate his own authority in the areas that mattered most to him. The most significant provisions of the 1954 reorganization reduced the design and construction staff and moved them out of the four regional offices into two new "branch offices of design and construction," soon known as the Western Office of Design and Construction (WODC), in San Francisco, and the Eastern Office of Design and Construction (EODC) in Philadelphia. This effectively returned the Park Service to the configuration of design offices it had had before the agency was regionalized in the 1930s. The entire 1954 reorganization, in fact, can be seen as part of a broader effort to dismantle federal bureaucracies, such as the regionalized Park Service design offices, which had been created to serve the New Deal. The idea of centralizing the design and construction staff of the Park Service, however, had not originated with McKay's study committee. Such a reorganization had actually been advocated for some time by Thomas Vint. Vint's position as "chief of design and construction" in Washington was greatly strengthened in 1954 as he assumed from the regional directors the supervision of agency design staff, now relocated in the WODC and EODC. The new organizational chart recalled the San Francisco and Philadelphia "field offices" that Vint had supervised from San Francisco between 1927 and 1933.[52] Sanford J. "Red" Hill headed the new WODC in San Francisco, while Edward S. Zim-

mer was chief of the EODC in Philadelphia. Like Vint, both men were landscape architects and had long experience with the Park Service, as did so many of the agency's planners and designers of the period. They now answered directly to Wirth through Vint rather than through the four regional directors.[53] If the reorganization purportedly reduced centralized bureaucracy, it also consolidated Vint's, and therefore Wirth's, direct control over planning and design in the parks. Once again Wirth had shown his bureaucratic ability to thrive under potentially threatening circumstances.

In hindsight, the 1954 management study and reorganization seemed to presage the introduction of Mission 66, which was proposed the following February.[54] But Secretary of the Interior McKay was attempting to improve bureaucratic efficiency throughout the Department of the Interior, not preparing for budget increases. On the contrary, his stated goal in 1953 was to do more with the resources already available. The reorganization was part of a broader effort to restructure the entire executive branch early in Eisenhower's first administration. Even though the formation of the WODC and EODC were crucial to the subsequent organization of Mission 66, they were established independently, almost a year before Wirth's initiative was conceived, and were not directly linked to proposed increases in construction budgets.

Political attitudes toward increases in Park Service appropriations were about to shift, however. Following the truce in Korea, a postwar downturn in the economy soon provided new reasons for Eisenhower to reconsider public works spending as a means of stabilizing the economy. Eisenhower greatly feared that a recession would be blamed on the Republicans, who now controlled Congress as well as the White House for the first time in two decades. There were other political reasons for him to back a new parks initiative. McKay, who advocated controversial policies such as bringing private power companies into partnership with public utilities, suffered from what historian Elmo Richardson describes as "foot in mouth affliction." McKay's bluntness exacerbated issues such as the controversy over the Echo Park dam, which Eisenhower supported, and contributed to a general perception that the administration was a poor steward of natural resources. Soon derided by opponents on conservation issues as "Giveaway McKay," the secretary became a lightning rod, and Eisenhower replaced him in 1956. In the meantime, any initiative at the Park Service that would help improve the administration's conservation image would clearly be politically useful.[55]

Eisenhower, like Truman, had little personal interest in national parks, recreational planning, or resource conservation. In his memoirs he acknowledges his "very considerable ignorance" on park issues. His priorities for public works were more likely interstate highways, the St. Lawrence Seaway, and federal dam projects. But Eisenhower also suggests in his memoirs that he and Secretary McKay had instigated Mission 66 early in 1954 after he received a letter from John D. Rockefeller Jr. Rockefeller had just read DeVoto's *Harper's* column and agreed that the condition of the parks was a "national tragedy." As a longtime park advocate and benefactor, he wanted to know why something was

not being done.[56] Rockefeller's status as a major political supporter deserved a quick response. In a memorandum to McKay, Eisenhower wrote that he had "been getting communications from people who seem to be genuinely concerned with what they believe to be the deterioration of our national parks," and that McKay should "take a second look." Eisenhower claims that the planning for what became Mission 66 began at that point, "early in 1954," after McKay and "his associates at the Department of the Interior began a survey" which led to the Mission 66 program.[57] But in his description of these events, Eisenhower conflates his memory of the "management study" of the Park Service, which McKay had just completed in December 1953, and the proposal for Mission 66 that Wirth brought to McKay on his own in February 1955. The two initiatives were not directly related. In his personal response to Rockefeller's letter at the time, Eisenhower referred only to McKay's recently completed study which would "permit more efficient use of existing manpower" at the Park Service. McKay's own response to the situation was to inform Rockefeller that a request for an additional $550,000 for park maintenance had been approved by the Bureau of the Budget.[58] More to the point, however, McKay also had a private meeting several days later with Rockefeller confidant Horace Albright, who explained at least one specific point of concern: the delayed completion of the final portion of the Colonial Parkway, running from the Williamsburg restoration to Jamestown, Virginia. McKay admitted to Albright that park construction money would actually be "considerably curtailed" under the administration's proposed budget for 1955. He assured him, nevertheless, that the parkway would get his "personal attention."[59] Rockefeller was satisfied by the response he received from the administration officially, and privately through Albright, and let the matter drop. Although Rockefeller would go on to participate in national park development of the 1950s through his philanthropy, neither he nor Eisenhower initiated Mission 66. Other than the very brief assertion in Eisenhower's memoirs, there are no other sources that contradict Wirth's own account of the origins of the program.

Between 1945 and 1955 the geographical, social, and political frameworks and assumptions for managing national parks had changed dramatically and permanently. As a Park Service chief planner since 1931 and director since 1951, Conrad Wirth understood these changes as well as anyone. Wirth's bureaucratic sense and timing had served him well in his career, and early in 1955 he decided that a dramatic proposal for greatly increased park appropriations would finally be more favorably received than they had been over the previous ten years. As it was crafted by Wirth and his staff, Mission 66 would be enthusiastically endorsed by the Eisenhower administration and approved by Congress, which was in fact in a mood to appropriate even more money, more quickly than requested.

For Wirth, Vint, and the other recreational planners of Mission 66, the modernization of the national park system was a necessary adjunct to the modernization occurring throughout the United States. For almost exactly one hundred years, since Central Park was acquired by the city of New York in 1856, park making had been an integral part of the modern landscape. The wave of urbanization, population growth, and highway construction following World War II demanded that the nation's park system be enlarged, adapted, and managed in ways that would allow it to continue to serve as a truly public park system, and as a functional component of evolving landscape patterns. The new American landscape demanded a new generation of national recreational planning.

Longtime Park Service officials such as Wirth and Vint understood the geographic and societal trends evident after World War II as a continuation of the changes that had followed World War I. They both involved rapid increases in the numbers of people coming to national parks in automobiles, in the context of a rapidly growing and urbanizing (or suburbanizing) society. Their task was to formulate as original and effective a vision for the park system in the 1950s as had been implemented under Mather and Albright in the 1920s. Such a renewal would demand, again, new architectural and landscape design, an expansion of the number and variety of parks in the system, further professionalization and diversification of Park Service staff, and a reiteration of the "master planning" process that Vint had first devised more than twenty years earlier. Mission 66 would require a reinvention of recreational planning, of the Park Service, and to some degree of the park system itself, to meet a vastly expanded public demand in a context of rapid social and geographic change.

There were, of course, other responses to the postwar dilemma. Wirth's and Vint's ideas of recreational planning did not appeal to wilderness advocates, who had concluded that too many people were already trying to use the parks. The parks were being "loved to death," it was agreed, but the answer could not be more development, no matter how well it "harmonized," because that would only mean more visitors. The postwar movement to establish congressional wilderness designations for public lands soon presented an alternative ideal to that of the modernized public park. For these wilderness advocates, the public park itself could no longer function truly effectively as a means of preservation. As long as preservation was for the purpose of "public enjoyment," it would require further development to accommodate a larger, more affluent, automotive public. Under the pressure of postwar levels of visitation, many came to feel that this price was simply too high to pay, and that recreational planning needed to move beyond the Olmstedian ideology which had traditionally guided the Park Service.

But there was never any doubt for Wirth, Vint, and the other organizers of Mission 66 that parks should continue to preserve scenic and historic places for public enjoyment. The national park under Mission 66 was conceived as a complementary and ameliorative component of the vast urbanizing landscapes that increasingly defined the patterns of daily life for millions of Americans. The essential challenge of the postwar dilemma that Drury had identified was to find a way to manage and redevelop the national parks so that they could effectively resume their role as true public landscapes while preserving their integrity, even in an era of greatly increased pressures on them. For landscape architects like Wirth, abandoning such purposes would profoundly diminish the entire endeavor, eviscerating it of social functionality and ideals. Without public access and enjoyment, parks would not allow a personal and societal communion with the natural world. And they would not function economically as part of the progress of the nation.

Changes in American society during the postwar period were so profound that the national park system inevitably would have changed in response. The questions of who would set new policies and what those policies would be intended to achieve developed into a struggle after 1955, as old conservation alliances began to break down and new ones formed. Perhaps no one—not the Park Service, not other federal officials, members of Congress, park concessioners, or early environmentalists—fully understood the degree to which the entire context of the modernizing American landscape was transforming, thereby establishing new conditions, new threats, and new possibilities for the national park system. In 1955 the principal question was simply: How would the Park Service finally respond to the postwar dilemma? Conrad Wirth had an answer.

CHAPTER 3

PLANNING PRINCIPLES AND
THE "MISSION 66 PROSPECTUS"

Bernard DeVoto described a crisis that, like Newton Drury's dilemma, involved "parks" rather than "wilderness" in that it concerned the condition of frontcountry landscapes, not the ecological health of the backcountry or the status of wildlife populations. If the postwar challenge were defined as a "parks" crisis, Wirth and his colleagues could present themselves as among the most experienced park planners in history. And after a decade of enforced idleness, the Park Service was ready to attempt once again to set national standards and policies for the development of public lands for recreational uses.

The creation of the Western and Eastern Offices of Design and Construction in 1954 was essential to the subsequent proposal for Mission 66. The two offices answered directly to Washington and created a centralized administrative structure. The architects, landscape architects, engineers, and other professionals in the new offices had hardly settled in before Wirth proposed his ten-year modernization and expansion of the park system, now unofficially estimated to cost at least $700 million. Landscape architect Red Hill headed the San Francisco office, with supervising architect Lyle E. Bennett, supervising engineer Percy E. Smith, and supervising landscape architect Robert G. Hall as his staff. In Philadelphia another long-time Park Service landscape architect, Edward Zimmer, had a staff that included John B. "Bill" Cabot, Robert P. White, and Harvey H. Cornell in the same positions. In Washington, Thomas Vint remained in his now strengthened role of chief of design and construction, with his long-time deputy Bill Carnes serving as his chief landscape architect, as he had since 1937.[1] All of these men—and at the time the Park Service still discriminated against women designers—had long careers as Park Service professionals.[2] Most of them had worked for Wirth or Vint since the

Conrad Wirth (right) with WODC chief Sanford "Red" Hill in Yellowstone in 1959. Photo by Jack E. Boucher, NPS Historic Photo Collection.

1930s, when so many young architects and landscape architects came to work for the agency. Because of the importance of planning and design within the Park Service throughout this period, many had also moved into administrative positions. Red Hill, Edward Zimmer, and Harvey Cornell, for example, had all been assistant regional directors in San Francisco, Richmond, and Santa Fe, respectively, before taking their assignments in the WODC and EODC.[3] Wirth surrounded himself with experienced longtime associates in Washington as well. In his summary of the history of the agency's organizational structures, Russell K. Olsen observes that Wirth's "cabinet" in Washington in the 1950s consisted mostly of people who had worked in his "CCC organization" during the 1930s, and that Mission 66 has often been characterized as

"the completion of Mr. Wirth's CCC program for the Service that was interrupted by World War II."[4]

The whole tenor of Mission 66—a sudden mobilization to address a national crisis—must have recalled the spring of 1933, when many of the same people had rapidly implemented emergency spending programs. This is certainly how a number of the employees and officials at the Park Service saw it at the time, and they described a similar sense of purpose and excitement. But in other ways the spring of 1955 could not have differed more from that of 1933. A popular Republican president now watched over a rapidly expanding economy. For many Americans, twenty years of hard work and sacrifice were giving way to unprecedented material comfort and security, to new houses, new cars, and growing families. In these ways the period suggested the 1920s more than the 1930s, and Mission 66 reflected this difference. Congress might finally be in a mood to appropriate money for parks, for example, but no one was even intimating that the CCC should be revived. And without the CCC or an equivalent, there could be no park planning or development of comparable breadth and ambition. The CCC had put hundreds of thousands of young men to work building national, state, and municipal parks, while hundreds of leading professionals joined the effort in supervisory roles. Without the CCC and the rest of the New Deal, Mission 66 could never match what the Park Service had accomplished in the 1930s. There would be no significant state park dimension to Mission 66, for example, or partnerships with other federal agencies beyond existing relationships with the Bureau of Public Roads, the Bureau of Reclamation, and the Army Corps of Engineers. Neither did the Park Service have the bureaucratic support of the National Resources Board or other New Deal national planning efforts. The New Deal had mobilized the entire federal government in a coordinated campaign of conservation programs. Now the Park Service would have to rely on its own human and fiscal resources to put Mission 66 into the context of a national plan for the use of public lands. The agency's role in this regard continued to be defined by the 1936 Park, Parkway, and Recreational-Area Study Act. The overall Mission 66 program was never affirmed by new legislation that would have redefined mandates for the agency or endorsed the Mission 66 program specifically.

In his memoirs Wirth describes the specific ideas and events that precipitated the rapid organization of his Mission 66 proposal. His own account of events is actually based on a history written in 1958 by agency historian Roy E. Appleman, which in turn was based in large part on interviews with Wirth in 1956 as well as Appleman's personal experience.[5] According to Wirth (and Appleman), one weekend in February the director was at his home in Maryland considering the reluctance of Congress to increase park appropriations since 1945. Congress had supported the Bureau of Public Roads, the Bureau of Reclamation, and the Army Corps of Engineers with multiyear authorizations for hundreds of millions of dollars that allowed these agencies to complete massive public works efficiently. Capital expenditures for national parks, meanwhile, were inadequate and fluctuated from year to year, making it difficult to plan large projects over extended periods. Wirth struggled to present the redevelopment of the national park system to Congress on the same terms, as a national priority requiring a long-term, major commitment of funds rather than the minimal and uncertain appropriations that allowed only a "patch on patch" approach to modernizing park facilities.[6]

Wirth does not mention Lucius Clay's interstate highway proposal, which had been published and submitted to Congress a month earlier. But while asking himself what a member of Congress would "want to hear," he apparently experienced an epiphany: the modernization of the national park system could indeed be presented as a ten-year program, requiring extensive coordination and planning nationwide, and achieved within one overall budget estimate. Wirth would present Congress with a total figure and a schedule for the entire job. He could argue that long-term, coordinated planning was necessary—just as it was to build highways and dams—in order to let larger contracts, benefit from economies of scale, and minimize the overall disturbance to parks and visitors by completing the work quickly. The alternative was to limp along with annual appropriations that allowed only endless incremental repairs to facilities that were not worth the investment because they would never be adequate for the numbers of people trying to use them.

This was the essence of "MISSION 66" (often all in capitals), a name Wirth hoped captured the urgency of the situation and evoked wartime zeal with the carefully chosen term "mission." Ten years was, he felt, the right balance between committing to unacceptably short-term planning and projecting too far into an uncertain future. Intensely aware of the tradition of his agency, Wirth also feared that under his administration the Park Service would fail to measure up to its own history. In the 1920s Mather and Albright had forged a powerful identity for the agency while developing a national park system that was admired all over the world. Thirty years later, Wirth knew that his Park Service was faced with challenges—and opportunities—that were just as great. By fixing Mission 66 to be completed in time for the fiftieth anniversary of the Park Service in 1966, he reminded himself and everyone else that living up to that legacy would require dedication, hard work, and equally successful responses to the new generation of problems besetting the park system.[7]

From the moment he was first taken with his idea, Wirth moved with single-minded alacrity. That Monday morning, February 8, when he called the regular "squad meeting" of his assistant directors, division chiefs, and other principal advisers, he announced that business as usual would end immediately in the Washington office. A new working group would be formed to begin outlining details and estimates for the ten-year program to modernize and expand the park system. The conference room they were meeting in, Room 3100, adjacent to the director's office in the Interior Department Building in Washington, would be given over to the group, who would be relieved of all other duties. By the end of the meeting, the squad had agreed on the individuals to be assigned to this "working staff" (later described as the "working committee") as well as the makeup of a "steering committee," consisting mostly of the supervisors of those in the first group. Wirth, as his choice of rooms for the project made clear, would maintain close control over and daily participation in every aspect of the plan. A strong administrator known for his direct style, Wirth did not lightly tolerate perceived incompetence or lack of enthusiasm; he would personally make sure that his mission stayed on its demanding course.[8]

The working committee, most of whom had not been present that morning, were quickly informed of their new assignments. Together with the steering committee and the assistant directors, they met in the same conference room with Wirth that afternoon. Wirth now expounded his goals at length and laid out the arguments for immediate action. Most of these must have been

Mission 66 "steering committee" in Yellowstone in 1957. Left to right: Jackson Price, Donald Lee, Harry Langley, Lon Garrison, Thomas Vint, John Doerr. NPS Historic Photo Collection.

Mission 66 "working committee" in Washington in 1956. Left to right: Howard Stagner, Robert Coates, Jack Dodd, Bill Carnes, Harold Smith, Roy Appleman, Ray Freeman. NPS Historic Photo Collection.

familiar to everyone in the room. The parks were being "loved to death," and the public and popular media had been calling for action for years. Budgets had stagnated at a level that had served 21 million visits annually, while in 1954 there had been 46 million visits recorded. The Park Service faced nothing less than "the destruction . . . of what it is charged with saving." The task was to "secure a reasonable protection of the parks and yet provide for increased public use in such a way as to not wear them out." Wirth charged the group to elaborate a "reasoned objective" for Mission 66 and to delineate a program to accomplish that objective. The solution "would not be [found] in the books and in regulations" and might not be possible within the terms of existing legislation; but he wanted answers, regardless of what the group determined would be necessary to implement them. According to Roy Appleman, who was a member of the new working committee, Wirth used the analogy of a poker game, suggesting that the Park Service had been "called." They needed to show their cards, and Wirth wanted theirs to be "a good hand." The Bureau of Public Roads had been planning its modern system of interstate highways at least since 1944. Wirth gave his working group eight months to have their proposal ready. He planned to present it at the General Service Conference of national park superintendents scheduled for that September in Great Smoky Mountains National Park.[9]

Wirth successfully imbued his staff with enthusiasm for their task of rapidly assembling and analyzing data, cost estimates, policy guidelines, and other features of what would be, eight months later, the Mission 66 proposal. The working staff felt they were about to make history, and the excitement was infectious, quickly spreading to park superintendents, field personnel, and eventually Interior officials and members of Congress. The two most important staff members working under Wirth during the eight-month effort were the chair of the steering committee, Lemuel A. "Lon" Garrison, and the chairman of the working committee, Bill Carnes.[10] Lon Garrison, a former ranger at Sequoia and Yosemite and former superintendent of Hopewell Village and Big Bend, had just moved to Washington to take the new position of chief of the "conservation and protection branch," making him the agency's "chief ranger." Garrison's field background and personal style appealed to Wirth, who had brought Garrison to Washington for other purposes but now would rely on him as his most trusted lieutenant guiding the early stages of Mission 66. Garrison was only four years younger than Wirth, but his memoirs suggest that he aspired to play the role of Albright to Wirth's Mather as together they strove to "dream up a contemporary National Park Service." After two years in Washington, Garrison felt that the Mission 66 steering committee, by now renamed the "advisory committee," had done its work. Following in Albright's footsteps, he accepted the position of Yellowstone superintendent. But just as Albright had in the 1920s, he maintained close contact with the Washington office, where he was considered a potential successor as director.[11]

Garrison was an interesting choice to head the Mission 66 steering committee, since as "chief ranger" he had impressive management experience but little design or planning background. Most of the other members of the steering committee had counterparts whom they supervised on the working committee. The chairman of the working committee was Bill Carnes, whom Vint had supervised as his chief landscape architect since 1937. One might have expected Vint, as the longtime chief of design and construction, to serve as the chairman of the steering committee. Mission 66 was, after all, mainly a design and construction program. The choice of Vint's protégé as the head of the working committee, on the one hand, did confirm Vint's continued influence. But on the other hand, Carnes's reassignment also deprived Vint of the services of his closest ally and associate, who had for decades handled the paperwork and bureaucratic functions Vint eschewed. Vint had always been a planner and designer more that a manager at heart, and he depended on Carnes as an assistant. As the head of the Mission 66 working committee, Carnes now assisted Wirth and Garrison, leaving Vint without his support. Vint remained in his position and exerted great influence on planning and design policy at this important time. Mission 66, however, was Conrad Wirth's program, and the director decided from the beginning not to put Vint in a position where he would share credit for the overall vision. Wirth later wrote that Carnes, because of his long association with Vint and his park planning methods, was "the logical chairman for the task force." Vint contributed, but less directly, as one of the steering committee members.[12]

By the end of the first week of planning Mission 66, the working committee prepared a memorandum signed by Wirth to be distributed throughout the Park Service. The "goal to which this Mission is directed," Wirth informed the field, was "nothing new; it was plainly stated in the Act of 1916 establishing the National Park Service." Those concepts were "as sound today as they were in 1916." Wirth decided that the essence of the problem was to "meet fully the responsibilities implicit in those concepts" and "to produce a comprehensive and integrated program of use and protection that is in harmony with the obligations of the National Park Service under the Act of 1916." All Park Service personnel were urged to send their "suggestions" directly to Lon Garrison, "particularly on the controversial subject of possible controls on overuse of park areas." Because of "the urgency of the project" the program was being initiated immediately, Wirth informed his employees, and suggestions were to be sent in by March 10. The Mission 66 planners were charged with "the development of a dynamic program," he added, for the approval of Secretary McKay and the Bureau of the Budget and Congress in time to affect appropriations for fiscal year 1957.[13]

Wirth's belief in the continued validity of the concepts expressed in the 1916 legislation would remain the ideological bedrock of Mission 66 until his retirement in 1964. From the outset, the organizers of the Mission 66 program found their most fundamental justifications in existing prewar legislation and policy. The working committee spent its first weeks researching historical documents, including the 1872 Yellowstone Act, the 1906 Antiquities Act, the 1916 National Park Service Act, the 1918 "Lane Letter," the 1933 executive reorganization, the 1935 Historic Sites Act, and of course the 1936 Park, Parkway, and

Recreational-Area Study Act.[14] Wirth would repeatedly refer to the 1916 act that established the Park Service, in particular, as the fundamental mandate of Mission 66. He felt secure in his interpretation of that legislation in part because of his close friendship and professional association with its author, Frederick Law Olmsted Jr. "The fundamental purpose" of the parks, Olmsted wrote in 1916, was "to conserve the scenery and the natural and historic objects and the wild life therein and to provide for the enjoyment of the same in such manner and by such means as will leave them unimpaired for the enjoyment of future generations."[15] This language clearly was influenced by the text of his father's 1865 Yosemite report, which stated that "the duty of preservation is the first," since "for the millions who are hereafter to benefit," preservation of the landscape was an obvious necessity. "Next to this" duty, the elder Olmsted continued, "is that of . . . aiding to make . . . [Yosemite Valley] available as soon and as generally as may be economically practicable to those whom it is designed to benefit."[16] Wirth and Frederick Law Olmsted Jr. both understood that the duty of preservation came first, since without it there would be nothing for the public to enjoy. But preservation without public enjoyment, as Olmsted reminded Wirth in 1949, was not what public parks—as described and developed by the two men's fathers—were intended to achieve.

The second most important policy document for Wirth was almost as old. In 1918 Horace Albright drafted a letter for the signature of Secretary of the Interior Franklin K. Lane describing policies and priorities for the new National Park Service. The essence of Albright's letter was contained in three points: first, the parks must be maintained "in an unimpaired form for the use of future generations" as well the present one; second, they were "set apart for the use, observation, health, and pleasure of the people"; and third, national, not local, interests must dictate all decisions concerning their management. Albright summarized the agency's management principles in a series of concise directives: to further the expansion and enjoyment of the park system, the letter advised, "you should diligently extend and use the splendid cooperation . . . among chambers of commerce, tourist bureaus, and automobile highway associations"; in planning additions to the system, "you should seek to find scenery of supreme and distinctive quality."[17] In March 1955 Wirth distributed the "Lane Letter" in another agency-wide informational memorandum. "With few exceptions," he wrote in the memorandum, the letter "could have been written yesterday."[18] Later critics would claim that the Mission 66 program moved too far away from earlier national park policy and tradition; in fact, from the beginning the program was completely rooted in the Progressive Era ideology—and in even earlier Olmstedian theory—which had served the agency so well to that point.

By the end of February, the Mission 66 working committee had asked every administrative department of the agency to submit a "recommended program" for its area of responsibility and was preparing surveys to be sent to every park in the system. Garrison and Carnes interviewed dozens of members of the Washington office, soliciting any and all opinions. Few experts outside the Park Service were consulted during these weeks. Within the agency, however, the planners suspended the usual protocols and requested employees at every level to address comments and suggestions directly to them. The lack of an official outreach to private conservation groups and park concessioners, in particular, would soon prove to be a major strategic error. But for the time being great enthusiasm was generated among Park Service office staff and field personnel, many of whom participated directly or indirectly in the effort. For his part, Wirth opened the door to his adjacent office many times a day, and he maintained personal oversight of the entire endeavor.[19]

On March 17 Wirth and his planners issued a second agency memorandum on Mission 66 "policies and procedures."[20] It had been a busy month, and the memorandum, with attachments, ran more than ten pages. The "steering committee and staff," Wirth announced, had three basic instructions for those who would be participating in Mission 66 planning: "Disregard precedents. . . . Be imaginative. . . . Bring up something effective in achieving the twin objectives of protection and optimum use." If Wirth venerated the documents that described the original mandate of his agency, he was also completely open to finding new ways to achieve that mandate. "The lid is off," he declared. "Only by giving full play to the imagination will we find solutions that will meet the problems of continuously increasing use of the parks by the American people." All Park Service personnel were again asked to participate and send in suggestions; some would be asked to come to Washington to give advice.

The "policies and practices as they might apply to a park" described in an attachment to the memorandum were just as radical in their tone. The policies perhaps also surprise today, considering the subsequent reputation of Mission 66 for "overdevelopment." The first policy recommendation, for example, was that travel to national parks "should not be actively encouraged," and that an "optimum visitor load" for both the present and future should be determined. Wirth and his planners then suggested four policies on "public use," all of which advocated the removal of development from within park boundaries, or at least from overcrowded and sensitive areas. They sought new strategies for relocating hotels and administrative facilities from "precious" areas—such as the rims of scenic canyons or the edges of geyser basins—to less sensitive sites. They noted that concessioners had sited many of these buildings before the Park Service was established in 1916, and since then the agency had made only partial progress in relocating or mitigating the effects of such development. At Sequoia, for example, there was a moratorium on building any more cabins in the Giant Forest, and at Yellowstone plans were under way to move existing development away from the rim of the Grand Canyon of the Yellowstone. But because of increased public use, the parks were now at a turning point. Further expansion of older developed areas would cause far greater damage and overcrowding around major park attractions and destinations. An unambiguous new policy was required: "It is imperative that the Service establish a guiding policy for correcting such existing encroachments, and preventing others in the future." Although "in certain areas the Service is on record" regarding the necessity of moving development to "less 'precious' and more advantageous locations," both "the Service and the concessioner continue to add developments in these locations to meet growing needs." In some cases even safety hazards from rockslides and floods had been ignored (for example, at Yosemite and Mount Rainier), and developed areas had been expanded as managers were forced into "compromising with a bad situation" while trying to meet the needs of visitors. But the Mission 66 planners were in no mood for further compromise. "There must be a definite policy . . . of 'getting out of the precious areas in the parks and on to the lesser areas,' both as to administrative facilities and visitor accommodations." What is more, "the eventual removal of overnight facilities from the parks, or from the most 'precious' areas therein, should be considered." Older lodge facilities, even such landmarks as the Old Faithful Inn and the Paradise Inn, might be demolished and replaced with lodging in less sensitive areas, or outside park boundaries altogether. Better roads and faster cars made it desirable, where practicable, to relocate overnight and administrative facilities to new "town sites" outside parks. These new "communities" would include residential districts for park employees, who would therefore have to commute to work in the parks (although their families would have easier access to schools and other services). Finally, new plans for national parks would have to weigh "completely revamping park transportation systems," particularly to increase the efficient use of buses.

A tremendous amount of new development would be required to achieve the kinds of goals that the Mission 66 planners instructed regional staff and superintendents to consider. Their instructions also implied the demolition of many historic hotels and park structures of all types. New strategies—and a huge amount of money—would be needed to reduce the impacts of growing numbers of visitors. If the idea of allowing essentially unrestricted numbers of people to enjoy the parks were to survive, a new set of priorities would be needed to guide revised master plans for every unit in the system. A "questionnaire" directed to park superintendents was therefore attached to the March 17 memorandum. The Mission 66 planners wanted to know first "what problems exist or are anticipated regarding the protection of natural conditions or in regard to animal populations, plant associations, forestry management, historic or scientific values, etc.?" They asked the superintendents to estimate "visitor volume," both present and projected for 1966. They wanted to know which management problems derived from "continuously increasing visitation" and how those problems impaired both "park values" and the "opportunity for proper park use by the public." Park managers were asked to assess and analyze their situation, using existing master plans as a starting point, but remembering that those plans "have been governed by existing laws, regulations, land holdings, or franchises more limiting in scope than is the study now in progress under Mission 66." Finally, "we must face the fact," Wirth continued, "that many park installations still in use are based on a stagecoach economy and travel patterns."

From the very start, Wirth described Mission 66 as an initiative for developing completely revised park master plans that would respond to the social, technological, and geographical trends of postwar American society. Armed with only the most rudimentary estimates for the costs of modernizing the entire park system, Wirth was also preparing to go directly to Congress for what he already knew would be the $500 million to $1 billion cost of implementing the entire program. Mission 66 was conceived entirely "in-house," by the Park Service, with very little significant participation by congressional staff, or by the agency's most vital private partners, conservation groups and park concessioners. Wirth and his staff obviously felt that they could invent a new approach to administering the national park system without much outside help. They could argue, with some basis, that no one had as much experience in dealing with the conflicting agendas of concessioners, conservationists, and the diverse, always demanding public. While Wirth recognized the eventual need for "better understanding, cooperation, and support of local and national civic and conservation groups" (the only mention made of outside groups at this point), for now he would look to the expertise within his own ranks.

Early Mission 66 policy statements reflected the contemporary sentiments of the most experienced park planner of all, Thomas Vint. Still the active and revered director of design and construction, Vint had invented the "master planning" procedures that had been the heart of Park Service development policies since the 1920s. During his long career with the Park Service he had worked closely with Mather, Albright, and Olmsted, and he had personally

Images taken by Mission 66 planners ca. 1955 showing new commercial services and facilities in "gateway towns" as well as increased traffic in and around parks. NPS History Collection.

trained (or "raised," as he sometimes put it) many of the senior planners and landscape architects in the agency.[21] Vint and Wirth had a long and complex relationship. They were close friends, and both had been given great responsibilities at the Park Service early in their careers. They held each other in high esteem, and in many ways each complemented the other. In the 1930s they had very separate roles in the Park Service, with Wirth in charge of his state park CCC organization and Vint overseeing planning and design within the national parks. In the 1940s Vint had little to do with the "river basin studies" and recreation area plans that occupied Wirth. Both men were popular figures within the agency, but they had very different personalities. Vint was gregarious and informal in his approach to management, and he inspired tremendous loyalty and affection among his staff. He was a designer rather than an administrator at heart (although Wirth nevertheless described him as "canny" in his bureaucratic style). When he and Wirth disagreed over the particulars of a park master plan, Vint reportedly agreed to the changes, then reversed them after Wirth left the room.[22] Vint took great pride in his master plans, and he also knew that his boss was busy with many other more pressing matters. For his part, Wirth was a former military school cadet, who in college enjoyed football and fraternal organizations more than his design apprenticeship. A masterly bureaucrat, he oversaw every detail of park operations with organized rigor. He was known for his ability to control a meeting and to deal quickly with any perceived incompetence or other distraction.

Wirth and Vint's professional relationship continued over three decades and was a productive partnership. They were always warm and friendly in their official duties, but there remained some measure of competition between them. They were both landscape architects with strong opinions on the details of planning and architectural design in the parks. In the 1930s their respective places in organizational charts—with separate responsibilities defined—apparently mitigated any tension between the older designer and the ambitious young administrator. As director, Wirth relied on Vint and enhanced his position through the 1954 reorganization of planning and design staff. In 1955, however, Wirth limited Vint's direct involvement in Mission 66, preferring to rely on younger men with whom he had less potentially competitive relationships. Given Vint's reputation within the Park Service, it would have been difficult for Wirth to claim Mission 66 as his own if he had put Vint, not Garrison, in charge of the steering committee.

The exact nature of Vint's early contributions to Mission 66 planning must be surmised. But with his trusted aide Bill Carnes heading the working committee, Vint clearly had a hand—directly or indirectly—in drafting the "policies and practices" issued in 1955. The idea of removing development to gateway communities outside parks, for example, had been advocated by Vint and members of his staff for more than ten years, ever since the postwar situation of the parks had begun to receive serious consideration. Vint understood that improved park roads, together with faster and more reliable cars, often eliminated the need for overnight accommodations in parks. Visitors could make a day trip, in many cases, leaving and returning home the same day. They could also stay in hotels and motels that were outside the parks but within practical driving distance of main park destinations.

In a memorandum to Newton Drury in 1945 on the subject of "development problems" at Yosemite, Vint insisted that it was time to "re-appraise" the agency's approach to planning and to "move some activities entirely out of the park." If Drury really wanted to reduce the presence of development on the floor of Yosemite Valley, Vint advised, the "convenience of the road system" that made it possible for so many people to visit also made it possible to move housing, maintenance, and concessioner facilities out of the park altogether. Vint pointed out that a whole program of development—including an expanded administration building, a new Yosemite Lodge, housing, and maintenance areas—was already considered necessary by the Park Service and the concessioner. In what became known at the time as the "Vint Plan," he suggested that none of the new buildings should be sited in Yosemite Valley itself but should instead be relocated to sites outside the park and to Big Meadows and Wawona, areas within the park but away from the crowded valley.[23] In 1947 Vint pressed his points to Drury, insisting that conditions at Yosemite were "as near to a clear slate" as would ever be likely to occur again, and that the "next step" would "determine the course to be followed for a long term of years." He knew that once a new commitment of capital investment was made, it would be many years— if ever—before they had a similar opportunity to reconceive the public's experience of Yosemite

Parking in Yosemite Village in the 1950s. Yosemite National Park Archives.

Valley. The Park Service could follow "Plan A" in the valley, he told Drury, and further expand and rebuild existing development, or it could follow what Vint called "Plan B," and build a new Yosemite Lodge in Wawona rather than in the valley, along with a new administrative center in either Wawona or Fresno. He knew that these would not be "popular" ideas, but he felt the time was drawing near when the Park Service would have to decide whether to accommodate increasingly destructive compromises or institute new planning policy that reflected the postwar social and geographic contexts of the national parks. "If you decide to rebuild Yosemite Lodge in the Valley," Vint warned Drury, "you will be following Plan A" and will continue to "drift in one direction, while hoping . . . to change to the other."[24] In 1949 Drury nevertheless approved building a new lodge in the valley, although a lack of construction funds delayed the project. Mission 66, however, soon revived these ruminations on park development policy for Vint and his colleagues.

Similar scenarios were taking place in many other parks in the 1940s, but Yosemite Valley held great significance for Vint, as it did for many others concerned with national park preservation. Vint had begun his Park Service career at Yosemite in 1922, and he remained particularly interested in the park while he headed the San Francisco field office of design and construction staff between 1927 and 1933. Vint had always worked closely with the Yosemite National Park Board of Expert Advisors, formed in 1928 with Frederick Law Olmsted Jr. as its first chairman. While his ideas for removing development from the valley might have seemed radical to some in 1945, they were actually a reiteration of a much older vision for the valley, described by the elder Frederick Law Olmsted in 1865. Even then, Olmsted knew that the number of visitors to the valley would "within a century" be in the "millions," and in his 1865 plan for the valley he therefore suggested minimal development: essentially a one-way loop road, trails, bathrooms, and campgrounds, which would serve as the only overnight accommodations.[25] The younger Olmsted had retained his father's interest in Yosemite, and as an influential member of the park's Board of Expert Advisors was an impor-

View of Yosemite Valley as seen entering from the west on Wawona Road. Author's photo.

tant supporter of Vint. Together they had considered such issues as the construction of the new Wawona Road (begun in 1930) and the proposed "ropeway" (or cable car) from the Happy Isles area of the valley to Glacier Point. While they believed that road construction was an appropriate and desirable modernization of the park landscape, they fought and defeated the visual intrusion of prominent "mechanical features" such as the ropeway.[26]

Through his own work and his association with Olmsted, Vint was well versed in the preservation issues of Yosemite Valley. In 1945 he was not only advancing a radical postwar vision for the management of the valley, he was asserting the priorities of the oldest national park plan of all: the elder Olmsted's 1865 plan. In March 1955 Wirth, Garrison, and Carnes made Vint's planning ideas the first policy framework for Mission 66. The new era of national park master planning was off to an optimistic start.

By that time the Mission 66 planners had decided to create a model master plan for a park selected as representative of many common problems and management considerations. That park would not be Yosemite, which was unique and too complex to serve the purpose effectively. Wirth chose instead to make Mount Rainier Na-

In 1865 Frederick Law Olmsted described Yosemite Valley as a unique juxtaposition of the sublime scenery of waterfalls and sheer granite walls and the pastoral beauty of the valley floor. Author's photo.

tional Park the "pilot study" for Mission 66 planning. There were many reasons why Mount Rainier was the perfect vehicle to showcase their ideas for developing a new program of accelerated redevelopment for each park, or, as it was soon described, a "Mission 66 prospectus." Larger parks had too many specific issues and interest groups to be instructive case studies. Mount Rainier was smaller and featured what the Mission 66 working committee described as "reasonably difficult problems, many of which would be typical of park problems in general."[27] The park offered a range of resources and superb scenery, including glaciers, mountains, forests, and rivers. Managers at Mount Rainier were also contending with a number of issues related to public use, including road construction, winter sports, and the renewal of concession contracts. Mount Rainier was the park where Mather had first demonstrated the benefits of his monopolistic concessioner contracts in 1915, and it was where Vint had first developed national park master planning in the late 1920s. Mount Rainier could again serve as a model park, in which a revised form of master planning—the Mission 66 prospectus—could be demonstrated.

The condition of many of Mount Rainier's public facilities in 1955 could be seen as an in-

Mount Rainier and the meadows of the Paradise area, as seen from the original approach to the Paradise Inn. Author's photo.

dictment of Park Service policies up to that point. Mather's organization of the Rainier National Park Company in 1915 had been held up as an example of how private concessioners could enhance federal management of the parks. By 1946, however, Drury described a dismal situation, in which once admired rustic lodges, such as the Paradise Inn (1917), were now overcrowded and "obsolete."[28] The Rainier National Park Company had suffered through the depression, and after the war its stockholders refused to invest new capital to expand and modernize its facilities. In 1952 Congress bought out the company's interest in its buildings, and the Park Service contracted with the company to run the hotels and restaurants. Many park administrators—even the conservative Albright—felt that this type of arrangement would eventually be necessary in most parks, although in 1955 the publicly owned concession facilities at Mount Rainier were still the exception to the rule. But this was another reason why the park would make an excellent demonstration project: Mission 66 planners would have a free hand in the proposed disposition of hotels and visitor facilities.

In 1955 Mount Rainier was already in the vanguard of several acrimonious policy debates with significance for the park system as a whole. Even before the war, skiers, local businessmen, and elected officials had been pressing the Park Service to develop the Paradise Valley area of the park into a commercial ski resort, complete with year-round accommodations and ski lifts. In 1946 Vint produced a plan illustrating what replacing the Paradise Inn with a hotel designed for year-round use might entail: a mas-

The Paradise Inn (1917) in the 1920s. NPS Historic Photo Collection.

sive $2 million concrete building with basement parking, one hundred guest rooms, dormitories, dining rooms, and enough capacity to serve crowds visiting Paradise only for the day as well as those staying at the hotel. Vint also observed that the year-round operation of such a hotel would still not break even and would have to be subsidized by the government. While dutifully producing schematic designs for a resort, Vint actually opposed the whole idea. For both Vint and Wirth, the prospect of permanent chair lift structures marching up the slopes of Mount Rainier, in particular, made a ski resort development utterly unacceptable. These were precisely the kinds of "mechanical features" that had been proposed at Yosemite Valley and elsewhere. Expanding the winter use of parks was considered desirable in part as a means to "spread" park use seasonally and reduce summer crowding; and limited ski operations had been developed elsewhere, notably at Badger Pass in Yosemite. But permanent ski lift towers on the slopes of Mount Rainier could not be countenanced. As historian Theodore Catton relates, by 1948 Vint had objected to Wirth in writing, and in 1953 Wirth expressed his opposition to Secretary of the Interior McKay, effectively threatening to resign. McKay backed his Park Service director, and the ski resort at Paradise was defeated, although the pressure to maintain year-round visitor use remained.[29]

The "pilot study" Wirth and his staff quickly assembled for Mount Rainier in 1955 further demonstrated that they were in no mood to compromise on the issue. The park's superintendent, Preston P. Macy, came to Washington, D.C., for a week in early April, and by April 11 the planners had in hand what they considered the first complete Mission 66 prospectus. The twenty-page report prominently featured the agency's new arrowhead logo. Several diagrams and schematic renderings of proposed facilities were interspersed with brief descriptions of policies and proposed development and a one-page estimate of costs. Prewar master plans, which had been the result of years, not weeks, of effort, were typically 30 by 40 inches and included detailed site plans, design renderings, and other studies at several scales. By comparison, the new prospectus, in 8½ by 11 inch format, was little more than an abbreviated summary. But what it described was a radical plan of park redevelopment.

The prospectus planners began by attempting to estimate how many park visits there would be by 1966. Almost 800,000 had been recorded in 1954, up from 35,000 in 1917, when the Paradise Inn opened, and 200,000 in 1927, when Vint was devising the first master plan. The planners' projection that within ten years annual visits would "exceed one million" was conservative.[30] The implications of this rise in the number of travelers nevertheless dominated all other considerations. In his foreword to the prospectus Wirth stated that, above all, "provision must be made to relieve impact on fragile areas by this ever increasing visitor use." Throughout the document the basic strategy for achieving this end was stated repeatedly: "Except for camping, Mount Rainier will be a day-use park . . . .With modern means of transportation it is no longer necessary that visitors remain in the park overnight to enjoy its scenic attractions and inspirational values. Areas immediately outside the park are available for the full development of visitor housing by private enterprise." Not even "trailer villages" were to be provided, because these represented not true camping but "another form of overnight housing," and so should also be relegated to neighboring towns. "Headquarters facilities" and staff housing too were to be moved to "more advantageous locations outside the park."[31] The 1955 Mount Rainier prospectus, the new model for Mission 66 planning, followed what Vint might have called "Plan B," business not as usual.

There were many implications for the conceptual transformation of national parks into strictly a day use and overnight camping destination. Eliminating park hotel concessions, for example, could not begin until existing contracts expired. Even then, concessioners could be expected to rally opposition, particularly in parks where their "possessory interest" had not already been purchased. This was a principal reason why Wirth conducted early Mission 66 planning within what he liked to call "the Park Service family," which is to say, in secret, at least as far as outside groups and the general public were concerned. The Mount Rainier prospectus also emphasized the idea of encouraging "private enterprise to develop overnight visitor housing outside the park, by eliminating such facilities within the park." Wirth was looking to get his agency out of the hotel business altogether at Mount Rainier, and he hoped to win political support for the plan by implying that park concessions were suppressing economic opportunities in gateway communities. The 1955 prospectus called for operation of the Mount Rainier hotels at Longmire, Paradise, and Ohanapecosh to be discontinued at the expiration of their contracts. The buildings would presumably then be demolished. The "lack of such competition within the park," the planners asserted, would "hasten the trend" they had already observed of new tourist development in nearby towns, and in this way meet the need for overnight accommodations.

The Mount Rainier prospectus delineated a program of redevelopment that would structure a new relationship between the park and its public. "Automobile campgrounds" would be removed from "fragile areas" at high elevations (the Paradise and Yakima Park areas), but new campgrounds at lower elevations would be built for significantly larger numbers of cars and campers. Day use areas (picnic grounds) would be retained, improved, and expanded in size and number. At Paradise and Cayuse Pass, Wirth would bow to the desire for winter access, but without any overnight facilities. "Ski tows" would be provided, but only of a type that could be completely removed in summer. The prospectus also featured a new system of "park interpretive centers," including a central "day-use building"

at Paradise that would replace the Paradise Inn and the Paradise Lodge. Each "interpretive center" would have a theme, for example, "glacial geology, flower and animal life" at the Paradise center. At Longmire a "public use building with auditorium" would replace the hotel there and serve as the main contact point, "strategically located on roads leading to nearby overnight accommodations outside the park." The prospectus acknowledged the changing social and geographic context of the park. Mount Rainier, like Rocky Mountain, Great Smoky Mountains, Shenandoah, and others, had always had large numbers of day trippers who drove from cities relatively nearby. Interstate highway construction, increasing use of cars, and suburbanization around Puget Sound cities guaranteed that this trend would only increase.

In this initial planning effort, a basic premise of the entire Mission 66 program immediately emerged: the impact of ever larger numbers of visitors in cars could be absorbed without "impairment" of the parks only if the patterns and types of public use were altered. The "difficult problem" of eliminating overnight accommodations in parks immediately arose as a central challenge. Overnight lodge visitors had to be turned into day visitors. In some cases, lodges and campgrounds only needed to be relocated and redesigned rather than removed from the park; but they definitely had to be sited away from overcrowded "precious" areas. Wirth exhorted his planners to make bold changes, reminding them that he had recently (and temporarily, it turned out) decided not to provide overnight facilities in the master plan for Everglades National Park.[32] He and his planners realized that soon all national parks would become more like Mount Rainier, with increased numbers of more mobile travelers. They had observed the growth of motels and other tourist businesses in "gateway towns" outside the entrances of many parks. As these towns grew, they would provide the shops, housing, schools, and other amenities that both staff and visitors once expected "park villages" to provide. They would also soon discover, however, a reality of park planning at any scale: public facilities are often easier to build than they are to remove. Public facilities in parks rapidly accrue strong constituencies of users and economic interests dependent on their continued operation. Local congressional delegations responded quickly to such concerns, and did not hesitate to involve themselves directly in proposals for parks in their districts. Some of the earliest and most fundamental policy inspirations of Mission 66 would also prove to be the most difficult to implement.

But in the spring of 1955, in the heady atmosphere of Room 3100, the "lid was off." The transformation of the national park system that was known as Mission 66 called for other measures, some of which would prove to be even more controversial than removing concessioner hotels. For example, in order for large numbers of cars and tourists to get in and out of parks efficiently, Mission 66 would require the modernization of hundreds of miles of park roads. To accommodate higher traffic volumes at greater speeds, winding routes would have to be straightened and widened, and bridges would need to be replaced. At Mount Rainier the prospectus called for finishing road projects un-

der way since before the war (the Stevens Canyon and West Side highways), and even expanding the road system with a low-speed "loop drive" around the Paradise area, an idea that conservation groups had opposed since the 1920s.[33] The Mission 66 planners also recommended an end to park transportation concessions, at Mount Rainier and in general. Since the nineteenth century, concessioners had provided transportation around parks for visitors arriving by train. These livery operations had often been more profitable than park hotels. In the 1940s concessioners at Mount Rainier, in particular, had objected to visitors arriving in "drive-yourself" rental cars, since this amounted to a violation of their monopoly for providing public transportation services. But the "majority of the [Mission 66 working] staff" felt that such restrictions were "not in the public interest" and should be specifically excluded in all future concession contracts. Appleman reported a "very strong feeling" that "any means of transportation a visitor might want to use for his own convenience should be allowed in the parks," as long as it met standards for "safety and protection." In the case of tour buses, the Mount Rainier concessioner had sought a more liberal policy allowing them in the park. In this case the planners agreed, recommending that "any bus or carrier" (including rental cars) be allowed, subject to regulations and fees.[34]

With passenger rail services all but ending nationally, the decisions to increase the capacity of park roads and end monopolistic protections for concessioner transportation services assured that the private automobile would strengthen its dominance as the only practical means of expe-

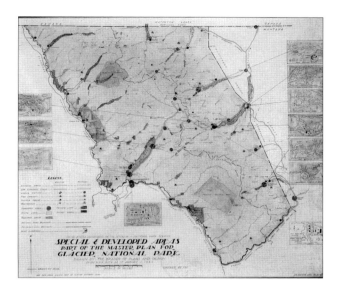

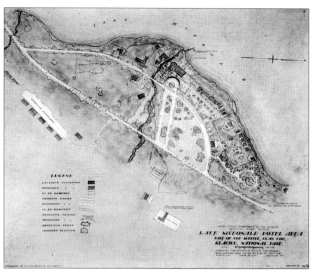

Plans from the 1930s Park Service master plan for Glacier National Park. These large format sheets featured carefully rendered drawings at several scales describing (and therefore limiting) all the development considered desirable for a given park. National Archives, RG 79.

riencing most parks. This dominance, however, was seen as part of the overall concept of reducing the impact of large numbers of visitors by making it easier for them to move through parks as efficiently—or at least as quickly—as possible. Maximizing the convenience of automotive tourism also meant providing more numerous picnic areas, comfort stations, interpretive centers, and other facilities. But wherever possible, this new development would be sited in less "sensitive" areas than earlier concessioner services had been and so would reduce the impact of crowds. Increasing the efficiency of park roads was an essential part of the strategy.

The model Mission 66 prospectus differed profoundly from the earlier master plans Vint and his staff had devised for Mount Rainier and every other park in the system.[35] Those plans had responded to the need to control the extent of park development—especially of new park roads—in the 1920s, when the first great wave of automotive tourism had arrived at many national parks. They often involved redeveloping and expanding existing concessioner areas, which in many cases had been established in close proximity to principal park destinations, such as the geyser basins of Yellowstone or the south rim of the Grand Canyon. Concessioners of the nineteenth and early twentieth centuries eventually built their most memorable hotels there. The park villages Vint and his staff designed in the 1920s and 1930s typically did not reject the locations of existing developed areas, but they did attempt to mitigate their presence even while expanding them. But even in cases where developed areas were having known deleterious effects on a park (such as the overnight cabins in Sequoia's Giant Forest), Vint rarely proposed relocating them altogether.[36] Concessioners during this era were seen as important partners who invested large amounts of capital in park facilities. As long as Mather and Albright embraced the partnership, it made little sense to recommend removing their improvements. Many of the hotels and other buildings in question had been built relatively recently, too, and returns on initial investments were still being made.

By the late 1930s, however, Vint had grown increasingly dissatisfied with his own master planning policy. If ever larger numbers of visitors were to continue to be accommodated, the necessary expansions of park villages would make it impossible to prevent them from overrunning and destroying park landscapes.[37] "Plan A," in other words, had reached the end of its usefulness. Those policies had effectively responded to a previous generation of challenges, but by the end of World War II, Vint was advocating a very different approach. Hotels built thirty or forty years earlier now required major rehabilitation, and demolition could be considered a reasonable—even desirable—alternative. A window of opportunity was opening, and Vint knew there would not be another for decades. Only at this point in the cycle of concessioner capital investment could the overall pattern of park development be seriously reorganized.

The Mission 66 prospectus for Mount Rainier did suggest the redevelopment of some of the same developed areas (such as Paradise and Longmire) that concessioners had established at the beginning of the century. The existing road corridors would also continue to determine the basic pattern of public access. But this latest iteration of national park planning would feature faster roads, larger campgrounds, "interpretive centers," and enlarged gateway communities. This new arrangement would allow for the demolition of overnight accommodations and other buildings in the park villages. In larger or more remote parks, where overnight accommodations would still be needed, new, redesigned lodges would be located in areas where they could be concentrated without damaging or encroaching on park scenery. The Mission 66 vision for national park planning indicated a genuinely innovative approach to accommodating the public. But the pilot prospectus for Mount Rainier was also the culmination of a process that the prewar master plans had begun: it was the final step in modernizing the frontcountry landscape to allow convenient and unrestricted automotive tourism while avoiding the "impairment" of park scenery and wildlife.

Out of the experience of creating the Mount Rainier prospectus, the Mission 66 team developed a generalized procedure for how other Mission 66 prospectuses should update and transform national park master plans. The first task was to "determine and state the important park resources." After this inventory, planners were to "fix a road and trail system" that would allow visitors to "see, experience, and enjoy the values to be derived from" the resources described in the list. In the great majority of cases, such road and trail corridors already existed but might require realignment, extension, or abbreviation. Planners should then "determine what visitor facilities, other than roads and trails," would be required in order to "provide a reasonable opportunity to enjoy the Park resources" and meet "administrative requirements . . . in terms of protecting [the park's] resources and providing visitor services." Finally, they were to decide what land acquisition (boundary expansions or inholdings) should be recommended.[38] The brief prospectuses were to be based on an analysis of the park master plans that had preceded them; but they were not to be in any way restricted by those plans or the assumptions implicit in them. The pilot study for Mount Rainier made it clear that a new set of priorities were to be considered. It was an approach that retained much of the traditional ideology of the Park Service—allowing access for public enjoyment—by radically altering the premises dictating how plans for ensuring that access and enjoyment should be made.

At a Park Service meeting that April in Shenandoah National Park, the Mount Rainier prospectus and the rest of the Mission 66 program were presented for the first time to the agency's four regional directors. Stripped of their regional design staff in 1954 and left out of Mission 66 planning in 1955, the directors were bound to have questions. Wirth, Garrison, and Carnes made a full presentation of Mission 66 goals and policies and discussed the results of the questionnaires sent out to parks the previous month. While the regional directors expressed their support, they also asked that their offices be kept more fully informed and more involved in plans. Garrison and Carnes went on the road that month to visit all four regional offices and the WODC and EODC to answer questions about the program and to meet with newly formed "Mission 66 committees" in each region. It was also agreed that further pilot studies should be done that would illustrate a "cross-section" of management concerns and park types. Wirth and his planners chose six more parks: Yellowstone and Everglades national parks, Chaco Canyon and Fort Laramie national monuments, Shiloh National Military Park, and the

Adams National Historic Site. A seventh pilot study, for Mesa Verde National Park, was added later; in this case the prospectus was to be prepared entirely by Region III staff in Santa Fe.

For the Mission 66 staff in Washington, work continued apace as the pilot study prospectuses were rapidly finished and further instructions were issued for regional offices and parks to prepare their own prospectuses for all the other parks in the system. On June 27, 1955, a third agency-wide informational memorandum reported on progress and set a deadline. The Mount Rainier prospectus was considered "completed," and the other pilot projects were well advanced. "Additional precepts" for Mission 66 planning, and brochures filled with "pertinent facts" for the public, were being written and designed. The goal remained to have the entire program outlined by that September. To accomplish this, Wirth insisted that a Mission 66 prospectus should be "made by, or for, each area . . . *not later than July 20.*"[39] Parks with adequate staff would prepare them themselves. Others would rely on regional, WODC, and EODC staff. The "studies" were to be initiated immediately and submitted to the Washington office and the appropriate regional and design offices for review. Any comments from the regions had to be made in writing by July 31 or the Mission 66 staff in Washington would assume that the prospectuses had been approved. Other instructions indicated the general outlines for the prospectuses. In a "narrative plan for protection, development, interpretation, and operation," superintendents were expected to make a statement of their park's "significance," inventory their "problems," record public use "patterns," and outline ideal interpretive, development, and operating plans. Superintendents were not to be limited by any "development requirements" their plans might incur, but they were to remember foremost the "necessity of preserving park values" that might be destroyed by excessive development. Once the prospectuses were approved, the Washington and regional offices were to coordinate the preparation of rough budget estimates.

A document titled "Principles Guiding Pilot Studies" was distributed as an attachment to the memorandum. The new principles indicated a change in emphasis from the initial planning guidelines distributed three months earlier. The first principle now listed was to secure "greater participation of private enterprise," especially for providing overnight accommodations. Presumably this referred to private development in gateway towns in addition to new concessioner investments in the parks. The second principle concerned "locating visitor accommodations" in attractive and accessible locations that would "not encroach on major park features," a policy that obviously implied only relocating, not removing, park concessions. There was no specific mention of converting parks to day use only; but new facilities were to be "geared to meet conditions imposed by modern means of transportation, and modern leisure time habits." The new principles also emphasized "spreading" park use seasonally and from overcrowded areas to less visited ones. The principles also specifically cited the need for a "coordinated nation-wide recreation plan leading to a nation-wide system of recreation facilities," the first time the Mission 66 planners had suggested how their work

might be coordinated with other federal and land management agencies. But they did not suggest that new legislation would be necessary, referring instead to the "intent" of the 1936 Park, Parkway, and Recreational-Area Study Act. These "principles" issued in June were decidedly less radical in tone than the initial policies outlined in March. The reactions to Mission 66 had already begun to reshape the program, if still only subtly at this point.[40]

The memorandum also gave an indication of the considerable political excitement the program had generated in less than six months. "Word of the objectives and purposes of Mission 66 has reached high places," Wirth intoned, and "the Service has been asked to present the subject to the President and his Cabinet." Although Wirth did not know it at the time, Maxwell M. Rabb, Eisenhower's secretary to the cabinet, had come up with the idea of a cabinet presentation on the subject of national parks after reading an editorial, "We've Been Starving Our National Parks," in the *Saturday Evening Post* that February.[41] Rabb's assistant, Bradley H. Patterson Jr., was taken with the idea and volunteered to work with Interior officials to arrange it. Patterson contacted Secretary McKay, and by May the Mission 66 staff had begun preparations for the meeting, which, after several postponements, finally occurred the following January.[42] Rabb's interest in national parks probably resulted from the steady barrage of negative press that was taking place, not any knowledge of the Mission 66 plans.[43] But whatever the reasons for it, after only six months of planning, the Park Service was asked to present its program directly to Eisenhower. Not since Roosevelt's involvement in the CCC had a chief executive potentially been so interested in Park Service operations. Wirth's bureaucratic facility, it seemed, was working again, putting his agency back into the forefront of federal recreational planning.

The excitement Wirth had generated also attracted interest—and concerns—from other groups. In the same June memorandum in which he reported Eisenhower's request, Wirth also warned that "rumours unfounded in fact . . . in connection with Mission 66" had come to his attention. These were harmless, he insisted, as long as they remained "confined to the Service family." But clearly they had not. Park concessioners and the residents of gateway towns, in particular, were susceptible to "misunderstandings." Conservation groups were also already troubled by a program that they knew nothing about, except that it would have enormous impact on the parks. Wirth then offered some arguments for assuaging these concerns. "We must not look upon the Mission 66 program merely as a convenient vehicle through which to secure maximum park developments in a minimum of time," he insisted. Each park would be considered individually. In some cases new developments would be "curtailed sharply," but in others they would not; in some parks "concessioners facilities [would] be removed," but in other cases they would be "recommended for considerable expansion."[44] Although these qualifications could hardly be described as backtracking in a program that still had not even been officially launched, they reinforced the less radical tone of the revised "principles" that were attached to the memorandum.

Rumors of the type that concerned Wirth were inevitable, though, since the Park Service had offered a compelling vision at this point but no specifics at all, at least not to anyone outside the "family." The director had been as indefatigable as his staff, traveling, speaking, and publishing on Park Service activities and priorities. In a number of public speeches and articles, Wirth described a "broad study" that was under way, but he did not go into details. One reason was clear: even with the great speed at which new plans were being drawn up, specific—and controversial—examples of just what the program would mean for individual parks were not available, or at least were not ready to be presented. Wirth also was not yet using the term "Mission 66" in speeches or published articles. Apparently the mission was to be a secret one until its official unveiling in September at Great Smoky Mountains National Park.[45] While many undoubtedly knew that something important was happening, the secrecy and speed with which Mission 66 was being assembled excited interest both in the government and among the press. But in some quarters it also spawned resentment. Wirth was succeeding with the Eisenhower administration, but vital partners, including conservation groups and park concessioners, already realized that the program was indeed being planned like a top-secret wartime mission, without any participation from them or the public.

Wirth did maintain close relationships with certain interest groups, however, a fact that may have further alienated wilderness advocates at the Sierra Club, the National Parks Association, and the Wilderness Society. Automobile clubs and oil companies, for example, had obvious interests in automotive tourism, and as Congress prepared to increase highway spending, they helped Wirth secure a share of federal aid highway appropriations specifically for park roads. The American Automobile Association (AAA) helped secure a $67 million authorization for national park road and parkway construction as part of the Federal Highway Act, signed in May 1954. The authorization was spread over the next three years, and as a result Congress made a $23 million appropriation for park highways in 1955. Though limited to road and parkway construction, the amount doubled the Park Service's total construction budget for fiscal year 1956 and presaged the greater increases to come under Mission 66.[46]

Wirth knew how effective the AAA and other allies could be on Capitol Hill, and he worked closely with AAA executive vice president Russell E. Singer and Michael Frome, the group's public relations director at the time. Already in December 1953 the AAA had hosted a private dinner at the Metropolitan Club at which Wirth presented a brochure, *National Park System: Present and Future*, which included the kind of statistics and policy analysis that would become the basis of Mission 66. The dinner was attended by Secretary of the Interior McKay, Laurance S. Rockefeller, *National Geographic* editor Melville Bell Grosvenor, and several influential members of Congress, including Gerald P. Nye of South Dakota and Burton K. Wheeler of Montana. The evening recalled the many dinners Mather had held in the 1920s at the Cosmos Club in order to enlist and develop park support. In this case, however, it was the AAA that organized the ef-

fort, which it followed up with another event in December 1954, themed as an "American Pioneer Dinner," held in another downtown hotel.[47] Again the AAA invited McKay, Wirth, and other officials to participate in a "new evaluation of the role of the parks in the pattern of our national life." Singer asked Wirth to give a presentation to "show the parks in their proper perspective and to bring the discussion into focus." Wirth responded with a thorough presentation of statistics, images, and proposed policy initiatives in a series of charts, graphs, and photographs. The material presented to the AAA and select members of Congress at these private dinners indicated the basic justifications and organization of what Wirth would soon describe as Mission 66.[48] There are no records of similar presentations to conservation groups in late 1954 or early 1955. At the time, perhaps, the political influence of the AAA made its friendship and support more valuable to Wirth in his dealings with a Congress that, at that point, had shown little willingness to fund any aspect of park improvements except road construction.

The Mission 66 planners assembling their program during 1955, however, did so independently, even secretly by today's standards, and no evidence suggests that the AAA or any private corporation directly influenced the preparation of prospectuses and policies any more than conservation groups did. The Mission 66 planners did employ at least one scientific survey of public opinion. In the spring of 1955 the Jackson Hole Preserve (a corporation funded by the Rockefeller family) agreed to pay for a professional "survey of the public concerning the national parks," conducted by a Princeton, New Jersey, market research firm. The survey was conducted that summer and published in December. The results further reinforced already strong convictions among Park Service planning staff about the general direction of the Mission 66 program. Among the more than 1,700 members of the public who filled out the ten-page Gallup survey, the three most common complaints about the parks concerned overcrowding, lack of overnight facilities, and shortage of restaurants and other concessions. Among people who had visited parks between 1951 and 1955, about 70 percent reported that their visit lasted one day or less, 50 percent were day trippers or had spent the night far from the park, and 20 percent had spent the night in nearby gateway towns. Of the 30 percent who had spent the night in a park, when asked what type of accommodations they would prefer, almost 80 percent said a motel or tourist cabin. Only 8 percent preferred hotels, while 14 percent wanted a campground.[49] Virtually all had traveled by car, and their preferences for park accommodations, like their travel arrangements in general, seemed to be determined mostly by considerations of expense and convenience. While the survey was under way, Mission 66 staff also received the various questionnaires and requests for comments that had been sent out to park superintendents that spring. Extensive interviews had also been conducted with chosen park managers. The working staff considered and summarized all of the concerns and opinions described.[50]

At least one other important survey, in this case regarding housing preferences among park staff and their families, was also available to the Mission 66 staff. At the 1952 park superintend-

ents' conference held in Glacier National Park, a group of Park Service employees' wives had formed the National Park Service Women's Organization. The women specifically wished to address the substandard housing conditions that prevailed in many national park residential areas. Herma Albertson Baggley, who as a Yellowstone ranger in 1931 had been the first woman to achieve permanent naturalist status in the Park Service, was elected national chair of the new organization. Married to the superintendent of Lake Mead National Recreation Area, Baggley, like so many of her colleagues, knew firsthand how inadequate staff housing could make it impossible to maintain good morale or retain qualified staff. As head of the women's group, she organized a systematic survey of existing housing data, gathered over the next year by women in almost every park that offered housing. In 1953 the organization submitted a report to Wirth which indicated that 10 percent of the agency's field employees were living in tents and 24 percent in one-bedroom houses or apartments. Of the latter group, 60 percent reported that the units were below "the standard of surrounding communities" in terms of size, basic utilities, and construction quality. Of the 40 percent lucky enough to be living in a two- or three-bedroom house or apartment, nearly half were in housing considered substandard by these measures. The majority of park housing had been built in the 1920s or by the CCC in the 1930s and sometimes lacked modern utilities, including even electricity and running water. The remainder of the housing stock consisted of dormitories, which housed 60 percent of seasonal employees, and a few "trailers,"

Substandard housing documented in Grand Teton (left and top right) and in Grand Canyon. NPS Historic Photo Collection.

which Baggley did not recommend as a replacement for "fixed housing." Baggley added that the statistics presented a "conservative" estimate of the problem; many Park Service women were proud of managing under difficult circumstances and wanted to avoid any appearance of complaining.[51] But at a time when many Americans were moving into their own ranch houses with attached garages, washing machines, and other conveniences, park staff and their families, not unlike military personnel, who were facing a similar crisis, were trapped in housing that represented an earlier set of expectations for the material setting of family life.

Wirth encouraged Baggley and the other women in her organization and instructed Vint to collaborate with them to produce model house plans for park families that would meet modern social requirements. These requirements were also indicated in Baggley's 1953 survey. Of the women surveyed, 94 percent preferred "individual buildings" to multi-unit buildings, citing play space for children and privacy as considerations. There was more diversity of opinion regarding whether "standard plans" for new two- and three-bedroom houses should be adopted over custom designs. But 76 percent favored standard plans, as long as there were adequate variations in construction and insulation to reflect regional climates. Standard plans provided some stability for women who moved their families so frequently, since they could be reasonably sure of what to expect at their next posting. At a minimum they could know that their furniture and other belongings would fit in their next residence. Attached garages were favored by 86 percent, and space for storage in a basement or utility room was a priority for 95 percent. Opinions were more evenly split on details such as the desirability of picture windows, plaster walls, and basements. In their recommendations for Park Service housing design, Baggley reported, the women agreed that a home's "architectural design should complement the area in which it is built," apparently despite standardized floor plans. No one was asking for any "luxuries," but "all expressed a desire for space," since cramped conditions exacerbated all other inadequacies. They wanted larger houses, and they wanted them sited on larger lots, farther apart from one another.[52]

The women managing households in sometimes remote and isolated settings were asking for nothing more than parity with the rest of the nation in terms of what was considered standard housing: the two- or three-bedroom, single-family detached home. It was hardly surprising that in 1955 Wirth and Vint endorsed standard plans for two- and three-bedroom ranch houses, a style that featured many of the architectural and site amenities Baggley's findings had specified.[53] The ranch house, probably more than any other type, symbolized a standard of material life that was consistent with what park staff and their families could see in surrounding communities.

Using a familiar building also ensured that local contractors could be found at reasonable cost, and that contemporary building materials and technology—from slab concrete foundations to manufactured windows—could be effectively employed. The ranch was also flexible: plans could easily be flipped into "right-handed" and "left-handed" versions; garages, entry portals, and other extras could be added; and different rooflines and siding materials could be applied to reflect local conditions and availability. By 1955 Wirth and Vint had concurred with the National Park Service Women's Organization on the basic outline for residential development in the parks. Over the next ten years the basic plans for park residences would be improved, altered, and reissued several times; but the standard would remain the single-family ranch house, built by area contractors who would be given some latitude on construction materials and techniques to reflect local conditions.

For the Mission 66 planners in Washington and their counterparts in the parks and regions, surveys of both park visitors and staff helped justify some of the decisions being made in the prospectuses they were rapidly preparing during the summer of 1955. The planning process, however, remained insular, within the Park Service "family." If this allowed for rapid progress, it also guaranteed different levels of confrontation with the full range of interest groups waiting to express their own preferences. In the meantime, the Washington staff soon discovered that in some cases they were trying to resolve management issues that had festered for years. The optimistic morale and policy statements of February soon came up against angry superintendents, opinionated regional staff, and WODC and EODC planners with their own ideas about what the prospectuses should contain.

Of the eight pilot studies under way, two incited no controversy. At the Adams National Historic Site in Quincy, Massachusetts, regional director Daniel J. Tobin, Hodge Hanson of the EODC, and the Mission 66 steering committee reviewed and accepted the working staff's prospectus with no changes. Wilhelmina Harris, the site's superintendent, was not present at the meeting but presumably agreed with the basic outline of the prospectus since it did not contradict the principles she had already espoused. In 1962 she would describe these goals as keeping "the house and grounds looking as if the Adamses had just stepped out. Modern intrusions and development facilities will be located on additional acquired property so as to leave the original gift of land and intact buildings [made in 1946] with their authentic flavor. . . . As long as this is continued, 'living history' will be felt." The site's exceptional integrity needed to be "preserved inviolate," and adjacent small parcels of land should be acquired as the postwar "megalopolis" of Boston encroached. The planners easily reached a consensus with Harris and others interested in the management of the property that had housed four generations of the illustrious Adams family between 1787 and 1927. The plans for Shiloh National Military Park in Tennessee also were quickly resolved. Superintendent Ira B. Lykes and regional staff quickly agreed with the Mission 66 staff on the proposed outline of management for the Civil War battlefield and cemetery.[54]

In other cases, strong-willed park superintendents forced the Mission 66 planners to reverse course that summer. At Fort Laramie National Monument (later redesignated a National Historic Site) in Wyoming, superintendent David L. Hieb and regional landscape architect Harvey P. Benson came to Washington to argue that the master plan they had developed should not be replaced by the new Mission 66 prospectus. In this case the working staff had attempted to simplify and accelerate the development of the park by converting an existing barracks for visitor use rather than acquiring additional land to build a new facility on the other side of Laramie Creek. The superintendent reacted angrily and won over the steering committee, including Vint. After "heated discussion," the working staff revised the prospectus to reflect the original master plan. In the discussions over plans for Chaco Canyon National Monument (later Chaco Culture National Historical Park) in New Mexico, superintendent Glen D. Bean and regional landscape architect Jerome C. Miller again took the working staff to task, demanding that the existing master plan be the basis of the new prospectus. In this case the original plan called for a road and visitor facilities on the canyon floor. The working staff suggested relocating both to the canyon rim, where they would be less obtrusive but would require visitors to hike down to the canyon floor for a closer look at the ruins. Once again, however, the steering committee capitulated and the prospectus reverted to the earlier plan.[55]

At Mesa Verde National Park in Colorado, the regional office in Santa Fe had apparently insisted that they would prepare the pilot prospectus themselves, bypassing the Mission 66 staff. The regional office in this case wanted to relocate the lodge, restaurant, headquarters, employee residences, and other facilities which since the 1920s had been centralized at Spruce Tree Point, near the site's most famous (and delicate) ruins. Since then the number of annual visitors had climbed to 42,000 in 1941 and 125,000 in 1952; it was expected that the latter figure would more than double by 1966. Regional staff decided that Mission 66 offered the "impetus necessary" to reverse conditions that were "stifling visitor enjoyment and causing deterioration of the physical environment at Spruce Tree Point." But Mission 66 working and steering committees were not able to agree with the regional staff on the overall strategy for redevelopment, and in 1955 the Mesa Verde prospectus was "kept under continuing study."[56]

Appleman reported that the three remaining pilot prospectuses, for Yellowstone, Everglades, and Mount Rainier national parks, were "accepted," subject to revisions. This characterization proved to be inaccurate in light of the contentious debate that would continue around Mission 66 planning for all of these parks for years to come. But as Appleman conceded drily in his 1958 history, the preparation of the first prospectuses in 1955 "showed all too clearly that it was not easy always to solve specific problems by the application of a fine-sounding principle."[57]

Yellowstone National Park best illustrated the long-standing difficulties of trying to cope with vastly increased numbers of visitors at a time when neither Congress nor park concessioners were willing to invest in new development. In 1948, 1 million visitors came to the park, up from 20,000 in 1920. The increase consisted almost entirely of people arriving in their own cars, who set their own agendas at hotels and campgrounds, and who increasingly found their own accommodations in towns outside park entrances. In 1948 Drury reported that "new development" was needed throughout the park system, but especially at Yellowstone. He claimed that the Old Faithful area was at "the saturation point" and that the facilities at the Grand Canyon of the Yellowstone were "obsolete." He proposed two new developed areas, West Thumb and Canyon Village, to be financed by combined concessioner and government funds. Drury backed the expansion of the Lake and Fishing Bridge areas and proposed a $3 million "administration-museum building" for Mammoth Hot Springs. To make the Grand Loop road system adequate for projected traffic volumes, he estimated that a $13 million road modernization program would be required.[58] But Drury knew that none of this would happen. In 1948 park concessioners were battling the Department of the Interior over the terms of new contracts and, for the time being, avoiding any new investments. Congress was preoccupied with the reconstruction of Europe and political turmoil in Asia. In contrast to a $20 million redevelopment program just for Yellowstone, construction in the entire park system totaled under $1 million that year.

The oldest and, at the time, largest national park, Yellowstone had always been the showcase of Park Service policies. But by the early 1950s the condition of visitor services—and the long delay in addressing them—were a national scandal. Wirth had begun to reform and centralize concession management when he became director in 1951, and he attempted to persuade the Yellowstone Park Company to invest millions of dollars in new development as part of a contract renegotiation. But he and the concessioner, William M. Nichols (the son-in-law of the company's founder, Harry W. Child), could not reach an agreement on the terms of such investments. Nichols's business situation had become more difficult in the 1940s. Railroad companies that in the past had made loans to the concessioner were now in the process of reducing and terminating passenger rail service to Yellowstone. The companies no longer had any reason to finance visitor accommodations, and banks balked at the notion of making large loans secured only by hotels that, because of their location, technically had their titles vested in the United States. Under the circumstances, Nichols was searching (unsuccessfully) for a buyer for his family's business. Nichols was in his seventies, worried about the future of his family's business, and was in no mood to sink any remaining assets into new construction.[59]

As the situation deteriorated, a group of Wyoming businessmen and elected officials organized an effort to buy and assume control of the Yellowstone Park Company, effectively asserting state control over this critical aspect of the federal park's management. On February 14, 1955, just a week after Wirth initiated Mission 66 planning, the Wyoming legislature passed a bill that would have authorized the state's acquisition of the Yellowstone concessions. Although such an action would have seriously undermined the Park Service's jurisdiction, there was no offi-cial response from Wirth or from the Department of the Interior; in any case, the proposal quickly sank under the weight of inherent legal and procedural difficulties. But the situation no doubt contributed to the "crisis" Wirth perceived that February, adding to the urgency with which Mission 66 was planned, particularly for Yellowstone.[60]

At about the time Mission 66 planning began, Wirth also organized a separate "working group" on the "concessioner needs" for Yellowstone. The Yellowstone Park Company's twenty-year contract was set to expire at the end of 1955, and Wirth anticipated the opportunity to require major capital investments as part of any new contract, whether with Nichols or a new concessioner. Headed by a special assistant, Phillip F. King, the concessions group included Yellowstone superintendent Edmund B. Rogers, park landscape architect Frank E. Mattson, chief ranger Otto M. Brown, and chief naturalist David de L. Condon. Their week-long meeting also involved members of the recently formed Mission 66 committees. The group debated the most basic assumptions about how Yellowstone should function as a public park. Should overnight accommodations in the park be continued, and if so under one or several concession contracts? Should increased demand instead be met by private businesses outside the park? Should older hotels in the park be "abandoned and removed" and replaced by "motel type" lodgings in less sensitive areas?[61]

The concessions group met while the Mission 66 planners were drafting their first policy statements; the two discussions overlapped and, to judge by the results, influenced each other.

The Yellowstone group concluded that there was still a need for several developed areas with accommodations within the park, and in fact they recommended greatly expanding overnight visitor capacity, from roughly 8,000 to 14,000. But they added that this expansion should never be exceeded, and that thereafter surrounding towns should meet any further demand for lodging. No new hotels should be built in the park since the public had shown a "decided preference for motel type accommodations." The new motels would be financed by issuing "prospectuses" that would invite private applicants to build and operate lodges in several areas of the park, preferably under separate concession contracts, with limited rights of preferential renewal.[62]

The concession plan specified that the Lake and Fishing Bridge area was to be enlarged, but that the boat docks were to be moved to a new development at nearby Bridge Bay. Bridge Bay would also include a new lodge. At West Thumb, landscape architect Mattson had advocated since at least 1946 relocating development that encroached on the geyser basin; with Vint's help and support, he planned a new visitor complex about a mile to the south, to be called Thumbay (later Grant Village).[63] At Old Faithful, the Old Faithful Inn and the roads around it would be razed, again to eliminate the "encroachment upon thermal features," and a new and expanded developed area to be named Wonderland (later Firehole Village) would be sited near Mallard Lake. The Mammoth Hot Springs area was to have its overnight capacity reduced "with the objective of the [nearby] town of Gardiner taking up the slack." At the Grand Canyon of

The Canyon Hotel, designed by Robert Reamer, was completed in 1911. NPS Historic Photo Collection.

the Yellowstone, again the existing lodge and cabins would be demolished and replaced by a new Canyon Village sited farther away from the canyon rim. The new village, which had first been planned in 1935, was a priority for Park Service planners because it could accommodate increased numbers without encroaching further on the rim of the canyon, where visitors traditionally enjoyed some of the most dramatic scenery in the park.[64]

Throughout Yellowstone, the concession planning group recommended expanding overnight accommodations and visitor services by demolishing old hotels and tourist cabins and replacing them with larger developments farther away from the geysers, important vistas, and other "sensitive areas." While the group recommended building several extensive new motel complexes, they also emphasized that these plans represented the ultimate development of the park. If demand for overnight accommodations continued to grow, it would have to be met by motels outside park boundaries. The overall pattern of use of the park, represented by the

This Yellowstone master plan sheet signed by Wirth in 1952 shows the location of the old Canyon Hotel and of the new Canyon Village that was to replace it. The idea for Canyon Village was first proposed in the 1930s, and it later became a centerpiece of the park's Mission 66 prospectus. Yellowstone National Park Archives.

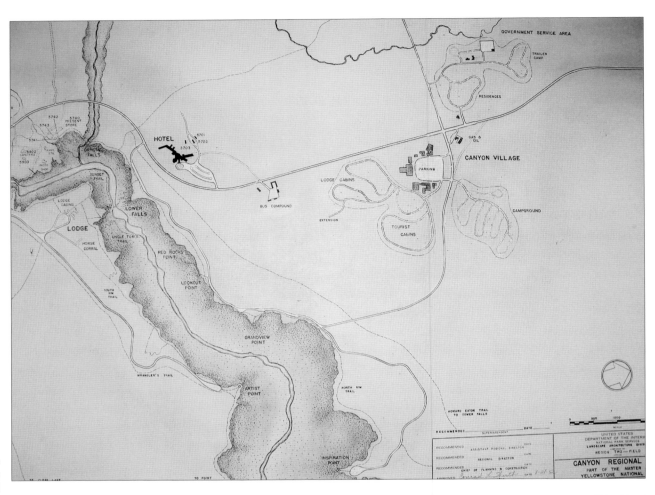

This pre-Mission 66 Yellowstone master plan drawing shows existing development around West Thumb and proposed locations for what would become Grant Village. Yellowstone National Park Archives.

Although the proposed postwar redevelopment of the Old Faithful area initially called for the demolition of the Old Faithful Inn and the Old Faithful Lodge, as seen here, these plans were quickly abandoned as Mission 66 got underway. Yellowstone National Park Archives.

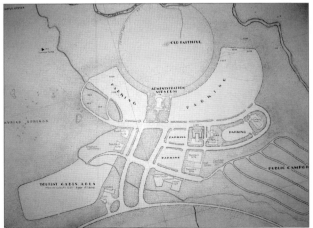

Grand Loop road system, should remain and be modernized but not expanded. These priorities mirrored the fundamental tenets of Mission 66, which were being drafted at the time. From the beginning, the success or failure of the overall project was linked to the fate of the new Yellowstone concession contracts and park redevelopment program. Under these circumstances, Yellowstone served as a flagship of Mission 66 planning, design, and policy.[65]

In April 1955 Superintendent Rogers and his staff were in Washington for a week-long discussion on the Mission 66 pilot prospectus for their park. Again there was a consensus that popular and sensitive destinations, especially Old Faithful and the Mammoth Hot Springs, were being overwhelmed. The Mission 66 committee agreed with the general ideas of the concession working group—which reflected the emerging philosophy of Mission 66 generally—that older developed areas should in many cases be demolished and replaced by more expansive facilities sited in less "sensitive" areas or else outside the park altogether. The initial prospectus resembled the recommendation of the concession group (although a minority of Mission 66 staff also wanted more development removed from Fishing Bridge because of the area's ecological significance). Most of the staff felt that camping facilities and day use areas should be greatly expanded, but they did not want "trailer courts" in the park, although they acknowledged that one (but no more) would have to be provided somewhere. They acknowledged as well an earlier study on the benefits of moving park headquarters out of Yellowstone to the nearby town of Gardiner, but the park staff and superintendent

nevertheless insisted that administration remain at Mammoth. The steering committee requested an inventory of tourist accommodations, campgrounds, and other recreation areas within one hundred miles of Yellowstone's entrances. There was also a general sentiment expressed that the park concessioner should be replaced.[66]

If the staff of Yellowstone and the Mission 66 planners agreed on a basic philosophy for the pilot prospectus for that park, the prospectus for Everglades National Park generated more dissent. Many Park Service officials believed Everglades to be the first true "wilderness park." In the 1934 legislation authorizing the park, Congress specifically mandated that it be "permanently preserved as a wilderness" and prohibited any development that would "interfere with the preservation intact of the unique flora and fauna and the essentially primitive conditions now prevailing."[67] The National Audubon Society and other conservation groups had already struggled for decades to preserve the Everglades as a unique and invaluable habitat, and they remained intensely involved in the fate of the park project. Land acquisitions were finally completed by the state of Florida in 1947. The park's first superintendent, Daniel B. Beard, ran the park on a shoestring for the next seven years, relying on the existing Ingraham Highway to provide access to the main visitor areas at Royal Palms, Coot Bay, and Flamingo. Several small concessions offered snack bar and tour boat services, but the highway often became impassable because of its poor condition, and even public restrooms were lacking. Conservationists, as well as local chambers of commerce and other

Florida state officials and members of Congress, eagerly awaited plans and funding for the development of the new national park. In the spring of 1953 Superintendent Beard traveled to Washington to consult with Vint, Wirth, and other staff on plans for Flamingo. But no major appropriations were made, and Beard was kept busy with property transfers, boundary expansions, and the efforts of oil companies to expand into the park. Park headquarters were housed in rented space in nearby Homestead.[68]

As was the case at Yellowstone, events at Everglades had reached a critical point just as Mission 66 was organizing. In October 1954 Secretary of the Interior McKay invited proposals from concessioners interested in building and operating a marina, motel, gas station, employee housing, stores, and other services at Flamingo. The contract required a private investment of at least $500,000, and the Park Service had already begun its contribution by making road improvements and dredging for future boat slips at the "chosen development site."[69] But while a concessioner was selected, the program for Flamingo continued to develop as the contract was negotiated. Following initial discussions with his Mission 66 committees that February, Wirth ordered a "special use study" that was conducted in the park. By March, Wirth had decided not to include overnight accommodations in the Flamingo development. He rather proudly exhorted his Mission 66 planners to make similarly difficult moves away from precedent at other parks.[70] Conservation groups, including the Audubon Society and the American Nature Association, had contacted Wirth and made clear their opposition to a "re-

sort" at Flamingo, implying that the 1954 program involved too much development. The initial organization of Mission 66 that February also had persuaded Wirth to heed Thomas Vint's advice and avoid "Plan A" at the Everglades. Given a clean slate, Wirth later explained, his agency intended to avoid a situation in which a small development in a sensitive area would grow to an unacceptable size as demand increased. He also pointed out that there was no shortage of motels nearby in Florida City and Homestead. Overnight accommodations would "constitute unnecessary intrusion into the natural scene" at Flamingo and take up too much of the very limited high ground in the park. Just as important, the elimination of the motel would "obviate the danger of the Flamingo development becoming just another Florida resort area. . . . Everglades National Park should not emulate or compete with those uses, but should stand as a distinctive feature itself."[71]

That July, Superintendent Beard returned to Washington to work on the Everglades prospectus with Mission 66 planners. The pilot prospectus they drafted contained no mention of any overnight accommodations and emphasized that the park was primarily a "biological area" and a "wilderness preserve." Interpretation, not recreation, was "requisite to the enjoyment and appreciation of the Everglades scene," and therefore the extent of development should be determined by the needs of the interpretive mission, not by recreation. In practice at Flamingo, this meant providing a "Public Use building" for visitor information, a restaurant, gas station, and even a marina (already under construction), but no motel. The plan characterized Everglades as a new kind of park, set aside for biological, not scenic, values, precariously set on the "very threshold of a major metropolitan area" that was sprawling rapidly. The prospectus emphasized the scientific mission of the park, and even suggested that the wildfire control policy should be based on "sound ecological facts," which might sometimes require that fire "be considered as part of the natural course of events, like hurricane." Beard, a Park Service field biologist since the 1930s and an Everglades researcher in his own right, helped give the prospectus its unprecedented ecological emphasis.[72]

But when the new concessioner, Robert Knight of the Everglades Park Company, realized that overnight accommodations would not be part of the Flamingo development, he immediately scaled back his interest. He felt that as a day use area Flamingo could not generate profits warranting the investment originally described. The terms of the contract were still under negotiation, and Knight made it clear that unless he was allowed to build a motel, he would not bear the cost of the large "Public Use" building the Park Service wanted. Local officials and important park supporters also wondered why overnight accommodations, which were part of the 1954 proposal, had been removed in the Mission 66 prospectus. At an October 1955 meeting in John D. Pennekamp's office at the *Miami Herald*, Wirth defended his decision to Florida's governor, congressional delegation, and other local officials.[73] The Park Service director insisted that overnight accommodations would not be part of the "initial development plan" at Everglades, although he did allow that they "could be provided later if deemed essential by the Service." Knight

agreed to the contract terms that fall, which now required him to invest only $250,000 in the overall development.[74]

That spring, however, the protest against Wirth's decision at Everglades became more organized and imposing. The Miami-Dade Chamber of Commerce addressed Assistant Secretary of the Interior Wesley D'Ewart directly, complaining that the draft prospectus was "a violation of the understanding of the people of this county . . . when they urged their state government to contribute . . . one million acres to the creation of the Everglades park . . . .The understanding was . . . that everything necessary would be done to make the Park a tourist attraction."

Parachute Key Visitor Center, Everglades National Park, as it appeared in the 1960s. NPS Photo by Jack E. Boucher.

The controversial motel complex in the Flamingo area of Everglades as it appears today. Author's photo.

The *Miami Herald* editorialized that Everglades deserved to be developed in a manner comparable to other parks in the system, which meant including the overnight accommodations that had been specified in the "original plans" but then "cancelled abruptly, without reason."[75] Wirth still supported his superintendent and planners, issuing a strong statement and a press release arguing that a motel was unnecessary and inappropriate and reminding his critics that his agency was spending $5 million on other development in the park, building a new road to Flamingo, picnic areas, interpretive centers, and the other features of a day use park. But "preservation of the scenic and scientific values of the Everglades while making them accessible to more and more visitors," he admitted, "presents one of the most challenging problems in our MISSION 66 program." Within a year Wirth acceded to political pressure and agreed to a motel at Flamingo with sixty units and a swimming pool.[76]

Like the Mount Rainier pilot prospectus, the first pilot to be completed just a few months earlier, the Everglades prospectus again indicated how difficult it would be to transform large national parks into day use destinations. Public expectations seemed to include overnight accommodations, even in a new park that had no previous tradition of large hotels. At Mount Rainier as well, the controversy over removing overnight accommodations was far from settled, even if the Park Service considered its prospectus for the park complete. Elected officials and local business interests in Washington angrily rejected the Mission 66 plans for Mount Rainier as soon as they learned of them. Despite the fact that winter use of the park had begun to decrease in the postwar period as the ski industry started to develop other, more suitable mountains, business leaders and public officials in Washington continued to believe that year-round use and overnight accommodations at Mount Rainier were linchpins of the state's tourist economy. In 1956 two congressional hearings were held in which both of Washington's senators, Henry M. Jackson and Warren Magnusen, denounced the Mission 66 prospectus and forced a complete reconsideration of plans for the park. Several new economic studies and planning proposals extended the controversy to 1960, when the senators introduced legislation that would have directed the Park Service to build a new hotel at Paradise whether it wanted one or not. In this case, Wirth continued to defend his agency's position successfully. The matter was only resolved in 1964, when Jackson and Magnusen finally relented and secured an appropriation for a new day use facility, or "visitor center," at Paradise. As a consolation prize for two powerful elected officials, the new visitor center was one of the

The Henry M. Jackson Memorial Visitor Center was completed in the Paradise area of Mount Rainier National Park in 1967. Author's photo.

largest and most elaborate designed under Mission 66. Completed in 1966 at a cost of $2 million, it was at the time the most expensive building the Park Service had ever built. But Mount Rainier, like Everglades, still never became a day use park. By the mid-1960s, historic preservationists urged the rehabilitation of the nearby Paradise Inn, which survived and continues to serve overnight guests today as a National Historic Landmark.[77]

As complex as the situations in the "pilot" Mission 66 parks may have been, they were only the beginning of the huge task of preparing the entire Mission 66 program for presentation to the press and public in September 1955. Wirth had instructed every superintendent and staff member in his agency to help prepare their own prospectuses that summer, using the guidelines that his staff had issued in March. In larger parks, superintendents and their staff took on the responsibility; smaller parks looked to the regional offices and WODC and EODC for assistance. Wirth maintained a system in which he personally reviewed and approved not just the "precepts for staff guidance" but the content of the individual prospectuses themselves. A naturally skilled bureaucrat, Wirth was also an experienced planner and landscape architect in his own right. Previous Park Service directors had

been businessmen and lawyers, but Wirth had both the training and the inclination to oversee the details of Mission 66. He also had personal precedent for such a large administrative undertaking. In the 1930s, when he organized the federal-state partnership of the CCC program, Wirth had orchestrated the delicate "cooperation" with state park agencies in which he effectively ensured, even dictated, policies and standards for park planning without alienating local authorities by infringing on their jurisdiction. In Mission 66, Wirth again imposed a strong, centralized administrative structure, and again he was able to review and control every aspect and detail of the program without making his partners (in this case superintendents and regional directors) feel that their authority had been usurped. Park Service staff joined enthusiastically in the Mission 66 planning process, in many cases working overtime without pay. By all accounts agency morale rose. But as the program moved from the preparation of pilot studies to determining the details that would affect virtually every unit of the park system, Wirth and his Washington staff retained a remarkable degree of centralized control over the details of individual park prospectuses as well as the general outlines of Mission 66 policies.

CHAPTER 4

PUBLIC POLICY AND "OUR HERITAGE"

Lon Garrison, the chairman of the steering committee, served as Wirth's most trusted lieutenant for the early planning of Mission 66. Thomas Vint of course had greater experience, and Bill Carnes, Vint's protégé and head of the working staff, was another landscape architect with decades of experience. But it was the former park superintendent and chief ranger, Garrison, who led the Mission 66 staff in Washington and became the most important early representative of the program, with the exception of Wirth himself.

Garrison may not have had experience in design and construction, but he had credibility with park managers, and he helped cast Mission 66 policy in terms that resonated with field personnel. Since at least March, Garrison had been drafting the "Guiding Precepts of Mission 66."[1] These reflected the views and contributions of many, but ultimately only Wirth had greater influence on the articulation of the ideas pre-sented. The precepts reiterated the basic themes of Park Service policy that informed the entire Mission 66 project: "Visitor enjoyment" of parks was the "best means of protecting them against exploitation or encroachment"; visitors must be "channeled to avoid overuse" and deterioration of certain areas; "channeling use" in this way required "proper development." Mission 66 would therefore be a "use and development program" that would achieve the "preservation objectives of the Service."

By August the "precepts" had reached a final form and become the first section of the "MISSION 66 Report" drafted in September for presentation at the Great Smokies conference. Additional "discussion sections" elaborated the precepts. "All visitors desiring to enter a national park," the planners had agreed, "may do so," whether in private vehicles, "drive-yourself" rentals, or permitted tour buses. "Limitations on numbers are not to be considered except for

Lon Garrison (in uniform) and Wirth (right) presenting a new interpretive display in Yellowstone to Secretary of the Interior Fred Seaton in 1958. Photo by Jack E. Boucher, NPS Historic Photo Collection.

certain . . . ruins or buildings which . . . require limits." In his draft, Garrison even crossed out "limits" and replaced the word with "restrictions." Wirth and his planners, who reexamined almost every aspect of national park operations at this time, never seriously discussed options for imposing limits on the numbers of people entering national parks.

The question of limiting the number of visitors had in fact been raised by field staff, including Eivind T. Scoyen, superintendent of Sequoia Kings Canyon.[2] Garrison addressed the matter—and quickly dismissed it—in the draft Mission 66 "precepts," as well as in subsequent published articles. Garrison, along with Wirth, Vint, Carnes, and probably almost all of the Mission 66 planners, strongly believed that expanded use of the parks could occur without impairing them. Success would require reconceptualizing how parks

should function as public places and redeveloping them accordingly. Making parks into day use destinations, for example, could be achieved with wider roads, larger parking lots, and expanded "visitor use centers" to provide ample interpretive displays, bathrooms, and administrative areas for larger numbers of people. Limiting public access to parks would therefore not be necessary. It would also betray the fundamental concept of what national parks, as public parks, were intended to achieve. But while visitors would not be turned away, neither would they be "guaranteed overnight or meal facilities" in every park. The new iteration of the national park idea was intended to maintain the parks as truly public parks, even under the greatly increased pressures of the postwar era.[3]

Other wide-ranging "discussions" were recorded by Garrison as the policy of the Mission 66 program matured that August. The "interpretive presentation" of a park or historic site should "take full advantage of the actual scene, object, or structure as the interpretive exhibit." On the one hand, this implied the location of roads, trails, and "visitor use centers" near the historic landscapes and natural features that were to be interpreted by the Park Service and enjoyed by the public. On the other hand, where concession hotels encroached on natural or historic scenes, they would be removed and replaced by businesses outside the park, or by new concessions sited in less sensitive areas. At parks where "public accommodations in the immediate vicinity" of the park were available or could be developed, hotels within park boundaries would eventually be demolished, depending on the limitations of existing concession contracts. When overnight accommodations were considered necessary in a park, because of remoteness or public "travel patterns" within parks, "competition in providing concession facilities" would be encouraged by seeking new concessioners, and sometimes multiple concessioners. Park Service administrative and maintenance buildings would be relocated according to the same priorities and removed from parks wherever it was deemed practicable.[4]

Wirth and Garrison described Mission 66 that summer in terms that seriously revised the logistical model Mather and Albright had created for how national parks should function. A new planning archetype was taking shape, one that responded to postwar travel patterns and social trends. Writing for magazines such as *American Forests* and *National Park Magazine,* Wirth and Garrison raised the curtain on Mis-

sion 66 that August, describing it as an accomplished fact. "MISSION 66 has been organized in the National Park Service offices," Garrison announced, "to produce a comprehensive and integrated program of uses and preservation that will harmonize with the Service's obligations under the Act of 1916." He went on to summarize the Mission 66 "precepts," addressing at greater length the question of visitor restrictions, particularly for the readers of *National Parks Magazine:* "One of the common suggestions in the MISSION 66 study is that quotas should be established to limit the number of people who may visit an area. Many of the historical areas are self-limiting; but it is the opinion of the committee and the staff of MISSION 66 that, in the great natural areas, quotas are not necessary at this time. Rather, modern traffic handling methods and proper development to achieve protection and interpretation will enable most existing visitor locations to accommodate the crowds anticipated in 1966." Wirth described his program in historical terms as "supporting the ideals and the vision of the pioneers of the national park movement" through an "intensive study of all the problems facing the National Park Service—protection, staffing, interpretation, use, development, financing, needed legislation, forest protection, fire." He and his staff had developed "experimental precepts to guide themselves and park staff in certain pilot studies to test the validity of their new thinking." Wirth firmly rejected the idea of "rationing park use," declaring emphatically, "The principle that is guiding the MISSION 66 Committee and Staff *is that the parks belong to the people, and they have a right to use* them." Redevelopment, and the "spread" of visitor use both geographically and seasonally, would make it possible.[5]

As word of the still mysterious Mission 66 program reached those outside the Park Service, concerns and questions immediately surfaced. C. Edward Graves of the National Parks Association responded to a presentation by Wirth that August by denouncing Mission 66 as a "secret effort to develop a body of policies on a bureaucratic basis without participation by the public." He doubted that the Park Service would be flexible enough "to be altered by the impact of public opinion" now that such advice was finally being sought. Wirth responded with a repetition of his manifesto, which Graves had already heard him present personally to National Parks Association board members. Wirth added curtly that since the program was about to be presented to the Bureau of the Budget and to Congress, "the details contained in it cannot be made public." Sounding all too officious, he informed Graves that his agency was not waiting for the "approval or disapproval" of "friends of the parks outside the Service." Although "the course of action to be followed" would be "affected considerably by public opinion," decisions affecting the park system "must rest with those specifically charged with responsibility." A similar response soon went out to the president of the Sierra Club, Alexander Hildebrand, who also expressed concerns about "secrecy" in a series of letters requesting detailed information on plans for the Sierran parks. Wirth needlessly offended the Sierra Club and other conservation groups by refusing to bring them into the planning process. Negotiations with both Con-

gress and park concessioners certainly did require some confidentiality, though the goodwill of the conservationists probably could have been won at the time with even perfunctory consideration. But Wirth responded to them with none of the solicitousness and warmth he showed other allies such as the AAA. Suspicion of secrecy soon hardened into an adversarial conviction that Wirth and his staff intended to retain absolute authority over Mission 66 plans and would not share details until all significant decisions had been made. A struggle over who had the right to participate in national park planning began as soon as Mission 66 became public knowledge.[6]

Wirth was understandably preoccupied, at the time, with the intense pressure he had put on himself and his staff to be ready to present Mission 66 at the Public Services Conference held at Great Smoky Mountains National Park from September 19 to 24. By this time Mission 66 was completely engaging Park Service staff all over the country, affecting their daily activities and duties as well as the entire institutional culture of the agency. Wirth had demanded that his Washington staff, with extensive help from regional and park staff, complete the eight pilot prospectuses, finalize the written "principles guiding the study," and draft any legislation considered necessary. He also asked for an "all-inclusive statement and budget" of the program in the form of a "brief, popular-style book," filled with charts, tables, and photographs, for distribution to the press, the public, and members of Congress. The details of the program would be assembled in a longer report with chapters covering every aspect of the initiative, which was intended to serve as the "bible" that would guide the program over the next ten years. "Everyone on the Staff felt that the Director had given a pretty heavy assignment," Appleman reported; but there was more. Wirth also asked that the entire program, including draft prospectuses and budget estimates for most of the 194 parks and historic sites of the park system, be in completed form by the end of the year in order to be submitted to the Bureau of the Budget for approval in December.[7] With approval from that office, the appropriations process could begin early in 1956, making it possible for Congress to act by the end June, in time to launch Mission 66 at the beginning of fiscal year 1957 (July 1, 1956). The overall costs of the program would need to be not only estimated but also broken down into annual appropriations requests covering the next ten years.[8]

Wirth and his staff presented their work on September 20. The conference of about two hundred superintendents and other officials was dominated by an extended discussion of the Mission 66 program. The mystery surrounding the details of the program, and perhaps word of Eisenhower's personal interest in it, made the conference a major public relations event. Newspapers from all over the country covered the story. The Mission 66 staff managed to have ready an illustrated booklet, *The National Park System,* and a longer "MISSION 66 Report," still in draft form and without the budget estimates.[9] All the pilot prospectuses were "complete" (if hardly completely settled), except for Yellowstone, where negotiations with the concessioner William Nichols had taken a sudden turn that August.[10] The staff also prepared Wirth's presen-

tation, which laid out the full scope of Mission 66 and emphasized arguments intended to support the huge budget requests soon to be submitted to the Bureau of the Budget and to Congress. Garrison and Carnes made a more technical presentation of the details contained in the draft "MISSION 66 Report," including the final "precepts." They also "set up shop" in an adjoining room where superintendents could be briefed individually by Mission 66 staff.[11]

Wirth began his keynote speech by quoting statistics from the AAA and the National Association of Travel Organizations on the postwar phenomenon of travel to national parks: 48 million people visited parks in 1954, and at Yellowstone alone they spent $20 million in and near the park. "Pleasure travel is big business today," Wirth observed, and in "preserving and properly using the National Parks we are perpetuating a saleable commodity," one that contributed enormously to both big and small businesses all over the country. Then Wirth expressed his own version of the "unique paradox" of national park management: "To the extent we preserve them . . . and use them for their own inherent, noncommercial, human values, to that same degree do they contribute their part to the economic life of the nation." In other words, parks were the one natural resource that could boost modern progress only if it was *not* "used," in the traditional sense of logging, grazing, dam construction, or private resort development. But use by tourists—within the context of "proper" park development—could go on indefinitely without unacceptable "impairment." It was time, however, for the federal government to understand the economics of the situation and make appropriate investments in this "important factor in the national economy." Low appropriations had rendered the Park Service incapable of protecting "irreplaceable features," and visitor enjoyment was suffering as well. "Masses of people" left the parks after visiting "with curiosity unsatisfied and enjoyment and appreciation incomplete—all because we do not have the facilities nor the personnel to help them know and comprehend what it is they see." By emphasizing the economic importance of the parks, Wirth implied that good business practices, if nothing else, demanded an investment before both the tangible and the intangible benefits of the park system were lost forever. He reiterated Progressive Era justifications for federal park making in a way that Stephen Mather would have admired, and added an indictment of budget policies that now threatened to destroy the parks and their very considerable economic and social dividends.[12]

Wirth's description of Mission 66 as a "fresh start" was based on three assumptions: first, that annual visitation would grow to 80 million by 1966; second, that the "visitor load" had to be "accommodated without undue harm to the parks"; and third, a new priority, that Mission 66 plans must "include all existing facilities that are usable."[13] The last item was most likely added to reassure lawmakers that the program, though expensive, would not be profligate. It may also have been intended to calm concessioner fears of widespread removal of their facilities. Wirth then listed "eight points" as the start of a "realistic development plan based on modern conditions." The first point listed was the need to

"secure greater participation of private enterprise," implying that a new generation of concessioners would be recruited to augment federal appropriations with private capital. Most of the other points reiterated the "precepts" and other policies that he and his staff had developed that summer, although he now stated as additional priorities the acquisition of private lands within park boundaries, the creation of a revolving fund to finance new staff housing in parks (this would have required its own legislation and never occurred), and the need for a "coordinated Nation-wide recreation plan . . . in accordance with the intent of the Park, Parkway, and Recreational-Area Study Act of 1936." Wirth had decided not to reveal estimates for the total costs of the program yet, although his planners had just confidentially suggested that the total for construction—not including increased annual operating costs—would be as much as $500 million.[14] Wirth decided to wait before presenting such figures, saying only that he had "a realistic business plan" that would require major federal investment in addition to concessioner investment. He ended with the inspirational observation that, as Americans experienced increased opportunities for leisure in the postwar era, "the way we use leisure will determine the kind of Nation we are tomorrow," and that national parks set "a national pattern for the most wholesome and beneficial kind of recreation," instilling in "the American people" a "pride in their government, love of the land, and faith in American tradition." He concluded, "To do this is worth all that we need to spend."

Although Wirth refrained from giving the details of proposed budgets, the broad scope and policy of the program was clearly delineated. The draft "MISSION 66 Report," which would be the basis of the report presented to Eisenhower and to Congress the following January, described much more than a "development program." In addition to chapters on roads, trails, concessions, housing, and other forms of capital development, the report outlined increased "operating needs" that would have to be met to run the modernized park system. While acknowledging that "personnel needs will not increase in direct proportion to increase in visitation" because of more efficient facilities and interpretive displays, the planners still estimated that a 10 percent increase in "employee man-years" would be required for each of the ten years of Mission 66. Park staff engaged in a wide range of "management, protection, and interpretation" would also need to be expanded. This meant not just a ten-year construction program but permanent increases in annual operating costs.

Park interpretation—the educational displays, materials, and presentations that rangers made available in every park—received a particular emphasis in the report. The planners wanted new audio-visual media, such as slide shows and films, to assist in the overwhelming task of interpreting the significance of parks to thousands of visitors. The number of publications available was also to be increased systematically, with brochures and booklets written for specific age groups as well as for the general public. Museum and scientific collections required new facilities and trained personnel, and the Historic Sites Survey and Historic American Buildings Survey, both inactive since 1941,

would resume with Mission 66 funding. The need for agency personnel development and training was still being studied, but a "comprehensive training plan" was proposed as part of the program. "Area Investigations" of potential additions to the park system and "Comprehensive Boundary and Scientific Studies" for every park would contribute to a "National Park System Plan," which would make recommendations to "round out" the park system and ensure that it represented a full range of "significant major types of areas," including "scenic, scientific, historic, seashore, etc." Existing "River Basin Studies" and "Reservoir Recreation Area Planning" would continue and increase, as would "Archeological Survey and Salvage" associated with them. Mission 66 would not merely physically redevelop the parks themselves; it would expand the national park system and return the Park Service to something that at least suggested its New Deal size and functions.

The setting of the September conference was particularly appropriate. Mission 66 planners often cited Great Smoky Mountains as an example of how a day use–only national park could work. Authorized in 1926, Great Smoky Mountains was the most heavily visited park in the system, but it had never had overnight accommodations other than campgrounds. Gateway communities, especially Gatlinburg, Tennessee, provided all the motels, shops, and restaurants the traveling public desired. Mission 66 plans for the park called for road improvements and visitor centers, but no new motel concessions were deemed necessary. The Public Services Conference, in fact, was not actually held in the park but in conference facilities in nearby Gatlinburg.

The press coverage of the September conference included stories in the *New York Times* and many other newspapers. The *Washington Post* editorialized that "Congress ought to give a sympathetic ear" to the Mission 66 proposal. Papers from Eugene to Salt Lake City to Baltimore echoed the positive response, and Secretary of the Interior McKay gave his assurance that the administration would support Mission 66.[15] Eisenhower, however, suffered a heart attack on September 23 while the Park Service conference was under way. The president, who had yet to give his official approval, remained in Denver convalescing for seven weeks. Already postponed for scheduling reasons, the cabinet presentation was now delayed at least until his return. The Mission 66 staff was busier than ever that fall, nervously preparing final budget figures for Congress, as well as the presentation for Eisenhower. Anticipating a positive reception in Congress, Wirth asked the Bureau of the Budget to approve sending a request for increased appropriations that fall, which would have launched Mission 66 within fiscal year 1956. The bureau demurred, however, insisting that the president first be given time to review the details of the program personally.[16]

By the end of the year, Wirth and his staff had accomplished a major bureaucratic and planning feat: the individual park prospectuses and other information and recommendations from the field all had been assembled in Washington and digested into a complete ten-year Mission 66 proposal, dated January 1956. Reviewed and approved by McKay, the report included an annual budget breakdown, with $66 million proposed for fiscal year 1957 and annual increases

building to $83 million in 1966. The total cost to the federal government, not including concessioner investments, would be $787 million over ten years. Only about $475 million of that total was for construction; the rest was for "management and protection" and "maintenance and rehabilitation" which the agency would need to do anyway. Mission 66 was presented not as a separate construction budget initiative, in other words, but as an overall increase in the agency's combined annual budget for operations and construction. In fact, it amounted to roughly doubling the agency's average combined annual appropriations. The agency's budget never returned to previous levels; as presented in 1956, Mission 66 entailed a permanent expansion of the park system, park staff, and all the activities of the Park Service.[17]

The report offered the most lucid summary of Mission 66 that would be made, truly serving as the "bible" that Wirth had envisioned. It identified the trends, needs, and expectations that the planners had identified in detail over the previous eleven months. According to the plan, the increase from 50 million to 80 million annual visits by 1966 could be accommodated. New public facilities and interpretive services would "improve the protection of the parks through visitor cooperation." Overnight accommodations would be expanded through "greater participation of private enterprise," meaning concessioner investments in the parks, or by private businesses outside park boundaries. Operating funds would be increased, and field staff would be expanded and provided with housing. Inholdings would be acquired, and "the protection and preservation of wilderness areas within the national park system" would be accomplished "in ways that will leave them unimpaired."[18] This last (eighth) point had not appeared in earlier draft versions. Appleman reported that "the Director and the Staff felt that Point 8 was superfluous," but they added it to assuage "the fears of certain conservationists" following the Gatlinburg conference. "Wilderness protection had never been an issue in the staff discussions," explained Appleman, because Wirth and his staff believed that Mission 66 already "guaranteed wilderness protection." The entire purpose of redeveloping the parks was to "channel" public use into less destructive patterns; in most cases, they felt, this would not involve significant encroachment on wilderness but would, on the contrary help preserve it. After Gatlinburg, however, Wirth began to hold monthly meetings with representatives of conservation groups. "Point 8" was added as a result.[19]

The final report did not contain the individual park prospectuses that had been so quickly prepared. Most of them were still under internal review and would not be released to the public until the following spring, or later in some cases. The larger part of the final Mission 66 report, in fact, did not address specific construction proposals at all; instead, it put forward an overall vision and budget for "managing and operating the system." The report introduced (or at least institutionalized) a new vocabulary for describing national park planning. The word "park" was defined specifically as any area administered by the Park Service, and "resources" were the "physical assets—historical, archeological, scenic, or scientific—contained in a park." Re-

sources could be either "primary resources" or "secondary assets," and "in general, the primary resources were "the scenic features that distinguish an area." Park "values" were the benefits that accrued through use of resources, and "park visitor experience" was the "sum total of the many things a visitor does, his impressions, new concepts, emotional reactions and responses." "Overuse" existed whenever a resource was destroyed or damaged "in excess of the ability to recover," for example, if a "basic alteration of the ecology of an area" resulted. Overuse also was indicated when there was an "impairment of opportunity of appropriate visitor experience (overcrowding of caves, historic houses, etc.)."[20]

The Mission 66 report indicated desired levels of staffing at the parks to achieve adequate "protection" and "interpretation" of their landscapes and resources.[21] The "services" of rangers, naturalists, and historians were deemed necessary to assure the vital distinction between merely using recreational parks (typically state or local parks) and "understanding national park values." For the first time the term "visitor center" was used consistently to describe the "hub of the park interpretive program," where "museum exhibits, dioramas, relief models, recorded slide talks, and other graphic devices" would "help visitors understand the meaning of the park and its features, and how best to protect, use, and appreciate them." Visitor centers, interpretive walks, audio-visual presentations, roadside exhibits, publications, park museums and collections all were described as coordinated and essential parts of the new national park experience—summarized as "enjoyment without impairment"—that Mission 66 would make possible. The Mission 66 report further (and somewhat repetitiously) outlined policies in another "program" of fourteen points, beginning unambiguously with the "preservation of park resources" as the "basic requirement underlying all park management." The second point reiterated that "substantial and appropriate use" of the parks was the best means to realize their "basic purpose" as stated in the 1916 Park Service legislation. "Adequate and appropriate developments" therefore were required for "public use and appreciation of any area, and for the prevention of over-use." Also, "an adequate information and interpretive service" was essential to "proper park experience."

The report discussed the situation of park concessioners in detail, particularly using the example of Yellowstone. The planners still asserted that "the only justification for a concession operation within a park is to supply needed visitor services that cannot be provided satisfactorily in any other way." They nevertheless called for new concession developments that would greatly expand the capacity of overnight accommodations in cases where they had determined these were needed. The stated reasons for such a determination were, first, the remoteness of certain park destinations, which were too far from gateway communities for easy access, and second, the "travel patterns" of visitors, which apparently referred to public expectations for overnight accommodations near certain popular destinations. The independent Gallup survey had reinforced the planners' conviction that the public wanted motel-type accommodations, not hotels. In twenty-six large parks in which

overnight accommodations were considered necessary or desirable, the Mission 66 planners called for increasing the total overnight lodging capacity from 23,797 guests to 58,797. This dramatic expansion was calculated to keep pace with the overall rise in visitation, as well as a predicted rise in the proportion of visitors seeking overnight accommodations, a ratio that the planners raised from 1 in 3.8 to 1 in 3. There was no explanation for this increase, except for the claim that it accurately predicted future demand on the part of the traveling public. The total cost of such an expansion in the concessioner "pillow count" in the park system would reach $62 million, with concessioners to provide $39 million of the total.

The proposed construction budgets in the final report also redressed an imbalance that Wirth and Garrison had repeatedly deplored. Because Congress had been willing to pass federal aid highway legislation, 80 percent of park construction budgets during the postwar period (up until 1956) had been dedicated specifically to park roads. While road spending would be slightly increased under Mission 66, most of the increase in construction would be in "buildings of all types, sewer, water, electric, and other utilities," addressing a "serious shortage in other types of [non-highway] development." The report emphasized the lack of overnight accommodations and dining facilities as top public concerns, as the Gallup survey had indicated. "Interpretive services, the results of which are a measure of protection," also fell short of what was required. Increased operations budgets were as necessary as new construction for a balanced program. "Concentration on building roads without providing facilities for those who use them, or developing a park fully without providing adequate operating resources, does not solve problems; it creates them," the report declared. Wirth also wanted it known that Mission 66 was "not a program for the construction of extensive road mileage." New roads would be built mostly in new parks; 90 percent of proposed road construction would consist of "reconstruction and realignment" of existing roads.

The planners also described a "modest program of scientific and historical investigations and studies" that would be necessary for the "management of park resources." Mission 66 would later be criticized for not including a major scientific research component in a program that was so ambitious in other ways. The report justified research only as necessary for interpretive programs and publications, and therefore related directly to park management and "protection." Wirth and his planners considered a program of pure scientific research beyond the agency's mandate and unjustified as a budget category; Congress and the Bureau of the Budget probably would have agreed. The final Mission 66 report did include proposals for "wildlife conservation," noting that "the maintenance of animal species in harmony with their environments is not simply a matter of 'letting nature take its course,'" and that the "techniques of managing wildlife in the islands of wilderness represented by the park areas are only partly developed." Much research needed to be done, the authors noted, particularly on the ecology of "overabundant hoofed animals and the maintenance of their range areas, the safeguarding of

rare and threatened species, the reintroduction of extirpated species, the control of exotic animals and plants," and other management problems. But if issues were identified, the remedies described were short and vague. "An adequate biological program" was to be achieved by "strengthening" existing staff and efforts, through "cooperative research agreements," and, where needed, through Park Service studies to "supplement cooperative activities." A budget for such biological research remained unspecified; it was included in the "over-all management and protection programs" of Mission 66.

The detailed $475 million construction budget, in comparison, makes it obvious that Mission 66 was devised by landscape architects and park interpreters, not scientists. The priorities of the program reflected the reality that the Park Service's legislative mandate was to protect parks while facilitating public use of them, not to function as a scientific research institute. Nevertheless, a historic opportunity to increase and emphasize the role of scientific research in the management of parks was not so much lost as never found.[22] The historian Richard West Sellars, in particular, deplores the failure of Mission 66 to fund scientific research and therefore to seize a historic opportunity to redirect Park Service policy. Sellars criticizes the agency's traditional approach to scenic preservation as "façade management," a set of policies and plans that enhanced public enjoyment of scenery but failed to safeguard the biological integrity of the parks.[23] There is no question that the final plan for Mission 66 as a program overtly committed to the priorities that Sellars identifies disappointed those who hoped for a more comprehensive and influential role of science in the bureaucracy and policies of the Park Service. By the early 1960s, those voices would swell into a powerful and scathing critique of the entire program. In 1956, however, the critical inadequacy of Mission 66 funding for park science went relatively unnoticed.

One major component of Mission 66 remained to be described in the final report: every decision and feature of the program needed to be put into the context of a larger national plan for meeting the postwar demand for outdoor recreational facilities. If Wirth failed to provide such a plan, Mission 66 would truly be no more than a "development" program, not a "conservation" program, as the planners repeatedly asserted it was. If there were no effort to coordinate state park and national forest development with proposed national park plans, aspects of Mission 66, such as the development of new concessioner motel complexes at Yellowstone, could easily be perceived as "overdeveloping" national parks without adequate study of alternatives to satisfy the postwar appetite for outdoor recreation. The lack of a meaningful component of public participation in Mission 66 planning only intensified the potential perception that Park Service planners, even if they were the most experienced park makers of their day, had failed to transcend the insular culture of their own agency and put their plans into a broader context of recreational land use. Unless Mission 66 were part of a convincing and coordinated strategy for national recreational planning, such a rapid and ambitious development program would be characterized as misguided and, finally, terribly destructive.

Wirth, however, had made his most important professional contributions as a national recreational planner. Since 1942 his ambition had been to resume the project of national recreational planning through whatever agency or funding was available. The final Mission 66 plan therefore included extensive descriptions of "Nationwide Recreation Planning," a project that had been "dropped before World War II" but would be "reestablished" through Mission 66. Wirth quoted extensively from the 1936 Park, Parkway, and Recreational-Area Study Act, which he insisted would suffice for the completion of a national plan that would serve as the context—and ultimately the justification—for whatever he proposed under Mission 66. But the 1936 legislation was not really a strong basis for the Park Service to continue to function as the nation's recreational planning agency. Wirth recognized this because, since at least early 1955, his staff had been drafting legislation that would have given the Park Service various new powers, for example, to authorize federal loans to concessioners, to establish a revolving fund to build park housing, or to build new facilities on federal lands that were not designated parklands.[24] Wirth had spent his career developing the Park Service as the nation's principal recreational planning agency, and he dearly wanted legislative authority to renew and expand that responsibility for the postwar era. But while Wirth had great success with appropriations subcommittees, he failed with the congressional legislative committees whose support he needed for such initiatives. "We prepared bills and they were introduced," he later wrote, "but try as we might, they were never called up for hearings.

Consequently we did the best we could without them."[25]

In his memoirs, the director describes his dealings with Congress in some detail. As Mather and Albright had done before him, Wirth personally presented and defended his agency's budget requests and any other proposed legislation in Congress. Throughout his career he was known for his close relationships with members of Congress and his skillful dealings with their staffs. His warm relationships with appropriations subcommittee chairmen, especially Michael J. Kirwan in the House and Carl Hayden in the Senate, made Wirth a powerful advocate in the mid-1950s. But in the end the director was forced to accept political limitations on what Mission 66 could aspire to be. Mission 66 never received a new legislative mandate that would have recast the agency's recreational planning authority. Legislation of that type was simply out of Wirth's reach politically, even as he attained greatly increased park appropriations. Wirth and his planners went ahead anyway, believing that Mission 66 could be "carried out under existing legislation." Congress tacitly approved of the idea of a "ten-year program," but only through the annual appropriations process. No other legislation authorized a ten-year total for Mission 66 spending or strengthened the Park Service's role as a national recreational planning agency. This would prove to be a relatively weak foundation for any claims Wirth could make for Mission 66 as a national plan for recreational land use.[26]

But in January 1955 the political future of the Mission 66 program still looked bright. Eisenhower had returned to Washington, and in his State of the Union address that month he found time to ask Congress to support a major national park budget initiative that his administration was about to submit. On January 27 Wirth, with Garrison, Carnes, and Howard R. Stagner (assistant director of the Mission 66 working staff), finally made their long-postponed cabinet presentation. Eisenhower's reaction at that point could hardly have been in doubt. Nevertheless, Wirth recalled that no presentation "made before the cabinet, or perhaps anywhere else . . . had ever received so much preparation." Wirth presented a carefully scripted "sixteen-minute" slide talk, and showed a "three-minute color movie." The images emphasized overcrowded national park frontcountry scenes, with a very brief summary of what Mission 66 was intended to accomplish. Eisenhower asked only one, rather good question: "Why was this request not made back in 1953?" McKay answered it, reminding the president that his own administration's budget policies had not allowed major new spending proposals for national parks. Indeed, as recently as 1954 McKay had reorganized the Park Service with the stated intention of addressing problems solely by "increasing efficiency." But the time was now right. Wirth's alacrity in bringing a fully elaborated program to Eisenhower as quickly as possible, once the tide had turned, validated his political instincts.[27]

Eisenhower gladly endorsed the program, but he had agreed in advance to write letters to Congress supporting only the 1957 annual budget request of $66 million, not the ten-year, $787 million figure. Mission 66 would be subject to the annual appropriations process and judged annually on its merits; there would be no separate authorizing legislation, as there soon would be for the Interstate Highway Act. Eisenhower officially endorsed the program, but if he or his administration officials subsequently felt that the money was not well spent, that endorsement would simply evaporate. Samuel Dodd, an official at the Bureau of the Budget who had been a principal supporter of Mission 66, later gave the Park Service some direct advice on how to secure continued budgetary support: make sure that Mission 66 resulted in public facilities—buildings, road improvements, and other public services—as advertised. If the money were diverted to other purposes, even well-justified ones, the

Bureau of the Budget and Congress would conclude that Mission 66 was merely building up a bureaucracy, or that it was a pretext for spending for other purposes. In either case, the increased level of funding would immediately be at risk in the next annual appropriation.[28]

On February 8, exactly one year after Wirth first presented Mission 66 to his staff at a Monday morning staff meeting, the Department of the Interior and the AAA jointly sponsored an elaborate dinner in the basement dining room of the Interior Building. Like the smaller 1954 dinner hosted by the AAA, the event was again themed as an "American Pioneer Dinner." The state parks department of South Dakota pro-

Wirth sampling elk and bison meat at the American Pioneer Dinner that launched Mission 66 in February 1956. American Automobile Association official Russell Singer is serving. Photo by Abbie Rowe, NPS Historic Photo Collection.

The dining room of the Department of the Interior building in Washington set for the 1956 American Pioneer Dinner. Photo by Abbie Rowe, NPS Historic Photo Collection.

vided the main course of elk and bison meat for the 350 guests. According to the *New York Times,* the evening was "the kick-off in a drive to win implementation" of the Mission 66 program as Congress began the fiscal year 1957 appropriations process. Among the guests were sixty members of Congress, various Interior and other administration officials, and Horace Albright and the rest of the board of the American Civic and Planning Association. Other attendees included the leaders of numerous outdoor recreation and conservation groups, heads of state parks departments, and representatives of travel and tourism organizations. The photographer Ansel Adams provided prints of Yosemite views for the guests. But at least some of those the Park Service criticized as "purists," including Devereux Butcher of the National Parks Association, were intentionally not invited.[29] American Automobile Association vice president Russell Singer served as "toastmaster," and spoke extensively about how he and his group had been "giving serious attention to the problems of the national parks," which could not be addressed just through increased appropriations, but also required reconsidering "the basic concept of these public lands" as represented by Mission 66. Wirth gave the slide and film presentation of his program and distributed copies of a new and expanded edition of the Mission 66 illustrated booklet aimed at a general audience. The booklet had been rewritten and redesigned by an outside public relations firm, all privately paid for along with the printing cost by unidentified "friends of the National Park Service." The full-color cover (a design suggested by Wirth himself) depicted the Liberty Bell, with the superimposed image of a man, woman, and two children. With professional illustrations and graphics, and a far snappier editorial voice, *Our Heritage, A Plan for Its Protection and Use: "MISSION 66"* was a powerful piece of promotional

The cover of *Our Heritage,* the brochure presented at the American Pioneer Dinner. NPS History Collection.

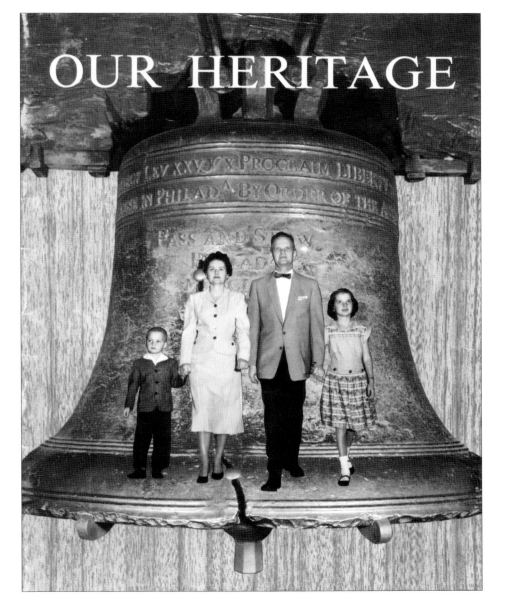

literature. The ideas and much of the text, however, were drawn from the earlier draft document, the final Mission 66 report, Wirth's Gatlinburg speech, and other Mission 66 reports and memoranda. The "8-point plan" and the annualized $787 million budget were included, as were the guiding "precepts," in a final section on "how the plan was developed."[30]

Wirth also arranged for the Walt Disney company to provide a short film for the occasion, "Adventure in the National Parks," which was a compilation of excerpts from "The Living Desert" and "The Vanishing Prairie" (from the True-Life Adventure Series), two short docu- mentaries that had been filmed in national parks. Wirth had genuine respect for Disney and for his company's nature films, which at the time were being broadcast as part of Disney's evening television show. He even hoped that Disney himself would endorse Mission 66 in the film's introduction, since he was already doing so much to popularize the parks.[31] The number of corporate sponsors, connections, and representatives at the 1956 American Pioneer Dinner illustrated Wirth's close relationships with tourist, automotive, and other private business interests. Since Stephen Mather's day, Park Service directors had formed alliances with leading business

Contemporary advertisements and brochures indicated the importance of the public-private partnerships fostered by Wirth during Mission 66. NPS History Collection.

groups and local "boosters" who helped per-suade members of Congress to support park legislation and appropriations. In the business-friendly climate of the Eisenhower years, Wirth cultivated this traditional convergence of inter-ests and formed close friendships not only with the AAA but also with individual state automo-bile associations and oil companies. Phillips Pe-troleum, for example, soon paid for an informational brochure on Mission 66 and also issued a road map series highlighting the na-tional park system. Sinclair Oil featured national parks in a series of print advertisements.[32] The center-spread image in *Our Heritage* (a full-color photograph of Jackson Hole and the Teton Range) was donated by Standard Oil of Califor-nia. While there was nothing new or unethical about such donations and friendships, there is also no doubt that other special interest groups—the conservation organizations—felt that they had lacked similar levels of access, and that their points of view had not significantly in-fluenced Mission 66 planning.

Rapid success in Congress followed on the heels of the American Pioneer Dinner. The Eisenhower administration submitted a $66 mil-lion Park Service appropriation request to the Senate in February. The Appropriations Com-mittee not only approved it but increased it to $68 million; the House approved the action be-fore the end of the month. In fact, members of Congress in both the House and the Senate had been following the progress of Mission 66 for some time, and a few members had begun to act on their own to secure funding. The House Sub-committee on Interior Appropriations approved the 1957 request and agreed to a supplemental

$17 million request that was made available immediately as part of fiscal year 1956.[33] Con-gress, it seemed, had rediscovered the national parks. Total Park Service budgets over the next ten years would exceed $1 billion. By this meas-ure, even critics of Mission 66 would have to ac-knowledge its success. Mission 66 introduced a new level of congressional support for the park system, one that has been maintained ever since.[34]

The Department of the Interior gave Wirth its Citation for Distinguished Service that March, and over the coming year many who participated in Mission 66 planning would re-ceive similar recognition. But even though Wirth and his planners had convinced Congress of the necessity of a new era of park moderniza-tion, many of the details of what this would mean to individual parks had not yet been de-cided. Mission 66 prospectuses for every park in the system had been submitted from the field by the end of 1955, but preparations for the cabinet meeting and American Pioneer Dinner had delayed the review, revision, and final ap-proval of the documents. As was the case with the pilot prospectuses, many of these plans in-volved heated debate and careful negotiation. In January 1956 Wirth had begun meeting with the Mission 66 staff in a series of Saturday and Sunday sessions dedicated to reviewing the draft prospectuses sent in by superintendents all over the country. By March the review had been completed, as it needed to be since Mis-sion 66 construction projects would begin that July with the new fiscal year. At that time, Wirth reminded his field staff that Mission 66 had "definitely gone beyond the stage of justification" and was "now in the action stage." Super-intendents were told to have concessioners in their parks prepare plans outlining how they intended to meet the investment responsibilities described for them in the prospectuses.[35] Through the rest of 1956 the Washington office was kept busy issuing press releases that accompanied the public "briefs," or summaries, of the Mission 66 prospectuses for every park. New revisions of the prospectuses in many cases were released over the coming years. But to a remarkable degree, Mission 66 planning for both Park Service and concessioner facilities was completed in 1956, although in most cases the details of architectural and landscape design were still to be elaborated.[36]

The administrative structure of the Park Service also began returning to normal as the initial planning of Mission 66 ended. Communications between the field staff and Washington once again had to be routed through the regional directors by March. In February, acting on a plan devised by Garrison, Wirth replaced the Mission 66 working staff with a smaller, permanent Mission 66 staff, still headed by Carnes, assisted by Howard Stagner. Garrison oversaw a similar reduction and institutionalization of the steering committee, which became the Mission 66 Advisory Committee, and which he continued to chair for the time being. The committee was intended to have a rotating membership with increased representation from regional offices and parks. Thomas Vint still served on it, and now was joined by one of his longtime colleagues, the architect Herbert Maier, who at the time was the assistant director of Region IV. Other members included superintendents, as well as design pro-

fessionals from the WODC and the EODC. Garrison himself, perhaps sensing that the most important challenges now awaited in the field, replaced Edmund Rogers as superintendent of Yellowstone in November 1956.[37]

Mission 66 was about to become a reality in scores of national parks. Although the program had been planned largely without public participation, by now it was essential to convince the public—not to mention concessioners, conservation groups, and everyone else concerned with conditions in the parks—that the huge disruptions and extensive construction activity they were about to witness represented a "conservation" not a "development" program. Wirth knew that public relations would now be paramount to continued political success. Public interpretive programs and brochures describing Mission 66 were quickly prepared, and Wirth himself oversaw the drafting of a scripted slide show, with recorded narration by him and other officials, to be made available in every park. The presentation was repeatedly revised and carefully planned down to the last image projected. The scripted slide show became a principal means of conveying the purposes and desired image of Mission 66 to park visitors.[38] The priority of almost all the public information prepared at the time was to present Mission 66 as a "conservation" effort. One of the earliest drafts of a public brochure, *Mission 66: Questions and Answers*, responded to the first question it posed, "What is MISSION 66?" with the answer, "MISSION 66 is a *conservation* program for the national park system." Park redevelopment was "simply one of the means by which 'enjoyment-without-impairment'" could be accomplished.

"Mission 66 in Action" was a Park Service slide show that featured these images and dozens of others, as well as an audio soundtrack of Wirth (left) and other Park Service officials describing the program. NPS History Collection.

Other means included educating visitors to cause less damage, and spreading "visitor load" geographically and seasonally. Mission 66 was not just a "construction program" but a "comprehensive program" that would provide "facilities and adequate staffing to permit proper protection, interpretation, maintenance, and administration."[39] A long struggle over the public image of Mission 66 had already begun.

Within the Park Service, Wirth worked hard to establish new traditions that would define the agency's identity for the next generation of its employees. The new arrowhead logo figured prominently everywhere, including on re-designed uniforms. Wirth also wanted to create holidays and celebrations specific to the Park Service. "Three permanent dates" were to be observed "with suitable ceremonies in each area of the system" in order to commemorate the agency's history. Campfire Day (September 19) recognized the 1870 campfire in Yellowstone around which the "national park idea" was supposed to have been first suggested. Each park was to have a celebration centered on a campfire. Founders Day (August 25), which marked the 1916 creation of the Park Service, is the only one of the three that continues to be observed by agency staff on a regular basis (mostly in the

Washington office). Establishment Day was to be celebrated by individual parks on the dates of their establishment.[40]

With the planning of Mission 66 completed, however, the reality of hundreds of millions of dollars of construction would soon determine exactly what Mission 66 was or was not. And what it was, above all, was a redefinition of how national parks would function as public places. The scores of Mission 66 prospectuses eventually prepared represented a new generation of park master planning, and a very different methodology for how that master planning was performed. Thomas Vint had described prewar Park Service master plans as "the counterpart of the city plan; everyone wants to get in the act, [and] the procedure calls for how they get in and out."[41] But Vint had not developed the Mission 66 prospectus, or the methodology of Mission 66 planning. Mission 66 prospectuses had been prepared in a manner more analogous to other public works projects of the 1950s, including the interstate highway program. No one, except arguably the AAA, had really got "in the act" at all. Mission 66 was a product of the planning culture of its day, and differed from prewar national park master plans, which had reflected town and regional planning practices of that era. If prewar planning had not included true public participation in a more recent sense of that term, it was at least a longer and more deliberate process in which concessioners, mountaineering clubs, and local business interests all had more significant opportunities to influence decisions. Mission 66 demanded efficiency, speed, and apparently extreme discretion. Inspired by the multiple-year funding awarded to

highway and dam construction agencies, Mission 66 had to some degree imitated their technocratic approach to planning public works, an approach that was the antithesis of the consensus among conflicting interests that prewar park master plans had tried to achieve.[42]

Another reality would soon be inescapable as Mission 66 put its physical imprint on the national park system. Thomas Vint's "Plan B"—removing overnight accommodations and administrative facilities from popular national park areas and converting those areas to day use only—may have inspired early articulations of Mission 66 policy, but in order to succeed, it required removing the remnants of "Plan A." Without the removal of older facilities, adding new developed areas, even if they were in less "sensitive" areas, did not solve the problem of overcrowding and encroachment on popular park attractions. But removing any kind of public facility from a public park is notoriously difficult. Almost any building or service located in an important public landscape develops a constituency of users and economic interests that will oppose its removal. Because of the nature of congressional politics in rural areas—and the power of congressional subcommittees over Park Service budgets and operations—even small interest groups could prevent the removal of favorite facilities from a national park. "Plan B," when combined with the perpetuation rather than the elimination of "Plan A," would add up to a lot of park development.

The Mission 66 prospectus nevertheless embodied a new idea of how national parks should be managed. It acknowledged postwar trends, such as the rise in population, encroaching low-density urbanization, new levels of automobile ownership, and the increased accessibility created by federal aid highway construction. Mission 66 concessioner facilities, visitor centers, administrative areas, and housing subdivisions all reflected the influence of contemporary trends in American planning and design, from shopping centers to ranch houses. The overall tenor of Mission 66, like that of contemporary interstate highway and urban renewal programs, was imbued with the "new spirit" of mid-century modernism: old and haphazard developments would be replaced through more rationally conceived construction, serving larger numbers more efficiently. At the same time, Wirth and his planners took great pains to establish that although this was a new kind of national park planning, it was nevertheless grounded in the ideology and legislation of the early twentieth century. Here too there was a parallel to a similar continuity in contemporary American housing and highway planning, illustrating the conceptual links between Progressive Era ideology and postwar modernist planning in the United States generally.

As practiced by Wirth, Park Service professionals, and soon a large number of their consulting architects, Mission 66 created a peculiarly American form of mid-twentieth-century design: the modernist national park. But while modernist architectural and planning ideas shaped Mission 66, this formal adoption did not imply a break with essentially Olmstedian justifications and goals for public park development. Nor did American modernism in general express the more radical intentions associated with its European precedents. Corporate America never intended its new suburban headquarters to be seen as endorsements of European socialism, and modernist shopping centers became the very temples of capitalist consumerism.

American modernist design evolved into a wide variety of responses to postwar social and geographic change. The Mission 66 park was one of those responses.[43] The story of Mission 66 as it moved from conceptual planning to physical development would in fact be the story of the limits of modernism in national park planning. Reactions to the program, as it actually took shape, would be particularly rich indicators of public attitudes toward modernism and its perceived association with the destruction of historical "landmarks" and natural "wilderness." Mission 66 soon incited deeply felt responses to modernist planning and architecture generally, both within and beyond park boundaries.

PART II

MISSION 66: DESIGN

CHAPTER 5

ARCHITECTURE

As Mission 66 moved from planning to reality, new design and interpretive programs manifested both continuity and change in the national park idea. Conrad Wirth had insisted that his staff, park concessioners, and professional consultants adopt radical solutions to the postwar parks "dilemma." But he was just as adamant that the fundamental challenge they faced had not changed: facilitating visits by ever larger numbers of people traveling in cars while avoiding the impairment of park landscapes and "values." Even while exhorting his planners to rethink the entire national park project completely, Wirth invoked the 1916 Park Service Act as the philosophical and legislative framework of their postwar redevelopment campaign. As embodied in the scores of park prospectuses prepared by 1956, Mission 66 continued a Progressive Era project—the modernization of park frontcountry for automotive tourism—that had begun thirty years earlier and was advanced by

the New Deal. But the prospectuses contained new strategies to achieve those established goals. The modernization of parks remained a general mandate, but in the postwar era, modernist theory and design influenced Mission 66 park planning and architecture specifically and decisively.

A new approach was needed primarily because of the extraordinary use that park landscapes were now expected to bear. Mission 66 anticipated 80 million visitors to the park system in 1966, a huge increase from 49 million in 1956. Even these figures drastically underestimated the trend: the actual 1966 figure would be 127 million.[1] New social and geographic contexts demanded a reexamination of how Park Service officials responded to their mandate. The decision to avoid "quotas" or "restrictions" on admission into parks had been made without public process or even meaningful internal discussion. But that decision now determined the essential challenge of the entire Mission 66 program: finding the means to enable tens of millions of people in cars to enter, experience, and leave parks efficiently, without impairing (as impairment was defined at the time) the landscapes and resources that this and all future generations of visitors were entitled to enjoy.

By January 1956 Wirth and his agency had elaborated their postwar model for achieving continued "enjoyment without impairment." It differed substantially from the prewar ideal of park planning such as in the 1929 master plan for Mount Rainier, which featured a series of park villages, most of which were located at the sites of earlier concessioner areas. Under Thomas Vint's guidance, these relatively haphazard areas had been redeveloped into planned "rustic" villages, with public plazas, administration buildings, museums, automotive campgrounds, and separate residential and utility zones. Coordinated with road improvements, a series of villages might (as at Mount Rainier, Yellowstone, or Grand Canyon) describe a dispersed pattern of use in which visitors stayed overnight at any of several locations near different park attractions. Since these villages could not grow to serve postwar levels of visitation without encroaching on the features near which they had originally been sited, Mission 66 proposed the intensified day use of parks in conjunction with the removal of hotels, administration buildings, and other buildings from the older park villages. To make the new model work, park roads would require wider lanes, new bridges, and flatter vertical and horizontal curves to move cars more efficiently. Automotive campgrounds would be relocated to less sensitive areas, but would grow to several

times their former size. Roadside overlooks, interpretive displays, short "nature walks," and low-speed "automobile trails" would proliferate and, it was hoped, enrich the visitor's experience. Larger parking lots would be provided everywhere, and in some cases new developed areas (relocated again to what were considered less sensitive areas) would be provided with extensive "motel type" accommodations. Day use "visitor centers" would centralize services such as restrooms, audio-visual presentations, museum exhibits, ranger contact points, and outdoor amphitheaters in one building complex, strategically sited to intercept "visitor flow" near park entrances, road intersections, and main destinations.

The new model for park planning represented both continuity and change, but it was the change that many people noticed first. Certainly the rhetoric of the day encouraged this perception. "Old traditions seemed to have determined standards far beyond their time," Wirth told his planners, and therefore "nothing was to be sacred except the ultimate purpose to be served."[2] Park Service staff and consulting designers had in fact already progressed beyond rustic village planning years before Mission 66 began. For example, Vint's "Plan B" proposal for removing development from Yosemite Valley, officially put forward in 1947, foreshadowed what would become the guiding precepts of Mission 66. In another important example, a dramatic new approach to park architecture was taking shape by the early 1950s at Grand Teton National Park in Wyoming, where events had their own momentum thanks to the philanthropic interest of John D. Rockefeller Jr.

The establishment and expansion of Grand Teton in the 1920s instigated more local controversy and congressional turmoil than any project the Park Service had undertaken up to that time. Mather and Albright had long hoped to extend Yellowstone National Park to the south in order to include the awesome Teton Range and the adjacent valley, Jackson Hole, which was an important winter habitat for elk. Congress established Grand Teton National Park in 1929, but with limited boundaries that protected only the mountains themselves, not the more valuable—and potentially developable—land of Jackson Hole. Since 1927 Rockefeller had collaborated covertly with Albright to finance the acquisition of much of the private land in the area. In 1930 Rockefeller's involvement was made public knowledge as he revealed his intent to donate what would eventually be more than 33,000 acres in order to extend Grand Teton National Park. Local residents and the Wyoming congressional delegation reacted violently to the subterfuge involved in the land acquisitions. The legislation necessary for the federal government to accept the gift became politically impossible. After two sets of congressional hearings and a decade of bitter dispute, the matter was finally resolved in 1943, when Franklin Roosevelt made the controversial decision to declare the area a national monument, thereby making it possible to accept Rockefeller's gift without congressional action. The national park extension did not occur until 1950, after much of the controversy had finally subsided.[3]

Rockefeller continued his involvement in the planning and development of the expanded national park by forming a new concessioner, the Grand Teton Lodge and Transportation Company, as a subsidiary of his private nonprofit organization, Jackson Hole Preserve, Inc. The company planned a $6 million lodge complex as part of what Rockefeller hoped would become a "pilot project" for postwar park development. Gilbert Stanley Underwood, the architect of the Ahwahnee and other prewar national park lodges, designed the new hotel and cabin complex, which Rockefeller personally sited on the shore of Jackson Lake, on a small plateau with sweeping views of the Teton Range. The elegant lodge, redolent of an earlier era of national park tourism, in some ways recalled the architect's prewar masterpieces. After entering the building at ground level under a massive porte cochere, visitors ascended a short flight of stairs to a spacious "lounge," more than two stories high, where they immediately encountered a wall of windows framing the dramatic views of the Tetons, with a vast expanse of willow flats serving as a foreground. This entry sequence, and much of the underlying planning and spatial design of the hotel, suggested similar devices Underwood had employed in his earlier rustic lodges such as the Ahwahnee or the Grand Canyon Lodge. But the novelty of the outward appearance of the Jackson Lake Lodge startled most observers. Underwood had worked extensively in concrete construction before, notably at the Ahwahnee. At that prewar hotel, however, the concrete had been formed and stained to resemble other materials, such as wood siding and beams. The concrete of the Jackson Lake Lodge was also given a wood-like texture and stained light brown; but in this case the "shadowood" plywood pattern impressed on the surface sug-

The Jackson Lake Lodge in Grand Teton National Park, designed by Gilbert Stanley Underwood, opened in 1955.

NPS Historic Photo Collection.

gested the rough wooden molds used in concrete construction rather than clapboard siding or timbers. This handling of concrete underscored the modernist inspiration of the building's massing, which Underwood conceived as an interlocking series of large rectangular boxes topped by shed roofs, directly expressing the functions and spaces of the interior volumes. Large horizontal bands of windows and the massive window wall of the main lounge further emphasized and confirmed the influence of American modernist architectural design.[4]

Underwood had come out of retirement for this last major commission of his career. While he showed his mastery of a building type he had done so much to develop—the national park lodge—he also made a striking statement about how postwar park architecture could adopt contemporary structural design and construction technology. While the results were dramatic, the architect had not abandoned many of the basic qualities that had made his earlier work seem so appropriate in its settings. The spatial sequence upon entering the building, and the importance of views of the surrounding landscape in that sequence, were reminiscent of his other lodges, as were the earth tones and rough textures of the building materials. The success of the project, which like Underwood's earlier lodges soon was frequented by celebrities as well as the general public, helped make the lodge an important indicator of future directions park architecture might take. Conrad Wirth, John D. Rockefeller Jr., and Rockefeller's son, Laurance, all spoke at the Jackson Lake Lodge dedication, held in June 1955, as Mission 66 planning was in full swing. As a "pilot project," Underwood's updated approach to national park architecture had won their support. The architect had taken some of the trends of mid-century American modernism—the extensive use of concrete, large windows, flat rooflines, geometric massing—and adapted them to the purposes, pro-

gram, and goals of postwar national park planning. The lodge was massive, but it was also partially set into the earth, given shed roofs with low angles, and constructed in earth-tone materials, all of which helped make it less visually obtrusive in its setting. Above all, it was conceived around the view showcased by its main windows. The entire building served as a viewing platform, with outdoor terraces oriented to the view as well. Unmistakably modernist in its inspiration, the Jackson Lake Lodge revised traditional assumptions about what made architecture "appropriate" in the setting of a national park. For Underwood, Wirth, and the Rockefellers, the new lodge succeeded by increasing the capacity for enjoyment of park landscapes while reducing the visual intrusion of the necessary facilities. The entire complex, including a large parking lot heavily planted with native trees that

The Jackson Lake Lodge featured decentralized motel units as well as the main lodge building. NPS Historic Photo Collection.

broke up and concealed its expanse, minimized its architectural presence while maximizing the program and services provided.

Not everyone agreed that the new lodge represented a positive direction for national park architecture. The Jackson Lake Lodge made passionate architectural critics out of many not previously known for their opinions on such matters. That August the *New York Times* reported on the "debate over national parks design" that the lodge had incited. "Those who bitterly deride the appearance of the . . . lodge," noted the article, "level their aesthetic barbs at the mammoth central structure chiefly because it does not look 'rustic.'" Unmoved by the building's efficient handling of large numbers of tourists, or by its minimized visual presence (it was mostly hidden from viewpoints elsewhere in the park), critics were outraged because the lodge did not look more like the Old Faithful Inn in nearby Yellowstone, or like other classic examples of rustic park architecture that they insisted were more effective in "blending with the scenery." Part of their concern stemmed from

indications that the lodge would serve as a design precedent for the still mysterious "10-year program" Wirth obliquely mentioned in his remarks at the dedication ceremony. Such a program apparently heralded more contemporary architecture that would completely redefine what it meant to "harmonize" with the unique settings of the national parks.[5]

Criticism of modernist design in national parks, like criticism of modernism in the United States generally, was already an established trend in 1955. Wilderness advocates were among the first to voice concerns about the "contemporary" appearance of postwar architecture in the parks. National Parks Association board member Martin Litton, who wrote on the deterioration of Yosemite Valley in 1952, also derided plans for a $2.5 million redevelopment of the "rustic, somewhat dilapidated" Yosemite Lodge. He suggested that the new lodge would consist of "government-approved modern structures that stand out like a sore thumb."[6] His fellow board member Devereux Butcher went much further in his denunciation of the trend.

The Old Faithful Inn, designed by Robert Reamer in 1903, was sited within viewing distance of the Old Faithful Geyser.

Yellowstone National Park Archives.

His 1952 article "For a Return to Harmony in Park Architecture" expressed outrage at the idea that the "gray, weathered Paradise Inn" at Mount Rainier, for example, might be replaced by a "typical businessman's hotel building like those in so many small towns—red brick, five to eight stories, flat roof, glass and iron marquee over the front door." A former architecture student and a trained artist and photographer, Butcher had been the executive director of the National Parks Association from 1942 to 1950 and still edited the organization's magazine. His article issued an impassioned plea—one that he and others would repeat throughout the Mission 66 period—for "an immediate return to the sound policies of park architecture that have prevailed these many years." The building that ignited his crusade was a dining room completed in 1951 in the Skyland concessioner area of Shenandoah National Park. What Butcher called a "picturesque and home-like" structure destroyed in a recent fire had been replaced by a new building with a flat roof and walls of almost floor-to-ceiling rectangular windows. He complained that the new building was designed "along modernistic lines" that were "out of tune with all the rest of the park's beautiful architecture." He was offended enough to undertake a national tour to observe other examples of recent construction. Although there was not much being built in parks at the time, there was enough for Butcher to ask, "Why has the Service abandoned its long-established policy of designing buildings that harmonize with their environment and with existing styles?" A new maintenance building at Big Bend National Park, he claimed, resembled a factory, and resi-

dences in Saguaro, Zion, and Glacier national parks were "ugly beyond words to describe" and "unsuitable" because they failed to achieve a "harmonious" relationship to their sites. Prewar park architecture that exemplified such harmony often stood nearby as a silent rebuke to the newer construction. Other negative examples included a comfort station at Glacier with a flat roof, and the new museum–office building in the administrative area of Everglades.[7]

Butcher's immediate suspicion was that the Park Service had "farmed out" the design work and that consulting architects, unfamiliar with national parks, had instigated the trend toward modernist materials and design. But Wirth, Vint, and their cadre of regional design staff and park superintendents very much retained their control over all planning and design in the parks. By the 1940s they had already begun to change Park Service design policies. Underwood's Jackson Lake Lodge was only the most spectacular result. The San Francisco architect

Designed by Eldridge Spencer in 1942, this employee residence is in the Middle Tecoya area of Yosemite Village. Author's photo.

Eldridge T. (Ted) Spencer, consulting for the Yosemite concessioner, designed what were probably the first clearly modernist buildings in a national park, a service station (1941) and employee residences (1942), using flat roofs, large windows, and no ornamentation.[8] In 1949 Newton Drury approved Spencer's plan for a new Yosemite Lodge, also in a modernist idiom, although the design was changed and was not built until later. There were other modest examples (including those cited by Butcher) of experiments in what was usually described as "contemporary" architecture, all of which at least tacitly met with the approval of regional directors, design staff, and Vint himself, who reviewed all design proposals in Washington. Butcher's critique of the new direction in park architecture struck a nerve, however, and was soon chorused by others, including Drury, who insisted in 1953 that while he was director he had never condoned the "modernistic structures . . . that were perpetrated on us by well-meaning but misguided architects." He went on to express complete confidence, however, in his "good friend and colleague, Tom Vint," with whom he had never disagreed on "any matter involving design."[9]

Butcher and those who supported his point of view felt that Park Service designers had lost their way and needed to be reminded of their architectural tradition. In his 1952 article Butcher went on to explain the principles of "harmonious" park architecture, presumably to officials such as Thomas Vint and Herbert Maier, who had developed the principles in the first place. Design, color, and site were the primary factors that needed to be considered so that a building could be "fairly hidden by features of the landscape." More to the point, Butcher declared that "pioneers" and "Indians" had built structures of materials "close at hand," employing the simplest construction, and "their rugged architectural styles" had therefore come to be associated with "great open spaces," just as "we associate the Swiss chalet with evergreen forests and big mountains" and the "Indian adobe" with the landscape of the Southwest, while "Spanish might fit the Big Bend country," and in the Appalachians, "the log cabin stands out in our minds as the original style." But "since we do not associate prefabricated building materials and modernistic styles with big open spaces," they created "inharmony in primitive landscapes." Butcher concluded with extensive quotations from architect Albert H. Good's 1935 *Park Structures and Facilities,* a Park Service catalog of depression-era design, which included a more nuanced "apologia" for prewar rustic design.[10]

Butcher's explanation for the appeal of prewar park development was simplistic but also accurate: the associations with pioneer and Native American cultures may have been mostly imaginary, but the architectural fantasy resonated with the public. Log and boulder construction in national parks bore little resemblance to any actual vernacular structures, but the architecture was never intended as a reconstruction of history so much as an invocation of mythic historical themes. Postwar modernist park architecture— epitomized in the Jackson Lake Lodge—often featured low profiles and horizontal massing, as well as materials with muted colors and rough textures that helped new buildings blend visually with their surroundings. But the new park architecture also assiduously eliminated the (admittedly spurious) historical associations of the rustic era, replacing them with architectural surfaces swept clean of the delightful decorative elements that had been so essential to Underwood's own prewar architecture, as well as that of Mary Elizabeth Jane Colter, Maier, Vint, and others. While the Jackson Lake Lodge actually was a more muted and less elaborate visual presence than a rustic lodge with the same capacity would have been, stripped of a decorative façade evoking pseudo-vernacular construction and traditional historical narratives, it struck Butcher and other critics as harsh, industrial, "inharmonious," and "urban."

As for the siting of buildings, Butcher's description of prewar park architecture as "fairly hidden by features of the landscape" was erroneous. These rustic buildings had been, above all, picturesque architecture. Far from being "hidden," Colter's Grand Canyon buildings, Underwood's Ahwahnee, Maier's park museums, and the park administration buildings designed by Vint all formed important compositional elements of perceived landscape scenes. Their complex, expensive, and usually nonstructural façades of overscaled timber and stone, carefully detailed adobe, or labor-intensive log construction were hardly intended to be unnoticed: they were powerful statements of both sober civic administration and vacation fantasy. They complemented and enabled an appreciation of place as picture. For many visitors such architectural imagery was a welcome and even necessary aspect of the aesthetic enjoyment of park scenery. For them, modernist architecture was inappropriate

Herbert Maier's Madison Junction trailside museum (1929) in Yellowstone, as illustrated in Albert H. Good's catalog of Park Service rustic design, *Park and Recreation Structures* (Washington, DC: Government Printing Office, 1938).

above all because it conflicted with their aesthetic conception and appreciation of the surrounding landscape. Modernist architecture—at least as Underwood and others adapted it to the requirements of the Park Service—did in fact offer the best means of accommodating growing numbers of visitors while truly minimizing the visual presence of a building. But in the end, the critics of the Jackson Lake Lodge were not really asking for less architectural presence; they wanted more. They missed the pseudo-vernacular associations and historical references—the entire picturesque conception of park architecture—that enhanced their aesthetic enjoyment of national park landscapes.

There were strong parallels between trends in postwar park architecture and those in park planning. Just as prewar rustic villages could not be expanded to meet increased demand without unacceptable encroachment on park features, the rustic architectural style (at least for Wirth, Underwood, and the Rockefellers) could not successfully accommodate the expanded capacity and programs of the postwar period. If park buildings continued to be conceived as picturesque architecture, they would not remain compositional components of the landscape but would grow into a far larger visual presence than they had been. They would dominate, not complement, their settings. The adapted modernism Underwood supplied in 1955 accommodated the new centralized programs more efficiently and economically. If decried as brutally utilitarian, such architecture nevertheless managed to remain "hidden" in a manner that rustic architecture had never been intended to accomplish. The massive Old Faithful Inn opened in 1904 with 140 rooms. The Jackson Lake Lodge complex, by contrast, had 300 rooms in addition to restaurants and other facilities. While its linear motel units sprawled over a larger area, the extent of the development was not immediately apparent, and it did not encroach visually on the surrounding landscape. The Old Faithful Inn may have been the most beloved of all national park lodges, but it was perched directly on the edge of rare thermal features and was hardly a "hidden" building.

Critics such as Litton, Butcher, and Drury failed to recognize that modernist architecture did not create the new and difficult realities of

The Old Faithful Inn and the Old Faithful geyser in 1929. Photo by George A. Grant, NPS Historic Photo Collection.

national park management but responded to them. Attempts to re-create rustic design would not have been successful, because it was impossible to return to the prewar social, economic, and geographic contexts on which that earlier idiom had been based. Underwood's new direction in the siting and design of park buildings logically complemented and implemented postwar park planning priorities. The public was also demanding new levels of convenience and material comforts, a fact confirmed by the Park Service's 1955 Gallup survey. And in a purely practical sense, true rustic architecture had ended with the CCC: a massive national park development program could not be economically undertaken if it meant paying postwar prices for the work previously done by CCC labor. The end of the Corps, which Wirth had fought to avoid more than anyone else, was the end of both the means and the aspirations of rustic park architecture.[11]

The trend toward modernist planning and architecture could no more be ignored in national parks than it could anywhere else in the United States. From the moment the program burst on the scene in the summer of 1956, Mission 66 expressed a fully developed commitment to progressive, sometimes striking modernist design. Mission 66 architecture embodied the recreational planning policies that had been developed as the heart of the entire program. Wirth and Vint, the officials most responsible for promoting and achieving rustic era design, now embraced the new architecture precisely because it reflected and made possible the response they had finally devised to mitigate the conditions that had plagued them through-

out the previous decade. For them, the resurrection of rustic design would have negated what they were trying to accomplish.

But the commitment to modernist architecture was hardly a radical or daring direction for the Park Service. In fact, it put the agency squarely in the mainstream of American design of the period. By the mid-1950s modernism had become the ubiquitous stylistic choice of corporations, government agencies, cultural institutions, housing developers, and retailers, who together were remaking the national landscape. Corporate clients all over the world—from roadside restaurant chains to multinational businesses—embraced various strains of modernist architectural style. New postwar building technologies made construction more rapid, economical, and efficient. No builder could afford to ignore labor-saving techniques such as the prefabrication of structural elements, innovative uses of steel and concrete, curtain wall construction, and extensive applications of glass. These technologies had been developed in conjunction with modernist architecture, which exploited their potential. Quite apart from stylistic associations and iconographic meanings, modernist architecture was simply a more efficient way of producing buildings, especially large ones. The United States, and much of the world, had "gone modern" for many of the same reasons the Park Service had: more labor-intensive, craft-oriented construction was no longer economically competitive, and therefore for most clients—including government agencies—it was no longer an option. The armed forces in particular had preceded the Park Service in the adoption of modernism. From the Wherry and

Capehart ranch houses being built around army bases to the vast new Air Force Academy designed by Skidmore, Owings and Merrill in Colorado Springs, the "government-approved modern structures" Martin Litton deplored in 1952 were in evidence everywhere by the mid-1950s.

Another major reason for the Park Service to adopt modernist architectural design was the general adoption of the idiom by professional consultants and in-house designers. As Mission 66 progressed from planning to construction, architects were rapidly set to work drawing up detailed designs, and the work they produced simply reflected the current state of their profession, just as earlier rustic-era building had reflected the influence of contemporary architectural practice. American architects had not been slow to capitalize on the trend toward modernist design, and in fact had been its leading instigators. Many architectural historians have described how a group of prewar European architects inspired the next generation of American practitioners to transform their profession. The Austrian architect Richard Neutra opened his office in Los Angeles in 1925, and over the next forty years produced a series of highly influential modernist residential and institutional buildings, employing extensive window walls, flat roofs, column grid construction, and elimination of ornamental details. In 1932 Phillip Johnson and the architectural historian Henry-Russell Hitchcock organized an exhibition of modernist architectural drawings and models at the Museum of Modern Art in New York and in their catalog described the International Style of architecture, exemplified in work by Neutra, Le Corbusier, and other, mostly European architects. According to Johnson and Hitchcock, the new style emphasized the composition of space rather than building mass, asymmetry in plan and elevation, and the organized repetition of individual building units. Ornamentation and historical references were completely eliminated, while new building technologies and materials were embraced. The architectural historian Leonardo Benevolo notes that, during the Great Depression, a group of "former masters of the Bauhaus" emigrated to the United States and soon found students and builders receptive to their architectural ideas. By 1937 the founder of that famous German design school, Walter Gropius, was heading the architecture department at the newly organized Harvard Graduate School of Design, while the German architect Ludwig Mies van der Rohe was in charge of the architecture department at the Illinois Institute of Technology. By 1940 other leading figures of European modernism were living, teaching, and building influential projects in the United States. Modernist icons such as Lovell House in Los Angeles (Neutra, 1929) and the Philadelphia Saving Fund Society Building (George Howe and William Lescaze, 1932) proclaimed the progressive trend in both residential and commercial architecture.[12]

By the late 1940s a generation of American professionals trained in the new approach had taken to the field. Architectural trade magazines were filled with examples of modernism in the United States, much of it more or less inspired by the International Style. The years immediately before Mission 66 were the apogee of the influence of modernism on American architectural practice. Architects and their clients favored modernist architectural designs for both practical and ideological reasons. In New York, the United Nations building (Wallace Harrison et al., 1950) and the Lever House office tower (Skidmore, Owings and Merrill, Gordon Bunshaft, 1952) manifested both government and corporate America's commitment to the new architectural expression. As Sarah Allaback observes in her history of Mission 66 visitor centers, it was inevitable that the influence of contemporary architectural practice would extend to national park architecture: "The forces at work—capitalism and a society obsessed with progress—were prevalent throughout the country; it was only a matter of time before they would enter the national parks."[13] For a generation that witnessed the irrational destruction and historicizing excesses of fascist regimes in Europe, modernism offered a means to rebuild the world rapidly along expressly rational lines, free of undesirable historical associations. Even before Mission 66 began, Park Service architects had already abandoned the imaginative allusions of rustic architecture in favor of a more technical and rationalized approach to building that, in the context of the national parks, could symbolize the more scientific and efficient park management that Mission 66 planning hoped to accomplish.

Because the Mission 66 program also generated a sudden increase in the amount of work expected from the in-house design force, the agency expanded its use of private design and engineering consulting firms. The increased use of consultants influenced Mission 66 design, but Park Service architects and administrators had already set the policies and outlines that, in almost all cases, consultants were expected to follow. Allaback describes how, by the early 1950s, even longtime Park Service architects (some of whom had produced important rustic buildings in the 1930s) had developed new approaches in response to postwar conditions. "We couldn't help but change," explained Park Service architect Cecil J. Doty. "I can't understand how anyone could think otherwise, how it could keep from changing." Allaback observes that this remark is "a key to understanding" the purpose of Mission 66 architecture, "which was not to design buildings for atmosphere, whimsy, or aesthetic pleasure, but for change: to meet the demands of an estimated eighty million visitors," and to do so in a reasonably efficient way, taking into account the availability of new building technologies and the higher costs of labor and materials.[14]

As a Park Service architect, Doty was a particularly important figure in the development of postwar park architecture. In his attitudes and background, however, he was typical of many of the agency's designers. An Oklahoman, he graduated in architectural engineering from Oklahoma A&M (now Oklahoma State) and in 1934 went to work for Herbert Maier in the Park Service CCC state park program in Oklahoma City. Maier and Vint trained the young designer into the kind of specialist they needed, giving him images and plans of their own rustic park buildings as examples to emulate. Doty was an adept designer and a talented illustrator, responsible for one of the finest prewar national park buildings, the adobe Region III headquarters in Santa Fe (1939). In 1940 Doty went to work in

Park Service architect Cecil J. Doty. NPS Southwest Regional Office, Santa Fe.

the Region IV headquarters in San Francisco, assisting regional architect Lyle E. Bennett, the designer of the Painted Desert Inn (1940) and other important rustic park buildings.[15] By 1948, when Doty was promoted to regional architect for Region IV, his preliminary designs for buildings at Olympic, Joshua Tree, and other parks featured flat or shed roofs, reinforced concrete construction, and other clear signs that, as Allaback observes, "Doty and his Park Service colleagues were moving in a progressive direction." For his part, Doty later observed that "when the CCC and all that labor ended, getting stone was out of the question." Strict limitations on the cost of buildings imposed by Congress necessitated more economical building techniques. The influence of consultants also was a factor: Doty worked with the architect Eldridge Spencer on his modernist designs for Yosemite in 1941 and 1942.[16] By the early 1950s Doty was at work on preliminary designs for the "public use" buildings at Grand Canyon and the

In 1937 Doty designed this massive adobe building, the NPS Region III Headquarters in Santa Fe, shown here as it appeared in 1939. NPS Southwest Regional Office, Santa Fe.

The Grand Canyon "public use" building (soon described as a "visitor center") designed by Cecil Doty and the WODC in 1954-1955. As was the case with the Region III Headquarters in Santa Fe, the geometric massing featured little ornamentation and the plan was organized around a central courtyard. Author's photo.

Flamingo area of Everglades. Their flat roofs, stark geometric massing, and contemporary materials confirmed that the architect's transition to modernist design was complete. Doty's story is instructive because it illustrates how Mission 66 architecture, despite the involvement of consultants, was controlled in-house, by Park Service designers. Doty's new approach to park architecture was influential on his colleagues, but it was consistent with their own contemporary work as well.

No extensive, official policy statement was ever made regarding the adoption of modernist design at the Park Service. During the New Deal, Vint and Maier had widely distributed plans and illustrations of appropriately rustic architecture, but Wirth made no comparably methodical efforts to standardize park architecture in the postwar period. Following the Great Smoky Mountains conference, where he had been asked to issue an official policy on architectural design, he responded only with a brief statement: "Structures should be designed to reflect the character of the area while at the same time following up-to-date design standards. Park structures are to conform, to some extent, with the trend toward contemporary design and the use of materials and equipment accepted as standard by the building industry. However, restraint must be exercised in the design so that the structures will not be out of character with the area and so that the structures will be subordinated to their surroundings."[17] In January 1957 Wirth participated by phone in a WODC conference and verbally issued the following "guiding principles" for architectural design: "Whatever we do in the line of development in the Parks, it must fit the terrain and be inconspicuous; Durability is an important attribute; Sound planning is basic to economic results; nothing should be built unless the need is already realized. . . . Don't try to lead your profession in fancy design."[18] Architectural design, in fact, was not a primary concern for Wirth. He felt that park development would succeed by "channeling" public use and therefore mitigating its impacts. In well-planned examples, he wrote in 1958, the result would be the same "regardless of decorative colors used, or the style of architecture selected." These were "details," important "in their way." But "park resources [were] neither destroyed nor preserved merely by application of a paintbrush or by a choice of . . . architectural décor." The role of architecture in the parks was changing, as was architecture itself. "Construction and maintenance today are machine jobs," Wirth observed. There were advantages to new building technology that would help minimize cost and construction time, and therefore impacts on surrounding landscapes.[19]

Compared to Wirth's long and detailed instructions on planning policy and process, his statements regarding architectural design were remarkably brief. The general sentiments Wirth expressed on appropriately "contemporary" design did not so much direct as reflect the gradual evolution among Park Service (and other) architects that had been under way since the late 1930s. The sudden burst of construction made possible by Mission 66 only made it seem as if there had been a sudden shift in design policy. Wirth, Vint, and other Park Service officials were fully aware of the work Doty and other architects were doing in the 1940s and early 1950s, and they approved of it, as confirmed by the fact that the work went forward. By the time architectural designs for Mission 66 were being finalized in 1956, adapted forms of "contemporary" architecture were already the desired style of architectural design in the national parks. Although there was occasional acknowledgement of critiques by Devereux Butcher and others, there was no more internal debate at the Park Service over the appropriateness of modernist architecture than there was over Wirth's fateful decision not to restrict access to popular parks.[20] In fact, as we have seen, the two important decisions were linked.

Even if modernist park architecture was vital to the implementation and success of Mission 66, it was the increased functionality and efficiency that could be achieved through modernist design, materials, and building technologies that primarily interested Wirth, Vint, and their planners. They did not adopt modernism as a style so much as they invented a distinctly modernist building type—the visitor center—and then used it extensively to implement their revised park planning ideas. A number of architects, landscape architects, historians, and interpreters contributed to the development of the visitor center. Like many modernist projects, the new buildings resulted from interdisciplinary cooperation and an increased emphasis on objective, efficient solutions to planning problems. The organization of the WODC and the EODC in 1954 brought Park Service designers, engineers, and historians together in their own offices in San Francisco and Philadelphia, independent of the regional administrative offices. In Washington, Vint re-

mained overall chief of design and construction, assisted by chief landscape architect Bill Carnes and chief architect Dick Sutton. In San Francisco, Sanford Hill headed the WODC, with Robert Hall as supervising landscape architect and Lyle Bennett as supervising architect. The EODC was headed by Edward Zimmer, with Harvey Cornell and John Cabot in the same respective roles. By 1960 Mission 66 had swelled the professional ranks in these two design offices to several hundred in-house landscape architects, architects, and administrative employees. Almost without exception, these managers were longtime Park Service employees who, regardless of where they received their academic training, had gained their most formative professional experience working in state and national parks during the New Deal.[21]

It was in the offices of the WODC and the EODC between 1954 and 1957 that the idea of the visitor center was elaborated as the successor to park museum and administration buildings. Early 1950s versions of visitor centers were first described as "administrative-museum," "public service," or "public use" buildings, reflecting the struggle to resolve complex, combined building programs. In February 1956, as initial plans for Mission 66 reached completion, Wirth issued a memorandum insisting that the term "visitor center" be used consistently. Wirth's terminology helps clarify the relationship of this new building type to contemporary trends in planning and architecture, particularly shopping center design. Visitor centers were predicated on the same assumptions as contemporary shopping centers: that large numbers of customers would be arriving by private car, and that both they and their vehicles needed to be efficiently handled as they shifted from the automotive realm to a strictly pedestrian environment, where they could conveniently find all services clustered together. In early designs for "public use buildings" at Carlsbad Caverns (1953) and Grand Canyon (1954), WODC architects (especially Cecil Doty) attempted to combine many of the functions of an entire park village in a single large building, described in one case as "a one-stop service unit." Park Service offices and interpretive display areas, as well as bathrooms, information desks, auditoriums, and generous lobbies, were all concentrated in efficient sequences of indoor spaces that were linked together in plan by a diagrammatic conception of "visitor flow."[22] Most of these spaces related to functions previously handled in separate structures, such as museums, comfort stations, and administration buildings; but new audio-visual media and increased numbers of visitors required larger (even multiple) auditoriums and spacious lobbies that could receive and organize floods of arrivals. The new buildings were planned in conjunction with extensive parking lots and new or realigned park roads. Congestion was to be avoided above all. "Circulation must be a continuous process of motion" for both vehicles and pedestrians, as Welton Becket advised for shopping center design (at the time he was also designing the Canyon Village Lodge complex at Yellowstone).[23] The concept of "one-stop shopping" took shape as the Park Service developed the visitor center, and for many of the same reasons. In fact, at a design conference in 1958, architect Lyle Bennett complained about the term "visitor center" because the public con-

fused the new and "unusual, specialized facility" with shopping centers, a far more familiar phenomenon for most park visitors at that time.[24]

The visitor center was more than an adaptation of the park museum idea. It was, as Victor Gruen characterized the shopping center, a new building type. The concept and planning process for visitor centers grew out of essentially modernist principles. As the "hub" and "focal point" of a park, the visitor center provided a control point and a center for arrival, orientation, and park interpretation. The new centers were strategically sited to intercept the flow of automobiles into and through a park, since more visitors now stayed in motels outside park boundaries and came to the parks on automotive day trips. The visitor center was intended to ensure that even under these circumstances, basic orientation, services, and core interpretive messages would be delivered to all. Otherwise the crowds of visitors might simply drive through the park without ever appreciating the significance of the scenery, history, or other resources, while perhaps resenting any negative aspects of their experience, including traffic congestion and overcrowded facilities. Managing "visitor flow" was the overwhelming reality of architectural design as well as park planning. And just as Gruen had civic aspirations for his "shopping towns," Vint insisted that the visitor center should serve as the new "city hall" of a park: a central public space that would be a common feature of every visitor's experience and a fixture of the daily pattern of life for the people who lived and worked there.[25]

New visitor centers were high on the list of desires in the majority of prospectuses drafted by park superintendents and Mission 66 planners. The final Mission 66 report (1956) insisted that "one of the most pressing needs for each [park] area is the visitor center." Wirth was particularly convinced that the idea would serve the park system well.[26] Before Mission 66, superintendents submitted proposals for new buildings or other facilities through a Proposed Construction Project (PCP), which detailed the need and program for a new building. The PCP was passed on to the regional office, where it was developed into a schematic plan with cost estimates. The regional director then prioritized the proposal for funding. The project might go into design development at that point, and eventually be finalized in construction drawings and sent out to bid once funding had been secured. The entire process usually occurred in-house, especially at the preliminary stages of design, although consulting architects and engineers might be used to produce final design drawings. After 1954, PCPs were sent directly to the WODC and EODC, although regional directors still prioritized construction budgets for their regions. The initiation of Mission 66 further changed the process by asking superintendents to assemble their wish lists of PCPs as Mission 66 prospectuses. The regional offices remained involved, but only through their participation in drafting and reviewing the prospectuses. In Washington, Wirth, Vint, and the Mission 66 planners already directly supervised the WODC and EODC; now they assumed much of the responsibility for prioritizing construction budgets as well. This assured a certain level of consistency in the priorities established for park construction. New visitor centers, for example, became a high priority for a majority of parks.[27]

With the 1956 appropriations secured, WODC and EODC staff anticipated at least ten funded visitor center PCPs per year over the next decade. In addition to preliminary designs, the first set of projects required immediate design development and construction drawings so that contracts could be assembled and projects bid out for construction that spring. Mission 66 called for increased levels of staffing for the Park Service generally, including the design offices. But the agency did not expect to handle all the new design work in-house, as it had for the influx of work during the New Deal. The need for architectural and engineering services was seen as a temporary demand; nor was there a need to relieve high unemployment as there had been in the 1930s. The situation was closer to that of the 1920s, when the Park Service had employed architectural consultants (including Myron Hunt, Gilbert Stanley Underwood, and Herbert Maier) to design many of the rustic park buildings of that era. Also, during the postwar period, any construction project estimated to cost more than $200,000 came under the supervision of the General Services Administration (GSA), a separate federal agency that received preliminary designs and contracted out for design development, construction drawings, and construction supervision. Two of the first visitor center projects handled by the EODC, the Yorktown and Jamestown visitor centers (1957) at Colonial National Historical Park, cost more than $300,000 apiece and so were supervised by the GSA. The Philadelphia architects Gilboy, Bellante, and Clauss developed the pre-liminary PCP and designed buildings with red-brick veneer (a concession to the historical setting) which otherwise suggested contemporary American institutional architecture, with large geometric volumes, open plans, large windows, and roof terraces. Park Service officials were unhappy with the results, perhaps for administrative as much as aesthetic reasons. After 1957 special approval was sought, and usually received, to keep even those projects costing more than $200,000 under Park Service supervision. The great majority of new visitor centers, in any case, cost less than that amount.[28]

Other projects, such as "comfort stations" or other small, utilitarian structures, received standardized plans rather than new designs. Housing had its own imposed cost limitations per unit, necessitating a level of standardization as well, although with flexibility for local conditions and materials. Visitor centers and park administration buildings, however, always required unique designs. Landscape architects and interpretive planners, both in the WODC and EODC and in individual parks, took the schematic idea for the project and worked it into the overall development context of each park's Mission 66 prospectus. The new visitor center was sited, integrated with the park road and trail systems, and planned as part of the overall interpretive strategy for the park. Often "secondary" visitor centers, smaller roadside structures or signs, and short "nature walks" near areas of particular interest composed complementary features of the overall interpretive plan. The landscape architects usually established the footprints of proposed visitor centers and even designed parking lots, paths, and outdoor amphitheaters that ex-

Ranger stations, such as this example in Big Bend National Park, could serve as secondary visitor centers. NPS Historic Photo Collection.

Entrance stations, such as these at the west entrance of Yellowstone (top right), in Shenandoah (middle left), and in Rocky Mountain (middle right) were also important points of public contact. Their designs reflected the need to serve larger vehicles and larger volumes of traffic. NPS Historic Photo Collection.

Visitor Centers in the West. Between 1956 and 1958 Craters of the Moon National Monument, Idaho (left) and Badlands National Park, South Dakota (right), received preliminary designs for visitor centers by Cecil Doty and the WODC and final designs for the buildings by consulting architects. These are typical of many low and medium cost Mission 66 visitor centers that created a new minimum standard of public service for parks and monuments in remote locations. NPS Historic Photo Collection.

ploited scenic views, historic sites, or other "park resources" in the surrounding landscape. At that point the architects and engineers (some of whom never saw the proposed visitor center site) would finish the set of "preliminaries" by developing schematic designs for the building itself, including rough cost estimates.

Cecil Doty did much of the preliminary visitor center design early in the Mission 66 program and contributed greatly to the development of this building type. Vint had already promoted Doty to the unusual post of "regional designer" in 1952, freeing him from the administrative duties of a regional architect and allowing him to concentrate solely on design. As the principal architectural designer of the WODC, Doty provided many preliminary design schemes, and in some cases developed those designs much further.[29] Allaback documents a total of 110 national park visitor center projects and sixteen "additions" to existing buildings with construction contracts let between 1956 and 1966. She also lists fifty-four preliminary visitor center design projects done by Doty while at the WODC during those years. Not all of Doty's preliminary designs were built, and many others were significantly altered by other architects as they progressed to final design and construction drawings. But Doty's contribution to Mission 66 visitor design in the mid-1950s, particularly at the initial, conceptual stage, was extremely significant. Wirth and Vint relied on Doty, much as they had in the 1930s on Doty's mentor, Herbert Maier, to provide architectural expressions of park planning goals that influenced not only buildings in the western parks but also, by example, visitor centers throughout the national park

system. But as the principal WODC designer, Doty also remained involved in project work and never rose from that level into the managerial ranks, as Wirth, Vint, Maier, and many other Park Service architects and landscape architects had done.[30]

There was no single designer in the EODC who played the same role as Doty in the WODC, although supervising architect John Cabot did exercise great influence on visitor center design both in his region and throughout the park system. Cabot later replaced Dick Sutton as the agency's chief architect in Washington, and in both capacities he established standards and procedures for the planning and design of visitor centers throughout the Mission 66 period. Like Doty, Cabot stressed the use of "spatial relationship diagrams" and "traffic flow diagrams" as starting points for preliminary design. For Cabot, the "freedom of expression in architecture during this postwar period" could not be ignored. He intended to make sure that the Park Service employed the best possible consultants, since "the cheapest investment is to hire the very finest design talent available."[31] After the first season of Mission 66 construction, Cabot traveled the country, reporting that new park buildings appeared "very refreshing designwise when viewed in comparison with the other [rustic] units in their immediate environment," but that the details of construction had not always been "given sufficient thought."[32] Construction contracts had been rushed, in some cases, with inadequately developed construction drawings, leading to shoddy or badly conceived workmanship. By 1957 Cabot sought a larger role for consulting architects, who increasingly would take preliminary Park Service designs and develop them into fully articulated, thoughtfully detailed construction contracts. The in-house design offices simply could not produce all the necessary construction documents. The consultants Cabot helped select were progressive, modernist designers, including some who were, or went on to become, leading figures in American architecture, such as Richard Neutra and Romaldo Giurgola. The role of the consultants varied according to the project. In some cases they did little more than produce construction drawings for developed designs; in others, particularly the larger, higher-profile cases, they were asked to develop the entire design. Even in these cases, however, the consulting architects were given the site, the program, and even the orientation and footprint for the new building, as determined by the Park Service landscape architects and interpretive planners.[33]

By the fall of 1957, the end of the second construction season of Mission 66, only three visitor centers had been completed: the two at Colonial National Historical Park and one at the south rim of the Grand Canyon, all of which had been initiated before Mission 66. But others were under construction—at Everglades, Carlsbad Caverns, Olympic, Yellowstone, and Dinosaur—and approximately ten additional projects per year were anticipated. The staffs of the WODC and EODC decided to conduct a thorough review of their work to that point and compare their experiences. Five days of meetings were held in Philadelphia that November, followed by three more days in February in San Francisco. The next month Washington chief of interpretation Ronald F. Lee and chief architect Dick Sutton issued a joint memorandum on visitor center planning and design, with attached notes on the discussions held as well as individual papers prepared by chief naturalist John E. Doerr and architects Bennett, Cabot, and Doty. The interpreters and architects emphasized the need for close cooperation "right from the early stages of planning" in order to serve the rapidly developing requirements for museum exhibits, interpretive displays, auditoriums, and office and storage space in the new buildings. Ronald

Visitor Centers in the East. Antietam National Battlefield, Maryland (left), was designed by EODC staff with consulting architect William Cramp Scheetz Jr. in 1962. Stones River National Battlefield, Tennessee (right), was designed by EODC staff in 1963. Seen here as they appeared in the 1960s, both are typical of the many Mission 66 visitor centers intended to help interpret historic landscapes.
NPS Photos by Jack E. Boucher.

Lee, who had been the chief instigator of the meetings, wanted more organization in the preparation of the "museum prospectuses" that determined the basic building program prior to the preliminary design stage. "Supplemental museum prospectuses" were called for by both the WODC and the EODC to elaborate more fully the considerable and obviously growing needs of curators and park interpreters.[34]

Some of the early problems identified included the desire of museum curators for spaces with few or no windows to protect objects from daylight, while architects and exhibition designers preferred sunny spaces with views of surrounding landscapes. The designers were also worried by the observation that already at Grand Canyon and Colonial, and soon elsewhere, lobbies, bathrooms, information counters, and exhibit spaces were becoming clogged with people waiting in lines, or simply "backtracking" rather than following a "circle" route through the facility. Inadequate space for the sale of publications, poorly located pay phones or water fountains, or an inefficient floor plan all could impede flow and drastically undermine the efficiency of the building. For the Park Service architects, the answer was "openness" in plan, including spacious entrance lobbies with high ceilings and large windows. Such spaces often typified modernist architecture, which employed steel and reinforced concrete construction that could span large uninterrupted areas with few vertical supports or load-bearing walls. Such construction enabled visual connections through large windows or window walls to outdoor spaces (often terraces) and surrounding views, another characteristic typical of mod-ernist design which naturally fit the programmatic and functional needs of the visitor center. Cabot recommended "openness of space and openness of plan," and suggested that outdoor spaces (which were less expensive to build) could be integrated with indoor spaces to accommodate even greater anticipated "visitor load." Views were to be "exploited," whether from the lobby, from roof terraces, or from outdoor terraces and amphitheaters directly incorporated into the circulation plan. Above all, Bennett, Cabot, and Doty agreed that "circulation [was] . . . the 'backbone' of any plan and should guide the visitor and help him make decisions." Cabot and Doty both provided numerous examples of conceptual "visitor sequence" and "visitor flow" diagrams, integrating indoor and outdoor spaces, which generated the design of ground-level floor plans.[35]

The visitor center adapted modernist ideas of architectural composition to the specific programmatic and functional purposes of national parks. The integration of indoor and outdoor space in a (usually) one-level public building evoked the pavilions of Mies van der Rohe; the flow diagrams developed by Cabot and Doty recalled Le Corbusier's use of architectural procession (a dramatic sequence of spaces and views) to organize the experience created by a building. As developed by the Park Service in the mid-1950s, the visitor center became a viewing platform, in which views from interior spaces, roof terraces, and adjacent outdoor terraces or amphitheaters were calculated as a flowing, sequential experience. The centers were buildings to see from, not to be seen. In this sense they reversed the premise of prewar park

MISSION **66** in action

The cover of a Mission 66 public information brochure illustrates an idealized visitor center as an almost transparent pavilion, offering a sequence of views through window walls and from outdoor terraces. NPS History Collection.

museum design. Those rustic buildings were sited to form elements of pictorial landscape compositions experienced by visitors moving through and around a park village. Great effort and expense went into the design of elaborate façades that evoked Swiss chalets, "pioneer" construction, or "Indian" culture. But the outward stylistic or aesthetic appearance of the Mission 66 visitor center—as long as it was minimal and did not visually contrast with its surroundings or call too much attention to itself—was almost inconsequential. The removal of most ornamentation and historical allusion was another aspect of modernism that fit the purpose of the new buildings perfectly, since they were meant not to have a powerful presence themselves but to recede visually even as they facilitated the appreciation of park landscapes and resources by ever larger numbers of people. The architecture, ideally, should be nearly transparent: a composition of functional, overlapping spaces and outward views, not of structural mass and decorative façades.

The best Mission 66 visitor centers achieved this adaptation of contemporary modernist ideas to the goals espoused by Park Service landscape architects and interpreters. Success-

ful examples included many smaller, less expensive buildings. Cecil Doty's Zion (1957) and Montezuma Castle visitor centers (1958) typify an unpretentious, functional approach to architecture that met pressing needs for visitor and administrative functions with dignified efficiency and minimal visual intrusion on the landscape. At Zion, from the public (front) side the visitor center appears to be a low, horizontal earth-tone structure. It was sited on a slope, however, so that two stories of maintenance and

From rustic to modern in Zion National Park. The park's rustic museum (top left), sited on a dangerous curve near the park entrance, was overwhelmed by postwar levels of use. The new visitor center (1957-1961) was built just inside the park. The public spaces featured window walls, an outdoor terrace, a contact desk, and other facilities, all well separated from the extensive office and maintenance areas attached in a long, low wing. Zion National Park Archives.

administrative space could be incorporated at the back of the building, unseen by most visitors. The building provided tremendous utility—office space and an attached maintenance yard—while leaving the public experience one of a light and spacious pavilion and terrace offering views of surrounding geological features. The visitor center thus was able to serve greatly enlarged administrative, maintenance, and curatorial programs without the public being aware of much of the real work the building was doing.[36]

While examples such as Zion were designed entirely in-house, with consultants producing only the working drawings, other visitor centers were true collaborations. The Flamingo visitor center at Everglades (1957) was partly funded by the new restaurant and motel concessioner, who hired his own architect, Harry L. Keck Jr., of Coral Gables. Doty (working in this case well outside his region) had earlier assisted Cabot and his EODC staff in drawing up preliminary designs for the building, and Vint had been closely involved, visiting the site several times and ap-

proving its location and conceptual design. Keck's office produced the final design and working drawings. Set high on columns to avoid flooding during storm surges, and featuring a ramped entrance, concrete construction, horizontal bands of windows, and plain geometrical massing, the building evoked the work of Le Corbusier and other modernists. But again, the architecture was not intended as merely a stylistic reference. The elevated structure accommodated far more program than it suggested, including office space at the ground level under the visitor center. Visitors entered by a ramp leading directly to the elevated level, where an unusual juxtaposition of airy public spaces—a restaurant and a visitor center connected by an open bridge—made the entire experience one of a raised viewing terrace oriented to Florida Bay. From the surrounding landscape, views of the bay were framed by the elevated bridge and terrace and the juxtaposed building masses, reinforcing the impression of an open pavilion, and somewhat belying the presence of a large restaurant and administrative complex.

The Flamingo Visitor Center in Everglades National Park was designed by Park Service staff in collaboration with Harry L. Keck Jr. in 1956-1957. NPS Photos by Jack E. Boucher.

The Quarry Visitor Center, Dinosaur National Monument, was a collaboration of the WODC and Anshen and Allen and opened in 1958. NPS Historic Photo Collection.

The collaboration that produced this result was typical of many visitor center projects. In other instances, particularly in the case of larger and more expensive buildings, architectural consultants were given greater responsibilities. Even in these situations, however, the private architects developed their designs after being given the "preliminaries" that established site, orientation, program, and surrounding landscape development. The Quarry Visitor Center at Dinosaur National Monument (1958), for example, was based on a preliminary concept developed by Doty and WODC colleagues. A remarkable bed of dinosaur fossils, discovered in 1909, was to be exposed, left *in situ,* and covered by a shed to protect it and provide public access and services. Put in the hands of consulting architects S. Robert Anshen, William S. Allen, and Robert Hein in 1957, the building, with its dramatic lines, became one of the unqualified aesthetic successes of Mission 66. Just a year earlier, the firm of Anshen and Allen had designed the Sedona Chapel in Arizona, a dramatic and widely published plan that incorpo-

rated the striking rock formations on which it was sited. The project probably helped the firm secure the Dinosaur commission, which also demanded a unique union with the geological setting. At Dinosaur, the architects suggested a series of steel trusses that carried an asymmetrical V-shaped roof over the exposed bed of fossils. While Park Service museum curators had originally proposed limiting natural light in the enclosure, the walls in Anshen and Allen's approved design were completely glazed in a rectangular grid of windows. Public services, offices, and interpretive space were located in a massive two-story concrete cylinder that contrasted to the light, angular shed structure attached to it. A sweeping entrance ramp led directly to the second level, and from there onto a terrace within the shed that gave a stunning view down onto the expanse of partially exposed fossils. An active paleontology laboratory was housed beneath the terrace, at the ground level of the shed extending behind the cylinder of the visitor center. The building opened in the spring of 1958 to a positive reception among

Park Service officials, architectural critics, and scientists, who appreciated the *in situ* interpretation of the resources as well as the active laboratory that was interpreted for the public.[37]

For Wirth, the successful development of Dinosaur was a priority for Mission 66. The positive critical assessment and clear architectural merit of the building served as a rejoinder to critics who objected to modernist design in national park settings. The building's minimalist aesthetic indeed "harmonized" with the forbidding landscape of northeastern Utah, and its frank expression of construction technology seemed appropriate in a facility dedicated to scientific research as well as public enjoyment. This was also the park that preservationists had

rallied to protect from the Echo Park Dam; the final victory in that controversy had just been achieved in 1956. Although the new visitor center was far from the Echo Park area, it nevertheless countered the claim that the park was unused by the public.

Mission 66 made it possible to fund substantial improvements at Dinosaur—and many other less well known parks and monuments with smaller numbers of visitors—virtually for the first time. Historian Hal Rothman points out that the Park Service did not give the same level of attention or funding to most national monuments as it did to more heavily visited and more famous landscape parks elsewhere in the system.[38] National monuments, set aside by presidential decree, not by

Picnic table shelters, White Sands National Monument, New Mexico. Author's photo.

congressional legislation, often preserved smaller areas and archaeological ruins that, at least initially, were of more interest to scientists and "pot hunters" than they were to the general public. The New Deal began to address the imbalance, providing development funds for sites such as Bandelier and White Sands national monuments in New Mexico (for which Bennett designed the park administration buildings).[39] The magnitude of Mission 66, however, and the outstanding need for visitor facilities in many smaller parks, brought an unprecedented level of consistency to all the units of the national park system. By the end of Mission 66, even the most remote parks enjoyed basic utilities, a visitor center, a maintenance yard, and standard housing for employees. This suite of basic facilities—above all the visitor center—became the sine qua non of a functional unit of the national park system. Without a visitor center, it seemed, no park could be expected to preserve and interpret its resources adequately, and a series of such buildings was considered necessary at larger parks. New visitor centers represented not only consistent standards for the convenience of visitors and staff but also a standard of administration in every park. The construction of visitor centers was linked to the expansion and training of staff to work in them, as well as the use of slide and movie projectors and other technological means of interpreting a park more efficiently to its public.

Thanks to Wirth and his staff of planners, as well as the scores of park superintendents who drafted Mission 66 prospectuses, the visitor center became the architectural and functional centerpiece of their reinvented National Park Service. More than 100 were planned, and by 1959, 35 had been opened, with many more under construction. By 1964 there were 72, and by 1966 there were 95, with 16 more let to contractors and under construction, for a total of 111 (at least by one agency count).[40] That year there were 254 units in the park system. Construction costs ranged from less than $100,000 (for example, Montezuma Castle, Hopewell Culture, Fredericksburg), to less than $200,000 (Arches, Canyon de Chelly, Eielson, Fort Sumter, Saratoga), to less than $400,000 (Sequoia and Kings Canyon, Colorado National Monument, Antietam, Rock Creek Park), to more than $400,000. In 1963 this last group included the Gettysburg Cyclorama and the Death Valley visitor centers (both around $500,000) and the $7.5 million Jefferson National Expansion Memorial Visitor Center in St. Louis. In 1966 the $2 million Paradise (now the Henry M. Jackson Memorial) Visitor Center at Mount Rainier joined this group as another very atypical project, in this case the result of an elaborate attempt to settle twenty years of controversy over hotels and winter use at Paradise. Of the ninety-nine visitor centers completed or "programmed" through fiscal year 1963, thirty-three cost less than $100,000, forty-three less than $200,000, twenty less than $400,000, and only three more than $400,000.[41] Some visitor centers involved the conversion or expansion of older buildings, but the great majority were new construction and established the functional center of a revised strategy for how a park should receive and serve visitors. The ubiquity of the new building type indicated the great faith national park planners and architects placed in the philosophical and practical approaches Mission

Many of the most successful and representative visitor centers were the less expensive, more typical examples. Cecil Doty was involved in the design of many in this category. Colter Bay Visitor Center in Grand Teton was designed by Doty with consulting architects Malone and Hooper, 1956-1958. NPS Historic Photo Collection.

Doty and WODC staff designed the Hoh Forest Visitor Center, Olympic National Park, in 1962. NPS Historic Photo Collection.

The Panther Junction Visitor Center in Big Bend National Park was designed by Doty and the WODC between 1964 and 1968. Author's photo.

The Sitka National Historical Park Visitor Center was a collaboration of Doty, the WODC, and John Morse and Associates. Author's photo.

Capitol Reef National Park Visitor Center was designed by Doty, the WODC, and Arthur K. Olsen and Associates in 1965–1966. NPS Historic Photo Collection.

66 represented. Considering the subsequent adoption of visitor center buildings by park agencies of all kinds all over the world, this new type of building must be considered one of the most influential public land management strategies ever devised.

The national park visitor centers also established the Park Service as an important architectural patron, willing to employ the most advanced contemporary design ideas that leading professionals had to offer. In 1954 Conrad Wirth had famously rejected Frank Lloyd Wright as the architect for a new restaurant in Yosemite Valley. Wirth derided Wright's proposal as a "mushroom-dome type of thing," a "thing to see, instead of being for service."[42] The very next year, however, Wirth dedicated the Jackson Lake Lodge, and at the same time his own design offices, the WODC and EODC, were producing modernist designs, some of which continued to startle and occasionally outrage at least some critics. In 1955 Cabot and EODC project architect Donald F. Benson designed futuristic shade structures for Coquina Beach at the Cape Hatteras National Seashore. The large metal louvers resembled a series of attached airplane wings. They attracted notice; the project was published in *Progressive Architecture* and won an American

Coquina Beach bathhouse and shade structure, Cape Hatteras National Seashore, designed by the EODC in 1955. NPS Historic Photo Collection.

Institute of Architects (AIA) national award.[43] The local newspaper reported, however, that "until people get used to the modern trend," the structures were likely to "cause as much comment as three nude men on a Republican Convention program." At least some critics wondered why the Park Service had abandoned the "wattle and daub" reconstructions of nearby historic sites.[44]

By 1957, as Mission 66 buildings started to appear in the parks, a debate of sorts arose between the architectural profession, which generally strongly supported the new architecture, and other groups, including the National Parks Association and some local newspaper editors and reporters. Devereux Butcher grew increasingly incensed, deriding Welton Becket's concessioner buildings at Yellowstone's Canyon Village, for example, as "colossal and of freak design." He insisted that the Park Service was violating "national policy governing our national parks" by creating "conspicuous park structures." Returning to Jackson Lake Lodge, he now condemned it as "Alcatraz" and the "ugliest building in the park and monument system." Later that year Butcher was supported by Ernest Swift, the director of the National Wildlife Federation, who charged that Mission 66 was "pros-

Canyon Village Lodge, Yellowstone, designed by Welton Becket and Associates in 1955–1956. NPS Historic Photo Collection.

tituting the scenic grandeurs of our national parks" by accommodating too many visitors in buildings like the Jackson Lake Lodge, which, he claimed, was "a concrete monstrosity built for that sub-species of Homo sapiens called the tourist." If John Steinbeck had needed source material in writing *The Grapes of Wrath*, Swift added, he "could have studied park visitors."[45] The virulent rhetoric often returned to the theme of "modernistic" design, which was associated with "overdevelopment" and inappropriate levels of use. There were simply too many people (and perhaps for some critics the wrong kind of people) using parks in ways the authors scorned. Modernist architecture—a potent symbol of Mission 66 policy and planning—manifested and facilitated the unconscionable trend.

Authors in architectural trade magazines, however, expressed delight that the Park Service had abandoned "associative rusticity" in favor of "better and more imaginative architecture." In January 1957 *Architectural Record* published a long defense of Mission 66 architectural design. "*Architectural Record* . . . undertakes a crusade," wrote author Emerson Goble. "We are happy to join in the current campaign of improvement . . . known as Mission 66." Goble understood the essence of the criticism of Mission 66, noting that postwar "mass use" was "both the reason for Mission 66 and the cause of concern to the protectors of the purist persuasion." The Park Service wanted to expand the capacity of the parks, but not too much, and there was "a neat question as to where to draw the line." While some might feel that no buildings at all should be allowed in parks, most understood the necessity. According to Goble, Mission 66's detractors felt that "if we must have buildings, let's have good,

Colter Bay tent cabin and campground area, Grand Teton, designed by Spencer & Ambrose in 1956. NPS Historic Photo Collection.

The visitor center for the Wright Brothers National Memorial, North Carolina, was designed by Mitchell/Giurgola, 1957–1960. The interior now features a reconstruction of the 1903 "Flyer." Author's photo.

Wright Brothers National Memorial Visitor Center as it appeared in the 1960s. NPS Photo by Jack E. Boucher.

safe, sentimental rustic stuff that everybody associates with scenery." But Goble saw the opportunity "for architects in the world's best building sites" to "add something to the nobility of nature in her most exalted moods." Citing new park concessioner projects, such as the Yosemite Lodge (Spencer & Ambrose), the Canyon Lodge at Yellowstone (Welton Becket and Associates), the Colter Bay developed area at Grand Teton (Spencer & Ambrose), as well as the Quarry Visitor Center, Goble hailed the "courage" of the Park Service in insisting that "man-made art is not necessarily sinful, [and] inspired architecture need not be egocentric or competitive" with the appreciation of scenery.[46]

This vein of critical appreciation of Mission 66 architecture continued through the 1960s and into the 1970s. In 1964 the architectural critic Wolf Von Eckardt concluded that "the Park Service dares to build well," commending the Wright Brothers Visitor Center (Mitchell and Giurgola), the Gettysburg Visitor Center and Cyclorama (Richard Neutra), and Cabot and Benson's shade structures at Cape Hatteras as "outstanding contemporary buildings by outstanding modern architects." Von Eckardt felt that each deserved "an award for architectural excellence," something he insisted could rarely be said of government buildings. Quoting at length from a conversation with Cabot (now chief architect in Washington), Von Eckardt compared the Park Service designs favorably to the "dreary mediocrity of federal architecture."[47] In 1970 the AIA awarded a citation to the Park Service as an organization for its "continuing effort to provide excellent design at all levels in our national parks." The next year the *AIA Jour-*

nal featured a portfolio of Mission 66 architecture, including the Quarry, Wright Brothers, and Everglades visitor centers, which had "serve[d] architecture well" and been the basis of the national award.[48]

At least in professional and critical circles, Mission 66 endowed the Park Service with the highest reputation for architectural patronage that the agency has ever enjoyed. To a great degree this reputation was based not so much on the typical visitor centers designed by in-house forces as on a few exceptional examples by well-known consulting architects. The firm of Anshen and Allen, for example, in part because of its early critical success with the Sedona Chapel and the Quarry Visitor Center, went on to design Eichler homes and other residences, schools, hospitals, and institutions in California and all over the country. The critical success of the Wright Brothers National Memorial Visitor Center, which opened in North Carolina in 1960, similarly helped launch the Philadelphia firm of Mitchell/Giurgola. Cabot recruited Ehrman Mitchell and Romaldo Giurgola shortly after they left the office of Gilboy, Bellante, and Clauss (the designers of the Yorktown and Jamestown visitor centers) to start their own firm. The architects went on to become major figures in the profession, with an international practice that won the AIA national award in 1976. Giurgola served as the chair of Columbia University's architecture school and won the AIA Gold Medal in 1982. Even Frank Lloyd Wright's firm, Taliesen Associated Architects, made a contribution to Mission 66, though five years after its founder had died. The Beaver Meadows Visitor Center in Rocky Mountain Na-

tional Park, which opened in 1967, indeed proved that great design could find appropriate uses and expression in a national park.[49]

The most renowned architect to work as a consultant to Mission 66 was Richard Neutra, one of the original figures of the International Style, who, with his partner Robert Alexander, was asked in 1958 to design two very different park projects. Mission 66 was under particular pressure to address Civil War battlefield parks because of the centennial commemorations being planned for the 1960s. No celebrations loomed larger than those planned for the Gettysburg National Military Park, the site of the war's greatest battle and Lincoln's famous ad-

dress in 1863. President Eisenhower also happened to own a home in Gettysburg and intended to retire there. Planning for a new museum to house a large nineteenth-century "cyclorama" painting of the battle had begun in the 1940s. Civil War historians, park managers, EODC planners and interpreters, and the Park Service Washington office all agreed that the Ziegler's Grove area of the battlefield—the viewpoint from which the huge circular painting had been executed—was a powerful location from which to interpret the history of the battle and make the most effective use the cyclorama painting. Given the location and the necessity of housing the painting, Neutra and Alexander's building, dedicated in 1962, took the form of a large, featureless concrete cylinder with a long, low wing extending from it. The minimalist geometric abstraction of the building, its overall low massing set partially in the trees, and its sensitive use of fieldstone masonry were intended to harmonize its visual presence with what was an extremely sensitive location in the middle of the battlefield. The procession through the building allowed visitors to experience the painting, and then to emerge onto a roof terrace and view the actual battlefield from the same reference point. Critics such as Von Eckardt praised the quality and sensitivity of the design. For the Park Service, the collaboration with a world-renowned architect on such an important public building marked the high point of the entire Mission 66 architectural design effort.[50]

The second Neutra and Alexander project for the Park Service was the Painted Desert Community, a combined visitor center, residential area, and maintenance facility in the Petrified Forest National Park in Arizona. In this case the architects produced the most unusual and atypical national park architecture of the entire era. Sited in a remote desert with a hostile climate, the new community was designed in a compact geometric layout, featuring row houses and apartments all directly attached to the visitor center and maintenance buildings in one large complex. The public buildings and apartments together defined a central, sheltered courtyard. The private gardens of the row houses were separated by masonry walls, which, like other walls in the complex, were intended to block the desert wind. The Painted Desert

The Painted Desert Community, Neutra and Alexander, as it appeared in the 1960s. NPS Denver Service Center, Technical Information Center.

Community was true International Style architecture, with unadorned rectangular massing, large featureless façades, and horizontal windows set in long bands. The dense little community situated in the vast open desert offered a complete contrast to typical ranch house subdivisions of the period. The entire project, a remarkable departure for the WODC and the entire Park Service, indicated the degree to which the agency was committed by the mid-1950s to employing the most progressive architectural ideas that the profession had to offer. Although there were indications that Wirth and Vint felt that the experiment had not been entirely successful, and that Neutra had not been receptive to suggested changes, the design nevertheless won a *Progressive Architecture* award in 1959, and the Park Service allowed construction

on the exceptional and essentially unchanged plan to proceed the following year.[51]

Administration buildings also continued to be built, although they rarely had the same importance they had before the war. At Grand Canyon and Mount Rainier, for example, rustic prewar administration buildings designed by Thomas Vint and his staff of landscape architects were sited directly on the village "plazas," where they imbued these central public spaces with a sense of the identity and civic administration of the park. A few administration buildings dating from the Mission 66 era, such as the Ash Mountain Administration Building (Cecil Doty, WODC, and Walter Wagner & Partners, 1962) in Sequoia and Kings Canyon National Parks, had similar importance. In these cases, as at Ash Mountain, the building might feature interpretive displays and a "public contact" area, comparable to the information desks of prewar examples. More often, however, new visitor centers combined administrative functions with those of the park museum, replacing the need for either of the older building types.

New "administrative areas" built outside park boundaries to replace the old administration and maintenance buildings in prewar park villages were a more noteworthy example of Mission 66 development for this purpose. The El Portal administrative complex outside Yosemite and the Tahoma Woods area outside Mount Rainier were intended to replace the administrative and maintenance functions in Yosemite and Longmire villages, respectively. At El Portal, the Mission 66 administration and residential area was later expanded and now includes a large office and maintenance complex, additional residences, and an elementary school. The Tahoma Woods administrative and residential area has also grown. In both cases, however, the prewar rustic villages that were to be replaced were never demolished. On the one hand, the overwhelming need for maintenance and administrative space, and perhaps the reluctance of park staff to leave their picturesque park villages, resulted in the dual administrative areas in these parks. On the other hand, at least the older villages did not grow to accommodate greatly increased maintenance and administrative needs. If this was only a partial victory for what Vint would later call "Plan B" master planning, these and other Mission 66 administrative areas outside parks established vital precedents for removing development from the parks themselves. These precedents have greatly influenced the siting of new park administration and maintenance facilities ever since.

At Olympic National Park, the intense controversies over timber management and wilderness preservation produced a distinctive approach for developing a national park administrative area. When the park was established in 1938, Secretary of the Interior Ickes and his assistant Irving Brant met with the new park's superintendent, Preston Macy, and other Park Service staff to determine "controlling development policies" for the park. This exceptional meeting indicated the degree to which controversies at Olympic held Ickes's and Brant's attention. The small group determined quickly (Ickes was there for only one day) that the new Olympic headquarters should be built outside the park boundaries, that existing roads were sufficient to provide "reasonable access," and

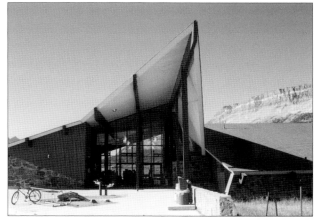

From rustic to modern in Glacier National Park. The rustic museum near Logan Pass (top, NPS Historic Photo Collection) was replaced by a new Logan Pass Visitor Center, a collaboration of the WODC/ Cecil Doty and Brinkman and Lenon, 1960-1963 (middle, author's photo). The same local consultants designed the St. Mary Visitor Center at the eastern entrance to the park in 1964 (bottom, author's photo).

A typical Mission 66 maintenance building. NPS Historic Photo Collection.

Mission 66 gas stations in Grand Teton (middle, NPS Historic Photo Collection) and Yellowstone (bottom, author's photo).

that no overnight accommodations would be necessary since nearby towns could provide them. In 1940 a new administration building and superintendent's residence were built in the nearby town of Port Angeles.[52] This was an early instance of Vint's "Plan B," but it had its own origins and inspiration. The U.S. Forest Service, which had administered the former Mount Olympus National Monument since 1909, had always placed its administration buildings in nearby communities rather than in the forests themselves, demonstrating the closer ties between national forest management and local economies and communities. The precedent of Forest Service examples influenced the decision to build in Port Angeles. The new building also revealed an interesting stylistic transition. Constructed mainly of wood, it nevertheless featured modernist design details and spatial composition, and perhaps more than any other single building demonstrated the gradual evolution from rustic to modernist park architecture.

Of the 257 "administrative and service buildings" built through Mission 66, the variety is considerable, from quasi–visitor centers that function as park headquarters to small modular buildings serving as office space. Mission 66 administration buildings were also often sited directly adjacent to maintenance yards, which were utilitarian areas usually defined by linear arrangements of sheds or garages delineating a central work area. The yards themselves were not functionally different from the utility areas built as part of rustic villages before the war; the buildings were now likely to be made of concrete blocks or metal siding, the economical construction materials that characterized most new buildings of these types in the park system (and elsewhere) during the postwar period. Wirth counted 218 new "utility buildings" built during Mission 66, a category that included storage buildings and workshops as well as structures that housed equipment for the extensive utility lines and other basic services being modernized, or provided for the first time, in many parks.[53] Administrative, service, and utility buildings all had either very limited public access or no public function at all. This was another reason why in many cases standardized plans were considered acceptable. Most examples of these building types, in any case, did not benefit from the level of design attention and detail that public facilities were likely to receive.

Perhaps the most appreciated category of Mission 66 architectural design from the point of view of park staff was employee housing: 743 single-family and semidetached houses were built, as well as 496 apartment units. These subdivisions were typically located near new visitor centers and administrative areas, or they expanded existing prewar bungalow-type residential areas, following the recommendations of Herma Baggley and the National Park Service Women's Organization. In addition to single-family units, other types of housing included dormitories and "housekeeping cabins." In some cases older housing, usually of a lower standard, reverted to "seasonal" use as new year-round housing became available. Many projects involved remodeling prewar "cottages" or other housing. In some situations, such as at Dinosaur and Petrified Forest, the architects designing visitor centers were also asked to design associated park housing. There were other exceptional

Mission 66 residential areas in Big Bend (top, NPS Historic Photo Collection), Yellowstone (middle, author's photo), and Everglades (bottom, author's photo).

cases that required "special design." But in general, single-family detached housing—soon known as the "Mission 66 ranch"—built through the use of standard (or "stock") plans, became the ubiquitous symbol of the effort to provide decent housing for Park Service families. The 1956 Mission 66 plan announced the goal of building a thousand units of park housing over the next five (not ten) years, at an average cost of $18,000. This large an effort, together with congressional cost limitations, required the use of standardized plans. Even using consultants, the Park Service could not hope to provide so many individual residential designs.[54] But despite the use of standardization, or perhaps because of it, Mission 66 raised the material conditions for family life in the parks to a level comparable to what most of the rest of the country was beginning to enjoy in the 1950s.

As was the case with the Capehart and Wherry housing built by the U.S. Army, federal standards and rules, whether specified by Congress in legislation or through policy at the Bureau of the Budget, set certain limits on Park Service housing construction. The Bureau of the Budget issued "design standards," for example, limiting two-bedroom residences to 1,080 square feet and three-bedroom houses to 1,260 square feet. Cost per unit was raised during the Mission 66 period to $20,000, but this was still a difficult requirement to meet, especially in remote areas where construction costs were high.[55] Within these limits, however, architect John Cabot in particular wanted to ensure that the Park Service developed the best possible standard designs. With dozens of units funded for immediate construction in the spring of 1956,

Cabot expressed concerns about the quality of the standard plans that had been quickly assembled following the regional directors' meeting in Washington in February of that year. Park housing had been a principal subject throughout a week of detailed discussions and presentations. Cabot felt that the resulting 1956 plans reflected "eastern city thinking" and suggested "mass produced developments surrounded by streets and sidewalks."[56] Park housing also remained the specific concern of the National Park Service Women's Organization. Wirth continued to support the organization's role advising on park housing, and this became the group's most important contribution to Mission 66. In response to Cabot's concerns, Herma Baggley reiterated the conclusions she had submitted to Vint on behalf of the organization three years earlier. Park Service women would accept and even welcome standard plans, she again pointed out, because such plans guaranteed at least decent housing even in remote areas and brought an element of consistency to a lifestyle that demanded frequent moves. Standardized plans, of course, did not have to mean that exterior sheathing, construction materials, or even rooflines all had to be the same everywhere, since local conditions and available materials required flexibility. Baggley reiterated that the women were willing to put up with rough conditions and "primitive" construction, but advised that they would like their housing to offer more storage space, separate entrance areas ("mud rooms"), larger kitchens, and more bedrooms.[57] Since the Park Service continued to discriminate against women professionals in its design offices (a policy that was only beginning to change in the 1950s), the influence of the Women's Organization on the design of Mission 66 housing is particularly notable.[58]

That fall Cabot issued his own memorandum on "the design of Park Service houses," in which he described the shortcomings of the housing that was being planned and built in the parks at that time. He was eager to build on the work of Baggley and the Women's Organization and felt that their recommendations had not yet been incorporated. Cabot cited the 1956 Women's Congress on Housing (organized that spring by the Housing and Home Finance Agency) as another opportunity to involve the women who lived and worked in the parks in the revision of house plans. The Women's Congress had recommended that homes be at least 1,200 to 1,500 square feet, with three bedrooms, one and a half bathrooms, a living room, a family room, a kitchen with eating space, and "as great an area of closet and storage space as can be contrived," according to Cabot. The architect did not seem to be concerned with the architectural style of new housing so much as with providing these minimal material amenities, within federal limitations, through efficient design. He urged that Park Service housing plans ought at the very least to meet contemporary expectations, especially among women, for a modern standard of living. He went on to state the "basic fundamentals" of successful housing, whether built by the federal government or by private developers: space should be enclosed to separate rest and quiet areas from daily activity areas, for example, and indoor and outdoor storage should meet both long-term and daily needs. "We have another duty," he reminded his colleagues, "be-sides the mass production of houses . . . to eliminate the distress of no housing at all," and that was to build houses that would meet the increasing demands and expectations of occupants for the next forty years. He then requested that existing "stock plans" be "held in abeyance" while the WODC and the EODC developed designs that would be "architecturally up to date with current national thinking." The two offices could "collaborate to work out plans solving actual conditions throughout the Country and, if possible, arrive at plans and designs that solve many varied conditions of climate and topography." The assumption was that park housing would necessarily be comparable in materials, construction, and general appearance to the vast majority of housing being so rapidly constructed at the time by builders all over the country.[59]

Cabot's efforts resulted in a set of revised "Standard Plans for Employee Housing" issued in time for the 1957 construction season. Included were five variations on a three-bedroom ranch, and six for a two-bedroom, as well as designs for a multiple unit, an apartment building, and a dormitory. The house variations included split-level floor plans and houses with and without basements. No further variations on the plans were to be allowed, except for the location of porches and garages and other "minor changes." "Left-hand" and "right-hand" versions of the plans were used as well. All construction was assumed to be "frame wall," but the choice of sheathing was left open, depending on local availability and construction practices. All units were to offer at least a minimum of material conveniences, including modern stoves and re-

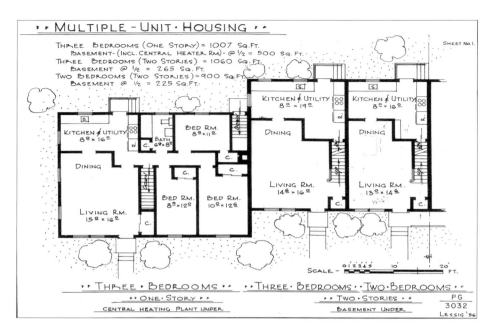

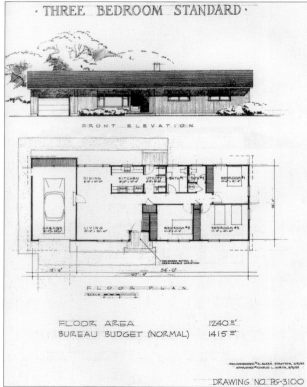

Standard housing plans for multiple units and the three-bedroom ranch. NPS Denver Service Center, Technical Information Center.

frigerators, linoleum floors in kitchens and bathrooms, central heating, and connections for washers and dryers. Superintendents were to pick preferred plans and submit them to their regional directors.[60]

In 1958 Wirth observed, "So far we have taken between 200 and 250 park service families out of rundown, outmoded—well, shacks is the right word—and put them in new houses and apartments more suited to the dignity of the job they are performing so ably." The next year the National Park Service Women's Organization again undertook a housing survey, this time under the direction of Inger Garrison, the wife of Yellowstone superintendent Lon Garrison. By February 1959, Garrison observed, 368 new housing units for permanent employees had been built. This put the program on schedule to complete 1,000 units in ten years (not the hoped-for five), although the total need was now estimated at almost 1,500 units. The tenor of the 107 survey responses that Garrison tabulated was very positive. About half of those questioned reported that Mission 66 housing had been built in their parks. In general that half responded positively at a ratio of about five to one to questions such as "Have the plans been adequate for site placement. . . . number of bedrooms. . . . number of bathrooms. . . . eating space. . . . traffic flow?" The general appearance of the houses was considered "fitting for the location and the Park" by a majority of twenty-five to three. The aesthetic, or style, of the houses was either widely approved or simply not a subject of comment; the major complaint was that the nearly flat roofs of the typical ranch were not appropriate in snow country. The respondents continued to show a strong preference for individual houses over multiple units, noting the need for privacy after working long days with fellow park staff who were also often neighbors. The three-bedroom ranch was widely favored, as was an additional dining area in the kitchen. The survey continued to show a strong consistency with the desires and expectations of Americans in general during the 1950s, as well as approval of Mission 66 housing policies.[61]

In February 1960 the 1957 standard plans were revised in an attempt to provide more space and amenities, still within the $20,000 per unit limit. Five types of housing were now offered: three-bedroom standard, four-bedroom standard, two-bedroom duplex (attached side by side), three-bedroom "superintendent" (slightly larger), and four-bedroom superintendent. The floor plans showed improvement in circulation and organization, with more storage, and a more defined entrance area, in addition to a slight increase (200 square feet) in overall size. Garages were now always attached (they had been detached in some of the 1957 plans). Two-bedroom houses were replaced by the two-bedroom duplex, consisting of two identical house plans (one reversed) linked by adjacent carports. Standard plans now included front elevation sketches, although the choice of siding remained open. The 1959 Women's Organization survey had affected the new plans, which now featured entry vestibules with closets, extra storage, and a dining area adjacent to the kitchen, as well as a garage with additional storage.[62] The standard plans served as the basis for quickly developing working drawings that necessarily were adapted to an individual building

Ranch house under construction in Grand Canyon in 1957. NPS Historic Photo Collection.

New ranch houses, 1957-1959, in Grand Teton National Park (middle) and Lincoln Home National Historic Site (bottom). NPS Historic Photo Collection.

One of the first Mission 66 comfort stations was built in Zion National Park in 1956. NPS Historic Photo Collection.

site. By the end of 1963, the process was further standardized with additional plans designed specifically for hillsides. New standard plans approved in 1964 closely resembled the 1960 ranch houses, although the average number of square feet of living space was reduced, reverting closer to the original 1957 size. By this time the three-bedroom, approximately 1,200-square-foot ranch with attached carport had become a ubiquitous standard.[63]

In terms of staff morale and the efficient administration of parks, Mission 66 addressed what had been a serious crisis caused by the dearth of staff housing. Housing, however, had

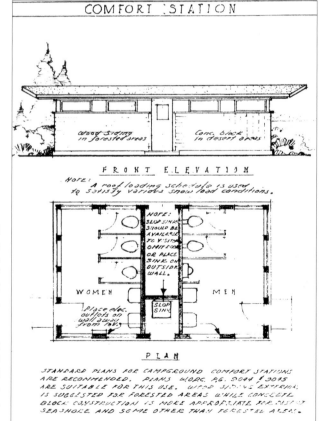

Several types of standard comfort station plans were produced during Mission 66, including this one by the Region IV office in 1959. NPS Western Regional Office, San Francisco.

Typical Mission 66 comfort stations in Big Bend National Park (top right) and Cape Cod National Seashore (bottom right). Author's photos.

no public function, and in fact was rarely ever seen by visitors. Park Service architects and members of the National Park Service Women's Organization felt that the overall appearance and construction of housing should be "appropriate" to its setting. but almost universally believed that the use of standard plans would not prevent this result. Other categories of Mission 66 architecture that also made use of standardized plans, to a greater or lesser degree, include "comfort stations," of which 584 were built, as well as other campground structures. Thirty-nine entrance stations were also built, often requiring individual design, but simple ranger kiosks and roadside interpretive structures could be produced from typical plans by the hundreds.[64]

The final category of Mission 66 architecture to be considered, concessioner lodges and stores, is discussed in chapter 8. As had always been the case, park concessioners hired their own architects to help plan and then build their visitor facilities. Park Service officials had the right to approve of the designs, and in fact had a tradition of working closely with concession architects to develop proposals that were true collaborations between private- and public-sector capital and design expertise. Architecturally, concessioner structures nevertheless differed from other types of park buildings. Concessions served the public, but could do so only if they continued to make a profit, and this reality affected programming and design. Concession capital augmented public spending during Mission 66 but did not reach the same level of importance that it had during the Mather era. While Wirth exhorted his concessioners to in-

Typical Mission 66 wayside interpretive displays in Great Smoky Mountains (top), Arches (middle), and Badlands (bottom). NPS Historic Photo Collection.

vest millions, the business of national park concessioning had changed dramatically since the
1930s, and managing park concessions became
one of the most problematic aspects of Mission
66. But some of the earliest and most high-pro-
file Mission 66 projects, such as the Canyon
Lodge in Yellowstone and the Yosemite Lodge,
were developed by concessioners and their architectural consultants. Concessioner architects
such as Gilbert Stanley Underwood, Welton
Becket, and Eldridge Spencer therefore contributed to the overall image of Mission 66 program to a degree that exceeded the relatively
small amount of private investment—about $33
million—that augmented the overall $1 billion
in federal park spending between 1956 and
1966.

CHAPTER 6

PRESERVATION AND INTERPRETATION

The dozens of modernist visitor centers that appeared in the first years of Mission 66 were the project's single most significant architectural product. But what made the visitor center a novel building type was its new programs and purposes as much as its innovative floor plans and construction. The development of interpretive programs and training under Mission 66 was therefore as much a part of the design effort as was architecture or landscape architecture. The emphasis on interpretation and preservation and the expansion of professional capabilities and activities in these fields made Mission 66 the most important federal historic preservation effort between the Historic Sites Act of 1935 and the National Historic Preservation Act of 1966.

For landscape architects like Wirth and Vint, historic preservation remained closely linked to scenic preservation, and both were subsumed under one larger project: national park making. "National parks and monuments fall into two groups," Vint explained in 1946, "natural and historical." In the former the primary purpose was "to preserve and protect one of the great works of nature." In the latter it was "to preserve and protect the scene at one of the great moments of our national history—to stop the clock and hold the scene of the moment in history that makes the area important." Whether in the case of scenic or historic preservation, providing for public access and enjoyment remained the essential task: "The development scheme [master plan] has to do with providing the facilities to permit the people to see and enjoy these areas," Vint maintained. "It is constantly working on the compromise that determines how far these facilities will intrude into the scenes that are to be preserved, as nearly as possible, as nature or history has left them to us."[1]

For Vint and the entire Park Service, preserving landscapes was the approach for both scenic and historic places. In either case, maintaining roads, visitor centers, and other facilities made it possible for the public to appreciate natural scenery and historic settings alike. In the process, the place was preserved through its transformation into a public park. In the late 1920s Vint successfully made the case to Albright that this transformation should be controlled by a unified aesthetic conception—the "master plan"—that controlled and limited the extent of development.[2] When he became director in 1929, Albright had two important goals for his agency: to expand into the management of historic sites, and to control all park development through the enforcement of master plans. These goals were linked, since the effectiveness of the Park Service as a historic preservation agency was to be achieved through the development of master plans for "national historical parks." Vint oversaw the development of the first such historical parks, including Colonial (Virginia), Salem Maritime (Massachusetts), and Hopewell Village (Pennsylvania). In 1933 Franklin Roosevelt transferred control over some forty battlefields and other historic sites and monuments from various other agencies to the Park Service, an executive order that Albright had personally sought as a means of balancing the park system functionally and regionally as well, since many historic sites were in the East.[3]

Until this point, the "house museum" had been the most typical form of historic preservation in the United States. Even the Williamsburg Restoration (a private undertaking funded by John D. Rockefeller Jr.) could be seen as a vast assemblage of individual house and garden reconstructions.[4] The national historical park, however, preserved entire landscapes through their transformation and improvement as public parks. Colonial National Historical Park, for example, consisted mainly of an automotive parkway across the peninsula between the York and James rivers in Virginia. The parkway connected national park properties at Yorktown and Jamestown and passed through the Williamsburg Restoration. While numerous historians, restoration architects, and other officials contributed to the overall concept of Colonial National Historical Park, it was the parkway itself that provided the physical context and continuity between the three separate historic sites. As Vint stated in the "Outline of Development" of 1933, the parkway would make the park a "single, coherent" entity, and would "transcend mere considerations of transportation . . . [and] contribute to the commemorative purposes of the monument."[5] The resulting landscape was in no sense a reconstruction of a colonial-era road corridor. Park Service landscape architects and engineers designed a modern automotive parkway like those that had been developed by landscape architects in Westchester County and elsewhere during the previous decade. As with the Mount Vernon Memorial Highway (which was under way by 1928), the Colonial project combined advanced roadway design with "appropriate" design details, in this case brick veneer over the concrete of the overpass bridges and culvert headwalls. The result was an entirely new landscape—a historical park—that combined new landscape design (the parkway) with the historic house reconstructions, archaeological excavations, and other "restorations" taking place at various sites along the corridor.[6] The Blue Ridge Parkway became the ultimate example of this type of park project by showcasing restored agricultural landscapes and vernacular architecture along a 469-mile route through Virginia and North Carolina. One of the great works of landscape architecture of the twentieth century, it is also one of the most ambitious historic preservation projects ever undertaken. Begun through the New Deal, the massive Blue Ridge project was later greatly advanced by Mission 66 funding.

The development of national historical parks owed more to the techniques of scenic preservation, or park making, than to historic house restoration or garden reconstruction. Depression-era historical parks and parkways might feature a restored landscape, house museum, or battlefield, but they did so in the context of a new designed landscape calculated to present to the public a series of what Vint called "historic scenes." And for Vint, these individual scenes could be best preserved by "stopping the clock" at a particular date of maximum significance. This would prove to be a problematic concept, since few landscapes (as opposed, perhaps, to individual buildings) had such discrete dates of significance. Neither were living, growing landscapes easily "stopped" in time.[7] During Mission 66, however, new historical parks continued established historic preservation practice at the Park Service. Mission 66 eventually funded dozens of important historical park developments of increased variety and scope, many of which had been begun before World War II.

In St. Louis, for example, preparation of the site for the Jefferson National Expansion Memorial began in the 1930s. Municipal leaders had been proposing the "revitalization" of the city's historic but decaying riverfront district for decades. Most of these plans called for the demolition of scores of nineteenth-century commercial buildings and warehouses, followed by the development of housing, municipal parking, or some kind of public park in their place. In an era before federal urban renewal programs, however, "slum clearance" on this scale was difficult for municipalities to achieve on their own. Seeing their chance to secure federal assistance, in 1933 local politicians and civic reformers conceived of a plan for a "national memorial" dedicated to the "men who made possible the western territorial expansion of the United States," including Thomas Jefferson, Lewis and Clark, and anonymous "hunters, trappers, frontiersmen, and pioneers." The memorial, to be designed and administered by the Park Service in partnership with local officials, would be the means of securing federal funding for the acquisition of the dilapidated riverfront. The intent was to eradicate "blight" by replacing it with an improved park landscape, thus attracting new private investment in nearby downtown business districts. Under the powers of the 1935 Historic Sites Act, Roosevelt declared "Old St. Louis" the first "national historic site." At that point, WPA and PWA dollars were to fund the demolition of the entire area. When Park Service architect Charles Peterson arrived in 1936, he was reduced to doing little more than researching and documenting structures as quickly as possible in advance of their being torn down. Drury supported the St. Louis memorial plans, against the advice of Peterson and other Park Service staff, and by 1942 all but three buildings of "Old St. Louis" had been razed.[8]

In 1937 Park Service landscape architects designed a memorial landscape for the riverfront consisting of a formal mall parallel to the riverfront levee, terminated at either end with neoclassical museum buildings. The central cross-axis was marked by an obelisk aligned with the city's Old Courthouse building, which was not demolished. But the St. Louis politicians and advocates of the project had grander aspirations for their memorial, and in 1945 they announced a national design competition. More than 170 entries were prepared, many by the

Mission 66 sign in St. Louis during Jefferson National Expansion Memorial construction. NPS Historic Photo Collection.

Eero Saarinen's Gateway Arch was designed in 1947 and completed in 1965 through Mission 66 construction funds. NPS Historic Photo Collection.

leading modernist architects of the day, including Walter Gropius, Charles and Ray Eames, and Louis Kahn. Richard Neutra served on the jury. In 1948 Eero Saarinen's dramatic concept for a slender 630-foot-high arch—a literal "Gateway to the West"—was selected. In the form of an inverted catenary curve constructed of stainless steel, the soaring arch became a modernist icon.[9] The Park Service now was in the position of managing a national historical park as unique as the distinctive arch itself. Forty blocks of historic downtown St. Louis had been demolished and replaced by a huge steel monument surrounded by a park designed by Saarinen's frequent collaborator, landscape architect Dan Kiley. The modernist landscape commemorated the history of westward expansion, while the original historic structures and landscape features associated with that history were completely erased.

Jefferson National Expansion Memorial had been the inspiration of local advocates who had been searching for the means to redevelop their riverfront since the Louisiana Purchase Exposition of 1904. The Park Service became involved as a result of Roosevelt's direct political interest; the agency never controlled the overall concept for the memorial, nor did it select the competition winner. In Philadelphia, however, the Park Service was drawn into the revitalization of another historic downtown, and in this case the agency was more comprehensively involved. Independence Hall and a cluster of other eighteenth-century buildings still stood in downtown Philadelphia, surrounded by two hundred years' worth of urban growth. Local civic leaders again sought to improve economic conditions and attract private developers to the declining core of the city by demolishing a considerable portion of it. Independence Hall had been the subject of pioneering preservation efforts since the nineteenth century, however, and the destruction of this national shrine and other historic buildings nearby was not contemplated. Instead, local advocates envisioned preserving and restoring the eighteenth-century buildings while removing only the nineteenth- and early-twentieth-century structures around them. New parks and open spaces would replace the more recent buildings, creating what was felt to be a more appropriate historical setting. By the 1920s, proposals had been made to raze three blocks of buildings immediately to the north of Independence Hall in order to create a monumental vista. In the 1930s, the New Deal and the Historic Sites Act seemed to offer opportunities to implement these ambitious plans, and by the end of the decade Park Service planners were studying the feasibility of establishing a national historical park.[10]

Agency officials, especially chief historian Ronald Lee, were supportive of the idea and worked in close partnership with Philadelphia's municipal government, businesspeople, and preservation advocates. In an exception to his wartime policy of suspending such designations, Roosevelt established the national historic site in 1943. When the war ended, Park Service planning quickly regained momentum. In 1947 architect Charles Peterson was reassigned to Philadelphia, joined by agency historian Roy Appleman, to research and document the affected area. In 1948 the Philadelphia National Shrines Commission, a coalition of local business inter-

ests, preservationists, and municipal officials, submitted a report to Congress recommending the creation of a national park. The plan, which called for extensive demolition of nineteenth- and twentieth-century buildings, featured a second open vista, or mall (this one extending east from Independence Hall), as well as other open spaces around the older buildings marked for preservation. Congress established Independence National Historical Park that year, and in 1949 authorized almost $4 million to fund the condemnation and demolition of buildings to create the new park landscape.[11] In this case, however, Lee and other Park Service officials had successfully offered legislative amendments that gave their agency more control over the planning and operation of the park. As the historian Constance Greiff observes, "They wanted to assure that the errors that had been committed at other sites," notably George Washington's birthplace and St. Louis, "did not recur in Philadelphia."[12]

Over the next decade, Ronald Lee in particular maintained close oversight of the planning for what was widely considered the nation's most significant historic shrine. But the process necessarily involved extensive collaboration with Philadelphia preservationists and city planners who were actively involved in other aspects of the urban renewal effort. In the early 1950s, for example, city and state government funded the demolition of the three blocks of buildings north of Independence Hall to make way for Independence Mall, which finally created the desired straight, open view back to the historic building. At the same time, Peterson was devising plans for Independence Hall and the historic areas immediately to the east. With the state-funded demolitions under way and his experience in St. Louis still fresh in mind, Peterson pointed out some basic problems with the existing approach to historical park design. The purpose of the new national park had been defined as interpreting and preserving buildings associated with eighteenth-century American history, and so the "period of significance" ended in 1800. But within the park's boundaries also lay significant works of nineteenth-century

American architecture that were now slated for demolition. Peterson felt that many of these buildings were worthy of preservation, and in any case, another formal mall looking back toward Independence Hall would be out of character with the dense pattern of streets and buildings that had always surrounded the building. In 1953, however, Wirth, Lee, and Vint came to Philadelphia, and in a conference with Peterson and local officials they reconfirmed the period of significance as 1774–1800. Following the Park Service reorganization of 1954, EODC chief Edward Zimmer and chief architect John Cabot supervised Peterson's master planning effort.

Once Mission 66 funding became available in 1956, much of the demolition for the national park proceeded during the next year, although further progress stalled over questions regarding the design of the new open spaces. Independence National Historical Park nevertheless became an emblem of Mission 66: the brochure introducing Mission 66 to the public (*Our Heritage,* 1958) featured a "typical" American family superimposed on an image of the Liberty Bell. Finally, in 1960 another Park Service conference was held in Philadelphia, during which the details of the master plan were finalized. Lee, now Park Service regional director for the Northeast, approved a compromise plan that retained some of the more intimate spaces of the original urban street pattern, even after many of the nineteenth-century structures had been removed. The restored eighteenth-century buildings were presented in a new park landscape, but that landscape did not feature a formal, open mall.[13]

Downtown Philadelphia before and after demolition associated with the creation of Independence National Historical Park. NPS Northeast Regional Office, Philadelphia.

Much Mission 66 historic preservation was characterized by the involvement of Park Service historians, landscape architects, and planners in major urban renewal projects of the postwar era. The Housing Act of 1956, coming the same year as the Interstate Highway Act and the launching of Mission 66, funneled hundreds of millions of dollars from the federal government to states and municipalities engaged in urban renewal. At the Park Service, Lee in particular recognized both the positive and the negative potential of these programs. Lee was another longtime Park Service official shaped by his New Deal experiences. He was pursuing his Ph.D. in history at the University of Minnesota in 1933 when he and a group of other graduate students received offers to go to work for the newly organized CCC. Lee worked as a historian for the CCC camp in Shiloh National Military Park, and in 1934 transferred to Washington to assist chief historian Verne E. Chatelain with the details of the Historic Sites bill. In 1935 he began working directly for Wirth as the chief historian of Wirth's CCC state park program, and while still in his twenties was in charge of a major historical research and education program. Lee became the Park Service's chief historian in 1938. Following service in World War II, he returned to Washington and quickly became involved in planning Independence National Historical Park. He also was an early organizer and instigator of the 1949 legislation establishing the National Trust for Historic Preservation. Although he did not serve on the Mission 66 steering committee in 1955, in the Park Service reorganization of 1954 Lee became chief of the newly created Division of Interpretation, a posi-

tion that would be of great significance in Mission 66 planning. Lee then moved to Philadelphia to serve as Park Service regional director from 1960 until his retirement in 1966. As important as his agency positions were, however, Lee also developed a network of private preservation advocates and pioneered new partnerships throughout his career, as exemplified by his work at Independence. He also headed the Park Service special task force on legislation beginning in 1961, and, through the many organizations and activities in which he participated, he was instrumental in developing the programs and policies that influenced the National Historic Preservation Act of 1966.[14]

For Ronald Lee, urban renewal programs of the 1950s represented both a grave threat and also an opportunity that could not be ignored. Shortly after becoming regional director in the Northeast in 1960, he outlined his hopes for an extensive program of historic preservation and urban park planning in a long memorandum on "Mission 66 in relation to historic preservation, open spaces, and urban renewal." Since 1949 Congress had made millions available for the demolition and redevelopment of American cities, Lee noted, and hundreds of millions more were on the way as cities and states lobbied for federal assistance. Unfortunately, "sweeping programs of slum clearance" could "carelessly or ignorantly destroy important landmarks and valuable examples of historic architecture." There had already been "mounting protests" against such actions in New York's Greenwich Village and elsewhere. Indeed by 1960 the destruction caused by urban renewal and urban highway construction had inspired editorial boards and preservation advocates all over the country to criticize the federally sponsored destruction of historic "landmarks." Lee went on to identify a corresponding need for "open space" preservation that was "as urgent as historic preservation" in urban renewal programs; but federal officials had not yet adequately addressed either concern.[15]

Neither the Park Service nor the National Trust was in a good position to deal with the enormous threat to American cities that the federal government had created. The Historic Sites Act, for example, authorized the acquisition of nationally significant landmarks, but that option remained very limited, expensive, and slow to implement. Some critics suggested that the Park Service was too preoccupied with its own properties (and with implementing Mission 66) to organize an effective response to the national crisis.[16] Lee pointed out, however, that the Park Service was already deeply involved in urban renewal plans not only in St. Louis and Philadelphia but in New York, Boston, and Washington as well. Philadelphia, Baltimore, and numerous other cities had also sought Park Service "advisory assistance on open space in metropolitan areas," which the agency's recreational planners were able to provide in only a very limited fashion through provisions of the 1954 Housing Act. Lee believed that this move into urban planning by the Park Service was justified in order to achieve the "preservation of historic monuments and natural landscape in urban areas where such cultural resources have enormous value, yet may be easily lost in vast programs of urban expansion."[17] If the results were limited, they were also significant. Under Mission 66,

Park Service participation in the New York City Shrines Advisory Board led to new or redesignated parks at Federal Hall, Grant's Tomb, Hamilton Grange, and Ellis Island, where Lee helped plan an "American Museum of Immigration." Similar participation with the Boston National Historic Sites Commission resulted in the eventual designation of Boston National Historical Park and Minuteman National Historical Park. In his 1960 memorandum, Lee suggested that the Park Service's "contributions to historic preservation and open space protection in urban areas" were becoming "a complementary program to wilderness preservation," and that this was a desirable direction in which the agency should grow. "The perpetuation of nationally recognized historic and cultural values of cities is a worthy objective for the National Park Service," he reasoned, "since it would broaden the "cultural basis" of the agency and make it "more fully national." It would also provide a "service to a tremendous portion of America's population which may never be privileged to visit a western national park."[18]

In 1959 Lee oversaw the publication of a large brochure on the Park Service's "nationwide historical program" titled *That the Past Shall Live*. It was intended to be a companion to another Mission 66 public relations booklet published two years earlier, *The National Park Wilderness*. In Wirth's introduction (probably drafted by Lee), he reminded readers that "more than two-thirds of the areas" in the national park system were cultural sites, and that the Park Service not only managed parks but also was "the primary Federal agency charged . . . with the preservation of America's historic sites and buildings." Setting a tone that captured the spirit of Lee's collaborative efforts, Wirth observed that historic preservation "must be a cooperative local, State, and national effort. . . . State historical societies, State park departments, and a host of State and local preservation groups" were collaborating with the Park Service and the National Trust "toward the common goal."[19] Lee was moving the Park Service into a national role in postwar historic preservation planning even as the agency was losing its

leadership in national recreational planning. He was doing it through collaborative partnerships, advocacy of new legislation, and ambitious historical park projects that tapped into congressional interest in urban renewal. Not all his recommendations were immediately acted upon, but his urban national park initiative suggested features of what Stewart L. Udall, soon to be named secretary of the interior, was beginning to describe as the "New Conservation." Much of the impetus for the National Historic

LEFT TOP:
Restoration of the Johnson home in 1957, Andrew Johnson National Monument (now National Historic Site), Tennessee. NPS Historic Photo Collection.

LEFT BOTTOM:
Restoration of a building in Appomattox Courthouse National Historical Park, Virginia, in 1959. NPS Historic Photo Collection.

RIGHT:
Mission 66 Reconstruction of the "slave cabin" in Booker T. Washington National Monument, Virginia. NPS Historic Photo Collection.

Preservation Act of 1966, as well as the urban national park programs of the 1970s, had roots in the experience of Mission 66 projects such as Independence National Historical Park.

Mission 66 historic preservation was not limited to large urban projects. The postwar period also saw widespread growth and refinement of park education and orientation programs, which Park Service officials now unfailingly described as park "interpretation." Mission 66 became the means of standardizing and implementing educational programs throughout the park system, particularly at scores of smaller historical sites and archaeological monuments that had not yet been fully developed. The ubiquitous Mission 66 visitor centers were the most tangible evidence of the provision of a new standard level of visitor programs. The development of uniform practices and professional training in park education and orientation was just as important: like the new buildings, they established the basis for explaining the significance of national park areas to the public. In addition, new methods and media for conveying this cultural significance to visitors helped institutionalize management priorities. The interpretation of a site thus became a fundamental part of the process of preservation.

The word "interpretation" used roughly in this sense had a long history, but by the late 1930s Park Service rangers and historians began to use it consistently to describe their goal of presenting enough scientific and historical information for visitors to appreciate the park landscapes and resources. While interpretive programs were essentially educational programs, Mission 66 officials used the term to convey their

own, perhaps somewhat revised intentions for park education. Earlier educational programs, which operated out of park museums, often gave broad instruction on themes of natural and cultural history. Mission 66 interpretive programs, by contrast, were intended specifically to convey the spirit and significance of an individual site to diverse groups of people. Whether described as education or interpretation, the activity was as old as modern tourism itself. Guidebooks and "nature guides" were common features of early-nineteenth-century tours of Great Britain's Lake District, the Swiss Alps, or New York's Catskill Mountains. By the late nineteenth century, national parks concessioners hired naturalists, who were often women, to give campfire talks, lead walks, and assist visitors in identifying local flora and fauna. From the earliest years of the Park Service, however, Mather and Albright felt that park educational programs needed to be more than amenities offered by hotel managers. The educational and inspirational potential of national parks set them apart from the merely recreational purposes of state and county parks and therefore helped justify federal rather than local management. Park Service educational programs were already under way in Yellowstone and Yosemite by 1920. The Yosemite educational program was started by a former educational director of the California Fish and Game Commission, Harold C. Bryant, who in 1925 went on to open the Yosemite School of Field Natural History. In 1923 Ansel F. Hall, the Yosemite "park naturalist," was given the new position of Park Service "chief naturalist" and established a new Education Division, with its office on the Berkeley campus. Bryant's Yosemite School trained many of the agency's early park naturalists, including many women. Women naturalists soon discovered, however, that despite their extensive and early participation in park educational programs, Park Service policy now barred them from being hired for the naturalist and ranger positions being created in many parks.[20]

Stephen Mather in particular realized the significance of educational activities and gave Hall's Education Division an equal place in the agency's organizational structure with the other two central divisions, landscape architecture and engineering. The emphasis on education made the creation of park museums a priority second only to the creation of park administration buildings during the 1920s. Congress, however, was reluctant to fund any federal educational programs, or even the construction of museums. The need was addressed instead through the auspices of the American Association of Museums and of John D. Rockefeller Jr. In 1923 Rockefeller funded the construction of a new museum at Mesa Verde, and the American Association of Museums received funding from the Laura Spelman Rockefeller Memorial to oversee the building of a new Yosemite museum, designed by Herbert Maier. Further grants from the Laura Spelman Rockefeller Memorial funded the Yavapai Observation Station on the south rim of the Grand Canyon and a remarkable series of "trailside museums" in Yellowstone. Designed by Maier and opened over the next four years, the Old Faithful, Norris Geyser Basin, Madison Junction, and Fishing Bridge museums in Yellowstone became landmarks of Park Service rustic style.[21] Museums in other parks, however, were difficult to fund

through regular appropriations, and were often operated out of old and inadequate structures. The situation changed dramatically after 1933, as New Deal programs funded a wide variety of museums and educational programs in state, local, and national parks.

National park educational efforts at first emphasized natural history and, in parks such as Mesa Verde, archaeology. But the addition of historical sites to the park system in the 1930s necessarily broadened the programs. In 1930 Albright established a Branch of Research and Education in Washington, headed by naturalist Harold Bryant and including geologist Wallace W. Atwood Jr. and, soon, historian Verne E. Chatelain. After the transfer of historic sites and monuments in 1933, historical research and interpretation were critical tasks for the Park Service, as the agency became the steward not only of some of the country's most revered historical shrines but a principal keeper of national historical memory as well. Park Service officials pointed out that while the aesthetic appreciation of scenery was certainly enhanced by natural history, many historic sites and battlefields could be indistinguishable from surrounding countryside without the benefit of historical context and interpretation. The Historic Sites Act of 1935 codified new historical research and education functions that the Park Service had already assumed. It directed the secretary of the interior to build and operate museums and to develop public educational programs pertaining to "historic and archeological sites, buildings, and properties of national significance." Under the title of chief historian, Chatelain, succeeded by Ronald Lee in 1938, oversaw historical research and educational programs throughout the park system.[22]

After World War II, many members of Congress continued to feel that it was inappropriate for the federal government to fund any kind of museum construction. According to historian Ralph H. Lewis, for some the word "museum" had "a negative connotation, much as 'education' had in the 1930s."[23] By the late 1940s Park Service officials were pursuing a number of strategies to reinvent the vocabulary and image of their educational activities. In 1941 the Branch of Research and Information became the Branch of Interpretation, and the term "interpretation" subsequently became the widespread replacement for "education." By the early 1950s the functions of old park "museums" were being programmed in the new "public use" and "public service" buildings, soon called "visitor centers." The new language reflected, and was contemporary with, the increasingly modernist idiom of park architecture. Park Service uniforms were also completely redesigned in 1947, doing away with the high boots, riding breeches, and closely fitting tunic of a more equestrian era in favor of shoes, trousers, and a looser, belted jacket. The new uniforms were styled after World War II military issue, just as earlier versions had suggested World War I era uniforms; the familiar round Stetson campaign hat, however, was retained.[24] In 1949 Drury organized an in-house competition for a new agency logo as well. The winning effort, by landscape architect Dudley C. Bayliss, was never used, but Wirth did not let the matter drop. Upon becoming director in 1951, he adopted a new design by Herbert Maier for what would become the familiar arrowhead logo. Used thereafter on publications, uniforms, signs, and buildings, the arrowhead became closely identified with Mission 66 and a powerful image of agency identity in general. In 1965 the arrowhead logo was registered as a trademark.[25]

Interpretation in the 1950s was differentiated by more than the new look and image of interpretive staff and facilities. When the reorganization of 1954 created a new Division of Interpretation under Lee, this function was once again at the highest organizational level, parallel with Vint's Division of Design and Construction.[26] This had been a specific recommendation in the 1953 report that preceded the reorganization, and Wirth fully supported the goal of creating a "unified interpretive organization" by combining the "natural history, history, museum, and information" offices.[27] Interpretation had become increasingly important for a number of reasons. The development of national historical parks had been an area of great growth since the 1930s, and obviously these parks required historical research and educational programs both to plan and to operate them. The historians in Lee's division collaborated with the planners and landscape architects in Vint's division and did the research necessary for historical park master planning. They also designed interpretive programs and provided the content for museum exhibits and interpretive displays. Lee pointed out, too, that as the national park system matured, interpretation grew more important generally. Many national parks were entering what he called an "interpretive stage," meaning that much of the work of acquiring, planning, and developing them was nearing completion. Even if parks still required modernization and expansion of facilities, the basic footprint of roads and other development had been decided. But the importance of operating and managing parks—and above all interpreting them to the public—constantly increased. Describing the mandate for parks as they entered this "mature phase," Lee quoted Aldo Leopold, who suggested that the essential task was to "improve the quality of park use." For Lee, "a boring interpretive program" made for a "low quality public use."[28]

Wirth shared Lee's conviction that improving and expanding the interpretation of the park system to the public should be a central goal of Mission 66. As Mather and Albright had in the 1920s, the director believed that the special, national significance of the park system needed to be carefully conveyed by his agency through programs, displays, and above all individual interpreters. Wirth made interpretation the single most important programmatic aspect of his postwar development campaign. Mission 66 did not sponsor major original historical research, nor did it initiate new scientific or ecological perspectives on the management of park resources; but it did provide more than one hundred visitor centers and myriad other facilities specifically designed around the needs of park interpretation. Wirth, Lee, and most of the planners and superintendents participating in Mission 66 planning all agreed that developing ranger programs, brochures, and audio-visual presentations and building roadside displays, amphitheaters, nature trails, and visitor centers would assure that park visitors found enjoyment and inspiration in their experiences of national

1950s interpretive display in Everglades National Park. Author's photo.

A campfire lecture in Big Bend featuring new audio-visual equipment. NPS Historic Photo Collection.

park landscapes and historic sites. Mission 66 was planned not only to avoid the physical damage caused by growing crowds but also to make sure that as many people as possible had a chance to experience and fully appreciate the special significance of every park in the system.

Interpretation was a particular concern for Wirth and Lee during the years immediately before Mission 66. Between 1953 and 1955 they published four instructional brochures for interpreters: *Talks, Conducted Trips, Campfire Programs,* and *Information Please.* The first two were written by Howard Stagner, who after 1957 became chief of the Branch of Natural History in Lee's Division of Interpretation. The short booklets offered mainly practical advice on the conduct of park programs.[29] But Wirth also had explicit intentions for using interpretation as an "offensive weapon in preventing intrusion and adverse use of areas." In a 1953 memorandum (probably drafted by Lee and other staff, such as chief naturalist John Doerr), Wirth outlined new goals that related directly to those soon formulated for Mission 66 itself. Interpretation, the memorandum stated, should serve both aspects of the agency's mandate: it should enhance visitors' enjoyment by providing information, but it should also protect parks from impairment by encouraging better appreciation of park resources and a more sympathetic understanding of the threats they faced. Interpretation should "point out specific ways in which the visitor should participate, to his own greater benefit, in proper park use and conservation." Harm was done out of ignorance, Wirth insisted, and rules were violated mainly because the need for them was not adequately explained. "Lessons in park use and conservation" in general could be drawn from instances and situations specific to a given park. If "threats to park integrity" were explained to visitors, they would be more likely to abide by restrictions, such as staying on trails and out of delicate meadows. The "conservation interpretation objective" was simple: "Give the visitor a personal knowledge of park and monu-

ment values, such as an awareness of park principles and values, and . . . an awareness of his own responsibility" so that "he may take intelligent action, whether it concerns his own behavior in the parks, or . . . after he leaves."[30]

After becoming a division chief in 1954, Lee was able to use his position to give Mission 66 its emphasis on interpretive facilities and programs. He continued to identify the goals of interpretation with those of Mission 66 itself. "The extent to which public use . . . can safely increase during the next ten years without adversely affecting the preservation [of the parks]," he wrote in 1955, "is directly dependent upon an effective program of information and interpretation." If the vast and changing public understood and appreciated the parks, they would "enjoy and use them wisely" and help protect them. Providing "information stations, publications, exhibits, campfire talks, conducted trips, roadside displays, audio-visual presentations, and other means" could improve the "mental attitude, appreciation, and understanding of the visitor." Two "twin" initiatives, "equally essential to accomplish MISSION 66," therefore were necessary: "planned physical development, and park interpretation for wise use." Lee was concerned that the postwar public's "higher education levels" and exposure to more sophisticated media (especially television) were challenging park interpreters to revise their methods and standards. Americans were also increasingly diverse and "city-bred," creating a greater imperative to instruct them in safe and appropriate behavior in wilderness areas.[31] Lee expressed concern as well over the fate of what had become, in some parks, extensive collections of historical, archaeological, and ethnographic artifacts. Most parks had never had the personnel or facilities to catalog and store adequately, much less properly display, their collections. There was an overwhelming need to develop "specialized technical treatment . . . to preserve these collections" as part of Mission 66.[32]

Wirth and Lee also strongly believed that increased "automation" and other new technologies would be needed to meet the challenge of providing basic levels of interpretive programs throughout the park system. Increased staffing was vital as well and was a planned aspect of Mission 66. But in light of the demands being placed on the Park Service, even if Congress made the requested increases in the number of employees, other strategies would still be needed to handle the anticipated numbers of visitors. Although nothing could replace personal contact with a ranger or interpreter, there simply would never again be enough of them in proportion to visitors to rely on personal interactions as the primary means of interpretation. Already in 1952 Lee had begun an audio-visual training program for interpreters, and the Jamestown and Yorktown visitor centers in Colonial National Historical Park were the first to feature auditoriums with projection rooms for showing interpretive films (a practice that had begun in nearby Williamsburg).[33] In 1955 he initiated "experimental" use of "audio-visual devices . . . to supplement the personal interpretive services" in a selected group of parks. By 1956 he was asking EODC chief Edward Zimmer to make sure that all preliminary planning for visitor centers be coordinated with the Division of Interpretation to ensure that the new facilities met the requirements of film and slide projectors.[34] By the next year, "self guiding tour systems" were available at a number of Civil War battlefields, and professionally printed "self-guidance publications" were replacing mimeographed handouts in many parks. At Yosemite, Great Smoky Mountains, and other parks, "self-guiding trails" were developed.[35] "Visitor-activated" interpretive devices (recorded interpretive talks) were designed, and by the early 1960s ninety parks featured "audio stations" and automatic movie or slide programs. Automatic audio or audio-visual presentations became standard features of new visitor centers, relieving personnel of the enormous task of giving thousands of visitors a basic introduction and orientation to a park.[36]

In the mid-1950s national park interpretation found its most eloquent literary voice, the journalist, novelist, and playwright Freeman Tilden. Wirth was particularly taken by Tilden's reflections on the national parks and their significance, beginning with *The National Parks: What They Mean to You and Me* (1951). Wirth arranged in 1953 to have Freeman's next book, *The Fifth Essence,* published through a private donation and distributed to all parks and field offices.[37] The "fifth essence" Tilden described was the spirit of place that the interpreter sought to evoke and convey to an audience. In 1955 the Park Service secured another private grant to support Tilden's "reappraisal of the basic principles which underlie the program of natural and historical interpretation."[38] Over the next year Tilden toured the park system observing programs and working as an interpreter. Ronald Lee oversaw the project, which culminated in 1957 with Tilden's next book, *Interpreting Our Heritage*; it became an essential text for national park interpreters from Mission 66 onward. In it Tilden further clarified the activity of interpretation—conveying the significance of a place to a diverse group of visitors—as opposed to conducting a class or lecturing on a broad theme. He established "six principles," including injunctions to "relate what is being displayed or described to something within the personality or experience of the visitor," and to "present a whole body, not a part." The "chief aim" of interpretation, for Tilden, was "not instruction, but provocation." If Wirth and Lee fashioned bureaucratic and functional tools for park interpreters, Tilden vividly described the inspirational spirit of their work.[39]

Tourism to historic sites grew enormously during the 1950s, a decade that became known for veneration of American "heritage." Park Service training and interpretive programs arose to support and respond to the popular trend.[40] Training a new generation of national park interpreters was a priority for Mission 66, and in 1956 Wirth instructed Lee to draw up plans for the operation of two "National Park Service schools" for park staff. In 1957 an agency task force identified a critical need for training "all uniformed employees (park rangers, naturalists, historians and archeologists)" and suggested a basic curriculum. A new National Park Service Training Center was established in Yosemite Valley that year, under the direction of Frank Kowski, who since 1951 had headed agency training programs from Washington.[41] The training center marked the first comprehensive

attempt by the Park Service to train its incoming uniformed employees, all of whom were to spend three months there "as soon as practicable after their appointment." This was not considered an adequate or permanent solution, however, and a larger training center was already being planned.[42] Mission 66 provided the funds, and the new training facility opened at Grand Canyon National Park in 1963. Named for Horace Albright, the Grand Canyon complex featured classrooms, offices, a library, and apartments for students. The next year an eastern counterpart opened on the campus of Storer College in Harpers Ferry, a historically African American institution that had closed in 1955. The eastern training center, dedicated to Stephen Mather, was housed in rehabilitated college buildings. Together the Albright and Mather training centers institutionalized the methods and intentions of natural and historical park interpretation as developed under Wirth, Lee, Tilden, and Kowski. For Wirth, the establishment of permanent institutions to train the next generation of Park Service interpreters and "stewards of our heritage" fulfilled one of his highest priorities for Mission 66.[43]

Even under Mission 66, however, getting substantial funding for personnel training apparently proved difficult, especially during the first half of Mission 66. Congress proved resistant to hiring adequate interpretive staff at all. By 1959 Park Service personnel assembled for a conference in Williamsburg unanimously agreed that "lack of sufficient personnel" remained the "most serious deficiency in NPS interpretation."[44] Mission 66 failed during these years to meet goals for increasing staff in general. In

1960, "cumulative staffing increases amounted to only a little more than half the number of additions scheduled during the first four years of MISSION 66," according to a training manual being developed in Lee's division that year.[45] John Doerr reported similar difficulties in 1960, noting that "interpretive services" in his natural history programs were up 54 percent, but that most of the increase "was attributable to self-guiding facilities" such as the "A-V cabinets" installed in thirty-seven visitor centers since 1956. "A-V presentations," "self-guided tours and trails," and "wayside interpretive devices" accounted for 67 percent of "interpretive contacts" in 1959; 22 percent of contacts were at information desks; and only 11 percent of contacts were "of the personal type" (ranger talks). Interpretive staffing "lagged seriously," said Doerr, and because of the need to staff visitor centers and deal with a 22 percent rise in visitation over the previous three years, he considered the personnel shortage "more acute now [1960] than in 1956." While a 372 percent increase in "naturalist personnel" had been called for under Mission 66, only a 7 percent increase had been realized.[46]

Doerr's complaints did not stop there, and probably reflected similar sentiments among natural historians and scientists both inside and outside the Park Service. Although he felt that Mission 66 had initially acknowledged the importance of sponsoring "research in natural history," no funds at all had been appropriated for this purpose before 1958, and only $28,000 annually had been funded for the subsequent two years. Doerr understood the political reality of the situation, suggesting that new legislation "comparable to the Antiquities Act and Historic Sites Act" would be needed to give the Park Service the mandate and budget to undertake "necessary" and "urgently needed" research. From "alpine wilderness ecology" to "Florida bay marine life" to "siltation studies" in Mammoth Cave, ongoing in-house research projects were not adequately funded. Outside agencies, including the U.S. Fish and Wildlife Service and the U.S. Geological Survey, were doing most of the research in parks, along with university and private nonprofit partners. But Doerr felt strongly that "it will be necessary to expand biologist staffing" in regional offices and parks so that the Park Service could identify its own research needs, initiate projects, and coordinate research by outside entities.[47]

Mission 66 obviously was planned and run by specialists in park design and interpretation who had their own expertise and priorities. But Doerr was probably correct in observing that new legislation would be needed if Congress were to see the Park Service no longer as primarily a park development and management agency but as a scientific research organization as well. Wirth could have been an effective advocate for new legislation, since he was well known for his relationships with members of Congress and his ability to secure appropriations. He had gained that reputation, though, by sensing and working within the political limitations of his time. Mission 66 exploited the willingness of Congress to fund construction projects; eventually it even succeeded in establishing professional training centers and gaining some increases in staffing. Wirth probably felt, however, that Congress would not approve major funding for Park Service scientific research, just as the lawmakers were unlikely to accept the new legislative mandate for national recreational planning authority. Under Mission 66 the Park Service did not fund scientific research; in fact, it is barely mentioned at all. Organizationally, scientific research fell under Ronald Lee in the Division of Interpretation. Wirth and Lee accepted the need for park naturalists to understand and contribute to natural history as part of their interpretive duties, but what little research was funded by the agency rarely extended beyond the studies required to enhance interpretive programs. The idea of ecological research guiding fundamental agency management policies and decisions was barely even discussed.

Even critics in the late 1950s, however, agreed that although new research remained unfunded, at least the construction of visitor centers and other interpretive facilities had proceeded efficiently. Park Service architects at the WODC and EODC had responded to the changing needs of interpreters and museum exhibit designers. Lee actively helped negotiate the exchange of ideas between interpreters and architects by organizing the two conferences that brought his division's personnel first to the EODC in 1957 and then to the WODC in 1958. The result of these conferences was, as noted previously, a reassessment of the entire visitor center concept in response to the programming requirements of park interpreters. Audio-visual and other "automatic devices" were seen as one answer to the dearth of interpretive staff, and architects accommodated them in the new buildings. Exhibit designers reconceived the purpose

and context of their displays, which now typically made up one part of the larger, more diverse functional programming of the visitor centers. Museum staff (also in Lee's Division of Interpretation) no longer designed exhibits as comprehensive illustrated narratives but rather as effective, concise orientations to specific parks. As national park historian Barry Mackintosh observes, older park museums "were viewed as supplemental to the visitor experience," but "visitor centers—multiple use facilities emphasizing orientation—were seen as integral to it."[48] The change was analogous to the difference that officials attempted to define between "education" and "interpretation." The visitor center and its exhibits were vehicles of the latter. Modernist design expressed the same shift in purpose and program.

A number of commemorative anniversary dates also shaped Mission 66 historic preservation and interpretation. The visitor centers at Jamestown and Yorktown had been completed because of funding made available in time for the 350th anniversary of the British settlement of Virginia. The Abraham Lincoln sesquicentennial was observed in 1957, and the Theodore Roosevelt centennial the next year, followed by numerous other anniversaries. Civil War battlefields were of particular interest during Mission 66 because of the events being planned for the centennial commemorations of that conflict. At many Civil War battlefields, the basic development and interpretation of the landscape had changed little since the late nineteenth century. Wirth and his Mission 66 planners intended to have every Civil War site ready for the increased attention and visitation they could expect in the coming decade. Planned improvements often included the acquisition of abutting land, as well as the construction of visitor centers and roads. A former general was in the White House, and Congress was in the mood to mark the nation's bloodiest war, creating a Civil War Centennial Commission in 1957. In their first report, the commissioners cited the goals of Mission 66, which they felt would "dovetail with the objectives of the Centennial." Between 1961 and 1965, local, state, and national commemorative events were held in forty states. At many of the most critical sites of the war, including Gettysburg, Antietam, Harpers Ferry, Chancellorsville, Appomattox, and others, Mission 66 visitor centers opened in time for centennial observances. At Harpers Ferry and Ford's Theater in Washington, extensive restorations of historic structures were initiated. Four new Civil War parks were acquired, and three thousand acres were added to the more than thirty national parks related to the conflict.[49]

In their final report the Civil War Centennial commissioners singled out "the imposing new Visitor Center at Gettysburg" as "one of the outstanding achievements made under the aegis of 'Mission 66.'"[50] Richard Neutra's Cyclorama and Visitor Center was dedicated in November 19, 1962, the ninety-ninth anniversary of Lincoln's address, and the critically acclaimed building served as the venue for commemorative events held in July and November 1963. Perhaps the most publicized of Mission 66 visitor centers, the Cyclorama also was erected at a central point on the battlefield, in Ziegler's Grove. Most historians and park managers at the time agreed that this would be a powerful way of interpreting the

battlefield, and that the encroachment on the historic scene was justified.[51] But the location of the "imposing" building raised the question whether the Mission 66 emphasis on interpretation was sometimes made at the cost of compromising park landscapes.

The locations of Mission 66 visitor centers were carefully considered. Ronald Lee and Dick Sutton outlined different strategies in their joint 1958 notes on visitor center design, as did Daniel Beard (the former Everglades superintendent), who succeeded Lee as the chief of the Division of Interpretation in 1960.[52] For interpreters, architects, and landscape architects (the last group usually being responsible for siting buildings), the importance of the views from the visitor centers was always stressed. Beard in fact criticized the Grand Canyon Visitor Center because it was "too far removed (1/3 mile) from the Canyon rim," and so failed to stimulate visitors to investigate the canyon's natural history and ask good questions of the visitor center staff. This emphasis put interpreters at odds with the intent of Vint's "Plan B," which suggested that visitor facilities should be relocated away from "sensitive" areas, such as the rim of the Grand Canyon. Lee and Beard both praised visitor centers that afforded "a good view of park features," such as those at Yorktown and Hopewell Village. The large visitor center window at Hopewell Village, for example, was "in itself a fine exhibit."[53] The outdoor or roof terraces at visitor centers such as Gettysburg were ideal for interpreters to conduct their programs, allowing visitors to observe the battlefield or other attraction directly in front of them, with supporting interpretive displays and visitor services nearby. Experienced interpreters knew that more distantly placed visitor centers—regardless of how artful the museum exhibits might be—could not compete with the power of interpreting a site while looking directly at the landscape being discussed.

Architect John Cabot described three specific strategies for locating visitor centers, which more or less echoed what Lee and Beard suggested: at park entrances, "en route" along a major park road or intersection, or at a "terminus" or major destination within the park.[54] In larger parks there were often several visitor centers at different entrances and destinations. There was a tension between the desire to remove visitor

centers from the "sacred" or "sensitive" areas (where older visitor services had congregated) and the wish to maintain the interpretive strength offered by proximity. At Yellowstone, for example, the Canyon Village and Grant Village developments replaced visitor services considered too close to scenic views and thermal features. But at Old Faithful a new visitor center was built with a direct view of the famous geyser. In smaller historic parks, where the role of interpretation was considered even more vital (and in which typically there was only one visitor center), the building was often located to provide an expansive view of the park landscape. This often meant that the visitor center was near or directly in the "historic scene" being interpreted. Since historic sites were considered more difficult for the public to appreciate, they were also often the subject of more elaborate interpretive plans. Reconstructions, "living history" reenactments, and other methods were sometimes promoted under Mission 66 to "bring history alive." At Fort Davis in Texas, a partial reconstruction

Mission 66 Restoration of Harper House in 1961, Harpers Ferry National Historical Park, West Virginia. Photo by Jack E. Boucher, NPS Historic Photo Collection.

Completed restoration of Hopewell Village, photographed in 1965, Hopewell Village (now Hopewell Furnace) National Historical Site. NPS Historic Photo Collection.

of a barracks served as the visitor center, and at Fort Union in New Mexico (and other similar sites) the visitor center was designed in a historically inspired idiom and placed immediately adjacent to the archaeological ruins. In historical parks in particular, interpretation was given priority over concerns for maintaining more absolute integrity of the setting.

Many preservationists, historians, and archaeologists would eventually deplore the location of some Mission 66 visitor centers, especially those at "terminus" sites, which came to be seen as encroachments on delicate natural features and historic settings. If the Gettysburg Cyclorama was a flagship of the Mission 66 program, it also became a symbol of what many came to see as a willingness to value interpretation and visitor experience above the stewardship of park landscapes and archaeological resources. Historian Robert M. Utley, who served as chief historian of the Park Service from 1964 to 1971, acknowledged in 1985 that "we weren't very conscious in those days of how we might be interfering with the preservation of the resources," noting that the Fort Union visitor center was set "practically right in the middle of the fort." Of Roy Appleman (the historian on the Mission 66 working staff), Utley recalled that "his interest was primarily in interpretation," and that he "believed in putting the visitor center right on top of the resource." At Chaco Canyon and elsewhere, Appleman "always argued that you had to see virtually everything from the visitor center." In 1985, echoing a general sentiment at the time, Utley concluded that such priorities were "outdated now."[55] But such reconsideration of policy on the part of Park Service historians and other staff

came mostly after Mission 66, especially in the 1980s, when modernist architecture was also being negatively reevaluated. During Mission 66, the architecture and siting of visitor centers—and the general emphasis on interpretation—were widely approved both within the agency and by others. And it should be noted that many Mission 66 visitor centers are not necessarily "on top of the resource" at all, but are near park entrances (sometimes on land outside the park and acquired for the purpose), within park administrative areas, or in other locations where visitors could be efficiently intercepted and oriented with minimal encroachment on "sensitive" areas.

The development of national historical parks and historic sites that were, or became, part of the national park system obviously dominated much of the Mission 66 historic preservation effort. The historian James Glass asserts that "during Wirth's tenure the Park Service operated an inward-looking preservation program . . . that enhanced its own historical monuments and parks" but failed to provide the leadership needed to curb the excesses of federal highway construction and urban renewal.[56] But there were Mission 66 preservation initiatives of consequence that involved historic resources outside the national park system. Vint, for example, grew increasingly interested in historic preservation later in his career. When Secretary of the Interior Oscar Chapman awarded him his department's Distinguished Service Award in 1952, Vint was cited for three achievements: the "inter-bureau agreement" with the Bureau of Public Roads in 1925, developing the "master plan idea" in the late 1920s, and organizing the Historic American Buildings Survey (HABS) in the 1930s.[57] HABS was discontinued in 1942, but under Mission 66 Vint arranged to reactivate HABS, which continued to be administered by his close friend and protégé Charles Peterson.[58] Lee was also able to continue the Historic Sites Survey (which had been initiated in 1936 under the provisions of the Historic Sites Act) briefly in 1946, although budget limitations in the late 1940s precluded progress or expansion. Lee then reactivated and expanded the survey in 1957 using Mission 66 funding. In the interim he reconceived the program as a centralized inventory of all nationally significant historical sites, not just those that might be potential additions to the park system, as had been the case originally. The distinction was an important one because it gave the Park Service responsibility for a national register of historic properties that were (and were intended to remain) outside the park system. In 1960 Lee succeeded in classifying these historically significant properties as "Registered National Historic Landmarks," and the Historic Sites Survey became the National Historic Landmarks Program, still under the authority of the Historic Sites Act. There were no federal legal protections for National Historic Landmarks, but the designations and distinctive bronze plaques became a means of identifying threatened landmarks anywhere in the country, assisting local preservation efforts, and generating a national inventory of sites that merited protection.[59]

The Historic American Buildings Survey and the National Historic Landmarks Program required not only documenting and researching historic buildings and sites but also assembling a federal preservation organization and a national network of preservation partners. These two

Mission 66 programs established the precedent of a federal list of significant historic resources, and despite their limitations, they maintained the Park Service's position as the nation's historic preservation agency. Mission 66 also created numerous opportunities for architects specializing in the documentation, preservation, and reuse of historic buildings. Historical "restorations and reconstructions" were a major category of Mission 66 activity at scores of national historical parks and monuments, from Philadelphia to Casa Grande. New standards and procedures for the restoration of historic buildings were established, and dozens of architects gained experience that led to the increased professionalization of "historical architecture" as a discipline.

Like Mission 66 itself, however, all of these preservation activities proceeded on the basis of New Deal legislation, in this case mainly the 1935 Historic Sites Act. Lee's strategy was analogous to Wirth's decision to use the Park, Parkway, and Recreational-Area Study Act of 1936 as the authority for Mission 66 recreational planning. In both cases, very capable New Deal bureaucrats utilized the legislative tools they knew so well to frame the renewed programs and activities of Mission 66. In both cases, critics outside the Park Service continued to point out the need for new legislation that would restructure and broaden federal efforts in these fields. While Wirth remained openly antagonistic to 1960s legislation such as the 1963 Outdoor Recreation Act and the 1964 Wilderness Act, Lee cultivated private-sector preservationists and supported the efforts that led to the 1966 National Historic Preservation Act. Wirth also opposed the early versions of that preservation legislation, however, since the acts implied that the Park Service would have to take responsibility for inventorying and monitoring historic resources that were only of state or local (not national) significance.[60] But largely as a result of Lee's efforts, the 1966 act placed the administration of a new National Register of Historic Places within the National Park Service. The Park Service retained leadership and administration of federal historic preservation programs, while in 1962 the agency was divested of similar authority for federal recreational planning in favor of the new Bureau of Outdoor Recreation.

Despite the controversial siting of some visitor centers and the perhaps "inward-looking" nature of its historic preservation program, Mission 66 advanced federal historic preservation at a crucial time when other federal agencies and Congress were engaged in massive destruction of historic buildings and landscapes. Mission 66 incubated the professional disciplines of interpretation and historical architecture and greatly advanced staff professionalization generally through the Albright and Mather training centers. Wirth counted 458 historic buildings "reconstructed and rehabilitated" under Mission 66 at a cost of more than $15 million. The projects varied from a Danish colonial sugar plantation on the Caribbean island of Saint John, to the Custis-Lee Mansion in Virginia, to Fort Davis in Texas. But the numbers only hint at the influence of projects such as those in St. Louis and Philadelphia that initiated later Park Service urban open space and historic preservation initiatives in Boston, New York, San Francisco, and other cities.[61] The invention of the Mission 66

visitor center and its integral interpretive programming was perhaps the most pervasive preservation concept of all, and has characterized efforts to orient and serve visitors not just by land management agencies but by institutions of all types ever since. Mission 66 today most often evokes a physical legacy of facility development, but the program's less tangible achievements in historic preservation policy and the practice of interpretation may in the end prove to have been more critical in the history of park management.

Restored Vanderbilt Mansion, Hyde Park, New York, in 1957. NPS Historic Photo Collection.

Reconstructed courthouse, Appomattox Courthouse National Historical Park, shown recently completed in 1964. NPS Historic Photo Collection.

CHAPTER 7

LANDSCAPE ARCHITECTURE

Mission 66 interpretive programming, like the visitor centers themselves, resulted from multidisciplinary collaborations at the Park Service during the mid-1950s. Ronald Lee's historians and interpreters, WODC and EODC architects and landscape architects, and many park superintendents and other staff supported most of the Mission 66 policies and priorities emanating from Washington. The sense of common values and goals—abetted by the lack of any public process—encouraged the productivity and high morale often described by participants. Mission 66 was above all an interdisciplinary endeavor, not unlike many other large-scale planning and development programs of the era. This collaboration was necessary and productive, but it also marked a change from an earlier era when Thomas Vint's landscape architects oversaw park "master planning" with more unilateral control. In the production of Mission 66 prospectuses, the emphasis on the visitor center,

as well as the fact that many parks were entering what Lee called an "interpretive stage," demanded greater participation by architects and historians. Urban historical park initiatives in Philadelphia and elsewhere also expanded roles for architects, interpretive planners, and historical architects more than for landscape architects. The agency's need for landscape architecture was changing. In the design implementation of Mission 66, landscape architecture was now only one element of a more multidisciplinary process.

National Park Service landscape architects traditionally had planned and designed on three scales. Master plans documents determined basic policies for the development of an entire park, whatever its size. The master plans included maps, in which one inch could equal a mile or more, with color-coded land use zones covering the whole park. More detailed site planning for individual developed areas (park villages) were also prepared, typically drawn at scales of one hundred to four hundred feet to the inch. Finally, the landscape architects also drew detailed designs for small structures such as individual parking lots and campgrounds, wayside interpretive areas and kiosks, building façades, guardrails, signs, and other landscape features. Construction documents were prepared as needed to convey to contractors the exact dimensions and character of construction and to provide the basis for detailed cost estimates.

During Mission 66, landscape architects continued to create and revise master plans under Vint's supervision. This work now entailed siting visitor centers and other facilities and integrating them into the new interpretive program for the park. While tension could develop between the provisions of earlier master plans and different ideas presented in Mission 66 prospectuses, more often the two planning processes converged. In some cases the same landscape architects were producing both documents. In others (particularly several of the "pilot prospectuses"), the participants met and attempted to reconcile their plans. Landscape architects in the WODC and EODC, in Washington, and in individual parks

In 1959 Region IV (San Francisco) landscape architects produced a manual for Park Service campground design. Mission 66 introduced new standards for utilities and sanitation, and more generous road and campground layouts for larger vehicles and trailers. In general, Mission 66 campgrounds had far greater capacities than prewar campgrounds but were sited in areas considered to be less sensitive. NPS Western Regional Office, San Francisco.

revised and developed both master plans and prospectuses, eventually producing consistent development strategies for virtually every park. The experience of rapidly preparing so many prospectuses eventually affected the master planning process. By the early 1960s some master plans, called "conceptual master plans," more closely resembled the shorter, smaller-format prospectuses, with more text and fewer drawings.

Landscape architects also continued to provide smaller-scaled designs for campgrounds, parking lots, waysides, and other site development. In addition to siting a park's visitor center, in other words, the designers might lay out the parking lots and paths and determine the general orientation of the building complex within the surrounding landscape. Or, once the decision to relocate a campground was made, landscape architects would locate and design the new campground, typically with the greater capacity and more generous dimensions demanded by the larger size and numbers of trailers and other recreational vehicles pouring into the parks.

But to a significant degree, the middle scale of landscape architecture—the scale of the park

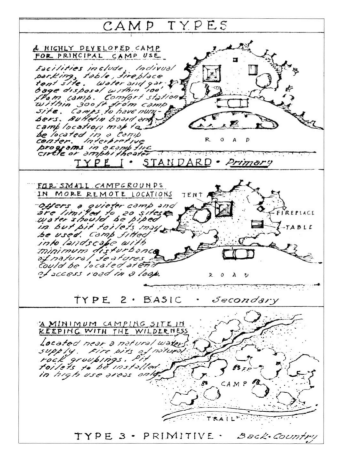

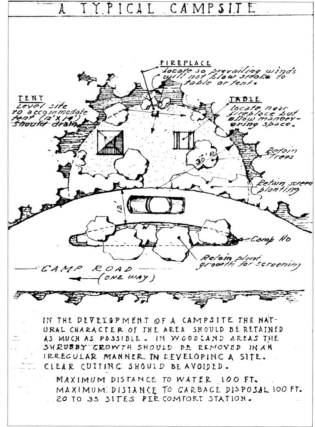

National park campers as illustrated in a slide from "Mission 66 in Action" in 1958. NPS History Collection.

village—was supplanted by visitor center planning and design as the visitor center complex centralized and replaced many of the public and administrative functions of the prewar rustic village. For obvious reasons, architects and interpreters were more essential than landscape architects in the design of visitor center buildings. There were a few new concessioner areas with overnight accommodations that were described as "villages" under Mission 66, but the rustic village idea had largely been superseded by the new day use facilities that embodied the strategy and priorities of Mission 66.

While landscape architects no longer controlled to the same degree the way parks were planned and developed, they had become more influential than ever within the Park Service. Wirth, Vint, EODC chief Edward Zimmer, chief of the Mission 66 working staff Bill Carnes, and many other agency designers and managers had

all been trained as landscape architects. As they reached senior administrative positions, they were running the agency many of them had joined over twenty years earlier. As a massive park modernization program, Mission 66 was essentially a landscape architectural project. Along with other agency officials, Park Service landscape architects were responsible for Vint's "Plan B," the "guiding principles" of the Mission 66 program, and other basic revisions of park planning procedures. In the broadest sense, Wirth's national recreational planning efforts, and the overall concept and implementation of the Mission 66 program itself, were the most important products of Mission 66 landscape architecture. The significance of landscape architecture under Mission 66 was clearly not limited to individual design projects, such as the layout of campgrounds and day use areas. Nevertheless, the role of the landscape architect in national park planning clearly changed, and even decreased, under Mission 66. This shift reflected parallel developments in the profession of landscape architecture as a whole, and in the long relationship between landscape architects and American park making.

"Landscape architecture" had historically meant the profession of park planning and design in the United States. Frederick Law Olmsted coined the term to describe his work with Calvert Vaux designing municipal parks and park systems in the 1860s. By the end of the nineteenth century, scores of municipalities, counties, and states had hired landscape architects to plan and design systems of parks and "scenic reservations" all over the country. The Department of the Interior began using landscape architects to plan the development of national parks in 1914. When the National Park Service was created in 1916, the agency's mandate, as it was understood by the framers of its legislation and its first directors, was to expand and modernize a system of federal scenic reservations for the enjoyment of an increasingly automotive public, and to do so in a manner that would allow future generations to enjoy the same privilege.

In the late 1920s, while he was convincing Albright of the importance of park master planning, Vint argued that landscape architecture was a profession that offered "a practical solution to the problem at hand" while also taking into consideration "the element of beauty." The latter could be attained in park development, he observed, only when the "congruity of parts gives harmonious form to the whole." The "first work" of the agency, therefore, was "the protec-

Mission 66 campground design in Yellowstone. Typical campground layout, comfort station, and amphitheater.
Author's photos.

tion and preservation of these landscapes." Its "second work" was to make the same areas "accessible to the people" so that they could be enjoyed. Vint ended his uncharacteristically effusive remarks with expressions of his most deeply held convictions: "What is the work of the Park Service but landscape work? What organization was ever given a nobler landscape problem?"[1]

Albright subsequently authorized Vint and his staff to assure that "comprehensive development plans" anticipated and controlled where and how public facilities would be provided in every park. Haphazard development by individual concessioners and park superintendents had proved to be destructive; by designing a park as a whole, with each developed area coordinated in an overall plan, the Park Service could hope to achieve a successful balance of scenic preservation and public use for the early automobile age. By the end of the 1920s national park master plans included drawings that defined overall land use zones for a park, site plans for individual developed areas (villages), and schematic designs for buildings and even for landscape construction details. By 1933 the public professional practice that Vint and his staff of landscape architects had instituted now positioned the Park Service to lead state and national park programs that had been vastly expanded under the New Deal. The result was a zenith in the history of American park making, and an experience that shaped the careers and sensibilities of Wirth and most of the professional colleagues he relied on during Mission 66.

But by the 1950s, Wirth, Vint, and other Park Service officials understood that the basic na-

ture of the "landscape problem" had changed. Mission 66 therefore offered a revised approach. As we have seen, visitor capacity was increased, usually by widening roads, expanding and relocating existing campgrounds and parking lots, and concentrating people and facilities into visitor center and overnight lodge complexes. In this sense Mission 66 was a redevelopment, not a development, campaign. Landscape architects now needed to collaborate more extensively with other professionals, especially architects and interpretive planners, to design the visitor centers and parkwide interpretive programs that were critical components of such redevelopment. The very appearance of the Mission 66 prospectuses indicated this shift in the relative importance of professional services. Prewar master plans had consisted of sets of large-format drawings done by Vint's landscape architects, featuring site plans at different scales, sometimes with perspective and sectional views, often rendered in colored pencil and pastels. The Mission 66 prospectuses were small-format, written building programs that typically included few plans or illustrations of any kind. Park villages and other developed areas of the rustic era would remain in many cases, but they would be redeveloped with new visitor centers, comfort stations, and interpretive kiosks as well as larger parking lots. This amounted to a list of mostly architectural and interpretive design features to be superimposed on an existing footprint of landscape development.

The relationship of the profession of landscape architecture to park commissions at the state and local levels underwent analogous changes during the postwar period. The new ge-

ographical context of regional, low-density urbanization and interstate highways affected the
functions of municipal and regional parks as
much as it did national parks. Since the turn of
the century, large municipal parks had begun to
be appreciated more for their potential to serve
the growing demand for active, organized recreation than as scenic reservations. In the postwar
years, increasing low-density urbanization
meant that many families now had yards, often
with enough room for small swimming pools,
picnic tables, and play areas for children, the
kinds of amenities that once drew the public to
parks. As the middle class abandoned older urban cores, many nineteenth-century parks
seemed increasingly unused and therefore available for new uses. Because they were already
publicly owned, municipal planners targeted
parks as potential locations for expressways,
public housing, or new hospitals and schools,
some of which perhaps seemed justified as
means of serving the disadvantaged communities that now surrounded the poorly maintained
parks. Regional scenic reservations in areas just
outside older cities often suffered similar fates as
regional park commissions began managing
their parks less as scenic reservations than as infrastructure to deliver recreational facilities and
services to the residents of vast metropolitan areas. By the 1950s, reservations around Boston
and elsewhere were being redeveloped with
recreational complexes including ball fields,
tennis courts, golf courses, ice rinks, indoor
swimming pools, and parking lots to meet the
demands of larger, more urban populations in
formerly rural counties. Interstate highways in
many cases bisected or ran along the edges of

Cover sheet for a typical prewar master plan, which consisted of dozens of large format, rendered plans at various scales. National Archives, RG 79.

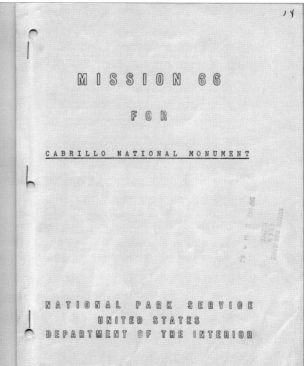

Cover of a typical Mission 66 prospectus, a letter-sized document with few or no plans or drawings. NPS History Collection.

Because of the legislative limitations of Mission 66, the Park Service did not undertake a major state park development initiative in the 1950s as it had in the 1930s. It did distribute a technical bulletin, *Grist*, that included design sheets, specifications, and landscape design suggestions for state and local park agencies. NPS History Collection.

parks that had once been bucolic retreats. Such redevelopment of existing park systems consisted largely of individual engineering and architectural projects, not the design of new parks or park systems.

Landscape architects were simply less essential as consultants for park agencies in the 1940s and 1950s than they had been in the 1920s and 1930s. The basic premises dictating how and why systems of public landscapes served the pub-

lic were shifting. At the same time, landscape architects were also dramatically adapting their profession to new social and economic conditions. During the Great Depression, up to 90 percent of the membership of the American Society of Landscape Architects (ASLA) had gone to work for public park commissions and other planning and development agencies at various levels of government. But the New Deal ended resoundingly in 1942, and when the private market for design services reemerged after the war, circumstances had changed. The opportunities for "country place" commissions would never again be as significant as they were before 1929, for example; but shopping center developers, residential builders, expanding universities, and relocating corporations all were potential new clients. While many professionals remained at agencies such as the Park Service (public agencies employed about one third of ASLA members in 1953), many more were eager to resume or begin private consulting firms.[2] To do so they needed to offer design services appropriate to the types of development then occurring, and they needed to create design strategies that were consistent with their clients' needs and tastes. And by the 1950s, many of those clients wanted modernist design.

The debate over whether landscape architecture should "go modern" had been under way since at least the early 1930s, and many members of the ASLA had resisted the trend.[3] As both residential and commercial clients patronized modernist architects after the war, however, contention over the meaning or desirability of modernist landscape design quickly faded. If they were to thrive in the new private market, landscape architects had to provide designs that were perceived as appropriate complements to the modernist architecture and planning that now often preceded their own involvement in projects. By the 1940s, articles in *Landscape Architecture* magazine, as well as more popular home and garden journals, indicated that "modern" had become a desirable characterization of new landscape design. Published projects such as Robert L. Zion's Roosevelt Field shopping center on Long Island or Sidney N. Shurcliff's work for Shoppers' World in Massachusetts indicates that mainstream professional practice had moved into a modernist design idiom.[4]

Postwar American landscape architects not only reinvented their profession in the context of an emerging private market for their services but also reinvigorated and expanded their activities by doing so. The move back to the private sector often meant adopting modernist theory and techniques, and in this regard landscape architects followed the lead of certain landscape designers who had been advocating modernist principles since the 1930s. The fate of the Harvard School of Landscape Architecture, which had begun under the direction of Frederick Law Olmsted Jr. in 1900, illustrates this professional trend. In 1936 the Harvard Graduate School of Design (GSD) was created under the overall direction of architect Joseph F. Hudnut, who in 1937 made Walter Gropius head of the architecture department. What had been separate schools of planning and landscape architecture now also became departments of the GSD. The reorganization implied many changes for design education generally, and for landscape architecture in particular. Hudnut and Gropius championed modernism and fostered a collaborative spirit in which "design" was considered to include "all those processes by which the visual arts are created." Their curriculum stressed unified training, interdisciplinary spirit, and preparation in new techniques of architectural design and construction. Hudnut eliminated most art history and other liberal arts courses, expecting his students to have acquired such foundations, to the degree they were needed, as undergraduates. Landscape architecture barely survived as a separate discipline at the new GSD. Hudnut reduced its faculty and gave the department a low priority. Academic education in landscape architecture, even more than in architecture, had depended on a knowledge of historical styles and precedent. The entire discipline as it had developed during the "country place" era was made irrelevant by the new educational model of the GSD. The few landscape faculty who remained, such as Bremer Pond, put up ineffectual resistance to the reformation taking place, but they were hopelessly out of step with what soon became a national trend in design education.[5]

As Hudnut and Gropius reorganized the future of American design education in Cambridge, the San Francisco Museum of Art mounted an exhibition of "modern landscape architecture" in 1937 that gave specific evidence of a modernist direction in the profession of landscape architecture. A counterpoint to the 1932 International Style exhibition in New York, the 1937 show was again co-curated by the architectural historian Henry-Russell Hitchcock. The basic premise, expressed by museum director Grace L. McCann Morely in the exhibition catalog, was that "landscape architecture, which is so

Mission 66 campground design in Big Bend National Park. While standardized designs were used for amphitheaters, picnic shelters, and comfort stations, different standard designs were specific to individual large parks or regions. Author's photos.

closely connected with architecture, should also have evolved a distinctly modern phase." Morely invited Hitchcock, architect Richard Neutra, and landscape architect Fletcher Steele, among others, to contribute their ideas on what the "principles of a contemporary style in landscape architecture should be." The exhibit featured models of recent California gardens by Thomas D. Church, Annette Hoyt Flanders, Lockwood De Forest, and Margaret Keeley Brown, as well as Steele and Neutra. The show also included the work of other landscape designers, photographs of European modernist gardens, garden ornament displays, and plans and renderings of historical gardens. The Pacific chapter of the ASLA put up a concurrent exhibition of recent work.[6]

In his catalog essay, Hitchcock offered persuasive guidance for how landscape architecture could reform itself along the lines of modernist architecture. Whether the "modern garden" was "a mere roof terrace [or] a national park," one principle could cover all of its manifestations: "the preservation of all possible values previously in existence in the landscape setting with the addition of only the simplest and most practical provision for specific human needs." For gardens and terraces adjacent to buildings, the landscape architect was to create "a sort of outdoor architecture" consistent with the materials, floor plan organization, and aesthetic of modernist buildings. Garden features such as screens, lattice walls, hedges, and trellises all served to extend the flowing, overlapping, and functional spaces of modernist domestic architecture, as well as the general integration of indoors and outdoors. On a larger scale, however, such "terraces should not be extended indefinitely into the natural setting." Buildings and garden should be one unit, ordered by the same "geometrical principles of design," and "set down on a well chosen site" that otherwise should be "almost completely untouched." The landscape architect should do as little as possible that might "interfere . . . with the natural virtue of the [larger] site" by concealing drives, swimming pools, and other "artificial features." Noting that "such a theory of modern gardening . . . may seem to limit the possibilities of the art," Hitchcock nevertheless reiterated that "modern gardening should preserve all the values of the existing natural environment, adding only necessary features," asserting that the same theory at "the other end of the scale" could guide "regional and even national planning."[7]

Hitchcock's remarks reflected his understanding of ideas suggested and illustrated by European modernists during the previous decade. Le Corbusier, for example, described the landscape around his high-rise building proposals of the 1920s as a "Virgilian dream," an uncorrupted pastoral vision that served as the visual and emotional setting of his architectural compositions. These undeveloped landscape designs were little more than abbreviated imitations of eighteenth-century English landscape parks, standing in for an idealized "nature."[8] The architectural historian Marc Treib suggests that modernists such as Le Corbusier regarded the landscape as "generic scenery . . . serving as the vegetal buffer between buildings."[9] Once the "natural" background for a work of art (the building) had been conceptualized along these lines, the best approach for the management of the landscape, apparently, was to do as little as possible to it. Any overt indication of design or manipulation would destroy the pastoral idyll and prevent the landscape from functioning as a neutral frame for appreciation of the building as a sculptural object.

If aspects of modernist architectural theory seemed problematic as the basis for a landscape design profession, the postwar adoption of modernism by institutional and corporate clients (and by design schools) nevertheless made it necessary or at least desirable for some landscape architects to develop modernist conceptual frameworks for their work. In 1937, while the San Francisco exhibition was being mounted, British landscape architect Christopher Tunnard published a series of articles also suggesting how modernist architecture might reform the practice of landscape design. In his 1938 book *Gardens in the Modern Landscape,* Tunnard established a manifesto for modernist landscape architecture and bewailed the fact that "gardens had remained aloof" from trends in architecture.[10] In 1939 Joseph Hudnut brought Tunnard to the GSD, where he and his publications provided both theory and practical examples for landscape design sympathetic to the new ethos. Tunnard soon insisted that "modern landscape design [was] inseparable from the spirit, technique, and development of modern architecture," and denounced the bifurcated model of "formal" and "naturalistic" styles, which he associated with "conventional methods of axial composition or of naturalistic arrangement of plant material." These were "design clichés . . . fatal to the uninhibited garden maker" and "the dying breath of the romantic age, long since broken down and already discarded by the sister art of architecture."[11] Photographs and plans of Tunnard's built work in England between 1936 and 1939 perfectly illustrated Henry-Russell Hitchcock's contemporary suggestions. Working with the architect Serge Chermayeff on the architect's own residence in Sussex, for example, Tunnard designed an architectonic terrace garden that created a defined, limited extension of the modernist, functional spaces of the house. The garden provided a viewing terrace for the surrounding parklike landscape, in which he made almost no

Mission 66 campground amphitheater, Big Bend National Park. NPS Historic Photo Collection.

Mission 66 campground entrance station in 1959, Mather Campground, Grand Canyon National Park. NPS Historic Photo Collection.

A lunch break in 1956 in Big Bend. Wayside interpretive kiosks, signs, and picnic areas were also designed by Mission 66 landscape architects. NPS Historic Photo Collection.

interventions.[12] In this project and others like it, the strategy of inserting of a unified building and terrace complex into a larger, "untouched" landscape was aided immeasurably by the fact that the "natural" setting was the product of eighteenth-century landscape gardening—a landscape park—that served admirably as the visual essence of a "Virgilian dream," with few modifications needed.

By the time Tunnard arrived at Harvard, at least some of the landscape students at the GSD were already chafing under the remnants of tra-ditional design education being offered there. Garrett Eckbo, for example, openly criticized Bremer Pond, who still taught "Beaux-Arts" principles of composition and required the study of historical precedents. Impressed by the newer faculty at Harvard, including Gropius, Tunnard, and the architectural historian Sigfried Giedion, Eckbo well understood the strength and potential of the new direction in design.[13] Eckbo and fellow students Dan Kiley and James C. Rose wrote three articles for *Architectural Record* in 1939 and 1940 in which they attempted to revise the theoretical foundations of their profession. Landscape design, they suggested, occurred in one of three "environments": urban, rural, or primeval. In their essay on landscapes in the "urban environment," they stressed the need for a "flexible [park] system distributing all types of recreation," citing Robert Moses's recent work in the New York area as the most advanced example. They then offered a typology of landscape types (from "play lot" to "parkways and freeways") that corresponded to the metropolitan park planning Moses had been engineering since the 1920s with landscape architect Gilmore D. Clarke, among other consultants and planners. Such a basic outline for a park system also accorded with the suggestions of the Regional Plan Association's *Regional Plan of New York and Its Environs,* compiled in the 1920s by planner Thomas Adams. In addition, the young Harvard modernists emphasized that urban parks should be functional parts of a "recreational environment" that would "integrate building and landscape," serve multiple uses, "exploit mechanization," and recognize the "decisive importance of 'the machine,'" by which of course they meant automobiles. Systems of automotive parkways and recreational complexes would "meet the new needs of urban society" and amount to an advance in landscape architecture comparable to that of modernism in architecture.[14]

Their essay on design in the "rural environment" similarly combined borrowed ideas with a flourish of modernist bravado. Reflecting on the dramatic changes in agriculture and rural life during the 1930s, they noted that recreation would have to suit the new needs of rural populations. Drawing especially on the ideas of the planner Benton MacKaye, they suggested that rural recreational centers should include outdoor theaters, ball fields, picnic grounds, community buildings, and other facilities that would consolidate rural populations in their recreational activities and thereby promote "social integration." Merely "rustic" or scenic parks were dismissed as of interest only to "urbanites," not "those who live on the land." In this case the examples cited were not parks but the new towns planned by the Tennessee Valley Authority, the Farm Security Administration (for which Eckbo worked), and the Resettlement Administration. In their article on the "primeval environment," the three essayists described the need for "establishing and then controlling an environmental equilibrium" between urban and rural landscapes by ensuring the continued existence of primeval areas "not inhabited by man." The justification for such a system of designated wilderness had been well elaborated by the Wilderness Society and other advocates by 1940; but the authors were forceful in their observation that preserving "natural scenery" would not suffice. Ecological science would be needed to guide management decisions in such areas. Providing "access" would only destroy them. "Wholesale invasion of the wilderness" was deplorable, and could not be "camouflaged out of existence by 'styles' of architecture . . . or by 'rustification' which is supposed to 'blend' with nature, and simulate the honest craftsmanship of the pioneers." Harmony, they noted, was "the result of contrast," and was no justification for park development in the primeval environment, where "the biological conception of environmental de-

Expanding road and parking capacities while minimizing the impacts of development created particular challenges for Mission 66 landscape architects. This 1950s view is of the Royal Palm developed area in Everglades.
Everglades National Park Archives.

Mission 66 parking lots often grew to considerable sizes. One-way circulation systems helped keep traffic flowing and allowed roadways to be narrower. Shaping parking lots to fit land contours and breaking them up with islands of vegetation were also common strategies to limit impacts, as seen here in Cape Cod (middle) and Yellowstone (bottom).
Author's photos.

sign" should be applied.[15] As derivative as these articles by Eckbo, Kiley, and Rose may have been, they were far more useful than vague references to a "Virgilian dream," and they were significant within the profession of landscape architecture for piecing together a set of fundamental ideas that could form the basis of a modernist practice. In 1950 many of these ideas were codified when Eckbo published *Landscapes for Living,* which became a standard textbook in professional education for years afterwards.

The most representative category of American modernist landscape design, however, had little to do with these ruminations on urban, rural, or primeval public landscapes. It was private garden design, particularly the design of the smaller gardens proliferating with the postwar housing boom. James Rose, in particular, wrote other articles in the late 1930s that explained how gardens could become a modernist art form, situated "between architecture and sculpture," through the use of asymmetric compositions, new materials, and design motifs that evoked contemporary fine arts and architecture. Above all, new residential landscapes should be "functional" outdoor living spaces rather than displays of formal horticultural composition, and they should exhibit seamless integration of interior and exterior space.[16] The fine arts also influenced garden design by the 1940s. The sculptor Isamu Noguchi's playground projects consisted of abstract earthform compositions, for example, and the landscape architect Roberto Burle Marx created striking garden plans inspired by abstract paintings.[17] By the end of the decade, a number of American landscape architects had developed successful new approaches to residential landscape design based on modernist principles, often in close association with architects building new residences in a related design idiom.

Much of the new spirit in residential design could be traced to California and the phenomenal low-density urban growth occurring there. The location of the 1937 San Francisco exhibition, and the fact that it was dominated by West Coast landscape architects, reflected the degree to which the postwar modernist garden was synonymous with the California garden. Thomas Church, in particular, defined the California garden as a mainstay of modernist landscape design, characterized by its relatively small size (usually attached to new single-family houses), asymmetric plan organization, use of wood decking and other hard surfaces, individual plants used for sculptural effect, and swimming pools or other features laid out in irregular, "biomorphic" shapes. Window walls and sliding doors integrated indoor and outdoor space, and sculptures or sculptural outdoor furniture served as centerpieces. Church produced some two thousand gardens during his career and influenced younger California landscape architects, including Garrett Eckbo and Lawrence Halprin, in their designs of both gardens and larger projects.[18] The sheer number of modernist gardens—Eckbo designed one thousand gardens himself in his lifetime—indicates the degree to which they were adapted to the mass production of housing taking place especially in California. Although the phenomenon of "outdoor living" was particularly suited to the mild climate of the West Coast, its appeal was nearly universal. Popularized in *California Sunset* and other design and consumer magazines, the modernist garden, as articulated by Church and others, embodied postwar material well-being as much as did the ranch house itself. The redwood deck and "kidney-shaped" pool proliferated into ubiquitous backyard clichés. In masterly examples of larger garden designs, such as Church's Donnell Residence (1949) or Dan Kiley's Miller House (with Eero Saarinen, 1955), the adept integration of house and garden confirmed the successful adaptation of modernist principles of spatial organization to garden design.

By the early 1950s landscape architecture was, as historian Melanie Simo describes it, "a profession in transition."[19] Most of the second generation of American landscape architects, who had established the ASLA and dozens of academic programs in landscape architecture in the first half of the century, were no longer practicing. Frederick Law Olmsted Jr., for example, retired from active practice in 1950 and died in 1957. By that time many other leading lights of the "country place" era were also gone.[20] Gilmore Clarke, who had overseen the development of Westchester County parks and parkways in the 1920s and the entire New York City park system in the 1930s, perhaps spoke for many of the remaining old guard when he wrote in 1947 that he saw "no Frank Lloyd Wrights or Le Corbusiers of landscape architecture" among the "thinning ranks" of students entering the field; what is more, he was at a loss to know whether this was "a liability or an asset."[21] The early 1950s were a nadir for many academic landscape architecture programs, which suffered from low enrollments, reduced budgets, and some doubt about what the future of the profession should be. Bremer Pond

Outdoor spaces, whether central courtyards or attached terraces, almost always were part of the "flow diagram" of Mission 66 visitor centers. Their design usually extended the plan and materials of the building itself. Geometrical planted islands, sometimes with seating walls, were common, as in this early example at Grand Canyon. Author's photo.

The site work around visitor centers reflected and supported the intended pattern of visitor movement, as well as the materials and construction of the architecture. Curving concrete paths, ramps, and geometricized seating walls sheathed in stone were all typical features of Mission 66 visitor center landscapes, as seen here at Bryce Canyon National Park, Utah. Author's photo.

Planting around visitor centers continued the established practice of using native plants in naturalized patterns and associations. The intent was to restore the landscape around the new construction as much as to create an aesthetic effect, as illustrated here at Zion. Author's photo.

lingered on in charge of landscape architecture at the GSD until 1950, indicating not so much tolerance of a venerable figure as indifference to what Hudnut and Gropius felt was an obsolete field. Older academics at other schools, such as Gilmore Clarke at Cornell, struggled to adapt to the dramatic developments in their professional world.

If academia had yet to adjust, a postwar practice of landscape architecture was nevertheless taking shape in the United States, and it was a modernist design discipline. Designers such as Dan Kiley were increasingly successful because they were preferred as subconsultants by leading modernist architects, such as Eero Saarinen. The postwar practice of landscape architecture also grew because it was responding to contemporary trends in land development and construction. By the mid-1950s, Garrett Eckbo, Lawrence Halprin, and other leading landscape architects had moved beyond garden design to take on larger and more complex projects, including the design of shopping centers, campuses, corporate parks, civic plazas, and large subdivisions described as "new communities." This typology of large landscape commissions expressed the dominant themes of postwar urbanization, such as low-density residential development, the relocation of corporate headquarters, and downtown "revitalizations." These kinds of large, complex projects, in turn, demanded larger practices with more employees trained to undertake a variety of design, engineering, and management tasks. Gropius himself created the model for large, integrated firms with The Architects Collaborative (TAC), the Cambridge office he established while at

Harvard. Other successful architectural firms of the 1950s, such as Skidmore, Owings and Merrill (SOM), also featured corporate business structures and large numbers of employees trained in various disciplines. Landscape architecture offices soon followed suit. In 1945 Eckbo formed a partnership with Robert Royston and Edward A. Williams in San Francisco, and Halprin founded his influential practice in the same city four years later. Another Californian, Hideo Sasaki, opened his first office in Boston in 1953 and soon "did for middle- and large-scale projects," according to Peter Walker and Melanie Simo, "what Thomas Church did for the West Coast house and garden."[22] He accomplished this by creating a large, multidisciplinary design office. In 1957 he and Walker formed Sasaki, Walker and Associates, a firm soon known for its urban renewal, campus planning, and large subdivisions. Major architectural firms on the East Coast sought out Sasaki and Walker as capable collaborators working along lines sympathetic to their own. Sasaki, Walker and Associates grew along the lines of SOM (where Sasaki had worked) and took on a corporate business structure that allowed the firm's principals to delegate management and design development tasks while reserving their own time for overseeing major decisions and working directly with clients. The firm was one of many multidisciplinary design firms that proliferated over the next two decades. As these design offices grew, many developed corporate structures, regionalized, and eventually split into new or renamed offices.[23]

This growth and change in the profession of landscape architecture affected educational programs, since new university instructors inevitably drew on their own experience to structure courses and curriculum. Sasaki, in particular, salvaged the landscape architecture program at the GSD. Beginning in 1953, when he became chair of the department, Sasaki reorganized training in landscape architecture to make it more closely resemble his own successful practice. He assembled graduate students and instructors into teams that solved design problems through an organized approach to "research, analysis and synthesis." Architects and planners were invited to join in collaborative design studios that simulated the structure of contemporary professional offices, and with landscape architects they were able to undertake the kinds of large-scale planning and urban redevelopment scenarios typical of the era. Some students went to work for Sasaki (Walker was one of his former students), while some of his employees came to teach in the collaborative design studios. Sasaki brought in an array of active planners and designers to participate in studios and other courses, and also invited government officials who were implementing urban renewal and other programs. Other academic landscape architecture departments went through similar transitions.[24]

Over the ten years following the establishment of Sasaki, Walker and Associates in 1957 (in other words, the period contemporary with Mission 66), dozens of new development projects all over the country demonstrated how much the reinvented profession of landscape architecture could accomplish. Sasaki and his project teams designed "new communities" such as Sea Pines Plantation on Hilton Head Island,

Road engineering at Yellowstone. While Park Service landscape architects had a tradition of minimizing the intrusions of road construction, the realities of postwar highway standards made this task increasingly problematic. The partial cloverleaf interchange in Yellowstone (left) indicates that sometimes Mission 66 planners were willing to go too far to accommodate higher traffic volumes. The Chittenden Bridge in the park (right) may have been a more beautiful piece of engineering when built in 1962, but it required the demolition of the old Chittenden Bridge (1903), a significant and historic landscape feature. Author's photos.

South Carolina, and "comprehensive downtown renewals," such as Constitution Plaza in Hartford, Connecticut. At new corporate parks, such as the John Deere Headquarters in Illinois and the Upjohn Headquarters in Michigan, the firm designed pastoral landscapes to serve as neutral settings for striking modernist architecture by Saarinen Associates and SOM. In Los Altos Hills, California, the firm planned the new Foothill College; in Boulder they designed the massive expansion of the University of Colorado. In San Francisco, Alcoa Plaza and Crocker Plaza were among dozens of "civic plazas" that featured extensive paving, modernist sculpture, and architectonic landscape elements such as geometricized concrete retaining walls and stairs (often used for seating), raised planting boxes, and elaborate fountains.[25] These few examples from just one firm's extensive portfolio only begin to indicate the range and scale of landscape planning and design projects that characterized the period. As the American landscape underwent the most sweeping changes in its history, there was much planning and design

work to be done. Soon an abundance of landscape architecture firms were working within a similar typology of project types, and often in the same context of large, multidisciplinary project teams.

Public parks were not a particularly important category of work for postwar landscape architecture firms. The public landscapes designed in the late 1950s and early 1960s often were "semipublic" urban spaces, owned or sponsored by private corporations or institutions. Many civic plazas fell into this category, as did the "bonus plazas" built by developers in New York after 1961, and the iconic Paley Park in Manhattan, designed by Robert Zion and Harold Breen in the early 1960s. M. Paul Friedberg and others reinvigorated small park design with fanciful, abstract "adventure" playgrounds later in the decade, but this remained a discrete and limited type of public landscape, usually attached to schools or housing projects. Walker and Simo observe that, at least in California, "by 1960, the design of neighborhood parks and gardens was no longer a mainstay" of leading landscape firms, which were taking advantage of the rapid urbanization occurring in the state by moving on to the design of "schools, college campuses, civic centers, and mixed-use projects with parking garages and roof gardens."[26] Certainly public landscapes remained an important element of what landscape architects were expected to be able to design. Large-scale urban renewal projects in St. Louis, Pittsburgh, and other cities called for new waterfront parks on what had been the sites of commercial or industrial development. But in fundamental ways, the older practice and ideology of park making was no longer a foundation of the postwar profession. Olmstedian theory—of the type that continued to inform Park Service landscape architecture during Mission 66—did not continue to have the same influence in a design profession that had adapted to modernist theory, a multidisciplinary context, and a new typology of commissions linked to postwar patterns of urbanization.

Neither did the extraordinary opportunities for park and parkway development made possible by the New Deal exist any longer. The Interstate Highway Act ensured that most new highway development would be engineered for combined commercial and noncommercial traffic. Unlike the noncommercial parkways that had been designed by landscape architects for park commissions in the prewar years, the interstate highways were planned by engineers for highway departments. Federal and state highway authorities never considered that systems of public landscapes should complement the new roads, as was the case with prewar park and parkway systems. Neither did Congress empower the

Park Service to embark on extensive "cooperation" with state and local governments to plan and design their park systems, as it had during the New Deal. In general, as new and enlarged patterns of land development and urbanization gathered momentum in the 1950s, few municipal and state governments implemented commensurate programs of park and parkway expansion. The new, low-density American city—the "metropolitan region"—offered the amenities of private residential landscapes, such as the California-type garden, as well as some new recreational parks, including ball-field complexes, playgrounds, or other facilities. But postwar urbanization was not typically conceived around systems of public landscapes and noncommercial parkways in the way much late-nineteenth- and early-twentieth-century urban expansion had been.

Mission 66 can be seen as at least a limited attempt to mitigate this historic shift in urban and regional planning priorities. As the country grew and urbanized at an unprecedented pace, the Park Service did attempt to expand and modernize the national park system (if not state and regional systems) at a scale comparable to the geographic and demographic trends of the day. At least in this sense, Mission 66 must be considered the most ambitious landscape architectural project of the postwar era. And in some ways, the same influences that shaped private landscape architecture firms helped determine Mission 66 design ideas and practice. For example, the WODC and EODC, established in 1954, could be described, in a sense, as regional offices of a multidisciplinary corporate design firm headed by Wirth and Vint in Washington.

Park Service landscape architects, like their in-house architectural colleagues, responded to the new artistic and technical context of the postwar period. The same geographic and social trends—interstate highways, low-density urbanization, new construction technology, and the popularity of modernist design—influenced Park Service landscape architects as much as they had the agency's in-house architects.

But in other ways, Mission 66 landscape architects proceeded in isolation from a larger professional context, at least to a greater degree than Mission 66 architects did. Insulated from both the vicissitudes and the refreshing opportunities of the private sector, the Park Service remained a haven for park planning and design informed by the old Olmstedian ideology. While Wirth and Cabot made a point of recruiting some of the most progressive architects of the day, private landscape firms did not participate in Mission 66, even in advisory capacities (Dan Kiley's participation in the Gateway Arch design being a notable but unique exception). Since the 1920s, in fact, the Park Service had relied almost exclusively on its own in-house force of landscape architects. Early Park Service administrators used architectural consultants, such as Gilbert Stanley Underwood, to design buildings. But they felt at the time that private landscape architects, many of whom were experienced mainly in "country place" design, lacked the training and sensibility needed to work in national park settings. Vint therefore trained a cohort of landscape architects who were longtime employees, and who continued to adapt their public practice to the agency's specific needs. In the 1920s and 1930s, however, Vint and Wirth had also maintained a healthy interaction with a broader private professional context, mainly through Frederick Law Olmsted Jr., who collaborated with them as a mentor and as a friend. The large number of private (and unemployed) landscape architects hired through the New Deal also guaranteed an infusion of creative thinking within the agency. But by the mid-1950s, the growing private sector within the profession of landscape architecture had less interest in the Park Service, and less useful advice to offer in any case. Private practitioners had moved away from traditional public park planning and were busy with other opportunities.

Given the enormous scope of Mission 66, and the fact that a landscape architect served as the director of the Park Service, it is striking that the ASLA and the rest of the profession did not take greater notice or become more directly involved in the program. In the 1940s leading figures such as Henry Hubbard and Olmsted continued to publish articles on national parks in *Landscape Architecture* magazine. The issues they addressed, such as "preservation and enhancement of natural scenery" and "the progressive encroachment of trees in certain meadows" of Yosemite Valley, reiterated traditional concerns and convictions regarding the role of the landscape architect in national park management.[27] At that time the ASLA "committee on national and state parks and forests" included Olmsted, Vint, Wirth, Carnes, as well as leading academics such as Philip H. Elwood and Ralph E. Griswold. First formed during the New Deal, the committee published regular reports in *Landscape Architecture* that covered public land management issues in detail. In 1955 Conrad Wirth made an important address to the ASLA on "the landscape architect in national park work," and the committee on national and state parks and forests reported extensively on the initiation of Mission 66 throughout the next year.[28] But little else appeared in *Landscape Architecture* on Mission 66, or national parks generally, over the next decade. In 1957 the magazine received a new, more contemporary graphic design, and in 1958 an energetic associate editor, Grady Clay, joined the staff. By 1960, when Clay took over as executive editor, he was bringing new authors to the magazine, such as the geographer J. B. Jackson, and publishing articles on a range of new issues from the "ecology of cites" and "urban sprawl" to "earth sculpture" and "cluster development." The profession was now prospering, with ASLA membership almost doubling between 1956 and 1966.[29] The few articles that appeared in *Landscape Architecture* on national parks, however, stressed only that parks were facing "ruin" from large crowds of automotive tourists, hardly an original or useful observation at that point.[30]

Even as Mission 66 construction began attracting attention in the popular press and architectural journals, no articles on the program appeared in the ASLA's official magazine. The renewed private sector of the profession understandably diverted the attention of a new generation of landscape architects. Clay represented the most innovative, dynamic segments of the profession that he covered, and the content of his magazine reflected their interests and concerns at the time. For whatever reasons, Wirth, Vint, and their colleagues did not benefit from constructive advice, involvement, or even criticism from leading landscape architects or the ASLA at a time when they greatly needed such support. Mission 66 went unheralded—almost unnoticed—by a profession that was "in transition," rapidly growing and moving on to new challenges.

But if Mission 66 landscape architecture proceeded without involvement from leading private-sector practitioners, the program nevertheless made its own significant contribution to postwar American landscape design. The revised national park master planning procedures, the "guiding principles" of the program, and the Mission 66 prospectuses together described a new ideal for the development of a national park system composed of parks of all types: large wilderness parks, historical parks, recreational parks, seashores (and lakeshores), parkways. The new ideal, or model, of park planning both revised and extended traditional goals for national parks. The fundamental principles of Mission 66 could be found in the Progressive Era policies and documents that Wirth venerated, but Park Service landscape architects had profoundly altered the basic premises governing how those principles should be implemented. New ideas and tools were used to reassert the viability of long-established ideology. The Mission 66 national park affirmed these priorities while devising new strategies for implementing them. These new planning strategies, together with modernist architectural design, created an overall ideal of national park development that differed from the prewar model for park master planning. The result can be described as the modernist national park.[31]

Mission 66 modernist national park planning dated back to Vint's concerns, already expressed in the late 1930s, that park villages and master plans (as he himself had devised them) in some cases could not sustain any further expansion of visitor capacity without causing unacceptable damage to and encroachment on park landscapes. This led to his "Plan B" (also called the "Vint Plan") for Yosemite Valley, which called for the heavily visited area to become a day use destination, with overnight accommodations and administrative facilities moved elsewhere. The same concerns shaped the first "pilot prospectus" for Mount Rainier and several of the other Mission 66 pilot projects. In the course of implementing Mission 66, this ideal was frequently compromised by the sometimes difficult negotiations that surrounded any dramatic change. But the essence of the new model remained: parks could be redeveloped to allow increased levels of use without causing unacceptable levels of damage or encroachments on park scenery, so long as the new policies were implemented. Park roads required widening and straightening, for example, for moving larger numbers of day use visitors in and out of parks. As overnight accommodations were phased out, the visitor center would centralize services and ensure a basic level of interpretation in every park. The locations of visitor centers would be chosen for the efficient interception of "visitor flow" and the avoidance of "sensitive" areas. The overall planning model of the modernist park was thus one of centralizing services in a large "one-stop" building rather than decentralizing development in numerous park villages, which themselves were decentralized complexes of smaller rustic structures such as museums, administration buildings, and comfort stations.

These ideas, codified in scores of Mission 66 prospectuses by the end of 1955, formed the basis of numerous construction projects under way by 1957. Together they determined new priorities for national park landscape architects. Rustic-era park construction had reflected an aesthetic conception of the national park in which associative architectural imagery helped "harmonize" development with its setting. Rustic buildings and villages were sited to serve as elements of larger landscape compositions that included nearby scenic features. By contrast, in the modernist park such associative imagery was useless, and siting large visitor center buildings near "sensitive" areas was potentially destructive. Landscape architects conceived of the visitor center as a viewing pavilion, not a picturesque element of a landscape scene. It was a building to see from more than to be seen, a composition of volumes and views, not of evocative façades and architectural mass.

This modernist building type also exhibited a modernist relationship between structure and site, and between visitor and landscape. As Hitchcock and Tunnard had suggested in the 1930s, the building and its terraces formed a discrete unit, set in an "untouched" landscape. This put the surrounding park in a new position conceptually; it was now seen less as a picturesque composition in which architecture and figures composed visual elements than as an abstraction, a pure, untouched "dream" that would only be degraded by the presence of any evidence of human activity.

The national parks that were built, or rebuilt, over the next ten years through the Mission 66 program demonstrated what a modernist national park could be in the context of postwar American society. No state, regional, or municipal park systems were redeveloped or expanded on a scale commensurate with the geographic and social transformations taking place in the United States. Perhaps the closest comparisons were two municipal park systems (both favorite examples of Sigfried Giedion), one developed in New York under Robert Moses and the other in Amsterdam, where the Dutch modernist Cornelis Van Eesteren oversaw major park improvements. But these were primarily prewar urban park projects. At the time when Wirth and his colleagues conceived their modernist national park model, there were few precedents in existence, and the question of what modernist theory implied for the design of national parks remained open.

One powerful suggestion was that large national parks should be managed more as "primeval parks" or wilderness areas, as outside advocates had argued since the 1920s. In 1940 landscape architects Eckbo, Kiley, and Rose effectively identified the modernist abstraction of the "Virgilian dream," in which the designer intervened as little as possible, with the need for primeval areas "not inhabited by man," in which "the biological conception of environmental design" should be applied and "rusticification" should be avoided. The Mission 66 modernist park at least initiated this conceptual transformation of the park landscape from picturesque scene into scientific wilderness. The relationship between the visitor center and its site, for example, implied a new basis for the changed relationship between the visitor and the park landscape. The visitor center was conceived as a

limited intrusion, separate and distinguishable from the "untouched nature" left undisturbed around it. The picturesque conception of the park had allowed for "improvement" of the landscape and the integration of rustic structures as parts of the scene. But in the modernist park the larger landscape was kept "unspoiled" by concentrating services in a central location from which the surrounding landscape was viewed, often through a large window or from a structured terrace. While this increasingly alienated perspective further removed people from the landscape both emotionally and literally, it also enabled larger numbers to "enjoy" the park while producing less impact upon it.

But the "wilderness" preserved in the Mission 66 park was a modernist abstraction, a "dream" that required only that it be directly encroached on as little as possible. This modernist concept of wilderness was an essential part of the Mission 66 park, because as long as the wilderness of the park landscape remained an abstraction, the expansion of the capacity of the parks for automotive tourism could be carried out without causing "impairment" simply by concentrating visitors in redeveloped frontcountry landscapes. As long as the visitor center complexes did not extend "indefinitely into the natural setting," as Henry-Russell Hitchcock put it in 1937, the "values of the existing natural environment" would be preserved. The implication was that doing nothing, not even research, was acceptable. As Wirth wrote in 1958, trying to assuage the concerns of contemporary wilderness advocates, wilderness preservation was not a specific "program item" in Mission 66 "because in a sense the less you have to do the better it [wilderness] is being preserved."[32]

Once environmental scientists and advocates began to understand and describe wilderness more fully in terms of ecological systems, it became clearer that the modernist concept of wilderness that guided Mission 66 park plans would not guarantee the biological integrity of the park landscape. As wilderness advocates developed their own, more scientific and sophisticated concept of wilderness and ways to protect its integrity, they also grew more disillusioned with the Mission 66 conviction that unrestricted access for "public enjoyment" could be provided without impairing parks. The most basic premises of the nascent environmental movement, in other words, would soon conflict with the most fundamental assumptions of the Mission 66 modernist park.

The environmentalist ideal of a wilderness defined in ecological rather than visual or aesthetic terms implied a postmodernist critique of the modernist concept of wilderness, and of postwar American modernism in general. Ultimately, the perceived success or failure of Mission 66 therefore depended on perceptions of postwar American modernism generally. Since the mid-nineteenth century, parks had served as idealized civic visions. Just as Central Park embodied an ideal of a more healthful and humane industrialized city, the national park master plans of the 1920s and 1930s exemplified regional and town planning principles of that era. No one could reasonably expect corporate parks, tract subdivisions, or shopping centers to apotheosize 1950s civic ideals; but Americans expected exactly that from their national system of public landscapes. Mission 66 arrived with great fanfare during a time when many Ameri-

cans were adapting to enormous social and geographic changes and felt a great need to rediscover or reinvent their historical and national identity. Mission 66 promised nothing less than to make the national park system—a coordinated system of scenic and historic places—a primary agent in establishing such identity through the creation, interpretation, and preservation of the nation's "heritage." Mission 66 promised to carry on the role of the American park, in other words, as a vital cultural institution and as an essential part of life and landscape in the United States, as they both underwent momentous change.

But as Mission 66 proceeded into the reality of construction, it would encounter far greater scrutiny and criticism than it had while being planned and designed. The essential deficiency of modernist theory as a basis for an adequate stewardship of wilderness became more evident as construction projects were completed and ever larger numbers of cars and tourists arrived. And while many Americans might have been generally indifferent to mid-century architecture, in the peculiarly significant setting of the national park, modernist buildings evoked strong reactions. This, as we have seen, was the case at the Jackson Lake Lodge in 1955, and the same critique intensified as Mission 66 projects began construction all over the country. The negative perception of modernist planning and design reinforced the characterization of Mission 66 as merely a development program, not a coordinated conservation effort. To some degree this was unfair, since many thousands of acres of parkland were being acquired, including new national seashores, lakeshores, recreation areas, and historical parks. But when critics saw what to them looked like a shopping center being built in Yellowstone, it reminded them of the "sprawl" outside the park's boundaries.

The reaction to modernist design in national parks inevitably was colored by reactions and attitudes to broader postwar urbanization and development trends. While in 1956 many conservation groups greeted Mission 66 plans with enthusiasm, as projects moved from design to construction, their attitudes hardened. Many advocates, who would soon be known as "environmentalists," would no longer tolerate further enlargement of park visitor facilities, widening of roads, or other expansions of the capacity of the parks to accommodate visitors. They no longer believed that parks could provide unlimited public access—regardless of how that access was designed—and still maintain their integrity in the present, much less the future. As the redevelopment of many national parks was implemented through a startling array of construction projects, the reactions to Mission 66 illustrated broad shifts in popular attitudes toward the changing American landscape generally, and toward the results of modernist planning and design specifically. For many, a visceral hatred of widespread low-density urbanization made it impossible to see Mission 66 construction as anything but an unacceptable extension of similarly flawed design into the sacred precincts of the national park system. Mission 66 aspired to embody a postwar ideal of progress, in which new aesthetic, conceptual, and technical designs addressed contemporary problems and mitigated the "dilemma" in which the parks—and perhaps society as a whole—had been trapped. But by 1957 many advocates no longer believed that modern progress in any form would produce an acceptable future. Environmentalists would not so much try to reform the Mission 66 park as try to stop it altogether. They would oppose expanding the capacity of parks under any pretext.

In the course of carrying out Mission 66, the Park Service discovered the limits of modernist theory, planning, and design as a means of reinventing the American national park. On the one hand, Mission 66 was not able successfully to capture the energy and vision that would soon be evident in Stewart Udall's "New Conservation," the establishment of the Bureau of Outdoor Recreation, the funding of the Land and Water Conservation Act, and ultimately the entire environmental movement, including the impressive array of federal and state legislation passed in the late 1960s and early 1970s.

On the other hand, neither the federal designation of many millions of acres of official wilderness, nor the new legal and administrative frameworks and procedures established through environmental legislation, were any more successful in solving what Newton Drury described so long ago as the "dilemma of our parks." Wilderness designations and environmental protections had enormous benefits, including the protection of vast areas from logging and mining, improved air and water quality, habitat conservation, and controls on destructive public works projects. But none of this ever amounted to a concrete plan that would make it possible for hundreds of millions of Americans to have meaningful, transcendent experiences of their national parks. Environmental quality is more closely monitored in parks today, and endangered species are better protected. But to a significant degree, as far as visitor experience is concerned, the national park system and the Park Service still function as artifacts of Mission 66. The logistical issues of traffic control, basic services, interpretation, and public safety are still managed within the conceptual framework of the modernist park. National park staff are still trained in the Mission 66 training centers, visitors are still oriented in (sometimes grievously altered) Mission 66 visitor centers, and the basic relationship between the automotive public and their parks remains what it has been since it was reconceived half a century ago. Parks have indeed become day use destinations to a greater degree than ever before, with the majority of visitors staying in gateway communities or traveling from nearby metropolitan areas. Mission 66 construction, if sometimes controversial, has proved

to be essential. Environmental ethics and laws have improved many aspects of park management, but they have not generally replaced Mission 66 infrastructure or the basic concept and development pattern of Mission 66 parks. Mission 66 park development remains today as much a part of the federal public landscape as its counterpart and contemporary, the interstate highway system.

In other words, the postwar "dilemma" persists today, and so does the only comprehensive design response that the Park Service has managed to make to address it: the Mission 66 modernist park. The story of the construction of Mission 66 parks, and the sometimes dramatic responses to this phase of the program, is a history of the developed areas of the national park system as we know them today.

PART III

MISSION 66: CONSTRUCTION

CHAPTER 8

CONCESSIONS AND CONTROVERSY

From the outset of Mission 66, Conrad Wirth insisted that his initiative was an integrated approach to "conservation," not just a "development" program. But construction—the physical redevelopment of parks—was the heart of the entire idea of the modernist national park. Parks could still be "for the people" only if they were redeveloped for a new pattern and pace of public use. Modernist planning and design, as absorbed and adapted by Park Service landscape architects and architects, offered new means of continuing the traditional national park project. A whole typology of redeveloped scenic reservations, historic sites, and recreational parks began to take shape as Mission 66 construction got under way in the summer of 1956.

A quickly planned and massive building program always had the potential for inefficiency or outright corruption. But in almost all cases Mission 66 construction was administered with competence and probity. Congress showed its confidence in the program by increasing its appropriations for national park acquisition and construction from $14 million in fiscal year 1955, to $45 million for 1957, to $51 million in 1961, and over $68 million in 1966. The annual operations budget (for maintenance, staff, and other regular agency functions) increased from about $18 million to $58 million during the same period. By 1956 Wirth could report that construction was proceeding, finally, on a "full-scale, rather than piecemeal, basis." The next year he asserted that Mission 66 was "the most significant undertaking of the National Park Service since its establishment."[1]

Park Service budgets continued to increase even as the reality of Mission 66 construction incited controversy among conservationists—and soon a wider public—who rejected the overall goal of making parks more accessible for automotive tourism. Prominent advocates from the

Sierra Club and other organizations denounced the "bulldozers of bureaucracy" as soon as Mission 66 put them into motion. By 1959 Mission 66 was embroiled in controversy, and Wirth instituted a period of reassessment and revision culminating in 1961 with the arrival of the Kennedy administration and new federal conservation priorities. In October 1963 Wirth announced his retirement, effectively forced from his position. Mission 66 itself survived and finished its construction phase in 1966. By that time the entire social and political context for managing national parks had shifted. The legacy of Mission 66 remained, however, in terms of physical development, institutional growth, and the expansion of the park system.

Mission 66 construction was funded mainly, but not exclusively, by the greatly enhanced appropriations that Congress could now hardly wait to make. Many national park concession contracts renegotiated under Mission 66 also required concessioners to make large capital investments. Between 1956 and 1966 park concessioners invested $33 million in new overnight accommodations, restaurants, and park stores, which was about $14 million less than called for in the 1956 Mission 66 final report. Concessioner investments had greater impacts than the figures suggest, however, because they resulted in some of the earliest and highest-profile Mission 66 construction projects. Concessioners hired their own architects and could initiate work quickly once they secured financing. Their facilities also were heavily used by the public and strongly affected early perceptions of Mission 66. And almost all overnight accommodations—the "motel type" park lodges that

quickly became controversial—were built through the investment of private capital.

The long and often difficult relationship between the Park Service and its private concessioners was an important factor in Mission 66 and needs to be considered in a historical context. Since the nineteenth century the federal government had enlisted entrepreneurs to provide visitor services in national parks. In 1864, when Congress gave Yosemite Valley to the state of California for public park purposes, the legislation stipulated that "leases not exceeding ten years" could be granted for portions of the valley and that income from the leases would be "expended in the preservation and improvement" of the park. In 1872 the Yellowstone legislation elaborated on this model, stipulating that ten-year leases could be granted by the secretary of the interior for areas of the park that required "buildings for the accommodation of visitors," with the proceeds again to be spent on park management and the construction of roads and trails.[2] Concession leases continued to be central to the management of federal scenic reservations at Sequoia, General Grant, Mount Rainier, Crater Lake, Grand Canyon, and other national parks. By 1907 Congress was authorizing twenty-year leases. Payments made by concessioners never covered the cost of managing the parks (as nineteenth-century legislators perhaps imagined they would), but private capital did finance the construction of remarkable hotels, such as Yellowstone's Old Faithful Inn (1903) and the Grand Canyon's El Tovar (1905). But the early concession system also suffered from chaotic management and abuse. For example, the park village at Yosemite Valley, under state administration until 1906, grew haphazardly, and by the early twentieth century the village was being criticized as an eyesore as well as the source of sewage and refuse that polluted the Merced River. At Yosemite, Mount Rainier, Grand Canyon, and other parks, multiple concessioners were authorized to do business, creating noisy competition for tourist trade under a system that did little to control these private enterprises or their impacts on surrounding landscapes.

By 1910 glaring inadequacies in the management of national parks had led to the movement to create a federal bureau to centralize and improve their administration. The reform of concession contracts and operations would be a first step for any new federal park agency. Stephen Mather's greatest successes as the first director of the new National Park Service arose from his ability to use his personal contacts and promotional skills to recruit investors and concession operators while consolidating and usually improving services. Earlier concession contracts had often been granted as political favors, or in any case outside the context of an overall plan for a park's development. Mather insisted that either a single concessioner in each park, or else one principal concessioner, should be granted a regulated monopoly. By limiting the number of contracts involved, the director could better control how these private businesses worked with his agency's staff. By eliminating competition, he could also anticipate that concessioners would invest capital willingly, since there was an expectation of ready profit. Under such terms, concessioners cooperated fully with the Park Service as partners in planning and designing new facilities.[3]

Mather quickly demonstrated how effective this policy could be. In 1915, the year he arrived at the Department of the Interior, concession management throughout the park system was confused at best. At Mount Rainier, forty-two separate concessioners competed for the very limited and seasonal tourist trade. That summer Mather persuaded a group of Seattle and Tacoma businessmen and park advocates to invest in the Rainier National Park Company, with the goal of having the new company take over all concession interests in the park. An initial capitalization of $200,000 in shares soon financed the construction of the Paradise Inn, a luxurious lodge in the tradition of the railroad hotels of the previous decade. Other concession contracts at Mount Rainier were soon bought out or discontinued, leaving the Rainier National Park Company the sole provider of accommodations and other services in the park. The change was generally perceived as a positive one, although by the 1920s some critics, in this case members of a local mountaineering club, accused the new concessioner of going too far to accommodate automotive tourists.[4] But in 1918 Mather could point to Mount Rainier and conclude that the "future was bright," and that events there so far had been "an object lesson that should guide the improvement of many other parks."[5]

The concession situation in each park varied, but in most cases Mather pushed for a concentration of business interests into a new or consolidated company to be favored with a monopolistic contract. In exchange, the Park Service gained increased control over business operations and oversaw large private investments in new or improved facilities. In some cases Mather struggled to replace concessioners who had powerful friends in Congress protecting their interests. At Yellowstone, where a network of concessions had developed since the 1880s, including hotels, stage coach services, and chains of tent camps, Mather began consolidating the array of businesses in 1916. After considerable strife (and the motorization of the stage coach lines), the concessions emerged mostly under the control of Harry Child by 1924. At Yosemite, Mather recruited a new concessioner, D. J. Desmond, who converted a U.S. Army barracks into the Yosemite Lodge in 1915 and began construction on a hotel at Glacier Point the next year. Desmond also began buying out other businesses in the valley in anticipation of a monopoly for his Yosemite Park Company. Another concession, Camp Curry, resisted consolidation until 1925, when finally a consolidated Yosemite Park & Curry Company gave the park a single concessioner. The combined company quickly financed the construction of the Ahwahnee, a rustic luxury hotel designed by Gilbert Stanley Underwood.[6]

Under Mather and Albright a generation of park concessioners learned to be comfortable with monopolistic contracts which ensured that their investments would be protected and would yield comfortable, if regulated, rates of return. Other grand lodges were built in the 1920s, for example, at Grand Canyon, Zion, and Bryce national parks, where Underwood again designed lodges and cabin complexes for the Fred Harvey Company and the Utah Parks Company. By 1929 private capital, complemented by public spending on roads and utilities, had provided a signif-

icant portion of the cost of developing what had become a unique and internationally admired national park system. Park hotels, restaurants, and stores, which Park Service officials—and probably most park visitors—considered essential services, were almost all built with private funds invested in monopolistic franchises.

But there were drawbacks to this strategy that soon became apparent as well. To a significant degree the system depended on personal relationships between Park Service officials and concession investors. Trust was needed, since the exact nature of the ownership of park hotels and other facilities could be subject to interpretation. Concessioners did not technically own property in the parks; rather they made "improvements" (such as buildings) on public property they leased. Legal title to the "improved property" was vested in the United States. Mather and Albright personally assured concessioners that they would be compensated for the value of any capital improvements they made (less depreciation) if for any reason their contracts were not renewed and their businesses were taken over by other companies. This implied that concessioners owned the value of their improvements, and that they could not be replaced by other concessioners without being compensated for that value.[7] The Park Service would therefore be in a far weaker position when renewing contracts than it had been when the concession policy had first been devised: replacing poorly performing concessioners might first require buying them out. Since many twenty-year concession contracts dated to the 1920s and 1930s, the implications of the policy complicated park management in the 1940s and 1950s.

During the Great Depression, the loss of paying customers, as well as a new philosophy at the Department of the Interior, had already strained the park concession system. Many concessions, suffering severe reductions in business, struggled to stay afloat. Large government investments in parks during the 1930s also meant that private capital was no longer needed. For many New Deal officials, neither was it any longer desirable. Mather and Albright were gone, and Ickes considered private park concessions an anachronism. He made no secret of his desire to buy out concessions so that they could be fully owned and run by the government. Congress proved unwilling to make such a radical (and expensive) change in policy, but the issue continued to be debated.[8] In 1942 many park concessioners effectively suspended operations and deferred maintenance for the duration of World War II. After the war, the sudden wave of visitors overwhelmed them. Drury detailed the conditions at Mount Rainier during the summer of 1946, which he suggested were typical. Over 1 million visitors had entered the park that year, more than twice the highest prewar figure. Meanwhile, the number of hotel rooms available was far below the prewar total, and almost all overnight accommodations were not just "obsolete" but "none too safe."[9]

Shocked at the dismal conditions at Mount Rainier—the park that had epitomized the benefits of the concession system—Drury called for action. Park concession policy had reached a turning point, as many concession contracts were coming due for renewal or were already operating on short-term extensions. A number of concession franchises changed hands through sale or inheritance. After almost twenty years of operating under these conditions, some operators had simply had enough. The Rainier National Park Company's contract, for example, was due for renewal in 1947, and the company's investors were not prepared to finance needed repairs and expansions as they would be asked to do under a renewed contract. Instead they lobbied for the federal government to buy out their interest and fund the necessary improvements directly. The company would operate the hotels on a contractual basis, but its buildings would be fully owned and maintained by the government. If this amounted to a considerable subsidy, they argued that there was no other way for the company to continue to provide services without going bankrupt. In 1950 Congress passed the necessary legislation, and the Paradise Inn and other concession buildings became federal property two years later.[10] But if many park concessioners were experiencing financial hard times during this era, very few were bought out by Congress. A window of opportunity to reform the park concession system through direct acquisitions, at a time when prices would be low, soon closed.

In 1946 some 275 national park concessioners operated facilities that represented $30 million of private investment.[11] Increased visitation, the poor condition of facilities, and the opportunity to revise the terms of renewed contracts combined to make concessions policy as critical an issue for Drury as it had been for Mather thirty years earlier. But Harry Truman's secretary of the interior, Julius A. Krug, took the issue out of the Park Service's hands. Krug attempted to reform the concession system by opening contracts up to competitive bidding as they expired. New concessioners would be selected if they offered better terms, and the new operators would then be required to buy out their predecessors. But the new agreements would have eliminated any government obligation to buy out existing concessioners upon termination of their contracts whether a new operator took over or not. Most concessioners denounced the policy as an attempt to nationalize their operations with no guarantee of compensation. They also objected to proposals for increases in franchise fees and shortened contract terms. Drury supported the concessioners, knowing they were necessary to the daily operation of many parks, and perhaps also feeling obligated by the informal agreements of the Mather era. When many operators refused to sign the contracts, Drury granted them extensions under the old terms. The stalemate continued for years, preventing the investment of private capital at a crucial time.[12]

But in 1946 Krug had appointed a "Concessions Advisory Group" made up of experts in tourism and conservation. In a 1948 report this group recommended that the Department of the Interior find a way to work with its concessioners under something like the policies Mather had negotiated. This included the continuation of monopolistic contracts and reassurances regarding the "security of investments in buildings, structures, and other improvements . . . while reserving in the United States formal legal title to such buildings." The group also added, however, that Congress should eventually acquire concessioner facilities and make them publicly owned and privately operated, as was about to be the case at Mount Rainier.[13] Park

concessioners, in the meantime, organized as the Western Conference of National Parks Concessioners and in 1948 put forward the legal idea of "possessory interest," which implied ownership in all but title of their improved properties. Congress also held hearings on park concessions in 1948 and 1949.[14] Perhaps most significantly, in October 1948 the federal comptroller general issued an opinion that park concessioners had rights "equivalent to equitable title in the facilities they have financed," an endorsement of the idea—if not the term—of possessory interest. Krug's successor, Oscar L. Chapman, issued a policy statement in 1950 that granted the concessioners most of what they had demanded. A new generation of contracts eventually extended the basic framework of traditional concession policy.[15]

But the business of park concessioning was changing, nevertheless. As passenger rail service to parks ended, railroad companies lost interest in financing concession companies. At the same time, massive investments were needed, at least if concessioners were to continue in anything like their traditional role. Patterns of travel and recreation now were dominated by automotive tourism at a greatly increased scale. The situation seemed to require replacing older hotels, which had been built for railroad and early automotive tourism, with "motel type" park lodges, which would more efficiently serve larger numbers of tourists and their cars and provide the "modern conveniences" the public demanded. Under these pressures, many concessions that had originally been family businesses or railroad subsidiaries began to reorganize or sell out, often to larger businesses that specialized in hotel and restaurant management. In 1954 the Santa Fe Railroad abandoned its businesses on the south rim of the Grand Canyon, donating many of its utility buildings to the government and selling its interest in El Tovar and the Bright Angel Lodge to the reorganized Fred Harvey Company. The Yosemite Park & Curry Company went through a series of management changes in the 1940s and 1950s, and the Great Northern Railroad sold out at Glacier National Park in 1960. Political and financial difficulties with the concession system persisted throughout Mission 66. After 1956 Congress required its own review and approval of all park concession contracts involving gross annual revenues over $100,000. Banks, which replaced railroad companies as a source of capital to finance improvements, were cautious about making loans secured only by possessory interest. In 1960 the Park Service prepared legislation that would have provided federal mortgage guarantees for concessioners, and the next year suggested the creation of a special federal fund to finance development directly. Neither scheme was enacted. Congress again conducted investigations into the concession system in 1962, and that year the Outdoor Recreation Resources Review Commission recommended maintaining the system of private construction and ownership "where feasible." In 1965 Congress passed the Concession Policy Act, which finally gave legislative recognition to possessory interest and the preferential renewal of contracts.[16] Once these rights were assured, banks more readily loaned money against the future earning potential of contracts. But at least some concessioners had difficulty securing loans to meet their investment obligations under Mission 66.

In 1953, 173 national park concessions grossed $32 million. Total concessioner assets were reported at $60 million in 1957.[17] When Wirth and his policy makers began Mission 66 planning, they never seriously considered abandoning the park concession system, despite its inherent problems. Such an effort would have been unlikely to succeed at a time when concessioners had just organized to protect their interests. The Eisenhower administration also sought to expand the role of the private sector, not eliminate it. But the Mission 66 policy memoranda and the "pilot prospectus" developed for Mount Rainier implied radical change for park concessions all the same. Converting parks from overnight destinations to day use suggested that many older park hotels would be bought out and demolished as contracts expired. In cases where visitors could easily find accommodations outside park boundaries, there would be no need for park lodges. The 1956 Mission 66 report stated that overnight concession services would be provided "only in those areas where required for proper and appropriate park experience, and where those services cannot be furnished satisfactorily in neighboring communities."[18] This goal conflicted directly with the interests of concessioners, for whom overnight stays were often considered desirable and even necessary aspects of their business models. Motel rooms brought in greater profits than stores, restaurants, and snack bars. Overnight accommodations ensured longer visits, too, which in turn increased business for these other services. The public also had expectations of not just visiting parks but staying overnight at or near favorite park destinations.

The political influence and contractual rights of park concessioners, often combined with the expectations of park visitors, made it difficult to remove overnight accommodations in many parks. In June 1955 Wirth had already begun to modify the tone of Mission 66 policy in this regard. The first of the "principles" distributed that month to guide the preparation of pilot prospectuses was to secure "greater participation of private enterprise." In part, this meant that demand for visitor services would be met by private businesses outside park boundaries; but it also provided assurance that new concessioner investments would be a major feature of Mission 66. The second principle listed in the memorandum stated that the relocation of overnight facilities away from "major park features" would be required in many cases. This policy stopped far short of suggesting that all hotels be removed from parks. Every situation would be considered "on its own merits," and while in some cases overnight concessions might indeed be removed, in others they would merely be relocated, and in fact "recommended for considerable expansion."[19]

The June 1955 "principles" not only reflected the political realities of dealing with the park concession system, but also were influenced by events already under way as Mission 66 was being planned. At Yellowstone, in particular, negotiations over the critical and expansive role of the park's concessioner would affect the future of the entire Mission 66 program. Since at least 1948, the year Yellowstone broke the 1 million visitor mark, Park Service officials had plans for a complete modernization of the park's roads and overnight facilities. But neither Congress nor the embattled concessioner, William Nichols, could be persuaded to make such investments at the time. Negotiations at Yellowstone, as previously noted, reached a critical point in the spring of 1955, just as Mission 66 planning got under way. With the Yellowstone Park Company's twenty-year contract set to expire at the end of the year, Wirth and the park's staff clearly hoped that Nichols would soon be replaced, possibly by several new concessioners, more willing to invest.

As Yellowstone historian Aubrey L. Haines observes, Nichols was "in a mood to sell out" in 1955 but had not found a buyer. But now he needed to renew his contract if his family's franchise were to remain salable, and the terms of any new contract would mean his becoming a full, if reluctant, partner in the implementation of Mission 66.[20] That August, Nichols secured a large bank loan and hired Welton Becket and Associates of Los Angeles to assemble proposals for three developed areas with motel complexes and other services. The proposed developments followed the outline of the draft Mission 66 prospectus for the park, and were in turn reflected in preliminary site designs from the park's master plan. A new developed area named Canyon Village would replace the Canyon Hotel, a massive wooden structure that encroached on the rim of the Grand Canyon of the Yellowstone. Thumbay (renamed Grant Village in 1956 in honor of Ulysses S. Grant) would enlarge and replace facilities considered too close to the West Thumb geyser basin. Bridge Bay was planned for an area near the Lake Hotel, again in order to expand capacity and allow the removal of some older development, in this case in the Fishing Bridge and Lake areas.[21] As Wirth prepared to unveil Mission 66 at the Smoky Mountains conference that September, the Yellowstone concessioner and his architect presented plans and received preliminary approval to proceed. That spring, Nichols signed a new twenty-year contract based on an initial commitment of $3.5 million to develop Canyon Village with five hundred motel units, employee dormitories, and a lodge building that would house a cafeteria, restaurant, and other services. On June 25, 1956, just days before the new fiscal year initiated the first official government spending on Mission 66 construction, Canyon Village became the first Mission 66 project to break ground. It was scheduled on a "fast track" to be opened the following summer. Indeed, the Park Service had already completed site preparation, including roads and utilities, and the contractor was working off-site on prefabricated motel units.

Wirth made the Canyon Village groundbreaking ceremony the first of many celebrations of Mission 66 progress. He also used the event to publicize the final version of the Mission 66 prospectus for Yellowstone, which had been delayed pending the results of negotiations with Nichols. In anticipation of 2 million annual visits by 1966 (the actual figure would be only slightly higher), the 1956 prospectus called for $17.5 million in government spending and a total concessioner investment of $13.5 million over ten years. After Lon Garrison took over as Yellowstone superintendent the next year, the estimates were revised upwards to $55 million and $15 million, respectively. The prospectus also "anticipated" an increase in the park's operations budget from $1.5 million to $2.2 million over the same period. On the government side, the number of campground sites would be increased from 490 to 1,420, serving up to six thousand campers at a time. Relocated and enlarged, the new campgrounds would feature amphitheaters, coordinated interpretive displays and activities, and modern comfort stations and utilities. Several "rental trailer courts" would finally be built, despite the misgivings of Park Service staff. The Grand Loop road system would not be extended (neither would it be significantly curtailed), but it would be widened and modernized everywhere. Many bridges were to be replaced, and some sections of roadway were to be relocated away from sensitive areas, such as Old Faithful and the shore of Yellowstone Lake. Several new visitor centers (including one at Canyon Village) and entrance stations would be built, and interpretive displays, trails, and signage would be erected in every developed area. Parking and roadside areas would be expanded, and some fifty new picnic areas were planned. Staffing would be increased, and the critical dearth of park housing would be addressed. Maintenance and shop buildings would be funded, and sewerage, power lines, and other utilities would be constructed throughout the park.

On the concessioner side, the total capacity for overnight accommodations in the park would rise from about eight thousand to about fourteen thousand, beginning with the motel complex at Canyon Village. Garrison pointed out that since visitors needed to stay in the park "at least a week" to appreciate it fully, overnight accommodations in the park were still considered necessary. They would also have to be expanded, just like the other facilities in the park, to serve the nearly twice as many visitors expected in 1966. But the new park "lodges" would not be "fancy hotels," like the Old Faithful Inn. The public wanted motels that were "simple, but as comfortable and convenient as possible." They were not to be attractions in themselves but a "means to an end" and would not compete with—or encroach on—the natural wonders of the park. The existing hotels would "remain during their useful life," but then they would be demolished along with their associated roads and development as new motels were completed. Stores, gas stations, and other commercial buildings would complement the motels. "Cafeterias, lunch counters, and coffee shop services" would be provided instead of expensive restaurants. All of this would be done, Wirth promised in his remarks at the groundbreaking, "without intrusion upon the sacred areas of scenic beauty and natural wonders, or the wilderness appeal of this vast area. In fact, the greatest contribution MISSION 66 will make to Yellowstone is the restoration, insofar as possible, of the natural setting in these [older hotel] areas."[22]

The Yellowstone prospectus described an entirely new "development pattern" for the park, one that had been conceived around the reality of high-volume, middle-class automotive tourism, and the decision that overnight accommodations were still necessary within park boundaries. Canyon Village became the first example of "motel type" concessioner lodgings planned as part of an entirely new, Mission 66 developed area. The project had been on the boards, however, for at least twenty years. Park Service officials had long considered the Canyon Hotel and the structures near it to be egregious intrusions on some of the most treasured scenery in the park. The developed area included the massive hotel itself (1911), as well as a store, cafeteria, campgrounds, horse corrals, and dozens of cabins, all clustered on both sides of the Grand Canyon immediately around the best points for viewing the spectacular Upper and Lower falls of the Yellowstone. Park staff, working with Vint's office, had made the removal of the Canyon Hotel and the development around it part of their master plans since 1935. At that time they suggested developing a new park village nearby that could provide services in a less conspicuous way. The basic concept was comparable to the plans made ten years earlier for replacing the "Old Village" in Yosemite Valley with the new Yosemite Village. But in the early 1920s, when Vint was helping chief landscape architect Daniel R. Hull plan Yosemite Village, they chose the new site in part because of its commanding views of Yosemite Falls and other famous features. The new Yosemite Village "harmonized" by being a picturesque element of the stunning landscape surrounding it in the heart of the valley.[23] Ten years later at Yellowstone, Vint and the park staff again sought to replace "poorly planned" development with a new village. But in this case the plans indicated a growing concern for more complete protection of park scenery, a change typical of Vint's attitudes by the late 1930s. The site for the new Canyon Village had no significant views, but it did have the virtue of being completely screened by stands of lodgepole pine. The awesome and "sensitive" scenery of the canyon could therefore be restored, at least visually, to "natural" conditions.

Park Service regional staff, together with park landscape architect Frank Mattson, devised the plans for Canyon Village, which Wirth and Vint, as always, reviewed in detail. The development was located about a mile away from the rim of the canyon, at an important crossroads. In Yellowstone's Grand Loop road system, a single transverse road connected the geyser basins on the west side of the loop to the canyon area

on the east side. Canyon Village was planned around the intersection on the east side. In postwar versions of the proposed plan, the intersection itself divided the developed area into functional zones: central parking and motel complex, campgrounds, and Park Service maintenance. A gas station was sited directly at the intersection, which also featured turning lanes. By the early 1950s the central plaza was described in master plan drawings as "parking," with a new lodge and other public buildings forming a

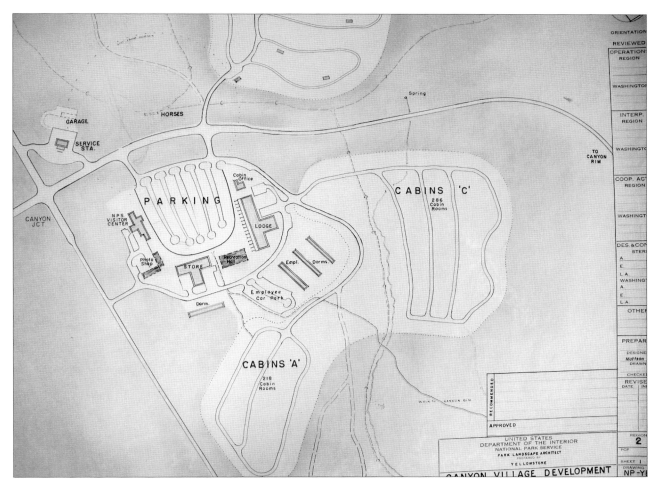

Master plan sheet showing Canyon Village development plans, Yellowstone. Yellowstone National Park Archives.

horseshoe around three sides of it.[24] Park village planning was gradually taking on a more efficient, automobile-oriented form. While it had clearly developed from earlier park village design, the need to accommodate larger numbers of cars, larger campgrounds, and up to five hundred motel units led to a more decentralized, sprawling plan. Every aspect of the development was predicated on the universal and pervasive use of automobiles.

In its location, scale, layout, and functionality, the early 1950s Park Service design for Canyon Village began to resemble a contemporary shopping center complex. This was done mainly in order to channel and serve large numbers of automotive tourists efficiently in one strategic location, and thereby minimize their impact on the scenery. The subsequent choice of a proven shopping center designer as the consulting architect for the project, however, indicated how the Yellowstone Park Company—and perhaps the Los Angeles bank lending millions of dollars—perceived the economic potential of the situation. Welton Becket was a pio-

neer in the design of postwar retail complexes in California. The Stonestown Shopping Center in San Francisco was an early and influential success for his office in 1949, and subsequently he planned many similar projects based on the model of "stores clustered around a central mall."[25] At Canyon Village, Becket designed the central lodge building with a massive shingled roof with eaves that extended down beyond the extensively glazed walls. Dramatic "glu-lam" roof beams extended beyond the eaves all the way down to concrete anchors set in the ground, forming a covered arcade around the exterior of the building. The prefabricated motel units, laid out along access drives behind the lodge, were assembled in attached radial clusters. Of inexpensive construction with rectangular plans and flat roofs, the motel units were unexceptional but convenient, and equipped with modern utilities. Two other park concessioners who invested in Canyon Village also hired Becket to design their buildings, the Hamilton Store and the Haynes Photographic Shop. Becket used the same materials and pitched roofs in these build-

Canyon Lodge, designed by Welton Becket and Associates, opened in Yellowstone in 1957.
Author's photo.

Canyon Lodge, Yellowstone.
Author's photo.

Lunch counter, Canyon Village, Yellowstone. Author's photo.

Canyon Village Visitor Center, Yellowstone, opened in 1958. Author's photo.

Canyon Village, Yellowstone. Author's photo.

Motel units, Canyon Village, Yellowstone. Author's photo.

ings as in the lodge, creating a unified visual theme. All the larger buildings of the complex featured high ceilings and extensive open floor space. The buildings featured little or no ornamental detail, and were similarly economical in their construction, which consisted of "slump block" precast concrete units, stone veneer over the concrete, and wood framing and sheathing. The massive, asymmetrically pitched roofs and unusually shaped large windows, especially in the gable ends of buildings, gave Canyon Village a "contemporary" look. In 1958 the Park Service

built a new visitor center in a complementary style, directly across the plaza from the lodge at the main public entrance to the horseshoe plaza.[26]

The Park Service completed site improvements at Canyon Village with a broad sidewalk connecting the main buildings, and with long islands planted with naturalized groups of native trees and shrubs in the parking lot. The planted islands separated and screened individual parking corridors, breaking up and concealing the lot's full extent. Park Service landscape architects also laid out an extensive campground, already opened by the summer of 1956, which Wirth was able to point to at the groundbreaking ceremony as an indication of things to come elsewhere in the park. Sewers, water and electric lines, roads, and lighting all were completed by Park Service contractors as the concessioner's builders went to work. The entire complex was, Wirth remarked hopefully at that time, a demonstration of "the ability of private capital to work in harmonious cooperation with the Federal Government to provide for the betterment of the parks." Indeed, with the concessioner supposedly committed to shouldering a significant portion of the cost of modernizing Yellowstone, Wirth had reason to consider the Canyon Village groundbreaking a major success. Newspapers from San Francisco to Denver picked up on the enthusiasm of the day, impressed by the extent of the commitment of private capital as well as the breadth and ambition of the redevelopment plans for the nation's oldest national park.[27]

But if the Canyon Village groundbreaking launched the construction phase of Mission 66 optimistically, the subsequent construction and operation of the Canyon Lodge ran into trouble from the start. Nichols had secured bank funding and hired an eminent architectural firm, but his Yellowstone Park Company, a family-directed business that had been operating in the park since 1891, proved incapable of supervising construction on such a large project. By the end of the summer, bank financing had to be increased to $5 million because of cost overruns. That fall Nichols stepped down as the head of the Yellowstone Park Company in favor of his son, and the

company board was reorganized to include non–family members. The next summer the official opening of the lodge was delayed from July 1 until August 31, the very end of the season. During the summer of 1958, Canyon Village was finally operational (if not entirely completed), but still had problems filling its motel rooms to capacity and making a profit. Demolition of the old Canyon Hotel began in 1959, in part to encourage the public to stay at the new Canyon Lodge instead. But the cost of the motel complex, as well as operational difficulties with running it, pushed the Yellowstone Park Company to the verge of bankruptcy. In 1959 the board was reorganized again, and now included a representative of the Los Angeles bankers worried about a default on their loan.[28] Continued financial and management woes at the Yellowstone Park Company made full participation in subsequent Mission 66 plans impossible.

In the fall of 1956 Lon Garrison replaced Edmund Rogers as superintendent of Yellowstone, indicating the importance Wirth placed on making progress there. Despite the Yellowstone Park Company's obvious difficulties, Wirth and Garrison tried to press on with the Mission 66 concession plans for the park, perhaps believing that the company could build its way out of its dilemma. The next motel complex in the prospectus was Grant Village, which Frank Mattson had first suggested in 1946 to replace the tourist cabins, store, campground, and other facilities located directly on the edge of the West Thumb geyser basin. Early 1950s master plans show the proposed West Thumb Lakeshore development about two and a half miles south of the geyser basin, and resembling Canyon Village in general layout. After it became part of the Mission 66 prospectus, clearing and grading of the site began in 1956. But further preparations were delayed as efforts were concentrated on Canyon Village. The prospectus suggested that the now renamed Grant Village would eventually be even larger than Canyon Village, with nine hundred motel units and lodge services such as a cafeteria, a coffee shop, and a gas station. In addition, the Park Service would build another extensive campground, a trailer court, employee housing, and a lakeshore marina for the growing numbers of boaters demanding access to Yellowstone Lake. But the Yellowstone Park Company, struggling to pay off the debt incurred at Canyon Village, could not (or would not) secure the millions of dollars of financing that would be required to develop Grant Village. Further site preparations and development paid for by the Park Service did get under way in 1961, and the campground and other public facilities were officially opened in the summer of 1963. Other structures, including employee housing, a gas station, and a marina services building, were soon added. The motel complex at Grant Village, however, would continue to be mired in controversy throughout Mission 66, and in fact for decades to come. While the Park Service put millions of Mission 66 dollars "into the ground" at Grant Village, preparing the site with roads, utilities, a marina, campground, and visitor center, the concessioner resisted making any investment. In 1966 the Nichols family finally managed to sell their remaining interest in their franchise, but the corporation that bought them out also avoided making any major capital investment at Grant Village or anywhere else in the park.[29]

In the meantime, most of the Mission 66 program for Yellowstone that did not involve concessioners went ahead as planned. But the situations at both Canyon Village and Grant Village indicated a broader problem with concessioner construction under Mission 66. The entire business of park concessioning had changed, and the collaborative relationship that had existed between the Park Service and private entrepreneurs had broken down. The Yellowstone Park Company was effectively bankrupted by the enormous strain of making

Bridge Bay marina, Yellowstone. Author's photo.

Road construction in 1958, Yellowstone. NPS Historic Photo Collection.

such a large investment at Canyon Village, and the company simply could not cope with the new scale and type of business operations it had undertaken. Mission 66 only exacerbated an already deteriorating situation; the inherent problems with the park concession system went back at least to the 1940s. But Wirth and his planners erred by maintaining a concession system that was in need of reform. Once again, Mission 66 proceeded within the political limitations of its day, without comprehensive new federal legislation that would have addressed fundamental problems. Reform came only later, in this case with the Concession Policy Act of 1965, and then finally with the federal purchase of the Yellowstone concessioner's possessory interest in 1979.[30]

But there was another, more profound problem with Mission 66 concessioner planning, and this involved how and when overnight accommodations were made part of park prospectuses. The final 1956 Mission 66 report confirmed a fundamental precept of prospectus planning: where possible, gateway towns, not park concessioners, should provide overnight accommodations. But the final report also stated that out of thirty large parks that together had an overnight capacity of 25,750, only four would have their lodgings phased out, since apparently only they were "favorably located to permit private enterprise to provide accommodations outside." In the other twenty-six, overnight concessions would not simply remain but be expanded in anticipation of the 80 million visitors expected in 1966. An overly simple formula was then used to determine future market demand. The existing ratio of overnight to day use visitors in the

twenty-six large parks with overnight concessions was about 1 to 3.8. But since "a greater proportion of all visitors would use lodgings if more were available," the ration of 1 to 3 was considered "more satisfactory." In the twenty-six parks, Mission 66 called for an increase in total overnight capacity from 23,797 to 58,797; in Yellowstone the figure rose from 8,417 to 13,891.[31]

This very limited analysis was used as the basis for investing both private and public funds in new "motel-type" park lodges. At Yellowstone and Yosemite, these lodges were among the earliest Mission 66 projects, and they made a considerable public impression. But the construction of massive motel complexes contradicted an original, central goal of Mission 66: to reduce the impact of large numbers of visitors by redeveloping parks more as day use destinations. Mission 66 planners had observed the growth of motels and other services in gateway towns, and they understood how improved highways would increase visitor mobility. Nevertheless, Mission 66 concession planning did not make a bold break from prewar policy. Instead it proposed greatly expanding the established concession system.

In the end, this expansion did not take place. Later market studies indicated that, at least at Yellowstone, such ambitions were not even supported by sound business plans. While visits to the park had doubled between 1940 and 1959, the Yellowstone Park Company found that the percentage of visitors staying in hotels and cabins had dropped by half, from 84 to 42 percent, during the same period.[32] The economics of park concessions—and of automotive tourism generally—had permanently changed. Park visitors had more options and mobility than ever before. While Wirth and Garrison pressured the Yellowstone Park Company to build additional motel units, the concessioner could not even profitably fill the reduced number of Canyon Village rooms that had already been built. As was the case in other parks, remote location and high elevation combined to create high construction costs and short seasons. Competitors in gateway towns, such as West Yellowstone, could offer lower prices and more luxurious conveniences. They also had lower construction costs, longer seasons, and full title to their property for mortgage purposes. Older park hotels of course had the advantage of being in the park, and—since they encroached directly on its wonders—they could offer the attraction of Yellowstone itself. But the less intrusive Canyon Lodge could not, since it was intentionally sited away from "sensitive" scenery. The Yellowstone motel complexes were planned merely as "a means to an end," intended to be convenient but otherwise unexceptional. As historian Mark Barringer observes, under Mission 66 the Yellowstone Park Company "stopped selling the park, their most valuable asset, and began selling motel rooms and cafeteria meals. And they lost the ability to make themselves part of the Yellowstone experience."[33]

National park hotels had never been a "means to an end." They embodied vacation fantasy and the appeal of mythic historical themes, and they were indeed part of the "Yellowstone experience." Welton Becket's Canyon Lodge, a masterly adaptation of modernist architectural design, served its functions efficiently. But it could not hope to "harmonize," specifically in this sense, because it was stripped of associative ornamentation and was purposefully located to avoid becoming a compositional element of park scenery. By protecting the scenery, in other words, Wirth and Vint had ensured that the new concession areas would never be accepted as part of it, at least not the way an earlier generation of hotels had. Mission 66 park development, which was planned in more remote areas to minimize its impact on park landscapes, ironically was criticized for not being more a part of those landscapes—for not "harmonizing." Devereux Butcher, in particular, blamed the modernist idiom of the architecture. But the increasingly alienated relationship of architecture to the surrounding landscape—arguably a central characteristic of modernist landscape design and planning—had far more influence on the perception of Canyon Village than the style or details of the structures themselves.

In any case, the Mission 66 goal of increasing the "pillow count" in Yellowstone to 14,000 never came close to being realized. The park's overnight capacity remained close to what it had been: 8,700 in 1964, and about 9,000 in 1972.[34] Other concession developments in other parks also provided the "motel type" lodges that the Park Service felt people wanted. In 1963, however, systemwide overnight concessioner capacity still stood at about 27,000. As at Yellowstone, Mission 66 concessioner developments in most cases did little more than replace older hotel rooms.[35] Mission 66 did not substantially increase the total capacity of overnight facilities in the parks, despite considerable efforts to do so. But why did Wirth and his planners try to expand concessioner accommodations to the extent they did? Barringer, a trenchant recent critic of Mission 66, insists that a blind adherence to agency "tradition" prevented them from embracing alternative approaches, such as limiting and eventually reducing lodging in Yellowstone.[36] But "traditional" Park Service planners, above all Vint, had argued for years that the agency should at all costs avoid the problems of "Plan A," typified by situations such as the Canyon Hotel and the Yosemite Lodge. Mission 66 planners had begun by making observations and gathering data that would have supported the policies Vint and others put forward. The only tradition Wirth, Vint, and their colleagues truly venerated was the conviction that parks were to be preserved for public enjoyment. At least in 1955, neither Wirth nor Vint believed that public enjoyment necessitated overnight lodgings, which were increasingly available outside parks. The landscape architects at the Park Service were in fact very willing to pursue alternative strategies as long as they allowed continued "enjoyment without impairment," and this spirit imbued the initial Mission 66 effort.

The realities of congressional and local politics in the 1950s, however, also influenced Mission 66 concession policy in its final form. This was the situation at Everglades National Park in 1955, when both the new concessioner and much of the public objected to Mission 66 plans that included a restaurant and marina but not a park lodge. Wirth held his ground, even when the concessioner halved the amount he was willing to invest. He reversed his decision, however, when he was attacked not only by local elected officials, business leaders, and newspaper edi-

tors but also by both Florida senators and the local congressman, all of whom demanded that the Everglades plan provide for a national park experience "comparable" to that of other national parks. Wirth could not resist that kind of pressure, at least not if he hoped to be successful with appropriations committees. And Wirth was, above all, skilled in congressional politics. He shaped Mission 66—including its concessioner policies—to reverse fifteen years of congressional indifference. In this sense his policies succeeded. But it was not Park Service "tradition" so much as the demands of the public, the influence and rights of concessioners, and the power of federal and local elected officials that perpetuated the national park concession system in the postwar period.

Concessioner developments were only a small part of Mission 66, but they had great impact on public perceptions of the program during its first years. For early critics of Mission 66, the construction of "motel type" lodges confirmed their fears that the Park Service had made too many compromises—or perhaps had never been on the right track at all—in facing the challenges presented by postwar automotive tourism. At Yosemite as well as Yellowstone, a new and expanded park lodge was the first substantial construction project begun under Mission 66. In this case, Vint had been arguing since 1945 for the removal, not the rebuilding, of Yosemite Lodge. The narrow confines of Yosemite Valley (about seven miles long and one mile wide) made the entire area a "sensitive" destination. As previously noted, Vint's postwar recommendations for Yosemite Valley constituted his "Plan B": the removal of the lodge, along with Park Service administrative offices and many other facilities, out of the valley and perhaps out of the park.

The negative effects of concessioner development in Yosemite Valley had been noted since the 1870s. The valley's remote location made transporting supplies expensive, and in order to serve their clientele, early hotel operators had drained, plowed, and planted many of the valley's meadows. To protect their buildings, they took steps to control flooding and suppress fires on the valley floor. In his 1865 management recommendations, Frederick Law Olmsted had foreseen how destructive such homesteading would be to the landscape, and he therefore urged the construction of an improved road for better access back to the steamboat docks at Stockton. If transportation costs were lowered in this way, both tourists and supplies could be brought in and out cheaply, making it less necessary to cultivate the valley floor or to build elaborate overnight accommodations. Visiting Yosemite would also be more affordable for all. But Olmsted's report was not implemented by the park's first board of state commissioners. The construction of the suggested road would be expensive, and the board did not want to eliminate potentially lucrative opportunities for private investors to build hotels and other establishments. Much of the valley floor soon became a pattern of cultivated fields surrounded by stands of ponderosa pine, which in the absence of fire rapidly colonized the now drier soils. By the 1880s the open landscape of scattered oaks and flood-prone meadows—the landscape Olmsted described and Watkins and Bierstadt made famous—had begun to disappear.

The larger Yosemite National Park was created around Yosemite Valley in 1890, and in 1906 the valley itself reverted to federal jurisdiction and became part of the national park. But the valley remained by far the principal attraction, and with the advent of automotive tourism complaints of overcrowding within its narrow confines became chronic. Stephen Mather's interest in the national park system, in fact, was first sparked by the scandalous conditions he found while visiting Yosemite Valley. The early policies he shaped for the Park Service attempted to correct the situation by reorganizing concession interests, by using concessioner capital to build the Ahwahnee and the Yosemite Lodge, and by planning a new Yosemite Village to replace the ramshackle "Old Village." The "All-Year" highway from the gateway town of El Portal into the valley was completed in 1926. The Park Service facilitated early automotive tourism, in other words, but also hoped to ameliorate its negative effects through planned developments that helped control how and where people drove, camped, hiked, swam, and enjoyed the scenery. This was what Thomas Vint described in the 1940s as "Plan A." But conditions of overcrowding in Yosemite Valley now promised to become unmanageable. Like Yellowstone, Yosemite was expected to record 2 million visits by 1966. But at Yellowstone those visitors would be spread over the hundreds of miles of roads and several major destination areas. At Yosemite, 95 percent of them were headed directly to the east end of the valley. For Vint, a radical change was in order, and he attempted to infuse Mission 66 with that new and controversial attitude. The inspiration for what became known as the "Vint Plan" (or "Plan B") captured the essence of Olmsted's 1865 report: make the valley a camping and day use destination, and rely on improved roads to get people and supplies in and out efficiently. Public access should not be restricted, and would not need to be, because the correct development plan would make it possible for millions to enjoy the landscape without destroying it.

Park planning at Yosemite, however, has always involved many interest groups and many points of view. The Yosemite Park & Curry Company, for example, wielded great influence through its director, Donald B. Tressider, who in 1943 stepped down to become president of Stanford University. Yosemite was also unique in that since 1928 it had its own Board of Expert Advisors (usually called simply the Advisory Board), made up of leading conservationists with tremendous experience. Over the years the three-member group included Frederick Law Olmsted Jr., the architect and developer Duncan McDuffie, the geologist John P. Buwalda, and longtime Sierra Club official William E.

Colby. In August 1945 Drury challenged the Advisory Board to consider Vint's proposal to remove development from the valley. But in 1946 the Advisory Board members reported that although they were "wholly in sympathy with the purposes of the Vint Plan," they could not endorse it. The valley was the "heart of the park," the primary destination for almost all visitors. Removing the lodge and other public facilities seemed "too great a sacrifice to make." By 1947 the Advisory Board was involved in discussing not whether the Yosemite Lodge should be rebuilt but where in the valley and how large the new lodge should be.[37]

In the spring of 1949, although Vint's master plan still called for the relocation of overnight accommodations, Drury approved designs for the reconstruction of the Yosemite Lodge in Yosemite Valley. The Yosemite Park & Curry Company, however, made it clear that it would not invest in new buildings until the contemporary controversy over concession contracts was settled. But unlike the Yellowstone Park Company, the Yosemite concessioner was eager to ex-

The new Yosemite Lodge, designed by Eldridge Spencer, opened in 1956 and replaced the former lodge on the same site. Author's photos.

pand, and general manager Hilmer Oehlmann asked architect Eldridge Spencer to continue revising plans for a new lodge. Spencer and his wife, the designer Jeannette Spencer, already had a long association with Yosemite. Jeannette Spencer had worked with Ansel Adams in the late 1920s designing the first Bracebridge pageants at the Ahwahnee. In the 1940s she redesigned these seasonal celebrations, and her husband oversaw the conversion of the Ahwahnee from naval hospital back to hotel. While the park's Mission 66 prospectus was still being prepared, Eldridge Spencer's plans for the new lodge, on the same site as the old one, were already complete. At that point Oehlmann moved quickly to secure over $1 million in bank financing and received approval to begin construction. The new Yosemite Lodge opened in time for the 1956 season. Like Canyon Lodge in Yellowstone, it featured a central service building with associated groups of motel units. Spencer designed a series of four low buildings with redwood sheathing, connected by covered walkways. Projecting eaves, large windows, and a dearth of ornamental details gave the complex a "contemporary" look. Some of the older cabins were retained in the new complex, and other motel units were later added, more than doubling the concessioner's investment. Yosemite Lodge suffered few of the financial and management problems that plagued Canyon Village, and since it was a redevelopment of an existing lodge (and remained close to the visitor facilities of Yosemite Village), it did not require extensive construction for utilities, roads, or other new services.[38]

Eldridge Spencer is best known today for his extensive work for the Yosemite concessioner,

particularly during Mission 66. Wirth and other Park Service officials admired Spencer's work, and in 1956 Rockefeller's Jackson Hole Preserve, Inc., hired him to lay out the Colter Bay development in Grand Teton National Park, a concession cabin and camping area that was intended to complement the services at the Jackson Lake Lodge.[39] Guided by Mission 66 plans, Yosemite concessioners also made significant investments to redevelop Yosemite Village at this time. In 1958 Degnan's, a restaurant and small food store, moved into a dramatic A-frame structure in the center of the village. A "merchandise center," including a market, clothing store, restaurant, and barber shop, was completed in the winter of 1959. Designed by Spencer, the building cost the Yosemite Park & Curry Company over $800,000. Spencer also designed staff

Degnan's store and restaurant, designed by Eldridge Spencer, opened in 1958 in Yosemite Village. Author's photo.

residences, a large warehouse, and other buildings. By the spring of 1959 the redevelopment of Yosemite Village allowed the Park Service to complete the demolition of the Old Village (on the other side of the Merced River), which had been a goal since the first new village plans were devised in 1914. That May, Wirth, Spencer, the park concessioner, and others celebrated the opening of the merchandise center, which was the centerpiece of the expanded Yosemite Village. In 1967 Spencer designed a large visitor center for the Park Service, completing the transformation of the area.[40]

Although the redevelopment of the Yosemite Lodge and Yosemite Village created exactly the kind of "drift" toward overdevelopment that Vint feared, aspects of the 1945 "Vint Plan" for the valley survived and were incorporated into the Mission 66 prospectus. Just as Mission 66 planning got under way, the Park Service had acquired 972 acres at the western entrance to the park, including the small former mining settlement of El Portal. Describing the acquisition as "a dream come true," the prospectus called for a major relocation of valley administrative offices, staff residences, and maintenance buildings to a new "operating base" to be located there. Many Park Service families had lived in El Portal for years, but the area was now to be expanded into a "model community" with all necessary services. The development of El Portal would make possible one of the primary goals described in the draft prospectus: to "move facilities out of Yosemite Valley . . . leaving only those facilities which are necessary and essential." Early drafts of the prospectus had a particularly preservationist tone. The first objective cited was the "freez-

ing of developments . . . not to exceed their present capacity." Final (1957) versions of the prospectus specified that "all accommodations for visitors and related services shall be limited to designated areas" and would not be allowed to sprawl beyond the established footprint of development. The Park Service and its concessioners could no longer "continue to build, construct and develop operating facilities on the Valley floor without seriously impairing and ultimately destroying" the unique landscape.[41]

These injunctions to freeze development obviously did not pertain to the redevelopment of the Yosemite Lodge and Yosemite Village, projects already under way thanks to concessioner capital. But even if the valley's "pillow count" (including campgrounds) remained at about 4,500, the prospectus acknowledged that the valley's day capacity would need to be expanded. "An adequate road and trail system; adequate facilities for the comfort and welfare of the visitor; and effective presentation and interpretation of the diversified resources of Yosemite" were all considered necessary to handle the anticipated influx. For its part the Park Service planned to spend over $22 million on road improvements, campgrounds, and other facilities throughout the park. To alleviate crowding in the valley, alternative destinations would be expanded. "Trailer courts" were planned for El Portal and Wawona. A "pioneer interpretive and information center" was developed at Wawona, involving the relocation of historic structures from different areas of the park into a "pioneer village." The number of campsites inside the valley was to remain at 2,500, but outside the valley campgrounds would be tripled to 2,400 sites.

Wirth (seated with glasses) examining Mission 66 plans for Yosemite in 1956. Lawrence Merriam is to Wirth's left and Superintendent John Preston is to his right, pointing. NPS Historic Photo Collection.

The potential of redirecting visitors to the Yosemite high country, along the Tioga Road corridor, was of particular interest. The White Wolf Lodge area was to be expanded, enhancing it as an alternate overnight destination. Soon there were plans for an enlarged campground and visitor center at Tuolumne Meadows as well, further relieving visitor pressure on the valley. "Perhaps no other area in the National Park System . . . [was] confronted with more difficult and complex problems," the prospectus planners noted. "The preservation and protection of the incomparable Yosemite Valley" was the foremost and most difficult problem of all.[42]

The Park Service relied on concessioner development at Yosemite, as at other parks, to implement key components of Mission 66 construction quickly. In general, concessioner development in Yosemite proceeded with few of

the problems being experienced at Yellowstone. At Mount Rushmore, Glacier, and Shenandoah, concessioners also built or expanded employee dormitories, public cafeterias, and other service buildings by 1957, apparently with relatively few problems. The controversial Flamingo development at Everglades was completed that year, and new motel units opened at Glacier as well. At Mount Rainier, the still contentious decision not to build new overnight accommodations at Paradise continued to be what Wirth described as the "major exception" to the "almost universally favorable" public reaction to Mission 66 that year. Much of the public response Wirth so hopefully characterized in this way was to construction projects that had been quickly undertaken by park concessioners.[43]

Other Mission 66 concessioner lodges included new complexes built at Grand Canyon,

Big Bend, and Glacier Bay national parks and the Blue Ridge Parkway.[44] On the south rim of the Grand Canyon, where Cecil Doty and other WODC architects designed one of the earliest examples of a visitor center, the Fred Harvey Company developed a new motel complex nearby, which also opened in 1957. Ninety-six motel units and a small central office building (replaced in 1972 by a larger lodge building) were sited along a loop road. Together with a vast campground and "trailer village" opened a few years later, the visitor center and lodge complex made up a new developed area, Mather Village (later called the Mather Business Zone), just east of the historic village of Grand Canyon.[45] Plans for shifting new visitor facilities to the east, away from the existing village—and away from the "sensitive" canyon rim—had been part of the park's master plan since at least 1950. The master plan also called for a relocation of the main automotive entrance to the area so that visitors would approach from the east, not the south. This realignment was completed in 1954. The master plan became the basis for the park's prospectus in 1956—the year that park visitation reached the 1 million mark—and construction continued throughout Mission 66 period, and in fact through the 1970s. By 1973 the "shopping plaza" between the visitor center and the Yavapai Lodge had been enlarged, completing what park historian Amanda Zeman documents as the park's "Mission 66 Village." Originally conceived in 1956 more along the lines of Canyon Village, the enlarged commercial area included a general store (1971), bank (1972), post office (1972), and several other buildings set around a large

and uninterrupted parking lot.[46] By the 1970s, however, it would have been difficult not to compare the Mather Business Zone with many other shopping plazas springing up across the country.

At both Big Bend and Glacier Bay national parks, relatively remote locations and low volume of visitors resulted in less construction of commercial concessioner lodges. Big Bend National Park was established in 1944, and initial development was minimal, although the CCC built park roads and a camp in the Chisos Basin while the area was still under state jurisdiction. Since the park was located in one of the most remote regions of the country, commercial possibilities for a concessioner were limited. Beginning in 1945 Ickes's nonprofit concessioner, National Park Concessions, Inc., provided overnight accommodations in the Chisos Basin, supplementing remaining CCC buildings with government surplus cabins. In 1950 the Park Service established an administrative area in the Panther Junction area by building staff residences and a maintenance area. But little else was done, and even the official dedication of the park was delayed until 1955. Soon thereafter Mission 66 called for $14 million in improvements at Big Bend, resulting in the first comprehensive scheme of development for the park. Over the next ten years the Park Service built a new visitor center, staff residences, and other facilities at Panther Junction, as well as secondary developed areas, roads, and utilities throughout the park. In 1966 the concessioner completed the new Chisos Mountains Lodge in the Chisos Basin, where the five thousand–foot elevation provided an island of cool moisture in the vast surrounding desert. The complex of modernist lodge building and surrounding motel units had an overnight capacity of 150. With an average of 80,000 visitors a year in the 1950s, and only 164,000 visits recorded in 1966, Big Bend never experienced the same visitor pressure—or the resulting controversies—as other big western parks. The Chisos Mountains Lodge, even after a later expansion, remains one of the best examples of the understated, efficient character that Mission 66 planners hoped such "motel type" lodgings could have.[47]

At Glacier Bay National Park, accessible only by boat and plane, plans for a park lodge went back at least to 1945. But again, the commercial potential for a concessioner was limited. Mission 66 built residences, local roads, and maintenance and administrative buildings in the Bartlett Cove area near the Gustavus airport, but lodge construction was delayed. In 1960 the Park Service invited potential concessioners to invest $150,000 in a lodge building, but none felt it was worth the risk. In 1964 Congress appropriated funds to pay directly for the construction of the Glacier Bay Lodge, the only example of public funding used to build overnight accommodations under Mission 66, and a private concessioner was then contracted to operate it. In many ways this was a more desirable scenario, since it removed the complications of possessory interest, bank loans, and the need to return profits on investments. Seattle architect John M. Morse, who had recently designed the Sitka National Historical Park visitor center, was hired to design what became perhaps the most striking of the Mission 66 national park lodges. Again the complex consisted of a

The expanded Chisos Mountains Lodge in Big Bend National Park opened in 1966. Author's photos.

Road construction in Big Bend in 1959. Photo by Jack E. Boucher, NPS Historic Photo Collection.

Glacier Bay Lodge, Glacier Bay National Park, Alaska, designed by John M. Morse in 1964. NPS Alaskan Regional Office, Anchorage.

central service building and surrounding motel units. In this case the surrounding rooms were connected by boardwalks that laced through the trees of the existing forest, helping to preserve the site and keep visitors dry in the exceptionally wet climate. The lodge building itself featured a massive pitched shingle roof and a large dining room with views across the cove to distant glaciers and mountains. The asymmetrical pitch of the roof (reminiscent of the outline of the Canyon Lodge in Yellowstone) cantilevered out over an outdoor deck. With its large windows, patterned wood sheathing, and period light fixtures and furniture, the Glacier Bay Lodge was a complete statement of modernist rusticity. More than any other Mission 66 lodge, it has retained the intended postwar aesthetic of Park Service architecture.[48]

Nevertheless, in many cases the question arose whether overnight concessioner lodges in national parks were not, as initially suggested by Mission 66 planners themselves, increasingly unnecessary and undesirable. While at truly remote locations, such as Big Bend and Glacier Bay, no alternative was likely to be available, this was less and less the case at Yellowstone, Everglades, Grand Canyon, Yosemite, the Blue Ridge Parkway, and other parks. When concessioner construction was combined with the improvement of park roads and the expansion of campgrounds, as well as new visitor centers, stores, and restaurants, it perhaps followed that as Mission 66 proceeded, more and more people saw the entire effort as a construction, not a conservation, program. As the economics of automotive tourism reached new heights in the postwar period, some critics felt that Mission 66 had given the tourist industry everything it could have asked for, all in the name of public "enjoyment."

To some degree, the idea of a "Mission 66 Village" that included concessioner accommodations contradicted some of the basic goals of the Mission 66 program. The prewar park village embodied that era's master planning strategy for dealing with what were then lower levels of automotive tourism. Postwar levels of use, everyone agreed, demanded new approaches. The business of park concessioning had changed, and the necessity for overnight accommodations in many parks was, arguably, disappearing. The Mission 66 modernist park—with its improved roads, expanded campgrounds, visitor centers, and roadside interpretation—offered a means of allowing a higher volume of automotive tourism without, it was hoped, sacrificing park resources. But the entire idea would be undermined if "Plan B" did not replace "Plan A" but instead was combined with it.

In hindsight, perhaps Mission 66 never should have been in the concession business. In fact, Wirth may have had no choice; the inherent compromises and intractable politics of the national park concessioner system, while exacerbated by Mission 66, were not created by it. In any case, compared to other aspects of the program, concessioner lodging was not a particularly large or significant category of development. In the end, there were just not that many new "motel type" lodges built in comparison, for example, to visitor centers, campgrounds, picnic areas, maintenance yards, or staff residences. But the expansion of the concessioner system struck at the heart of what Mission 66, at least in its most idealistic form, was intended to achieve. It also resulted in some of the worst examples of what critics cited as "overdevelopment."

It is worth considering, however, that the alternative to providing overnight accommodations in parks soon showed evidence of another, possibly even more destructive set of problems. At Great Smoky Mountains and Rocky Mountain national parks, where no overnight accommodations were built, the gateway towns of Gatlinburg and Estes Park grew into resorts anyway, limited only by the few land use regulations that local governments imposed. The development of West Yellowstone into a regional tourism center makes Canyon Village today seem quaint by comparison. Similarly, the fiercely debated sixty-unit motel at Flamingo seems innocuous enough compared to the general trends of urbanization in South Florida since then. Perhaps the greatest shortcoming of Mission 66 planning was that it failed to anticipate what regional economic development—especially the growth of gateway towns—would mean to the integrity of the national parks themselves in the long run. Where overnight accommodations were kept out, the result was simply more development pressure immediately outside the parks. National parks, as national attractions, generated economic activity in surrounding towns and counties; but Mission 66 planning usually stopped at park boundaries. While boundary expansions and the acquisition of private inholdings were often recommended and implemented, Park Service planners never anticipated that the future health of the park system would depend on engaging local communities as active partners in preserving larger ecosystems and regional scenic character. The concession system, and the whole problem of how and where postwar levels of automotive tourists would find lodgings, needed to be completely reconsidered on a regional basis. But it would have been asking a lot of Wirth and his planners to do so in the political and social climate of the 1950s. Such regional planning remains an elusive goal even today.

Wirth soon had other problems, in any case, that threatened to derail Mission 66 entirely. Concessioner developments such as Canyon Village generated a backlash, particularly among conservation groups. This negative reaction matured into a broader disapproval not just of a few concessioner motel complexes but of the entire Mission 66 program. In 1957, as the first products of Mission 66 were completed, the tone of criticism shifted. Devereux Butcher's shrill pronouncements on architectural aesthet- ics gave way to broader, more thoughtful, and more damaging judgments coming from other conservationists, many of whom had initially supported Mission 66. For this group, modernist architecture might or might not be appropriate; their concern was with preserving what they described as "wilderness" in the national park system. Wilderness had many definitions and connotations, which were endlessly parsed on both sides of the debate. But for wilderness advocates, in both common usage and legislative language, the term meant above all an area that was and would remain free from roads and the automotive tourists they conveyed.

For this group of advocates, therefore, Mission 66 road projects would be the target of their most intense denunciations. And after 1957, Mission 66 roads, more than any other type of development, generated controversy over the entire philosophy that underlay the Park Service's response to the postwar crisis in the parks.

CHAPTER 9

PARK ROADS AND WILDERNESS

Road construction had always shaped public park development plans. This was true in nineteenth-century municipal park designs, conceived around overlapping carriage drives and pedestrian paths, and it was true of prewar national park master planning, which to a considerable extent was the result of efforts to determine and limit the character and extent of roads in national parks.

In the late 1920s, when Horace Albright was setting Park Service "comprehensive planning" policy for future development in national parks, Thomas Vint asked that his division be put in charge of producing "master plans" through which every aspect of land use and development would be controlled—especially roads. Park development could proceed "on a Landscape or an Engineering basis," he told Albright. But if highway engineers were in charge, he warned, they would pursue an independent program of road construction outside the context of more

comprehensive plans for public use and landscape preservation. Roads were too important to be left to the engineers: they defined the overall pattern of public use and had enormous implications for how that use would affect parks. Roads themselves could be profoundly destructive, particularly if they were built to overly high standards or were located in ways that failed to minimize their presence, at least visually. Park roads, in other words, were not merely infrastructure to be efficiently engineered. They determined the level and location of access and use, and they were a principal mode of public perception of park landscapes. They were integral and essential components of design and needed to be planned as such.

Albright agreed, and Vint's landscape architecture division eventually became a division of planning, design, and construction, overseeing all aspects of park development. Throughout his career, many of Vint's most important design projects (and controversies) involved decisions about whether, and how, to build park roads. It was Vint's involvement in the Going-to-the-Sun Road, in Glacier National Park, in fact, that first established early policy on national park road design and construction standards. Vint personally persuaded Stephen Mather, while they were visiting the proposed road location in 1924, to adopt an alternative alignment that would reduce landscape scarring and create stunning experiences of park scenery for motorists. Going-to-the-Sun Road was the first major test of whether the Park Service would be able to control large and potentially destructive construction projects in the parks. Largely as a result of Vint's suggestions, observations, and protests, Mather fired his chief engineer and then entered into an "interbureau agreement" with the Bureau of Public Roads. This partnership with the federal road-building agency proved to be a successful collaboration between Park Service landscape architects, who maintained their priorities for how and where roads should be built, and the Bureau of Public Roads engineers, who made sure that roads were well conceived and that construction was carefully supervised. Vint's advance to become chief landscape architect in 1927 and the subsequent enforcement of his master planning procedures assured that most park road construction would proceed on a "Landscape basis." The roads built in the 1920s and 1930s, such as Going-to-the-Sun Road, Trail Ridge Road in Rocky Mountain National Park, and the Zion–Mt. Carmel Road in Zion National Park, survive as evidence of how successful these policies were.[1]

As noted earlier, Vint trained his own cadre of landscape architects in the Park Service, many of whom had strong preservationist tendencies. At Mount Rainier, Yosemite, and many other places, park superintendents or concessioners with ambitious plans for "scenic drives" or other development schemes found that agency landscape architects could be quick to oppose them, and that Vint would back up his staff from Washington. In a 1940 letter to Newton Drury, Vint reassured the incoming director that although Park Service landscape architects certainly dealt with "park development" (a subject Vint knew made Drury uneasy), they had their own peculiar ethos: "As a group each man feels he is a 'Non-Developer.' We take as much pride in heading off a project as we do in designing and building a necessary piece of work as best we can."[2]

Many of the projects Vint's park planners had "headed off" were roads. One of the principal characteristics of the national park master plan, as it took shape in the 1920s and afterwards, was that it amended earlier (pre-automobile) ideas about national park circulation systems. At Yellowstone, for example, the Grand Loop was built at the beginning of the century as just that: an extensive circuit of wagon roads that reached most of the popular destinations in the park. At Mount Rainier, in particular, Vint recognized that this type of road pattern would need to be rethought for the automotive age. Automobiles had a greater impact than horse-drawn wagons both on the roads themselves and on surrounding landscapes. More heavily engineered automotive roads required a wider corridor of excavation, and they conveyed larger numbers of tourists, resulting in higher levels of public use. A complete loop road around Mount

Rainier, as it was planned at the beginning of the century, would have far more deleterious effects in the 1920s than originally anticipated, since obviously by that time it would be engineered for cars, not wagons. As a result, Vint made sure that the new master plan for the park truncated the planned road system, and the "round-the-mountain" road was never built. A new road policy took shape in many other park master plans as well,. Each park would indeed need at least one great automotive road that would provide access to significant destinations and a meaningful overall experience of the park's landscape; but the parks would not be "gridironed" by highways. One scenic road would often be enough. A carefully planned road through a park could strike the necessary compromise between automotive access and landscape preservation.[3]

This was the context for the original planning of Tioga Road in Yosemite National Park, a project destined to become the single most controversial project of the Mission 66 program. The first Tioga Road had been scratched and blasted out of the High Sierra granite as a turnpike in 1883. The turnpike never succeeded commercially, but in 1890 it remained a private inholding when Congress established Yosemite National Park. The road cut directly across the middle of the new park, and there were soon calls to acquire and improve it in order to open the scenic High Sierra to access for recreation. Tolls were not being collected on the road, but neither was it being maintained by its private owners. To become a reliable route, it would have to be acquired and made part of the park. By 1909 this suggestion was picked up by the Sierra Club, the organization founded by John Muir and others in 1892 to "explore, enjoy, and render accessible the mountain regions of the Pacific Coast . . . [and] to enlist the support and cooperation of the people and the government in preserving . . . the Sierra Nevada Mountains." Sierra Club members were interested because Tioga Road offered access to Tuolumne Meadows, Tenaya Lake, and other high-country destinations. In 1915, when Stephen Mather arrived at the Department of the Interior, the acquisition and improvement of Tioga Road became a priority for him. In one of his earliest, signature successes, Mather talked a group of fellow national park advocates, local automobile clubs, and others into contributing money for the acquisition and maintenance of the road. Mather donated half of the needed $15,000 himself. Later that year the federal government received the road as a gift and opened it to automobiles.[4]

The old Tioga Road was an adventurous drive, only thirteen to fifteen feet wide, with no paving and extremely steep grades. The Park Service kept it passable for cars, however, and soon small tourist camps were built at Tuolumne Meadows, Tenaya Lake, and the White Wolf area. As traffic increased in the 1920s, more substantial improvements followed. Some curves were straightened, sections were widened, and a complete realignment of the eastern end of the road began to be investigated. By 1931 the Park Service had made plans with the Bureau of Public Roads to reconstruct the entire road and realign portions of it. The plans divided the road into three sections: a twelve-mile section from the park's eastern entrance to Tuolumne Meadows; an eleven-mile section at the other end of the road, from its intersection with the Big Oak Flat Road to the White Wolf area; and a twenty-one-mile section in the middle, crossing over the high country through more difficult, mountainous terrain. Construction on the two end sections began in the early 1930s and continued with New Deal funds. By 1938 the two sections at either end had been completed; in these areas the old wagon trail became a paved automotive road, twenty feet wide with three-foot paved shoulders and maximum grades of 6 percent. The reconstruction of the more rugged middle section of Tioga Road, however, was not even begun. It remained narrow, twisting, and unpaved, with 15 percent grades in places.[5]

Reconstructing an old wagon road to modern automotive standards was typical of the prewar projects accomplished through the partnership of the Park Service and the Bureau of Public Roads. Where such an old right-of-way existed, it might be used for a new road, particularly in cases where the original location and structure were sound. In other cases it was desirable to abandon all or parts of the old alignment and find a new route better suited to the more demanding standards (greater width, easier hills, wider curves) of an automotive road. Although Tioga Road was a particularly important example, the plans for its modernization were typical of this era of national park road making. The rebuilt road also nicely served the overall goals of park master planning: one good road across the heart of the park would be adequate for access, and it would also help stifle other development schemes. As the Tioga Road widening project went ahead in the 1930s, for example, proposals for the Glacier Point "ropeway" and for a new road connecting the east end of Yosemite Valley to Tuolumne Meadows were rejected.

The Tioga Road situation, in fact, typified how Vint and other Park Service officials felt automotive road making should be incorporated into a comprehensive park plan. It bore similarities to other park road projects of the era, including the first of this type, Going-to-the-Sun Road. That road was another important trans-mountain route, in this case over the Rocky Mountains in northern Montana. Like Tioga Road, it had three sections: one on either side of the mountains and one very difficult section in the middle. This central portion of Going-to-the-Sun Road crossed the Continental Divide in one of the most scenic areas of the park, surrounded by views of high peaks and glaciers. Vint (and soon Mather) worried that building this section of road with multiple switchbacks, as the Park Service engineers first suggested, would cause massive destruction of the landscape and would discredit the Park Service as a preservation agency during its first major road-building attempt. Vint's solution at Glacier, which Mather adopted in 1924, was to build a longer, more expensive, but less visually intrusive road. The result was a success, not just because it minimized damage to the scenery, but because it established the credibility of the Park Service as an agency that developed parks but also was a responsible steward of them. Going-to-the-Sun Road legitimized the partnership with the Bureau of Public Roads and validated Vint's ideas for how landscape architecture could improve and curtail road construction in national parks.

Going-to-the-Sun Road, Glacier National Park, Montana. Author's photo.

Now, about ten years later, the central section of Tioga Road raised similar concerns. The two sections of the road approaching the high country were built with little controversy (as they had been at Glacier). But the choice of how to reengineer the middle section over and across the heart of Yosemite's high country again demanded careful consideration. Beginning in 1931 Vint, park landscape architect John B. Wosky, and their Bureau of Public Roads partners began studying alternatives. Since the existing wagon road followed a slow and winding path, at least some realignment would be needed. One option, in fact, was to abandon the road almost completely and locate a new road to the north, along a "high line" between Tuolumne Meadows and White Wolf, running north of Mount Hoffman and through the Ten Lakes region. Although these areas were previously undisturbed wilderness, the route would allow for less destructive construction and would avoid direct encroachment on Tenaya Lake. As an alternative, Vint, Wosky, and their colleagues were able to identify a feasible "low line," which stayed close to the existing wagon road while not following it exactly in some places. As with any major development proposal for the park, the Advisory Board was asked to participate. For this group there was no question that the distur-bance of a large area of previously untouched High Sierra wilderness would do far more dam-age than realigning the existing road, even if the "low line" required blasting and excavation along the existing Tioga Road corridor. A spe-cial committee of directors of the Sierra Club agreed in a report they made in 1934. Appar-ently Vint had felt the same way, or at least he was easily convinced. By the late 1930s, an ap-proved "low line" strategy had been identified for the reconstruction of the final section of Tioga Road. But consideration of the alterna-tives had taken time, and World War II pre-vented construction from getting under way.[6]

After the war, Wirth, Vint, and the Yosemite Advisory Board all felt that they had already de-cided the question of how the Tioga Road re-construction should be completed. The treatment would be comparable to other proj-ects that had resulted in roads that the public (and conservation groups) considered to be sce-nic, sensitive, and appropriately limited in ex-tent. But precedent would not be a reliable guide in this case; too much was in the process of changing. By the time Mission 66 finally pro-vided the funding to finish the Tioga Road proj-ect, the battle over how—and whether—the reconstruction should go forward had become a contest between different visions of what a na-tional park should be.

At their August 1947 meeting the Advisory Board issued a statement reiterating their sup-port for completing the Tioga Road widening. They felt that it was needed because serious op-position to the project had already organized. Until that time the Advisory Board had served as the principal conduit for conservation groups, especially the Sierra Club, to influence Yosemite management policies. Advisory Board members William Colby and Duncan McDuffie, for exam-ple, were also Sierra Club directors, and had been part of the 1934 committee approving the "low line" for Tioga Road. Colby was a particu-larly venerated figure in the club's history. Born in 1875, in 1901 he organized the first Sierra Club "high trips" into the mountains and led these famous group outings for decades. A suc-cessful lawyer, he worked closely with Muir op-posing the Hetch Hetchy Dam, and he later facilitated the transfer of ownership of Tioga Road for Mather. But now certain Sierra Club members and directors dissented from the con-sensus on Tioga Road expressed by Colby and the Advisory Board. Harold C. Bradley, in partic-ular, pointed out that once the road was im-proved, more people would use it, and the high country it traversed would lose the sense of iso-lation and remoteness that were essential quali-ties of wilderness. A retired professor of chemistry only a few years younger than Colby, Bradley described his position in an article that David Brower, then editor of the *Sierra Club Bul-letin*, presented to the club's board to be ap-proved for publication. Bradley and Brower wanted the Park Service to consider making only minor improvements to the Tioga Road so that it would not serve larger volumes of traffic. They suggested that a second, parallel roadway designed to the same low standards as the exist-ing road could be built, and that each roadway could then carry traffic in one direction. They also wanted the "high line" option to be revis-ited because it at least avoided encroaching directly on the shores of Tenaya Lake and would not require blasting remarkable examples of glacially polished granite along the Tioga Road corridor.[7]

The Sierra Club board demurred from publishing the article for the moment, noting that the road project was already more than half complete (referring to the work done in the 1930s), and that the plan for the "low line" reconstruction had been developed with their participation and approval. For their part, the Advisory Board issued their 1947 statement summarizing why they rejected the "high line" in the first place, and why the suggestion for a second, parallel roadway was "based on several misconceptions." A second one-lane road, they pointed out, would cause almost as much landscape damage as the construction of a new two-lane road. In combination with at least some improvements to the existing road (which everyone agreed were needed), the result would be very close to having two trans-mountain highways rather than one, doubling the amount of disturbance. They remained convinced that the best way to minimize the impact of the road project was to widen the existing road as planned. As for concern over the increased use of Tuolumne Meadows, they insisted that the area had long ago "ceased to be a primitive or wilderness area." On the contrary, the site was already popular with campers and hikers, and increasing the level of use would not mean disturbing a formerly pristine area. The completion of Tioga Road would bring more visitors, but this was an appropriate location for this kind of use and would help reduce visitor pressure on Yosemite Valley. In 1948 Vint issued his own written statement in which he supported his conclusions and those of the Advisory Board. "The road would not open up a new section of the park to motor traffic," he pointed out. As for anticipated damage to rock formations and other features, the "preservation of the immediate landscape along the route" was a high priority "in keeping with long-established practices." Other options, such as a second roadway, would cause greater construction disturbance than their backers realized. And while Vint knew that the completion of Tioga Road "would materially increase the number of visitors and the attendant disturbance to the area adjacent to the road," the "solitude of the primeval" would still be available in "the surrounding untouched wilderness of 700,000 acres."[8]

From the beginning of the Tioga Road controversy, in other words, there were really two discussions taking place. The first was about how best to build a park road according to the policies and standards developed by the Park Service in the 1920s and 1930s. Vint, Colby, the Yosemite Advisory Board, and later Wirth all argued this position effectively. The Sierra Club board, however, soon split. Colby and other club members continued to accept the basic need and justification for completing the road project. Their reasons were essentially unchanged: the improved road would make the Yosemite high country more accessible in a controlled and appropriate way. Secure in this philosophical position, they simply disagreed with technical suggestions (the "high line" and the second roadway) that seemed ill-advised. They agreed with Vint that one automotive road across the park was not too many, and they trusted him to ensure that the location and construction of the road would minimize scarring of the landscape.

Bradley, Brower, and soon a group of other, mostly younger club members, however, were really arguing that Tioga Road should not be rebuilt at all, at least not to the same standards as the prewar sections of the road. Debate over their proposed alternatives gave Brower and Bradley time to pursue the real work of opposing the project: capturing public concern and influencing perceptions of the situation. If the project became enough of a political liability, the Department of the Interior would step in and tell the Park Service what to do. This strategy, versions of which would become so important to environmental activism and litigation in the coming decades, above all was the contribution of Brower. It later would constitute a critical component of his leadership in the struggle to preserve Dinosaur National Monument. Technical challenges to complacent (and sometimes mistaken) technocrats would become Brower's trademark, and would serve him well when he challenged Bureau of Reclamation engineers and defeated the Echo Park dam. It was the experience of the Tioga Road controversy that enabled Brower to develop this technique, and in the process transform the Sierra Club into a modern environmental advocacy group.

Bradley was perhaps the most honest in stating his opposition to the entire idea of modernizing Tioga Road. The Sierra Club finally published his article (now co-authored by Brower) in 1949, and others soon followed. Bradley simply felt that the increased access the road would create was no longer a good idea. Access to national park area should not be ex-

panded in general, he argued, and the Park Service should instead start finding ways to curtail it. Bradley had his own suggestion for Yosemite: leave Tioga Road in its "primitive state" and thereby prevent the thousands of visitors to Tuolumne Meadows and Tenaya Lake from becoming millions. The condition of Tioga Road had "served to screen out those who must have speed to be happy; those who are not sufficiently interested to invest the time and effort; those who require a house on wheels when they rough it; those who are timid, or incompetent and realize it." The "check on traffic" created by the twenty-one miles of old road had been "sufficient so that the high country has survived with little deterioration or loss of charm," while more accessible areas, above all Yosemite Valley, exemplified the loss of everything national parks were supposed to preserve. Bradley insisted that what he was supporting was a form not of "exclusion" but of "voluntary screening." Those willing to "pay the price in terms of effort and time" would have access; other visitors could "elect to drive somewhere else." The policy was no more "punitive" or "snobbish" than a library's demanding quiet so that readers could enjoy their books. "Park roads determine park history," he accurately observed. Roads themselves "could be designed to diminish excessive trampling, overcrowding, and vandalism by filtering out those motorists who cannot tolerate being slowed down by scenery."[9]

This was the essence of the Tioga Road debate, but rarely would it be expressed so clearly. Tioga Road did indeed curtail access: about thirty thousand motorists drove it in 1955, just a year before the park recorded 1 million visits.[10]

But opponents of the reconstruction were careful to frame their argument as one of appropriate "road standards for national parks," emphasizing the direct damage to park landscapes done by road construction even if planned by the most conscientious landscape architects. Vint, Colby, and others made the mistake of allowing themselves to be drawn into a debate about the degree to which the road widening would desecrate the landscape, not whether it was sound and ethical policy to "filter" visitors to the Yosemite high country down to thirty thousand out of 1 million. In 1951 Colby personally investigated (on foot, at the age of seventy-six) a modified "high line" proposal made by the project's opponents, comparing it to the "low line" alignment. This new "high line" was a shorter detour away from Tenaya Lake, via Polly Dome Lake. Colby's report to the Advisory Board, illustrated with photographs and firsthand observations, nevertheless reasserted that introducing a road anywhere to the north of Tenaya Lake would constitute an unwarranted "invasion" of an "untouched wilderness area." The new proposal would have avoided directly encroaching on Tenaya Lake and the remarkable glacially polished granite around it; but, Colby pointed out, the new proposal would result in similar or greater impacts to Polly Dome Lake, which until then, unlike Tenaya Lake, had been unaffected by automobile access.[11]

Bradley and Brower, however, kept the discussion focused on such proposals, and above all on "road standards" as the direct cause of "overcrowding." Everyone agreed that Yosemite Valley was overcrowded, and the two authors shifted the

Tioga Road congestion in the early 1950s. NPS Historic Photo Collection.

discussion to conditions there. They concluded that there were six reasons for overcrowding in the valley: California's increasing population, more leisure time, more disposable income, the widespread use of cars, improved highways, and the presence of artificial "attractions imported from urban life" in the valley. Of these, only the last two could be affected by park managers. Artificial attractions (such as evening entertainments organized by concessioners) could "gradually be eliminated" through simple changes in policy. That left highway construction as the one "controllable factor" to be addressed. Not only did modernized highways bring in too many people, but also, like artificial entertainments, they attracted the wrong sort of people: "merely the restless driver and . . . the trailer tourist." The character as well as the size of crowds was determined by "the quality of the roads provided to and within the park." The difference between a true national park—a wilderness park—and an "overcrowded . . . recreational resort" depended on the width, alignment, and capacity of park roads. Roads that were easy and convenient to drive brought in the merely curious, people who were not really interested in appreciating the natural wonders of Yosemite. Once there, they became bored and sought out "urban" distractions, which concessioners were happy to provide for a fee. More "primitive" and difficult roads would "screen out" the kind of visitor who would not be willing to drive them and "filter" the public into a far smaller number of more appreciative individuals.[12]

Bradley and Brower succeeded in striking a nerve among many Sierra Club directors, such as Colby and Bestor Robinson, who felt that they would be accused of elitism if they argued against road improvements in the hope that "primitive" roads would keep most visitors away. But the idea also quickly found advocates among other members. The Sierra Club board was split, but the momentum was with those protesting the Tioga Road widening. This group included Richard M. Leonard, a lawyer who would soon become club president, and Ansel Adams, on his way to becoming one of the most famous photographers in the country. Adams had been publishing photographs of Yosemite since the 1920s and had been a Sierra Club board member since the 1930s. He now turned his formidable artistic skill to the defense of Tenaya Lake, which he felt would be grievously harmed by the proposed "low line" road location. It had been Adams and Leonard who proposed the alternate "high line" route investigated by Colby in 1951. In 1952 Leonard dutifully reported on the ongoing controversy in the *Sierra Club Bulletin,* choosing his words carefully. He noted that the club's board had asked for further investigation of a "relatively short bypass north of Tenaya Lake . . . thus avoiding the heavy and rapid traffic at the lake and the possibility of construction scars in one of the park's most treasured scenic areas." But both the Park Service and the Advisory Board, after further investigation, had rejected the idea. Leonard added, however, that the "low line" also traversed "areas heretofore untouched," since it would not follow the old wagon road exactly. "The choice," he concluded tendentiously, "would seem to be between (1) invading a primitive area and changing the mood of Tenaya Lake and (2) invading a different primitive area [Polly Dome Lake] and sparing Tenaya Lake." No consensus came out of the discussion in the early 1950s. The Sierra Club board remained split and tabled the question.[13]

Leonard was one of a group of younger activist Sierra Club members whom he described as "young Turks." For this group of club directors, including Brower and Adams, the realities of postwar recreational trends demanded a complete reconsideration of how and where the Park Service provided access to parks. They may not have managed to change the club's policy on Tioga Road in 1951, but they did succeed in changing the wording of the club's bylaws from "explore, enjoy, and render accessible the mountain regions of the Pacific Coast" to "explore, enjoy, and preserve the Sierra Nevada and other scenic resources of the United States." The Tioga Road corridor around Tenaya Lake was destined to become a battleground for opposing philosophies of access. As Sierra Club historian Michael Cohen observes, "The issue of access separated the newer generation from many of the old," and by the early 1950s, the "young Turks" were beginning to represent the mainstream of the Sierra Club's membership. Leonard and Brower were elected to the club's board, and in 1952 Leonard became president. He immediately proposed that Brower be hired in a new position, as the club's executive director. At the time Brower was editing the *Sierra Club Bulletin,* but his public relations, writing, and organizational skills were soon put to better use. With the backing of their board, he and Leonard moved the Sierra Club onto a national stage, broadening its mission and greatly expanding membership along the way. The nationwide public attention drawn by the Echo Park controversy increased the club's profile, and the 1956 defeat of the dam was, Cohen observes, "a crucial turning point" that determined the "nature of the club's organizational structure and aims." Encouraged by their success and growing strength, Brower and the Sierra Club now joined with the Wilderness Society and other groups in support of their next priority: federal legislation to create a "national wilderness preservation system."[14]

The Tioga Road controversy involved the question of greater public access to a relatively unvisited (although not roadless) area of Yosemite National Park. It therefore was a debate about wilderness, and how wilderness would be defined, designated, and protected in the postwar period. This made the fate of Tioga Road of signal importance to conservation groups, and tied the road project—and all of Mission 66—to early efforts to pass the National Wilderness Preservation Act. As it took shape in 1956, the draft wilderness act was the culmination of decades of concern for "primeval" areas in the national parks, and especially in the na-

tional forests, where most of the potential wilderness designations would be made. Invigorated by the victory over the Echo Park dam, advocates felt that the dream of a federal system of wilderness preserves was now within reach. The system would be created through legislation that conferred special protected status on federal lands that met certain criteria, regardless of what agency had jurisdiction over them. Congress would directly mandate that the areas be left undisturbed, undeveloped, and roadless forever. In the final 1964 version of the act, "a wilderness" was defined "an area where the earth and its community of life are untrammeled by man, where man himself is a visitor who does not remain." Official wilderness would be "undeveloped Federal land retaining its primeval character and influence, without permanent improvements or human habitation," and with "the imprint of man's work substantially unnoticeable."[15]

This postwar ideal of wilderness required, above all, the absence of people and of any significant trace of human occupation or history. The concept was perhaps more poetic than scientific, since human culture and its influence on even remote landscapes had been pervasive in North America for thousands of years. Postwar wilderness also evoked the modernist idyll of the "Virgilian dream": an untouched, pristine, and stable nature that would be violated by any signs of human presence. The best management plan for such areas, as modernist theorists such as Henry-Russell Hitchcock suggested, was to interfere as little as possible with them and avoid any suggestion of human influence on the inherent stability and balance of what appeared to be "undisturbed" nature. The emotional appeal of this wilderness ideal had great power in the postwar decades, capturing the national imagination at a time when Americans were experiencing overwhelming alteration and modernization of the national landscape.

In many ways, this postwar ideal of wilderness should have been consistent with many of the goals of the Mission 66 modernist park. Both models implied an increased separation—a modernist alienation—between park landscapes and park visitors. The roads, roadside interpretation, and visitor centers of the Mission 66 park enforced a passive, visual relationship to surrounding landscapes that helped prevent the public from directly disturbing them. Mission 66 planning enforced this separation between people and wilderness by making it possible for visitors to enjoy the natural or historical resources of a park without ever leaving frontcountry areas, and in some cases without ever leaving their cars. There were many ways in which Mission 66 could, indeed, be seen as a development program that would enable the preservation of wilderness, as it was being defined in the postwar era. But there was also one profound difference between the wilderness advocated by the conservation groups and the wilderness to be preserved in the Mission 66 park: the continued facilitation of public enjoyment of whatever it was that was being preserved. Wirth and his planners would not abandon the basic notion that a national park was intended to allow people, millions of them if they chose to visit, to experience the benefits and pleasures of what the Park Service now often described not as scenery and history but as wilderness and heritage.

But the presence of people—crowds of noisy and perhaps all too unappreciative automotive tourists—created an irreconcilable conflict for wilderness advocates, even if those people were restricted to a frontcountry corridor of roads, overlooks, and visitor centers. Those advocating wilderness preservation in the 1950s were defining wilderness specifically as an absence of humanity and its influences. Millions of people therefore could not enjoy—or even be anywhere in the vicinity of—wilderness without destroying it, regardless of master plans, prospectuses, or any other park design scheme that purported to achieve "enjoyment without impairment." Any road construction or improvement simply could not be part of a strategy for wilderness preservation. Tioga Road was only one Mission 66 project, but it dramatically revealed the contrasting wilderness ideals of the Park Service and conservation groups in the mid-1950s. The planned "low line" would require the blasting and excavation of a High Sierra landscape held dear, personally, by Brower, Adams, and other leading advocates. But even worse, the road widening would result in easy public access to an entire corridor of what were then still remote, relatively unvisited areas of the park.

As a result of the Tioga Road controversy, wilderness advocates mistrusted Wirth and Mission 66 from the start. As soon as they got a complete picture of the project, they responded by stepping up their campaign for a national system of wilderness preserves, which they now characterized as a counterpoint—and an antidote—to Mission 66. Brower and Howard C. Zahniser, director of the Wilderness Society, met with Wirth early in 1956 and asked him to back their draft wilderness legislation, which was first introduced in the Senate later that year. Wirth found reasons to deny support. At first he claimed that by the time interest groups had watered down the provisions of the bill, official wilderness designation would actually offer less protection than parks and monuments would have without it. Later, there were other similarly contrived objections. But neither legalistic critiques nor the protection of bureaucratic "turf" fully explained Wirth's opposition to the wilderness bill. The entire concept of congressionally designated wilderness, at least as it was being presented to Wirth in 1956, conflicted with his own ideas about how and why his agency was preserving landscapes as public parks. How would the public be served by wilderness preservation unless it was coupled with some form of access? This was the essence of national park design. Road corridors and developed areas served as mediating landscapes, making it possible to appreciate the surrounding wilderness visually as scenery, or serving for those so inclined as the starting point for backcountry trips. But to designate wilderness for its own sake, unaccompanied by park planning and even limited development, eliminated the public in any significant numbers from the entire undertaking. The art of national park design involved assuring meaningful public experiences of wilderness. Advocates of federal wilderness designation implied that the Park Service had dramatically failed its basic mandate by allowing too much access: the national park wilderness was being destroyed by an excess of visitors. Mission 66 would not solve the problem but make it

many times worse. Wirth understood that the new landscape ideal of wilderness was being presented not as a complement to the model of the national park as he understood it but as a replacement for it.

If both models—the Mission 66 park and postwar wilderness—were influenced by contemporary modernist theory in planning and design, they were two very different responses. The critics of Tioga Road had begun to describe a new kind of national reservation that cut its ties to Olmstedian justifications and social purposes. Designated wilderness, in this sense, was not a public park, at least not in the same sense the term had been used in the United States for a hundred years. The concept of postwar wilderness, as advocated in the 1950s and then enacted in 1964, would mark the end of the dominance of public park ideology in the management of American national parks. As Wirth sensed, the rise of the postwar ideal of wilderness implied much more than a reduction of his agency's jurisdictional authority.

Wirth, Vint, the Yosemite Advisory Board—an entire generation of national park planners—revered a tradition of public service that had been established, above all, by the elder Olmsted. In his 1865 Yosemite report Olmsted justified government sponsorship of park making in terms of an obligation to protect the right to the "pursuit of happiness." Because experiencing landscape scenery was necessary for human fulfillment, preserving opportunities for everyone to do so was "justified and enforced as a political duty." Government therefore had to make sure that the "enjoyment of the choicest natural scenes in the country and the means of recreation associated with them" were "laid open to the use of the body of the people," because without government action, private interests would monopolize "all places favorable in scenery to the recreation of the mind and body." Those places would become unavailable to the public at large.[16] This rhetoric justified municipal, regional, state, and national park making in the United States for the hundred years immediately preceding Mission 66. But a small, self-selected ("filtered") group no longer constituted the "body of the people." Designated wilderness areas, when planned without access by the public (meaning large and diverse groups of people), would not function as public parks, and park commissions could not make the same claims for government's having a "political duty" to preserve landscapes. The politics of preservation—and the role and responsibilities of government in park making—were changing. While Wirth was always careful to insist that he fully endorsed the overall goals of the wilderness bill (that is, landscape preservation), he never really supported the legislation, and he never positioned his agency in the new political and philosophical context it represented. Instead, Wirth conducted parallel operations intended to address some of the same concerns through a theoretical framework of national park planning that he understood and supported. And his very first task, he felt, was to define wilderness in terms that made sense for what his agency was trying to accomplish through Mission 66.

Wirth was a sensitive observer of federal politics, and he knew by 1956 that the wilderness advocates were gaining sympathy and leverage in Congress in a way that the prewar "purists" never had. That is why he met with Zahniser and Brower, and why he subsequently scheduled monthly meetings with the wilderness advocacy groups. He also brought Sequoia and Kings Canyon National Parks superintendent Eivind Scoyen to Washington as associate director and asked him to "set up procedures . . . so that wilderness preservation groups will feel their interests are better protected." Wirth noted that for years Scoyen had been having "conversations" with Brower, Zahniser, Leonard, Bradley, and George Marshall (of the Wilderness Society) "relative to the problems of wilderness protection in the parks." The superintendent had developed constructive relationships with these early environmentalists.[17] Born and raised in Yellowstone National Park, Scoyen had worked as a backcountry ranger beginning in 1919. He had been one of Mather's original cadre of superintendents in the 1920s and had run a series of western parks in the 1930s and 1940s.[18] As superintendent at Sequoia in 1955 he urged that "some means to limit use and development" in the parks be made part of Mission 66 planning. He also warned that the Sierra Club and other groups should be asked to participate in the planning process.[19] Since 1949 he had attended the Sierra Club's biennial wilderness conferences, where much of the early planning for the Wilderness Act was taking place. But Scoyen also had a profound sense of duty to the public and a genuine affection for what he called the "tin can tourist" in the "disreputable flivver." Like Garrison, Scoyen had field experience that appealed to Wirth, and as associate director he became a close adviser, often acting for the director.

Scoyen had responsibility for a public rela-

"Roadside wilderness" as depicted for the "Mission 66 in Action" slide show in 1958. NPS History Collection.

tions effort that was intended to make it clear that the Park Service knew what wilderness was, and knew how to preserve it. He worked closely with Howard Stagner, assistant director of the Mission 66 working staff and later chief of the Branch of Natural History. Later that year Stagner produced a draft document, "Preservation of Natural and Wilderness Values in the National Parks," which assembled arguments and observations from various sources and offered an alternative to the definition of wilderness that Zahniser, Brower, and others advocated. The first point was that in considering wilderness, the Park Service was "as much concerned with the whole park as with any special area within it." This was because the "national park philosophy" was itself a "wilderness philosophy"; the two could not be separated. The same attitudes prevailed in the preservation of large roadless areas, as in the management of "wilderness values along a roadside." The successful preservation of roadless areas of a park also depended directly on "how the more accessible, developed, more heavily used portions of the park are treated." Throughout the document, Stagner resisted the bifurcation of the park into backcountry wilderness areas and frontcountry developed areas. Wilderness could be defined, as its postwar advocates proposed, in physical terms as a vast area in which human influence was minimal or absent; but Stagner insisted that "wilderness also needs to be regarded as a quality—defined in terms of personal experience, feelings, or benefits," and not solely in terms of physical attributes. The "quality of wilderness" could indeed be appreciated in a preserved roadless area, but it could be experienced under other circumstances as well. It could even exist "close to a major highway," as long as the road, the visitor, and the overall experience were "shielded from the effects of mechanized civilization." The "quality" or "value" of wilderness could be manifest in a "scene or a vista of . . . beauty unaffected by obvious man-made intrusions" or simply a "spot where one can feel personally removed from civilization." Wilderness certainly was a physical, "ecological condition," but it also was "a state of mind." The first concept was important for the successful protection of physical wilderness; the second was vital to understanding how people enjoyed wilderness and how best to plan for the "intelligent and beneficial use of this important cultural and recreational resource." In this sense, the park as a whole—backcountry and frontcountry—was one landscape, imbued throughout with the same "quality." The physical wilderness of the backcountry could coexist with the wilderness "state of mind" in the front country. The vitality of both was essential to the national park experience.[20]

If this definition of wilderness seemed broad, Stagner pointed out that "pure wilderness," as its advocates were describing it, did not exist in the United States, with the possible exception of the Brooks Range in Alaska. The more one knew about the ecology of a region, the more evident it became that human history had influenced it. "Time tends to paint our memory in rosy hues," the natural historian observed, but many parks had been "abused lands" in which overgrazing, extensive poaching, and predator exterminations had radically altered natural systems. This was a favorite theme of Wirth's as well, who liked to point out that some wilderness areas had histories of grazing, hunting, mining, and even logging. "Many times it has been said that a wilderness once destroyed is gone for-

ever," he wrote to Bestor Robinson, a sympathetic Sierra Club director. "If this were true, then virtually all the High Sierra passed out of this category before the beginning of the century." Wirth felt that at the Park Service, "our wilderness concept" was more adaptable to local conditions and acknowledged that natural processes could restore wilderness over time.[21] It was a less rigorous definition, but a more generous one. Park Service wilderness had seen human activity in the past, and had survived. The implication was that it could see a little more history—like a road widening—without being hopelessly and permanently desecrated.

Stagner's draft document identified the goals of wilderness preservation with those of public park making. Preservation and use were the single "true purpose" of a national park, which "indistinguishably" combined both in a single concept. Wilderness was not restricted to backcountry areas that few visitors ever experienced directly. "Qualities of wilderness" extended "beyond the wilderness proper" and pervaded even "the most used portion" of a park. "Comparatively few park visitors experience true wilderness," he pointed out. By contrast, "millions profit from those qualities of wilderness which are available to them in the near vicinity of park roads and developed areas. But who may say that the latter gain less than the former?" Many of these arguments had been elaborated in the 1920s in response to the first wave of criticism of national park development.[22] It was difficult to combine use and preservation—or people and wilderness—in a national park; but one without the other failed to fulfill the fundamental mandate. Yellowstone was "envisioned as a *public* park," Stagner emphasized, recalling the 1870 campfire around which the idea for a national park had supposedly first been discussed. "And the *public* park proposal came as a counter proposal *after* private ownership was suggested." What is more, "it was the *whole* of the area they sought to set aside . . . the total scene."[23] That was what a national park—and what Stagner called "the national park wilderness"—was: the total scene; backcountry and frontcountry; roadless and with roads; vast untouched areas and developed areas; physical wilderness and "wilderness qualities." The public was part of the overall scene, and that was the essence of the challenge the Park Service faced. The "few—in this case meaning the wilderness lovers—are well provided for as far as the parks are concerned," Wirth wrote Brower in 1958. "The over-riding

problem of the Park Service is the millions, not the few. Our concern is to give the millions of good, sincere citizens and their families, who wish and intend to exercise their right to visit their national parks, an opportunity to do so."[24]

Stagner's draft text was circulated to conservation groups and others, edited, and published in 1957 as a color brochure (paid for by Jackson Hole Preserve, Inc.), *The National Park Wilderness*.[25] Wirth felt that it fully expressed how the Park Service understood wilderness in the postwar era and often spoke of it, with *Our Heritage*, as the two guiding documents of Mission 66. But for wilderness advocates, and above all Brower, the document quickly became fodder for their own public relations and legislative campaign. Brower responded to the draft and the published text with outrage, but also almost with

Pages from *The National Park Wilderness*, a 1957 Park Service publication that particularly incensed David Brower and other wilderness advocates. NPS History Collection.

man is a part of the scene—wilderness has little human value without him.

and wilderness reaches outward from the roadside to be experienced fully by those who penetrate it.

man's enjoyment springs from the quality of wilderness that invests even the most visited spectacles and reveals itself to all who regard it . . . . .

glee at the rich opportunities they presented for criticism. For Brower, writing in *National Parks Magazine,* Mission 66 had been planned without even considering the preservation of the "primary value of the parks, their wilderness." He disparaged the idea of "wilderness values along the roadside" as a confirmation of his worst fears that the Park Service wanted to "blur the distinction" between "the real wilderness" and places that had been compromised by development, even if they seemed scenic. Noting that the Park Service had been no use in the Echo Park fight and now did not support the wilderness bill, Brower disdained the agency's concern for "wilderness values." The very idea seemed to suggest that development would not harm wilderness, since the "quality of wilderness" could somehow "extend" into areas developed with roads and other facilities. "A road—or a reservoir—could be fully rationalized" by such a philosophy. Brower went on to threaten that "some of our best-informed law-makers . . . see the situation somewhat differently," specifically naming Senator Hubert H. Humphrey and Congressman John P. Saylor, powerful backers of the wilderness legislation. Congressional politics had always been Wirth's strength; Brower was announcing a direct challenge. Brower's critique heralded the new position of the Sierra Club, the National Parks Association, the Wilderness Society, and other groups as a coalition that not only offered advice to the Park Service but also drafted legislation intended to direct the agency's policies and actions.[26]

Brower ended his acerbic line-by-line critique of *The National Park Wilderness* by calling for a "Mission 65"—honoring the date of Olmsted's 1865 Yosemite report—to replace Mission 66. Brower quoted the portion of the report stating that at Yosemite "the first point to be kept in mind . . . is the preservation and maintenance as exactly as is possible of the natural scenery." All improvements for public access, wrote Olmsted, should be kept to a minimum and should not be "inharmonious." But if Brower understood Olmsted the preservationist, he ignored Olmsted the humanist. Olmsted was interested in preserving human as well as natural resources; public park landscapes manifested this combined concern. By identifying landscape preservation with social reform and public health, Olmsted established the intellectual, rhetorical, and political foundations for national park making up to and including Mission 66. Public parks served the "body of the people," and Olmsted anticipated and welcomed the fact that millions would eventually enter Yosemite Valley every year. If the valley were developed along the lines he suggested, those millions would enjoy, but not impair, the landscape. But Olmsted's report, after all, had been ignored by the managers of Yosemite Valley ever since it was written. Even Vint would have agreed that Mission 66 continued the "drift" toward overdevelopment in the valley and compounded the earlier mistake of allowing hotels and other development there in the first place. For Vint in particular, Brower's "Mission 65" gibe must have been galling, since it unwittingly echoed the landscape architect's own attitudes and proposals dating back to the "Vint Plan" of 1945. Vint did not respond in writing at this point, but Wirth did not conceal his frustration and contempt. "As far as you are personally concerned," he wrote Brower, "your need for clarification" of Mission 66 policy "will continue as long as you subject what we say to a microscopic search for hidden meanings and equivocations." In a separate letter to the editor of *National Parks Magazine,* Wirth deplored the timing of Brower's article (it appeared in the same issue as one of Wirth's own articles, "Mission 66 in the Headlines") and declined to respond directly, noting that he "could not conceive that anything we have to say would be acceptable to Mr. Brower."[27]

As scores of parks became Mission 66 construction sites in the next several years, Wirth continued to struggle to control the popular definition of wilderness and the public's perceptions of Mission 66. Between January and May 1956, the *Christian Science Monitor* published a series of feature articles, "Our National Parks: A Heritage Worth Saving," by reporter (and former park ranger) Max K. Gilstrap. While the series may have been originally conceived as one more exposé of deteriorating conditions in the parks, it coincided with the public presentation of Mission 66 and the official start of construction that July. As he did for other articles in newspapers and magazines at the time, Wirth provided quotations, information, and illustrations. While the series described a severe "crisis" in the parks, its overall tone was still sympathetic to Park Service efforts, characterizing Mission 66 as a "Crusade to Preserve."[28] Potential negative publicity from the Tioga Road debate, however, already worried the director. In his own written statement on Park Service policy, which Gilstrap used to conclude the series, Wirth wrote that "from time to time we hear it said" that the Park Service was "permitting the wilderness to be destroyed, principally by building roads that invade the wilderness." But park roads were only being made "safe for today's travel." They were not becoming superhighways, nor were they being extended into roadless areas. One of the first "precepts" of Mission 66, he now insisted, "related specifically to wilderness protection."[29]

Scoyen coordinated other public information efforts in order to sustain the "enthusiastic support" he felt had launched the program. He directed staff to prepare "prospectus briefs" and accompanying press releases for wide distribution. All construction projects were to have somewhat enigmatic signs stating, "This is a MISSION 66 Project," or just "A MISSION 66 Project," which he hoped would "stimulate curiosity" about the program and encourage visitors to ask questions and look at the informational posters and other materials that were being distributed to parks before the end of the first construction season.[30] By 1957 these relatively modest efforts were replaced by more expensive, professionally designed brochures such as *MISSION 66 in Action* (paid for by the Jackson Hole Preserve, Inc.) and *Your MISSION 66 and the National Parks: Passport to Adventure* (paid for by Phillips Petroleum, and featuring its corporate logo on the cover).[31] Like *Our Heritage,* the brochures reiterated, in a more popular idiom, the basic principles of Mission 66.

The most ambitious public relations effort of 1956, however, involved some of the new technology that park interpreters were just beginning to use. Color slides and 35 mm slide projectors were features of the "automated" interpretive services being offered, especially in

Eivind Scoyen, as depicted in the "Mission 66 in Action" slide show, on a backcountry trip in Yellowstone. NPS History Collection.

new visitor centers, amphitheaters, and campground circles that had been designed to accommodate them. Bill Carnes and the Mission 66 staff in Washington assembled a slide show with over seventy images, mostly of park scenery and historic sites. Sets of the slides were distributed to parks, along with a tape recording of Wirth and his staff describing Mission 66, personally, for the public. Scripts of the narration were also provided, indicating the points at which the slides should be advanced. A great deal of effort went into the production of these audio-visual presentations, and over the next several years at least four updated versions were created with both images and text being altered to reflect progress. Howard Stagner served as narrator, but Carnes was in charge of production and distributed memoranda detailing the kinds of information and images he wanted from the field.[32] Carnes himself, in his increasingly important role as "Chief of MISSION 66 Staff" in Washington, began the presentations with a description of park conditions in 1955. Wirth then explained how Mission 66 had been planned, and the general goals of the program. Ronald Lee described interpretive programs and progress in historical parks. One of the longest and perhaps most personal verbal presentations was by Eivind Scoyen, who related the story of his childhood and early rangering in Yellowstone as a preamble to his defense of Mission 66 wilderness policies. He remembered Yellowstone as it was in 1915, when there were 52,000 visitors. It was astonishing to him that visitors in the 1950s still found accommodations basically within the footprint of development that had been established by 1908. At Yellowstone, he insisted, this precedent would be maintained. Millions of dollars were being spent on new facilities to accommodate millions of visitors, but "the job will be accomplished without taking another acre from the wilderness," and this was true for other national parks as well. "When MISSION 66 is completed," Scoyen promised, "the wilderness will still be there."[33]

In the meantime, Wirth pressed ahead with Mission 66 construction, knowing that public relations were vital, but that Congress and the Bureau of the Budget would now judge his program on the efficiency with which construction money was spent. With some exceptions, progress in this sense was good. In the initial years of Mission 66 construction, concessioner lodges, visitor centers, campgrounds, and other facilities opened, and many other projects were under way. The widening of Tioga Road, however, remained controversial.

The final, central portion of the road was scheduled to be one of the first Mission 66 projects to go to construction in the summer of 1956, but flooding in Yosemite caused superintendent John C. Preston to shift priorities and delay construction for a year. Work on the approved "low line" route finally began the following summer. The delay had allowed time for the project's opponents to protest, and for Wirth to respond. For years, even moderate Sierra Club board members had been writing angry letters to Wirth expressing their suspicions that Tioga Road was to become a "speedway" or even a commercial highway. Alex Hildebrand, for example, pointed out to Wirth that "a highway down the center aisle of a cathedral would enable more people to go through it, but it would not enable more people to come there for peace and spiritual inspiration."[34] At the same time, Wirth was under pressure from Bureau of Public Roads engineers to widen the road to twenty-eight feet (two ten-foot travel lanes flanked by four-foot paved shoulders). Wirth responded by asking a sympathetic Sierra Club board member, Walter Huber, to investigate the situation. Huber was a former Sierra Club board president and a respected mining and road engineer who had worked extensively in the High Sierra. He recommended that two-foot shoulders would be adequate almost everywhere along the road, for a total width of only twenty-four feet. The difference was significant and would help reduce the amount of excavation and scarring the project would inevitably produce. With Huber's help, Wirth persuaded the Bureau of Public Roads to compromise on three-foot paved shoulders.[35]

The change, however, did not come close to mollifying the project's opponents. Their complaints also involved the horizontal and vertical alignments of the road (the specifications that determined the tightness of curves and steepness of hills). These were critical factors in determining both the "design speed" of the road and the total extent of excavation and filling that would be required. Less rigorous standards would result in a slower road with less capacity, but one that caused less disturbance. The Park Service maintained standards in terms of width and alignments comparable to the prewar sections of the road, at what the engineers described as a "40-mile per hour design speed," in this case horizontal curves with a minimum radius of four hundred feet and maximum grades of 7 percent. As construction began that July,

Tioga Road along Tenaya Lake in the Yosemite high country. Author's photo.

Some of the results of the controversial Tioga Road rock blasting. Author's photo.

Mission 66 bridge on Tioga Road. Author's photo.

the Sierra Club's still divided board made no formal objection.[36] Ansel Adams, however, was urging fellow Sierra Club directors to oppose the project. His immediate concern was Tenaya Lake, and the fact that the "low line" of Tioga would now result in excavation and filling directly on its shore. By the end of the summer the split on the Sierra Club's board had widened, with more board members convinced that the impacts of construction were too destructive.[37]

The short construction season in the High Sierra soon brought work to a halt. Using the *Sierra Club Bulletin* as a vehicle, and with his board's approval, Brower now openly and fiercely condemned the construction of the "new speedway" that would encourage high-speed driving and despoil the shores of Tenaya Lake. He accused Park Service officials of deceit and continued to press them to reconsider the purpose of park roads and the standards for their construction. The road had already been "irrevocably carved," Brower lamented, into "one of the park's finest areas." The charm of the old road was destroyed. "Tenaya Lake, the Yosemite Indians' 'Lake of the Shining Rocks,' is strung on a highway now," he angrily protested, "and you will be able to skirt its very edge in 35 seconds' less time, not noticing, perhaps, that some of the shine is gone." Furthermore, "variations on the same theme" could be found wherever Mission 66 was at work.[38]

The location and construction standards for the Tioga Road development that took place in 1957 had been decided in the 1930s. The project was essentially comparable, with changes in the design of culverts and other structures, to the sections of the road that had been completed before the war. But many Sierra Club members and directors, as well as other conservationists and park advocates, now came to see these standards—at least when applied in the austerely beautiful High Sierra landscape—as a disastrous form of overdevelopment that illustrated the misguided priorities of Mission 66. By the start of the next construction season in July 1958, the two sides were committed to irreconcilable positions. Sierra Club advocates deluged the Park Service and the Department of the Interior with demands to stop the project, or at least to consider further alternative proposals. Near Tenaya Lake, work planned for that summer included creating a parking area and overlook at a point where the road would cross over a prominent granite formation, or dome. While the views would be spectacular from the overlook, the granite feature itself would be seriously scarred by blasting. Brower and Adams, leading the opposition, proposed an alternative. They wanted the road relocated to the base of the dome, which would still allow visitors to climb up to see the view, while preventing more visible scarring. That August they pressed Wirth and Secretary of the Interior Fred Seaton to order a stop to construction to allow time to consider their proposal. Wirth either was still hopeful of salvaging his relationship with the Sierra Club or, more likely, was directed by Interior Department officials; in any case, he agreed on August 5 to halt the work and meet the advocates on-site.[39]

On August 19 Wirth walked the site with Brower and Adams and other Sierra Club and Park Service officials. There was no meeting of minds. Brower and Adams remained adamant that the road should be relocated to the base of the rock formation, even if it meant far steeper grades and tighter turns than the standards allowed. Wirth's engineers told him that the resulting alignment would create an unacceptable hazard, and he might as well also "build a hospital at the foot of the hill" to handle victims of the wrecks it would cause. Wirth apparently tried to reach some kind of détente with Brower, engaging in lengthy discussion and making a show of ordering his staff to investigate the issues being raised. At one point, perhaps regretting his agency's increasingly confrontational relationship with the conservation groups, Wirth asked Brower why the Sierra Club leaders had "changed their minds," reversing decades of support for the road project and the underlying philosophy it represented. According to Wirth, Brower responded curtly that "it was a different Sierra Club now."[40] Indeed, it was the Tioga Road construction that, as much as anything, had transformed the club and set it on the path of modern environmental advocacy.

Following this cool exchange, Wirth ordered work to resume. He did relocate the 1.2-mile section of road in question, but only partway down the granite formation. It was a compromise that pleased no one, since it created a less scenic road but still required highly visible blasting across the dome. The entire episode, including the dramatic meeting near Tenaya Lake and the subsequent blasting and excavation that August, was a disaster for the image of Mission 66. If the Sierra Club lost the battle over Tioga Road, it began winning the public relations war. In his report on that summer's events, Brower

A portion of Tioga Road cutting through the High Sierra. Author's photo.

characterized Park Service officials as intransigent and duplicitous.[41] The images of blasted granite rubble and excavated borrow pits provided Adams with a wealth of material for elegizing the scarred landscape and documenting the "Tenaya tragedy." The failure to stop the Tioga Road widening galvanized advocates as no victory ever could have. "There is no use fooling ourselves that nature with a slick highway running through it is any longer wild," Adams wrote. "What possessed the minds and hearts of road people . . . to maintain ruinous standards in this priceless area? . . . The Tenaya tragedy stands as an example of what must never happen again in national park or other wild areas. . . . The bulldozers of bureaucracy have bypassed the gentle persuasions and advice of our conservation spokesmen."[42]

Adams published his harshest criticisms that December. The "failure in basic planning" at Yosemite, he wrote, should "stand out as a warning against future depredations of the natural scene." Adams condemned not just the Tioga Road project but Park Service planning in general. He demanded "the basic right to explore programs such as Mission 66 while they are being formulated," insisting, "I have the right to penetrate the 'paper curtain.'" Adams felt that "a complete re-evaluation of park and wilderness definitions and procedures" was urgently needed. "The National Gallery of Art . . . exists for those who desire to experience the great masterworks in an appropriate environment. . . . I believe this is the way national parks should be presented." He gladly accepted some of the Mission 66 prospectus, including the development of El Portal and the removal of some services from the valley; but he condemned the contemporary construction of the "merchandise center" and other buildings that seemed to negate any advances. The "supreme problem" faced by the Park Service, he declared, was to find ways to "depressurize the parks and return them to their logical status." But Mission 66 was "built upon a definition [of parks] which justifies the urge to expand and to manage." Adams wanted "a reorganization of approach and planning within government . . . based on the establishment of a sound and enforceable definition of park and wilderness qualities, values, and functions" and a "reformation of the park service." He soon called for a complete halt to Mission 66 so that the "whole scheme" could be "studied afresh." In the meantime, Adams felt that "all we can say is, 'Father forgive them for they know not what they do.'"[43]

If nothing else, Tioga Road put the issue of park road standards under intense scrutiny. By 1959 Wirth had announced that road policy was going through a review, noting that his agency was now getting as much criticism from the Bureau of Public Roads for underbuilding as it was from conservation groups for overbuilding. The relative positions of the Park Service and the Bureau of Public Roads had changed. In 1924, Going-to-the-Sun Road was the biggest project the roads bureau had ever undertaken, and the Park Service was their biggest client. But with interstate highway construction in full swing in the late 1950s, national park roads were no more than a minor subcategory of federal road building. The Park Service had less leverage to influence engineering standards and details, which the federal highway engineers were busily updating for postwar conditions. By 1962 Wirth was exploring the possibility of backing out of the partnership with the Bureau of Public Roads altogether in order to gain complete control over park road construction. But Congress had made appropriations for roads since 1924 on the assumption that the roads agency, as a full partner, would assure that construction was efficiently engineered and supervised. The legislators gave no indication that they would pay for park road projects under any other arrangement. The Park Service was locked into the "interbureau agreement" that Mather had originally negotiated.

At the same time, Harold Bradley and other conservation advocates continued to deplore Mission 66 and to publish their own ideas for park road standards. Bradley, who was elected president of the Sierra Club board in 1957, framed the controversy as one of competing road standards: high-speed "roads for access" versus low-speed "roads for display."[44] By keeping the discussion on the impacts of road construction, Bradley and others also deflected analysis of their central proposition: that Yosemite and other parks should be enjoyed by those who could and would appreciate them, not by the public at large. One effective and perhaps even democratic means of limiting access was to avoid widening park roads. The public would then self-select into those willing and able to be inconvenienced by narrow and congested roads, and those who would, as Bradley had put it earlier, "elect to drive elsewhere."

Increasing the capacity of park roads, however, was an indispensable strategy for Mission

Tioga Road and Tuolumne
Meadows. Author's photo.

66, because the program was dedicated to making the parks work—as public parks—for the public at large. Bradley, Adams, Brower, and others had approved of the idea of Yosemite as a public park before the war, but they could no longer do so in the 1950s, after the public had become so numerous. It also must be said that the public had become more diverse. Postwar demographic changes in California, in particular the doubling of the population and the growth in relative affluence of Central Valley communities, made Yosemite not only a more crowded place but also one that was less dominated by the Bay Area professional classes that traditionally had provided the Sierra Club with its most active members. Put another way, Brower and Adams had not been against prewar park development, which had made their youthful experiences of Yosemite possible, but they vigorously opposed postwar development, which opened the park to a larger, broader public.[45] For all their outrage over the "Tenaya tragedy," they also deplored the planned visitor center and expanded campground for Tuolumne

Meadows, and in general regretted the fact that the high country would now be more accessible to a wider range of people.

Such conclusions did not escape at least some Park Service officials, who were deeply angered by what they saw as hypocrisy and narcissism. John Preston, the embattled Yosemite superintendent during these years, was frustrated (or tactless) enough to put his opinions into written statements. In 1959 he vigorously defended his handling of the Tioga Road project to his fellow park superintendents. He also suggested that Adams suffered from a messianic complex, and that Brower had "excessive love for himself" and was using the situation to advance personal ambitions at the expense of sound policy for the organization he led.[46] The Tioga Road controversy had colored perceptions of the entire Mission 66 program. Park Service officials knew it and resented it.

One of the striking things about the 1958 meeting of Brower and Wirth to discuss Tioga Road was the fact that Thomas Vint was not there. In some ways the meeting recalled another similarly dramatic meeting when, in 1924, Vint had persuaded Mather to accept an alternate route for Going-to-the-Sun Road. That conference had also taken place at the site of a disputed road alignment, at high elevation, surrounded by magnificent scenery. The outcome, however, had been very different. In 1924 Vint had succeeded in altering Park Service road policy, and from that point he had assumed increased responsibilities within the agency and had overseen a new era of park road construction. But Vint had been increasingly silent on Tioga Road since issuing his 1947 written statement backing the "low line" strategy. He was un-involved in the 1958 controversy, and now became even less engaged in Mission 66 as a whole. The two road controversies—at Glacier and Yosemite national parks—were bookends to Vint's career. In 1961, the year Tioga Road was dedicated, Vint retired. He left no record of what he thought of the events of 1958. In one sense, Wirth's actions that summer validated the prewar road policies that Vint had established. But Wirth's decision also failed to meet the standard that Mather had set in 1924. Mather had recognized at that time that things needed to be done differently, and he took considerable risk in doing so. In hindsight, 1958 was another watershed moment that called for taking chances and devising fresh approaches; but Wirth chose to stay firmly within the intellectual framework he had created for Mission 66. The Tioga Road debate caused a further hardening of attitudes, not the broad reassessment of the situation critics demanded. The effect of Wirth's decision was exactly the opposite of Mather's: it drastically eroded Park Service credibility at a crucial moment. Blasting and excavation for Tioga Road proceeded as planned but undermined the reputation of Mission 66 and its planners in the process.

Wirth misjudged the great change taking place in the American conservation movement. He thought that he, and Mission 66, could ride out the growing storm over Tioga Road. "We are aware," he wrote to *New York Times* columnist John B. Oakes in one of many attempts to control the unfolding public relations debacle, "—at least in our own minds we think we are aware—of the pitfalls that are ahead of us in connection with taking care of the large numbers of people that are coming to the parks."[47] Wirth pointed out that one thousand projects had been begun or completed between 1956 and 1958, representing a $62 million commitment. But only eight miles of new roads had been built, while 130 miles had been rebuilt. Nine visitor centers, 3,200 campsites, and many "behind-the-scenes facilities" had been built as well. "I make no apology for the construction included in Mission 66," he insisted. "It's the people's right to visit their parks, and they do so in large numbers." The press and the conservation groups emphasized the "construction aspects of Mission 66" without acknowledging that it was all done for the purpose of preservation. "There is no surer way to destroy a landscape than to permit undisciplined use by man," he repeated, not for the first or last time. "Roads, trails, campgrounds, and other developments are one means, perhaps the most important one, of localizing, limiting, and channeling park use." There were other Mission 66 accomplishments to herald: fifty thousand acres of parkland had been acquired and 750 employees hired. "But you can't hang a sign on a new ranger saying 'I'm a Mission 66 project,'" and the "headlines" inevitably stressed construction. That May, Wirth published a lavishly illustrated seventy-page article in *National Geographic* showcasing the national "heritage of beauty and history," as well as the "'new look' in park architecture."[48] Wirth's most ambitious piece of publicity yet, it was a high-water mark for Mission 66 in terms of public image.

By 1959 the tide was turning. Wirth issued agency memoranda admitting that it was "increasingly apparent that a greater effort must be made . . . to present the MISSION 66 program to the public in its true light." There was a "misapprehension" among the public that "MISSION 66 is somehow damaging the Parks or that it is inimical to the purpose for which the Parks were created." Wirth asked all staff who came into contact with the public to "redouble" their efforts to explain that almost all construction would take place within the envelopes of existing development in the parks. "All utterances, oral or written, relating to MISSION 66," Wirth ordered, "should place stress on such benefits as protection, preservation, and enjoyment of the parks, with lesser emphasis being given to the total dollars spent." The "*use* rather that the *cost*" of new facilities was to be emphasized. Wirth wanted more public relations events to be planned and more articles to be written. But there was an underlying sense that control over "the MISSION 66 story" had been lost. There were even "indications" that in some cases park staff did not understand "the concept behind MISSION 66." More informational materials were distributed to parks so that "*all* employees" might better appreciate the "basic purpose of the National Park Service" and how Mission 66 was a "tool to carry it out." Wirth asked that park staff tell the public less about construction progress and more about efforts such as "research studies in regard to use of back country." But there was little to tell with regard to such limited aspects of Mission 66, while construction in the upcoming 1959 season would soon be reaching a peak.[49]

As for Wirth, his staff in Washington, and many of his superintendents, adverse publicity seems to have stiffened their resolve. Bill Carnes, for example, distributed a short essay on the subject of Mission 66 written by Robert M. Coates, Park Service "public policy analyst." Describing the program as a "Renaissance movement in parks," Coates explained why he (and Carnes) felt it was increasingly resented. Mission 66 was "returning to the basic fundamentals" of the park movement, and therefore was "destroying the false convictions, distortions, and teachings of those who were working the park idea around to a narrow and selfish exploitation for the select few—a doctrine that is the very antithesis of our democratic principles." Mission 66 was in fact "a crusade" that carried on the ideals, first described by Andrew Jackson Downing and the Olmsteds, of American parks as the great public spaces of the nation. Regardless of the benefits of new construction, "without such a revival and resurgence" of "zeal, enthusiasm, and conviction," the parks would be "doomed."[50]

Notwithstanding these effort to control public perceptions, by the time Tioga Road was dedicated in 1961—the midpoint of the Mission 66 program—Wirth and his planners had been forced into a major "reassessment" of their efforts. Mission 66 would never again enjoy the optimism of its enthusiastic beginning. Wirth held the dedication ceremony for Tioga Road at the controversial overlook near Tenaya Lake, now named in honor of Frederick Law Olmsted Jr. Olmsted had died in 1957, and William Colby was too old and sick to attend the ceremony. The Yosemite Advisory Board had disbanded, and Vint was retiring. The tone of Wirth's comments was defensive. The project had caused a controversy, he admitted, and the greatest problem had occurred "right here where we stand." He was making a point: "large numbers of park visitors" could now enjoy the beautiful views that surrounded the gathered dignitaries. "Look at it!" he exclaimed. "Have you ever seen anything more beautiful? . . . We have been criticized for this location. I hope our good friends, the critics, will forgive us for not following their advice."[51]

The principal speaker at the ceremony, however, was John A. Carver Jr., the new assistant secretary of the interior. Just as the arrival of the Eisenhower administration had set the stage for the beginning of Mission 66, the arrival of the Kennedy administration, and the appointment of Stewart L. Udall that January as secretary of the interior, put in motion the events that would lead to the announcement of Wirth's retirement late in 1963. Udall's philosophy of "New Conservation" differed from that of Mission 66. The Park Service provided a draft speech for Carver, which, if he ever read, he completely ignored. "Tension mars this occasion, and I feel trepidation," he began. "I'm tempted here to treat my delicate task as did the politician called to comment on the unlovely child. 'Say,' he exclaims, 'that is a baby.' For it is a fact, for good or ill, that here there is a road." While he urged all sides to end their recriminations for the common good of shared goals, he made it clear that the change of administration meant that conservation groups now had a sympathetic ear at the Department of the Interior. In the meantime, he said, "Connie Wirth's reputation stands on a base of public service broader than this road," and no one could suggest that he had ever been motivated by anything but the "highest aspirations." Nevertheless, from the beginning there

was intense mutual distrust between Wirth and the outspoken assistant secretary.[52]

Tioga Road was not the only Mission 66 road project to generate heated debate. Plans for Mount McKinley (later Denali) National Park in

Olmsted Point and controversial road cuts through granite, Tioga Road. Author's photo.

View from Olmsted Point. Author's photo.

Alaska were quickly opposed by scientists and conservation advocates worried that a park known for its frontier wilderness character would be devastated by an influx of automotive tourists. In this case the conservationist Olaus J. Murie became another fierce critic of Mission 66. As a field biologist, Murie had done pioneering studies of the wildlife of Mount McKinley beginning in the 1920s. His younger half-brother, Adolph Murie, was also a field biologist who produced his own major studies of Rocky Mountain and Alaskan fauna over a twenty-year career with the Park Service. Olaus was more the activist, and in the 1950s he was a key figure in drafting and advocating proposed wilderness legislation.[53] As president of the Wilderness Society, he also wrote Wirth a series of letters condemning Mission 66 projects all over the country, and he became as potent an adversary as Brower and Adams.[54] Wirth and Scoyen were kept busy writing long letters back, explaining details of park plans and defending their overall commitment to preserving wilderness. But these were the kinds of efforts that would have had better results in 1955, when conservationists had been anxious to join in early Mission 66 planning.

Both Olaus and Adolph Murie particularly opposed Mission 66 plans for Mount McKinley, where they had done so many years of research over their long careers. Established as a park in 1917, Mount McKinley had only begun receiving visitors in the early 1920s, when the Alaska Railroad opened. The Park Service and the Alaska Road Commission then extended a road into the park, allowing a concessioner to meet tourists at McKinley Station and bring them into the park in touring cars. In 1929 Vint drew up a plan calling for the road to be extended to the site of a proposed rustic lodge at Wonder Lake. By 1938 the unpaved road was completed, but it remained rough by prewar national park standards. Annual visitation to the park, remained in the hundreds in the 1920s and reached a high of only 2,200 in 1939. There was little pressure on the park from visitors, and little interest from Congress or concessioners in further investment. The rustic lodge and other elements of Vint's master plan were never built.[55]

The situation changed for the park, and for all of Alaska, after the Alcan Highway was built during World War II. After the war, local officials proposed the construction of the Denali Highway (not to be confused with the park road, later known as Denali Road), which connected Mount McKinley to Alaska's highway system. Mission 66 planners anticipated that the road's opening in 1957 would move the park from the old model of "package-type train and bus tour" to a situation comparable to that in parks in the rest of the country: "mobile visitors" in private automobiles would demand campgrounds, roadside visitor centers, and other car-friendly services. The prospectus characterized the existing park road as a "95 mile substandard gravel highway" that would be inadequate for the private automobile traffic that would begin arriving when the Denali Highway opened. The entire park road would need to be rebuilt and realigned where necessary "to reduce hazards or improve views." It also would be brought up to "paving standards" with a twenty-foot-wide roadway and three-foot paved shoulders. The road would not be extended, however, nor would any new roads be proposed for the park. The prospectus also canceled plans for a lodge at Wonder Lake. Campgrounds, a park store, and other day use services would be available, but "private enterprise would provide . . . [overnight lodgings] beyond park boundaries" as the need arose. Existing concession operations would continue, however, and several new visitor centers were planned. "Behind-the-scene improvements" would include housing, maintenance areas, and utilities, mostly in the administrative area near the park entrance. After ten years and about $10 million in planned construction, visitors would find the "remote and untouched aspect" of the park unaffected, but they would also be "impressed by the comfortable and well located" campgrounds and "well integrated interpretive program." The overall "theme of the park," as expressed in the prospectus, was "the maintenance of wilderness integrity."[56]

Some of the preservationist tone of the final park prospectus resulted from Adolph Murie's comments and involvement. In 1956 Murie condemned earlier Mission 66 proposals that included overnight lodging (not at Wonder Lake but near the Savage River, closer to the park entrance) as well as other aspects of proposed plans. In a long personal letter to Sanford Hill at the WODC, Murie worried that the park could become "another Yellowstone or Yosemite" unless Hill took advantage of the opportunity "for some planning along idealistic lines." He insisted that "wilderness standards in McKinley must be maintained to a higher level than anything we have attempted in the States." But although the final prospectus called for no overnight lodgings and made other changes,

Murie and others were not completely satisfied. In an echo of the Tioga Road debate, they called for the park road to remain in its existing condition and for basic priorities to be reconsidered. They wanted the park to stay essentially undeveloped, with only the unpaved road and perhaps a few carefully sited campgrounds to serve the public. The proposed widening and modernization of the road, in particular, threatened to destroy the very "wilderness integrity" that the Mission 66 planners had so dutifully described. The wilderness character of this most famous Alaskan park needed complete protection; even roadside interpretive signs were an unwelcome indication of civilization. As park historian William E. Brown observes, Mission 66 "brought the first phase of McKinley Park's preservation-versus-development debate to a head."[57]

Work proceeded slowly (by Mission 66 standards) at Mount McKinley, but by the early 1960s the construction program was well under way, with work on the Eielson Visitor Center, improvements in the park administrative area, and significant road construction completed. By 1963, however, state highway plans again changed the situation. Another state highway was under construction between Anchorage and Fairbanks, roughly along the route of the Alaska Railroad. This would open the park to an even higher level of automotive tourism, and concern over Mission 66 plans quickly took on great urgency. Writing in *National Parks Magazine*, Olaus Murie warned readers that "the prevailing enthusiasm for what the bulldozer can do" had come to Alaska, and particularly to Mount McKinley, where a "speedway was under construction." Murie noted that the Park Service was still under pressure from local interests to build a lodge in the park, adding (perhaps fearing another reversal, as at Everglades) that the agency had not categorically ruled out the possibility. Architectural aesthetics were an issue as well. The Eielson Visitor Center—an unassuming but decidedly modernist building completed in 1960—was characterized as a "monstrosity" (and

The Eielson Visitor Center under construction in 1960 in Mount McKinley (now Denali) National Park. NPS Historic Photo Collection.

The Eielson Visitor Center in 1964. NPS Historic Photo Collection.

later, by Adolph Murie, as "the Dairy Queen"). The editors of *National Parks* agreed, calling again for a "complete reform of park road construction" and of park planning in general. Other articles, editorials, and letters to the editor echoed the sentiments.[58]

The situation recalled the Tioga Road controversy. But Secretary Udall apparently was not interested in repeating that experience. Wilderness and wildlife protection had always been priorities at Mount McKinley, and relatively low numbers of visitors made arguments for accommodating public demand less persuasive. When the intensity of the opposition to Mission 66 plans for the park became clear in 1963, Vint's successor as director of design and construction, A. Clark Stratton, announced a major change in plans. The Mount McKinley park road would be completed according to what Stratton described as "telescoping standards." The first thirty miles, mostly completed already, would be a paved road twenty feet wide with three-foot paved shoulders. The next forty miles, however, would be an unpaved twenty-foot-wide surface with minimal shoulders. The final eighteen miles to Wonder Lake would remain a "primitive gravel road." Wherever possible, the new road would retain its existing alignment.[59] The "telescoping standards," in other words, amounted to a termination of the Mission 66 road project in mid-construction. Work continued for several years before it officially halted, but the "telescoping" road, known today as Denali Road, remains as a physical record and expression of the changing fortunes of the Mission 66 program.

The reactions to the Tioga Road and later the Denali Road projects were intense and changed the climate in which the public, the Department of the Interior, and some employees of the Park Service received Mission 66. But the controversies around these roads were not typical. Hundreds of less dramatic road improvements and realignments were undertaken throughout the park system, and the majority did not incite opposition. Many in fact were welcomed as needed improvements. By Wirth's own estimate, 1,570 miles of roads were "reconstructed" under Mission 66, while 1,197 miles of new roads were built, "mostly in new areas" of the rapidly expanding park system.[60] But the ambitious pace and scope of Mission 66, initially considered its virtue, now worked against its public image. The "bulldozers of bureaucracy" were active everywhere by the late 1950s, leading Ansel Adams, Olaus Murie, and other activists to suggest that the bulldozer should be the symbol of Mission 66. By the early 1960s they had succeeded in characterizing the program, at least for a significant and influential segment of the public, as one of rampant overdevelopment.

But for Wirth and his Mission 66 staff, road projects remained critical to their modernist concept of the park. Plans for overnight accommodations, for example, could be canceled, as they were at Mount McKinley. Leaving roads in a "primitive" state, however, meant restricting not just overnight use but day use as well. That left little of the public park idea; a park became a reservation to be used by a small, self-selected group. There was also an important distinction, at least for Wirth and his staff, between building a new road and improving an existing one. Park Service officials repeatedly observed that neither the Tioga Road nor the Denali Road proj-

Typical Mission 66 road construction. NPS Historic Photo Collection.

ect involved the invasion of a previously roadless area. For conservationists, however, this was a distinction without a difference; increasing the capacity of a road could be almost as bad as building a new one.

In cases where new roads had been proposed in roadless wilderness areas, however, Wirth and his planners were willing to cancel prewar road construction plans. They often described Mission 66 as a plan of redevelopment, not development, that would typically remain within the overall existing footprint of development in parks. Exactly what constituted an existing footprint of development was, of course, subject to interpretation. Scoyen insisted, for example, that Canyon and Grant villages in Yellowstone were within the park's 1908 development footprint because they were sited along the corridor of the park road system, which had been laid out by that date. But in other cases, where new road development would undeniably penetrate existing wilderness, Mission 66 planners in fact tried to be true to their own policies.

At Olympic National Park, for example, numerous road proposals had been put forward for decades. As the bitter contest over whether valuable rain forests would be preserved or sent to the mills continued through the 1950s, conservationists, elected officials, and park planners also debated how this "wilderness park" should be developed for public use. Initial Mission 66 plans called for the construction of a scenic highway in the "coastal strip" portion of the park, where a road had been planned since the 1930s. But conservationists now objected to a new highway along the spectacular and undeveloped coastline, and in the spring of 1957 Wirth permanently removed the project from the park's prospectus. Mission 66 paid for the completion of the spur road to the Hurricane Ridge Lodge (1952) in the park, but in 1959 Wirth decided that the lodge should be converted to a day use facility rather than expanded for increased overnight use. Olympic's Mission 66 development plan ended up as a series of improvements to existing spur roads into the park, with visitor centers, campgrounds, and other facilities along or at the ends of the roads.

The vast majority of the park remained roadless, as it had been before Mission 66. The park administrative area (as described earlier) had already been built outside the park in the nearby town of Port Angeles.[61]

At Kings Canyon National Park, another of Ickes's "wilderness parks," Mission 66 plans called only for a minor extension to the prewar road into Kings Canyon, which had been built by the Forest Service. The rest of the park remained roadless. In neighboring Sequoia National Park, plans called for some improvements to the Generals Highway, but not for any significant new roads. At Everglades, the new park road to Flamingo was, again, technically a reconstruction of the old Ingraham Highway, and the Mission 66 prospectus characterized the park as primarily a "biological area" and a "wilderness preserve." Major new road construction under Mission 66 usually occurred, as Wirth repeatedly asserted, in parks that were being added to the system, especially new national seashores, recreation areas, and historical parks. In addition, the

A contemporary cartoon by Dave Bixby. Operation Outdoors was a Forest Service program begun in 1957. Courtesy Desert Protective Council, Inc.

relocation of existing roads considered inadequate (such as the approach road to Paradise at Mount Rainier) and the completion of projects begun before the war (such as the Stevens Canyon Highway, also at Mount Rainier) made up significant categories of new road construction. A large amount of new mileage also fell into the category of "access roads" for new residential areas, maintenance yards, and concessioner developments. At least according to Wirth and his planners, none of these new roads invaded or reduced wilderness.

But by the early 1960s, as the Park Service efficiently spent the enormous construction appropriations Congress continued to make, for many people the bulldozer had indeed become the symbol of Wirth's program. The controversies aroused by Mission 66 construction obscured some of the profound contributions to the national park system that the program was making, even as conservationists condemned it. Much of this legacy has already been described. For example, visitor centers and the revised approach to park interpretation that they facilitated, and the increased hiring, training, and professionalization of uniformed staff, were physical and institutional foundations of the postwar Park Service that were created through Mission 66.

The most significant products of Mission 66, however, remain to be discussed. Considering Wirth's career and interests, these achievements were appropriately in the fields of recreational planning, new park acquisition, and recreational and historical park developments. These categories of Mission 66 planning and development will outlast even the program's built legacy of roads, utilities, residences, and visitor centers.

The dramatic typological expansion of the park system and the addition of new parks and thousands of acres of parkland occurred at a crucial moment in American landscape history, when private development was rapidly covering the nation's last undeveloped seashores and lakeshores. Mission 66 made big plans for public access and recreation at a time when such schemes could still be implemented. The new parks and new types of parks created through Mission 66 constitute the most vital—and often forgotten—category of the program's accomplishments.

But after 1958, national recreational planning at the Park Service went ahead in tandem with another federal initiative. That year Congress established the Outdoor Recreation Resources Review Commission, which was charged with reporting on the state of outdoor recreation resources in the United States and making recommendations for federal legislation or other actions to meet the growing demand for access to parks and other recreation areas. The commission's mandate, in other words, was to make suggestions as to how to accomplish much of what Wirth had organized Mission 66 to do. Wirth had not led—nor did he support—the initiative to create the Outdoor Recreation Resources Review Commission. As with the contemporary campaign to pass the Wilderness Act, the group continued its work as Mission 66 went ahead on a parallel track. In the early 1960s Mission 66 construction moved from groundbreakings to ribbon-cuttings; but the great social and political changes of the era demanded that Wirth reformulate Mission 66 for its second half.

CHAPTER 10

"PARKS FOR AMERICA"

When Stewart Udall resigned from Congress in 1960 to become John F. Kennedy's secretary of the interior, a new era in federal conservation began. From a prominent Arizona family, Udall had served on the House Committee on Interior and Insular Affairs since 1955 and was already informed and influential on federal conservation issues. Over the next nine years Udall helped secure the passage of the Wilderness Act (1964), the Land and Water Conservation Fund Act (1964), the National Historic Preservation Act (1966), and the Wild and Scenic Rivers Act (1968), just to name some of the legislative accomplishments of the era.[1] Through the remaining years of Mission 66 and for three years following, Udall oversaw a massive expansion of the national park system. His book on conservation policy, *The Quiet Crisis,* became a best-seller in 1963, a year after Rachel Carson's *Silent Spring* marked the onset of a broad social and political movement becoming known as environmental-

ism. Not since Harold Ickes oversaw New Deal programs in the 1930s had any secretary of the interior accomplished so much or been so well known a public figure as Stewart Udall in the 1960s. Youthful and passionate, Udall contrasted with Eisenhower's more staid secretary, Fred Seaton, who had given his department's full support to Conrad Wirth since 1956.

The second half of Mission 66, during the Kennedy and Johnson administrations, was played out in a completely changed political setting at the Department of the Interior. In his 1963 book describing "the quiet conservation crisis of the 1960s," Udall observed that Americans were living "in a land of vanishing beauty, and of an overall environment that is diminished daily by pollution, noise, and blight." The book was a call to action: "We must act decisively—and soon—if we are to assert the people's right to clean air and water, to open space, to well-designed urban areas, to mental and

physical health." But the action Udall had in mind did not sound much like Mission 66, nor did the secretary mention the ongoing program in his book. Udall called for a "preservation-of-environment" initiative based on the coordination of federal policies, including the acquisition of land for conservation and recreation areas. He urged the immediate passage of the Wilderness Act and other legislation. Invoking Aldo Leopold, the biologist and conservationist who died in 1948, he proposed a "land ethic for tomorrow" which would be the basis of a "balanced conservation program" and a "higher ideal of conservation" that would "make the earth a better home both for ourselves and for those as yet unborn."[2] Even before the 1960 election Wirth knew that he needed to act if he

and his agency were to remain in step with the changes occurring in the political and philosophical culture of American conservation.

Many government officials and much of the public, however, still considered Mission 66 an outstanding success story. Other federal and state agencies imitated the program. In 1957 the Forest Service started its own five-year program, "Operation Outdoors," and realized increased appropriations for its own roads, campgrounds, and visitor centers.[3] By 1960, a year when over 72 million people visited the national park system, Mission 66 had developed 7,000 individual campsites and rehabilitated another 4,000. Over 650 miles of old roads had been improved and 140 miles of new roads and 880 new parking areas had been built. Fifty-four visitor centers were opened or under construction, and over 1,000 visitor center interpretive displays and 1,500 "wayside" interpretive exhibits had been designed and installed. Over 160 miles of new trails had been built and another 120 miles rebuilt. Hundreds of campfire circles and outdoor amphitheaters complemented the campgrounds and visitor centers. Millions of dollars had been spent on water lines and sewage treatment plants, and power lines connected many parks to regional grids for the first time. About $180 million had been spent on construction, and projects under way represented $60 million more. Concessioners had invested $20 million. Land acquisitions totaled 227,000 acres. Park staffing had admittedly lagged, as Congress proved less willing to fund new personnel than to build roads and facilities; but by 1959 the agency had 8,000 permanent and seasonal employees, up from 7,200 in 1956. Operations budgets had risen from $20 million to $37 million. Over 700 units of housing, much of it new ranch houses, were available for park staff.[4] In 1959 Wirth claimed that, at least in terms of visitor and staff facilities, the national park system was "in the best condition in its history."[5]

Changes were in order, nevertheless. Almost from the beginning Park Service officials had planned a "top-level review" of Mission 66 for 1960, an election year in which the program would also reach its halfway point.[6] The objections of wilderness advocates and the creation of the Outdoor Recreation Resources Review Commission (ORRRC) in 1958 increased the urgency of such plans. By 1959 "a restudy of the original Mission 66 program" was already under way.[7]

The creation of the ORRRC, in particular, had left Wirth with little option but to reconsider Mission 66. For three years, as the recreation commission assembled data and prepared its final report, Wirth struggled to retain the Park Service's role as the nation's recreational planning agency. But Congress had never really believed that Mission 66 was a "national recreational plan" rather than merely a development program requiring no legislative consideration beyond annual appropriation bills. Mission 66 therefore relied on the authority of New Deal legislation, such as the 1935 Historic Sites Act and the 1936 Park, Parkway, and Recreational-Area Study Act. In many ways Mission 66 was the last New Deal park initiative. Among the Park Service directorate (director, associate director, assistant and regional directors) in 1960, none had begun working for the government after 1934. Many Mission 66 projects, including Canyon Village and Tioga Road, had been planned in the 1930s, and the program held fast to the basic ideology of prewar national park making as well as many specific plans.

Wirth never secured a broad new legislative mandate for his agency in the postwar era. Increased annual appropriations meant construction progress, but they did not authorize Mission 66 to coordinate an overall federal and state initiative for the recreational use of public lands. Mission 66 assistance to state park systems was limited to technical bulletins—design sheets and specifications for typical park facilities—issued through the National Conference on State Parks. This was a far cry from the role the agency had played in the expansion of state park systems during the New Deal.[8] Neither did Mission 66 appropriations fund what many conservationists increasingly felt was needed: a massive program of federal land acquisition for new public park areas of all types. When it created the ORRRC, however, Congress began consideration of a new generation of broad legislation that would replace New Deal–era policies and bureaucracies with new planning organizations and funding methods. Mission 66 had opened congressional purse strings for national park development. But the ORRRC heralded a new willingness to legislate a more comprehensive approach to the conservation and recreation issues of the day.

The advocates of the ORRRC were responding to the fact that all public lands—not just national parks—were overcrowded and overwhelmed by the demand for recreational access to lakes, seashores, forests, and mountains. Outdoor recreation was a huge industry by the 1950s, involving not only cars and roadside motel and restaurant development but motor boats, camping trailers, and other equipment as well. Recreation rivaled logging, ranching, mining, and dam construction in terms of social and economic impact; it had become a primary function of federal and state public lands, including those, such as the national forests, in which recreation had never been a foremost consideration. Every federal and state land management agency had increased obligations to provide public access and facilities for recreation. Coordination across federal departments and with state and local governments was more vital than ever. The Park Service had provided this kind of coordination during the New Deal. The creation of the ORRRC indicated that Mission 66 had not continued that function.

The origins of the ORRRC legislation were somewhat obscure. The idea was first suggested by the conservationist Joseph W. Penfold of the Izaak Walton League of America. Penfold and an assistant chief of the Forest Service, Edward C. Crafts, drafted the first versions of the recreation legislation and soon attracted the backing of Brower and the Sierra Club. The precedent of Mission 66 helped inspire the ORRRC proposal, but from the beginning it set forth an alternative vision and implied a criticism of Wirth and his agency. Many government officials and private conservationists saw the professional culture of the Park Service as inimical to the spirit of interagency cooperation that they hoped the ORRRC would achieve. As the agency with the most to lose, the Park Service took exception to the entire ORRRC effort, reinforcing the impression that it would neither share authority nor cooperate in a multi-agency endeavor. The ORRRC legislation gathered broad support in Congress, however, thanks to the inclusive process it described, as well as the recognized economic and social importance of outdoor recreation to a variety of interests all over the country. Some of the legislators interested in the bill also backed wilderness legislation as a complementary measure. For a while "wilderness" and "recreation" bills—both opposed by the Park Service—were being considered in Congress simultaneously. Congressman Wayne N. Aspinall of Colorado, who chaired the House Public Lands Committee, and Senator Joseph C. O'Mahoney of Wyoming endorsed the recreation plan. In the fall of 1957 President Eisenhower sent a special message to Congress supporting it. According to historian Robin W.

Winks, Nelson A. Rockefeller (Laurance's brother) also lobbied at a crucial point, persuading House Speaker Sam Rayburn to move the legislation forward quickly, with little debate. Eisenhower signed the bill in June 1958.[9]

The ORRRC consisted of eight designated members of Congress and seven outside experts in recreation. The latter were appointed by Eisenhower, who also named the commission chairman. A large and inclusive advisory council brought in representatives from federal, state, and local governments, business interests, and conservation groups. The new commission was empowered to survey all the nation's "non-urban" recreational resources (those not associated with municipal park systems), and to assess what the nation's recreational needs would be for the remainder of the twentieth century. The commission was then to "determine what policies and programs should be recommended to assure that the needs of the present and the future" were met. Appointments were made, staff was hired, and the commission got to work early in 1959. Special research studies—on wilderness, on hunting and fishing, on "metropolitan areas," and many others—were commissioned. The Census Bureau conducted a national survey of public activities and preferences. The scope of the undertaking was impressive, and the open meetings and broad partnership of federal, state, public, and private interests contrasted with the way Mission 66 had been planned four years earlier. Charged with making their report and then disbanding by January 1962, the ORRRC had funding, a legislative mandate, and broad support.[10] A new era of federal conservation and recreational planning had been set in motion, but not by the Park Service. In fact, as inclusive as the ORRRC was, it all but excluded the Park Service from participation. The backers of the legislation made sure that Wirth and his staff, regardless of their experience in park planning, would not be in a position to control the commission's process, activities, or recommendations.

Wirth's one consolation, he thought, was that Laurance Rockefeller had been appointed commission chairman. Rockefeller's long association with the Park Service and close friendship with Albright, Wirth, and other officials made him a member of the "family." By the 1950s Laurance had assumed his father's interest in conservation issues, beginning with the planning and construction of the Jackson Lake Lodge and other developments at Grand Tetons. In 1956 he gave the federal government over five thousand acres on the island of St. John to create Virgin Islands National Park, which was dedicated that December. The national park surrounded Rockefeller's newly opened hotel and resort complex, Caneel Bay, in which he anticipated the low-impact, nature-oriented experience later described as "eco-tourism."[11] Although the new Virgin Islands park had been planned independently of Mission 66, it greatly boosted the program during its first year. Rockefeller also financed other projects and publications for the Park Service, many through his family's nonprofit organization, Jackson Hole Preserve, Inc., of which he was president. His appointment to lead the ORRRC (apparently at Albright's suggestion) solved a sensitive problem. The Park Service had decades of recreational planning data and surveys that the ORRRC would need to consult and use. Rockefeller's appointment helped ensure that Wirth would cooperate with the ORRRC and share his agency's information and expertise, even as he was left out of the process. "An earlier recreational study program, started by the National Park Service in 1936 . . . and accelerated under the Mission 66 program," Wirth reported in 1959, was now "tied in closely" with the ORRRC.[12]

Wirth hoped that the Park Service could act as a consultant to the ORRRC, as it had in the 1930s for the National Resources Board, producing the data and analysis for the acquisition of proposed national seashores, recreation areas, historical parks, and state parks. Above all he did not want to surrender his agency's responsibility to plan for the expansion of the national park system itself. So while his staff cooperated with the ORRRC, Wirth began to envision changes to Mission 66 that would improve the program's image, certainly, but that also would make it a better fit with the priorities being set by the new commission. In 1959 Wirth initiated a revision of Mission 66. "As we enter a year of study and reappraisal of our MISSION 66 status," he wrote to his staff, "certain changes of staffing and handling of the effort must be made. We will be in another period in which the efforts and best ideas of the whole Service 'family' will be required." At a staff meeting in Washington in February 1960, Wirth announced that the agency faced the task of "re-analyzing our entire MISSION 66 program to revitalize it." The director tried to conjure up the urgency of the first meetings, held almost exactly five years earlier in the same room. He wanted to repeat the original Mission 66 planning process, on a

reduced scale, in order to come up with a renewed vision in time for it to be unveiled to the public at the next Park Service conference, scheduled for April 1961 at Grand Canyon. The revised Mission 66 program would be presented to a new administration (Eisenhower, completing his second term, could not run for reelection), but still nine months before the ORRRC presented its final report. Whether he was dealing with Republicans or Democrats, he said, he wanted a renewed Mission 66 "locked" and "ready to roll." Some things, however, had not changed. "There is to be no publicity," the director warned; everything was "to be kept in the 'family.'" The revision of Mission 66, like the original, was to be planned by his staff behind closed doors and then dramatically sprung on the public and press.[13]

Even while changes were being made, Wirth recommitted his agency to the basic philosophy and convictions of Mission 66. The program, and the name itself, retained a powerful image in Congress and for much of the public. Wirth asked every park superintendent to reassemble the 1955 Mission 66 memoranda and other documents, including *Our Heritage, The National Park Wilderness,* and *That the Past Shall Live,* in order to make them available to park staff. He hoped to rekindle enthusiasm and "renew our memories" of the "philosophy and intent" of Mission 66 even as an "intensive reappraisal" determined how it should adapt.[14] He also began replacing the Mission 66 park prospectuses with "master plans in a new format." Beginning in 1959 the new master plans replaced both park prospectuses and "development outlines," and to some degree were a return to the more detailed, longer-term park plans.[15] Simplified in format and reduced in content, however, the new master plans exhibited the pervasive influence of Mission 66. Wirth directed every park to develop new master plans over the next three years, combining prospectuses, previous master plans, and other research. The result was to be a "sounder basis for development planning" and would "extend the Master Plan concept into the management field." The master planning process continued to evolve in the early 1960s as the term "prospectus" was abandoned. By 1963 the "package system" of master plan preparation had been devised. Park staff met with professionals from the regional and design offices in the park being planned, and for a period of days or weeks they worked together on-site. The package system accelerated master planning by creating an early consensus among all agency reviewers and contributors. A "professionally qualified natural scientist" was also assigned to each "package master plan team." These revisions in park master planning greatly affected how Mission 66 was conducted in its second half.[16]

As his reappraisal proceeded, Wirth repeatedly stated his commitment to contribute to the work of the ORRRC. The recreation commission promised to usher in an array of federal legislation that had eluded Wirth for years, including measures to fund the direct acquisition of new federal park land and to provide grants-in-aid to state park systems. If the ORRRC threatened his agency's bureaucratic position, it also promised the achievement of legislative goals that Wirth had long wanted to make part of Mission 66. But since the Park Service did not directly participate in the ORRRC, Wirth had lit-

tle opportunity to shape the recommendations it would make. He therefore created his own commission, of sorts, intended to support and help implement the ORRRC's proposals but also to upstage the commission's final report. To do this, he drew on an extensive network of municipal, state, and federal park officials, most of whom had worked together on New Deal park programs. In the winter of 1956, Wirth later recalled, a group of these colleagues had already formed what they called the Committee of Fifteen. Made up of five members from each level of government, they discussed the coordination of recreational plans and possible means of renewing federal grants for state parks. Wirth characterized the committee as a continuation of an informal "discussion group" begun in the 1930s among agencies and individuals involved in the administration of the CCC.[17] Whatever its origins, Wirth's network of state and municipal park executives suddenly became very active in 1959 as they became aware that the ORRRC would make recommendations directly affecting them. In August 1960, at Secretary of the Interior Seaton's invitation, officials from the American Institute of Park Executives and the National Conference on State Parks were asked to join the Park Service to initiate a new park planning organization. Under the combined aegis of the three groups representing three levels of government, the initiative was named "Parks for America."[18]

Wirth insisted that Parks for America would "neither conflict [with] nor duplicate" the ORRRC but be an effective partner in advocating legislation to fund new federal and state parks. The ORRRC itself did not intend to make specific recommendations for land acquisition; Wirth and his municipal and state partners, however, had a huge backlog of specific proposals waiting to be implemented. "Approximately 40 bills were introduced in the last Congress, to authorize the acquisition of national seashores . . . [and] state seashore areas as identified in the seashore survey reports," the Committee of Fifteen wrote. "None of these were enacted." Congress up to that point had never funded the direct acquisition of land for new national parks, and Parks for America welcomed the prospect that the ORRRC might change that attitude. But they also felt that they already had their own plans for park system expansions and so did not need advice as much as political support. Wirth and Benjamin H. Thompson, Park Service director of land planning, stressed that their agency had been compiling "seashore reports and other data" since the 1930s and had continued these efforts through river basin studies in the 1940s. These surveys of recreational needs and opportunities had been elaborated under Mission 66 and now could "provide the basis for an immediate acquisition program" for national and state parks. Parks for America could begin its public relations campaign immediately; there was no need to wait for the ORRRC to publish its final report. Wirth even wanted another event "somewhat similar to the Pioneer Dinner" to kick off the legislative campaign to fund an unprecedented wave of direct federal acquisition of national parkland and grants-in-aid to states for the same purpose.[19]

In December 1960, as the transition to the Kennedy administration was under way, *Parks & Recreation* magazine published an article describing Parks for America as the Committee of Fifteen met in Washington to further their plans. Knowing that Kennedy and Udall strongly supported the ORRRC and the proposals expected to come from it, Wirth told the group that they had "the real opportunity of the century now." Parks for America would seek "a new vitality in park land acquisition programs," and the new administration would help them realize their goals in Congress. Early in 1961 the group met with Udall, "who expressed his approval of the aims and objectives of the **PARKS FOR AMERICA** program." The executive director of the ORRRC, Francis W. Sargent, attended the March meeting of the Committee of Fifteen and told the group that he considered them a "working unit" of the recreation commission. Wirth and Thompson were ready to give Sargent specific numbers for necessary state and local park system land acquisition: by 1970 the federal government should acquire over 9.6 million acres for state and local parks at a cost of $6.3 billion. By putting these numbers forward in 1961, Parks for America helped assure that the ORRRC would not fail to make ambitious proposals for federally funded state and local park expansion.[20]

Parks for America was meant to complement, implement, and perhaps upstage the ORRRC. If some of the municipal, state, and national park executives who made up the campaign were threatened by the new recreation commission, they also intended to make sure that they were not left out of federal spending programs that might result from it. On the national park side, Wirth used his plans for a revised Mission 66 to similar ends. Early in 1960 he built up anticipation for the "second stage of MISSION 66," which was to be "launched" at the Park Service conference at Grand Canyon in 1961. The new Mission 66 would increasingly emphasize land acquisition: the first two priorities of the program, as they were being drafted at the beginning of 1960, were "new areas" and the "expansion of the system." Wirth began suggesting that construction had proceeded so well in the first half of Mission 66 that new priorities could now be addressed. By 1960 the agency was "over the hump, or at least 85% complete, in the repairs, reconstruction, [and] replacement of facilities." The second half of Mission 66 would emphasize acquisition and expansion of parks in anticipation of new legislation made possible by the ORRRC. Wirth also anticipated other potential ORRRC recommendations, for example, by experimenting with the idea that separate national park and national recreation systems should be defined, each with its own management policies.[21] Wirth worked hard to show the incoming administration that he could adapt his agency, and Mission 66, to changing times. In the briefing paper he prepared for Udall at the end of 1960, he summarized some of the revised priorities being readied for presentation at the Grand Canyon conference that spring. "Rounding out the national park system" was the first priority, and he listed over fifteen national seashore, recreation area, and historical park proposals for which legislation was already drafted.[22]

Wirth was not yet sixty-two and had already served as director for Republican and Democratic administrations. It was a testament to the perceived stature of the Park Service's professional tradition, and to Wirth's personal reputation,

that Kennedy and Udall apparently did not consider replacing him in 1961. Although the ORRRC threatened the Park Service's position in the federal government, the Parks for America campaign demonstrated the strength and support of Wirth's network of state and local park commissions and executives. Mission 66 construction had incited controversy over the previous five years, but in its "second stage" the program promised to be more in harmony with New Conservation. Wirth was careful to show full support for the ORRRC, which Kennedy and Udall strongly supported, but he also protected his agency's bureaucratic position. At least for the time being, Wirth and Mission 66 seemed to have made a successful transition to become part of the new spirit at the Department of the Interior.

But the strong image of Mission 66 cut both ways. Negative publicity about Mission 66—and therefore about the Park Service itself, which was now completely identified with the program— surged in the popular press just as the new administration was settling in. In 1961 the *Atlantic* magazine dedicated most of its February issue to withering criticisms of Park Service policy. The timing of the issue was damaging, as was its content. In a long letter to Udall, Wirth tried to mitigate the impact of the bad publicity. On the one hand, he acknowledged that Paul Brooks, who wrote on "The Pressure of Numbers," was right: "We wholeheartedly endorse what Mr. Brooks has to say. . . . Overdevelopment and more roads is not the answer. The pressures of numbers can only be relieved by the establishment of additional park and recreation areas on all levels." On the other hand, Wirth rejected Devereux

Butcher's claim that "to popularize the national parks is to cheapen them and reduce them to the level of ordinary playgrounds." Wirth pointed out that "the parks belong to the people and the people are determined to visit them. . . . The people cannot be unreasonably restricted or excluded from the parks and the parks must provide for them." The litany of defensive responses was familiar: few new roads (as opposed to road improvements) had been built; the basic footprint of development in the parks had (arguably) not changed much since the 1920s; Mission 66 development was more efficient and therefore had allowed the restoration of older, more destructive developed areas to "natural" conditions; the parks could not be "insulated" from the public, who had a right to visit them.[23]

Udall's reply to Wirth became the basis of an article the secretary published that summer, also in the *Atlantic*. The secretary defended Mission 66, but he emphasized that "a new administration [had] come to power" and that this was an "opportune moment to review the scope of the program and assess its work." Udall's strategy was to write off certain experiences—such as Tioga Road—as "mistakes" that would not be repeated. A modernist, ramped observation tower at Clingman's Dome in Great Smoky Mountains (similar to the Shark Valley observation tower in Everglades) was another "mistake" that was now often cited as an example of inappropriate architectural design in the parks. Other errors, such as the Flamingo motel in Everglades, had been forced on the Park Service. Some unfortunate situations, such as the amount of development on the south rim of the Grand Canyon, had resulted from historical patterns over which

the agency could have only limited control. "When you view the many Mission 66 projects in perspective," the new secretary observed, "it is amazing that so few egregious errors have been committed."[24]

This fair-minded defense of the Park Service was possible because Udall had already secured the reorientation of Mission 66 along lines consistent with his goals. His confidence resulted from the "launch" of the "second stage" of Mission 66 at Grand Canyon that April. Named the "Mission 66 Frontiers Conference," the event was described as a "reappraisal"; but it really served to unveil the previous year's work reinventing Mission 66 which Wirth, Carnes, and the rest of the Park Service staff (in this case mostly in Washington) had already prepared. The event marked a change in tone, and to some degree a reconciliation between the Park Service and the larger conservation community. Conservation organizations were ready, in some cases, to temper their criticisms. The National Parks Association officials, for example, now insisted that they had "concurred from the beginning on the importance of making reasonable provision for the great increase in the number of visitors." They had fairly condemned "excesses" such as Tioga Road and "inappropriate architecture" such as the Clingman's Dome observation tower. But Mission 66 was nevertheless "a grand idea," especially now that they anticipated that the "balance" was to be shifted toward increased funding for management, protection, and research.[25]

The Park Service strategy at the Frontiers Conference was to stress how well Mission 66 design and construction had proceeded, while at the same time acknowledging that priorities were being changed. In his opening address, Wirth insisted that Mission 66 was a "good and sound" success, but that he and his staff *"did not plan it big enough!"* The real opportunity was now before them, and the urgency was greater than ever. He quoted Kennedy and Udall and picked up the tone of emerging environmentalist rhetoric: "Unless the American people can act quickly, they and future generations will lose forever the opportunity to save a few remaining remnants of the natural shoreline, vast wilderness areas of scenic beauty, and simple open spaces for men to enjoy." As for interagency cooperation, the national parks could "never again be islands standing isolated and lofty." Their fate was linked to the management of other public and private recreational areas, and his agency was ready "in its thinking, planning, and actions" to "stand shoulder to shoulder" with other land management agencies, as well as conservation organizations of all types. Wirth described how Parks for America would advocate a "broad national plan for parks and recreation areas and an acquisition plan covering all levels of government which would incorporate the forthcoming recommendations of the Outdoor Recreation Resources Review Commission." The Park Service "share of the program" would "probably call for as many as 25 new national parks . . . and a sizable number of new recreational areas." Mission 66 was still the "long-range program it was before," but its scope was being "widened greatly to meet the needs of rapidly changing times." The "first part" of the job, addressing the "shameful physical facilities in the parks," was well under way and would continue. But the new emphasis would be on hiring

Clingman's Dome observation tower in Great Smoky Mountains National Park, seen here in the 1960s, was often cited as inappropriate architectural design by critics of Mission 66. NPS Photo by Jack E. Boucher.

and training staff for those facilities, on improving "protection and management" of parks, and above all on vastly expanding the federal park and recreation system. "I do not believe the climate has ever been better for the fulfillment of the National Park idea than it is right now," the director concluded. The new administration had indicated the great urgency it placed on conservation and recreation issues, and beyond that "everyplace you go throughout the country, people are talking about the protection of our natural resources." There was a strong feeling among the public that it was "absolutely necessary for the advancement of a free society . . . to appreciate and know what this earth of ours means to us."[26]

Eivind Scoyen gave the "oldtimer's" perspective at the Frontiers Conference, which was probably appreciated considering that many of those present had been with the Park Service thirty years themselves. Lon Garrison attended the conference but did not make a presentation. Thomas Vint, who retired that November, did not attend. William Carnes, still the head of the Mission 66 working staff in Washington, had assumed most of the responsibility for the reappraisal and reorientation of the program in its second half. Wirth described Carnes as "the guiding factor . . . Mr. Mission 66 himself." Carnes's talk, however, was mainly a historical summary of public park ideology.[27] Wirth himself concluded the conference by giving the clearest indication of what the revised priorities of Mission 66 would now be. In the excitement of the hour, exact figures seemed to vary somewhat, but they got the idea across: at least ten seashore areas, forty to fifty historical areas, fifteen recreation areas, and fifteen national parks all were to be added to the system. The partnership with Parks for America would be instrumental in getting the necessary legislation passed. In addition, the director wanted at least $1 million a year for "research," increased funds for hiring and training staff, and a complete "revamp" of publications and interpretive displays.[28]

Secretary of the Interior Udall attended the Grand Canyon conference and offered an inspiring vision of his conservation priorities. The Truman and Eisenhower administrations, he noted, had managed to add only 92,000 acres to the national park system; the Kennedy administration would reverse this dismal record and emulate the accomplishments of Theodore Roosevelt and Franklin Roosevelt. Mission 66 had a remarkable record of achievement, but it had also "brought into sharp focus what we call the quiet crisis that confronts our nation today. The need to set aside—before it is gone—open spaces to meet the recreational needs of the future. . . . What we save now may be all that is saved." At the Frontiers Conference, and then in his article for the *Atlantic,* Udall urged all parties to move on, put aside resentment and rivalries, and join in a historic effort to expand all types of landscape reservations at a critical moment in American history.[29]

Following the reappraisal and the Frontiers Conference, the Washington and regional offices of the Park Service began a reorganization. In the Washington office, Vint and Scoyen both retired by the end of the year. Vint's position was raised to the level of assistant director, and he was replaced not by an architect or engineer but by an administrator, Clark Stratton. Separate divisions of construction and master planning were added, parallel to those for landscape architecture, architecture, and engineering. Scoyen's replacement as associate director (just below director on the organizational chart) was seen at this point as a potential successor to Wirth. For the next year, however, that position remained vacant. Garrison, who might have been a logical choice for the post, had been somewhat distanced from events in Washington and had not played a role in Parks for America or the Mission 66 reappraisal. He remained superintendent of Yellowstone until 1963, when he became a regional director in Omaha, and later in Philadelphia.[30] Carnes, who had been so instrumental on the Mission 66 working staff since 1955, left in 1962 to take a position on the landscape architecture faculty at the University of Illinois.[31] Regional directors started to regain some of the authority that they had lost under the 1954 reorganization, and to an even greater degree under Mission 66. Plans for concession developments, as well as site plans and working drawings for other projects, could be approved in the regional offices after 1961.[32]

The Park Service personnel changes occurring at the beginning of the Kennedy administration probably had more to do with timing than politics: the New Deal generation was reaching retirement age just as New Conservation arrived. The Park Service was also adapting, Wirth hoped, to accommodate the vision of the new secretary of the interior and the upcoming recommendations of ORRRC's final report. But there were further changes in order. The

ORRRC embodied a new approach not just to park planning but to government itself. Rockefeller had a capable executive director of the ORRRC, Francis Sargent, who had trained as an architect at MIT and who would go on to be elected governor of Massachusetts. Sargent directed partnerships, public meetings, extensive use of outside researchers and consultants, and in general a planning process unlike anything occurring at the Park Service. The ORRRC's re-

Signed group photograph of Park Service staff in Washington in 1960. Wirth is seated center, with Vint behind him. Eivind Scoyen is to Wirth's right and Hillory Tolson is to his left. All would be retired within a few years. NPS Historic Photo Collection.

port described a "national outdoor recreation policy" that relied on extensive collaboration between local and state governments and among federal agencies to acquire or otherwise preserve large areas for outdoor recreation. Even the vocabulary used in the report indicated a new kind of thinking about recreation on public lands. "Outdoor recreation resources" were divided into six categories, including "high-density recreation areas," "natural environment areas, "unique natural areas," and "historic and cultural sites." The commissioners anticipated that "outdoor recreation activity" would "*triple* by the year 2000." The extensive data on this "demand" were broken down into types of recreation and analyzed in relation to demographic trends and patterns of urbanization. The "supply" was analyzed in terms not of acres but of "effective acres" that were accessible and appropriate for the kinds of recreation the public was seeking. Recreation needed to be more available near "metropolitan areas," the commissioners determined, where "the typical subdivision of postwar suburbia" had "squandered the recreation potentials" with houses "splattered . . . all over the countryside." Suggestions for "cluster development," therefore, were also included in planning effectively for outdoor recreation, and local governments were to be encouraged to use their zoning powers as part of the solution. The ORRRC recommended not just major programs of land acquisition but new ways of thinking about how federal and state governments should manage and pay for "recreation resources." The commission recommended that land management agencies "adopt a system of user fees designed to recapture a significant por-

tion of the operation and maintenance costs." Congress should also enact a major federal grants-in-aid program for state park acquisition.[33]

The ORRRC ushered in a new era in state and federal governments' thinking about the general issues of conservation and recreation. The commission's recommendations led to a federal emphasis on recreation in "metropolitan areas," which was where the people were but the "effective acres" of recreation opportunity were not. The ORRRC urged spreading out recreational use on a wider variety of public lands. Above all, the proposed policies and initiatives the ORRRC described implied that Congress should pass a variety of measures to address the situation. Considering the legislation that followed in the 1960s, the ORRRC must be seen as one of the most effective congressional commissions ever convened.

The new framework for conservation and recreational planning, however, largely excluded the Park Service. In fact, one of the ORRRC's major recommendations was the creation of a new federal agency, the Bureau of Outdoor Recreation, which would assume the responsibilities for national recreational planning that Congress had conferred on the Park Service in 1936. Udall, despite his early support for Wirth and Mission 66, did not even wait for Congress to act on the recommendation. Through an administrative order he established the Bureau of Outdoor Recreation (BOR) in April 1962, with the co-drafter of the ORRRC legislation, Edward Crafts, as its director. Adding insult to injury, Crafts was a Forest Service employee; most of the new agency's personnel, however, along with most of its first year's operating budget, came from the Park Service.

Many experienced landscape architects and planners in the Washington office, in particular, were transferred to the BOR.[34]

The creation of the BOR obviously was a huge blow to Wirth personally, and one from which he would not recover professionally. Rockefeller remained part of the "family," but he had demonstrated that his family's alliance with the Park Service, if not at an end, went only so far. The creation of the BOR further transformed how the Park Service and Mission 66 operated in the new decade. More than any other factor, it was Wirth's subsequent inability to embrace the BOR fully that caused Udall to lose confidence in him. The creation of the BOR represented a huge policy initiative at the Department of the Interior, and Wirth's lack of cooperation with and continued hostility toward the new agency could only be interpreted as counterproductive disloyalty. The stakes were high for Udall. When Congress passed the 1963 Outdoor Recreation Act authorizing the Department of the Interior to continue the planning and surveys of the ORRRC, the secretary assigned these responsibilities to the BOR. The still tiny agency now "coordinated" planning among more than twenty federal agencies and various state and local organizations. Although it had no land management responsibilities, the BOR would have significant influence over where and how new national and state parks were created once the means of funding such acquisitions was established. This potential came to fruition in 1964, when Congress passed the Land and Water Conservation Fund (LWCF) Act, which authorized grants to federal agencies for the acquisition and development of new parks and recreation areas. The act also authorized grants-in-aid to the states (on a fifty-fifty matching basis) for the same purpose. The funds were to be supplied through a national system of park "user fees," the sale of surplus federal property, and federal gasoline taxes. Under a later amendment, revenues from offshore oil drilling were added for a total authorization of up to $200 million annually. The LWCF finally created a dedicated fund—analogous to the "trust fund" that financed interstate highway construction—for the acquisition of new national and state parks. The act was an unprecedented commitment to acquire property directly for a massive expansion of federal and state park systems. Congress and Udall had not made the program part of Mission 66, however, nor even of the Park Service.[35]

The LWCF was also unprecedented in the new role it prescribed for user fees to cover the cost of acquiring and developing park and recreation areas. From 1918 until 1965, when the LWCF went into effect, the national park system had been supported entirely through "general treasury" funds. Park funding came from the taxation of the general public, in other words, not through fees paid by users or through any other income (such as concession fees) generated in the parks. In many parks the public paid a fee at an entrance station, but technically these charges were for permits to allow tourists to use their cars in the parks, not an admission fee. In any case, beginning in 1918 these permit fees went, like concession revenue, directly into the general treasury. Annual park appropriations therefore had no direct relationship to income generated in the parks. But this philosophy began to change by 1953, when Congress increased the automobile permit fees, which the legislators now referred to simply as "entrance fees."[36] By that time other observers, such as the park historian John Ise, felt that the "entrance fees" should be raised further. Ise observed that there were too many visitors in the parks anyway, and "too many particularly who do not really care much for what they see."[37] Higher charges for admission might help weed out those tourists who, as Harold Bradley put it, were not willing to "pay the price" and were better off elsewhere. But with the creation of the LWCF in 1965, a system of true "user fees" for federal public lands created an alternative source of funding, set aside in a fund earmarked for the purpose of supporting outdoor recreation. Funding parks through general taxation had been justified by the assertion that a national park system was necessary for the health and welfare of the American public as a whole. The LWCF began a shift toward paying for parks through fees instead, suggesting that the users rather than the general public were the ones who benefited, and therefore should be the ones to provide funding. The difference implied a changing definition of "public" parks.

The ORRRC and the legislation that followed it defined a watershed in the history of American parks and in the institutional history of the Park Service. Wirth was severely disappointed but could hardly have been surprised by the ORRRC's recommendations. Shortly after the publication of the commission's final report, he wrote his old friend Laurance Rockefeller to congratulate him, but also to express regret that the Park Service would lose the national plan-

ning functions that had been the basis of the director's career since 1931. He tried to convince Rockefeller that he agreed with the ORRRC's suggestions, writing, "We are all more interested in an adequate and sound park and recreation program . . . than we are in building up our own little organizations, so if this is the way to do it let's all join together and put it across."[38] Despite such attempted reassurances, however, he did not give the new agency the cooperation and support it needed. Within months Udall was considering who should replace Wirth as director. After an encouraging start with the Kennedy administration in 1961, by the end of 1962 Wirth was planning his retirement.

The ORRRC report and the creation of the BOR were not the only instigators of change in the early 1960s. The advocacy for a federal system of designated wilderness, the maturing science of ecology, and the political movement of environmentalism all combined to shape New Conservation at the Department of the Interior. The Wilderness Act, after a long and fitful legislative history that had begun in 1956, was finally signed into law by President Lyndon Johnson in September 1964. The act allowed the eventual designation of many national park backcountry areas as official wilderness, ensuring that they would remain roadless and completely undeveloped. But the act did more than provide another level of protection for wild places; it set down a new landscape ideal and new purposes for landscape preservation. Setting aside official "wilderness areas" out of federal lands could not be justified in Olmstedian terms, for the benefit of public enjoyment. These areas qualified as wilderness precisely because they were inaccessible to the public.[39] Although large national parks, especially in the West, continued to be the icons of wilderness for the American public, they in fact represented a very different kind of landscape reservation. Wilderness designation did not involve park making but prohibited it. Wilderness areas were designated for their own sake, primarily as biological reserves, not necessarily for the use of the public. Such preserves were described by advocates as necessary for a healthy society, as parks had been; but the social functionality of wilderness did not entail tourism or enjoyment. Its value to society was its intrinsic biological integrity, and that integrity was understood in scientific, not scenic, terms.

The ideas inherent in the Wilderness Act reflected the maturing scientific discipline of ecology and its increasing influence among scientists, policy makers, and preservation advocates. An awareness of the biological importance of national parks had been building since the 1930s gained momentum in the postwar era. But Mission 66 had never included a significant scientific research component, at least in part because Congress would probably not have funded such an effort. Nevertheless, by the late 1950s prominent scientists and others were arguing that the Park Service had failed to exploit a historic opportunity by not even trying to persuade Congress to fund scientific research in the parks.[40] By the early 1960s, the dearth of reliable information on wildlife populations—and the resulting lack of consistent wildlife policies—resulted in public outrage and additional bad publicity for the Park Service. In Yellowstone, for example, biologists had long supported culling the park's elk herd, since without "direct reductions" the population would grow beyond the "carrying capacity" of the park's northern range. Public hunting was advocated by local sportsmen and elected officials, but was resisted by Garrison and others who did not want to establish such a precedent in a national park. Trapping and transporting the animals proved to be inefficient. With the elk population increasing to what scientists believed to be unsustainable numbers in the winter of 1961, Garrison ordered his rangers to shoot more than four thousand of the animals. Park and conservation advocates all over the country were enraged by what seemed to them a brutal and senseless action. Garrison, Wirth, and Udall were drawn into a national debate over whether and how elk should be hunted or otherwise reduced in Yellowstone.[41]

Although Garrison had acted on the advice of scientists, the incident made clear the degree to which the Park Service was trying to manage wildlife with little or no program of consistent scientific research on which to base decisions. Although Mission 66 planning documents had acknowledged the need for such a program, it had remained almost completely unfunded. Following the Yellowstone elk incident, Howard Stagner (now chief of the Branch of Natural History) made a report on the overall condition of "wildlife management in national parks." Stagner outlined many of the ecological subjects that required better and more scientific research if park managers were to make the best decisions. He also clarified key wildlife policies, including the prohibition of public hunting, the protection of predators, the elimination of exotic species, the reintroduction of extirpated species, and the shooting of "hoofed animals" by rangers to bring their numbers within the carrying capacity of range lands.[42] Following Stagner's report—and the damaging controversy over the Yellowstone elk—Udall initiated a broad and deep review of the entire subject of scientific research and wildlife management policies in the national parks. He asked the National Academy of Sciences to review the state of the Park Service's research activities and needs. Chaired by biologist William J. Robbins, the academy's committee reported in 1963 that "research by the National Park Service . . . lacked continuity, coordination, and depth." What is more, they were unconvinced that "the policies of the National Park Service have been such that the potential contribution of research and a research staff . . . [was] recognized and appreciated." The report sounded an unprecedented note of severe criticism of the Park Service by a respected outside organization.[43]

At the same time Robbins and his committee were assessing the lack of effective Park Service scientific research, another group appointed by Udall was analyzing the agency's wildlife management policies. Headed by the biologist A. Starker Leopold (the son of Aldo Leopold), this committee also made its report in 1963. The Leopold report took on a life of its own, reprinted by conservation organizations and read and admired extensively. The report acknowledged that most national parks had been through "periods of indiscriminate logging, burning, livestock grazing, hunting and predator control." After becoming parks, they then "shifted abruptly to a regime of equally unnatural protection from lightning fires, from insect

outbreaks, absence from natural control of ungulates" (including elk) and other side effects of preservation. Parks therefore did not represent "primitive America." But "restoring the primitive scene," if impossible to do completely, should be the objective of park management. Literate and persuasive, the Leopold report crystallized for many readers a new vision of a national park ideal: "The goal of managing the national parks and monuments should be to preserve, or where necessary to recreate, the ecologic scene as viewed by the first European visitors." The basis for preserving and restoring ecosystems obviously needed to be scientific, not scenic. "Mass recreation facilities" were also "incongruous" with this goal, and Leopold urged the Park Service to "reverse its policy of permitting these non-conforming uses, and to liquidate them as soon as possible (painful as this will be to concessionaires)."[44]

If detached from the political complexities of national park management, the Leopold report captured a vital and idealistic expression of preservation philosophy that had eluded Wirth and his staff at the time. Richard West Sellars, in his authoritative history of natural resource management in the national parks, describes the Robbins and Leopold reports together as a "kind of ecological countermanifesto that marked the beginning of renewed efforts to redefine the basic purpose of the national parks." Sellars notes that Mission 66 was "the culmination of the vision of Stephen Mather and Horace Albright, who had sought to develop the parks and make them accessible for the benefit and enjoyment of the people. The program was the high point of what might be termed the 'landscape architecture approach.'" But after the scientific research reports of 1963, the Park Service entered "a new era, in which park management would be judged far more on ecological criteria."[45]

Ecological science, of course, did not immediately gain the funding and bureaucratic power that Robbins, Leopold, and others advocated. But the cumulative effects of their reports, along with the ORRRC report, the creation of the BOR, the establishment of the LWCF, and the signing of the Wilderness Act, permanently changed the political and ideological context in which the Park Service operated. Neither the director nor any other Park Service official would ever again set the national conservation agenda to the degree that Wirth had attempted through Mission 66. The Mission 66 modernist park had been conceived around older assumptions about the value of parks: about the right of the public to enjoy them, about the meaning of wilderness, about what activities constituted impairment. The new generation of park advocates had pursued and won major legislative and administrative victories that redefined those assumptions at precisely the time Mission 66 construction was reaching its climax. This circumstance inevitably colored the perception of Mission 66 as just a "development program," and that is exactly how Congress treated it. Mission 66 appropriations for construction (and, after 1961, land acquisition) kept rising; but far more significant discussions about the future of federal outdoor recreation policy, about public land use and acquisition, and about the management of parks as ecosystems all took place outside the Park Service. The new agenda and

vision for national parks was being set among a diverse group of federal agencies, environmental advocates, and private partners, not just among a network of aging New Dealers. By 1963 the entire world had moved on, leaving Wirth, his colleagues, and Mission 66 behind. Congress, conservation organizations, and higher-level officials at the Department of the Interior would set the course of action for the Park Service to a far greater degree than they had done previously. In the future, directors of the Park Service would increasingly implement, not initiate, policy.

With his situation deteriorating fast, Wirth reported that on August 22, 1962, "the one billionth visit to the national parks was recorded since the first visit [was recorded] in 1904." If the trend held, the second billionth visitor would arrive in just eleven years. Although this was an ominous statistic, Wirth did not seem to find it regrettable. The parks were still "opportunities to enjoy great scenic and inspirational areas of the country," and their experiences would help visitors "better comprehend the physical and spiritual links that bind America's past to its present and future." In private, Wirth was even more out of step with contemporary environmentalist sentiment. "I still maintain," he said in one interview, "that the parks are for the people and not for the animals alone." By the end of 1962, Mission 66 construction had exceeded that for any previous year: 2,343 individual projects totaling $152 million.[46]

Wirth later insisted that his retirement was his own idea and undertaken on his own schedule. But there is no reason to believe that he wanted to retire before 1966. That year he would be over sixty-five, in his thirty-fifth year with the agency, and he could celebrate the completion of Mission 66 and the fiftieth anniversary of the Park Service as he stepped down. But less than six months after the creation of the BOR, Udall and Carver were actively considering who should be the next Park Service director. By August 1962 Udall knew whom he wanted to appoint: George B. Hartzog Jr., a Park Service concessions lawyer and former superintendent of the Jefferson National Expansion Memorial. Udall had met Hartzog the previous summer while visiting the proposed Ozark Rivers National Monument in Missouri. Hartzog made a positive impression, and in October 1962 Udall offered him the position of director. Hartzog suggested, however, that he be made associate director instead (filling Scoyen's vacant position), with the understanding that he would be promoted to replace Wirth once the director retired. This interim appointment would allow a smoother transition and would help to avoid the impression that Wirth was being forced out.[47]

The exact circumstances and timing of Hartzog's selection to replace Scoyen soon became a subject of some controversy, with different individuals telling slightly different versions of the story through speeches, interviews, and later in published memoirs. In 1961, after Scoyen told Wirth that he intended to retire at the end of the year, the director assembled a small group of close associates to draw up a list of "career men" with enough experience to qualify for the job. Apparently Wirth and Udall agreed that the position should be considered an apprenticeship, and that whoever was selected would succeed

Wirth as director. The meeting was held in Annapolis and included, besides Wirth himself, Thomas Vint, Ronald Lee, and Yosemite superintendent John Preston. Later, Scoyen would insist that Hartzog's name had been the first on the list. But Wirth recalled in 1974 that the list was not even been completed until "October or November of 1962." In any case, Wirth did not forward the "Scoyen list" of candidates to Udall until October 1962—that is, after Hartzog had been offered the job and Wirth had learned of his selection. The secretary made his choice, in other words, without the director's advice. Wirth subsequently claimed, as Scoyen did, that Hartzog had always been on the list. But he never specified when Hartzog's name had been added or why. According to Hartzog himself, the other names "were much senior to me in rank and years of service." In fact, it seems likely that Wirth added Hartzog to the list of acceptable candidates only after he learned that Udall had already selected the young lawyer to be the next Park Service director. But no one involved wanted to admit that Hartzog had not been on the "Scoyen list" all along. In any case, by November 1962 Hartzog was definitely on the list, which Wirth then shared with Udall for the first time. In January, Hartzog accepted the position of associate director after Wirth privately assured him that he would retire following the next Park Service conference in October 1963.[48]

Intelligent and affable, Hartzog was a talented government lawyer with over fifteen years' experience at the Park Service, including valuable field duty as a superintendent. But while he would easily qualify for a career appointment to an assistant or regional director position, he probably was not Wirth's choice to become the seventh Park Service director. Hartzog had never been a member of the agency's directorate, and although he had supervised much of the Gateway Arch construction in St. Louis, he had played no major role in Mission 66. In August 1962, when Hartzog had asked Wirth about possibilities for career advancement, Wirth informed him that no suitable promotions were available. Hartzog then resigned from the Park Service and took a private-sector job in St. Louis that he had been offered.[49] For Udall and Carver, Hartzog's resignation was another point in his favor since it proved his independence. They approached him within months of his departure about the possibility of returning to the Park Service. The surprising move required promoting Hartzog over a number of higher-level candidates—Garrison, Stratton, and Beard, for example—with more experience.[50]

Hartzog had quickly developed, as he recalls in his memoirs, "a trusting, warm, personal friendship" with Udall at their initial meeting in the Ozarks, which had been characterized by "tremendous camaraderie." Hartzog was the same age as the secretary, and he felt that they shared similar "rural small town" backgrounds. Fed up with Wirth's failure to support the BOR, Udall and Carver decided that Hartzog had the qualities they needed in a director. He had enough fortitude and intelligence to stand up to Wirth, and so, they hoped, he would not be intimidated by Wirth's allies, who would still be running much of the Park Service. Although Hartzog certainly was a "career man," politics also figured in his selection. Neither party affiliation nor reward for political services was di-

rectly involved, but Udall and Carver knew that he was a staunch Democrat. Wirth, meanwhile, was supported by Republicans, even though he had been appointed under Truman and, like previous directors, tried to remain above partisan politics. Hartzog's limited professional experience did not fully qualify him over other, more accomplished candidates; but the young lawyer would be a formidable and energetic advocate, and his views were more compatible with those of the Kennedy administration. These were the qualifications that mattered most to Udall and Carver.[51] And whether or not he was originally on the "Scoyen list," over the next nine years Hartzog's legislative accomplishments would make him one of the most successful directors in the history of the Park Service.

The 1963 Park Service conference, titled "Conference of Challenges," would be Wirth's last. Held in Yosemite Valley, it featured summaries of Mission 66 progress over the previous eight years as well as the unveiling of a major agency policy document, soon known as "Road to the Future." Wirth wanted to emphasize continuity at the conference, where Hartzog would be introduced to the assembled superintendents as the next director. The appearance of continuity was important because it implied that even if Wirth was stepping down, Mission 66 had been a success, and Udall approved of its basic (if modified) policies and accomplishments. If the incoming director were painted as an outsider, it would imply that Udall had completely repudiated Mission 66. Even worse, if Hartzog were not seen as a "career man," it would suggest that the position of Park Service director had become a purely political appointment, to be filled by partisans interested mainly in advancing the current administration's agenda. Not only Wirth but also Albright, Scoyen, and other agency supporters desperately wanted to avoid even the appearance of such a precedent. Since Mather's day a broad consensus about national park policy and a high esteem for the professional expertise of Park Service staff had allowed the agency to occupy the bureaucratic high ground, above the appearance of political motivations. If the position of director was always political in nature, it also had always been filled by career conservationists and administrators, not political partisans. Events of the early 1960s, however, were eroding this practice. If Hartzog were perceived as less than a completely qualified professional, the position of Park Service director would begin to lose its exceptional status. For his part, Udall also did not want to appear to be politicizing the Park Service.

On the first full day of the conference at Yosemite, however, the outspoken Assistant Sec-

Assistant Secretary of the Interior John Carver (second from left) arriving at the Conference of Challenges in Yosemite Valley in October 1963. Yosemite superintendent John Preston is on the far right, and George Hartzog is between them. NPS Historic Photo Collection.

retary Carver quickly disrupted the anticipated scenario and revealed how much had changed at the Department of the Interior. If he had been unrestrained at the Tioga Road dedication, he now unleashed pure invective. "The entire Park Service is resolutely shutting its eyes to the fact of the creation of the Bureau of Outdoor Recreation," he charged, undoubtedly waking up some of his early morning audience. He accused the assembled superintendents and agency officials of treating the question of the BOR as "idle conversation" that they hoped would just "go away." When all else fails, he observed, "the Park Service seems always able to fall back upon mysticism, its own private mystique." Referring to an agency job description that called for a sense of the "'rightness' of National Park Service philosophy," Carver claimed that the document had "the mystic, quasi-religious sound of a manual for the Hitler Youth Movement." The Park Service was a branch of government, he reminded his listeners. "It isn't a religion and it shouldn't be thought of as such." Noting that he had been caught in a "vicious cross-fire" over Yellowstone elk policy, he praised the Leopold report as "solid backing for a good position." But "to credit the Park Service with the Leopold Report is like crediting a collision at sea for a dramatic rescue effort—the captain of the offending ship is hardly likely to get a medal for making the rescue effort possible."[52]

What was "mystique" to Carver, however, was a tradition of professionalism to many among his audience. What Carver was really attacking was the Progressive Era idea that experts could administer a federal agency detached from politics, justifying their decisions by the prestige (and perhaps the effectiveness or value) of their professional knowledge and opinions. Carver announced that the world had changed, and the Park Service would not be able to use the purported "rightness" of its professional culture to exempt it from more participatory and cooperative—and inherently political—processes, as exemplified by the ORRRC. Wilderness advocates and environmentalists could cheer this derogation of Park Service professional culture, which at the time was dominated by landscape architects and other "development" experts. In the future, however, they would find it difficult to claim a similar position of detached, unassailable expertise for their own professional group: natural scientists. The changes being made in 1963 had been brought about through the dynamic and powerful influence of environmental politics. Once the Park Service was politicized, it would in the future be run by politicians, such as assistant secretaries of the interior, with various allegiances. Professional experts—including scientists as well as landscape architects—would never again have the same bureaucratic power once Udall and Carver discredited the notion of such "mystique" and brought the agency fully into the political arena alongside environmentalists and their opponents.

Carver wisely left the Conference of Challenges, and the park, immediately after his speech. He had not spent all his arrows, however. He was one of a few officials who knew that Udall planned to announce Wirth's retirement at the end of the conference. While this development was hardly in doubt, the timing and nature of Wirth's departure held great symbolic significance. Immediately upon his return to Washington, Carver met with a *New York Times* reporter, taking the opportunity to suggest that Wirth was being fired specifically for his resistance to the BOR and for being out of step with administration policy on scientific research. The "semi-autonomous status assumed by the Park Service" would soon come to an end, reported the *Times*. Officials at the Department of the Interior felt that the agency had become "'inbred' and so professional that it has lost sight of its obligations to the public." Hartzog had been chosen mainly because he enjoyed "closer relations with Secretary Udall." The story appeared on October 17, the fourth day of the conference, a day before Udall was scheduled to arrive and make his address. Carver's tactic worked; Wirth, Scoyen, Albright and others spent months, and eventually years, trying to dispel the impression that Wirth had been fired and that Hartzog had been appointed primarily because he would do what he was told.[53] Scoyen, who expressed the sentiments of many at the conference, reacted to the *Times* account with dismay. While addressing the assembled conference the following day, he denied that Wirth "was being precipitously forced out" and that Hartzog "was being given the job because he would be more cooperative with the Secretary's Office." The fact that many people now believed exactly that was "one of the most demoralizing things that has happened to the National Park Service since it was established." Scoyen and Wirth both insisted that Hartzog had "been on the list" all along and that they fully supported him. Scoyen in particular insisted that while the secretary could never "afford to ignore entirely the political aspects of the situation" when appointing a director, he was "deeply thankful" that Udall had chosen someone "capable of handling the job." Udall himself addressed the group later that day and tried to mend fences; he was effusive in his praise of the outgoing Wirth and of Park Service "tradition." Wirth retired at the end of the year, and Hartzog replaced him in January 1964.[54]

The drama at the Conference of Challenges deflected attention from the main purpose of the event: to announce the results of a study of "long range requirements" prepared by a "special task force." The "long range plan," soon known as the "Road to the Future," had been prepared over the previous year by a different group of Washington staff, including Hartzog, Howard B. Stricklin, William C. Everhart, Myron D. Sutton, Charles E. Shedd Jr., and Robert M. Sharp. When the final report was published in 1964, it did not mention Mission 66. The Road to the Future described Udall's vision for the national park system as implemented by Hartzog. It replaced *Our Heritage* and the other Mission

66 publications as a summary of the agency's policies and priorities.

The most significant aspect of the new "framework for planning" was the division of the park system into three categories: "natural areas," "historical areas," and "recreational areas."[55] A series of new "objectives" was also defined for the agency, each with a set of "goals" divided under the separate headings for each of the three park types. The first objective, "to provide for the highest quality and use of the National Park System," for example, was followed by a list of specific goals along with suggested actions to accomplish them. Many key policy statements throughout the plan established continuity with Mission 66: "Parks are preserved for people" and "increased use . . . should therefore be welcomed." There was no need to "limit entry" in "natural areas," since "crowding" in the parks usually occurred only in certain areas at certain times of peak demand. The document was prepared, after all, while Wirth was still director. But if Hartzog denied that there were too many people in the parks, he did insist that there were too many cars, as well as too few non-automotive experiences. Hiking, walking, and bicycling would be encouraged; methods of alternative transportation from buses to monorails would be explored. "Determining park capacity" was another goal for "natural areas," as was encouraging backcountry use through "wilderness threshold" areas that made "less primitive" wilderness areas more accessible for day hikes. "Historical areas" and "recreation areas" received their own (much briefer) sets of goals under the same general objective.[56]

The next general objective, "to conserve and

Secretary of the Interior Stewart Udall speaking at the Conference of Challenges in 1963. He is announcing that George Hartzog (seated behind him) would be the next director of the Park Service. NPS Historic Photo Collection.

manage for their highest purpose the natural, historical and recreational resources of the National Park System," further illustrated both continuity with Mission 66 policy and a fresh emphasis on new ideas. Udall's enthusiastic support for the goals set out in the Leopold report, for example, were fully elaborated as both natural resource management policies and a commitment to seek an expanded scientific research program. Leopold later served briefly as the agency's chief scientist. But the role of science and scientists in the Park Service bureaucracy would continue to be limited, even with Hartzog's support as director. As Richard Sellars documents, integrating scientific research into national park management proved almost as difficult during the environmental era as it had been previously.[57]

The Road to the Future adopted the ORRRC's typology of six outdoor recreation resource types. Master planning was restructured around six "resource classifications," including "high-density recreation areas," "natural environment areas," "primitive areas," and "historic and cultural sites." Some of these resource classifications could potentially occur in more than one type of park: natural environment areas, for example could be found in the natural, historical, and recreational areas of the park system. The new language was calculated to integrate more smoothly with planning efforts at other agencies, especially the BOR. Hartzog also emphasized that the Park Service had a broader responsibility to consider the state of the "total environment" that extended beyond park boundaries. Referring to Udall's book *The Quiet Crisis,* Hartzog described the need for "park management to find ways to widen the park's influence on its surroundings and . . . on the region as a whole in an ever-broadening circle of involvement. . . . Secretary Udall's challenge to the nation is for every citizen to be aware of this interlocking responsibility to take part in applying this land ethic—to be concerned about the land and waters, its animals and plants; the air we breathe; our total environment." The "concept of the total environment" was "a protest against ugliness, whether . . . in the cities or the countryside." It implied that park master planning should be "comprehensive land planning . . . on the part of all agencies and organizations, in and outside the park," which could help "reduce the impact of use upon park resources and better serve the public need." The fourth objective of the Road to the Future was "to cooperate with the Bureau of Outdoor Recreation" and "to participate actively with organizations of this and other nations in conserving, improving and renewing the total environment."

But the Road to the Future also carried on many of the basic assumptions of Mission 66 policy. "Conservation through development design" guided by "master plans," for example, would "assure balanced relationships between preservation of the park resources and visitor needs." The third objective entailed continued expansion of the national park system. In this case Mission 66 planners had been preparing the necessary plans and legislation for years and simply continued their activities. The final two objectives of the Road to the Future referred to commitments in the areas of park interpretation and the development of professional staff, both of which had already been greatly advanced through Mission 66, and again were retained without radical redirection. Visitor centers would continue to be built, and their architectural style would continue to reflect contemporary trends in American design. The basic planning and organizational structure of the agency, at least as it had been adapted since 1959, would remain intact.

The Road to the Future restated and revised Mission 66, however, in order to make it consistent with Udall's New Conservation and the broader environmental movement. At least in some respects, it also marked an end to Mission 66. Although Wirth's program remained in existence until it officially came to a close in 1966, Udall and Hartzog rarely mentioned it. With a new director and a new rhetoric of park planning in place by the end of 1964, Mission 66 existed mainly as a budgetary entity, as compilations of construction statistics, and in the memories of Wirth and his fellow Park Service "alumni."

During his last year as director, Wirth prepared a "Progress Report" that summarized Mission 66 statistics. In part such a report was needed because the format and content of Department of the Interior annual reports changed under Udall, and now included much less specific information. But Wirth also took the opportunity to create a complete record of what Mission 66 accomplished in eight years under his direction. Twenty-seven new areas had been added to the national park system, and one hundred visitor centers had been built or were under construction. The two new agency training centers held particular significance for Wirth, as he looked to the professional prepara-

tion of the next generation of rangers and park staff. Other projects of particular note were the "relocations necessary to protect park features from human impact" that had taken place at Yellowstone and Yosemite and were under way at Mount Rainier and Mesa Verde. The list of construction accomplishments was, of course, long and impressive; few had ever cast doubt on the efficiency of Mission 66 as a design and construction program. But Wirth now quantified the results of the agency "research program" with similar precision: "45 projects and 77 reports, and the establishment of 15 current research projects partly or wholly funded by the Service." The Historic American Buildings Surveys (HABS), reactivated under Vint in 1957, had documented over two thousand structures, and the reinvigorated activities of the Historic Sites Survey included plans for a sixteen-volume series of thematic studies of American history and prehistory.[58]

Above all, on his retirement Wirth emphasized the ongoing planning and acquisition program that was expanding the national park system, which had been and would continue to be the emphasis of Mission 66 in its second half. Wirth insisted that Mission 66 recreational planning had been conducted "in cooperation with" the BOR. In fact, Wirth had gone ahead with his expansion program without paying much attention to the fledgling agency. The Park Service had lost much of its most experienced planning staff—including many of its landscape architects—to the BOR, but it had nevertheless completed up to two hundred "comprehensive studies" of potential additions to the park system. Wirth also reported that he and his staff had completed their own national recreational plan, which surveyed 4,800 existing and 2,800 potential "parks and related types of recreation areas" throughout the United States. "Hereafter," the director noted dryly, "this type of planning will be the responsibility of the Bureau of Recreation." The recreational plan was published in 1964 as *Parks for America: A Survey of Park and Related Resources in the Fifty States, and a Preliminary Plan*. The five hundred–page inventory, which recalled Wirth's 1941 recreational plan in methodology and format, was the last report of its type produced at the Park Service. In his foreword Udall rather acerbically observed that the report "should prove valuable to the Bureau of Outdoor Recreation" but that it did not represent that agency's (or Udall's) own opinions or conclusions regarding potential additions to national or state park systems. The BOR was under way with its own studies, the secretary insisted, and *Parks for America* was published as the Park Service's "last report in the field of nationwide park planning" only because it had already been largely completed at the time the BOR was established.[59]

The twenty-seven additions to the national park system made during the first eight years of Mission 66 included Virgin Islands National Park; Booker T. Washington and Grand Portage national monuments; Fort Davis, Fort Smith, and Sagamore Hill national historic sites; City of Refuge and Minute Man national historical parks; and Arkansas Post, Fort Clatsop, and Lincoln Boyhood national memorials. But no categories of national park expansion loomed larger in Mission 66 and Road to the Future planning than national seashores and national recreation areas. Three new national seashores, Cape Cod, Padre Island, and Point Reyes, had been created, and others were under way. Along with Lake Mead, Glen Canyon, and Flaming Gorge national recreation areas, these parks embodied how Mission 66 expanded the range and purposes of the national park system. Mission 66 planning for national seashores and recreation areas anticipated the work of the BOR and even preempted it to the extent that by 1963, an expansive scope and vision for these types of parks had already been thoroughly described.

As with so much of Mission 66 planning, the origins of national seashores and recreation areas were firmly rooted in the New Deal. In this case Wirth had been personally involved from the outset. In 1934 and 1935 his land planning branch conducted extensive studies of undeveloped seashore areas along the Atlantic, the Gulf of Mexico, and later the Pacific shorelines. The result was a recommendation that twelve to fifteen areas would qualify as new national parks and another thirty as state parks. Congress authorized only one new seashore park, however, and in 1937 Cape Hatteras National Seashore became the first of its type. But as in other cases in which Congress created new parks in areas not already under federal ownership, land acquisition lagged. Congress had never appropriated funds for the direct acquisition of private property to create a new park. Western parks had typically been set aside out of lands already in the public domain simply by retaining them in federal ownership. But creating a new national park out of private lands required that a state government or an individual first acquire the land and then give it to the federal government as a gift. In the case of Cape Hatteras, the Mellon family stepped in to provide over half the cost of the needed land, with North Carolina providing the balance. The national seashore was finally established in 1953. Developed through Mission 66, the new park was dedicated in 1958.[60]

By the early 1950s, the limited amount of undeveloped coastline left in the United States was rapidly disappearing. The other potential national seashores identified in 1935 were all lost to private resort, second home, and residential development. Recognizing the urgency of the situation, Paul Mellon also agreed to fund Park Service studies that would pick up where New Deal plans had left off. As Park Service planners assembled data over the next several years, Mission 66 anticipated national seashores as an important category for expansion. But authorizing legislation for seashore parks did not material-

ize during the first half of Mission 66. Unless Congress proved willing to break with tradition and fund the acquisition of land for the creation of new park areas, there was no way to proceed with ambitious plans for national seashores.

The first Mission 66 seashore report funded by Mellon, *Our Vanishing Shoreline*, published in 1957, covered only the East and Gulf coasts. The survey team included a biologist, a historian, and two landscape architects who surveyed 3,700 miles of coastline between Maine and Texas by air and in the field. They concluded that only 6.5 percent of the shoreline was in public ownership, a figure that should be increased at least to 15 percent. The planners identified fifty-four undeveloped areas with enough recreational potential to become federal, state, or local "public seashores," including Cumberland Island (Georgia), Fire Island (New York), and Cape Cod (Massachusetts). One

The Great Beach of Cape Cod National Seashore. NPS Historic Photo Collection.

third of the total shoreline suitable for parks was in Texas. The report recommended immediate federal legislation to acquire not only waterfront land for recreational purposes but also "ample quantities of hinterland of marsh and swamp" to preserve habitat and ecological systems. *Our Vanishing Shoreline* was followed by further studies that by 1959 covered the Pacific Coast and Great Lakes shorelines. Wirth also used the 1959 Park Service conference at Colonial National Historical Park to publicize national seashore and lakeshore planning goals.[61] "The lesson is all around us," he wrote in a press release. "We can no longer depend on private philanthropy, [and] State donations . . . to meet our park and recreational requirements. . . . We got our national park system the easy way. . . . From now on [parks] are going to cost money, and a great deal of it. . . . The time is now. Ten years will be too late."[62]

In August 1961, after years of contentious consideration, Congress authorized the Cape Cod National Seashore and appropriated $16 million to initiate the purchase of what would eventually be over 44,000 acres. Point Reyes (California) and Padre Island (Texas) national seashores followed in 1962. By the end of 1966 Congress had authorized nine national seashores and lakeshores, and by 1972 four more that had been planned under Mission 66 followed. In all, 718 miles of shoreline were eventually protected through the acquisition of over 700,000 acres.[63] Cape Cod had set a historic precedent for direct federal acquisition of private land for park purposes. From 1961 to 1966 Congress authorized fifty-four additional na-

Salt Pond Visitor Center, Cape Cod National Seashore. Author's photo.

Bathhouse, Cape Cod National Seashore. Author's photo.

Overlook shelter, Cape Cod National Seashore. Author's photo.

tional park areas, and in almost all cases the legislators included money for the purchase of land.[64]

National recreation areas had a parallel history. The recreational potential of reservoirs being built by the Bureau of Reclamation had been recognized since the 1920s. Wirth had begun planning recreation areas in cooperation with the dam builders in 1934. Lake Mead National Recreation Area was the first of its type when Congress authorized it in 1936. The Park Service was given responsibility for developing the recreation area (which was administered jointly with the Bureau of Reclamation until 1964) for boating, camping, and water-oriented recreation. Land for national recreation areas was usually already under public ownership since it had to be for dam construction purposes. At Lake Mead, therefore, the CCC was able to begin road construction and other park development as soon as the reservoir filled. After World War II, however, the use of the area intensified enormously, with over 2 million annual visits recorded in 1951. Mission 66 called for a complete redevelopment plan, including large campgrounds, visitor centers, employee housing, maintenance areas, utilities, marinas, and other features that would become typical of postwar national recreation areas.[65]

Mission 66 initiated the growth of federal recreation areas with the redevelopment of Lake Mead, followed by the establishment of Glen Canyon (Utah and Arizona, 1958), Whiskeytown (California, 1962), and Flaming Gorge (Utah and Wyoming, 1963) national recreation areas. Obviously the establishment of the BOR and the funds made available through the LWCF greatly accelerated the process. Between 1952 and 1972 the Park Service developed twelve federal reservoirs as national recreation areas. As national park historian Barry Mackintosh observes, of one hundred additions to the national park system made between 1952 and 1972, thirty-two were primarily devoted to recreation (including national seashores and lakeshores). The increase vastly expanded the recreational dimension of the national park system. Soaring demand for such areas drove the expansion of national recreation areas and national seashores and lakeshores during the second half of Mission 66. But it was also true that remaining opportunities for large new parks in the "natural area" category had diminished. Virgin Islands National Park remained the most significant Mission 66 addition in the natural areas category until Canyonlands (Utah, 1964) and Guadalupe Mountains (Texas, 1966) national parks were established.[66] After 1964 official wilderness designation also became an alternative to national park establishment for preservationists seeking more complete protection. The wilderness preservation system grew dramatically; but fewer large natural areas would be added or transferred to the Park Service from other federal agencies once wilderness designation was an option.

The expansion of the number of historical areas in the park system was prodigious under Mission 66, perhaps for some of the same reasons. As with recreation areas and seashores, this was where opportunities for expanding the system (especially east of the Mississippi) were most available. Between 1952 and 1972, fifty-nine historical areas were added, including eleven sites associated with former presidents. Military history sites, as always, were well represented. In addition to the Minute Man National Historical Park (Massachusetts, 1959), Horseshoe Bend National Military Park (Alabama, 1956), and several Civil War battlefields, a series of frontier forts, including Fort Clatsop (Oregon, 1958), Arkansas Post (Arkansas, 1960), and Fort Davis (Texas, 1961), were established and developed as historic sites. The proliferation of historical areas, some of them representative of themes not previously represented in the park system, was an important contribution of Mission 66. The homes of Booker T. Washington (Virginia, 1956) and Frederick Douglass (Washington, D.C., 1962) became part of the park system, as did the memorial to the Johnstown Flood (Pennsylvania, 1964) and the Hubbell Trading Post (Arizona, 1965). The trend was continued during the Hartzog years as the themes of American history included in the park system further diversified.[67]

Another major land acquisition program funded through Mission 66 involved the national parkway system. Congress had been more forthcoming with funds for park road and parkway construction in the early 1950s than it had with appropriations for other purposes. The 1954 Federal Highway Act, for example, authorized $32 million for parkway construction over three years. The money was used mainly to help finish national parkway projects that had been begun during the 1930s, including the Blue Ridge (Virginia and North Carolina), Colonial (Virginia), George Washington Memorial (Virginia and Maryland), and Natchez Trace (Tennessee, Alabama, and Mississippi) parkways.

Mission 66 immediately increased funding for these projects and fueled hopes that the national parkway system would be significantly expanded. By 1957 parkway construction was at its "highest volume" since the program began in 1933. Mission 66 work on Colonial Parkway had been particularly intense in order to finish it (along with two of the first Mission 66 visitor centers) in time for the 350th anniversary of the settlement of Jamestown. That year Dudley C. Bayliss, the landscape architect who headed the Park Service parkway program out of the Washington office, reported that the Blue Ridge Parkway was about "three-fourths complete" and the Natchez Trace Parkway was "nearing the halfway mark." Both of these linear parks were over four hundred miles long. The Blue Ridge would be substantially finished under Mission 66, although the last, controversial seven miles would not be completed until 1987. Most of the Natchez Trace was also completed under Mission 66, although that parkway was not officially dedicated until 2005.[68]

Bayliss also described six other projects that were part of his program, including the Chesapeake and Ohio Canal Parkway, which had been authorized in 1950 but had just been "restudied" and was about to be completely reconceived. The Foothills Parkway, planned to skirt the Tennessee foothills of Great Smoky Mountains National Park, was also in an early stage of land acquisition and construction. The parkway program came under the Landscape Architecture division in the Washington office and so was administered by Clark Stratton after he replaced Vint in 1961. Stratton had great hopes for a national parkway system that would com-

plement the interstate highway system and would similarly benefit from Congress's apparent willingness to fund road construction. The most ambitious Mission 66 parkway proposal was for the Mississippi River Parkway, or Great River Road, which would follow both banks of the Mississippi from Minnesota to Louisiana. The parkway had been planned since 1951, but Stratton and Bayliss hoped that it would now be financed directly "as part of the Federal Aid Highway System," in other words, with interstate highway money.[69]

There were other ambitious, and ultimately unrealized, proposals: the Allegheny Parkway between Harpers Ferry and the Cumberland Gap; an extension of the Blue Ridge Parkway to Georgia; parkway connections between the George Washington Memorial, Colonial, and Blue Ridge parkways and Harpers Ferry; the Cumberland Parkway connecting Great Smoky Mountains National Park, the Cumberland Gap, Mammoth Cave, and the Natchez Trace Parkway.[70] Whether or not a national system of noncommercial parkways connecting national parks and historic sites all over the country would have

Mission 66 funding moved the Blue Ridge Parkway substantially towards its completion, as documented in these 1960s photographs: the Mabry Mill reconstruction (top); a parkway bridge (middle); the Peaks of Otter Lodge (left); and the Pinnacle overlook (right). NPS Photos by Jack E. Boucher.

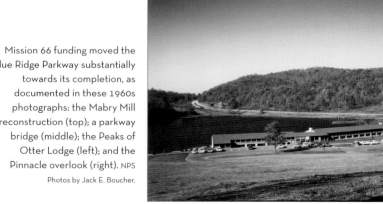

been desirable, these and other ambitious Mission 66 parkway proposals were never implemented. Congress continued to make appropriations to complete the Blue Ridge, Natchez Trace, and George Washington Memorial parkways, all of which were nearing completion. But the Great River Road and the others remained in the planning or "advisory" stage. National parkway proposals were not part of the ORRRC's recommendations, nor did they fit well within New Conservation. The BOR did not assume parkway planning responsibilities, which remained at the Park Service as one of the most important remaining activities of the now greatly reduced Landscape Division. But already in 1959 the Advisory Board on National Parks, Historic Sites, Buildings and Monuments had suggested that the Park Service get out of the parkway business altogether. That did not happen; but neither did the growth of the national parkway system that Stratton and Bayliss had hoped for under the second half of Mission 66. The stagnation of the parkway program, and the eventual failure to institute it as a complement to the interstate highway system, would remove a last bastion of significant influence among landscape architects at the Park Service.[71]

National parkways aside, the enormous expansion of the national park system that occurred during the 1960s and early 1970s may be the most substantial legacy of the Mission 66 program, particularly in its second half. But was this great moment in American conservation history the result of Mission 66 or of the new priorities set by the ORRRC, Udall's New Conservation, and the creation of the BOR? George Hartzog certainly must be given much of the credit. As Mackintosh points out, during Hartzog's nine years as director (1964–1972), "69 of today's park units were added to the System— nearly three-quarters as many as had been permanently added in the preceding 30 years."[72] The second half of Mission 66 obviously benefited from the fresh attitude in Congress that the ORRRC had managed to inspire. Without Kennedy and Udall, for example, it is doubtful that the landmark Cape Cod legislation would have succeeded in 1961.

But it is also apparent that the accomplishments of New Conservation would not have been as impressive had it not been for the foundation of recreational planning provided by Mission 66, which itself was based on decades of research and surveys by Wirth and his staff. The revised second half of Mission 66 and *Parks for America* put specific plans and detailed legislation into the hands of lawmakers just as the political climate began to warm to such proposals. The result was richly productive for the national park system. Udall and Hartzog achieved political consensus; but they also came to Congress armed with detailed, impeccably prepared proposals for new parks and recreation areas. Hartzog himself noted that "it was my good fortune to become director at a most propitious time in the history of the National Park System." He was referring mainly to the "great waves of environmental concerns" that were "beginning to move."[73] He might have also noted, though, that no incoming director had ever had a path more thoroughly prepared than he had when he assumed control over the last two years of Mission 66.

As the official conclusion of Mission 66 approached, Hartzog did not organize an extensive commemoration of the event. Wirth had moved to New York and taken a position as a consultant to Laurance Rockefeller (as Albright had for Laurance's father). Working out of an office in Rockefeller Center, Wirth remained active in public affairs, including contemporary national park plans such as the proposed Adirondack national park. In 1966 *National Geographic* magazine published a long article by Wirth about Mission 66 which was the most extensive published commemoration of the completion of his program.[74] For his part, Hartzog organized a series of "fiftieth anniversary celebrations" for the Park Service that diverted attention from Mission 66 as much as they celebrated it. In the agency's official anniversary brochure, the director briefly noted the "dramatically successful close" of Mission 66, but described at length the even greater challenge of "improving the total environment" that remained. Udall was also generous in his praise of the "amazingly successful program."[75] But these sentiments were not broadly published in 1966. Most Park Service press releases and events emphasized the overall history of the Park Service, not the completion of the ten-year program, and the dozens of newspapers and magazines that picked up on the story usually echoed the "Fifty Years of Parks" theme, mentioning Mission 66 in passing, if at all.[76] Other fiftieth anniversary events include lecture series, commemorative calendars and stationery, and scores of tributes in individual parks and communities all over the country.[77]

Twenty-two conservation organizations sponsored a "Golden Anniversary Dinner" held that August in a Washington hotel. Some eight hundred "distinguished friends" attended the event, but Wirth was not among them. Hartzog used the evening not to recall Mission 66 but to help inaugurate his own park development and expansion program, "PARKSCAPE, U.S.A." First described as the "Centennial Challenge," Parkscape was to be completed in time for the Yellowstone centennial in 1972. The new initiative was calculated to retain the strong public image—and increased budgets—of Mission 66 while leaving behind the controversies. Mission 66, which had been "brought about by a desperate need to catch up with work," was "now in the history books." In a series of memoranda and magazine articles, Hartzog outlined his priorities for Parkscape, many of which were drawn from the Road to the Future. The program had five major goals: "completing" the park system by 1972; developing "cooperative programs with other agencies"; "utilizing the national park concept" to improve life in American cities; better "communicating the values of park conservation"; and developing an international assistance program in anticipation of the second World Conference of National Parks, scheduled to be held in Yellowstone and Grand Tetons in 1972.[78]

Many aspects of Parkscape essentially continued the work of Mission 66, at least as the program had been modified since 1959. In hindsight, the most successful of the five initiatives Hartzog described was the first, which entailed the ongoing, massive expansion of the park system with new national parks, recreation areas, seashores, lakeshores, and historic sites. As noted, the growth of the park system under Hartzog was a prodigious feat completed in a relatively short time. As the system expanded, the idea of exactly what constituted a national park did as well. Building on the precedent of the Ozark National Scenic Riverways established in 1964, Congress passed the Wild and Scenic Rivers Act in 1968. The act identified eight rivers to be designated as the first components of a "wild and scenic rivers system," assuring they would remain in a "free-flowing condition" and that they and their "immediate environments" would be preserved undeveloped for future generations. Like designated wilderness areas, most wild and scenic rivers were not under the jurisdiction of the Park Service. But under Hartzog, five new wild and scenic rivers joined the national park system. The National Trail System Act, also signed in 1968, made the 2,100-mile Appalachian Trail part of the park system and set up a process for identifying and adding other historic and recreational corridors

to the "national trails system." Hartzog's interest in urban national parks also had major results. In 1972 Congress established Golden Gate (San Francisco and Marin County) and Gateway (New York and New Jersey) national recreation areas, giving the Park Service a greatly increased role in the management of metropolitan park systems. The 1966 National Historic Preservation Act also gave Hartzog the opportunity to "expand the National Register of Historic Landmarks to include properties of state and local significance," thereby creating "a record of all that merits preservation and a yardstick against which to measure the rightful roles of all concerned in the preservation movement."[79]

The Parkscape program itself, however, did not represent the same scale or level of original planning effort that Mission 66 or the ORRRC had. Parkscape was intended not to redo the

Sign celebrating the fiftieth anniversary of the National Park Service in 1966. NPS Historic Photo Collection.

National
Park Service
1916-1966

5ᶜ
U.S.

Parkscape logo commemorative
stamp, 1966. NPS History Collection.

work of the ORRRC but to implement it. Another central purpose was to change the name and image of Mission 66 activities while essentially continuing many ongoing plans and construction projects. Over the previous ten years the Park Service had become completely identified with Mission 66. Parkscape was meant above all to change that identity. The rhetoric of New Conservation—and a new agency logo—were therefore essential aspects of Parkscape. Hartzog hired a prominent New York graphic design firm, Chermayeff & Geismar Associates, to devise the "symbol of PARKSCAPE U.S.A." Bold and geometric, it consisted of two interlocking triangles with three black dots in the center. The logo represented the three types of national park areas: the triangles stood for a mountain (natural) and a tent (recreational), and the black dots for cannon balls (historical). While the design was effective and won professional awards, Hartzog immediately found himself defending it from critics. He did not intend to re-

place the arrowhead, he assured them; but the Parkscape symbol did supplant the arrowhead on stationery, on agency reports and documents, and in interpretive park brochures and displays. The Post Office used the symbol on a five-cent stamp commemorating the agency's fiftieth anniversary, and other commemorative events and publications featured it in 1966. In 1968 Udall hired the same firm to produce a new Department of the Interior logo in a similar abstract graphic style; it replaced the department's familiar "buffalo seal" that year. At the same time Hartzog announced that the Parkscape symbol would indeed now replace the arrowhead on all badges, uniforms, signs, and publications.[80]

Park rangers, superintendents, and other agency supporters rose up angrily at this point, urging Udall and Hartzog to reject their new logos and return to the buffalo seal and arrowhead. The dispute may seem trivial; but Parkscape was essentially a symbolic initiative intended to revamp the public image of the Park Service and its activities. Many employees, including former directors Wirth and Albright, felt that the agency's tradition (its "mystique") was being erased. The new image generated a genuine outpouring of dismay. When Secretary of the Interior Walter J. Hickel replaced Udall in 1969, he immediately disposed of the short-lived Department of the Interior logo and restored the buffalo seal. Hartzog followed suit and brought back the arrowhead as the Park Service's official symbol.

This misadventure in graphic design revealed a deeper problem with Parkscape: it never captured the imagination of agency staff or the public the way Mission 66 had. Hartzog was, it turned out, a "career man" fully "capable of the job." His nine years of accomplishments put him comfortably in the company of Mather, Albright, Cammerer, Drury, and Wirth. But Parkscape did not survive long as a public relations entity. Soon the Park Service was preparing instead for the nation's bicentennial, which became the next major deadline for agency preparations and expansions. Hartzog also delegated planning and design decisions to a greater degree than his predecessors (particularly Wirth), and so he was not personally involved in design and construction. His interests were more in the political and legislative arena, where he achieved tremendous success. In his memoirs, Hartzog neglects even to mention Parkscape.

The BOR also had great success in the 1960s but withered as the political climate changed. Many of its early projects and activities began under Mission 66 and accelerated as appropriations were made through the provisions of the LWCF and other park legislation. After 1963 the agency also benefited from increased cooperation from the Park Service. But in 1969 it still had only five hundred employees of its own.[81] The BOR was something of an experiment in government: an agency whose primary mandate was to coordinate the work of other agencies. With no land management responsibilities, the BOR never gained the bureaucratic momentum it needed to survive in the long term. With the arrival of the Nixon administration in 1969, Edwin Fitch reported that his agency was "at a crossroads in its existence." Since it had been created through administrative, not legislative, authority, the new secretary of the interior could do away with the BOR as quickly as Udall had created it. But the BOR survived until 1978, when the Carter administration replaced it with the Heritage Conservation and Recreation Service, which was abolished in turn in 1981 by Reagan's first secretary of the interior, James G. Watt. What was left of the federal government's recreational planning expertise at that point was given back to the Park Service. But the move was hardly intended to stimulate a new generation of park and recreational planning. On the contrary, the era of big federal recreation plans, which had begun with the Cape Cod legislation, was ending. Neither the Reagan administration nor Congress typically supported ambitious park plans during the next decade, particularly if they might involve federal acquisition of private property.

There were major changes as well for the planners and designers who had not been transferred to the BOR and remained at the Park Service after 1962. Hartzog understandably never had the close relationship with the WODC and EODC that Wirth had. With Mission 66 over, the BOR functioning, and the regional offices taking on more responsibility for design and construction, the Park Service design offices were now subject to cutbacks. Hartzog also established the precedent of using outside management consultants, in this case James A. Kittleman and Associates of Chicago, for "organizational studies" and recommendations. In 1969 the Philadelphia office was replaced by a new Eastern Service Center in Washington. The San Francisco office was renamed the Western Service Center. In 1971 the combined service centers still had over 580 employees. That year they were abolished, however, and replaced by a new Denver Service Center, in Lakewood, Colorado, which had only 350 employees. The remainder of the Park Service planning, landscape architecture, architecture, engineering, and historian positions were eliminated or transferred to parks, regional offices, or other federal agencies.[82] The Denver Service Center's first priority involved the design of various site developments and interpretive facilities planned to commemorate the events of 1776.

Compared to the events and changes of the early 1970s, the completion of Mission 66 in 1966 was an anticlimax. While there was a significant amount of continuity between the Wirth and Hartzog years, Hartzog's departure at the end of 1972 truly ended a period of national park history that had begun in 1945. Following the 1972 election, Nixon's second secretary of the interior, Rogers C. B. Morton, fired Hartzog for unexplained but clearly political reasons and replaced him with a political appointee with no

professional qualifications for the job. Ronald H. Walker was only thirty-six, and though a trusted political lieutenant in the White House, he had no experience with state or national parks. He lasted only two years and was followed by a series of Park Service directors with diverse backgrounds (some indeed "career men"), who served relatively short terms and who came and went with the political winds at the Department of the Interior.[83]

By the time Hartzog was fired, new public attitudes and congressional legislation had profoundly changed the federal administration of natural resources and public lands. Environmentalism as a political movement had assumed great influence in Washington. Besides the legislation already described, including the Wilderness Act, the LWCF Act, the National Historic Preservation Act, the Wild and Scenic Rivers Act, and the National Trail System Act, by 1973 Congress had also passed the Water Pollution Control Act, the Clean Air Act, the Endangered Species Act, and the National Environmental Policy (NEPA) Act. At the Park Service, organizational change, combined with prescribed procedures for assessing the "environmental impacts" of proposed actions, necessarily changed park management and agency culture. Park master planning, for example, continued to be revised until finally in the 1970s it was replaced by the "general management plan." The new park plans were far less specific, some featuring little or no actual site design at all. The general management plan did include, however, the environmental review now required under NEPA. The plans therefore studied different strategic "alternatives" for future management, assessed the potential benefits and impacts of each, and selected a preferred alternative for implementation. With public process and other forms of review and participation also required by NEPA, by the 1970s national park planning and design required new sets of professional training and skills and a completely revised planning procedure.

Even as the Park Service went through these profound organizational, political, and professional changes, Congress continued to increase the size and diversity of the national park system. Over forty new park areas were established between 1973 and 1980. The 1978 National Parks and Recreation Act alone authorized fourteen additions. While the vast majority of these new parks were vital and worthwhile enhancements, critics began to sense that the entire process was driven by congressional politics, not national recreational planning.[84] "Park barrel legislation," such as the 1978 act, had become a means for Congress to deliver federal largesse to its constituencies. The lawmakers had little interest in "rounding out the system" or maintaining standards of national significance; nor did they necessarily care if the Park Service staff was stretched thin in the management of an ever larger and more diverse collection of federal reservations and sites. But the BOR and the Park Service seemed no longer to be in a position to control the legislators' enthusiasms by providing authoritative recreational studies and plans. More park legislation, critics began to suggest, was not the same as good park legislation.

According to historian Ronald A. Foresta, the Park Service suffered a "loss of steering capacity" in the 1970s. "Those who formerly sus-

George Hartzog (arms folded) inspecting new Park Service women's uniforms in 1972. Lon Garrison is standing to the far left; his wife Inger Garrison is modeling the dress. NPS Historic Photo Collection.

tained the agency in the pursuit of its goals," including members of Congress and conservation groups, "increasingly imposed their own wills on it." Agency supporters sensed that the Park Service was pursuing outdated goals that were not adapted to the ever intensifying crisis of public use in the parks. "Udall made this point when he established the Bureau of Outdoor Recreation and forced Wirth's resignation," writes Foresta. "Environmental groups implied it when they criticized the agency for what they saw as a lack of commitment to environmental principles." Subsequent directors of the Park Service continued to believe that the organization had "fallen prey to bureaucratic hardening of the arteries" and needed to be "brought in line with modern times." This was the "central task," Foresta concludes, that has "occupied, and sometimes even obsessed, Park Service leadership in the modern era." If the Park Service could "understand exactly what the modern era demanded from the Park System and Service, its problems of internal control and external dependence would be mitigated and both the parks and their keepers would be restored to their former high places in American life."[85]

In 1991, on the occasion of the seventy-fifth anniversary of the Park Service, a large conference was held in Vail, Colorado. The participants included park managers, scientists, and other experts from inside and outside the Park Service, who together endorsed a 1992 policy statement known since as the "Vail Agenda." While the group stood by the 1916 mandate to "conserve . . . and provide for the enjoyment" of the park system, they also noted that the "purposes" of the Park Service had "evolved." The agency's "primary responsibility . . . must be protection of park resources." Access and interpretation for enjoyment also "should be provided," as long as park resources were not impaired. The participants concluded that a major program of sustained scientific research should be pursued; but again this would be greatly aided by new legislation, since Congress had still never conferred such a mandate on the agency. While the Park Service should "minimize development of visitor facilities within park boundaries," it should also "embark on an innovative program of facility planning, design, and maintenance to prepare the 'front country' of each park for visitor needs, while protecting the unique features of each park." Wherever possible, visitor needs should be taken care of in "gateway communities," and the Park Service should engage in cooperative planning efforts to help those communities prosper and cope with continued growth.[86]

The 1992 policy statement summarized what many still feel are sound "strategic objectives" for the national park system. For those with long enough memories, many of those objectives also might have recalled the Vint Plan of 1945, the early policy directives of Mission 66, the revised Mission 66 priorities of 1959, the Road to the Future, and Parkscape. If there were similarities between these earlier documents and the Vail Agenda, they perhaps can be best explained by the inescapable persistence of the condition described by Newton Drury in 1949 as the "dilemma of our parks." The essence of the dilemma still exists. The only viable response therefore does as well: if the public is to enjoy parks without impairing them, that use must somehow be accommodated, controlled, channeled, choreographed, or otherwise designed. Creative new approaches to site planning and park development are still needed. To deny this is to evade the requirements and responsibilities of stewardship.

Opponents of Mission 66 claimed victory when Wirth retired and the program came to an end. But it was not a victory for the Park Service, at least in the sense that the agency never fully recovered its independence and prestige within the federal government. To a significant extent the Park Service lost the ability to set its own course. The Denver Service Center has since suffered further reductions and reassignments of planning and design staff, as Congress apparently came to believe that planning and design are not necessary in-house functions of the Park Service at all and should be assumed almost entirely by private consultants. Although the Park Service had certainly used design consultants in the past—notably during Mission 66—it did so as a knowledgeable and effective client. Mission 66 consultants acted as partners, complementing experienced multidisciplinary teams of in-house staff. Without that in-house professional capacity, the Park Service cannot maintain design standards and consistent design identity throughout the park system. The agency will no longer be a strong client; with its private partners, it will in fact be many different clients, with varying priorities, opinions, and motivations, some of which may or may not be particularly well informed or justified. The identity of the system, as a diverse set of significant scenic and historic places managed and interpreted according to consistent and high standards, will itself break down.

The Park Service is criticized for adhering to its tradition. But that tradition has been in decline for forty years. Continuing to blame it for current woes is becoming more difficult to defend. There has been plenty of time for new traditions to be formed. Whatever may have prevented that from happening, it has not been the ghosts of Mission 66.

"THE CAPACITY TO PROVIDE ENJOYMENT"

For motorists driving Tioga Road today, it is not always easy to feel the outrage that Brower, Adams, and others felt in 1958. A noncommercial two-lane park road, it was not, in fact, engineered to the "speedway" standards of contemporary interstate highways. Most would even agree that it is one of the most stunning scenic roads in North America. But there are few alive today who remember the high country along the Tioga Road corridor in the 1920s, as Adams knew it, coming upon Tenaya Lake in its splendid isolation. Such moments were "magic," Adams wistfully recalled.[1] But it was a kind of magic that was easily destroyed. The controversies that so affected the course of Mission 66 ultimately involved the realities of increased public use. People disrupted Adams's idyll more than the blasting of a few granite formations. Arguments about "road standards" or "modernistic architecture" usually came down to disagreement over how accessible parks

should be. Lower numbers of visitors along the old Tioga Road were acceptable; the higher numbers that the widened road would bring were not.

In 1968 these sentiments found the support of a scientific theory when ecologist Garrett Hardin wrote an essay titled "The Tragedy of the Commons." Hardin described how individuals inevitably would attempt to exploit communal resources—including national parks—in order to maximize personal gain or enjoyment. As a given population increased, this would result ultimately in the destruction of the common resources (metaphorically, "the commons") being used. There was no way to stop this process, since people predictably pursued their individual benefit even at the cost of disaster for the larger group or society. The only possible prevention of the tragedy was to control population. The theory fit perfectly with the desire to limit the number of visitors to national parks.

Tioga Road approaching Tenaya Lake. Author's photo.

People would keep coming in ever larger numbers—despite the consequences—unless the population were controlled, which is to say, unless limits were imposed on access. "Plainly we must soon cease to treat the parks as commons," he wrote, "or they will be of no value to anyone."[2] For many contemporary environmentalists, national parks could no longer function as truly public places without being destroyed.

But as Hardin later acknowledged, there were perhaps other means of averting the tragedy: managing the commons. Managing the commons of the national park system was the essence of the Progressive Era project begun by Mather and Albright, of which Mission 66 was the last consistent, systemwide result. While Hardin insisted that there were no "technical" solutions to the tragedy (because eventually population increase would negate them), Mission 66 planners insisted there were: redesigned frontcountry roads and developed areas. While the ability of the parks to support increased access would not be infinite, the postwar crisis in demand would not be beyond the park system's capacity to yield enjoyment sustainably.

Statistical summations of the expansion and modernization that resulted from this conviction vary slightly among different reports and accounts. During his long retirement, Wirth made a project of assembling figures and records, many of which ended up in his personal papers at the University of Wyoming's American Heritage Center. He published his own summary in his 1980 memoir, *Parks, Politics, and the People*.[3] In one analysis, Wirth added the initial $17 million appropriated to the Park Service in fiscal year 1956 to the $884 million appropriated in fiscal years 1957 through 1966 (July 1956–June 1966), and the $110 million in LWCF money appropriated to the BOR and transferred to the Park Service (in 1965 and 1966) for land purchases, to arrive at a total of over $1 billion ($1,001,534,000) in Mission 66 spending. Concessioners invested another $33 million. The increase in total funding amounts (from the original $787 million estimate) reflected the expansion of the park system itself. According to the Park Service's 1966 Mission 66 progress report, seventy new park areas of all types and sizes had been authorized between 1956 and 1966. A total area of 2.1 million acres had been acquired through donations, transfers, exchanges, and purchase. Congress had appropriated over $76 million for Mission 66 land purchases, in addition to the amount supplied through the LWCF. Total visits to the park system had risen from 61.5 million to 124.1 million. Total authorized Park Service staffing had grown from 8,061 to 13, 314. Other Mission 66 statistics, such as the total mileage of roads and trails reconstructed or constructed, and the numbers of visitor centers, utility buildings, campgrounds, picnic areas, residences, training facilities, and other Mission 66 structures built, have been cited in earlier chapters.

The efficiency of Mission 66 as a park development and expansion program was impressive. More significantly, however, the program permanently enlarged the range and funding of Park Service activities. The agency's size and budgets, in other words, did not return to a previous level after 1966. According to author Dwight F. Rettie, total funding per unit of the park system in constant 1990 dollars rose from about $410,000 in 1949, to $1.8 million in 1959, to $2 million in 1966. Appropriations continued to rise after Mission 66, to $2.2 million per unit of the system in 1973 and $2.9 million in 1995.[4] Mission 66 permanently altered the sense of what level of funding was appropriate for national parks. The program also permanently increased the number and diversity of park areas in the system and the degree of professionalization of a much larger Park Service.

Was all this construction and institutional expansion, in the end, a good idea or not? The national park system today, despite the threats that continue to besiege it, cannot be fairly characterized as a tragedy of the commons. One of the reasons it has survived is that most "technical" of management solutions: Mission 66. Even today in parks all over the country the public relies on roads, parking lots, campgrounds, visitor centers, bathrooms, and utilities built through Mission 66. The Park Service is able to do its job thanks to maintenance buildings, residences, entrance stations, and administrative headquarters that often date to the Mission 66 era. This development, arguably, has made it possible for increased numbers to enjoy the national park system while averting the tragedy. Since 1973 there has been no comparable systemwide improvement of frontcountry facilities. In an era of new environmental regulation and the "general management plan," the Park Service and the American public have continued to rely on the extensive, and now aging, infrastructure built largely under Mission 66.

It is also worth noting that since the 1980s, at least in some parks, the population (that is, the visiting public) shows signs of stabilizing. The situation varies widely. At Glacier, Mount Rainier, and Shenandoah, visitation has leveled off since 1980. At others, including Yellowstone and Yosemite, numbers continued to rise through the 1990s but have been more irregular since then. In other cases, such as Grand Canyon, numbers continue to rise to levels that seem impossible to sustain. According to the Park Service, total "recreation visits" systemwide rose from 220 million to almost 277 million between 1980 and 2004, but these figures also reflect an increase in the number of park areas.[5]

The question how, and where, numbers of park visitors continue to increase is of central importance, as it has been since the postwar dilemma began. Increased numbers of visitors, more than any other factor, drove the concepts, planning, funding, and construction of Mission 66. If the numbers of park visitors in fact do not increase, or even decrease, in many parks in coming decades, the crisis of the national parks will have entered a new, and perhaps less virulent stage. In that case, Mission 66 may prove to

have been a good bet. The program expanded frontcountry capacity to a maximum, which it was hoped would be the ultimate level of development necessary. While a price was paid—with Tioga Road and projects like it—the idea of national parks as public parks survived.

But this is true only if the redevelopment and expansion of the park system turns out to be sufficient to meet demand. If, on the one hand, the numbers of visitors continue to grow indefinitely (as it often seems they will), then no amount of redevelopment or expansion will ever meet the demand in the long term. Hardin will be proved correct; technical solutions will eventually be negated by sheer numbers. In that case, park managers will be forced to do what advocates outside the agency wanted to do in 1956: curtail access to the most popular parks and destinations, whether through advance reservations, permits issued by lottery, or some other method. Such restrictions on access, together with increased user fees and other changes in management, would turn public parks into essentially semiprivate reservations. If this transformation were going to be necessary anyway, then perhaps it should have occurred in the first place, as the Sierra Club directors and others urged. From this point of view, attempting to evade this change through a massive construction program in the 1950s and 1960s was a destructive, ultimately futile stopgap.

On the other hand, it also seems possible that the basic strategy of Mission 66—redevelopment to meet immediate postwar demand, and reliance on gateway communities to meet future pressures—may have succeeded in averting the tragedy of the commons while still keeping national parks open to the public at large. If we accept that the pressures of use, even today, are being handled without impairment of the parks, then Mission 66 did exactly what its planners hoped: it saved the national park system as a public park system, open to "the body of the people." It maintained the functionality of the park system as an essential and healthful mitigation of modern life, accessible to all, which preserves the natural and historical heritage of the nation.

Coming to any conclusions about Mission 66 also demands a consideration of "preservation" itself, and how the meaning of the term changes. The 1916 Park Service Act famously stated that "the purpose [of the national parks] is to conserve the scenery and the natural and historical objects and wild life therein and to provide for the enjoyment of the same." In an examination of that text, the 1956 Mission 66 final report remarked on "the singular use of the word *purpose.*" The act "defined one purpose, a single objective, not several." That one purpose was a "concept that at once embraces and indistinguishably combines both use and preservation." Protection was an absolute requirement but not an end itself. "The primary justification for a National Park System lies in its capacity to provide enjoyment in its best sense, now and in the future."[6]

Mission 66 proceeded under the assumption, in other words, that the preservation of scenic and historic places was best achieved by making them into public parks. This implied that a plan for improvement was necessary. Without planned development, the public would not fully appreciate the parks; they would also de-stroy them through "unchanneled" use. Preservation and improvement therefore were part of the same project: making a park. Compared to the alternatives of private commercial or industrial uses, Park Service officials believed, park development preserved landscapes. But environmentalists rejected park making as preservation. Facing the realities of the postwar crisis, a growing group of advocates insisted that automotive tourism had emerged as the greatest threat of all. Preservation and improvement therefore were no longer part of one project; they were antagonistic opposites. Wilderness designation, not park making, became their model of preservation. Wilderness was identified by the absence of any improvement, and its designation demanded a prohibition of such plans.

Wilderness, as a landscape ideal or model, implied changes for national park management, even in frontcountry and historical areas that would never qualify as official wilderness. Wilderness was not a public landscape, in the same sense, and certain assumptions of public park ideology (which Mission 66 attempted to enshrine) soon were devalued. The basic justification for government funding of parks described by Olmsted in 1865 was that access to scenic landscapes was necessary to the health and happiness of individuals and of society as a whole. But the Sierra Club directors who suggested that visitors to Yosemite should be "filtered" down to those capable of truly appreciating the scenery did not feel that the experience was necessary for everyone; nor was it needed for the general public's health and well-being. The "user fees" recommended by the OR-

RRC and implemented through the LWCF suggested that completely public (general treasury) funding was no longer fully justified to support park systems. The use of fees and diverse private funding sources soon increased, and by the 1980s private nonprofit partners and private donations became more and more significant in park management. In 1996 Congress began a "fee demonstration program," which allowed parks to charge higher entrance fees and retain most of the money for their own operations. While park managers can be expected to embrace any source of new funding, these trends may eventually privatize national parks, in the sense that private contributions and user fees will become their major sources of operating funds.

These developments are occurring in municipal and state park systems as well as national parks, and they reflect broad social and political trends. But they also reflect the influence and implications of the postwar landscape ideal of wilderness. If a national park is being conceived of as a wilderness, it is not expected to have the same social functionality that it did as a public park. This has led to a different sense of how and why parks should be funded. While public park ideology justified public funding through taxation, since the 1960s the prevalence of user fees and public-private partnerships has increased. The determination of what constitutes an "impairment" of park resources has also been affected by the postwar ideal of wilderness, defined by an absence of any indication of human activity. The postwar explosion of recreational use of public lands therefore represented a more egregious form of impairment to environ-

mentalists than it did to Park Service officials. Determining the limit of what the Mission 66 final report described as the "capacity to provide enjoyment" proved to be a particularly divisive point. Wilderness advocates borrowed a term from ecologists to attempt to determine the "carrying capacity" of parks, or the number of visitors they could serve without negative consequences. The term referred originally to the numbers of hoofed animals a given range could support before its condition declined precipitously. But park visitors were not elk, and the resource they consumed, "enjoyment," could not be easily quantified. For Wirth and his planners, the carrying capacity analogy made no sense. While the amount of grass a range produced was a function of constants (rainfall and soil), a park's capacity to provide enjoyment could be vastly increased. That was what Mission 66 was designed to do.

But clearly that capacity cannot be increased indefinitely. The reality of 4 million visits recorded at Yosemite in 1996 no doubt reduced the quality of the experience of the "incomparable valley" for everyone. But at the same time, one would have a hard time convincing many of those visitors that the difference between the effects of 2 million people a year, as opposed to 4 million, would justify keeping them out altogether.

A historical consideration of Mission 66 very quickly hits on some of the most hotly contested topics in park management today. This helps explain why many park advocates, environmentalists, and current Park Service staff often hold negative opinions about Mission 66: it represents the "tradition" that many of them have spent their professional careers overcoming. The denigration of Mission 66 among Park Service officials serves a purpose. The philosophy it represents—parks are "for the people" and therefore presumably not for the "resources"—must continue to be guarded against. It is a sad fact that armies of commercial interests surround parks and historic sites throughout the system. Whatever their purported ideological convictions, these interests are, as they always have been, ready to exploit parks in profoundly damaging ways for commercial purposes. These interests also fully understand how to influence congressional politics and public opinion. The situation makes it imperative for Park Service officials to continue to be wary of slogans, like "parks are for the people" (a favorite of both Wirth and Hartzog), which can be misconstrued and exploited by their adversaries.

But less thoughtful critiques of Mission 66, since Butcher's day, have often also been based on misconceptions about what the program and its motivations actually were. Many at the Park Service remain convinced that Mission 66 design was too hurried and standardized, that materials were substandard, and that climate or other local conditions were not considered. This book should prove that these charges are usually false. Mission 66 planning, design, and construction were carried out to high standards and with an efficiency that would be remarkable if duplicated today. Building techniques and materials were comparable to those used in other construction of the era. While standardized designs (virtually mandated by congressional cost restrictions) were used for some building types, all major buildings, and certainly all visitor centers,

were individually planned and designed for their parks and locations. And while certain visitor centers were sited near principal destinations ("on the resource," for critics), this was done consciously, with awareness of the compromise being made, and with an understanding of the enormous interpretive power of being able to refer directly to a landscape—a battlefield perhaps—through a window wall or from the terrace of a visitor center. Where Mission 66 planners erred, such as in the location of Grant Village on important wildlife habitat, it was usually done in ignorance, not out of lack of concern for resources. Neither should Mission 66 be held accountable for decades of underfunded maintenance. A roof may leak because it was poorly designed; it may also leak because it is fifty years old.

But the most consistent indictment of Mission 66 has been that it abandoned "traditional" rustic design in favor of modernist architecture that was "inharmonious" and "urban." There is tremendous irony in this criticism. Wirth, Vint, Maier, Doty, and Underwood—presumably some of the principal culprits in this aesthetic crime—were, with others, the inventors of Park Service rustic design. They were far more aware of what "rustic" was, what it was not, and why it needed to be replaced than anyone alive today. But since the 1980s, rustic design has come to be associated with a more ecological approach to park management, despite the fact that it was not particularly energy-efficient or "sustainable" design. Rustic builders often used park resources, such as stone and logs, in its construction. But the rustic style has nevertheless come to represent the values of environmentalism for many today, who feel that it "harmonizes" in ways Mission 66 modernism does not. As discussed earlier, the horizontal massing, unornamented elevations, and (usually) unobtrusive siting of Mission 66 buildings actually did minimize their visual presence, particularly in light of the increased floor space and amount of program being provided. The exceptions to this generalization, such as the Jackson Visitor Center at Mount Rainier, are notable and striking. But other, more numerous examples, at Rocky Mountain, Zion, Big Bend, Cape Cod, and many other parks, bear out the observation. More efficient and in a way more scientific, Mission 66 architecture should have appealed to those who desired to see a greater influence of the sciences in the management of the parks. But science, efficiency, and visual unobtrusiveness were not really the main points being considered; the emotional appeal of rustic architecture was.

In addition, while Mission 66 is accused of abandoning Park Service tradition, more of that "tradition" was constructed during the Mission 66 era than many realize. The arrowhead logo and redesigned uniforms are the most notable examples. But so are Founders Day and other agency events; the training centers that inculcate the meanings and techniques of "interpretation"; the increased training and professionalization of uniformed employees; and the size and diversity of the park system itself. Above all, the visitor center continues to serve as the hub not only of visitor experience but of daily life and work for park staffs as well.

Criticism of Mission 66 of course is justified in many cases. Mistakes were made; tastes change; and the sheer ubiquity of Mission 66 era construction was sure to result eventually in dissatisfaction with aspects of the program and its built legacy. The ranch house as a type has proved to be durable and flexible; but many families today may consider them spartan, plain, or simply not up to current standards. Park managers often complain that Mission 66 visitor centers are too small. Designed for fewer visitors than experienced today, they certainly are at times crowded. But if the numbers of visitors has grown, the amount of programming shoehorned into Mission 66 visitor centers has increased even more. Bookshops, for example, have become considerable retail enterprises that produce significant revenue (for a nonprofit partner). More employees are needed for new responsibilities, such as compliance with NEPA and the National Historic Preservation Act, and they require more office space, as do universities and nonprofit partners engaged in research programs. Trying to fit fifty years' worth of such programmatic growth—along with larger numbers of visitors—into a Mission 66 visitor center can of course prove impossible.

But there are vital reasons, today, to come to a more considered historical appreciation of Mission 66. Above all, it was the last consistent, ambitious, systemwide redevelopment of the national park system. Parkscape and the bicentennial initiative were not in the same category, in terms of the scope of centralized planning and the consistent expression of design and amount of construction. The elimination of the WODC and the EODC, and the additional requirements and procedural changes brought about by environmental legislation, also changed the way the Park Service operated. Mission 66 could not have been attempted again the same way after 1973 even if it were considered desirable, which it would not be, since expectations of public process and environmental protections have increased. As the last systemwide program of its type, however, Mission 66 determined the general configuration of much of today's national park frontcountries and historic sites. The development plans of the 1950s and 1960s still often determine the levels and patterns of visitor use and therefore to some degree the content of visitor experiences. For those involved in current park planning, redevelopment, and interpretation efforts, a better understanding of the history of these frontcountry landscapes is an absolute necessity.

Another reason to reconsider Mission 66 is that the program introduced the levels of Park Service funding, staffing, training, and professionalization that are the necessary foundations of national park stewardship. With these requirements, there are concomitant minimum expectations of public service—visitor center, roads, staff residences, utilities, and so on—for any element of the national park system. In this sense Mission 66 reconfigured the place of the national parks and the Park Service in American society. But it did so from a more powerful position within the federal government than the Park Service has enjoyed since. This political reality puts the agency in a position of being permanently outmatched. It must act as the steward of a system that was mainly developed during the Park Service's first fifty years, when the agency could more effectively set its own course. It must now manage a park system that demands the institutional ability and political

strength of the more influential organization it once was.

Mission 66 also has a unique and important place in the history of American preservation. Preservationists—whether they are preserving natural or cultural resources—need a better grasp of their own past, including the recent past. The history and theory of preservation have been neglected by preservationists, many of whom seem to think that their profession began with the National Historic Preservation Act. Mission 66 is an essential bridge in preservation theory and practice between the New Deal and the present historic preservation bureaucracy, which was born in 1966. Preservation has involved more than good versus greed, more than saving landmarks from the inexorable progress of modernity; it has utilized compromise, development, and massive demolitions, as in St. Louis and Philadelphia. Mission 66, which fostered the professionalization and expansion of historic preservation much as the Williamsburg Restoration did in the 1920s, is an essential chapter in this rich and complex history.

Assessing, finally, the significance of Mission 66 in the American landscape should perhaps be done in tandem with consideration of its contemporary, the interstate highway system. Mission 66 attempted—successfully or not—to provide park planning and expansion that could match Eisenhower's roads. Success was unlikely, given the difference in the nature of the legislation and the level of appropriations Congress gave each. But the effort was essential and bold; and if it had come later, it would have been too late. The last seashores and lakeshores would have been out of public reach, and existing parks would have been completely overwhelmed. If Mission 66 was not able fully to counter and complete the modernization of the American landscape represented by the 1956 Interstate Highway Act, it nevertheless achieved many important accomplishments. It also inspired Congress to create the ORRRC, and that commission, thanks to Congress's willingness, finally, to pass the necessary legislation, did begin to undertake the massive expansion and reconfiguration of public recreation policy that the reality of the interstate highways demanded.

In short, the national park system as it is experienced today owes much to Mission 66. Will the essential assumptions and planned patterns of use established through Mission 66 ever change? That is for current park managers to decide. The national park system today is undergoing a new period of redevelopment that will be the most pervasive and significant since Mission 66. But where Mission 66 was centralized and widely publicized, the new wave of park redevelopment is relatively decentralized and has attracted almost no public notice. The Park Service as an agency has itself become more decentralized, for a number of reasons. Much of the new construction taking place is being funded by private partners, or by user fees retained by individual parks. What is being built? Often, whether the continuities or ironies are recog-

nized or not, first on many superintendents' priority lists is a new—and much larger—visitor center. It seems, perhaps, that Mission 66 does live on. Many new park buildings reflect the basic assumptions of the program. Their sheathing in neo-rustic veneers should not disguise the similarities. Even the *New York Times* editorialized that what was needed today to address a multibillion-dollar "backlog of deferred maintenance" in the parks was "another Mission 66."[7] But what would that be? At this point it would likely continue the current trend toward decentralized, local initiatives, with significant private funding and partnerships, but without consistent, systemwide policies for building programs or design standards: a kind of Mission 66 without the "mission." And without detailed (and enforced) park master plans, the dangers of ad hoc construction projects, whether put forward by Congress, superintendents, or local partners, always remain.

The most important reason to examine Mission 66, then, is to help decide what the next mission should be. By no means should we wish that Mission 66 could be replicated; but to truly move beyond it, it must be understood first. The national park, as a public park, has not turned out to be a tragedy of the commons. It is alive and well, if besieged. And it is necessary to the future well-being of American society.

NOTES

INTRODUCTION

1. See Dwight F. Rettie, *Our National Park System: Caring for America's Greatest Natural and Historic Treasures* (Urbana: University of Illinois Press, 1995), 250–251, for a comparison of Park Service budgets in 1990 constant dollars.
2. Visitor statistics are available from the National Park Service through the agency website. See www.nps.gov/refdesk. Also see the appendixes of Rettie, *Our National Park System.*
3. Alfred Runte, *National Parks: The American Experience* (1979), 2nd ed., rev. (Lincoln: University of Nebraska Press, 1987), 156, 158–159, 171.
4. David R. Brower, *For Earth's Sake: The Life and Times of David Brower* (Salt Lake City: Peregrine Smith Books, 1990), 220; Richard West Sellars, *Preserving Nature in the National Parks: A History* (New Haven: Yale University Press, 1997), 174.
5. Bernard DeVoto, "Let's Close the National Parks," *Harper's* 207, no. 1241 (October 1953): 49–52.
6. Conrad L. Wirth, *Parks, Politics, and the People* (Norman: University of Oklahoma Press, 1980), 9–22, 66–168.
7. Rettie, *Our National Park System*, 251–252. It is difficult to compare total expenditures on the national park system during the New Deal to the cost of Mission 66, but there is no question that New Deal programs represented a greater overall commitment. For example, the Department of Labor's and the U.S. Army's adjusted costs of recruiting, housing, and feeding the Civilian Conservation Corps alone may have exceeded the Mission 66 total. Mission 66 also did not include the massive state park expansions overseen by the Park Service in the 1930s, nor was it complemented by other federal programs (such as the Public Works Administration or the Resettlement Administration, among others) that greatly augmented Park Service activity during the New Deal.
8. Wirth, *Parks, Politics, and the People*, 262–274; R. Bryce Workman, *National Park Service Uniforms: The Developing Years, 1932–1970* (Harpers Ferry, W. Va.: National Park Service, Harpers Ferry Center, 1998), 31, 33–38; "Mission 66 Progress Report," March 1966, National Park Service History Collection, Harpers Ferry Center.
9. See Sarah Allaback, *Mission 66 Visitor Centers: The History of a Building Type* (Washington, D.C.: Government Printing Office, 2000).
10. Thomas C. Vint, "Development of National Parks for Conservation," in *American Planning and Civic Annual,* ed. Harlean James (Washington, D.C.: American Planning and Civic Association, 1938), 69–71. The words are inscribed on the Roosevelt Arch (1903) at the Gardiner entrance to Yellowstone, and are a quotation from the 1872 legislation which created that park.
11. Wirth, *Parks, Politics, and the People*, 242.

12. A transcript of Olmsted's letter is in Conrad Wirth's personal papers at the University of Wyoming (American Heritage Center, Conrad L. Wirth Collection) and is reprinted in part in Wirth, *Parks, Politics, and the People*, 21–22, as well as in several articles authored by Wirth beginning in the mid-1950s.

13. In 2000 several Mission 66 visitor centers were designated National Historic Landmarks for their architectural significance. These include the Quarry Visitor Center, Dinosaur National Monument; Wright Brothers National Memorial Visitor Center; and Beaver Meadows Visitor Center, Rocky Mountain Park. Others Mission 66 visitor centers have been determined eligible for listing in the National Register of Historic Places.

1. NEWTON DRURY AND THE "DILEMMA OF OUR PARKS"

1. Richard H. Stroud, ed., *National Leaders of American Conservation* (Washington, D.C.: Smithsonian Institution Press, 1985), 129–130.

2. John B. Dewitt, *California Redwood Parks and Preserves* (San Francisco: Save-the-Redwoods League, 1985), 9–15; Joseph H. Engbeck Jr., *State Parks of California: 1864 to the Present* (Portland, Ore.: Graphic Arts Center Publishing Company, 1980), 41–45, 47–55.

3. There is also reason to believe that Ickes was simply confused about what direction the Park Service should take in 1933. At first he hoped that Albright would continue; then he proposed Drury, who represented a very different direction. Robert Shankland, *Steve Mather of the National Parks*, 3rd ed. (New York: Alfred A. Knopf, 1970), 302; Ronald A. Foresta, *America's National Parks and Their Keepers* (Washington, D.C.: Resources for the Future, 1984), 47–49; Horace M. Albright, *The Birth of the National Park Service: The Founding Years, 1913–1933* (Salt Lake City: Howe Brothers, 1985), 309; John Ise, *Our National Park Policy: A Critical History* (Baltimore: Johns Hopkins University Press, 1961), 443–444; Barry Mackintosh, "Harold L. Ickes and the National Park Service," *Journal of Forest History* 29, no. 2 (April 1985): 78–84.

4. See Paul S. Sutter, *Driven Wild: How the Fight against Automobiles Launched the Modern Wilderness Movement* (Seattle: University of Washington Press, 2002). Sutter demonstrates that the wilderness ideal, as it took shape especially in the 1930s, was more a reaction to the ef-fects of increased automotive recreation than the result of conflicts over natural resource exploitation: "The modern wilderness idea emerged as an alternative to landscapes of modernized leisure and play, and it was preeminently a product of the discordant internal politics of outdoor recreation" (20).

5. See Carsten Lien, *Olympic Battleground: The Power Politics of Timber Preservation* (San Francisco: Sierra Club Books, 1991), 60–83; Alfred Runte, *Yosemite: The Embattled Wilderness* (Lincoln: University of Nebraska Press, 1990), 135–159; Ethan Carr, *Wilderness by Design: Landscape Architecture and the National Park Service* (Lincoln: University of Nebraska Press, 1998), 115–138, 219–225.

6. William C. Tweed, *Recreation Site Planning and Improvement in National Forests, 1891–1942* (Washington, D.C.: Government Printing Office, 1980), 8–13; Donald N. Baldwin, *The Quiet Revolution: Grass Roots of Today's Wilderness Preservation Movement* (Boulder: Pruett Publishing Company, 1972) 29–36; Roderick Nash, *Wilderness and the American Mind* (1967), 3rd ed. (New Haven: Yale University Press, 1982), 185–187, 191; Dennis M. Roth, *The Wilderness Movement and the National Forests* (College Station, Tex.: Intaglio Press, 1988), 1–12; Mark W. T. Harvey, *A Symbol of Wilderness: Echo Park and the American Conservation Movement* (Albuquerque: University of New Mexico Press, 1994), 51–75; Sutter, *Driven Wild*, 19–53.

7. Vint, "Development of National Parks for Conservation," 69–71.

8. The Park Service master plans also employed a more restrictive (and more controversial) zone, the "research area," which limited access of any type. Ibid.; Thomas C. Vint, "National Park Service Master Plans," in *Planning and Civic Comment* 12, no. 2 (April 1946): 21–40.

9. James F. Kieley, "A Brief History of the National Park Service," unpublished report, U.S. Department of the Interior, Main Interior Library, 1940, 23; U.S. Department of the Interior, *1940 Annual Report*, 203, and *1941 Annual Report*, 203; Conrad L. Wirth, *The Civilian Conservation Corps Program of the United States Department of the Interior* (Washington, D.C.: Department of the Interior, National Park Service, 1944); Wirth, *Parks, Politics, and the People*, 65–93. Also see Harlan D. Unrau and G. Frank Williss, *Administrative History: Expansion of the National Park Service in the 1930s* (Denver: Government Printing Office, 1983); John C. Paige, *The Civilian Con-*

servation Corps and the National Park Service, 1933–1942 (Denver: Government Printing Office, 1985).

10. Ise, *Our National Park Policy*, 437–439; Unrau and Williss, *Expansion of the National Park Service in the 1930s*, 267–269; John C. Miles, *Guardians of the Parks: A History of the National Parks and Conservation Association* (Washington, D.C.: Taylor & Francis in cooperation with the National Parks and Conservation Association, 1995), 86–95, 124. For analysis of the wilderness movement and the founding of the Wilderness Society as reactions to the effects of modern outdoor recreation, see Sutter, *Driven Wild;* for an account of early wilderness proposals and ideas, see Melanie Simo, *Garden and Forest: Traces of Wilderness in a Modernizing Land, 1897–1949* (Charlottesville: University of Virginia Press, 2003). Joseph Sax has described "reflective recreation" as the highest use for national parks, requiring limitations on "conventional recreation" activities, including motorized recreation and tourism. Joseph L. Sax, *Mountains without Handrails: Reflections on the National Parks* (Ann Arbor: University of Michigan Press, 1980), 18–24, 61–64.

11. Foresta, *America's National Parks*, 47.

12. Donald Worster, *Nature's Economy: A History of Ecological Ideas* (1977), 2nd ed. (New York: Cambridge University Press, 1994), 258–290.

13. Sellars, *Preserving Nature in the National Parks*, 85–87; James A. Pritchard, *Preserving Yellowstone's Natural Conditions: Science and the Perception of Nature* (Lincoln: University of Nebraska Press, 1999), 37–39.

14. Donald C. Swain, "The National Park Service and the New Deal," *Pacific Historical Review* 41, no. 3 (August 1972): 312–332.

15. Quoted in T. H. Watkins, *Righteous Pilgrim: The Life and Times of Harold L. Ickes* (New York: Henry Holt and Company, 1990), 550.

16. Harold L. Ickes to Jens Jensen (copy), March 18, 1938, Personal Papers of Arno B. Cammerer, entry 18, RG 79, National Archives. The letter is typical of many that Ickes sent on this topic.

17. Mackintosh, "Harold L. Ickes," 80–83.

18. Robert W. Righter, *Crucible for Conservation: The Struggle for Grand Teton National Park* (1982; reprint, Moose, Wyo.: Grand Teton Natural History Association, 2000), 40.

19. Ise, *Our National Park Policy*, 332–336; Harold L. Ickes to Jens Jensen (copy), March 18, 1938, Personal Papers of Arno B. Cammerer, entry 18, RG 79, National Archives.

20. Ise, *Our National Park Policy*, 371–376.

21. John Jameson, *The Story of Big Bend National Park* (Austin: University of Texas Press, 1996), 30, 70–84.

22. Quoted in Lien, *Olympic Battleground*, 200.

23. Lary M. Dilsaver and William C. Tweed, *The Challenge of the Big Trees: A Resource History of Sequoia and Kings Canyon National Parks* (Three Rivers, Calif.: Sequoia Natural History Association, 1990), 202–225.

24. For the role of Franklin Roosevelt and Harold Ickes in 1930s wilderness protection efforts at Olympic and elsewhere, see Irving Brant, *Adventures in Conservation with Franklin D. Roosevelt* (Flagstaff, Ariz.: Northland Publishing Co., 1988).

25. Barry Mackintosh, *The National Parks: Shaping the System* (Washington, D.C.: Government Printing Office, 1991), 55–56.

26. Mackintosh, "Harold L. Ickes," 80; U.S. Department of the Interior, press release, June 19, 1940, "Selection of Newton B. Drury for the Post of Director of the National Park Service . . . ," Personal Papers of Newton B. Drury, entry 19, RG 79, National Archives.

27. David R. Brower, *For Earth's Sake: The Life and Times of David Brower* (Salt Lake City: Peregrine Smith Books, 1990), 219–220.

28. U.S. Department of the Interior, National Park Service, *1941 Annual Report.*

29. Newton B. Drury to Robert Sterling Yard, undated draft (ca. 1943), Personal Papers of Newton B. Drury, entry 19, RG 79, National Archives. By 1949 Drury was more receptive to the idea of congressional designation of wilderness areas.

30. Newton B. Drury, "National Park Service War Work, December 7, 1941, to June 30, 1944," confidential report, Personal Papers of Newton B. Drury, entry 19, RG 79, National Archives. The protocol, first described in a 1940 memorandum, bears a notable resemblance to the environmental review process established thirty years later through the National Environmental Policy Act.

31. Lien, *Olympic Battleground*, 213–253. Ickes's personal dislike and abuse of Cammerer was well known. See, for example, Ise, *Our National Park Policy*, 442; Donald C. Swain, *Wilderness Defender: Horace M. Albright and Conservation* (Chicago: University of Chicago Press, 1970), 218, 250.

32. Newton B. Drury, "National Parks in Wartime: A Review of the Year," in *American Planning and Civic Annual,* ed. Harlean James (Washington, D.C.: American Planning and Civic Association, 1942), 68–74; idem, "National Parks Look toward the Peace," in *American Planning and Civic Annual,* ed. Harlean James (Washington, D.C.: American Planning and Civic Association, 1943), 19–23; Carl P. Russell, "The National Parks in Wartime," *Outdoor America* (July 1943); Harold Butcher, "Our National Parks in Wartime," *Travel Magazine* 83, no. 4 (August 1944): 26–27; Ise, *Our National Park Policy,* 449–451.

33. U.S. Department of the Interior, National Park Service, *1946 Annual Report,* 307–310.

34. Ibid., 308.

35. U.S. Department of the Interior, National Park Service, *1947 Annual Report,* 327–328; *1948 Annual Report,* 318; *1949 Annual Report,* 302; Ise, *Our National Park Policy,* 455; Rettie, *Our National Park System,* 251.

36. The next three of the five priorities set by Drury also relate to park development, including an injunction on any attempt to "'gild the lily' or try to improve on nature's design." Providing "interpretive aids" was another requirement, since otherwise visitors might not achieve a "full appreciation of the parks," and accommodations needed to be provided, though only "to the extent that near-by outside enterprises do not adequately meet public needs." Newton B. Drury, "Park Conservation: A Report on Park and Outdoor Recreational Resources in the United States for the Secretary of the Interior," January 28, 1946, confidential report, Personal Papers of Newton B. Drury, entry 19, RG 79, National Archives.

37. See Newton B. Drury, "The National Park Concept," *National Park Magazine* 23, no. 97 (April–June 1949): 28–34; idem, "The National Park Service: The First Thirty Years," in *American Planning and Civic Annual,* ed. Harlean James (Washington, D.C.: American Civic and Planning Association, 1946), 29–37; idem, "Planning for National Parks and Parkways," in *American Planning and Civic Annual,* ed. Harlean James (Washington, D.C.: American Civic and Planning Association, 1948), 1–9; idem, "Preserving Nature . . . Our National Park Policy," *The Living Wilderness* 17, no. 40 (Spring 1952): 1–4.

38. Drury, "Planning for National Parks and Parkways," 7.

39. Newton B. Drury, "The Dilemma of Our Parks," *American Forests* 55, no. 6 (June 1949): 6–11, 38, 39.

40. Conrad L. Wirth, "The Aims of the National Park Service in Relation to Water Resources," transcript of address to National Citizens Conference on Planning and Resources, May 19, 1952, Conrad L. Wirth Collection, University of Wyoming, American Heritage Center.

41. Conrad L. Wirth, "The Aims of the National Park Service in Relation to Water Resources," in *American Planning and Civic Annual,* ed. Harlean James (Washington, D.C.: American Planning and Civic Association, 1952), 11–18. Also see Newton B. Drury, "Recreation Plan for Lake Texoma," *Pencil Points* (June 1945): 58–68; Conrad L. Wirth, "Recreational Use of Water," transcript of address to United Nations Scientific Conference on the Conservation and Utilization of Resources, May 3, 1949, Conrad L. Wirth Collection, University of Wyoming, American Heritage Center; U.S. Department of the Interior, National Park Service, *1948 Annual Report,* 352–353, and *1950 Annual Report,* 305–307; Ise, *Our National Park Policy,* 468–470.

42. In 1951 Secretary of the Interior Oscar L. Chapman barred the Bureau of Reclamation from undertaking any further surveys in national parks. Ise, *Our National Park Policy,* 470–473.

43. Drury argued with Ickes over the Park Service's role in managing recreation areas in the so-called "Black Magic–Ivory Tower" correspondence. See Sellars, *Preserving Nature in the National Parks,* 174–177.

44. See Elmo Richardson, *Dams, Parks, and Politics: Resource Development and Preservation in the Truman-Eisenhower Era* (Lexington: University Press of Kentucky, 1973); Clayton R. Koppes, "Environmental Policy and American Liberalism: The Department of the Interior, 1933–1953," *Environmental Review* 7 (Spring 1983): 17–53; Mark W. T. Harvey, *A Symbol of Wilderness: Echo Park and the American Conservation Movement* (Albuquerque: University of New Mexico Press, 1994); Jon M. Cosco, *Echo Park: Struggle for Preservation* (Boulder: Johnson Books, 1995).

45. Conrad L. Wirth and Frederick Law Olmsted Jr., *A Survey of the Recreational Resources of the Colorado River Basin* (1946; reprint, Washington, D.C.: Government Printing Office, 1950), 199. Apparently the 1941 interagency memorandum that authorized the study specifically allowed for the consideration of a new reservoir and recreation area in Dinosaur National Monument. Harvey, *A Symbol of Wilderness,* 31–32.

46. See Susan Rhoades Neel, "Irreconcilable Differences: Reclamation, Preservation, and the Origins of the Echo Park Controversy" (Ph.D. diss., University of California, Los Angeles, 1990).

47 Although the exact circumstances of Drury's departure are not fully known, most historians have concluded that his continued opposition to the Echo Park dam after 1950 was a deciding factor. Ibid., 488–493; Harvey, *A Symbol of Wilderness*, 31–35, 100–104; Cosco, *Echo Park*, 42–53.

2. CONRAD WIRTH AND POSTWAR "RECREATIONAL PLANNING"

1. Harvey, *A Symbol of Wilderness*, 104–105; Foresta, *America's National Parks*, 52.

2. Theodore Wirth, *Minneapolis Park System, 1883–1944* (Minneapolis: Board of Park Commissioners, City of Minneapolis, 1945); James H. Husted, "Park Family . . . in Three Generations of Wirths," *Park Maintenance* (January 1952): 5–7; "Conrad Louis Wirth, Former NPS Director, Dies at 93," *National Park Service Courier* (Summer 1993): 22–23; Wirth, *Parks, Politics, and the People*, 4–10.

3. Wirth, *Parks, Politics, and the People*, 11–15.

4. All this was in addition to the other CCC work being done in the national parks themselves. See Kieley, *A Brief History of the National Park Service;* Wirth, *The Civilian Conservation Corps Program of the United States Department of the Interior;* Wirth, *Parks, Politics, and the People*, 65–93; Unrau and Williss, *Expansion of the National Park Service in the 1930s;* Paige, *The Civilian Conservation Corps and the National Park Service.*

5. In 1936 the number of CCC state park regions was reduced back to four. Wirth, *Parks, Politics, and the People*, 127, 130–131; Paige, *The CCC and the National Park Service*, 48–51; Unrau and Williss, *Expansion of the National Park Service in the 1930s*, 252.

6. National Resources Board, *Recreational Use of Land in the United States*, pt. 10 of *Report on Land Planning* (Washington, D.C.: Government Printing Office, 1938).

7. U.S. Department of the Interior. National Park Service, *A Study of the Park and Recreation Problem of the United States* (Washington, D.C.: Government Printing Office, 1941).

8. See Thomas C. Vint and J. R. Thrower, eds., *Report on the Building Program from Allotments of the Public Works Administration, Eastern Division, 1933–1937* (Washington, D.C.: National Park Service, n.d. [1937]), 1; Unrau and Williss, *Expansion of the National Park Service in the 1930s*, 249.

9. Harold L. Ickes, "Report on the Committee of the Department of the Interior on Permanent Civilian Conservation Corps," September 22, 1936; and Robert Fechner to Conrad L. Wirth and Fred Morrell, April 8, 1937, Conrad L. Wirth Collection, University of Wyoming, American Heritage Center.

10. Wirth, *The Civilian Conservation Corps Program of the United States Department of the Interior.* Much of the text of the report appears in "exhibits" and drafts prepared in 1936 and 1937 by Wirth that are now in the Conrad L. Wirth Collection, American Heritage Center, University of Wyoming.

11. Drury, "National Parks Look toward the Peace," 22.

12. Conrad L. Wirth, "Parks and Their Uses," in *American Planning and Civic Annual*, ed. Harlean James (Washington, D.C.: American Civic and Planning Association, 1935), 156–161.

13. Wirth's opposition to the Echo Park dam was unequivocal: "There will be no turning around, or turning from, the fundamental concept of the national park system. . . . I shall not consent to the building of a dam in a national park." "Director Wirth on Park Policy," *National Parks Magazine* 26, no. 110 (July–September 1952): 101, 134. Also see Wirth, "The Aims of the National Park Service in Relation to Water Resources," 18; Cosco, *Echo Park*, 49–51.

14. Harvey, *A Symbol of Wilderness*, 81–84.

15. George Thomas Kurian, *Datapedia of the United States, 1790–2000: America Year by Year* (Lanham, Md.: Bernan Press, 1994), 17, 79, 111–112, 267.

16. U.S. Department of Commerce, *Two Hundred Million Americans* (Washington, D.C.: Government Printing Office, 1967), 51.

17. See Kenneth T. Jackson, *Crabgrass Frontier: The Suburbanization of the United States* (New York: Oxford University Press, 1985); Robert Fishman, *Bourgeois Utopias: The Rise and Fall of Suburbia* (New York: Basic Books, 1987); Adam Rome, *The Bulldozer in the Countryside: Suburban Sprawl and the Rise of American Environmentalism* (New York: Cambridge University Press, 2001).

18. House & Home, *Housing Facts and Trends* (New York: McGraw Hill/Dodge Publication, 1965), 21.

19. Jackson, *Crabgrass Frontier,* 326; Kurian, *Datapedia,* 239; House & Home, *Housing Facts and Trends,* 18.

20. Under the terms of the 1949 Wherry Act, private developers built housing on land leased to them by the government and then managed the properties and rented them to military personnel. The Wherry program was replaced in 1955 under the Capehart Act, under which developers again built housing, but with the government assuming ownership and management responsibilities directly. Nearly 250,000 units of housing were built under the two acts. Because of their special situation as rental housing associated with military bases, the Cape and Wherry neighborhoods have changed less than many other tract developments of the 1950s See R. Christopher Goodwin & Associates, "Neighborhood Design Guidelines for Army Wherry and Capehart Era Family Housing," draft, government report, U.S. Army: Fort Detrick, Md., 2002. Also see Congressional Quarterly Service, *Housing a Nation* (Washington, D.C.: Government Printing Office, 1966), 21; Chester Hartman and Robin Drayer, "Military-Family Housing: The Other Public Housing Program," *Housing and Society* 17, no. 3 (1990): 67–78; William C. Baldwin, "Wherry and Capehart: Army Family Housing Privatization Programs in the 1950s," *Engineer* (April 1996): 42–44.

21. Victor Gruen and Lawrence P. Smith, "Shopping Centers: The New Building Type," *Progressive Architecture* (June 1952): 66–109.

22. Nancy E. Cohen, *America's Marketplace: A History of Shopping Centers* (Lyme, Conn.: Greenwich Publishing Group, 2002), 28, 52, 55.

23. On shopping center design and designers, see Richard Longstreth, *City Center to Regional Mall: Architecture, the Automobile, and Retailing in Los Angeles, 1920–1950* (Cambridge: MIT Press, 1997), 307–347.

24. Eugene Weston Jr., "Has the Automobile Made the Skyscraper Obsolete?" *Architectural Record* 102 (October 1947): 124–145.

25. "Should Management Move to the Country?" *Fortune* (December 1952): 142.

26. See Louise A. Mozingo, "The Corporate Estate in the USA, 1954–64: 'Thoroughly Modern in Concept, but . . . Down to Earth and Rugged,'" *Studies in the History of Gardens and Designed Landscapes* 20, no. 1 (January–March 2000): 25–56.

27. "Rural Insurance Plant," *Architectural Forum* (September 1951): 104–107; Mozingo, "The Corporate Estate," 28–36.

28. "General Motors Technical Center: To Unite Science with Its Application," *Architectural Record* 98 (November 1945): 98–117; "General Motors Technical Center," *Architectural Forum* 95 (November 1951): 111–123; "GM Nears Completion," *Architectural Forum* 101 (November 1954): 206–224.

29. "The Corporate Neighbor in the Suburb," *Progressive Architecture* (June 1959): 146–164; "Big Business Moves to the Country," *Architectural Record* (September 1951): 160–163.

30. Allaback, *Mission 66 Visitor Centers,* 17–18.

31. National forest roads received about 10 percent of the total authorization; national parks received none. Bruce E. Seely, *Building the American Highway System: Engineers as Policy Makers* (Philadelphia: Temple University Press, 1987), 46–59.

32. Stephen T. Mather, "The Ideals and Policy of the National Park Service Particularly in Relation to Yosemite National Park," in *Handbook of Yosemite National Park,* ed. Ansel F. Hall (New York: G. P. Putnam's Sons, 1921), 81; U.S. Department of the Interior, National Park Service, *1924 Annual Report,* 11–12; U.S. Congress, House of Representatives, Committee on the Public Lands, *Construction of Roads, etc. in National Parks and Monuments: Hearings before the Committee on the Public Lands,* 68th Cong., 1st sess., February 7, 8, 12, and 14, 1924.

33. See Linda Flint McClelland, *Building the National Parks: Historic Landscape Design and Construction* (Baltimore: Johns Hopkins University Press, 1998), 195–242; Carr, *Wilderness by Design,* 139–187.

34. Seely, *Building the American Highway System,* 141–149.

35. Ibid., 187.

36. Tom Lewis describes the consensus behind highway improvements at the time in terms of support from elected officials, unions, private trade groups, lobbyists, and newspaper editorialists. Tom Lewis, *Divided Highways: Building the Interstate Highways, Transforming American Life* (New York: Viking Penguin, 1997), 98–123.

37. Kurian, *Datapedia,* 267.

38. Mark H. Rose, *Interstate: Express Highway Politics, 1939–1989,* rev. ed. (Knoxville: University of Tennessee Press, 1990), 70–93; Lewis, *Divided Highways,* 98–122.

39. Wirth, *Parks, Politics, and the People,* 238–239. According to a 1958 in-house history of the Mission 66 program, Wirth conceived of the initiative on February 6 and 7,

primarily as a means of addressing the inadequacies of annual appropriations, by seeking authorization for a ten-year construction program. Roy E. Appleman, "A History of the National Park Service Mission 66 Program," January 1958, unpublished report, National Park Service, Denver Service Center, Technical Information Center.

40. The report was presented to Congress in January and published in February. Seely, *Building the American Highway System,* 214–215.

41. Russell went on to describe his solution, in which all park development would be removed to the Big Meadows area and only day use would be allowed in Yosemite Valley. Martin Litton, "Yosemite's Beauty Fast Disappearing," *National Parks Magazine* 26, no. 111 (October–December 1952): 164–168, reprinted from *Los Angeles Times,* September 1, 1952.

42. Paul Shephard Jr., "Something Amiss in the National Parks," *National Parks Magazine* 27, no. 115 (October–December 1953): 150–151, 187–190.

43. Bernard DeVoto, "Let's Close the National Parks," *Harper's* 207, no. 1241 (October 1953): 49–52.

44. Jerome B. Wood, "National Parks: Tomorrow's Slums?" *Travel* 101, no. 4 (April 1954): 14–16.

45. Charles Stevenson, "The Shocking Truth about Our National Parks," *Reader's Digest* 66, no. 393 (January 1955): 45–50; Robert M. Yoder, "Twenty-four Million Acres of Trouble," *Saturday Evening Post,* July 3, 1954, 32, 78–80.

46. Stevenson, "The Shocking Truth," 50; Yoder, "Twenty-four Million Acres of Trouble," 80.

47. Wirth, *Parks, Politics, and the People,* 234.

48. Anthony Netboy, "Crisis in Our Parks," *American Forests* 61, no. 5 (May 1955): 24–27, 46–47. A transcript of Wirth's February 1954 statement to the House Subcommittee on Interior Appropriations is in box 12, Conrad L. Wirth Collection, University of Wyoming, American Heritage Center. In addition to these arguments, Wirth also narrated a slide show of decrepit and overcrowded facilities in the parks.

49. Yoder, "Twenty-four Million Acres of Trouble," 80.

50. U.S. Department of the Interior, National Park Service, *1953 Annual Report,* 333–336; Conrad L. Wirth, Memorandum to Washington Office and All Field Offices, July 27, 1954, box 12, Conrad L. Wirth Collection, University of Wyoming, American Heritage Center.

51. Wirth, Memorandum to Washington Office, July 27, 1954.

52. U.S. Department of the Interior, National Park Service, *1954 Annual Report,* 335–336. Wirth credits Vint with the idea of creating the Western and Eastern Offices of Design and Construction. Wirth, *Parks, Politics, and the People,* 292.

53. Vernon L. Hammons, "A Brief Organizational History of the Office of Design and Construction, National Park Service, 1917–1962," unpublished report, Department of the Interior, National Park Service, Washington, D.C., n.d., 4–5; Russell K. Olsen, *Administrative History: Organizational Structures of the National Park Service, 1917–1985* (Washington, D.C.: Government Printing Office, 1985), 19–22, 73; Hillory A. Tolson, *Historic Listing of National Park Service Officials* (1964), rev. Harold P. Danz (Denver: Department of the Interior, National Park Service, 1991), 19, 32, 37; "National and State Parks and Forests," *Landscape Architecture* 38, no. 4 (July 1948): 106–107.

54. A 1977 agency history of the National Park Service's Denver Service Center describes the 1954 reorganization (erroneously) as the first step of the Mission 66 program. This claim subsequently appears in other sources, but without any further documentation. U.S. Department of the Interior, National Park Service, "Denver Service Center," 1977, unpublished report, National Park Service, Technical Information Center, Denver.

55. Elmo Richardson, *The Presidency of Dwight D. Eisenhower* (Lawrence: Regents Press of Kansas, 1979), 33.

56. John D. Rockefeller Jr. to Dwight D. Eisenhower, December 10, 1953, Rockefeller Archives Center, Pocantico Hills, N.Y.

57. Dwight D. Eisenhower, *Mandate for Change, 1953–1956* (New York: Doubleday & Company, 1963), 549–550.

58. Dwight D. Eisenhower to John D. Rockefeller Jr., January 8, 1954; Douglas McKay to John D. Rockefeller Jr., January 11, 1954, Rockefeller Archives Center, Pocantico Hills, N.Y.

59. Horace M. Albright to John D. Rockefeller Jr., January 14, 1954, Rockefeller Archives Center, Pocantico Hills, N.Y.

3. PLANNING PRINCIPLES AND THE "MISSION 66 PROSPECTUS"

1. Hammons, "A Brief Organizational History," 3.

2. In 1957 Laura Wilson became the first woman to work as a landscape architect for the Park Service. Mission

66 helped break down some of the barriers for women in the agency, but only because the greatly increased amount of work created more open positions. There was no official policy at the time to integrate women into the professional ranks, and in fact women faced significant obstacles at the Park Service, as they did in the design professions elsewhere. On the subject of women designers at the Park Service, see Polly Welts Kaufman, *National Parks and the Woman's Voice: A History* (Albuquerque: University of New Mexico Press, 1996), 172–175.

3. Tolson, *Historic Listing of National Park Service Officials,* 19, 32, 37.

4. Olsen, *Organizational Structures of the National Park Service,* 19.

5. Roy E. Appleman, "A History of the National Park Service Mission 66 Program," unpublished report, 1958, National Park Service, Denver Service Center, Technical Information Center. Appleman, who was a member of the team that planned Mission 66, explains that his history was based almost entirely on written notes that he took continuously: "[I] kept an informal diary . . . [and] made notes at the time discussions were in progress and often took down literally verbatim the words spoken. . . . Almost nothing presented herein is based on unsupported memory" (10). His account provides an excellent summary by a professional historian who was also a participant in the events described. Wirth relied heavily on the account when writing his memoirs.

6. Wirth, *Parks, Politics, and the People,* 237–239; Appleman, "A History of the Mission 66 Program," 4–5.

7. Wirth, *Parks, Politics, and the People,* 238–239.

8. Ibid., 239; Appleman, "A History of the Mission 66 Program," 7–8.

9. Appleman, "A History of the Mission 66 Program," 8–10.

10. The other members of the steering committee were Thomas C. Vint, Harry Langley, John E. Doerr, Donald E. Lee, Keith Neilson, and Jackson Price. The other members of the working committee were Harold G. Smith, Robert M. Coates, Howard R. Stagner, Jack B. Dodd, Roy E. Appleman, and Raymond L. Freeman. Appleman, "A History of the Mission 66 Program," 7.

11. Lemuel A. Garrison, *The Making of a Ranger: Forty Years with the National Parks* (Salt Lake City: Howe Brothers, 1983), 256–267.

12. Conrad L. Wirth "The History and Concept of the Master Plan," n.d. (ca. 1975), box 28, Conrad L. Wirth Collection, University of Wyoming, American Heritage Center. For Bill Carnes's ideas on master planning (which closely reiterate Vint's), see William G. Carnes, "Landscape Architecture in the National Park Service: Its Contribution to Preservation and Development," *Landscape Architecture* 41, no. 4 (July 1951): 145–150.

13. "Informational Memorandum No. 1, Mission 66," February 18, 1955, box A8213, National Park Service History Collection, Harpers Ferry Center. The seven Mission 66 informational memoranda released by Wirth between February 1955 and November 1956 amount to a manual for planning procedures. The documents are available at the National Park Service Harper's Ferry Archive, as well as the Yellowstone National Park Archives and the Conrad L. Wirth Collection, American Heritage Center, University of Wyoming.

14. All of these documents are collected and described in Lary M. Dilsaver, ed., *America's National Park System: The Critical Documents* (Lanham, Md.: Rowman & Littlefield Publishers, 1994), 28–52, 135–136.

15. For the text of the act, see ibid., 46–47. The "Organic Act" for the National Park Service was drafted with the participation of Representative William Kent (California), Robert Sterling Yard, J. Horace McFarland, Frederick Law Olmsted Jr., Robert B. Marshall, and Horace M. Albright. Albright and McFarland both credited Olmsted with drafting this essential paragraph of the bill. See Carr, *Wilderness by Design,* 78–79.

16. For the text of the report, see Dilsaver, *America's National Park System,* 12–27. Key portions of the 1865 report, which had been fragmented and all but lost, were nevertheless available to the younger Olmsted, who began officially editing his father's papers at about the time he was writing the National Park Service legislation. We know he read and appreciated portions of the 1865 report because he quoted from them in a 1914 article (Frederick Law Olmsted Jr., "Hetch-Hetchy," *Landscape Architecture* 4, no. 2, 37–46). The complete report was reassembled from these fragments by the elder Olmsted's biographer, Laura Wood Roper, in 1952 (*Landscape Architecture* 43, no. 1, 14–25).

17. For the text of the letter, see Dilsaver, *America's National Park System,* 48–52.

18. "Informational Memorandum, Statement of National

Park Policy—1918," March 21, 1955, box A8213, National Park Service History Collection, Harpers Ferry Center.

19. "Informational Memorandum No. 1, Mission 66," February 18, 1955, box A8213, National Park Service History Collection, Harpers Ferry Center; Wirth, *Parks, Politics, and the People*, 241–243; Appleman, "A History of the Mission 66 Program," 9–18.

20. All quotations are from "Informational Memorandum No. 2, Mission 66—Policies and Procedures," March 17, 1955, box A8213, National Park Service History Collection, Harpers Ferry Center.

21. For Vint's life and the significance of his prewar work with the National Park Service, see Linda Flint McClelland, "Vint, Thomas Chalmers," in *Pioneers of American Landscape Design*, ed. Charles A. Birnbaum and Robin Karson (New York: McGraw-Hill, 2000), 413–416; Carr, *Wilderness by Design*, 189–195.

22. Wirth much later acknowledged these observations in a conversation with Charles Peterson. Charles E. Peterson, "Memo for VINT File," January 9, 1981, Thomas C. Vint Collection, Papers of Charles E. Peterson.

23. In a contemporary memorandum on Kings Canyon National Park, Vint warned against siting any buildings at all in the canyon, because once the agency followed the "same course as in the past," it would eventually "have a duplicate Yosemite problem in the Kings Canyon." Thomas C. Vint, "A Brief Discussion of Development Problems in Yosemite National Park," April 14, 1945; and "A Brief Discussion of Development Problems in Sequoia–Kings Canyon National Parks," April 14, 1945, both in Personal Papers of Newton B. Drury, entry 19, RG 79, National Archives.

24. Thomas C. Vint to Newton B. Drury, November 10, 1947, memorandum, Personal Papers of Newton B. Drury, entry 19, RG 79, National Archives. Vint was supported in the particulars of his suggestions for Yosemite by park landscape architect Alfred C. Kuehl, another professional recruited in the 1930s, who had previously worked at Grand Canyon.

25. For the complete text of the Yosemite report, see Victoria Post Ranney, Gerard J. Rauluk, and Carolyn F. Hoffman, eds., *The California Frontier, 1863–1865*, vol. 5 of *The Papers of Frederick Law Olmsted* (Baltimore: Johns Hopkins University Press, 1990), 488–516.

26. While Vint did not write many long reports or explanations of his professional practice, in 1930 he did write a detailed justification for denying the ropeway project at Yosemite, because he knew the decision would set a precedent for similar "mechanical features in all parks." Thomas C. Vint, "Report on Yosemite Ropeway Application," November 21, 1930, Thomas C. Vint Collection, Papers of Charles E. Peterson.

27. Appleman, "A History of the Mission 66 Program," 18–19.

28. U.S. Department of the Interior, National Park Service, *1947 Annual Report*, 320–323.

29. Theodore Catton, *Wonderland: An Administrative History of Mount Rainier National Park* (Washington, D.C.: Government Printing Office, 1996), 413–435.

30. All quotations are from "1966 Prospectus, Mount Rainier National Park," cover memorandum dated June 9, 1955, entry A1-1, RG 79, National Archives. There were more than 1.7 million visitors to Mount Rainier in 1966.

31. The park landscape architect Ernest A. Davidson had been advocating the removal of administrative facilities from the park since at least 1943. Catton, *Wonderland*, 496. Davidson worked for Vint from 1926 until his death in 1944, mostly as the Mount Rainier landscape architect. Vint particularly appreciated not only his design work but his preservation sensibilities as well. See Carr, *Wilderness by Design*, 231.

32. Appleman, "A History of the Mission 66 Program," 20.

33. Vint had opposed it as well. The drive was never built. See "1966 Prospectus, Mount Rainier National Park."

34. Appleman, "A History of the Mission 66 Program," 19–20; Catton, *Wonderland*, 392.

35. Many of these master plans are conserved in the cartographic division of the National Archives in College Park, Md. For descriptions of the master planning process, see Vint, "National Park Service Master Plans," 21–22.

36. Yosemite Village was one early "park village" that replaced the old, more ramshackle town in Yosemite Valley. In this case, the new village was removed to the other side of the Merced River as part of the elimination of multiple concessioners to make way for Mather's chosen monopoly, the Yosemite Park and Curry Company. The proposed relocation of Yellowstone's Canyon Village in the late 1930s was another important exception. Construction of the new Canyon Village was delayed, however, and in fact would end up becoming the first substantial accomplishment of the Mission 66 program.

37. Vint's convictions in this regard were subsequently proved correct in cases where prewar park villages were expanded to meet postwar demand. At Yosemite Village, for example, the existing village plan kept most buildings (except the Ahwahnee and the Yosemite Lodge) out of the park's main viewsheds. Postwar expansions of village facilities, however, created significant visual intrusions. This observation was proved through research and analysis by landscape architect John Reynolds and Park Service general management planning staff in the 1970s. See National Park Service, *Draft Environmental Statement: General Management Plan, Yosemite National Park, California* (Washington, D.C.: Government Printing Office, 1978).

38. Appleman, "A History of the Mission 66 Program," 22.

39. "Informational Memorandum No. 3, Mission 66, Progress and Procedures," June 27, 1955, box A8213, National Park Service History Collection, Harpers Ferry Center.

40. Ibid.

41. "We've Been Starving Our National Parks," *Saturday Evening Post*, February 12, 1955, 10.

42. Appleman, "A History of the Mission 66 Program," 65–66.

43. Wirth, *Parks, Politics, and the People*, 252.

44. "Informational Memorandum No. 3, Mission 66, Progress and Procedures," June 27, 1955.

45. For examples of speeches in which Wirth hints at but does not use the term "Mission 66," see "Parks, Their Planning, and Some of Their Problems," a speech given at the Annual Recreation Conference at the University of Massachusetts, Amherst, March 11, 1955; "An Adequate Park System for 300 Million People," given at the National Citizens Planning Conference on Parks and Open Spaces in Washington, D.C., May 24, 1955; and "The Landscape Architect in National Park Work," given in Detroit to the American Society of Landscape Architects in June 1955 and later published in *Landscape Architecture* 46, no. 1 (October 1955): 13–18. All these and other speeches by Wirth are in box 4 of the Conrad L. Wirth Collection, American Heritage Center, University of Wyoming.

46. Conrad L. Wirth to Russell E. Singer, June 30, 1955, box 25, Conrad L. Wirth Collection, American Heritage Center, University of Wyoming; U.S. Department of the Interior, National Park Service, *1954 Annual Report*, 339–340; Rettie, *Our National Park System*, 251.

47. Michael Frome, *Greenspeak: Fifty Years of Environmental Muckraking and Advocacy* (Knoxville: University of Tennessee Press, 2002), 15.

48. Russell E. Singer to Conrad L. Wirth, December 1, 1954; Conrad L. Wirth, "The National Park System Present and Future," presentation text, box A8213, National Park Service History Collection, Harpers Ferry Center; Conrad L. Wirth to Russell E. Singer, June 30, 1955, box 25, Conrad L. Wirth Collection, American Heritage Center, University of Wyoming.

49. Audience Research, Inc., "A Survey of the Public Concerning National Parks," unpublished report, Princeton, N.J., 1955, National Park Service Technical Information Center; Appleman, "A History of the Mission 66 Program," 55–57; Wirth, *Parks, Politics, and the People*, 244–249.

50. Appleman includes a ten-page summary of the concerns of Park Service managers and staff in "A History of the Mission 66 Program," 22–32.

51. Herma A. Baggley, "Report of the National Park Service Housing Survey," unpublished report, 1953, National Park Service History Collection, Harpers Ferry Center; Kaufman, *National Parks and the Woman's Voice*, 113–115.

52. Baggley, "Report of the National Park Service Housing Survey."

53. Wirth, *Parks, Politics, and the People*, 244.

54. "Master Plan for the Preservation and Use of Adams National Historic Site," December 1962, National Park Service History Collection, Harpers Ferry Center; Katherine Lacy, *Cultural Landscape Report: Adams National Historic Site* (Brookline, Mass.: National Park Service, Olmsted Center for Landscape Preservation, 1997), 63–64; Appleman, "A History of the Mission 66 Program," 50–51.

55. "Tentative 1966 Prospectus for Fort Laramie National Monument," June 22, 1955; "Tentative Prospectus for Chaco Canyon National Monument," July 20, 1955; and "Draft Mission 66 Prospectus for Chaco Canyon National Monument," August 8, 1955, all in National Park Service History Collection, Harpers Ferry Center; Appleman, "A History of the Mission 66 Program," 50–53.

56. Eventually the approved Mission 66 plan called for five decentralized day use areas, including an "archeological area of equal interest" at Wetherill Mesa. Spruce Tree Point would be converted to one of this series of

day use areas, retaining only some of its employee residences and administrative functions. New lodgings and the majority of visitor services would be located away from the sensitive archaeological sites, but not out of the park altogether, at a new developed area on Navajo Hill. Overnight park accommodations would thereby be tripled, but removed completely from the sensitive Spruce Tree Point. The planners relocated park headquarters to the entrance area, also away from any known archaeological sites. The complete plan for Mesa Verde called for many miles of new roads, several major buildings (some to be paid for through a new concessioner contract), land acquisitions, and other development that would significantly increase the visitor capacity of the park. It would also, however, remove older development from more sensitive areas (closer to the major visitor attractions) and, it was hoped, eliminate the overcrowding and damage to the landscape occurring there. "Outline of Plan for the Development of Mesa Verde National Park," n.d. (1962), National Park Service History Collection, Harpers Ferry Center.

57. He made the comment regarding Everglades National Park specifically. Appleman, "A History of the Mission 66 Program," 49.

58. U.S. Department of the Interior, National Park Service, *1948 Annual Report*, 320–321;

59. Aubrey L. Haines, *The Yellowstone Story*, 2 vols. (Boulder: Yellowstone Library and Museum Association in cooperation with Colorado Associated University Press, 1977), 2:372.

60. Ibid., 2:373; Mark Daniel Barringer, *Selling Yellowstone: Capitalism and the Construction of Nature* (Lawrence: University Press of Kansas, 2002), 117–119.

61. The group also included the head of Yellowstone concessions management, Benjamin F. Dickson, and a young Park Service lawyer named George B. Hartzog Jr. "Determination of National Park Service Objectives in Its Concessioner Contracts at Yellowstone for the Next Twenty Years," n.d. (handwritten date "Feb. 55") entry A1, box 16, RG 79, National Archives. The group's recommendations were written up in a slightly different version in a memorandum by park staff to Wirth that April. See Mary Shivers Culpin, *"For the Benefit and Enjoyment of the People": A History of Concession Development in Yellowstone National Park, 1872–1966* (National Park Service, Yellowstone National Park, Wyo.: Yellowstone Center for Resources, 2003), 105–107.

62. The use of the term "prospectus" in this case may have suggested the term "Mission 66 prospectus," subsequently used for all Mission 66 development plans. Earlier the concessioner Nichols had also used the term to describe his own development proposals. "Determination of National Park Service Objectives in Its Concessioner Contracts at Yellowstone for the Next Twenty Years."

63. Robin Smith, "The History of Grant Village," unpublished report, 1988, 18, Vertical Files, Yellowstone National Park Archives.

64. "Determination of National Park Service Objectives in Its Concessioner Contracts at Yellowstone for the Next Twenty Years." Also see Culpin, *"For the Benefit and Enjoyment of the People,"* 107–116.

65. "Determination of National Park Service Objectives in Its Concessioner Contracts at Yellowstone for the Next Twenty Years." This planning document states emphatically that while overnight capacity should be increased to "about 14,000 people," in the future any additional need for accommodations should be "absorbed . . . in communities adjacent to the park." Later Yellowstone prospectuses were consistent with this recommendation.

66. Edmund B. Rogers to Conrad L. Wirth, "MISSION 66, First Submission Prospectus," memorandum, November 10, 1955, entry A1, box 16, RG 79, National Archives; "Mission 66 Prospectus," 1957, National Park Service History Collection, Harpers Ferry Center; Appleman, "A History of the Mission 66 Program," 37–45. A 1945 report claimed that half a million dollars could be saved annually without loss of efficiency by moving park headquarters to Gardiner. Fred T. Johnston to Edmund B. Rogers, memorandum, January 9, 1945; and "Mission 66, Recreation Inventories," May 6, 1955, both in box A8213, National Park Service History Collection, Harpers Ferry Center.

67. Mission 66 documents and even press releases quoted the legislation, which Wirth characterized as a "positive injunction." See, for example, "Improving Visitor Uses of Everglades National Park," May 10, 1956, entry A1, box 5, RG 79, National Archives.

68. "Superintendent's Monthly Narrative Report," May 1953, Everglades National Park Collections Management Center.

69. "Proposals Sought for Construction and Operation of Visitor Facilities in Everglades National Park," press re-

lease, October 14, 1954, National Park Service History Collection, Harpers Ferry Center; "Superintendent's Monthly Narrative Report," April 1954 and June 1955, Everglades National Park Collections Management Center.

70. Appleman, "A History of the Mission 66 Program," 20.

71. Eivind T. Scoyen to Wesley A. D'Ewart, "Concession Facilities, Everglades National Park," memorandum, April 3, 1956; and Conrad L. Wirth, "Improving Visitor Uses of Everglades National Park," May 10, 1956, both in entry A1, box 5, RG 79, National Archives.

72. "Prospectus, Mission 66, Objectives for Everglades National Park for 1966 and Beyond," draft, July 15, 1955, National Park Service History Collection, Harpers Ferry Center. The prospectus also originally stated that park headquarters would be outside the park in Homestead or Florida City, a decision that was later reversed after the superintendent and regional director argued in favor of the Parachute Key location near the park entrance.

73. "Superintendent's Monthly Narrative Report," October 1955 and January 1956, Everglades National Park Collections Management Center.

74. In the end, the Park Service paid more than half the cost of the $350,000 Public Use building. Daniel B. Beard to Edward Zimmerman, "Mission 66 in Relation to Concession Planning," memorandum, July 21, 1955, entry A1, box 5, RG 79, National Archives; "Proposed Contract for Operation of Visitor Facilities in Everglades . . . Submitted to Congress for Review," press release, September 21, 1955, National Park Service History Collection, Harpers Ferry Center.

75. Alfred Canel to Wesley A. D'Ewart, April 26, 1956, entry A1, box 5, RG 79, National Archives; "Why Discriminate against Everglades?" editorial, *Miami Herald,* May 22, 1956.

76. Wirth, "Improving Visitor Uses of Everglades National Park"; "Mission 66 Improvement Program Is Announced for Everglades," press release, May 20, 1956, entry A1, box 5, RG 79, National Archives; Herbert Maier to Lemuel Garrison, "Report to the Regional Director on the Everglades Meeting," memorandum, April 15, 1957, box A8213, National Park Service History Collection, Harpers Ferry Center.

77. Catton, *Wonderland,* 476–490.

4. PUBLIC POLICY AND "OUR HERITAGE"

1. All quotations are from "Steering Committee Precepts for Staff Guidance," unsigned draft (Lemuel A. Garrison), March 1955, box A8213, National Park Service History Collection, Harpers Ferry Center.

2. Eivind T. Scoyen to Lemuel A. Garrison, March 8, 1955, box A8213, National Park Service History Collection, Harpers Ferry Center.

3. Lemuel A. Garrison, "Guiding Precepts Mission 66," draft memorandum, August 29, 1955, box A8213, National Park Service History Collection, Harpers Ferry Center.

4. Ibid.

5. Lemuel A. Garrison, "Mission 66," *National Parks Magazine* 29, no. 122 (July–September 1955): 107–108; Conrad L. Wirth, "Mission 66," *American Forests* 61, no. 8 (August 1955): 16–17.

6. C. Edward Graves to Conrad L. Wirth, September 10, 1955; Conrad L. Wirth to C. Edward Graves, October 31, 1955; Conrad L. Wirth to Alexander Hildebrand, November 7, 1955; Alexander Hildebrand to Conrad L. Wirth, November 22, 1955, all in box A8213, National Park Service History Collection, Harpers Ferry Center.

7. Mission 66 planners counted 180 units of the park system in 1955; Dwight Rettie's 1995 study suggests that there were 194. The discrepancy is apparently the result of the way certain "affiliated areas" and national cemeteries were and are counted. Rettie's figures are used here for the sake of consistency. Rettie, *Our National Park System,* 252–253.

8. Wirth, *Parks, Politics, and the People,* 250–251; Appleman, "A History of the Mission 66 Program," 58–63.

9. *The National Park System,* National Park Service brochure, n.d. (1955); "MISSION 66 Report," September 1955, National Park Service History Collection, Harpers Ferry Center.

10. Lemuel A. Garrison to Edmund B. Rogers, August 6, 1955, box A247, Yellowstone National Park Archives. Developments at Yellowstone are discussed in chapter 6.

11. Appleman, "A History of the Mission 66 Program," 62.

12. "Public Services," agenda, September 20, 1955, box 6, Conrad L. Wirth Collection, University of Wyoming, American Heritage Center; "Statement by Conrad L. Wirth, Public Services Conference," September 20, 1955, box 4, Conrad L. Wirth Collection, University of Wyoming, American Heritage Center.

13. All quotations are from "Statement by Conrad L. Wirth, Public Services Conference."

14. "MISSION 66 Report," September 1955.

15. Sydney Gruson, "U.S. Park Service Plans Expansion," *New York Times,* September 20, 1955; "Mission 66," editorial, *Washington Post,* October 17, 1955; "Digest of Newspaper Comment," November 9, 1955, National Park Service History Collection, Harpers Ferry Center.

16. Sydney Gruson, "M'Kay Reassures U.S. Park Experts," *New York Times,* September 25, 1955; Wirth, *Parks, Politics, and the People,* 252.

17. In 1955 the combined agency budget had been less than $33 million; with federal highway money the 1956 total was raised to almost $49 million. In presenting the cost of Mission 66 in his final report, Wirth took the proposed 1957 budget of about $66 million (assumed to be a normal or "base" budget), multiplied by ten, and subtracted it from the $787 million estimated total for the ten-year program. The difference, he suggested was the actual increase, or true cost, of Mission 66. The $787 million figure ended up being used anyway despite this effort to minimize the apparent cost. "Mission 66: To Provide Adequate Protection and Development of the National Park System for Human Use," January 1956, unpublished report, National Park Service, Denver Service Center Library).

18. Ibid.

19. Appleman, "A History of the Mission 66 Program," 75–76. David Brower describes a meeting with Wirth in late 1955 in which he and Howard Zahniser asked for a greater emphasis on the preservation of wilderness as "the primary value of the parks." David R. Brower, "'Mission 65' Is Proposed by Reviewer of Park Service's New Brochure on Wilderness," *National Parks Magazine* 32, no. 132 (January 1958): 3–6, 45–47.

20. Howard R. Stagner, "Mission 66 Definitions," draft memorandum, July 18, 1955, box A8213, National Park Service History Collection, Harpers Ferry Center.

21. All quotations are from "Mission 66: To Provide Adequate Protection and Development of the National Park System for Human Use."

22. For a more thorough discussion of the failure of Mission 66 to fund scientific research, see Sellars, *Preserving Nature in the National Parks,* 168–173.

23. Ibid., 4.

24. "Mission 66: To Provide Adequate Protection and Development of the National Park System for Human Use"; Appleman, "A History of the Mission 66 Program," 59.

25. Wirth, *Parks, Politics, and the People,* 322.

26. Ibid., 315–352.

27. Ibid., 254; Appleman, "A History of the Mission 66 Program," 63–70, 78–87.

28. Appleman, "A History of the Mission 66 Program," 97.

29. Frome, *Greenspeak,* 16.

30. Appleman, "A History of the Mission 66 Program," 91–94; William M. Blair, "Saving the Parks," *New York Times,* February 12, 1956; "Pioneer Dinner Launches Mission 66," *National Parks Magazine* 30, no. 125 (April 1956): 59–60; National Park Service, *Our Heritage, a Plan for Its Protection and Use.*

31. Conrad L. Wirth to Ben Sharpsteen, December 29, 1955, box 25, Conrad L. Wirth Collection, University of Wyoming, American Heritage Center.

32. Department of the Interior, *1956 Annual Report,* 303.

33. "Mission 66," *New York Times,* February 26, 1956; Wirth, *Parks, Politics, and the People,* 262 Appleman, "A History of the Mission 66 Program," 89.

34. Using Dwight Rettie's statistical index, combined appropriations per unit of the park system in constant 1990 dollars rose (in round figures) from about $629,000 in 1929 to $1.2 million in 1939, and then dropped to $410,000 in 1949. They rose again to $1.8 million in 1959 and to $2 million at the end of Mission 66 in 1966. Appropriations continued to rise after Mission 66 to $2.2 million per unit of the system in 1973 and $2.9 million in 1995. Rettie also reports, however, that the total number of visits recorded to the park system rose from 127 million to 383 million between 1966 and 1995. From these visitation figures one could argue that federal support for the parks has waned. Rettie, *Our National Park System,* 251–253.

35. Appleman, "A History of the Mission 66 Program," 91. Between October 1955 and November 1956 Wirth sent out four additional "informational memoranda" all on the subject of "procedures for preparing final prospectuses": "Memorandum No. 4, MISSION 66, Procedures for Preparing Final Report," October 7, 1955; "Memorandum No. 5, MISSION 66, Procedures for Preparing Final Prospectuses," March 16, 1956; "Memorandum No. 7, MISSION 66, Preparation of Prospectus Briefs," November 9, 1956, all in box A8213, National Park Service History Collection, Harpers Ferry Center.

36. Many of these press releases are conserved at National Park Service History Collection, Harpers Ferry Center.

37. Lemuel A. Garrison to Conrad L. Wirth, August 17, 1955, box A8213, National Park Service History Collection, Harpers Ferry Center; Appleman, "A History of the Mission 66 Program," 95–97.

38. Several versions of the slide show, sets of numbered slides, and at least one of the audio tapes are conserved at the National Park Service's Harpers Ferry Center Archive.

39. National Park Service, *Mission 66: Questions and Answers,* n.d. (1956), National Park Service History Collection, Harpers Ferry Center.

40. Conrad L. Wirth to All National Park Service Personnel, January 3, 1956, box A8213, National Park Service History Collection, Harpers Ferry Center; U.S. Department of the Interior, *1956 Annual Report,* 302.

41. Herbert Evison, interview with Thomas Vint, 1960, transcript, 10, Thomas C. Vint Collection, Papers of Charles E. Peterson.

42. For more on prewar Park Service master planning, see Carr, *Wilderness by Design,* 189–247.

43. The term "modernist" is used throughout this book to refer to works of design influenced by twentieth-century architects and fine artists associated with modern, or modernist, movements. "Modernization"is used to refer to the application of technology and capital in the transformation of land in the modern historical era. Modern landscapes, in other words, are the products of modernization (including urbanization, mechanization of agriculture, industrialization, etc.); modernist landscapes are discrete works of twentieth-century design.

5. ARCHITECTURE

1. The larger number was partly due to a rise in the number of units in the system from 195 to 254. Nevertheless, the researcher Marion Clawson, who reviewed the initial Mission 66 plans for the Eisenhower administration, correctly forecast that the 1966 figure would be closer to 120 million, and Mission 66 planners were consistently conservative in their estimates of future numbers of visitors to parks. Rettie, *Our National Park System,* 252; Garrison, *The Making of a Ranger,* 258–259.

2. Wirth, *Parks, Politics, and the People,* 242.

3. Righter, *Crucible for Conservation,* 47–65, 85–102.

4. Paula S. Reed and Edith B. Wallace, "Jackson Lake Lodge, National Historic Landmark Nomination," 2003. This National Historic Landmark nomination form is available through the National Register of Historic Places, National Park Service, Washington, D.C. (http://ww.cr.nps.gov/nhl/designations/samples). The Jackson Lake Lodge was designated a National Historic Landmark in 2003, in part for its significance as an influential precedent of modernist architectural design in the parks.

5. Jack Goodman, "Controversy over Lodge in the West," *New York Times,* August 7, 1955.

6. Martin Litton, "Yosemite's Beauty Fast Disappearing," *National Parks Magazine* 26, no. 111 (October 1952): 164–168.

7. Devereux Butcher, "For a Return to Harmony in Park Architecture," *National Parks Magazine* 26, no. 111 (October 1952): 150–157; Miles, *Guardians of the Parks,* 132–133, 162–164.

8. Spencer published the designs in *Pencil Points,* an architecture magazine. See *Pencil Points* 23 (1942): 43–46; and *New Pencil Points* 24 (1943): 70–71.

9. Newton B. Drury, letter to the editor, *National Parks Magazine* 27, no. 2 (January–March 1953): 39. See Jonathan Searle Monroe, "Architecture in the National Parks: Cecil Doty and Mission 66" (master's thesis, University of Washington, 1986).

10. Butcher quoted Harvard Graduate School of Design dean Joseph Hudnut—who did as much as anyone to bring architectural modernism to the United States—in support of his contention regarding the importance of associations in architecture. Butcher, "For a Return to Harmony in Park Architecture," 153–154.

11. For the best summary of such aspirations, see Albert H. Good, *Park and Recreation Structures* (1938; reprint, New York: Princeton Architectural Press, 1999).

12. On the adoption of European modernism in the United States, see Leonardo Benevolo, *History of Modern Architecture,* 2 vols. (1960; reprint, Cambridge: MIT Press, 1977), 2:629–683; William H. Jordy, *The Impact of European Modernism in the Mid-Twentieth Century* (New York: Oxford University Press, 1972), 87–164; Anthony Alofsin, *The Struggle for Modernism: Architecture, Landscape Architecture, and City Planning at Harvard* (New York: Norton, 2002).

13. Allaback, *Mission 66 Visitor Centers,* 10.

14. Ibid., 12–14.

15. "Interview with Cecil J. Doty, Retired National Park Architect, March 10, 1985," conducted by Laura Soullière Harrison, transcript, 20, Oklahoma State University Library; Allaback, *Mission 66 Visitor Centers*, 215–221. The Region III headquarters building in Santa Fe and the Painted Desert Inn in Petrified Forest National Park were designated National Historic Landmarks in 1987 for their significance in American architecture. See Laura Soullière Harrison, *Architecture in the Parks: National Historic Landmark Theme Study* (Washington, D.C.: Government Printing Office, 1987), 411–424, 441–450.

16. "Interview with Cecil J. Doty, Retired National Park Architect, March 10, 1985" 21; Allaback, *Mission 66 Visitor Centers,* 221.

17. Conrad L. Wirth, "Design of Structures," memorandum, February 13, 1956, box 6, Conrad L. Wirth Collection, University of Wyoming, American Heritage Center.

18. These statements were transcribed and distributed to WODC design staff. Conrad L. Wirth, "Excerpt from Telephone Conference between the Director and Chief, WODC, . . . January 9, 1957," box 7, Design & Construction File, RG 79, National Archives. The comments were subsequently read to the Advisory Board on National Parks, Historic Sites, Buildings and Monuments, at their March meeting in Washington, D.C. The Advisory Board was discussing the issue of architectural design quality as a result of criticism, and praise, appearing in different journals. "Summary Minutes, 36th Meeting, Advisory Board on National Parks, Historic Sites, Buildings and Monuments, March 5, 6, 7, 1957, Washington, D.C.," Yosemite National Park Archives.

19. Conrad L. Wirth, "Mission 66 in the Headlines," *National Parks Magazine* 32, no. 132 (January 1958): 8–9, 36–37.

20. As was the case with the decision not to limit access to the parks, there were individual objections from superintendents and other Park Service officials to Wirth's policy to proceed with modernist architectural design. There is no evidence of a sustained debate of any kind on the subject, however, during the early years of Mission 66.

21. Hammons, "A Brief Organizational History of the Office of Design and Construction," 3; "Interview with A. Clark Stratton," March 1, 1962, conducted by S. Herbert Evison, transcript, 2, National Park Service History Collection, Harpers Ferry Center.

22. Allaback, *Mission 66 Visitor Centers,* 17–21.

23. Welton Becket, "Shopping Center Traffic Problems," *Traffic Quarterly* 9 (April 1955): 162–172.

24. Allaback, *Mission 66 Visitor Centers,* 18.

25. U.S. Department of the Interior, National Park Service, "Visitor Center Planning: Notes on Discussions Held in EODC November 18–22, 1957, and WODC February 4–6, 1958," unpublished report, n.d. (1958), National Park Service Denver Service Center Library; Allaback, *Mission 66 Visitor Centers,* 222; Barry Mackintosh, *Interpretation in the National Park Service* (Washington, D.C.: Department of the Interior, National Park Service, 1986), 49–51.

26. At the opening of one of the first visitor centers in 1957, at Yorktown (Colonial National Historical Park), Wirth's prepared remarks included the statement, "Throughout the Nation, 170 (?) National Park Visitor centers are either under construction, in the final stages of planning, or firmly fixed in our comprehensive program." There were 195 units in the park system at the time. Wirth scratched out the questionable number and wrote in "more than 100" by hand. A collection of Wirth's speeches, including many prepared remarks for visitor center dedications, are conserved at the University of Wyoming American Heritage Center, Conrad L. Wirth Collection, box 7.

27. "Interview with Cecil J. Doty," conducted by Jacilee Wray, February 26, 1990, transcript, 3–4, catalog no. GRCA 52220, Grand Canyon National Park Archive; Allaback, *Mission 66 Visitor Centers,* 26.

28. "Interview with A. Clark Stratton," conducted by S. Herbert Evison, March 1, 1962, transcript, 2–3, National Park Service History Collection, Harpers Ferry Center.

29. "Interview with Cecil J. Doty," conducted by S. Herbert Evison, October 26, 1962, transcript, 4, National Park Service History Collection, Harpers Ferry Center; "Interview with Cecil J. Doty," February 26, 1990, 4; U.S. Department of the Interior, National Park Service, *Visitor Center Planning,* 45.

30. Conrad Wirth gives a total of 114 new visitor centers during Mission 66. Wirth, *Parks, Politics, and the People,* 270. The precise definition of what constitutes a new visitor center (as opposed to an addition or a remodeling) makes it difficult to specify an exact number. Allaback's totals reflect what she could confirm through project records at the Technical Information Center,

National Park Service, Denver Service Center. See Allaback, *Mission 66 Visitor Centers,* 255–265.

31. John B. Cabot, "Creative Park Architecture," *Park Practice Guidelines,* Department of the Interior, National Park Service (July 1963), 53–55.

32. John B. Cabot, "Notes Gathered Traveling," October 12, 1956, memorandum, box 29, RG 79, National Archives, Mid-Atlantic Region.

33. Allaback, *Mission 66 Visitor Centers,* 24–33.

34. U.S. Department of the Interior, National Park Service, *Visitor Center Planning,* 1–5; Ralph H. Lewis, *Museum Curatorship in the National Park Service, 1904–1982* (Washington, D.C.: Department of the Interior, National Park Service, 1993), 150.

35. See U.S. Department of the Interior, National Park Service, *Visitor Center Planning,* 1–20, 45–48; Lewis, *Museum Curatorship,* 151.

36. Allaback, *Mission 66 Visitor Centers,* 228–246.

37. Ibid., 39–60. The Quarry Visitor Center was designated a National Historic Landmark in 2001 for its significance in American architecture.

38. See Hal Rothman, *America's National Monuments: The Politics of Preservation* (Lawrence: University Press of Kansas, by arrangement with University of Illinois Press, 1989).

39. The complex of park buildings at Bandelier National Monument was designated a National Historic Landmark district in 1987 for its significance in American architecture. Harrison, *Architecture in the Parks,* 355–382.

40. According to a 1973 Park Service account, 6 Mission 66 visitor centers opened in calendar year 1957, 10 in 1958, 19 in 1959, 7 in 1960, 5 in 1961, 11 in 1962, 11 in 1963, 9 in 1964, 10 in 1965, and 7 in 1966. Sixteen more had contracts let (gone to construction) before 1966 and opened between 1967 and 1969, for a total of 111. "Visitor Centers Completed under Mission 66," memorandum, n.d. (1973), box A8213, National Park Service History Collection, Harpers Ferry Centers. Allaback lists 110, confirmed through the records of the National Park Service Technical Information Center, Denver Service Center, with locations and attributions. Allaback, *Mission 66 Visitor Centers,* 255–262. The final Mission 66 "Progress Report" in 1966 listed only 100 "new" visitor centers, probably indicating a discrepancy between new buildings and projects involving substantial additions and alterations to existing buildings. U.S. Department of the Interior, National Park Service,

"Mission 66 Progress Report, March 1966," National Park Service Technical Information Center, Denver.

41. "Analysis Visitor Centers Mission 66," memorandum, n.d. (1963), box A8123, National Park Service History Collection, Harpers Ferry Center. All figures represent the original, unadjusted costs.

42. Allaback, *Mission 66 Visitor Centers,* 11.

43. "Award Citations," *Progressive Architecture* 37, no. 1 (January 1956): 92; "Bathing and Public Facilities," *Progressive Architecture* 39, no. 7 (July 1958): 88–89.

44. Dan Morrill, "Coquina Beach at Nags Head to Feature Modern Trend in Architectural Ideas," *Virginian-Pilot,* July 22, 1956.

45. Devereux Butcher, "Sunshine and Blizzard," *National Parks Magazine* 31, no. 128 (January 1957): 24–33; Ernest Swift, "Parks—or Resorts?" *National Parks Magazine* 31, no. 131 (October 1957): 147–148.

46. Emerson Goble, "Architecture (?) for the National Parks," *Architectural Record* 121, no. 1 (January 1957): 173–185.

47. Wolf Von Eckardt, "The Park Service Dares to Build Well," *Washington Post,* March 29, 1964.

48. Robert E. Koehler, "Our Park Service Serves Architecture Well," *AIA Journal* 1 (January 1971): 18–25.

49. The Quarry, Wright Brothers, and Beaver Meadows visitor centers were all designated National Historic Landmarks in 2001 for their significance in American architecture. See Allaback, *Mission 66 Visitor Centers.*

50. Ibid., 95–144.

51. Ibid., 145–180.

52. "Statement of Controlling Development Policies," n.d., Olympic National Park Archives; Irving Brant, *Adventures in Conservation with Franklin D. Roosevelt* (Flagstaff, Ariz.: Northland Publishing Co., 1988), 117; Guy Fringer, *Olympic National Park: An Administrative History* (Seattle: National Park Service, 1990), 92.

53. Wirth, *Parks, Politics, and the People,* 266–267.

54. The final and official decision to use "stock" housing plans in Mission 66 was made at the Regional Directors Conference in February 1956. John B. Cabot, "The Design of Park Service Houses," October 19, 1956, memorandum, box 29, RG 79, National Archives, Mid-Atlantic Region, Philadelphia.

55. U.S. Department of the Interior, National Park Service, "Standard Plans for Employee Housing," 1957, unpublished report, National Park Service Technical Information Center, Denver.

56. John Cabot to Supervising Architect, WODC, March 27, 1956, box 29, RG 79, Regional Archives, Philadelphia.

57. George F. Baggley to John B. Cabot, October 16, 1956, box 29, RG 79, National Archives, Mid-Atlantic Region, Philadelphia). George Baggley was writing on behalf of his wife, Herma. Also see Kaufman, *National Parks and the Woman's Voice*, 113–117.

58. Kaufman, *National Parks and the Woman's Voice*, 172.

59. John B. Cabot, "The Design of Park Service Houses," October 19, 1956, box 29, RG 79, National Archives, Mid-Atlantic Region, Philadelphia.

60. U.S. Department of the Interior, National Park Service, "Standard Plans for Employee Housing," 1957, unpublished report, National Park Service Technical Information Center, Denver.

61. Inger Garrison, "Report of National Park Service Housing Survey," 1959, unpublished report, National Park Service History Collection, Harpers Ferry Center.

62. E. T. Scoyen, "New Standard Plans for Permanent Employee Housing," February 17, 1960, National Park Service History Collection, Harpers Ferry Center.

63. U.S. Department of the Interior, National Park Service, "Standard Plans for Employee Housing," 1957.

64. Wirth, *Parks, Politics, and the People*, 267.

6. PRESERVATION AND INTERPRETATION

1. Vint, "National Park Service Master Plans."

2. This essentially Olmstedian theory continued to guide Vint and other officials during Mission 66. Frederick Law Olmsted Jr. in particular had influenced Park Service historical park planning. His 1929 state park plan for California became a procedural blueprint for planning a park system that included both scenic and historic landscapes. See Frederick Law Olmsted Jr., *Report of State Park Survey of California* (Sacramento: California State Printing Office, 1929).

3. Since the 1906 Antiquities Act, Congress had taken steps to preserve a number of archaeological sites in the West as national monuments, some of which came under the care of the Park Service when it was first created. Albright began acquiring historic sites in the East beginning in 1930 with George Washington's birthplace in Virginia. The Park Service became the leading federal historic preservation agency, however, only after Roosevelt's 1933 executive order. See Foresta, *America's National Parks*, 129—145; Mackintosh, *Shaping the System*, 24–43.

4. Many of these gardens, such as the grounds of the Governor's Palace, were designed by Arthur A. Shurcliff, a preeminent historical landscape architect of his day, who typified the academic interest in colonial garden research and design. See Elizabeth Hope Cushing, "Shurcliff, Arthur Asahel (Shurtleff)," in Birnbaum and Karson, *Pioneers of American Landscape Design*, 351—356.

5. Quoted in Historic American Engineering Record (HAER), "Colonial National Historical Park Roads and Bridges, HAER no. VA-115," Michael G. Bennett, project historian, 21, unpublished government report, 1995.

6. For the mutual influence of historic preservation and parkway design, see three works by Timothy Davis: "Mount Vernon Memorial Highway and the Evolution of the American Parkway" (Ph.D. diss., University of Texas at Austin, 1997); "Mount Vernon Memorial Highway: Changing Conceptions of an American Commemorative Landscape," in *Places of Commemoration: Search for Identity and Landscape Design*, ed. Joachim Wolschke-Bulmahn (Washington, D.C.: Dumbarton Oaks, 2001), 123–177; and "'A Pleasing Illusion of Unspoiled Countryside': The American Parkway and the Problematics of an Institutional Vernacular," in *Constructing Image, Identity, and Place: Perspectives in Vernacular Architecture*, vol. 9, ed. Kenneth Breisch and Kim Hoagland (Knoxville: University of Tennessee Press, 2003), 228–246.

7. Just as early wilderness advocates questioned national park development in the 1930s, some historians wondered whether the new historical parks of that era did not restrict the educational usefulness of historic sites as much as preserve them. See Foresta, *America's National Parks*, 130. Recent critics have pointed out that freezing a landscape not only is a practical impossibility but also serves as a justification for the removal of later, often significant landscape features and limits the interpretive potential of a site to a single narrative directly associated with the chosen scene or historical moment. This has been particularly the case in battlefield parks. See Martha Temkin, "Freeze-Frame, September 17, 1862: A Preservation Battle at Antietam National Battlefield Park," in *Myth, Memory, and the American Landscape*, ed. Paul A. Shackel (Gainesville: University Press of Florida, 2001), 123–140.

8. Regina M. Bellavia, *Cultural Landscape Report for Jefferson National Expansion Memorial, St. Louis, Missouri* (Omaha: Government Printing Office, 1996), 11–25.

9. The St. Louis Arch, completed in 1965, was designated a National Historic Landmark in 1987 for its significance in American architecture. Harrison, *Architecture in the Parks,* 471–482.

10. Constance M. Greiff, *Independence: The Creation of a National Park* (Philadelphia: University of Pennsylvania Press, 1987), 29–52.

11. Ibid., 40–69.

12. Ibid., 65.

13. Ibid., 96–112.

14. Papers of Ronald F. Lee, biography, National Park Service History Collection, Harpers Ferry Center. Charles B. Hosmer Jr. documents Lee's career extensively in *Preservation Comes of Age: From Williamsburg to the National Trust, 1926–1949,* 2 vols. (Charlottesville: University Press of Virginia, 1981).

15. Ronald F. Lee, "The National Park Service and MISSION 66 in Relation to Historic Preservation, Open Spaces, and Urban Renewal," July 28, 1960, binder 7, National Park Service History Collection, Harpers Ferry Center.

16. See James A. Glass, *The Beginnings of a National Historic Preservation Program, 1957 to 1959* (Nashville, Tennessee: American Association for State and Local History, 1990), 3–15. Glass points out Wirth's reluctance to involve his agency in any inventory of historic sites of local or state significance, since they would not qualify as eventual additions to the national park system.

17. Lee, "The National Park Service and MISSION 66 in Relation to Historic Preservation, Open Spaces, and Urban Renewal."

18. Ibid.; Ronald F. Lee, "Accomplishments and Future Requirements in the Historical Program of the National Park Service under MISSION 66," September 14, 1960, binder 7, National Park Service History Collection, Harpers Ferry Center.

19. U.S. Department of the Interior, National Park Service, *That the Past Shall Live* (Washington, D.C.: Government Printing Office, n.d. [1959]), 8, 32–33.

20. On the history of national park museums and educational programs, see Harold C. Bryant and Wallace W. Atwood Jr., *Research and Education in the National Parks* (Washington, D.C.: Government Printing Office, 1936); C. Frank Brockman, "Park Naturalists and the Evolution of National Park Service Interpretation through World War II," *Journal of Forest History* 22, no. 1 (January 1978): 24–43; Barry Mackintosh, *Interpretation in the National Park Service* (Washington, D.C.: Department of the Interior, National Park Service, 1986); Barry Mackintosh, "The National Park Service Moves into Historical Interpretation," *Public Historian* 9, no. 2 (Spring 1987): 51–63; Ralph H. Lewis, *Museum Curatorship in the National Park Service, 1904–1982* (Washington, D.C.: Government Printing Office, 1993); Kaufman, *National Parks and the Woman's Voice,* 65–87.

21. See Lewis, *Museum Curatorship,* 29–66. In 1987 the Mesa Verde Museum was made part of a National Historic Landmark district, and the three remaining Yellowstone museums (Fishing Bridge, Madison Junction, and Norris Geyser Basin) were designated National Historic Landmarks, all for their significance in American architecture. Harrison, *Architecture in the Parks,* 211–228, 311–330.

22. Brockman, "Park Naturalists," 40–43; Mackintosh, *Interpretation in the National Park Service,* 18–37. Lee performed his duties as chief historian under several titles, including chief of the Branch of Historic Sites.

23. Lewis, *Museum Curatorship,* 117. Lewis was also the long-time head of the Park Service's museum branch.

24. Workman, *National Park Service Uniforms: The Developing Years,* 25–30.

25. R. Bryce Workman, *National Park Service Uniforms: Badges and Insignia, 1894–1991* (Harpers Ferry, W. Va.: National Park Service, Harpers Ferry Center, 1991), 25–30. Wirth recalled in 1968 that Maier prepared the prototype for the arrowhead logo and presented it at the Park Service conference held at Yosemite in the fall of 1950. It was adopted by widespread approval at the conference and then officially approved by Drury. Conrad L. Wirth to George B. Hartzog Jr., June 5, 1968, box 33, Conrad L. Wirth Collection, University of Wyoming, American Heritage Center.

26. Olsen, *Organizational Structures of the National Park Service,* 77.

27. Conrad L. Wirth, "Objectives for Service Program of Interpretation in 1954," February 16, 1954, box 12, Conrad L. Wirth Collection, University of Wyoming, American Heritage Center.

28. Ronald F. Lee, "Comments on the Role of Interpretation in the National Park Service," February 16, 1961, Personal Papers of Conrad L. Wirth, box 22, RG 79, National Archives.

29. Mackintosh, *Interpretation in the National Park Service,* 85. The brochures are available at the National Park Service's Harpers Ferry Center Archive.

30. Mackintosh reprints the entire memorandum in an appendix in *Interpretation in the National Park Service,* 105–111.

31. Ronald F. Lee, "Interpretation," draft memorandum, October 17, 1955, National Park Service History Collection, Harpers Ferry Center.

32. Ronald F. Lee to Roy E. Appleman, December 6, 1955, National Park Service History Collection, Harpers Ferry Center; Ronald F. Lee, "Special Objectives for Interpretation in the National Park System in 1956," January 10, 1956, box 6, Conrad L. Wirth Collection, University of Wyoming, American Heritage Center.

33. Lewis, *Museum Curatorship,* 145; Mackintosh, *Interpretation in the National Park Service,* 85.

34. Ronald F. Lee, "Audio-Visual Space Requirements in Visitor Center Buildings," memorandum, November 9, 1956, box 29, RG 79, National Archives, Mid-Atlantic Region.

35. U.S. Department of the Interior, *1957 Annual Report,* 328.

36. Mackintosh, *Interpretation in the National Park Service,* 38–45.

37. Conrad L. Wirth to John D. Rockefeller Jr., December 3, 1953, box 23, Conrad L. Wirth Collection, University of Wyoming, American Heritage Center.

38. Mackintosh, *Interpretation in the National Park Service,* 85–86.

39. Freeman Tilden, *Interpreting Our Heritage: Principles and Practices for Visitor Services in Parks, Museums, and Historic Places* (Chapel Hill: University of North Carolina Press, 1957).

40. See John Bodnar, *Remaking America: Public Memory, Commemoration, and Patriotism in the Twentieth Century* (Princeton: Princeton University Press, 1992), 194–205.

41. Eastern National Park & Monument Association, *National Park Service: The First Seventy-five Years* (1990), 42.

42. Task Force on Professional and Technical Training, "Survey of Employee Training," March 7, 1957; and Conrad L. Wirth, "National Park Service Training Center," June 18, 1957, both in box 12, Conrad L. Wirth Collection, University of Wyoming, American Heritage Center; "Selecting and Training the Stewards of Our Heritage: An Improved Personnel Program for the Na-

tional Park Service," draft, n.d. (1960), National Park Service History Collection, Harpers Ferry Center; U.S. Department of the Interior, *1957 Annual Report,* 312; Mackintosh, *Interpretation in the National Park Service,* 85.

43. Amanda Zeman, "Grand Canyon Village Master Planning Effort," draft National Register of Historic Places multiple properties nomination, February 24, 2003, National Park Service, Grand Canyon National Park.

44. "Staffing Requirements: SUPER MISSION 66," September 14, 1960, Personal Papers of Conrad L. Wirth, box 22, RG 79, National Archives.

45. "Selecting and Training the Stewards of Our Heritage."

46. "Condensation of Visitor Services, Natural History Program," October 17, 1960, National Park Service History Collection, Harpers Ferry Center.

47. Ibid.

48. Mackintosh, *Interpretation in the National Park Service,* 45–54; Lewis, *Museum Curatorship,* 150–156.

49. U.S. Civil War Centennial Commission, *Guide to the Observance of the Centennial of the Civil War* (Washington, D.C.: Government Printing Office, 1959), 5; "Mission 66: To Make Your Civil War Tour Memorable," *Civil War Times* 3, no. 3 (June 1961): 12–14; U.S. Civil War Centennial Commission, *The Civil War Centennial: A Report to Congress* (Washington, D.C.: Government Printing Office, 1968), 34–35.

50. U.S. Civil War Centennial Commission, *The Civil War Centennial,* 35.

51. The Ziegler's Grove site for a new park building had first been put forward in the 1940s; landscape architect Edward Zimmer and the park superintendent finalized the choice in 1957, long before Richard Neutra was involved. Allaback, *Mission 66 Visitor Centers,* 95–143.

52. U.S. Department of the Interior, National Park Service, "Visitor Center Planning: Notes on Discussions Held in EODC, November 18–22, 1957; and WODC, February 4–6, 1958," unpublished report, n.d. (1958), both in National Park Service, Denver Service Center Library; Daniel B. Beard, "Report on Visitor Center," January 29, 1960, National Park Service History Collection, Harpers Ferry Center.

53. Beard, "Report on Visitor Center."

54. U.S. Department of the Interior, National Park Service, "Visitor Center Planning."

55. Richard W. Sellars and Melody Webb, "An Interview with Robert M. Utley on the History of Historic Preservation in the National Park Service, 1947–1980," Sep-

tember 24, 1985–December 27, 1985, transcript, National Park Service, Denver Service Center, Technical Information Center.

56. Glass, *The Beginnings of a New National Historic Preservation Program,* 6.

57. Oscar L. Chapman, "Citation for Distinguished Service, Thomas C. Vint," Papers of Charles E. Peterson.

58. Charles E. Peterson, "HABS: In and Out of Philadelphia," in *Philadelphia Preserved: Catalog of the Historic American Buildings Survey,* ed. Richard Webster (Philadelphia: Temple University Press, 1976), xxi–xlvi.

59. Barry Mackintosh, "The Historic Sites Survey and the National Historic Landmarks Program: A History," unpublished report, National Park Service, Washington, D.C., 1985, 27–41.

60. Glass, *The Beginnings of a New National Historic Preservation Program,* 6.

61. Wirth, *Parks, Politics, and the People,* 267.

7. LANDSCAPE ARCHITECTURE

1. Thomas Vint to Horace Albright, May 22, 1929, Papers of Horace M. Albright, entry 17, RG 79, National Archives.

2. In 1953, out of 907 members of ASLA, 297 worked in the public sector, 46 of them at the National Park Service, down from 93 in 1947. "National and State Parks and Forests," *Landscape Architecture* 37, no. 3 (April 1947): 105–106; Leon Zach, "Landscape Architecture in Government Agencies," *Landscape Architecture* 43, no. 4 (July 1953): 150–153.

3. See "Contemporary Trends and Future Possibilities in Landscape Design," *Landscape Architecture* 22, no. 4 (July 1932): 288–303.

4. See, for example, Thomas J. Baird, "There *Is* a Modern Way to Look at Gardening," *American Home* 33, no. 1 (December 1944): 18–20; M. E. Bottomley, "Landscape Design in the Modern Manner: Based on the Controls of Common Sense and Good Taste," *Landscape Architecture* 37, no. 2 (January 1947): 43–49. Also see Sidney N. Shurcliff, "Shoppers' World: The Design and Construction of a Retail Shopping Center," *Landscape Architecture* 42, no. 4 (July 1952): 145–151; Robert L. Zion, "The Landscape Architect and the Shopping Center: An Unusual Opportunity at Roosevelt Field, New York," *Landscape Architecture* 48, no. 5 (October 1957): 7–12.

5. Alofsin, *The Struggle for Modernism,* 121–130; Melanie Simo, *The Coalescing of Different Forces and Ideas: A History of Landscape Architecture at Harvard, 1900–1999* (Cambridge: Harvard University Graduate School of Design, 2000), 21–36.

6. San Francisco Museum of Art, *Contemporary Landscape Architecture and Its Sources,* exhibition catalog (San Francisco: San Francisco Museum of Art, 1937).

7. Henry-Russell Hitchcock Jr., "Gardens in Relation to Modern Architecture," ibid., 13–19.

8. See Caroline Constant, "From the Virgilian Dream to Chandigarh," *Architectural Review* 181, no. 1079 (January 1987): 66–72.

9. Marc Treib, ed., *Modern Landscape Architecture: A Critical Review* (Cambridge: MIT Press, 1993), ix.

10. Christopher Tunnard, *Gardens in the Modern Landscape* (London: Architectural Press, 1938), 75.

11. Christopher Tunnard, "Modern Gardens for Modern Houses," reprinted in Treib, *Modern Landscape Architecture,* 159–165.

12. See Lance M. Neckar, "Christopher Tunnard: The Garden in the Modern Landscape," ibid., 144–158.

13. Alofsin, *The Struggle for Modernism,* 159–170; Simo, *A Coalescing of Different Forces and Ideas,* 21–36.

14. Probably the most direct influence on this vision of a modernist urban park system was the architectural historian Sigfried Giedion, who gave an influential series of lectures at Harvard in 1938 and 1939, later expanded into his book *Space, Time, and Architecture* (Cambridge: Harvard University Press, 1941), which became a standard textbook at the GSD and elsewhere.

15. The articles are all reprinted in Treib, *Modern Landscape Architecture,* 68–91.

16. James C. Rose, "Freedom in the Garden" (1938), reprinted in ibid., 68–72. Also see Marc Treib, "Axioms for a Modern Landscape Architecture," ibid., 36–67; Dean Cardasis, "Space, Time, and Landscape Architecture: Fusion in the Works of James Rose," in *Preserving Modern Landscape Architecture: Papers From the Wave Hill—National Park Service Conference,* ed. Charles A. Birnbaum (Cambridge: Spacemaker Press, 1999), 24–28 .

17. See Peter Walker and Melanie Simo, *Invisible Gardens: The Search for Modernism in the American Landscape* (Cambridge: MIT Press, 1994), 56–91.

18. Michael Laurie, "Thomas Church, California Gardens, and Public Landscapes," in Treib, *Modern Landscape Architecture,* 166–179; Walker and Simo, *Invisible Gardens,* 92–115.

19. Melanie Simo, *One Hundred Years of Landscape Architecture: Some Patterns of a Century* (Washington, D.C.: ASLA Press, 1999), 129–143.

20. For example, Charles A. Platt, Ferruccio Vitale, Percival Gallagher, James L. Greenleaf, Henry V. Hubbard, Warren H. Manning, Charles Downing Lay, Albert D. Taylor, Marjorie Sewell Cautley, Kate Olivia Sessions, Ellen Biddle Shipman, Arthur A. Shurcliff, and Alfred Geiffert Jr. all died between 1933 and 1957. See Birnbaum and Karson, *Pioneers of American Landscape Design.*

21. Quoted in Simo, *One Hundred Years of Landscape Architecture*, 131.

22. Walker and Simo, *Invisible Gardens*, 212.

23. See ibid., 224–257.

24. Ibid., 209–223.

25. Ibid., 230–257.

26. Ibid., 141.

27. Henry V. Hubbard, "The Designer in National Parks: The Preservation and Enhancement of Natural Scenery" (1941), *Landscape Architecture* 38, no. 2 (January 1948): 58–60; Frederick Law Olmsted Jr., "The Significance of Decisions in Park Work: Need for Discretionary Judgment in Policy Interpretation," *Landscape Architecture* 37, no. 3 (April 1947): 85–87.

28. Conrad L. Wirth, "The Landscape Architect in National Park Work," *Landscape Architecture* 46, no. 1 (October 1955): 13–18. In his address Wirth quoted at length from the 1949 letter Olmsted had written him following the death of Wirth's father.

29. The ASLA estimated that there were 2,500 active landscape architects in 1957 (1,462 were ASLA members). In 1966 the organization estimated that there were more than 4,000 active professionals, 2,900 of whom were members. See "Selected 1957 ASLA Committee Reports," *Landscape Architecture* 48, no. 3 (April 1958): 169–176; "Universities: Bracing for the New Student Tide," *Landscape Architecture* 57, no. 1 (October 1966): 8.

30. See, for example, Raymond A. Wilhelm, "Station Wagon 'Pioneers' Invade Parks," *Landscape Architecture* 51, no. 2 (January 1961): 90–91.

31. The use of the term "modernist" may be problematic for those who reserve this term to refer specifically to landscape design directly inspired by modernist architecture. The term is used here, however, in the belief that different groups of planners and designers varied in their responses to postwar social and aesthetic trends, resulting in multiple "modernisms" in landscape architecture. Mission 66—a unique blend of Olmstedian park planning, Progressive Era ideology, and modernist landscape theory and architectural design—constitutes one form of postwar modernist landscape architecture, distinct from the work of contemporary professionals better known as "modernists," such as Garrett Eckbo or Dan Kiley.

32. Quoted in Sellars, *Preserving Nature in the National Parks*, 167.

8. CONCESSIONS AND CONTROVERSY

1. Rettie, *Our National Park System*, 251–252; U.S Department of the Interior, *1956 Annual Report*, 300; U.S. Department of the Interior, *1957 Annual Report*, 308.

2. For the texts of the legislation see Dilsaver, *America's National Park System*, 11, 28.

3. To justify the elimination of free competition, Mather referred to Progressive Era public utility theory which suggested that regulated monopolies were legal and desirable government policy when they were the only practical means to provide public services such as electric and phone lines. Providing for adequate park accommodations through private enterprise, in other words, required the elimination of destructive forms of competition. In their annual reports, Mather and Albright began to refer to concessioner operations in the parks as "public-utility services," a term that emphasized the analogy to public utilities that functioned as regulated monopolies.

4. Arthur David Martinson, "Mountain in the Sky: A History of Mount Rainier National Park" (Ph.D. diss., Washington State University, 1966), 83, 91–94; Catton, *Wonderland*, 248–255; Carr, *Wilderness by Design*, 220–228.

5. U.S. Department of the Interior, National Park Service, *1918 Annual Report*, 60.

6. For summaries of early park concession history, see Shankland, *Steve Mather of the National Parks*, 114–127; Ise, *Our National Park Policy*, 606–618; William C. Everhart, *The National Park Service* (New York: Praeger Publishers), 112–132; Don Hummel, *Stealing the National Parks: The Destruction of Concessions and Public Access* (Bellevue, Wash.: Free Enterprise Press, 1987), 56–67; Peter J. Blodgett, "Striking a Balance: Managing Concessions in the National Parks, 1916–33," *Forest and Conservation History* 34, no. 2 (April 1990): 60–68.

7. In a 1928 amendment to the 1916 act creating the Park Service, the secretary of the interior was formally granted the authority to award concession contracts without competitive bidding and to allow concessioners to execute mortgages and issue shares of stock to finance improvements. The policy of "preferential renewal" of contracts (without competitive bidding) was put in writing in a department policy document signed by Ickes in 1933. Preferential renewal was intended to assure the security of private investments without granting actual title to properties. "Briefing Meeting . . . Concerning Concessioner Activities," memorandum (copy), September 6, 1962, box 5, Personal Papers of Conrad L. Wirth, RG 79, National Archives.

8. Ickes did manage to start a nonprofit concession corporation, National Park Concessions, Inc., that opened or took over concessions at Mammoth Cave, Isle Royale, Olympic, and Big Bend, parks for which private concessioners apparently could not be found. Elsewhere private businesses remained the mainstay for providing overnight accommodations through the 1930s. U.S. Department of the Interior, National Park Service, *1946 Annual Report*, 310–317. In a 1938 report completed for the National Resources Board, however, the Park Service recommended that all concession services be acquired and operated through contracts with private companies or directly by the government. National Resources Board, *Recreational Use of Land in the United States*, pt. 10 of *Report on Land Planning* (Washington, D.C.: Government Printing Office, 1938), 29.

9. U.S. Department of the Interior, National Park Service, *1947 Annual Report*, 320–323.

10. Catton, *Wonderland*, 437–457.

11. C. Girard Davidson to Julius A. Krug, "Concession Policies of the National Park System," memorandum, November 1, 1948, Main Interior Library, Washington, D.C.

12. "Briefing Meeting . . . ," September 6, 1962; Ise, *Our National Park Policy*, 463; Hummel, *Stealing the National Parks*, 130–140, 156–161; Barringer, *Selling Yellowstone*, 104–106.

13. Dale E. Doty, "Concession Policies of the National Park System," memorandum, October 13, 1950, Main Interior Library, Washington, D.C.

14. U.S. Congress, House, Committee on Public Lands,

80th Cong., "Concessions in National Parks," Hearing no. 41, 1948; U.S. Congress, House, Committee on Public Lands, 81st Cong., "Concessions in National Parks," Hearing no. 28, 1949.

15. "Briefing Meeting . . . ," September 6, 1962; C. Girard Davidson to Julius A. Krug, "Concession Policies of the National Park System," memorandum, November 1, 1948, Main Interior Library, Washington, D.C.

16. A. C. Stratton to Conrad L. Wirth, "Concessioners' Mortgage Guarantees," memorandum, April 18, 1960, box 5, Personal Papers of Conrad L. Wirth, RG 79, National Archives; Hummel, *Stealing the National Parks*, 182, 185, 192; Barringer, *Selling Yellowstone*, 180; Outdoor Recreation Resources Review Commission, *Outdoor Recreation for America: A Report to the President and to Congress by the Outdoor Recreation Resources Review Commission* (Washington, D.C.: Government Printing Office, 1962), 164.

17. Everhart, *The National Park Service*, 119; Ise, *National Park Policy*, 615.

18. "Mission 66: To Provide Adequate Protection and Development of the National Park System for Human Use," January 1956, unpublished report, National Park Service, Denver Service Center Library.

19. "Informational Memorandum No. 3, Mission 66, Progress and Procedures," June 27, 1955, box A8213, National Park Service History Collection, Harpers Ferry Center.

20. Haines, *The Yellowstone Story*, 2:375–376. The concessioner's reluctance to enter into his investment obligations was expressed, for example, in a long letter to the park superintendent that June, shortly after the new contract had been signed. W. M. Nichols to Edmund B. Rogers, June 15, 1956, box A248, Yellowstone National Park Archives.

21. By 1957 Wirth and Garrison had backed away from the other initially proposed development, Firehole Village, which would have replaced the inn and lodge at Old Faithful. "Draft Mission 66 Prospectus Brief," August 28, 1957, Mission 66 Prospectus Files, National Park Service History Collection, Harpers Ferry Center.

22. "MISSION 66 PROGRAM FOR YELLOWSTONE . . . ," press release, June 24, 1956, box A248, Yellowstone National Park Archives; "Address by Conrad L. Wirth . . . Canyon Village," prepared remarks, June 25, 1956, box 6, Conrad L. Wirth Collection, University of Wyoming, American Heritage Center; "Draft Mission 66 Prospec-

tus Brief," March 21, 1957, and "Draft Mission 66 Prospectus Brief," August 28, 1957, both in Mission 66 Prospectus Files, National Park Service History Collection, Harpers Ferry Center.

23. It is also true that by keeping the new Yosemite Village in a relatively compact form in the east end of the valley, views of the west end of the valley (including those from Inspiration and Discovery points) remained unaffected. The site selected for the new village also did not encroach on the historic scenic views of the valley, as shown by later park planners through their analysis of nineteenth- and early-twentieth-century paintings and photographs; see the "Historic Viewpoint Analysis" of the *Draft Environmental Impact Statement, General Management Plan, Yosemite National Park* (Washington, D.C.: Government Printing Office, 1978), 102–106. But the central public buildings of Yosemite Village were intended to be seen in the context of their extraordinary setting. The major public space, or "plaza," of the village was surrounded by the rustic façades of the museum, administration, and other buildings, with dramatic views of Yosemite Falls, Sentinel Rock, Half Dome, and other features of the surrounding cliff walls in the background.

24. "Canyon Regional Plan," 1952 Yellowstone National Park Master Plan, Yellowstone National Park Archives.

25. Becket was also well known by the 1950s for large office and hotel buildings for corporate clients, including the Hilton Hotel chain. His office was on its way to becoming one of the largest in the country. See Welton Becket, "Shopping Center Traffic Problems," *Traffic Quarterly* 9 (April 1955): 162–172; William Dudley Hunt Jr., *Total Design: Architecture of Welton Becket and Associates* (New York: McGraw-Hill, 1972).

26. See Lon Johnson, "Determination of Eligibility, Canyon Village (Horseshoe Plaza) Historic District," unpublished report, 2000, Yellowstone National Park.

27. "Address by Conrad L. Wirth . . . Canyon Village," prepared remarks, June 25, 1956, box 6, Conrad L. Wirth Collection, University of Wyoming, American Heritage Center; "$31 Million 10-Year Yellowstone Project Set," *Denver Post*, June 25, 1956; "U.S. Reveals Program for Yellowstone," *San Francisco Chronicle*, June 27, 1956.

28. Barringer, *Selling Yellowstone*, 132–150.

29. The controversies around Yellowstone concessions continued long after Mission 66 ended. It was not until 1979 that Congress finally purchased the possessory interest of the Yellowstone Park Company. The Park Service then prepared to use public funds to build a Grant Village motel complex, to be operated by a new concessioner on a contract basis. By that time, however, merchants and motel owners in the rapidly growing town of West Yellowstone denounced what they perceived as government-sponsored competition. In 1981 Secretary of the Interior James Watt responded and stopped construction. Building resumed shortly thereafter, but Grant Village remained far smaller than originally planned. By the time the first two hundred motel units opened in 1984, it was difficult to see the entire episode as anything but a long and destructive fiasco. For accounts of later concessioner woes at Yellowstone, see Richard A. Bartlett, *Yellowstone: A Wilderness Besieged* (Tucson: University of Arizona Press, 1985), 365–379; Barringer, *Selling Yellowstone*, 141–144; Haines, *The Yellowstone Story*, 2:375–379; Robin Smith, "The History of Grant Village," unpublished report, 1988, Vertical Files, Yellowstone National Park Archives.

30. The Concession Policy Act of 1965 gave legislative sanction to the preferential rights of renewal and possessory interest, and therefore gave banks a more secure basis for making large loans to concessioners. The purchase of the Yellowstone Park Company's possessory interest in 1979 allowed the government to own, improve, and expand facilities directly, rather than attempt to coerce a private partner to invest. Since the 1970s, numerous concession companies throughout the park system have been consolidated by corporations specializing in "guest services," operating franchises on a contractual basis. Concession facilities themselves, however, remain a patchwork of full federal ownership and concessioner ownership (possessory interest).

31. "Mission 66: To Provide Adequate Protection and Development of the National Park System for Human Use," January 1956.

32. Smith, "The History of Grant Village."

33. Barringer, *Selling Yellowstone*, 179.

34. Haines, *The Yellowstone Story*, 2:383. Today there are around 2,238 rooms and cabins in Yellowstone. Camping has been expanded above the original suggested Mission 66 level to about 2,200 sites.

35. "Mission 66 Progress Report," October 1963, 13, National Park Service, Denver Service Center, Technical Information Center.

36. See, for example, Barringer, *Selling Yellowstone,* 130–131.

37. At the time the Advisory Board consisted of Colby, Buwalda, and McDuffie. Minutes of the Yosemite National Park Board of Expert Advisors, August 24–30, 1946; August 23–29, 1947, n.d. (August, 1949), Yosemite National Park Archives. Also see Runte, *Yosemite: The Embattled Wilderness,* 189–192.

38. Runte, *Yosemite: The Embattled Wilderness,* 187; Shirley Sargent, *Yosemite's Innkeepers: The Story of a Great Park and Its Chief Concessionaires* (Yosemite, Calif.: Ponderosa Press, 2000), 134, 148.

39. The Colter Bay development eventually included a visitor center, cafeteria, stores, trailer camping area, and eighty-five cabins, a number of which had been moved from other locations in the park. Colter Bay had its own detractors, who deplored its visible lakeshore location and its facilities for power boat access to Jackson Lake. Conrad L. Wirth to Eldridge T. Spencer, April 18, 1958,

40. box 7, Personal Papers of Conrad L. Wirth, RG 79, National Archives; Sargent, *Yosemite's Innkeepers,* 146–148. "Yosemite Valley and Mission 66," draft prospectus, n.d.,

41. National Park Service, Harpers Ferry Center; "Mission 66 for Yosemite National Park," prospectus, July 9, 1957, National Park Service, Harpers Ferry Center. "Mission 66 for Yosemite National Park," prospectus,

42. July 9, 1957. U.S. Department of the Interior, *1956 Annual Report,*

43. 301; U.S. Department of the Interior, *1957 Annual Report,* 310, 344. The Peaks of Otter Lodge (Johnson, Craven and Gib-

44. son, architects) opened in 1964 on the Blue Ridge Parkway in Virginia. U.S. Department of the Interior, *1959 Annual Report,*

45. 328. The extensive Mission 66 construction at the south rim

46. of Grand Canyon National Park also included the Albright Training Center complex, the Shrine of the Ages, a new maintenance area, a high school, a clinic, many residences, and significant road and utility development. For a full account, see Amanda Zeman, "Grand Canyon Village Mission 66 Planning Effort: National Register of Historic Places Multiple Property Nomination Form," 2003, unpublished report, Grand Canyon National Park.

47. John Jameson, *The Story of Big Bend National Park* (Austin: University of Texas Press, 1996), 75–81; Ross A. Maxwell, *Big Bend Country: A History of Big Bend National Park* (Big Bend National Park, Tex.: Big Bend Natural History Association, 1985), 69–75.

48. Bonnie S. Houston, "Determination of Eligibility, Glacier Bay Lodge Complex," draft, unpublished report, National Park Service, 2005; Theodore Catton, "Land Reborn: A History of Administration and Visitor Use in Glacier Bay National Park and Preserve," government report, National Park Service, 1995, 264–283.

9. PARK ROADS AND WILDERNESS

1. See Timothy Davis, Todd A. Croteau, and Christopher H. Marston, *America's National Park Roads and Parkways: Drawings from the Historic American Engineering Record* (Baltimore: Johns Hopkins University Press, 2004).

2. Thomas C. Vint to Newton B. Drury, July 6, 1940, Personal Papers of Newton B. Drury, entry 19, RG 79, National Archives.

3. Carr, *Wilderness by Design,* 215–235.

4. Richard H. Quin, "Yosemite National Park Roads and Bridges," Historic American Engineering Record (HAER no. CA-117), 1991, 2–10, Library of Congress; Michael P. Cohen, *The History of the Sierra Club, 1892–1970* (San Francisco: Sierra Club Books, 1988), 9.

5. Quin, "Yosemite National Park Roads and Bridges," 11–16; Keith A. Trexler, "The Tioga Road: A History," *Yosemite* 40, no. 3 (June 24, 1961): 31–58.

6. Quin, "Yosemite National Park Roads and Bridges," 102; Cohen, *History of the Sierra Club,* 95.

7. Minutes of the Yosemite National Park Board of Expert Advisors, August 23–29, 1947, Yosemite National Park Archives; Cohen, *History of the Sierra Club,* 97–100.

8. Minutes of the Yosemite National Park Board of Expert Advisors, August 23–29, 1947; Thomas C. Vint, "Statement Concerning Road Development in the High Sierra Section of Yosemite National Park," November 1, 1948, Yosemite National Park Archives.

9. Harold C. Bradley and David R. Brower, "Roads in the National Parks," *Sierra Club Bulletin* 34, no. 6 (June 1949): 31–54; Harold C. Bradley, "Yosemite's Problem Road," *Pacific Discovery* (January 1950): 3–8.

10. Quin, "Yosemite National Park Roads and Bridges," 17.

11. William E. Colby, "Report to the Yosemite Advisory Board on Relocation of Tioga Road," November 15, 1951, Minutes of the Yosemite National Park Board of Expert Advisors, n.d. (1952), Yosemite National Park Archives.

12. Bradley and Brower, "Roads in National Parks," 31–54; Bradley, "Yosemite's Problem Road," 3–8.

13. Richard M. Leonard, "The Tioga Road at Tioga Lake," *Sierra Club Bulletin* (September 1952): 8–9.

14. Michael P. Cohen, *The History of the Sierra Club, 1892–1970* (San Francisco: Sierra Club Books, 1988), 93, 103, 149–163, 173.

15. For summaries of the legislative history of the Wilderness Act, see Craig W. Allin, *The Politics of Wilderness Preservation* (Westport, Conn.: Greenwood Press, 1982), 102–142; Dennis M. Roth, *The Wilderness Movement and the National Forests* (College Station, Tex.: Intaglio Press, 1988), 1–12.

16. For the complete text of the Yosemite report, see Ranney, Rauluk, and Hoffman, *The California Frontier, 1863–1865*, 488–516.

17. Conrad L. Wirth to Howard Zahniser, March 19, 1956, copy, box A248, Yellowstone National Park Archives.

18. Tolson, *Historic Listing of National Park Service Officials*, 9, 28, 69, 113, 132, 172, 194.

19. Eivind T. Scoyen to Lemuel A. Garrison, March 8, 1955, box A8213, National Park Service History Collection, Harpers Ferry Center.

20. Howard R. Stagner, "Preservation of Natural and Wilderness Values in the National Parks," March 1957, unpublished draft report, National Park Service, Denver Service Center Library. Some of these ideas were presented by Wirth at the Fifth Biennial Wilderness Conference, sponsored by the Sierra Club and other groups that month in San Francisco. See Conrad L. Wirth, "Wilderness in the National Parks," *Planning and Civic Comment* 24, no. 2 (June 1958): 1–8.

21. Conrad L. Wirth to Bestor Robinson, May 8, 1958, box 25, Conrad L. Wirth Collection, University of Wyoming, American Heritage Center.

22. As park superintendent at Zion in 1927, for example, Eivind Scoyen wrote Mather regarding "purist" criticism of the Park Service's road building program. "The man who overcomes nature's obstacles to reach some [roadless] point that thrills his nature loving instinct may be a nature lover," he wrote. "However, at the same time we have a family rattling along in a disreputable flivver bound for a similar place. The father and mother have slaved and saved for 20 years for this opportunity, and only through the blessing of good roads have they been able to reach their goal. Considering these two, which is the true nature lover? Has one a right to condemn the other? I think it is the duty of the parks to find a place for both." Eivind T. Scoyen to Stephen T. Mather, October 23, 1927, copy, Papers of Horace M. Albright, entry 17, RG 79, National Archives, Washington, D.C.

23. Howard R. Stagner, "Preservation of Natural and Wilderness Values in the National Parks," March 1957, unpublished draft report, National Park Service, Denver Service Center Library.

24. Conrad L. Wirth to David R. Brower, May 7, 1958, box 25, Conrad L. Wirth Collection, University of Wyoming, American Heritage Center.

25. Howard R. Stagner, *The National Park Wilderness* (Washington, D.C.: Government Printing Office, 1957). For a contrasting analysis of this document, see Sellars, *Preserving Nature in the National Parks*, 187–189.

26. David R. Brower, "Mission 65 Is Proposed by Reviewer of Park Service's Brochure on Wilderness," *National Parks Magazine* 32, no. 132 (January 1958): 3–6, 45–48.

27. Conrad L. Wirth to David R. Brower, May 7, 1958, box 25, Conrad L. Wirth Collection, University of Wyoming, American Heritage Center; Conrad L. Wirth to Bruce M. Kilgore, February 18, 1958, box A8213, National Park Service History Collection, Harpers Ferry Center.

28. Max K. Gilstrap, "Our National Parks: A Heritage Worth Saving," feature article series, *Christian Science Monitor*, January 26–August 17, 1956.

29. Conrad L. Wirth, "Policy and Practice in the National Park Service," May 1, 1956, box 6, Conrad L. Wirth Collection, University of Wyoming, American Heritage Center. A shortened version of Wirth's statement was published in the *Christian Science Monitor*, May 3, 1956.

30.

31. Eivind T. Scoyen, "Keeping the Public Informed about MISSION 66," November 21, 1956, box 12, Conrad L. Wirth Collection, University of Wyoming, American Heritage Center.

32. These and other brochures are conserved at National Park Service History Collection, Harpers Ferry Center. William G. Carnes, "New MISSION 66 Slide Talk," memorandum, June 14, 1956, box A248, Yellowstone National Park Archives.

33. Several versions of these slide shows, with their written texts and reel-to-reel tape recordings, can be pieced together at National Park Service History Collection, Harpers Ferry Center.

34. Quoted in Runte, *Yosemite,* 195. Alfred Runte suggests that Park Service plans for the Tioga Road widening in the 1950s were made at least in part at the behest of business owners in the gateway town of Lee Vining, who hoped to see more traffic cross the park and go through their town. Local businesses certainly attempted to influence park policies (as always). But the Park Service had other, long-standing reasons to complete Tioga Road, and the decision to proceed had already been made in the 1930s.

35. Quin, "Yosemite National Park Roads and Bridges," 18.

36. John C. Preston, "Statement before the Region Four Conference Held in Death Valley National Monument, January 11–16, 1959," Yosemite National Park Archives.

37. Quin, "Yosemite National Park Roads and Bridges," 19; Cohen, *History of the Sierra Club,* 141.

38. David R. Brower, "Mission 66, Roads, and the Park Idea," *Sierra Club Bulletin* (January 1958): 14–15.

39. "Parks Director Will Check on Tioga Road Dispute," *Fresno Bee,* August 13, 1958; Roy Taylor, "Park Director Orders Tioga Work Resumed," *Fresno Bee,* August 20, 1958; David R. Brower, "Tioga Protest: What Happened below Tenaya," *Sierra Club Bulletin* 43, no. 8 (October 1958): 3–7.

40. "Yosemite Hassel [sic] Settled," *San Francisco Chronicle,* August 21, 1958; Quin, "Yosemite National Park Roads and Bridges," 19–20; Wirth, *Parks, Politics, and the People,* 359.

41. Brower, "Tioga Protest."

42. Ansel Adams, "Tenaya Tragedy," *Sierra Club Bulletin* 43, no. 9 (November 1958): 1–4; Ansel Adams and David R. Brower, "The Tioga Road and Tenaya Lake: Twenty-two Photographs," *Sierra Club Bulletin* 43, no. 9 (November 1958).

43. Ansel Adams, "Yosemite—1958: Compromise in Action," *National Parks Magazine* 32, no. 135 (October 1958): 166–175, 190; "Adams Urges Halt to Sierra Development," *Fresno Bee,* January 25, 1959.

44. "On Park Shrines and Highways," editorial, *National Parks Magazine* (April 1959): 10–11; Harold Bradley, "Roads in Our National Parks," *National Parks Magazine* 33, no. 137 (February 1959): 3–6.

45. John A. McPhee makes similar observations about Brower in *Encounters with the Archdruid* (New York: Farrar, Straus and Giroux, 1971).

46. Preston, "Statement before the Region Four Conference Held in Death Valley National Monument."

47. Conrad L. Wirth to John B. Oakes, February 12, 1958, box A8213, National Park Service History Collection, Harpers Ferry Center. Oakes, an influential environmental journalist, criticized the Park Service for construction at Yellowstone and elsewhere. In 1955 he had replaced Bernard De Voto on the Advisory Board on National Parks, Historic Sites, Buildings and Monuments.

48. Conrad L. Wirth, "Mission 66 in the Headlines," *National Parks Magazine* 32, no. 132 (January 1958): 8–9, 36–38; Conrad L. Wirth, "Heritage of Beauty and History," *National Geographic Magazine* 113, no. 5 (May 1958): 587–663.

49. Conrad L. Wirth, "Telling the Story of MISSION 66," memorandum, February 27, 1959; and Hugh M. Miller, "Need for All Employees to Understand MISSION 66," memorandum, March 9, 1959, both in box A8213, National Park Service History Collection, Harpers Ferry Center.

50. Coates also served on the Mission 66 working committee. Robert M. Coates, "MISSION 66: The Start of a Renaissance Movement in Parks," cover memorandum by William G. Carnes, September 30, 1959, box A307, Yellowstone National Park Archives.

51. Conrad L. Wirth, "Remarks at the Tioga Road Dedication," June 24, 1961, Yosemite National Park Archives.

52. "Program Set for Tioga Road Dedication," Yosemite National Park press memorandum, June 19, 1961; "Interior Department Urges Conservationists to Support Goals," U.S. Department of the Interior Press Release, June 25, 1961; "Draft Speech for Assistant Secretary Carver at the Tioga Road Dedication," May 29, 1961, all in Yosemite National Park Archives.

53. Stroud, *National Leaders of American Conservation,* 276–277.

54. Olaus J. Murie to Conrad L. Wirth, December 10, 1957, and January 7, 1958, both in box A8213, National Park Service History Collection, Harpers Ferry Center.

55. William E. Brown, *Denali: Symbol of the Alaskan Wild* (Denali National Park: Denali Natural History Association, 1993), 99–100, 135, 157, 164–169.

56. "Mission 66 for Mount McKinley National Park," n.d. (1957), National Park Service History Collection, Harpers Ferry Center.

57. Adolph Murie, "Comments on Mission 66 Plans and Policies Pertaining to Mount McKinley National Park," memorandum, November 8, 1956; Adolph Murie to Sanford J. Hill, September 21, 1957, marked personal;

and "Mission 66 for Mount McKinley National Park," n.d. (1957), all in National Park Service History Collection, Harpers Ferry Center; Brown, *Denali,* 198–199, 200–201.

58. Olaus J. Murie, "Mount McKinley: Wilderness Park of the North Country," *National Parks Magazine* 37, no. 187 (April 1963): 4–7; "The Editorial Page: Implications of McKinley," *National Parks Magazine* 37, no. 189 (June 1963): 2; Adolph Murie, "Roadbuilding in Mount McKinley National Park," *National Parks Magazine* (July 1965): 4–8.

59. The concept of "telescoping standards" apparently was worked out by Sanford Hill at the WODC. Brown, *Denali,* 195–204; Paul M. Tilden and Nancy L. Machler, "The Development of Mount McKinley National Park," *National Parks Magazine* 37, no. 188 (May 1963): 10–15.

60. Wirth, *Parks, Politics, and the People,* 262.

61. Lien, *Olympic Battleground,* 204, 302–303; Fringer, *Olympic National Park,* 154–155.

10. "PARKS FOR AMERICA"

1. Robert M. Utley and Barry Mackintosh, *The Department of Everything Else: Highlights of Interior History* (Washington, D.C.: Department of the Interior), 1989, 43–44.

2. Stewart L. Udall, *The Quiet Crisis* (New York: Holt, Rinehart and Winston, 1963), vii, 172, 180, 190–191.

3. U.S. Department of Agriculture, Forest Service, *Operation Outdoors,* pt. 1, *National Forest Recreation* (Washington, D.C.: Government Printing Office, 1957).

4. "MISSION 66 PROGRESS REPORT," draft, April 1961, box A8213, National Park Service History Collection, Harpers Ferry Center; U.S. Department of the Interior, *1959 Annual Report,* 323–324; Rettie, *Our National Park System,* 251.

5. Department of the Interior, *1959 Annual Report,* 323; "National Park Service Officials to Hold Planning Conference at Grand Canyon," press release, April 23, 1961, box A8213, National Park Service History Collection, Harpers Ferry Center.

6. In 1957 the architect (and at the time assistant western regional director) Herbert Maier hoped that the review would be conducted by a panel including leading architects and landscape architects from private practice, biologist Olaus Murie, Horace Albright, and experts in public education. Herbert Maier, "Half-way Point Evaluation of MISSION 66," September 6, 1957, box 7, Conrad L. Wirth Collection, University of Wyoming, American Heritage Center.

7. U.S. Department of the Interior, *1959 Annual Report,* 324. In 1960 Secretary of the Interior Seaton also performed a review of all design and construction procedures in his department. The review was conducted in response to inquiries from congressional committee staff concerned about costs and efficiency. The final report suggested increasing the use of standardized plans and reducing the amount of "design review" conducted. "Report of the Committee on Design and Construction in the Department of the Interior," Ralph C. Meima, chairman, 1960, Personal Papers of Conrad L. Wirth, RG 79, National Archives.

8. The bimonthly "information letter" called "Grist," included design sheets, specifications, and suggestions for "operational procedures . . . and 'tricks of the trade.'" See U.S. Department of the Interior, *1957 Annual Report,* 335.

9. Edwin M. Fitch and John F. Shanklin, *The Bureau of Outdoor Recreation* (New York: Praeger Publishers, 1970), 60–63; Robin W. Winks, *Laurance S. Rockefeller: Catalyst for Conservation* (Washington, D.C.: Island Press, 1997), 121–139.

10. Outdoor Recreation Resources Review Commission (ORRRC), *Outdoor Recreation for America: A Report to the President and to the Congress by the Outdoor Recreation Resources Review Commission* (Washington, D.C.: Government Printing Office, 1962).

11. Rockefeller initially contacted Wirth regarding the creation of Virgin Islands National Park in 1955 after seeing a park proposal for the areas prepared by the Park Service in 1939. His interest in Caneel Bay as the site of his resort development, however, was what had originally brought him to the area. Wirth, *Parks, Politics, and the People,* 52–53.

12. U.S. Department of the Interior, *1956 Annual Report,* 313; Winks, *Laurance S. Rockefeller,* 63–65; Department of the Interior, *1959 Annual Report,* 325.

13. "Excerpts from Director's Staff Meeting Minutes, Feb. 11, 1960," typescript; and "Meeting February 10, 1960, Concerning Re-study of the National Park System and Re-evaluation of MISSION 66," typescript, both in box A8213, National Park Service History Collection, Harpers Ferry Center.

14. Conrad L. Wirth to Washington and All Field Offices,

memorandum, April 28, 1960, box A248, Yellowstone National Park Archives.

15. Conrad L. Wirth to MISSION 66 Advisory Committee, memorandum, March 3, 1960; George F. Baggley to Superintendents, Region Two Field Areas, memorandum, March 9, 1960, both in box A219, Yellowstone National Park Archives.

16. He also attempted to address a serious problem: because of the accelerated pace of Mission 66, Proposed Construction Projects (PCPs) had gone ahead without ever having been part of a park master plan. Master plans required a longer process, and so PCPs had gone to construction while a backlog of approved master plans grew. U.S. Department of the Interior, *1959 Annual Report,* 329; "Mission 66 Progress Report," October 1963, Denver Service Center, Technical Information Center, 8; George B. Hartzog Jr., "Remarks . . . Conference of Challenges," October 18, 1963, box 26, Conrad L. Wirth Collection, University of Wyoming, American Heritage Center.

17. "An Analysis of the MISSION 66 Program Made by C. L. Wirth at a Meeting at the Grand Canyon in 1961," May 27, 1974, box 33, Conrad L. Wirth Collection, University of Wyoming, American Heritage Center; Wirth, *Parks, Politics, and the People,* 281.

18. "Parks for America, Organizational Meeting," October 31, 1960, minutes, box 22, Conrad L. Wirth Collection, University of Wyoming, American Heritage Center.

19. "Parks of the Future (Discussion Paper)," October 31, 1960, National Park Service, Harpers Ferry Center; "Parks for America, Organizational Meeting," October 31, 1960, minutes, box 22, Conrad L. Wirth Collection, University of Wyoming, American Heritage Center.

20. "PARKS FOR AMERICA, The Committee of Fifteen, Minutes of December 5, 1960, Meeting, Washington, D.C.," box 22, Conrad L. Wirth Collection, University of Wyoming, American Heritage Center; "Parks for America," *Parks & Recreation* 43, no. 12 (December 1960): 528–529, 541–543.

21. Conrad L. Wirth, "A Report on MISSION 66—Its Accomplishments—Its Future," September 1960, box 27, Conrad L. Wirth Collection, University of Wyoming, American Heritage Center.

22. "A Brief on the National Park System and the National Park Service Prepared for Secretary Stewart L. Udall," December 15, 1960, box 27, Conrad L. Wirth Collection, University of Wyoming, American Heritage Cen-

ter; "An Analysis of the MISSION 66 Program Made by C. L. Wirth at a Meeting at the Grand Canyon in 1961," May 27, 1974.

23. Paul Brooks, "The Pressure of Numbers," *Atlantic* 207, no. 2 (February 1961): 54–56; Devereux Butcher, "Resorts or Wilderness?" *Atlantic* 207, no. 2 (February 1961): 45–51; Conrad L. Wirth to Stewart L. Udall, March 10, 1961, National Park Service, Harpers Ferry Center.

24. Stewart L. Udall to Conrad L. Wirth, March 20, 1961, box 33, Conrad L. Wirth Collection, University of Wyoming, American Heritage Center; Stewart L. Udall, "National Parks for the Future," *Atlantic* 207, no. 6 (June 1961): 81–84.

25. "Mission 66 Reappraised," editorial (inside front cover), *National Parks Magazine* 35, no. 163 (April 1961).

26. "Report of the National Park Service Mission 66 Frontiers Conference, Grand Canyon National Park, April 24–28, 1961," transcribed tape recording, 10–18, AC 2886, National Park Service History Collection, Harpers Ferry Center.

27. Carnes quoted from Andrew Jackson Downing, Frederick Law Olmsted, and many other early park advocates whom he believed were "far more liberal in their outlook than many of their latter day disciples might realize. They believed in public parks for the benefit of the whole people." He reminded the group that these ideas were the foundation of Mission 66, for which three "basic considerations" had evolved: "preservation of park resources"; "substantial and appropriate use of the National Park System"; and "adequate and appropriate developments" that made it possible to use the parks without impairing them. He spoke again of the "renaissance" of traditional public park values which he hoped Mission 66 had sparked. "Report of the National Park Service Mission 66 Frontiers Conference, Grand Canyon National Park, April 24–28, 1961."

28. Ibid.

29. Ibid.; Udall, "National Parks for the Future."

30. Tolson, *Historic Listing of National Park Service Officials,* 9, 21; Olsen, *Organizational Structures of the National Park Service,* 83.

31. Conrad L. Wirth to William G. Carnes, July 20, 1962, box 24, Personal Papers of Conrad L. Wirth, RG 79, National Archives.

32. Master plans and plans for historic structures were still reviewed in Washington. "Interview with A. Clark Stratton," March 1, 1962, conducted by S. Herbert Evison, transcript, 22, National Park Service History Collection, Harpers Ferry Center.

33. ORRRC, *Outdoor Recreation for America,* 1–10, 83.

34. Fitch and Shanklin, *The Bureau of Outdoor Recreation,* 79–85, 92.

35. Ibid., 86–89. For the text of the LWCF Act, see Dilsaver, *America's National Park System,* 287–297.

36. See Barry Mackintosh, *Visitor Fees in the National Park System: A Legislative and Administrative History* (Washington, D.C.: Department of the Interior, National Park Service, 1983).

37. By 1959 park entrance fees equaled only 6 percent of the agency's appropriated budget. Ise, *Our National Park Policy,* 625.

38. Conrad L. Wirth to Laurance S. Rockefeller, February 5, 1962, box 24, Personal Papers of Conrad L. Wirth, RG 79, National Archives.

39. For the text of the act, see Dilsaver, *America's National Park System,* 277–286.

40. See Stanley A. Cain, "Ecological Islands as Natural Laboratories" (1959), ibid., 200–210.

41. Pritchard, *Preserving Yellowstone's Natural Conditions,* 201–205; Sellars, *Preserving Nature in the National Parks,* 198–199.

42. For the text of the 1962 Stagner report, see Dilsaver, *America's National Park System,* 217–223.

43. For the text of the Robbins report, see ibid., 253–262.

44. For the text of the Leopold report, see ibid., 237–252.

45. Sellars, *Preserving Nature in the National Parks,* 200–203, 214–217.

46. U.S. Department of the Interior, *1963 Annual Report,* 95, 107; "Interview with Director Wirth on November 1, 1962," Personal Papers of Conrad L. Wirth, RG 79, National Archives.

47. George B. Hartzog Jr., *Battling for the National Parks* (Mount Kisco, N.Y.: Moyer Bell, 1988), 71–78; "An Analysis of the MISSION 66 Program Made by C. L. Wirth at a Meeting at the Grand Canyon in 1961," May 27, 1974, box 33, Conrad L. Wirth Collection, University of Wyoming, American Heritage Center; Eivind T. Scoyen, "Remarks . . . Conference of Challenges," October 18, 1963, box 26, Conrad L. Wirth Collection, University of Wyoming, American Heritage Center; Conrad L. Wirth to Stewart L. Udall, October 18, 1963, Personal Papers of Conrad L. Wirth, RG 79, National Archives; telephone interview with George B. Hartzog Jr., December 14, 2005.

48. Hartzog, *Battling for the National Parks,* 71–78; "An Analysis of the MISSION 66 Program Made by C. L. Wirth at a Meeting at the Grand Canyon in 1961."

49. Hartzog, *Battling for the National Parks,* 76, 79. In a 1965 interview Hartzog said that when he approached Wirth in 1962 before leaving the Park Service, Wirth told him he was "on the list" for associate director but gave no indication that he would be chosen. Either way, Wirth made no effort to keep him from leaving the agency. "George B. Hartzog: The National Parks, 1965," interview by Amelia R. Fry, Bancroft Library, University of California, Berkeley, Regional Oral History Office, 10.

50. Hartzog, *Battling for the National Parks,* 72, 90.

51. Whatever conclusions one comes to with regard to Hartzog's appointment, Udall politicized the Park Service in other ways. Until the 1960s the Advisory Board on National Parks, Historic Sites, Buildings and Monuments in Washington was made up of members whose appointment (made by the secretary of the interior) was approved by the Park Service director. The Advisory Board served as a means for directors to cultivate a group of influential supporters, who were usually knowledgeable about or at least involved in national park affairs. But Udall made appointments to the Advisory Board without consulting the Park Service, in part to reward political supporters. Foresta, *America's National Parks,* 71–74.

52. John A. Carver Jr., "Remarks . . . Conference of Challenges," October 14, 1963, box 26, Conrad L. Wirth Collection, University of Wyoming, American Heritage Center.

53. Carver also told the reporter that the position of director had been "regarded as a professional and career one" until 1953, when Eisenhower turned it into a political appointment. He was referring to the fact that in 1953 Secretary of the Interior McKay put the agency director, and one assistant to the director, into "Schedule C" civil service status. This action (which Wirth resisted) allowed for these positions to become political rather than career appointments. Wirth continued to fight the increased politicization of the Park Service throughout his retirement years. William M. Blair, "Park Service Due for Big Changes," *New York Times,* October 17, 1963; "An Analysis of the MISSION 66 Pro-

gram Made by C. L. Wirth at a Meeting at the Grand Canyon in 1961"; Wirth, *Parks, Politics, and the People,* 364–365.

54. Scoyen, "Remarks . . . Conference of Challenges"; Stewart L. Udall, "Remarks . . . Conference of Challenges," October 18, 1963, box 26, Conrad L. Wirth Collection, University of Wyoming, American Heritage Center.

55. The division of the park system into three park types was made official Park Service policy with the adoption of Hartzog's park system plan of 1972. Hartzog credited the original concept to a suggestion by Robert Coates; but different versions of the idea dated back to the 1930s. Hartzog, *Battling for the National Parks,* 102.

56. Quotations throughout this discussion are from "The Road to the Future: Long Range Objectives, Goals and Guidelines for the National Park Service, Department of the Interior," 1964, Personal Papers of Conrad L. Wirth, RG 79, National Archives.

57. Sellars describes the resistance of "traditional management culture" to scientific research at the Park Service. Sellars, *Preserving Nature in the National Parks,* 226–229.

58. "Mission 66 Progress Report," October 1963, National Park Service, Denver Service Center, Technical Information Center.

59. U.S. Department of the Interior, National Park Service, *Parks for America: A Study of Park and Related Resources in the Fifty States, and a Preliminary Plan* (Washington, D.C.: Government Printing Office, 1964).

60. U.S. Department of the Interior, National Park Service, *Our Vanishing Shoreline* (Washington, D.C.: Government Printing Office, n.d. [1959]); Wirth, *Parks, Politics, and the People,* 55–58, 192–193.

61. U.S. Department of the Interior, National Park Service, *Our Vanishing Shoreline;* Robert W. Ludden, "Nationwide Recreation Planning," December 1, 1960, typescript conference presentation, National Park Service, Harpers Ferry Center.

62. "Parks for America Is Our Common Concern," June 8, 1961, press release, National Park Service History Collection, Harpers Ferry Center.

63. U.S. Department of the Interior, National Park Service, *Our Vanishing Shoreline;* Wirth, *Parks, Politics, and the People,* 192–200.

64. "An Analysis of the MISSION 66 Program Made by C. L. Wirth at a Meeting at the Grand Canyon in 1961"; Wirth, *Parks, Politics, and the People,* 198–200.

65. "Summary of Mission 66 Objectives and Program for Lake Mead National Recreation Area," May 4, 1956, entry A1, box 9, Personal Papers of Conrad L. Wirth, RG 79, National Archives.

66. Mackintosh, *The National Parks,* 71–78.

67. Ibid., 62–78.

68. U.S. Department of the Interior, *1956 Annual Report,* 318; U.S. Department of the Interior, *1957 Annual Report,* 321; Dudley C. Bayliss, "Planning Our National Park Roads and Our National Parkways," *Traffic Quarterly* (July 1957): 417–440.

69. "Interview with A. Clark Stratton," conducted by S. Herbert Evison, 22.

70. Phillip R. Smith Jr., "Fifty Years of Parks," *New York Times,* May 8, 1966.

71. U.S. Department of the Interior, *1959 Annual Report,* 360; U.S. Department of the Interior, *1961 Annual Report,* 382; U.S. Department of the Interior, *1963 Annual Report,* 110.

72. Mackintosh, *The National Parks,* 63.

73. Hartzog, *Battling for the National Parks,* 88.

74. Wirth was also a trustee of the National Geographic Society. Wirth began the article with an extensive defense of Tioga Road, a project he knew had cost him dearly but which he continued to feel had been justified and successful. Conrad L. Wirth, "Today in Our National Parks: The Mission Called 66," *National Geographic* 130, no. 1 (July 1966): 7–46.

75. U.S. Department of the Interior, National Park Service, *The National Park Service: 1916–1966* (Washington D.C.: Department of the Interior, National Park Service, 1966); Stewart L. Udall, "A Salute and a Challenge," *Park Maintenance* (March 1966): 12–14.

76. See, for example, "National Park Service Developing Plans for 50th Anniversary," press release, December 29, 1965, National Park Service, Harpers Ferry Archive; Smith, "Fifty Years of Parks"; Stanley A. Cain, "Fiftieth Anniversary of the National Park Service, 1916–1966," *The Living Wilderness* 30, no. 94 (Autumn 1966): 16–18.

77. See *National Park Courier* 5, no. 8 (August 1966). The American Society of Landscape Architects also held its annual meeting in Yosemite Valley in 1966 and organized a "panel presentation" with Albright, Drury, Wirth, and Carnes. The program in *Landscape Architecture* magazine mistakenly refers to the panel's topic as "Project '66."

78. George B. Hartzog Jr., "To Each National Park Service Employee," January 2, 1967; and "PARKSCAPE U.S.A.,"

memorandum, January 3, 1967, both in National Park Service History Collection, Harpers Ferry Center.

79. Mackintosh, *The National Parks,* 75–78; George B. Hartzog Jr., "Mission 66 and Parkscape," *Historic Preservation* 18, no. 4 (August 1966): 140–143; George B. Hartzog Jr., "Tomorrow in Our National Parks: Parkscape USA," *National Geographic* 130, no. 1 (July 1966): 48–92; George B. Hartzog Jr., "Parkscape USA," *Parks & Recreation* 1, no. 8 (August 1966): 616–620.

80. R. Bryce Workman, *National Park Service Uniforms: The Developing Years, 1932–1970* (Harpers Ferry, W.V.: National Park Service, Harpers Ferry Center, 1998), 44–46.

81. Although many of these had been transferred from the Park Service, Udall was careful not to place any former Park Service officials in top management positions at the BOR. Fitch and Shanklin, *The Bureau of Outdoor Recreation,* 92–93, 189, 200–201.

82. U.S. Department of the Interior, National Park Service, "Denver Service Center," 1977, unpublished report, National Park Service, Denver, Technical Information Center; Harlan D. Unrau, "A History of the Denver Service Center," 1999, draft unpublished report, Denver Service Center; Hartzog, *Battling for the National Parks,* 100.

83. Hartzog, *Battling for the National Parks,* 239–248.

84. Mackintosh, *The National Park System,* 86–100. The story of the Alaskan parks (the national monuments declared by President Carter in 1978 and the Alaska National Interest Lands Conservation Act of 1980) is a history in itself and is not considered here.

85. Foresta, *America's National Parks,* 90–91.

86. *National Parks for the Twenty-first Century: The Vail Agenda,* 2nd ed. (Washington, D.C.: National Park Foundation, n.d.[1994]), 19, 83–86.

CONCLUSION

1. Ansel Adams, "Tenaya Tragedy," *Sierra Club Bulletin* 43, no. 9 (November 1958): 1–4.

2. Garrett Hardin, "The Tragedy of the Commons," *Science* 162 (December 1968): 1243–48.

3. In addition, Park Service staff assembled a March 1966 "Progress Report" replete with statistics. A "20th Anniversary" celebration was also held in Gatlinburg, Tennessee, in 1975 (National Park Service, Harpers Ferry Center). In 1976 Wirth prepared "Mission 66 Revisited," an unpublished history submitted to the Park Service (National Park Service, Denver Technical Information Center).

4. Rettie, *Our National Park System,* 251–253.

5. For complete statistics as kept by the Park Service, see www.nps.gov/refdesk.

6. "Mission 66: To Provide Adequate Protection and Development of the National Park System for Human Use," January 1956, unpublished report, National Park Service, Denver Service Center Library.

7. "Fixing Up the National Parks," editorial, *New York Times,* June 26, 2004.

Abbey, Edward. *Desert Solitaire: A Season in the Wilderness.* New York: Ballantine Books, 1968.

Adams, Ansel. "Yosemite—1958: Compromise in Action." *National Parks Magazine* 32, no. 135 (October 1958): 166–190.

Albrecht, Donald, ed. *World War II and the American Dream: How Wartime Building Changed a Nation.* Cambridge: MIT Press, 1995.

Albright, Horace M. "The Everlasting Wilderness." *Saturday Evening Post* 201, no. 13 (September 1928): 28, 63–68.

Allaback, Sarah. *Mission 66 Visitor Centers: The History of a Building Type.* Washington, D.C.: Government Printing Office, 2000.

Allin, Craig W. *The Politics of Wilderness Preservation.* Westport, Conn.: Greenwood Press, 1982.

Alofsin, Anthony. *The Struggle for Modernism: Architecture, Landscape Architecture, and City Planning at Harvard.* New York: Norton, 2002.

Ames, David L., and Linda Flint McClelland. *Historic Residential Suburbs: Guidelines for Evaluation and Documentation for the National Register of Historic Places.* Washington, D.C.: Government Printing Office, 2002.

Appleman, Roy E. "A History of the National Park Service Mission 66 Program." Unpublished report. U.S. Department of the Interior, National Park Service, 1958.

Audience Research, Inc. "A Survey of the Public Concerning National Parks." Unpublished report for National Park Service, Denver, Technical Information Center, 1955.

Baldwin, William C. "Wherry and Capehart: Army Family Housing Privatization Programs in the 1950s." *Engineer* (April 1996): 42–44.

Barringer, Mark Daniel. "Mission Impossible: National Park Development in the 1950s." *Journal of the West* 38, no. 1 (January 1999): 22–26.

_____. *Selling Yellowstone: Capitalism and the Construction of Nature.* Lawrence: University Press of Kansas, 2002.

Bartlett, Richard A. *Yellowstone: A Wilderness Besieged.* Tucson: University of Arizona Press, 1985.

Bayliss, Dudley C. "Parkway Development under the National Park Service." *Parks & Recreation* 20 (February 1937): 255–299.

_____. "Planning Our National Park Roads and Our National Parkways." *Traffic Quarterly* (July 1957): 417–440.

Becket, Welton. "Shopping Center Traffic Problems." *Traffic Quarterly* 9 (April 1955): 162–172.

Bellavia, Regina M. *Cultural Landscape Report for Jefferson National Expansion Memorial, St. Louis, Missouri.* Omaha: Government Printing Office, 1996.

Benevolo, Leonardo. *History of Modern Architecture.* 1960. 2 vols. Cambridge: MIT Press, 1977.

Bishop, M. Guy. "Mission 66 in the National Parks of Southern California and the Southwest." *Southern California Quarterly* 80 (Fall 1998): 293–314.

Blair, William M. "Saving the Parks: Ten-Year Program Is Urged to Bring Overtaxed Facilities Up to Date." *New York Times,* February 12, 1956.

Bradley, Harold C. "Yosemite's Problem Road." *Pacific Discovery* (January 1950): 3–8.

Bradley, Harold C., and David R. Brower. "Roads in National Parks." *Sierra Club Bulletin* 34, no. 6 (June 1949): 31–54.

Branyan, Robert L., and Lawrence H. Larsen. *The Eisenhower Administration, 1953–1961: A Documentary History.* New York: Random House, 1971.

Brockman, C. Frank. "Park Naturalists and the Evolution of National Park Service Interpretation through World War II." *Journal of Forest History* 22, no. 1 (January 1978): 24–43.

Brooks, Paul. "The Pressure of Numbers." *Atlantic* 207, no. 2 (February 1961): 54–56.

————. *The Pursuit of Wilderness.* Boston: Houghton Mifflin, 1971.

Brower, David R. *For Earth's Sake: The Life and Times of David Brower.* Salt Lake City: Peregrine Smith Books, 1990.

————. "Mission 65 Is Proposed by Reviewer of Park Service's Brochure on Wilderness." *National Parks Magazine* 32, no. 132 (January 1958): 3–6, 45–48.

Brown, Sharon A. *Administrative History: Jefferson National Expansion Memorial Historic Site.* U.S. Department of the Interior, National Park Service, 1984.

Brown, William E. *Denali: Symbol of the Alaskan Wild.* Denali National Park: Denali Natural History Association, 1993.

Butcher, Devereux. "For a Return to Harmony in Park Architecture." *National Parks Magazine* 26, no. 111 (October 1952): 150–157.

————. "Resorts or Wilderness?" *Atlantic* 207, no. 2 (February 1961): 45–51.

————. "Sunshine and Blizzard: Afield with Your Representative." *National Parks Magazine* 31, no. 128 (January 1957): 24–33.

Butcher, Harold. "Our National Parks in Wartime." *Travel Magazine* 83, no. 4 (August 1944): 26–27.

Cabot, John B. "Creative Park Architecture." *Park Practice Guideline.* U.S. Department of the Interior, National Park Service, July 1963. 53–55.

Cameron, Jenks. *The National Park Service: Its History, Activities, and Organization.* Institute for Government Research, Service Monographs of the United States Government, no. 11. New York: D. Appleton and Company, 1922.

Carnes, William G. "Landscape Architecture in the National Park Service." *Landscape Architecture* 41, no. 4 (July 1951): 145–150.

Carr, Ethan. *Wilderness by Design: Landscape Architecture and the National Park Service.* Lincoln: University of Nebraska Press, 1998.

Carson, Rachel. *Silent Spring.* Cambridge: Riverside Press, 1962.

Catton, Theodore. *Wonderland: An Administrative History of Mount Rainier National Park.* Seattle: U.S. Department of the Interior, National Park Service, 1996.

Chase, Alston. *Playing God in Yellowstone: The Destruction of America's First National Park.* New York: Harcourt Brace Jovanovich, 1986.

Clawson, Marion. *Land and Water for Recreation: Opportunities, Problems, and Policies.* Policy Background Series. Chicago: Rand McNally & Co., 1963.

Clawson, Marion, and Jack L. Knetsch. *Economics of Outdoor Recreation.* Published for Resources for the Future, Inc. Baltimore: Johns Hopkins University Press, 1966.

Clay, Grady. "Ruin Our Parks? How to Survive 40,000,000 Tourists." *Landscape Architecture* 49, no. 2 (Winter 1958): 71.

Cohen, Lizbeth. *A Consumers' Republic: The Politics of Mass Consumption in Postwar America.* New York: Alfred A. Knopf, 2003.

————. "From Town Center to Shopping Center: The Reconfiguration of Community Marketplaces in Postwar America." *American Historical Review* 101, no. 4 (October 1996): 1050–81.

Cohen, Michael P. *The History of the Sierra Club, 1892–1970.* San Francisco: Sierra Club Books, 1988.

Cohen, Nancy E. *America's Marketplace: The History of Shopping Centers.* Lyme, Conn.: Greenwich Publishing Group, 2002.

Colby, William E. "Yosemite's Fatal Beauty." *Sierra Club Bulletin* 33, no. 3 (March 1948): 79–108.

Collins, Peter. *Changing Ideals in Modern Architecture.* Montreal: McGill University Press, 1965.

Congressional Quarterly Service. *Housing a Nation.* Washington, D.C.: Government Printing Office, 1966.

Constant, Caroline. "From the Virgilian Dream to Chandigarh." *Architectural Review* 181, no. 1079 (January 1987): 66–72.

Contemporary Landscape Architecture and Its Sources. Exhibition catalog. San Francisco: San Francisco Museum of Art, 1937.

Cox, Elbert. "MISSION '66': A Program to Develop Our National Parks." *Virginia Forests* (Spring 1960): 5–12.

Cox, Laurie Davidson. "The Green Mountain Parkway." *Landscape Architecture* 25, no. 3 (April 1935): 117–126.

Craig, Lois, et al. *The Federal Presence: Architecture, Politics, and Symbols in United States Government Building.* Cambridge: MIT Press, 1979.

Cramer, Sterling S. "Crisis in Yosemite." *National Parks Magazine* 101, no. 24 (June 1950): 41–50, 77.

Cronon, William, ed. *Uncommon Ground: Rethinking the Human Place in Nature.* New York: W. W. Norton and Company, 1996.

Culpin, Mary Shivers. *"For the Benefit and Enjoyment of the People": A History of Concession Development in Yellowstone National Park, 1872–1966.* National Park Service, Yellowstone Center for Resources, YCR-CR-2003-01, Yellowstone National Park, 2003.

_____. *The History of the Construction of the Road System in Yellowstone National Park, 1872–1966.* Selections from the Division of Cultural Resources, Rocky Mountain Region, no. 5. Denver: Government Printing Office, 1994.

Davis, Timothy. "Rock Creek and Potomac Parkway, Washington D.C.: The Evolution of a Contested Urban Landscape." *Studies in the History of Gardens & Designed Landscapes* 19, no. 2 (Summer 1999): 123–237.

Davis, Timothy, Todd A. Croteau, and Christopher H. Marston. *America's National Park Roads and Parkways: Drawings from the Historic American Engineering Record.* Baltimore: Johns Hopkins University Press, 2004.

DeVoto, Bernard. "Let's Close the National Parks." *Harper's Magazine* 207, no. 1241 (October 1953): 49–52.

_____. "Shall We Let Them Ruin Our National Parks?" *Saturday Evening Post* 223, no. 4 (July 1950): 17–19, 42–46.

Dilsaver, Lary M. *America's National Park System: The Critical Documents.* Lanham Way, Md.: Rowman and Littlefield, 1994.

Dilsaver, Lary M., and William C. Tweed. *Challenge of the Big Trees: A Resource History of Sequoia and Kings Canyon National Parks.* Three Rivers, Calif.: Sequoia Natural History Association, 1990.

Doell, Charles E., and Gerald B. Fitzgerald. *A Brief History of Parks and Recreation in the United States.* Chicago: The Athletic Institute, 1954.

Douglas, Marjory Stoneman. *The Everglades: River of Grass.* New York: Rinehart & Company, 1947.

Drury, Newton B. "The Dilemma of Our Parks." *American Forests* 55, no. 6 (June 1949): 6–11, 38–39.

_____. "The National Park Concept." *National Parks Magazine* 23, no. 97 (April 1949): 28–34.

_____. "The National Park Service: The First Thirty Years." In *American Planning and Civic Annual.* Ed. Harlean James. Washington, D.C.: American Planning and Civic Association, 1946.

_____. "National Park Service Grazing Policy." *National Parks Magazine* 16, no. 70 (June 1944): 16-17.

_____. "The National Parks." In *American Planning and Civic Annual.* Ed. Harlean James. Washington, D.C.: American Planning and Civic Association, 1950.

_____. "The National Parks in Wartime: A Review of the Year." In *American Planning and Civic Annual.* Ed. Harlean James. Washington, D.C.: American Planning and Civic Association, 1942.

_____. "The National Parks Start Back." In *American Planning and Civic Annual.* Ed. Harlean James. Washington, D.C.: American Planning and Civic Association, 1947.

_____. "Planning for National Parks and Parkways." In *American Planning and Civic Annual.* Ed. Harlean James. Washington, D.C.: American Planning and Civic Association, 1948.

_____. "Preserving Nature . . . Our National Policy." *The Living Wilderness* 17, no. 40 (Spring 1952): 1–4.

Dunlap, Thomas R. *Saving America's Wildlife.* Princeton: Princeton University Press, 1988.

Eisenhower, Dwight D. *Mandate for Change.* Garden City, N.Y.: Doubleday & Co., 1963.

Ernst, Joseph W., ed. *Worthwhile Places: Correspondence of John D. Rockefeller Jr. and Horace M. Albright.* New York: Fordham University Press, 1991.

Everhart, William C. *The National Park Service.* 1972. Boulder: Westview Press, 1983.

Ferguson, Bruce K. *Landscape Architecture Magazine Cumulative Index, 1910–1986.* Mesa, Ariz.: PDA Publishers Corporation, 1988.

Fitch, Edwin M., and John F. Shanklin. *The Bureau of Outdoor Recreation.* New York: Praeger Publishers, 1970.

Flader, Susan L. *Thinking Like a Mountain: Aldo Leopold and* the *Evolution of an Ecological Attitude toward Deer, Wolves, and Forests.* Columbia: University of Missouri Press, 1974.

Foresta, Ronald A. *America's National Parks and Their Keepers.* Washington, D.C.: Resources for the Future, 1984.

Frampton, Kenneth. *Modern Architecture: A Critical History.* Rev. and enlarged ed. New York: Thames and Hudson, 1985.

Frome, Michael. *Greenspeak: Fifty Years of Environmental Muckraking and Advocacy.* Knoxville: University of Tennessee Press, 2002.

Garrison, Lemuel A. *The Making of a Ranger: Forty Years with the National Parks.* An Institute of the American West Book. Salt Lake City: Howe Brothers, 1983.

————. "Mission 66." *National Parks Magazine* 29, no. 122 (July 1955): 107–108.

Giedeon, Sigfried. *Space, Time, and Architecture: The Growth of a New Tradition.* 1941. 5th ed., rev. and enlarged. Cambridge: Harvard University Press, 1970.

Gilstrap, Max K. "Our National Parks: A Heritage Worth Saving." *Christian Science Monitor,* January 1956–May 1956.

Glass, James A. *The Beginnings of a National Historic Preservation Program, 1957 to 1959.* Nashville: American Association for State and Local History, 1990.

Glover, James M. *A Wilderness Original: The Life of Bob Marshall.* Seattle: The Mountaineers, 1986.

Goble, Emerson. "Architecture (?) for the National Parks." *Architectural Record* 121, no. 1 (January 1957): 173–185.

Goodman, Jack. "Controversy over Lodge in the West." *New York Times,* August 7, 1955.

Graham, Frank, Jr. *The Audubon Ark: A History of the National Audubon Society.* New York: Alfred A. Knopf, 1990.

Greene, Linda Wedel. *Yosemite: The Park and Its Resources.* 3 vols. Washington, D.C.: Department of the Interior, National Park Service, 1987.

Greiff, Constance M. *Independence: The Creation of a National Park.* Philadelphia: University of Pennsylvania Press, 1987.

Gross, Michael, and Ron Zimmerman. *Interpretive Centers: The History, Design, and Development of Nature and Visitor Centers.* Stevens Point, Wis.: UW-SP Foundation Press, 2002.

Gruen, Victor, and Larry Smith. *Shopping Towns USA: The Planning of Shopping Centers.* New York: Reinhold Publishing Corporation, 1960.

Gruen, Victor, and Lawrence P. Smith. "Shopping Centers: The New Building Type." *Progressive Architecture* (June 1952): 66–109.

Haines, Aubrey L. *The Yellowstone Story.* 2 vols. Boulder: Yellowstone Library and Museum Association in cooperation with Colorado Associated University Press, 1977.

Hammons, Vernon L. "A Brief Organizational History of the Office of Design and Construction, National Park Service, 1917–1962." Unpublished report. U.S. Department of the Interior, National Park Service, n.d.

Hardin, Garrett. "The Tragedy of the Commons." *Science* 162 (December 1968): 1243–48.

Harrison, Laura Soulliere. *Architecture in the Parks: National Historic Landmark Theme Study.* Washington, D.C.: Government Printing Office, 1986.

Hartzog, George B., Jr. *Battling for the National Parks.* Mount Kisco, N.Y.: Moyer Bell, 1988.

————. "Mission 66 and Parkscape." *Historic Preservation* 18, no. 4 (August 1966): 140–143.

————. "Parkscape USA." *Parks & Recreation* 1, no. 8 (August 1966): 616–620.

————. "Tomorrow in Our National Parks: Parkscape USA." *National Geographic* 130, no. 1 (July 1966): 48–92.

Harvey, Mark W. T. *A Symbol of Wilderness: Echo Park and the American Conservation Movement.* Albuquerque: University of New Mexico Press, 1994.

Hays, Samuel P. *Beauty, Health, and Permanence: Environmental Politics in the United States, 1955–1985.* New York: Cambridge University Press, 1987.

————. *A History of Environmental Politics since 1945.* Pittsburgh: University of Pittsburgh Press, 2000.

Heald, Weldon F. "Urbanization of the National Parks." *National Parks Magazine* 35, no. 160 (January 1961): 7–9.

Hitchcock, Henry-Russell, and Phillip Johnson. *The International Style: Architecture since 1922.* 1932. New York: W. W. Norton & Co., 1966.

Holt, W. Stull. *The Bureau of Public Roads: Its History, Activities, and Organization.* Institute for Government Research, Service Monographs of the United States Government, no. 26. Baltimore: Johns Hopkins University Press, 1923.

Hosmer, Charles B., Jr. *Preservation Comes of Age: From Williamsburg to the National Trust, 1926–1949.* 2 vols. Charlottesville: University Press of Virginia, 1981.

Hubbard, Henry V. "The Designer in National Parks: The Preservation and Enhancement of Natural Scenery." *Landscape Architecture* 38, no. 2 (January 1948): 58–60.

————. "Landscape Development Based in Conservation as Practiced in the National Park Service." *Landscape Architecture* 29, no. 3 (April 1939): 105–121.

Hummel, Don. *Stealing the National Parks: The Destruction of Concessions and Public Access.* Bellevue, Wash.: Free Enterprise Press, 1987.

Huth, Hans. *Nature and the American: Three Centuries of Changing Attitudes.* 1957. Lincoln: University of Nebraska Press, Bison Books, 1990.

————. "Yosemite: The Story of an Idea." *Sierra Club Bulletin* 33, no. 3 (March 1948): 47–78.

Ise, John. *Our National Park Policy: A Critical History.* Baltimore: Johns Hopkins University Press, 1961.

Jackson, Kenneth T. *Crabgrass Frontier: The Suburbanization of the United States.* New York: Oxford University Press, 1985.

Jameson, John. *The Story of Big Bend National Park.* Austin: University of Texas Press, 1996.

Jofuku, Tracey Lynne. "That the Past Shall Live: Conrad Wirth and the National Park Service, 1951–1963." B.A. thesis, Harvard University, 1991.

Jones, Holway R. *John Muir and the Sierra Club: The Battle for Yosemite.* San Francisco: Sierra Club, 1965.

Jordy, William H. *The Impact of European Modernism in the Mid-Twentieth Century.* Vol. 5 of *American Buildings and Their Architects.* New York: Oxford University Press, 1972.

Kaufman, Polly Welts. *National Parks and the Woman's Voice: A History.* Albuquerque: University of New Mexico Press, 1996.

Kieley, James F. "A Brief History of the National Park Service." Unpublished report. Washington, D.C.: Department of the Interior, Main Interior Library, 1940.

Koehler, Robert E. "Our Park Service Serves Architecture Well." *AIA Journal* 1 (January 1971): 18–25.

Koppes, Clayton R. "Environmental Policy and American Liberalism: The Department of the Interior, 1933–1953." *Environmental Review* 7 (Spring 1983): 17–53.

Krueckeberg, Donald A., ed. *Introduction to Planning History in the United States.* New Brunswick, N.J.: Center for Urban Policy Research, Rutgers University, 1983.

Kurian, George Thomas. *Datapedia of the United States, 1790–2000: America Year by Year.* Lanham, Md.: Bernan Press, 1994.

Lee, Ronald F. *Family Tree of the National Park System.* Philadelphia: Eastern National Park and Monument Association, 1972.

————. *The Origin and Evolution of the National Military Park Idea.* Washington, D.C.: Department of the Interior, National Park Service, 1973.

————. *Public Use of the National Park System: 1872–2000.* Washington, D.C.: Department of the Interior, National Park Service, 1968.

Leopold, Aldo. *A Sand County Almanac, with Essays on Conservation from Round River.* 1949. New York: Ballantine Books, 1966.

Lewis, Ralph H. *Museum Curatorship in the National Park Service, 1904–1982.* Washington, D.C.: Department of the Interior, National Park Service, 1993.

Lewis, Tom. *Divided Highways: Building the Interstate Highways, Transforming American Life.* New York: Viking Penguin, 1997.

Lien, Carsten. *Olympic Battleground: The Power Politics of Timber Preservation.* San Francisco: Sierra Club Books, 1991.

Litton, Martin. "Yosemite's Beauty Fast Disappearing." *National Parks Magazine* 26, no. 111 (October 1952–December 1952): 164–168.

Longstreth, Richard. *City Center to Regional Mall: Architecture, the Automobile, and Retailing in Los Angeles, 1920–1950.* Cambridge: MIT Press, 1997.

————. *The Drive-In, the Supermarket, and the Transformation of Commercial Space in Los Angeles, 1914–1941.* Cambridge: MIT Press, 1999.

Mackintosh, Barry. *Historic Sites Survey and National Historic Landmark Programs: A History.* Washington, D.C.: Department of the Interior, National Park Service, 1985.

————. *Interpretation in the National Park Service.* Washington, D.C.: Department of the Interior, National Park Service, 1986.

————. "The National Park Service Moves into Historical Interpretation." *Public Historian* 9, no. 2 (Spring 1987): 51–63.

————. *The National Parks: Shaping the System.* Washington, D.C.: Government Printing Office, 1991.

————. *Visitor Fees in the National Park System: A Legislative and Administrative History.* Washington, D.C.: Department of the Interior, National Park Service, 1983.

Madrid, Christine L. "The Mission 66 Visitor Centers: Early Modern Architecture in the National Park Service, 1956–1976." Master's thesis, University of Virginia, 1998.

Maier, Herbert, and Albert H. Good. "Structures in State Parks—An Apologia." In *American Planning and Civic Annual.* Ed. Harlean James. Washington, D.C.: American Planning and Civic Association, 1935.

Martinson, Arthur David. "Mountain in the Sky: A History of Mount Rainier National Park." Master's thesis, Washington State University, 1966.

Maxwell, Ross A. *Big Bend Country: A History of Big Bend National Park.* Big Bend National Park, Tex.: Big Bend Natural History Association, 1985.

McClelland, Linda Flint. *Building the National Parks: Historic Landscape Design and Construction.* Baltimore: Johns Hopkins University Press, 1998.

McPhee, John. *Encounters with the Archdruid.* New York: Farrar, Straus and Giroux, 1971.

Mickel, Ernest. "Mission 66, A New Challenge to Architects: Long-Range Building Plan for National Parks." *Architectural Record* 120, no. 2 (August 1956): 32.

Miles, John C. *Guardians of the Parks: A History of the National Parks and Conservation Association.* Washington, D.C.: National Parks and Conservation Association, 1995.

Monroe, Jonathan Searle. "Architecture in the National Parks: Cecil Doty and Mission 66." Master's thesis, University of Washington, 1986.

Mozingo, Louise A. "The Corporate Estate in the USA, 1954–64: 'Thoroughly Modern in Concept, but . . . Down to Earth and Rugged.'" *Studies in the History of Gardens and Designed Landscapes* 20, no. 1 (January 2000): 25–56.

Murie, Adolph. "Road Building in Mount McKinley National Park." *National Parks Magazine* (July 1965): 4–8.

Murie, Olaus J. "Mount McKinley: Wilderness Park of the North Country." *National Parks Magazine* 37, no. 187 (April 1963): 4–7.

Nash, Roderick. *Wilderness and the American Mind.* 1967. 3rd ed. New Haven: Yale University Press, 1982.

National Parks Magazine. "Mission 66 Reappraised." *National Parks Magazine* 35, no. 163 (April 1961): inside front cover.

Neel, Susan Rhoades. "Irreconcilable Differences: Reclamation, Preservation, and the Origins of the Echo Park Controversy." Ph.D. diss., University of California, Los Angeles, 1990.

Netboy, Anthony. "Crisis in Our Parks." *American Forests* 61, no. 5 (May 1955): 24–27, 46–47.

Newhall, Nancy. *A Contribution to the Heritage of Every American: The Conservation Activities of John D. Rockefeller Jr.* New York: Alfred A. Knopf, 1957.

Noll, William N. "Mission 66: The National Park Service Program for the Revitalization of America's National Parks, 1955–1966." Master's thesis, Kansas State University, 1997.

Oelschlaeger, Max. *The Idea of Wilderness: From Prehistory to the Age of Ecology.* New Haven: Yale University Press, 1991.

Olmsted, Frederick Law, Jr. *Report of State Park Survey of California.* Sacramento: California State Park Commission, 1929.

Olsen, Russell K. *Administrative History: Organizational Structures of the National Park Service, 1917–1985.* Washington, D.C.: Government Printing Office, 1985.

Outdoor Recreation Resources Review Commission. *Outdoor Recreation for America: A Report to the President and to Congress by the Outdoor Recreation Resources Review Commission.* Washington, D.C.: Government Printing Office, 1962.

Pack, Anthony Newton. "Practical Idealism in Our Parks." *Nature Magazine* 32, no. 2 (February 1939): 97–98.

Packard, Fred M. "An Appraisal of Mission 66." *National Parks Magazine* 30, no. 125 (April 1956): 61–62, 91–95.

Peterson, Charles E. "HABS: In and Out of Philadelphia." In *Philadelphia Preserved: Catalog of the Historic American Buildings Survey,* xxi–xlvi. Ed. Richard Webster. Philadelphia: Temple University Press, 1976.

Pritchard, James A. *Preserving Yellowstone's Natural Conditions: Science and the Perception of Nature.* Lincoln: University of Nebraska Press, 1999.

Rettie, Dwight F. *Our National Park System: Caring for America's Greatest Natural and Historic Treasures.* Urbana: University of Illinois Press, 1995.

Richardson, Elmo. *Dams, Parks, and Politics.* Lexington: University Press of Kentucky, 1973.

————. *The Presidency of Dwight D. Eisenhower.* Lawrence: Regents Press of Kansas, 1979.

Ridenour, James M. *The National Parks Compromised: Pork Barrel Politics and America's Treasures.* Merrillville, Ind.: ICS Books, 1994.

Righter, Robert W. *Crucible for Conservation: The Struggle for Grand Teton National Park.* 1982. Moose, Wyo.: Grand Teton Natural History Association, 2000.

Rose, Mark H. *Interstate: Express Highway Politics, 1939–1989.* Rev. ed. Knoxville: University of Tennessee Press, 1990.

Roth, Dennis M. *The Wilderness Movement and the National Forests.* College Station, Tex.: Intaglio Press, 1988.

Rothman, Hal. *America's National Monuments: The Politics of Preservation.* Lawrence: University Press of Kansas by arrangement with the University of Illinois Press, 1989.

Runte, Alfred. *National Parks: The American Experience.* 1979. 2nd ed., rev. Lincoln: University of Nebraska Press, 1987.

————. *Yosemite: The Embattled Wilderness.* Lincoln: University of Nebraska Press, 1990.

Sax, Joseph L. *Mountains without Handrails: Reflections on the National Parks.* Ann Arbor: University of Michigan Press, 1980.

Schullery, Paul. *Searching for Yellowstone: Ecology and Wonder in the Last Wilderness.* Boston: Houghton Mifflin, 1997.

Scott, Mel. *American City Planning since 1890.* Berkeley: University of California Press, 1969.

Seely, Bruce E. *Building the American Highway System: Engineers as Policy Makers.* Philadelphia: Temple University Press, 1987.

Sellars, Richard West. *Preserving Nature in the National Parks: A History.* New Haven: Yale University Press, 1997.

————. "The Rise and Decline of Ecological Attitudes in National Park Mangement, 1929–1940: Part 1." *George Wright Forum* 10, no. 1 (1993): 55–78.

————. "The Roots of National Park Management." *Journal of Forestry* 90, no. 1 (January 1992): 16–19.

————. "Science or Scenery?" *Wilderness* 52, no. 185 (Summer 1989): 29–34.

————. "The University of California: Present at the Creation." *Courier: Newsmagazine of the National Park Service* 35, no. 2 (February 1990): 4.

Shephard, Paul A., Jr. "Something Amiss in the National Parks." *National Parks Magazine* 27, no. 115 (October 1953–December 1953): 150–151, 187–190.

Shurcliff, Sidney N. "Shoppers' World: The Design and Construction of a Retail Shopping Center." *Landscape Architecture* 42, no. 4 (July 1952): 145–151.

Simo, Melanie. *The Coalescing of Different Forces and Ideas: A History of Landscape Architecture at Harvard, 1900–1999.* Cambridge: Harvard University Graduate School of Design, 2000.

————. *Forest and Garden: Traces of Wilderness in a Modernizing Land, 1897–1949.* Charlottesville: University of Virginia Press, 2003.

————. *One Hundred Years of Landscape Architecture: Some Patterns of a Century.* Washington, D.C.: ASLA Press, 1999.

Sontag, William H., ed. *National Park Service: The First Seventy-five Years.* Philadelphia: Eastern Park and Monument Association, 1990.

Spence, Mark David. *Dispossessing the Wilderness: Indian Removal and the Making of the National Parks.* New York: Oxford University Press, 1999.

Stagner, Howard R. *The National Park Wilderness.* Washington, D.C.: Government Printing Office, 1957.

————. "Preservation of Natural and Wilderness Values in the National Parks." Unpublished report. U.S. Department of the Interior, National Park Service, 1957.

Steen, Harold K. *The U.S. Forest Service: A History.* Seattle: University of Washington Press, 1991.

Stegner, Wallace, ed. *This Is Dinosaur: Echo Park Country and Its Magic Rivers.* New York: Alfred A. Knopf, 1955.

Stevenson, Charles. "The Shocking Truth about Our National Parks." *Reader's Digest* 66, no. 393 (January 1955): 45–50.

Stroud, Richard H., ed. *National Leaders of American Conservation.* Washington, D.C.: Smithsonian Institution Press, 1985.

Sullivan, Timothy Allan. "The Visitor Centers of the National Park Service Mission 66 Era: A Historical Analysis and Reuse Proposal." Master's thesis, Columbia University, 1998.

Sutter, Paul S. *Driven Wild: How the Fight against Automobiles Launched the Modern Wilderness Movement.* Seattle: University of Washington Press, 2002.

Swain, Donald. L. *Wilderness Defender: Horace M. Albright and Conservation.* Chicago: University of Chicago Press, 1970.

Swift, Ernest. "Parks—Or Resorts?" *National Parks Magazine* 31, no. 131 (October 1957): 147–148.

Tilden, Freeman. *Interpreting Our Heritage: Principles and Practices for Visitor Services in Parks, Museums, and Historic Places.* Chapel Hill: University of North Carolina Press, 1957.

_____. *The National Parks: What They Mean to You and Me.* New York: Alfred A. Knopf, 1951.

Tilden, Paul M., and Nancy L. Machler. "The Development of Mount McKinley National Park." *National Parks Magazine* 37, no. 188 (May 1963): 10–15.

Tolson, Hillory A. *Historic Listing of National Park Service Officials.* 1964. Rev. 75th anniversary ed. Ed. Harold P. Danz. Denver: Department of the Interior, National Park Service, 1991.

_____. *Laws Relating to the National Park Service, the National Parks, and Monuments.* Washington, D.C.: Government Printing Office, 1933.

Treib, Marc, ed. *The Architecture of Landscape, 1940–1960.* Philadelphia: University of Pennsylvania Press, 2002.

_____. *Modern Landscape Architecture: A Critical Review.* Cambridge: MIT Press, 1993.

Trexler, Keith A. "The Tioga Road: A History." *Yosemite* 40, no. 3 (June 1961): 31–58.

Tunnard, Christopher. *Gardens in the Modern Landscape.* London: Architectural Press, 1938.

Tunnard, Christopher, and Boris Pushkarev. *Man-Made America: Chaos or Control? An Inquiry into Selected Problems of Design in the Urbanized Landscape.* New Haven: Yale University Press, 1963.

U.S. Department of Agriculture. Forest Service. *Operation Outdoors.* Part 1. *National Forest Recreation.* Washington, D.C.: Government Printing Office, 1957.

U.S. Department of Commerce. Bureau of the Census. *Two Hundred Million Americans.* Washington, D.C.: Government Printing Office, 1967.

U.S. Department of the Interior. National Park Service. *Annual Report of the Director of the National Park Service to the Secretary of the Interior.* Washington, D.C.: Government Printing Office, 1941–1963.

_____. *Draft Environmental Statement, General Management Plan, Yosemite National Park, California.* Washington, D.C.: Government Printing Office, 1978.

_____. *EODC Handbook.* Washington, D.C.: Department of the Interior, National Park Service, 1963.

_____. *Future Parks for the Nation.* Washington D.C.: Department of the Interior, National Park Service, n.d. [ca. 1962].

_____. "The Master Plan Handbook." Unpublished report. U.S. Department of the Interior, National Park Service, 1959.

_____. *Mission 66 in Action.* Washington, D.C.: Department of the Interior, National Park Service, n.d. [ca. 1957].

_____. *Mission 66 for the National Park System.* Washington, D.C.: Government Printing Office, 1956.

_____. *Mission 66 Progress Report.* Washington, D.C.: Department of the Interior, National Park Service, 1963.

_____. *Mission 66 Progress Report.* Washington, D.C.: Department of the Interior, National Park Service, 1966.

_____. *Mission 66: Questions and Answers.* Washington, D.C.: Department of the Interior, National Park Service, 1956.

_____. "Mission 66 Report." Unpublished report. U.S. Department of the Interior, National Park Service, 1955.

_____. *The National Park Service: 1916–1966.* Washington D.C.: Department of the Interior, National Park Service, 1966.

_____. *National Park Service Administrative Manual.* Vol. 4. *Design and Construction.* Washington, D.C.: Department of the Interior, National Park Service, 1962.

_____. *The National Park System.* Washington D.C.: Department of the Interior, National Park Service, n.d. [ca. 1955].

_____. *Our Heritage, a Plan for Its Protection and Use: "Mission 66."* Washington, D.C.: Government Printing Office, 1956.

_____. *Our Vanishing Shoreline.* Washington, D.C.: Government Printing Office, n.d. [1957].

_____. *Park Use Studies and Demonstrations.* Washington, D.C.: Government Printing Office, 1941.

_____. *Parks for America: A Study of Park and Related Resources in the Fifty States, and a Preliminary Plan.* Washington, D.C.: Government Printing Office, 1964.

_____. "Report of the National Park Service Mission 66 Frontiers Conference." Unpublished report. U.S. Department of the Interior, National Park Service, 1961.

_____. "Standard Plans for Employee Housing." Unpublished report. U.S. Department of the Interior, National Park Service, n.d. [1957].

_____. *A Study of the Park and Recreation Problem of the United States.* Washington, D.C.: Government Printing Office, 1941.

_____. *That the Past Shall Live.* Washington, D.C., n.d. [1959].

_____. "Visitor Center Planning: Notes on Discussions Held in EODC November 18–22, 1957, and WODC February 4–6, 1958. Unpublished report. U.S. Department of the Interior, National Park Service, n.d. [1958].

_____. *Your Mission 66 and the National Parks: A Passport to Adventure.* Washington, D.C.: Phillips Petroleum Company, n.d.

Udall, Stewart L. "National Parks for the Future." *Atlantic* 207, no. 6 (June 1961): 81–84.

_____. *The Quiet Crisis.* New York: Holt, Rinehart and Winston, 1963.

_____. *The Quiet Crisis and the Next Generation.* Salt Lake City: Peregrine Smith Books, 1988.

Van Fleet, Clark C. "Nature Out of Balance." *Atlantic* 207, no. 2 (February 1961): 52–53.

Vint, Thomas C. "Development of National Parks for Conservation." In *American Planning and Civic Annual.* Ed. Harlean James. Washington, D.C.: American Planning and Civic Association, 1938.

_____. "National Park Service Master Plans." In *Planning and Civic Comment.* Washington, D.C.: American Planning and Civic Association, 1946.

Von Eckardt, Wolf. *Mid-Century Architecture in America: Honor Awards of the American Institute of Architects, 1949–1961.* Baltimore: Johns Hopkins University Press, 1961.

_____. "The Park Service Dares to Build Well." *Washington Post,* March 29, 1964.

Walker, Peter, and Melanie Simo. *Invisible Gardens: The Search for Modernism in the American Landscape.* Cambridge: MIT Press, 1994.

Ward, Henry Baldwin. "What Is Happening to Our National Parks?" *Nature Magazine* 31, no. 10 (December 1938): 611–615.

"We've Been Starving Our National Parks." *Saturday Evening Post* 227, no. 33 (February 1955): 10.

Whiting, E. C., and W. L. Phillips. "Frederick Law Olmsted, 1870–1957." *Landscape Architecture* 48, no. 3 (April 1958): 145–157.

Wilhelm, Raymond A. "Station Wagon 'Pioneers' Invade Parks." *Landscape Architecture* 51, no. 2 (January 1961): 90–91.

Winks, Robin W. *Laurance S. Rockefeller: Catalyst for Conservation.* Washington, D.C.: Island Press, 1997.

Wirth, Conrad L. "An Adequate National Park System for 300 Million People." In *American Planning and Civic*

Annual. Ed. Harlean James. Washington, D.C.: American Planning and Civic Association, 1955.

_____. "The Aims of the National Park Service in Relation to Water Resources." In *American Planning and Civic Annual.* Ed. Harlean James. Washington, D.C.: American Planning and Civic Association, 1952.

_____. *The CCC and Its Contribution to a Nation-Wide State Park Recreational Program.* Washington, D.C.: Department of the Interior, National Park Service, n.d. [ca. 1940].

_____. *Civilian Conservation Corps Program of the United States Department of the Interior, March 1933 to June 30, 1943.* Washington, D.C.: Government Printing Office, 1944.

_____. "Federal Aid for State Parks: The NPS." In *American Planning and Civic Annual.* Ed. Harlean James. Washington, D.C.: American Planning and Civic Association, 1939.

_____. "Heritage of Beauty and History." *National Geographic* 113, no. 5 (May 1958): 587–663.

_____. "The Landscape Architect in National Park Work." *Landscape Architecture Magazine* 46, no. 1 (October 1955): 13–18.

_____. "Mission 66." *American Forests* 61, no. 8 (August 1955): 16–17.

_____. "Mission 66 in the Headlines." *National Parks Magazine* 32, no. 132 (January 1958): 8–9, 36–38.

_____. "The National Parks in Wartime." In *American Planning and Civic Annual.* Ed. Harlean James. Washington, D.C.: American Planning and Civic Association, 1943.

_____. *Parks, Politics, and the People.* Norman: University of Oklahoma Press, 1980.

_____. "Parks and Their Uses." In *American Planning and Civic Annual.* Ed. Harlean James. Washington, D.C.: American Planning and Civic Association, 1935.

_____. "Parks and Wilderness." In *Origins of American Conservation.* Ed. Henry Clapper. New York: Ronald Press Company, 1966.

_____. "The Story of Grand Teton National Park." In *American Planning and Civic Annual.* Ed. Harlean James. Washington, D.C.: American Planning and Civic Association, 1956.

_____. "Today in Our National Parks: The Mission Called 66." *National Geographic* 130, no. 1 (July 1966): 7–46.

Wirth, Conrad L., and Frederick Law Olmsted Jr. *A Survey of the Recreational Resources of the Colorado River Basin.* 1946. Washington, D.C.: Government Printing Office, 1950.

Wirth, Conrad L., and Howard Stagner. "Mission 66 Revisited." Unpublished report. U.S. Department of the Interior, National Park Service, 1976.

Wood, Jerome B. "National Parks: Tomorrow's Slums?" *Travel* 101, no. 4 (April 1954): 14–16.

Workman, Bryce R. *National Park Service Uniforms: Badges and Insignia, 1894–1991.* Harpers Ferry, W.Va.: National Park Service, Harpers Ferry Center, 1991.

————. *National Park Service Uniforms: The Developing Years, 1932–1970.* Harpers Ferry, W.Va.: National Park Service, Harpers Ferry Center, 1998.

Worster, Donald. *Nature's Economy: A History of Ecological Ideas.* 1977. 2nd ed. New York: Cambridge University Press, 1994.

Yoder, Robert M. "Twenty-four Million Acres of Trouble." *Saturday Evening Post* 227, no. 1 (July 1954): 32, 78–80.

Zach, Leon. "Landscape Architecture in Government Agencies." *Landscape Architecture* 43, no. 4 (July 1953): 150–153.

Zahniser, Howard. "The Need for Wilderness Areas." In *American Planning and Civic Annual.* Ed. Harlean James. Washington, D.C.: American Planning and Civic Association, 1955.

Zaitlin, Joyce. *George Stanley Underwood: His Rustic, Art Deco, and Federal Architecture.* Malibu, Calif.: Pangloss Press, 1989.

Zenzen, Joanne Michele. "Promoting National Parks: Images of the West in the American Imagination." Master's thesis, University of Maryland, College Park, 1997.

Zube, Ervin H., Joseph H. Crystal, and James F. Palmer. "Visitor Center Design Evaluation." Unpublished report. U.S. Department of the Interior, National Park Service, 1976.

Page numbers in *italics* refer to illustrations or material contained in their captions.

at, *172*; concessioner development in, 250–51, *251*, 364n8; dam construction projects and, 36; establishment of, 27; housing at, *167*; interpretive displays at, *210*; land acquisition for, 27; modernist architecture at, 133, *146*, 340; road construction in, *251*; visitor center at, *156*; as wilderness park, 26, 27

Big Meadows (Yosemite), 75, 349n41

Bixby, Dave, *288*

Blue Ridge Parkway (Va./N.C.): concessioner development along, *322*, 366n44; construction of, 25, 33, 321, *322*, 323; extension proposals for, 322; as historic preservation project, 176–77; Ickes and, 25; Mission 66 concessioner lodges along, 250, 252

boating, 36

Booker T. Washington National Monument (Va.), 317, 321

Boston (Mass.), 182, 197, 205

Boston National Historical Park, 182

Boston National Historic Sites Commission, 182

Bradley, Harold C., 260–61, 262, 263–64, 268, 279–80

Branch of Plans and Designs, 42

Brant, Irving, 165

Breen, Harold, 216

Bridge Bay (Yellowstone), 234–35, *241*

Bright Angel Lodge (Grand Canyon), 233

Brooks, Paul, 299

Brower, David R.: contradictory stances of, 280; Drury and, 30; Echo Park dam opposed by, 262; Mission 66 criticized by, *271*, 271–73, 276, 277–78; opposition strategy of, 262; ORRRC and, 294; as Sierra Club board member, 265; Tioga Road project opposed by, 260–61, 262, 263–64; as wilderness advocate, 265, 266–67; Wirth and, 355n19

Brown, Margaret Keeley, 208

Brown, Otto M., 94

Brown, William E., 285

Bryant, Harold C., 184–85

Bryce Canyon National Park (Utah), *214*, 230

bungalow, 48

Bunshaft, Gordon, 49, 139

Bureau of Public Roads (BPR): congressional appropriations for, 65; criticism of, 52; NPS interbureau agreement with, 195, 256, 258, 279; pre-WWII road construction and, 51–52, 258; Tioga Road project and, 275

Bureau of Reclamation: congressional appropriations for, 35, 65; Echo Park dam proposal of, 36–37, 43–46, 262;

NPS interbureau agreement with, 37, 320; park surveys of banned, 346n42

Bureau of Outdoor Recreation (BOR): decline of, 327–28, 329; establishment of, 223, 304–5, 309, 312; funding of, 335; national parkways and, 323; national recreation areas and, 197, 320; Udall and, 315, 373n81; Wirth's opposition to, 313

Bureau of the Budget, 59, 106, 107, 116, 168, 275

buses, 82

Butcher, Devereux: misconceptions of, 136–37; modernist architecture criticized by, 132–35, 158, 243, 254, 356n10; NPS and, 142; Wirth and, 117, 299–300

Buwalda, John P., 246, 366n37

cabins, 167

Cabot, John B. ("Bill"): Cape Hatteras shade structures designed by, 157–58; consultants hired by, 147–48; as EODC supervising architect, 63, 142; staff housing design by, 161, 168–70; visitor center design by, 149, 152, 194

California: interstates and demographics in, 53; landscape architecture in, 213, 216–17; state parks, 35, 359n2

California State Park Commission, 20

California Sunset magazine, 213

Cammerer, Arno B.: CCC programs consolidated by, 41; Ickes and, 25, 345n31; as "Mather man," 39; as NPS director, 19, 21; retirement of, 19, 30

Camp Curry (Yosemite), 230. *See also* Yosemite Park & Curry Company

Campfire Day (NPS holiday), 121

campfire talks, 184, *187*, 293

campgrounds, *159*; concessioner development and, 248–49; construction of, 281, 292; Forest Service, 292; landscape architecture at, *200–201*, 201, *203*, *208*, *210*; in Mission 66 prospectus, 81; in NPS promotional material, *202*; policy recommendations for, 81, 84, 89, 128; post-WWII deterioration of, 55, 56

Canyon Hotel (Yellowstone), *95*, *96*, 234, 236, 240

Canyonlands National Park (Utah), 320

Canyon Village (Yellowstone): automobile orientation of, 237–38; campground at, 240; concessioner development at, 235–37, 238–39, *239*; development of, 234–35; groundbreaking ceremony for, 235, 236, 240; landscape architecture at, 239–40; master plan for, 236–37, *237*, 293; modernist architecture at, 238–39, 243; opening of, 240; proposal for, 93, 95; road construction and, 287; siting of, 95; visitor center at, 194, 239

porate consolidation of, 365n30; day use parks and, 109; economics of, 242–43; educational programs of, 184; haphazard development by, 204; investment by, 293, 335; lack of official outreach to, 71; in Mission 66 proposal, 110, 112; Mission 66 rumors and, 87; modernist architecture and, 132–35; monopolistic contracts of, 78, 82, 229–30, 363n3; policy recommendations for, 71–72, 75, 82–83, 84, 86, 105; political influence of, 234; preferential contract renewal, 364n7; public complaints about, 89; public-private partnerships and, 173–74; as "public-utility services," 363n3; railroad investment in, 232–33; transportation services, 82–83. *See also* lodges; *specific park*

Concession Policy Act (1965), 233, 241, 365n30

"Concessions Advisory Group," 232

Condon, David de L., 94

Conference of Challenges (Yosemite; 1963), 311–14, *312, 314*

Connecticut General Life Insurance Company, 49

conservationists, 71; as coalition, 272; contradictory stances of, 280; Kennedy administration and, 283, 291–92; Mission 66 criticized by, 106, 223, 227–28, 254, 276–78; Mission 66 fiftieth anniversary celebrations, 324; Mission 66 revision and, 300, 309; Mission 66 rumors and, 87; modernist architecture criticized by, 132–35, 158–59; wilderness parks and, 97–98; Wirth's alienation of, 87–88, 106, 117, 119, 266–67, 277, 281; Wirth's meetings with, 111, 355n19. *See also* environmentalism/environmentalists; National Parks Association; New Conservation; Sierra Club; Wilderness Society; *specific organization*

Constitution Plaza (Hartford, Conn.), 216

construction industry, 50

construction of Mission 66: contracts for, 147–48; criticism of, 227–28, 252–54, 289, 367n22; current public reliance on, 335–36; first groundbreaking, 235–36; funding of, 227, 228; impact of Tioga Road controversy on, 273, 280, 281; NPS public relations campaign for, 273–75; press coverage of, 240, 281; public perception of, 278, 286–87, *288,* 289; signage, *287;* start of, 227; statistics, 292–93, 309, 316–17; underfunded maintenance of, 339. *See also* concessioners; roads; *specific facility type; specific park*

conurbation, 47

Coot Bay (Everglades), 97

Coquina Beach (Cape Hatteras), *157,* 157–58

Cornell, Harvey H., 63–64, 142

corporations: landscape architecture and, 206, 214–15, 216; modernist architecture and, 137; suburban moves of, 49–50

corruption, 227

county parks, 41

Cox, Elbert, *13*

Crafts, Edward C., 294, 304–5

Crater Lake National Park (Ore.), 228

Craters of the Moon National Monument (Idaho), *146*

"Crisis in Our Parks," 57

Crocker Plaza (San Francisco, Calif.), 216

Cumberland Gap National Historical Park (Ky./Tenn./Va.), 322

Cyclorama and Visitor Center (Gettysburg, Pa.), 193

dam construction, 35–36. *See also* Echo Park dam proposal

Davidson, Ernest A., *23,* 351n31

day tripping, 81, 89

day use areas, 81, 122, 128, 202, 352–53n56

Death Valley National Park, 31, 155

De Forest, Lockwood, 208

Degnan's store and restaurant (Yosemite), *247,* 247–48

Demaray, Arthur E., 39

Denali Highway, 284

Denali National Park (Alaska). *See* Mount McKinley National Park

Denali Road (Mount McKinley), 284–87

Denver Service Center, 328, 330. *See also* Western Office of Design and Construction

Depression, Great: concession system during, 231

design of Mission 66. *See* architecture, Mission 66; interpretation; landscape architecture, Mission 66

Desmond, D. J., 230

Detroit (Mich.), 49–50

DeVoto, Bernard, 6–7, 55, 56, 59, 63, 368n47

D'Ewart, Wesley, 99

Dickson, Benjamin F., 353n61

"Dilemma of Our Parks, The" (Drury), 34–35

Dinosaur National Monument, 167. *See also* Echo Park dam proposal; Quarry Visitor Center

Disney, Walt, 118

Dodd, Jack B., *67,* 350n10

Dodd, Samuel, 116

Doerr, John E., *67,* 148, 188, 191, 350n10

Donnell Residence, 213

dormitories, 167

Doty, Cecil J., *23, 140;* administrative buildings designed

chitecture at, *140*, 140–41, 143; observation stations at, 185; park villages in, 128; post-WWII deterioration of, *8*, 21, *90*; press criticism of, 55; rustic architecture at, 135, 164; staff housing in, *90*; visitation at, 336; visitor center at, 148, 149, 193, *214*, 250

Grand Canyon of the Yellowstone, 95, 234, 236–37

Grand Portage National Monument (Minn.), 317

Grand Teton Lodge and Transportation Company, 129

Grand Teton National Park (Wyo.): concessioner development in, 247, 366n37; establishment of, 129; modernist architecture at, 128–32, *159*; post-WWII deterioration of, *90*; service buildings at, *166*; staff housing at, *90*, *171*; visitor center at, *156*; wilderness protection in, 26; World Conference on National Parks at (1972), 324. *See also* Jackson Lake Lodge

Grant, Madison, 19

grants-in-aid programs, 304

Grant's Tomb (New York, N.Y.), 182

Grant Village (Yellowstone), 194, 234, 240–41, 287, 339

Graves, C. Edward, 106

Great Northern Railroad, 233

Great River Road, 322, 323

Great Smoky Mountains National Park (N.C./Tenn.): as day use-only park, 109, 253; interpretive programs at, *173*, 189; modernist architecture at, 300, *301*; parkway proposal for, 322; Public Services Conference at (1956), 68, 87, 103, 106–10, 111, 235

Greenwich Village (New York, N.Y.), 181

Greiff, Constance, 179

Grist (NPS technical bulletin), *206*, 369n8

Griswold, Ralph E., 218

Gropius, Walter, 138, 178, 207, 210, 214–15

Grosvenor, Melville Bell, 88

Gruen, Victor, 48, 144

Guadalupe Mountains National Park (Tex.), 320

guidebooks, 184

"Guiding Precepts of Mission 66," 103–6

habitat conservation, 223

Haines, Aubrey L., 234

Hall, Ansel F., 184

Hall, Robert G., 63, 142

Halprin, Lawrence, 213, 214, 215

Hamilton Grange (New York, N.Y.), 182

Hanson, Hodge, 92

Hardin, Garrett, 333–34, 336

Harper House (Harper's Ferry, W.Va.), *194*

Harper's Ferry (W.Va.), 190, 193, 373n3

Harper's Ferry National Monument (W.Va.), *194*

Harper's magazine, 6–7, 55, 59

Harris, Wilhelmina, 92

Hartford (Conn.), 40, 49

Hartzog, George B., Jr., *329*; at Conference of Challenges (1963), *312*, 313; firing of, 328; management consultants hired by, 328; as NPS associate director, *292*, 310–12; as NPS director, 313–14, *314*; NPS fiftieth anniversary and, 323–24; Parkscape and, 326–27; park system growth under, 324–25; relations with design offices, 327–28; Wirth and, 371n49; Yellowstone concessions and, 353n61

Harvard Graduate School of Design (GSD), 138, 207, 209, 210–11, 362n14

Harvard School of Landscape Architecture, 207, 215

Hayden, Carl, 115

Hein, Robert, 153

Hetch Hetchy Valley (Yosemite), 36, 44, 260

Hickel, Walter J., 327

Hieb, David L., 92

highways: congressional appropriations for, 88; consensus behind, 348n36; dilemma caused by, 263; federal aid program, 50–52; historic preservation and, 181–82; Mission 66 prospectus and, 122, 123; parks developed in tandem with, 51, 53–54, 60; post-WWII overcrowding on, 52. *See also* interstate highway system

Hildebrand, Alexander, 106, 275

Hill, Sanford J. ("Red"), *13*, 285; road design by, 369n59; as WODC chair, 58, 63–64, *64*, 142

Hilton Head (S.C.), 215–16

historical parks. *See* national historical parks

Historic American Buildings Survey (HABS), 109, 195–96, 316

historic preservation: automotive parkways and, 176–77; commemorative anniversaries and, 192–93; Mission 66 and professionalization of, 341; national historic site development and, 195–97; New Deal efforts, 359n3; NPS public relations campaign for, 182–83; in Philadelphia, 178–80, *180*; restorations/reconstructions, *183*, 193, *194*, 194–95, 196, *197*; scenic preservation and, 175–76, 177; in St. Louis, 177–78; urban renewal and, 181–84

historic sites. *See* national historic sites

Historic Sites Act (1935), 175, 191; Historic Sites Survey and, 196; Lee and drafting of, 181; as Mission 66 ideological foundation, 69, 293; national historical parks designated under, 179; national historic sites designated under, 177; NPS educational programs codified under, 185; passage of, 29; river basin studies and, 36; urban renewal and, 182

Historic Sites Survey, 109, 196, 316

Hitchcock, Henry-Russell, 138, 207–9, 220, 221, 265–66

Hoh Forest Visitor Center (Olympic), *156*

Hopewell Village (Furnace) National Historic Site (Pa.), 29, *29*, 68, 176, 193, *194*

Horseshoe Bend National Military Park (Ala.), 321

hotels, 72, 74–75, 79, 83–84, 230

housing, park staff: Mission 66, 167–73, *170*; multiple-unit, *170*; NPS Women's Organization recommendations for, 89–91; post-WWII deterioration of, 47–48, 55, *90*; standardization of, 145, 358n54

Housing Act (1954), 182

Housing Act (1956), 181

Howe, George, 138

Hubbard, Henry, 218

Hubbell Trading Post National Historic Site (Ariz.), 321

Huber, Walter, 275

Hudnut, Joseph F., 207, 209, 356n10

Hull, Daniel R., 236

Humphrey, Hubert H., 272

Hunt, Myron, 145

hunting, 34, 270, 307

Hurricane Ridge Lodge (Olympic), 288

Ickes, Harold L.: Cammerer and, 25, 345n31; CCC institutionalization and, 43; concessioner contracts and, 231, 364n7; Drury and, 21, 344n3, 346n43; NPS director chosen by, 30, 344n3; Olympic development and, 165; as preservationist, 25–26; WWII park exploitation and, 31

Illinois Institute of Technology, 138

impairments, 45–46, 127–28; recreational use of public land and, 338

Independence National Historical Park (Philadelphia), 29–30, 178–80, *180*, 181, 184, 197

inefficiency, 227

Ingraham Highway (Everglades), 97, 288

International Style, 138, 164, 207–8

interpretation: artifact collections and, 188–89; displays, *104*, *173*, 173, *187*, 193–94; educational programs as precedent for, 184–86; goals of, 188; at historical parks, 359n7; improvements in, 187–89; "interpretive centers," in Mission 66 prospectus, 81, 83, 84; landscape

architecture and, 204; literary voice for, 189–90; in Mission 66 proposal, 109, 111; modernist planning model and, 224; NPS reorganization and, 186–87; Road to the Future recommendations, 315; significance of, 340; staffing for, 189, 190–91, 192; standardization of, 184, 190; technological innovations and, 189, 273–74; use of term, 184; visitor center siting and, 193–95

Interpretation Division. *See* National Park Service Interpretation Division

Interpreting Our Heritage (Tilden), 189–90

Interstate Highway Act (1956), 115–16, 181, 217, 342

interstate highway system: construction of, 279; impact on Mission 66, 13, 81, 122, 341–42; landscape architecture and, 205–6, 217; legislation for, 53

invasive species, 307

Ise, John, 306

Isle Royale National Park (Mich.), 26, 364n8

Jackson, Henry M., 100–101

Jackson, J. B., 219

Jackson Hole (Wyo.), 129

Jackson Hole Preserve, 88–89, 129, 247, 273, 295

Jackson Lake Lodge (Grand Teton), *130*; criticism of, 135, 158–59, 222; decentralized motel units at, *131*; dedication ceremony for, 157; modernist architecture of, 129–32, 134–35; as National Historic Landmark, 356n4; NPS design policies and, 133

Jackson Visitor Center (Mount Rainier), 340

James A. Kittleman and Associates, 328

Jamestown (Va.), 145, 176, 192

Jefferson National Expansion Memorial (St. Louis, Mo.), 29, 155, 177–78, *178*

Jensen, Jens, 25

John Deere Headquarters (Ill.), 216

John Morse and Associates, *156*

Johnson, Andrew, *183*

Johnson, Lyndon B., 291, 306

Johnson, Phillip, 138

Johnson, Craven, and Gibson, 366n44

Johnstown Flood National Memorial (Pa.), 321

Joshua Tree National Monument (Calif.), 140

Kahn, Louis, 178

Keck, Harry L., Jr., *152*, 152

Kennedy, John F./Kennedy administration: conservationist influence on, 228, 291–92; Mission 66 revision and, 228; national parks and priorities of, 302, 323; NPS re-

Louisiana Purchase Exposition (1904), 178
Lovell House (Los Angeles, Calif.), 138
Lykes, Ira B., 92

Mabry Mill reconstruction (Va.), *322*
MacKaye, Benton, 211
Mackintosh, Barry, 192, 320, 323
Macy, Preston P., 80, 165
Madison Junction (Yellowstone), *135*
Magnusen, Warren, 100–101
Maier, Herbert, 147; Doty and, 139; as Mission 66 Advisory Committee member, 120; Mission 66 revision and, 369n6; museums designed by, 185; NPS logo designed by, 186, 360n25; as rustic architect, 134, *135*, 135, 141, 145, 339; standardization and, 141
maintenance buildings, *166*, 166–67, 248
Malone and Hooper, *156*
Mammoth Cave National Park (Ky.), 36, 322, 364n8
Mammoth Hot Springs (Yellowstone), 93, 95, 97
Marshall, George, 268
Marshall, Robert B., 23, 350n15
Marx, Roberto Burle, 212
Massachusetts Agricultural College, 10, 40
Mather, Stephen T.: BPR and, 256; commons management and, 334; concessioner contracts of, 78–79, 83, 229–30, 363n3; dam construction projects and, 36; Drury and, 20, 21; educational programs and, 184; interagency agreements negotiated by, 279; lobbying efforts of, 50–51; as NPS director, 19, 30; NPS identity shaped by, 66; road construction standards set by, 280–81; Vint and, 73; Yellowstone expansion and, 129; Yosemite conditions and, 245
Mather Village (Grand Canyon), 250
Mattson, Frank, 94, 95, 237, 240
McDuffie, Duncan, 246, 260, 366n37
McFarland, J. Horace, 350n15
McKay, James Douglas, 86; Colonial Parkway and, 59–60; Everglades concessions and, 98; Mission 66 proposal and, 110; NPS politicized by, 371–72n53; NPS reorganization and, 57–58, 115; Wirth and, 57, 80
McLaren, Donald, 40
McLaren, John, 40
media: Mission 66 launching as covered by, 117; Mission 66 proposal as covered by, 110; national park system criticized by, 6–7, 54–57, 86
megalopolis, 47
Mellon, Paul, 318

Merriam, John C., 19
Merriam, Lawrence, *13, 249*
Mesa Verde Museum, 360n21
Mesa Verde National Park (Colo.), 85, 92–93, 185, 352–53n56
metro city, 47
Miami-Dade Chamber of Commerce, 99
Miami Herald, 99, 100
Mies van der Rohe, Ludwig, 138, 149
Miller, Hugh, *13*
Miller, Jerome C., 92
Miller House, 213
minimalism, 163
mining, 31, 34, 45–46, 223, 270
Minneapolis (Minn.), 40
Minute Man National Historical Park (Boston, Mass.), 182, 317, 321
"Mission 65," Brower's call for, 272
Mission 66: administrative structure of, 101; CCC compared to, 64–65; as commons management, 334–35; completion of, 328; controversy over, 13–15, 252–54, 338–40; efficiency of, 335; estimated cost of, 108–9, 110, 112–13, 355n17; facilities of, 15; funding of, 115–16, 118, 119, 180, 191–92, 335; goals of, 3, 31, 85, 187, 188, 337; guiding precepts of, 103–6, 202, 219; housing styles, 48; ideological foundations for, 293; implementation of, 46, 73, 82, 119–22; influence of, 323; as in-house program, 87, 91, 114, 199; as interdisciplinary endeavor, 199; interstate highway system and, 341–42; launching of, 14, 38, *116*, 116–19; legacy of, 223–24, 289, 323, 340; modernism and, 123; naming of, 10, 66; New Deal park expenditures compared to, 343n7; NPS "Progress Report" on (1966), 373n3; NPS role in, 65, 73; official unveiling of, 87; origins of, 348–49n39; park improvements through, 10–12, *12*, 110–14; political limitations on, 115; post-WWII demographic trends and, 46–49, 60–61, 222; press coverage of, 219, 299–300; public perception of, 12–13, 87, 299–300; public-private partnerships and, 173–74, 330–31; recreational planning and, 29; as redevelopment plan, 287, 336–37; research funding inadequate in, 191–92; road modernization in, 54, 279–80; scope of, 10–12, 217, 218; shortcomings of, 253–54; significance of, 15, 289, 340–42; standardization and, 155; statistics, 316–17, 335; as ten-year program, 65–66; timing of, 66; twentieth anniversary celebration for, 373n3; use of term, 87; visitor centers as centerpiece

National Association of Travel Organizations, 107

National Audubon Society, 97, 98

National Capital Park and Planning Commission, 40

national cemeteries, 354n7

National Conference on State Parks, 293, 297

National Environmental Policy (NEPA) Act (1969), 328–29, 340, 345n29

national forests, 22, 51, 166, 348n31

National Geographic, 281, 324

National Geographic Society, 88, 372n74

national historical parks: educational usefulness of, 359n7; first, 179–80; interpretation at, 194–95; land acquisition for, 302, 320–21; master plans for, 176; road construction in, 288. *See also specific park*

National Historic Landmarks: Gateway Arch as, 360n9; Mission 66 administrative buildings as, 358n39; Mission 66 lodges as, 356n4, 357n15; Mission 66 visitor centers as, 344n13, 358n37; park museums as, 360n21; program established, 196

National Historic Preservation Act (1966), 175; environmentalist influence and, 328; Mission 66 influence on, 183–84; New Conservation and, 46; park staff required for compliance with, 340; passage of, 196–97, 291; professionalization of historic preservation begun with, 341

national historic sites: first, 177–78; interpretation at, 190; inventories of, 360n16; Mission 66 and development of, 195–97; post-WWII overcrowding at, *7*; preservationism and, 23; recreational planning and, *29*, 29–30; visitation at, 190. *See also specific site*

national monuments, 154–55. *See also specific monument*

National Park Concessions, Inc., 250–51, 364n8

National Park Magazine, 105, 272

national park master plans: landscape architecture in, 204; large-format appearance of, 204, *205*; PCPs and, 370n16; planning principles of, 222; "research areas" in, 344n8; revisions of, 219–20, 370n16, 371n32

National Parks, The (Tilden), 189

National Parks and Recreation Act (1978), 329

National Parks Association: Echo Park dam opposed by, 37; Ickes and, 30; Mission 66 criticized by, 106; Mission 66 revision and, 300; modernist architecture criticized by, 132–35, 158; NPS and, 272; post-WWII parks dilemma and, 54–55; wilderness advocacy of, 23–24; Wirth's alienation of, 87–88, 117

National Park Service (NPS): as architectural patron, 156–64, 330–31; arrowhead logo of, *12*, 12, 80, 121; 186, 326–27, 340, 360n25; BOR and, 304–5, 373n81; budgets of, 3–6, *4*, 32–34, 43, 51, 54, 57, 88, 108, 119, 227–28, 348–49n39, 355n17; bureaucratic expansion of, 42; CCC activities of, 10, 40–42; consultants hired by, 330–31; criticism of, 22–23; dam construction projects and, 37–38; decentralization of, 342; declining influence of, 329, 330–31, 340–42; educational programs of, 184–86; establishment of, 36, 45, 121; fiftieth anniversary of, 66, 323–24, *325*, 372n77; goals of, 176; historic preservation planning by, 182–83, 196–97; holidays specific to, 121–22, 340; insular culture of, 87, 91, 114, 141, 144, 199, 294, 313; interagency cooperation of, 258, 279, 295–96; interagency influence of, 36, 38, 51–52; interest group influence on, 118–19; landscape architects at, 362n2; leadership of, *13, 303*; legislation for, 350n15; mandate of, 203; Mission 66 "Progress Report" prepared by, 373n3; Mission 66 role, 65, 73; modernization campaigns of, 3, 137–39; during New Deal, 343n7; office moved, during WWII, 31, 33; ORRRC and, 295–96; parks dilemma caused by, 21–22; philosophy of, 31, 61, 70, 103, 309; politicization of, 312–13, 371n51, 371–72n53; preservationism and, 23–25; press criticism of, 6–7, 55–56, 307; prewar master plans of, 122; priorities of, 34; recreational planning and, 35–36, 41–42, 183, 289; Region III headquarters (Santa Fe), 139, *140*, 357n15; Region IV headquarters (San Francisco), 139–40; reorganization of (1954), 57–58, 69, 186, 349n54; reorganization of (1961), 302–3, 371n32; scientific research unfunded by, 191–92, 307–8, 372n57; seventy-fifth anniversary of, 330; sexism in, 168–69, 185, 349–50n2; uniforms of, 186, *329*, 340; wilderness preservation and, 272; wildlife management policies of, 307–8; WWII resources and, 31–32. *See also* Albright, Horace M.; Drury, Newton B.; Hartzog, George B., Jr.; Mather, Stephen T.; Wirth, Conrad L. *entries*; *specific branch*; *director*

National Park Service Act (1916), 69–70, 112, 127, 337, 350n15; amended (1928), 364n7

National Park Service Design and Construction Division, 186

National Park Service Education Division, 184–85

National Park Service Interpretation Division, 181, 186–90, 192, 193

National Park Service Research and Education Branch, 185–86

National Park Service Training Center, 190

Offices of Design and Construction. *See* Eastern Office of Design and Construction; Western Office of Design and Construction

oil industry, 88, 119

Old Faithful area (Yellowstone), 93, 95, *96*, 97, 194

Old Faithful Geyser (Yellowstone), *132, 136*

Old Faithful Inn (Yellowstone): construction of, private investment in, 228; policy recommendations for, 72, 95, *96*, 364n21; as rustic architecture, 132; siting of, *132, 136*, 136

Old Faithful Lodge (Yellowstone), *96*, 364n21

Olmsted, Frederick Law: Brower and, 272; "landscape architecture" coined by, 203; park philosophy of, 267, 370n27; road construction and, 245, 246; Yosemite report of (1865), 70, 76, *77*, 245, 246, 267, 350n16

Olmsted, Frederick Law, Jr., 10, *45*; ASLA and, 218; California state parks and, 20, 359n2; Colorado River basin study and, 35, 44; Echo Park dam opposed by, 44–46; Harvard landscape architecture program begun by, 207; NPS legislation and, 350nn15–16; park philosophy of, 14, 46, 70, 267; retirement/death of, 213, 282; Vint and, 73, 76–77, 218, 359n2; Wirth and, 40, 45, 218, 363n28; as Yosemite Expert Advisors Board chair, 76–77, 246

Olmstedian theory: Mission 66 as legacy of, 282, 363n31; NPS landscape architecture influenced by, 217, 218; post-WWII wilderness ideal and, 267–68; Vint and, 359n2

Olmsted Point (Yosemite), 282, *283*

Olsen, Russell K., *64*

Olympic National Park (Wash.): administrative area at, 165–66; controversies over, 27–28, 31; Mission 66 development plan for, 288; modernist architecture at, 140; nonprofit concessions at, 364n8; road proposals at, 287–88; visitor center at, 148, *156*; as wilderness park, 26, 27–28

O'Mahoney, Joseph C., 294

openness, 149

Operation Outdoors, *288*, 292

Our Heritage (NPS publication), *4*; controversy over, 271; first presentation of, 117, *117*; Independence National Historical Park and, 180; interest group influence on, 119; as Mission 66 promotional literature, 117–18; Mission 66 revision and, 296; Road to the Future as replacement of, 314

Our Vanishing Shoreline (Mission 66 report), 318–19

Outdoor Recreation Act (1963), 196, 305

Outdoor Recreational Resources Review Commission (ORRRC): concession policy and, 233; establishment of, 289, 293, 294–95, 342; goals of, 295; members of, 295–96; Mission 66 revision and, 293, 301, 303–5, 309, 337–38; national parkway proposals and, 323; Parkscape and, 325–26; Parks for America and, 297–99; recreation resource typology of, 315; Wirth and, 289, 296, 297

overcrowding, 89

overlooks, *322*

Ozark National Scenic Riverways (Mo.), 325

Pack, Arthur Newton, 23

Padre Island National Seashore (Tex.), 317, 319

Painted Desert Community (Petrified Forest), 163–64, *164*

Painted Desert Inn, 140, 357n15

Paley Park (New York, N.Y.), 216

Panther Junction area (Big Bend), *156*, 250

Parachute Key Visitor Center (Everglades), *99*

Paradise Inn (Mount Rainier), 72, *79*, 101, 133, 229, 231, 289

Paradise Valley (Mount Rainier), 79–80, 81, 100–101, 249

Paradise Visitor Center (Mount Rainier), 155

Park and Recreation Structures (Good), *135*

parking, 104, 128, 201, 204, *212*, 237–38, 292

park museums/collections, 111, 143, 150–51, *151*, 185, 192, 360n21

Park, Parkway, and Recreational-Area Study Act (1936): as Mission 66 ideological foundation, 69–70, 86, 108, 114, 196, 293; NPS planning role expanded in, 41–42, 65; passage of, 41; river basin studies and, 36

Parks & Recreation magazine, 298

Parkscape, U.S.A., 324–27, *326*, 330

Parks for America, 297–99, 301

Parks for America, 323

Parks, Politics, and the People (Wirth), 335

park staff: for interpretation, 189, 190–91; Mission 66 expansion of, 110; Mission 66 expansion plans for, 111, 145, 189; professionalization of, 175, 189, 190, 197, 316; Road to the Future recommendations, 315; understaffing, 190–91, 293. *See also* housing, park staff

Park Structures and Facilities (Good), 134

park superintendents: haphazard development by, 204; Mission 66 prospectuses and, 85–86; Mission 66 questionnaires submitted to, 72

park villages: automobile use and, 237–38, 253; conces-

sion 66 proposal and, 114; New Conservation and, 323; NPS and, 183; ORRRC policy recommendations for, 303–5; wilderness advocates opposed to, 61. *See also* Wirth, Conrad L., as recreational planner

Recreational Use of Land in the United States (NPS), 42

recreation areas. *See* national recreation areas

"redwoods national park," activism for, 23–24

reenactments, 194

Regional Directors Conference (1956), 358n54

regional economic development, 253–54

Regional Plan Association, 211

Regional Plan of New York and Its Environs, 211

research, scientific, 113–14, 191–92, 307–8, 372n57

reservations, advance, 336

reservoirs, 35–36, 43, 320, 346n45

Resettlement Program, 211

resort development, 45–46, 79–80

restaurants, 157, 230

restorations, *183*, 193, *194*, 196, *197*

Rettie, Dwight F., 335, 354n7, 355n34

revision of Mission 66, 369n6; completion of, 328; conservationist support of, 300; goals of, 301, 302; launching of, 300–302; negative publicity and, 299–300; NPS plans for, 293; ORRRC policy recommendations for, 303–5, 337–38; parks added during, 317–23, *322*; Parkscape and, 324–27; Parks for America and, 297–99; prospectuses replaced with new master plans, 296–97, 370n16; Road to the Future and, 314–16; Vail Agenda and, 330; wildlife management in, 307–8; Wirth's initiation of, 296–99

river basin studies, 35–36, 43, 346n45

Riverside Park (New York, N.Y.), 40

road design: automobile use and, 256–57; interstate highway system and, 13; telescoping, 286, 369n59

roads, 56, 284; congressional appropriations for, 348n31; consensus behind, 348n36; criticism of, 367n22; Forest Service, 292; importance of, and park planning, 255, 279–80; landscape architecture and, 258; master plans for, 255–56; Mission 66 construction statistics, 287, 292; Mission 66 policies, 288–89; parks as day use destinations and, 104; policy recommendations for, 74–75, 82–83, 84, 353n56; wilderness preservation and, 163–64, 267. *See also* Going-to-the-Sun Road (Glacier); highways; interstate highway system; Tioga Road (Yosemite)

roadside exhibits, 111, 128, 187

Road to the Future: objectives of, 314–16; Parkscape and,

324; park types in, 314, 372n55; unveiling of, 311, 314; Vail Agenda and, 330

Robbins, William J., 308, 309

Robinson, Bestor, 264, 270

Rockefeller, John D., Jr., 59–60, 128–29, 131, 176, 185

Rockefeller, Laurance S.: at Mission 66 events, 88, 131; as ORRRC chair, 295–96, 303, 306; Virgin Islands park and, 295, 369n11; Wirth as consultant to, 324

Rockefeller, Laura Spelman, 185

Rockefeller, Nelson A., 295

Rocky Mountain National Park (Colo.): as day use-only park, 253; modernist architecture at, *146*, 340; press criticism of, 55; road construction in, 25, 51, 256; visitor center at, 161–62, *162*, 344n13

Rogers, Edmund B., *6*, 94, 97, 120, 240

Roosevelt, Franklin D./Roosevelt administration: CCC institutionalization and, 43; Grand Teton expansion and, 129; historic preservation efforts of, 176, 178, 359n3; national parks and priorities of, 8, 302; NPS transformed under, 40, 176. *See also* New Deal

Roosevelt, Theodore, 192, 302

Roosevelt Arch (Yellowstone), 343n10

Roosevelt Field shopping center (N.Y.), 207

Rose, James C., 210–12, 221

Rothman, Hal, 154

Royal Palms area (Everglades), 97

Royston, Robert, 215

Runte, Alfred, 368n34

Russell, Carl P., 54, 349n41

Saarinen, Eero, 49, *178*, 213, 214

Saarinen Associates, 216

Sagamore Hill National Historic Site (N.Y.), 317

Saguaro National Park (Ariz.), 133

Salem Maritime National Historical Park (Mass.), 176

San Francisco (Calif.): civic plazas in, 216; historic preservation in, 197; NPS regional headquarters in, 140; post-WWII demographic trends in, 47; Wirth in, 40; WODC office in, 58

San Francisco Museum of Art, 207

Santa Fe (N.M.), NPS regional headquarters in, 139, *140*, 357n15

Santa Fe Railroad, 232–33

Sargent, Francis W., 298, 303

Sasaki, Hideo, 215–16

Sasaki, Walker and Associates, 215

Saturday Evening Post, 55, 56, 86

conservationist influence in, 268; dam construction projects and, 35; educational programs unfunded by, 185; environmentalist influence on, 328; highway appropriations, 88, 279; interstate highway legislation, 53; land acquisition and, 298; Mission 66 as viewed by, 12–13; Mission 66 budget and, 10, 73, 116, 119, 227, 228; Mission 66 planning and, 50; Mission 66 presented to, 106, 107; museum construction unfunded by, 186; national historical parks established by, 179; national park economic interests and, 82; national park road appropriations, 50–51; national park system expanded by, 329; New Deal programs terminated by, 8, 42; ORRRC legislation and, 294–95, 342; parkway appropriations, 323; post-WWII park appropriations, 33–34; recreational planning and, 305; scientific research and, 191–92; urban renewal appropriations, 181; Wirth's relations with, 114–15

user fees, 305–6, 336, 337–38, 371n37

U.S. Fish and Wildlife Service, 191

U.S. Forest Service, 22, 166, 292

U.S. Geological Survey, 191

U.S. House of Representatives, Subcommittee on Interior Appropriations, 119

U.S. Interior Department: American Pioneer Dinner at, *116*, 116–19; concessioner contracts and, 93, 364n7; conservationist influence at, 283, 306; design review at, 369n7; Eisenhower administration and, 57, 58; logo of, 326–27; Mission 66 planning at, 66; Truman administration and, 8; Vint awarded by, 195; Wirth awarded by, 119. *See also* Chapman, Oscar L.; Ickes, Harold L.; Krug, Julius; McKay, James Douglas; Seaton, Fred; Udall, Stewart L.; *specific secretary*

U.S. Labor Department, 41

U.S. Post Office, 326

U.S. Senate Appropriations Committee, 119

U.S. War Department, 41

Utah Parks Company, 230

Utley, Robert M., 195

Vail Agenda (1992), 330

Vanderbilt Mansion (Hyde Park, N.Y.), *197*

Van Eesteren, Cornelis, 221

Vaux, Calvert, 40, 203

Vint, Thomas C., *13*, 48, *303*; administrative buildings designed by, 164; architectural style of, 134, 135; ASLA and, 218; awards received by, 195; bureaucratic style of, 74; concessioner development and, 236; as Design and Construction Division chief, 186; design staff of, 22, *23*; Doty and, 141, 147; Everglades prosepectus and, 98; highway modernization and, 53–54; historic preservation and, 175–76, 195–96; master planning policy of, 84, 176, 195, 199, 200–201, 219–20, 255–56, 351n23; as "Mather man," 39; on Mission 66 Advisory Committee, 120; Mission 66 controversies and, 13–14; Mission 66 policy recommendations and, 73–76; as Mission 66 steering committee member, *67*, 69, 74, 350n10; modernist architecture and, 137; Mount Rainier master plans and, 83–84, 128; Mount Rainier ski resort proposal and, 79–80; on national parks, purpose of, 28; as NPS landscape architect, 42, 202, 203–4, 256; NPS landscape architects trained by, 218; NPS reorganization and, 58, 63; Olmsted and, 73, 76–77, 218, 359n2; park design controlled by, 133, 142; "Plan A" of, 244, 245; retirement of, 281, 301, 302; road construction and, 255–56, 258–60, 280, 284; rustic architecture and, 141, 339; staff housing and, 90, 91; Tioga Road controversy and, 260, 261–62, 263, 280–81; wilderness zoning by, 22; Wirth and, 74, 310

"Vint Plan" ("Plan B"): concessions relocated to gateway towns in, 75, 122, 244–46; Mission 66 influenced by, 122, 128, 165, 202, 220, 248; necessity of replacing "Plan A" with, 253; origins of, 220; Vail Agenda and, 330

Virgin Islands National Park, 295, 317, 320, 369n11

visitor centers: commemorative anniversaries and, 192–93; construction of, 147–48, 155, 281, 292–93, 357n26; controversies over, 285–86; cost of, 145, 155, *156*; critical acclaim of, 157–58, 159–61; criticism of, 158–59; early development of, *143*; first use of term, 111; Forest Service, 292; as historic landmarks, 344n13, 358n37; historic preservation and, 197; influence of, 155–57; institutional review of, 148–49; interpretive programs in, 175, 184, 187, 189, 192; landscape architecture at, 201–2, 204, *214*, 220, 221; modernist planning model and, 220; opening of, 192–93, 357n26, 358n40; origins of, 142–43; park museums reprogrammed as, 186; parks as day use destinations and, 100–101, 104; PCPs for, 144–45; preliminary design of, 145–47; problems of, 149, 340; public-private partnerships and, 152–53; purpose of, 144, 149–50; Road to the Future recommendations, 316; rustic museum design reversed in, 149–52; significance of, 50, 192, 197, 340; siting of, 193–95, 339; staffing for, 145, 191; stan-

ceived by, 348–49n39; implementation and, 119–20; informational memoranda released by, 350n13, 355n35; interest group influence on, 87–88, 106, 118–19; interpretation and, 186, 187–88; at Jackson Lake Lodge dedication, 131, 157; landscape architecture background of, 202; modernist architecture and, 137, 157, 357n20; modernist planning model and, 123; national seashore planning goals and, 319; NPS Women's Organization and, 168; ORRRC and, 289, 296, 297; park design controlled by, 133; policy documents selected by, 70, 114; program revision, 296–99, 301, 370n16; proposal by, 3, 14, 38; prospectus and, 77–78; public presentations of, *104*, 105–6, 107–10, 116–19, 349n48; public relations campaign, 120–22, *121*, 273–74, 281–82; road policy and, 279, 288; rustic architecture and, 339; scientific research and, 191–92; staff housing and, 91, 168; statistics assembled by, 335, 357–58n30; Tioga Road controversy and, 260, 266–67, 275, 277, 282–83, 372n74; unpublished history by, 373n3; Virgin Islands park and, 369n11; visitor center concept and, 50; wilderness preservation and, 221, 266–68, 270, 284; at Yellowstone groundbreaking, 235–36

Wirth, Conrad L., as recreational planner, *41*, 202; CCC institutionalization and, 43; CCC park work directed by, 22, 28, 40–42, 44, 74, 101, 181; concessioner contracts and, 56; concessioner development and, 79–80; dam construction projects and, 37, 45–46, 347n13; highway modernization and, 53–54; national recreation areas planned by, 35–36, 43–44; negative publicity and, 55, 56–57; Olmsted and, 218, 363n28; philosophy of, 44; staff housing shortages and, 48; Vint and, 74

Wirth, Theodore, 8–10, 14, 39–40

WODC. *See* Western Office of Design and Construction

Women's Congress on Housing (1956), 169

Wonder Lake (Mount McKinley), 284

Works Progress Administration (WPA), 22, 177

World Conference of National Parks (Yellowstone/Grand Tetons; 1972), 324

World War I, 60

World War II: concessions suspended during, 231; demographic trends following, 38, 46–49, 60–61, 122–23, 217–18, 222, 263; impact on park budgets, 28, 42; impact on park priorities, 30, 31–32

Wosky, John B., 259

Wright, Frank Lloyd, 157, 161

Wright Brothers National Memorial (N.C.), *160*, 161, 344n13

Wyoming legislature, 94

Yakima Park (Mount Rainier), 81

Yard, Robert Sterling, 22–23, 30, 350n15

Yavapai Lodge (Grand Canyon), 250

Yavapai Observation Station (Grand Canyon), 185

Yellowstone Act (1872), 69

Yellowstone Lake, 93, 235

Yellowstone National Park: accommodations at, 365n34; Campfire Day at, 121; campgrounds at, *203*, 365n34; concessioner controversies in, 240, 241, 252, 364nn20–21, 365n29; concessioner development in, 72, 83, 93–97, *95, 136*, 228, 234–44, *241*, 243–44; dam construction projects and, 36; educational programs at, 184; first Mission 66 groundbreaking at, 235–36; housing at, *167*; interpretive programs at, *104*, 190; land acquisition for, 129; landscape architecture at, *212, 216*; master plan for, *96*, 236, *237*, 240–41; modernist architecture at, *158*; motel complexes in, 241; museums at, 185, 360n21; park villages in, 128; policy recommendations for, 71; post-WWII deterioration of, *9*, 93–94; post-WWII overcrowding at, 4, *5*; press criticism of, 55; prospectus for, 85, 93–97, *96*, 234–36, 241, 353nn65–66, 364n21; rail service terminated in, 94; road construction in, *241*, 256, 287, 368n47; road design at, 97, *216*, 237; Roosevelt Arch, *21*, 343n10; rustic architecture at, *132, 135*, 136; service buildings at, *166*; visitation at, 234, 336; visitor centers at, 148, 194; wilderness in, 270–71; wildlife management at, 307, 308, 312; World Conference on National Parks at (1972), 324. *See also* Canyon Village; Old Faithful Inn

Yellowstone Park Company, 94, 234, 238, 240, 241–43, 365n29–30

Yorktown (Va.), 145, 176, 192, 193

Yosemite Lodge, 75, 132, 134, 161, 230, 244–49, *246*

Yosemite National Park, 245, 338. *See also* Tioga Road; Yosemite Valley

Yosemite National Park Board of Expert Advisors: disbanding of, 282; members of, 45, 76–77, 246, 366n37; Olmstedian tradition and, 267; Tioga Road controversy and, 259–60, 261, 263, 264

Yosemite Park & Curry Company, 230, 233, 246–47

Yosemite Park Company, 230

Yosemite School of Field Natural History, 184–85

Yosemite Valley, *76, 77*; accessibility of, 337; administrative complex at, 164–65, 351n31; Ahwahnee Hotel, 32, *32*, 135; ASLA conference at (1966), 372n77; automobile use in, *5*, 5, 54; campgrounds at, 280; concessioner development in, 72, *75*, 132, 228–29, 236, 242, 244–49, 365n23; Conference of Challenges at (1963), 311–14, *312*, *314*; controversies over, 252, 259–66; dam construction projects and, 36, 44, 260; as day use-only park, 349n41; educational programs at, 184–85; interpretive programs at, 189, 190; landscape architecture in, 218; modernist architecture at, *133*, 134, 140; Olmsted and, 76–77; Olmsted report on (1865), 70, 76; policy recommendations for, 75, 128; post-WWII deterioration of, *7*, 21, 263; press criticism of, 55, 56; prospectus for, 248–49, *249*; as public park, roads and, 279–80; ropeway proposal at, 351n26; Vint and, 76, 128; visitation at, 245, 336; visitor centers at, 248, 280; WWII park exploitation and, 31–32

Yosemite Valley Railroad, 5

Yosemite Village, *133*, 245, 247–48, 352n37, 365n23

Your Mission 66 and the National Parks (NPS brochure), 273

Zahniser, Howard C., 266–67, 268, 269, 355n19

Zeman, Amanda, 250

Zimmer, Edward S., *13*; as EODC chair, 58, 63–64, 142; as landscape architect, 202; Philadelphia historic preservation and, 180; visitor center planning and, 189, 361n51

Zion, Robert L., 207, 216

Zion-Mt. Carmel Road (Zion), 51, 256

Zion National Park (Utah): architectural transition at, *151*; CCC facilities at, *8*; comfort stations at, *172*; concessioner development in, 230; landscape architecture at, *214*; modernist architecture at, 133, 340; post-WWII deterioration of, *8*; road construction in, 51, 256; visitor center at, *151*, 151–52, *214*